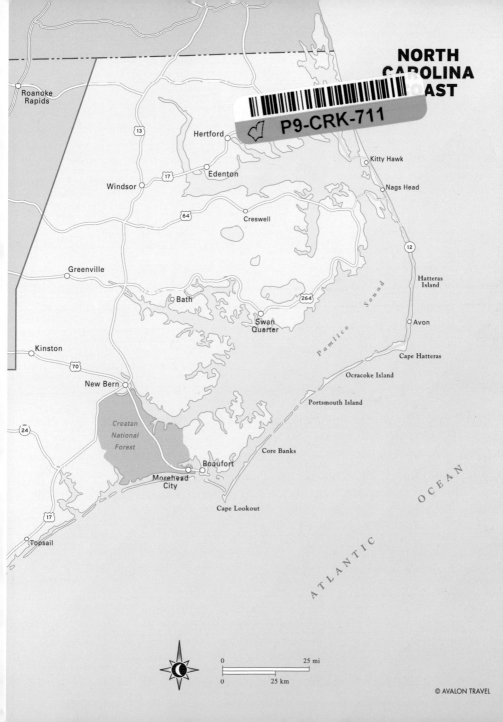

NORTH CAROLINA COAST

P9-CRK-711

Roanoke Rapids

13

Hertford

Kitty Hawk

17

Edenton

Nags Head

Windsor

64

Creswell

12

Greenville

Hatteras Island

Bath

264

Avon

Swan Quarter

Pamlico Sound

Cape Hatteras

Kinston

Ocracoke Island

70

New Bern

Portsmouth Island

Croatan National Forest

24

Core Banks

Beaufort

Morehead City

17

Cape Lookout

Topsail

ATLANTIC OCEAN

0   25 mi

0   25 km

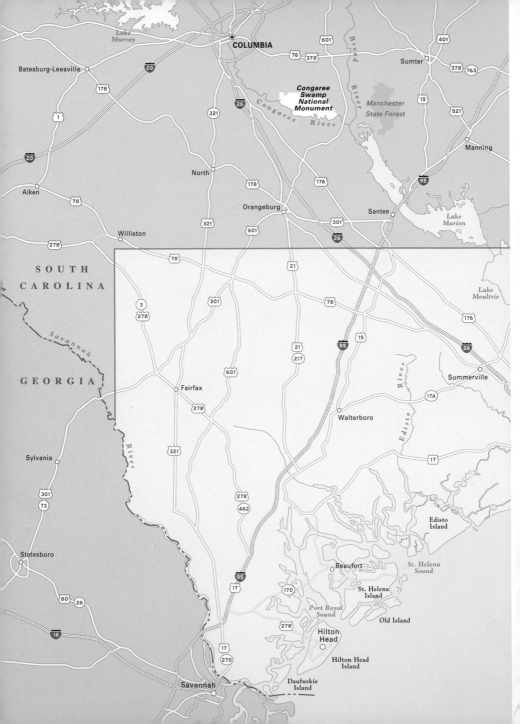

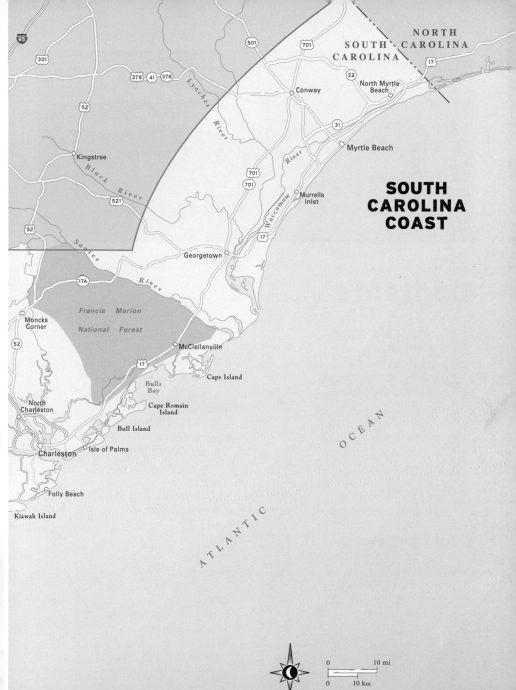

SOUTH CAROLINA COAST

NORTH
SOUTH CAROLINA
CAROLINA

Conway

North Myrtle
Beach

Myrtle Beach

Kingstree

Murrells
Inlet

Georgetown

Moncks
Corner

Francis Marion

National Forest

McClellanville

Cape Island

Bulls
Bay

Cape Romain
Island

North
Charleston

Bull Island

Charleston

Isle of Palms

Folly Beach

Kiawah Island

ATLANTIC

OCEAN

Lynches River

Black River

Santee River

Waccamaw River

0   10 mi

0   10 km

© AVALON TRAVEL

Contents

Discover
the Coastal Carolinas

From the wide, deep waterways of North Carolina on down to the South Carolina Sea Islands, there's a shared, effortless mystique over the 500-mile stretch of Carolina coast – a sense of time standing still that is both poignant and palpable. No mere poet's license, it's something you feel here, whether in the bracing tang of the sea breeze or the oddly comforting whiff of pluff mud at low tide.

The chronicle of this stretch of the Eastern seaboard includes some of the United States' oldest and most important recorded history. The names from its past echo on today: Sir Walter Raleigh, Blackbeard, Francis Marion, Fort Sumter, the Wright Brothers.

But outdoor recreation is by far the chief passion, almost all of it having to do with the waterways that virtually define the region. Swept by a constant, cooling breeze off the Atlantic and crisscrossed by hundreds of rivers, creeks, and marshes, the Carolina coast is an aquatic wonderland for boaters, kayakers, and naturalists alike.

If you want family-themed vacationing, there are the commercial areas of Myrtle Beach, Hilton Head Island, or Wrightsville Beach, with their user-friendly stretches of sand and tourist infrastructures. For a more challenging journey, put the kayak on top of the car and head to the Great Dismal Swamp of North Carolina or the blackwater ACE Basin

of South Carolina. For a remote, laid-back beach experience, hang out on the Outer Banks, or take a jaunt down to Edisto Island or Hunting Island and enjoy the beachfront life, South Carolina-style.

Locals and visitors alike also enjoy the fruits of the sea in the fresh catch that exemplifies the coastal Carolina plate. From Elizabeth City to Charleston to Port Royal, from fried to grilled to boiled, you can be assured of a tasty nautical treat at nearly every meal – though the barbecue around here is not too shabby, either!

Another common denominator along the Carolina coast is the people themselves. All have their distinctive identities, and they go by many names: the "wreckers" of the Outer Banks, the Down Easterners of the Core Sound, the Gullah of the South Carolina islands, even the "snowbirds" of Hilton Head. But the thread linking them all together – and infusing the atmosphere of the coastal Carolinas – is a gusto combining a gregariousness of spirit with a love of the simple pleasures of life.

Planning Your Trip

▶ WHERE TO GO

The Outer Banks

This windswept area includes the first English colony in America and the hiding ground of pirates and retains its poignant mystique to this day. Nags Head has a well-developed tourist infrastructure and boasts attractions like sandy Jockey's Ridge State Park and the Wright Brothers National Memorial. But along Cape Hatteras National Seashore, the towns start seeming smaller, with Ocracoke Island, accessible only by ferry, embodying the remoteness associated with the Outer Banks. Across the sounds, the Great Dismal Swamp draws kayakers and naturalists.

Tryon Palace gardens in New Bern

North Carolina Central Coast

Beaufort (BO-furt), North Carolina—not to be confused with Beaufort (BYOO-furt), South Carolina—boasts a long pedigree and beautiful old homes and cemeteries. A burgeoning tourist hotspot, New Bern also features a large historic district and the gorgeous Tryon Palace. With many sunken ships offshore, Morehead City is a diver's mecca, while Cape Lookout National Seashore features fantastic, uninhabited beaches and wild horses.

Wilmington and the Cape Fear Region

A great blend of old and new, Wilmington, North Carolina, combines an exquisite historic district with a young, happening vibe and plenty of shopping and dining opportunities. Enjoy its beautiful homes and gardens, but don't miss the excellently preserved World War II battleship, USS *North Carolina*. To the east and the south are great oceanfront recreational areas like Wrightsville Beach and Kure Beach.

Myrtle Beach and the Grand Strand

The 60-mile Grand Strand of South Carolina focuses on the resort and beach activity of Myrtle Beach, and to an increasing extent, North Myrtle Beach. Down the Strand are the more peaceful areas of Pawleys Island and Murrells Inlet, with the historic Georgetown area and its scenic plantations anchoring the bottom portion. Because of the Strand's long, skinny geography, always budget more time than you think you'll need to get around.

Charleston

One of America's oldest cities and an early national center of arts and culture,

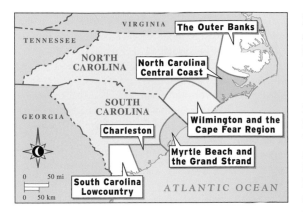

laurels. Situated on a hallowed spit of land known as "the peninsula," the Holy City is now a vibrant, creative hub of the New South.

South Carolina Lowcountry

The South Carolina Lowcountry's mossy, laidback pace belies its former status as the heart of American plantation culture and the original cradle of secession. Today, it combines the history of Beaufort and Bluffton and the natural beauty of the ACE Basin with the resort development of Hilton Head and the relaxed beaches of Hunting Island.

Charleston's legendary taste for the high life is matched by its forward-thinking outlook. The starting point of the Civil War is not just a city of museums resting on its historic

► WHEN TO GO

You can't go wrong hitting the Carolina coast in the spring, when the azaleas are in bloom and there's still a little dryness in the air. It is the absolute best time to visit Charleston and the Lowcountry, and this is when most love affairs with the area are born.

While a spring visit to the Grand Strand will avoid the crowds, the heat, and the jacked-up summer hotel prices, water temperatures will still be quite chilly at this time. Ditto for the North Carolina Outer Banks.

Memorial Day weekend is a good time to visit anywhere in the coastal Carolinas; however, the beaches will be jammed. Despite Myrtle Beach's efforts to discourage big biker rallies during this period, there is still likely to be plenty of biker activity, which is harmless but can be intrusive.

Summer gets a bad rap in the South. The truly oppressive heat doesn't come until August, and the coast's sea breeze makes it much more endurable than sweltering inland areas.

IF YOU HAVE . . .

- **A WEEKEND:** Enjoy the old-world charms of Charleston and the more modern appeal of Myrtle Beach.

- **FIVE DAYS:** Add a jaunt south to Beaufort and Hilton Head, South Carolina, or north to Wilmington and New Bern, North Carolina.

- **A WEEK:** Add the Outer Banks.

old rice paddy gate at Magnolia Plantation

Late summer in the coastal Carolinas means two things: humidity and hurricanes. Not until well after Labor Day will you be reasonably assured that a gathering storm will not spoil your vacation plans. To me, this is the least recommended time to visit.

September right after Labor Day is a perfect time to hit Myrtle Beach and the Grand Strand—lodging prices are cut dramatically and the crowds are much thinner, but the beach weather remains ideal.

My own favorite time to travel up and down the coast is late October/early November, when the kids are back in school, crowds are down, the weather is wonderful, prices are low, but there are still plenty of places open for business.

▶ BEFORE YOU GO

If you're headed to the Outer Banks—or anywhere on the North Carolina coast north of Wilmington for that matter—keep in mind that the wind can whip up and things can get pretty chilly pretty fast. Bring a windbreaker or sweater, even in the height of summer.

For trips to South Carolina at almost any time of year, wear natural fabrics if at all possible. It's likely to be hotter and more humid than where you come from, and breathable cotton on your skin will help raise your comfort level.

Overall, dress is quite casual in the coastal Carolinas, with Charleston and Hilton Head being the most fashion-conscious areas by far. However, with the notable exception of Myrtle Beach, keep ostentatious displays of unclothed flesh to a minimum—this is still the South, after all.

Contrary to media stereotypes, you will have access to any type of modern amenity during your trip to the coastal Carolinas. The one exception is cell phone coverage on the Outer Banks, which can get sketchy to nonexistent at times.

Harbour Town in Hilton Head

Explore the Coastal Carolinas

▶ THE BEST OF THE COASTAL CAROLINAS

From Nags Head to Hilton Head, here's a car journey down the coast hitting all the hot spots and highlighting the region's culture, history, natural beauty, and rich maritime legacy.

Day 1
Begin at Nags Head on North Carolina's Outer Banks, your home base for the next couple of days, and enjoying the beach and the key local sights, Jockey's Ridge State Park and the Wright Brothers National Memorial.

Day 2
This morning head down to windswept Cape Hatteras National Seashore and climb the historic lighthouse. Then, in the afternoon, head to Roanoke Island's Fort Raleigh National Historic Site. At night, perhaps take in a performance of "The Lost Colony" historical drama.

Beaufort's Old Burying Ground

Day 3
This morning enjoy the exquisite historic district in New Bern, with a visit to the gorgeous gardens at Tryon Palace. After a tasty lunch downtown, head to the ocean again and walk the waterfront at Beaufort. Don't miss a visit to the North Carolina Maritime Museum and the Old Burying Ground. Tonight drive down to Wilmington for the first of two nights at a fine B&B, such as the Rosehill Inn.

Day 4
This morning tour Wilmington's historic homes: Bellamy Mansion, the Burgwin-Wright House, and the Zebulon Latimer House (save with a three-house ticket). After lunch, walk the decks of the USS North Carolina. Tonight have a quality meal downtown at any one of the fine eateries on and around Water Street.

Day 5
After breakfast at your B&B, head out to the ocean for some fun at Wrightsville Beach. This afternoon head into Myrtle Beach, South Carolina, for the first of two nights, perhaps taking in a delightfully cheesy, utensil-free dinner show at Medieval Times at Broadway at the Beach. Alternately, you could stop for fried seafood along the way at Calabash, North Carolina, on the border.

BEST BEACHES

Best Scenery
Cape Hatteras National Seashore (The Outer Banks)
Sullivan's Island (Charleston)
Hunting Island State Park (South Carolina Lowcountry)

Best for Families
Wrightsville Beach (Wilmington and the Cape Fear Region)
Kure Beach (Wilmington and the Cape Fear Region)
Myrtle Beach (Myrtle Beach and the Grand Strand)
Isle of Palms (Charleston)
Hilton Head Island (South Carolina Lowcountry)

Carolina Beach

Best for Water Sports
Nags Head (The Outer Banks)
Myrtle Beach (Myrtle Beach and the Grand Strand)
Hilton Head Island (South Carolina Lowcountry)

Best for Solitude
Cape Hatteras National Seashore (The Outer Banks)

Ocracoke Island (The Outer Banks)
Topsail Beach (Wilmington and the Cape Fear Region)

Most Local Character
Carolina Beach State Park (Wilmington and the Cape Fear Region)
Edisto Beach State Park (Charleston)
Folly Beach (Charleston)

Day 6

Today is your big Myrtle Beach day. Claim your patch of sand along the miles of beaches in the morning, and after lunch visit Ripley's Aquarium, shop at Barefoot Landing, or have a round of miniature golf. Tonight enjoy some down-home entertainment by catching a show at the Carolina Opry, quaffing an adult beverage or two at The Bowery, or perhaps learning how to do the Shag at Ocean Drive Beach.

Day 7

Work your way southward with a stop at Brookgreen Gardens on the Grand Strand, having lunch at the waterfront in nearby Georgetown. This afternoon visit gorgeous

Hampton Plantation, then it's down to Charleston. After checking into your room at the Vendue Inn or the Andrew Pinckney Inn, walk the French Quarter, including looks at St. Philip's Episcopal Church and the French Huguenot Church. Enjoy a classic Charleston dinner at one of any number of amazing restaurants nearby, such as Tristan, Peninsula Grill, or High Cotton.

Day 8

This full day in Charleston includes some shopping on King Street and a walk along the Battery and nearby Rainbow Row for a snapshot of these photogenic mansions. For an afternoon historical road trip, cross the Cooper River to Mount Pleasant, and

MARINE MORSELS

The Coastal Carolinas are awash, literally, in seafood. Here are some epicurean highlights for the seafood lover.

MAY RIVER OYSTERS
The legendary freshness and taste of May River oysters are available right off the docks in the South Carolina Lowcountry at the **Bluffton Oyster Company** or in area seafood restaurants.

LOWCOUNTRY SIGNATURES
The Lowcountry's two signature dishes, **shrimp & grits** and **she crab soup,** are both available in delicious abundance in the Charleston area. Try **Poogan's Porch** for shrimp & grits and **Hyman's Seafood** north of town for she crab soup.

Enjoy fried herring at Cypress Grill.

CALABASH SEAFOOD
The seaside North Carolina town of **Calabash,** just north of the state line with South Carolina, has given its name to an entire genre of seafood. Enjoy these fried delectables at one of about a dozen Calabash restaurants in the town itself, or at their equivalent throughout the Myrtle Beach area, such as **Original Benjamin's.**

FRIED HERRING
If the idea of fried herring sounds a bit weird, head straight to the **Cypress Grill** in Jamesville, North Carolina, east of Williamston in the Albemarle or Inner Banks region (Feb. - Apr.), and see how it's done. You can eat every part of the fish except for the backbone, and it's all crispy and delicious.

visit Boone Hall Plantation and the nearby Charles Pinckney Historical Site. For more recent history, visit the Patriots Point Naval and Maritime Museum. Tonight eat and drink in style in the Upper King area, perhaps with dinner at La Fourchette and late-night tapas at Raval.

Day 9
You have a full array of choices for this full day in Charleston, including a walk along the Battery and nearby Rainbow Row, a ferry ride to Fort Sumter, a jaunt across the Cooper River to Boone Hall Plantation and the Patriots Point Naval and Maritime Museum, or across the Ashley River to visit one of the historic plantations. If it's a weekend, you can head up to North Charleston to see the Confederate submarine CSS *Hunley* at the repurposed Charleston Navy Yard.

Day 10
Finish your tour by spending the morning in historic Bluffton on the relaxing May River, browsing the art galleries. Then jaunt down to Hilton Head Island to relax on the beach, with a visit to Sea Pines Forest Preserve and Harbour Town.

▶ COASTAL CAROLINAS FOR COUPLES

With lovely beaches, charming cities, and evocative historic districts, the Carolina coast offers up some ideal spots for a couples' getaway, whatever your romantic style.

Outdoor Romance

Hunting Island is far more than a state park, it is also a state of mind, with beautiful, windswept beaches and an awesome view from the top of the lighthouse. Outdoor activities include kayaking the inlet where parts of *Forrest Gump* were filmed and birdwatching for loons, herons, egrets, and more. Share a tentsite, or hole up in one of the cabins (there's a minimum week-long stay in high season).

Although Myrtle Beach proper isn't necessarily one's first thought when one thinks of romance, Huntington Beach State Park boasts a great stretch of beach, several nature trails, and a fanciful "castle" mansion and grounds. Camp at the park, then go right across the highway to Brookgreen Gardens, America's largest collection of outdoor sculpture, which is perfect for strolls through the various nooks and crannies on the sprawling, verdant grounds.

City Romance

Charleston is one of the most romantic cities in the world, so you really can't go wrong there. Although it's not in the center of town, one of the most romantic spots in Charleston is Middleton Place and its magnificent gardens. Couples can even stay on the grounds, at the Inn at Middleton Place, in a room with floor-to-ceiling windows overlooking the gardens and the Ashley River.

For a little bit of Paris in the South, try the atmospheric French Quarter. Take a carriage ride or just enjoy the intimate streetscape. More social, young-at-heart couples will want to head to the hip Upper King area—stop at Raval or Basil for drinks and food.

a fine example of a Charleston single house in the French Quarter

CAROLINA LIGHTHOUSES

Often treacherous for sailors due to its geography and susceptibility to storms, the Carolina coast is chock-a-block with historic lighthouses. Generally speaking, most have public visiting hours, including "climbing" availability, from late spring to early fall. Sometimes the grounds remain open when the lighthouses are closed to the public. It's always a good idea to call ahead.

NORTH CAROLINA

- **Currituck Beach Lighthouse:** Still active, open to the public for climbing Easter–November.

- **Bodie Island Lighthouse:** Still active, closed to the public. Keeper's building is open to the public.

- **Cape Hatteras Lighthouse:** Still active, open to the public for climbing the third Friday in April until Columbus Day. Gorgeous view.

- **Ocracoke Lighthouse:** Still active, closed to the public. Grounds are open to the public.

- **Cape Lookout Lighthouse:** Still active, closed to the public. Keeper's quarters and grounds are open to the public.

- **Bald Head Island Lighthouse:** Inactive, open to the public year-round. State's oldest light.

SOUTH CAROLINA

- **Georgetown Lighthouse:** Still active, closed to the public.

- **Morris Island Lighthouse:** Inactive, closed to the public. You can get a great view of it from the north end of Folly Island.

- **Hunting Island Lighthouse:** Inactive, open to the public year-round for climbing. It's located within a popular state park and offers a stunning view.

- **Harbour Town Lighthouse:** Technically not a real lighthouse at all, but a tourist attraction within Sea Pines Plantation. Open to the public year-round for climbing.

Cape Hatteras Lighthouse

the waterfront of historic Wilmington

Equal parts evocative antebellum seaport and trendy college town, Wilmington is also a great choice for a romantic trip. Choose from an abundance of B&Bs, like the Graystone Inn, and spend a weekend soaking in the city's beautiful 19th-century architecture and well-restored waterfront.

Historical Romance

New Bern is a handy little getaway for those who like strolling through a large and tastefully restored historic district.

For those seeking a smaller, more poignant historic town, try Beaufort, North Carolina, which has a palpable vestige of its very old seaport past. You can rent a houseboat for the weekend and spend the entire time floating on the water. Or on land, you can stroll through the Spanish moss and live oaks in the beautiful Old Burying Ground.

Just Us

Of course to really get away from it all—and I mean just about *all*—head to the Outer Banks of North Carolina and get on a ferry to windswept, sparsely populated Ocracoke Island. If that seems like too much, you can drive to Rodanthe or Cape Hatteras National Seashore, which also offer a sense of solitude.

▶ NATURAL ADVENTURES

You could devote a lifetime to experiencing the diverse and evocative ecosystems of the Carolina coast. Here's a week-long trip covering the highlights.

Day 1

Begin up in the Great Dismal Swamp of North Carolina, where you'll spend the morning kayaking amid this anything-but-dismal ecosystem. Then head down to Nags Head on the Outer Banks, where you can stay in a beachfront motel for the night. If you have a four-wheel drive, on the way, you can drive onto the beach near Corolla and see the fabled herd of wild horses there.

Day 2

Spend the morning hang-gliding off the huge sand dune of Jockey's Ridge State Park, or head down to Pea Island National Wildlife Refuge on Hatteras Island for some bird-watching. This afternoon on your way down to Beaufort, North Carolina, stop at Mattamuskeet National Wildlife Refuge for some more bird-watching on this important flyway.

Day 3

Today in Beaufort you begin with a ferry ride to Harkers Island and a tour of Cape Lookout National Seashore, courtesy of Coastal Ecology Tours, where you'll enjoy the protected scenery and habitat. This afternoon visit the North Carolina Aquarium in back in Beaufort, where you'll spend one more night.

Day 4

Today you get up bright and early to head down the South Carolina coast to the blackwater Edisto River, where you'll take a waterborne tour with Carolina Heritage Outfitters, based northeast of Beaufort, South Carolina, and spend the night in a tree house upriver.

Day 5

This morning you paddle back down the Edisto River to your vehicle. From here, you can take the drive inland to fascinating Francis Beidler Forest, where some of the oldest-growth cypress stands in the world still remain.

Pea Island National Wildlife Refuge

AFRICAN AMERICAN HERITAGE

The life and contribution of the coastal Carolinas' African American population is a testament to resilience, resourcefulness, and authentic culture. Here are the key sights in the region: You can see them all in a five- or six-day road trip with stays in Wilmington, Charleston, and Beaufort, South Carolina, or combine them with other sights when you're headed to just one area.

WILMINGTON

- **Bellamy Mansion:** This historic mansion features extensive interpretive programming on African American history, as well as one of the few intact slave quarters in the United States.

- **Louise Wells Cameron Art Museum:** At this nationally renowned museum, you'll find artwork of notable regional African American artists.

GEORGETOWN

- **Rice Museum:** This museum has several exhibits on the contributions of African Americans in building the rice culture of the Lowcountry and the way they lived.

CHARLESTON

- **Old Slave Mart Museum:** This structure that once held an indoor slave market today re-creates what happened during those actions and traces the history of the slave trade.

- **Old City Market:** On land donated to the city with the stipulation that no slaves were ever to be sold here, the City Market was once and still is a place for African American vendors to ply their wares.

- **Avery Research Center for African American History and Culture:** Those of an academic bent can visit this research center at the College of Charleston and view exhibits that sample from its permanent archives. While on this gorgeous campus, don't miss a visit to the Cistern area in front of historic Randolph Hall, where Barack Obama spoke before a large crowd during the 2008 presidential campaign.

- **Philip Simmons Garden:** View the wrought-iron art of Charleston's most beloved artisan in the garden of St. John's Reformed Episcopal Church.

- **Drayton Hall Plantation:** At this authentically preserved plantation building in West Ashley, you can take a tour and visit the old African American cemetery on the grounds.

- **Boone Hall Plantation:** Visit this former cotton plantation and still-active agriculture facility to see the excellent restored slave quarters and the well-done interpretive exhibits. While on Mount Pleasant don't miss the sweetgrass basket-maker stands all along Highway 17.

BEAUFORT, SOUTH CAROLINA

- **Robert Smalls House:** View the home of the African American Civil War hero Robert Smalls, who later served in Congress.

- **Tabernacle Baptist Church:** Robert Smalls attended this church, which today hosts a memorial sculpture of him on the grounds.

- **Beaufort National Cemetery:** This burial ground contains a memorial to African American Civil War troops.

THE LOWCOUNTRY

- **Penn Center:** Located on St. Helena Island, this is a key research and cultural site in the study of the Gullah culture and people.

- **Daufuskie Island:** The Historic District here is where Pat Conroy taught African American children at the still-standing Mary Field School.

- **Tuskegee Airmen Memorial:** Located inland in Walterboro, this monument is dedicated to the African American fighter pilots who trained here during World War II.

- **Union Cemetery:** This small but evocative cemetery on Hilton Head Island serves as the final resting ground of several soldiers of the Civil War Colored Infantry.

THE OUTER BANKS

The Outer Banks are like a great seine net set along the northeastern corner of North Carolina, holding the Sounds and inner coast apart from the open ocean, yet shimmying obligingly with the forces of water and wind. The Outer Banks can be—and on many occasions have been—profoundly transformed by a single storm. A powerful hurricane can fill in a centuries-old inlet in one night, and open a new channel wherever it pleases. As recently as 2003, Hatteras Island was cut in half—by Hurricane Isabel—though the channel has since been artificially filled. This evanescent landscape poses challenges to the life that it supports, and creates adaptable and hardy plants, animals, and people.

The Sounds are often overlooked by travelers, but they are an enormously important part of the state and region. Collectively known as the Albemarle-Pamlico Estuary, North Carolina's Sounds—Albemarle, Pamlico, Core, Croatan, Roanoke, and Currituck—form the second-largest estuarine system in the country (second only to the Chesapeake Bay). They cover nearly 3,000 square miles, and drain more than 30,000. The diverse marine and terrestrial environments shelter crucial plant and animal communities, as well as estuarine systems that are essential to the environmental health of the whole region, and to the Atlantic Ocean.

Sheltered from the Atlantic, the Inner Banks are much more accommodating, ecologically speaking, than the Outer Banks. Wetlands along the Sounds invite migratory birds by the hundreds of thousands to shelter and rest, while pocosins (a special kind of bog found in the region) and maritime forests have nurtured

© JIM MOREKIS

HIGHLIGHTS

◖ **Wright Brothers National Memorial:** This American treasure provides a fun, educational, and ultimately stirring chronicle of one of the greatest achievements in history: powered flight (page 25).

◖ **Jockey's Ridge State Park:** The largest sand dune in the eastern United States is a great place to romp, relax, enjoy the view, or fly a kite (page 26).

◖ **Fort Raleigh National Historic Site:** Here at the site of the Lost Colony, the mysterious first chapter of English settlement in the New World unfolded in the 1580s (page 33).

◖ **Ocracoke Island:** On this remote island, you'll find a historic village that is the home of one of America's most unique local communities, as well as some serious water sports and walking opportunities (page 40).

◖ **The Great Dismal Swamp:** This natural wonder straddling the Virginia/Carolina line is an amazing place for canoeing or kayaking, bird-watching, and sightseeing (page 43).

◖ **Somerset Place Historic Site:** The graceful architecture and exotic setting of this early plantation contrast with the tragic history of its slavery days (page 47).

◖ **Pettigrew State Park:** Lake Phelps, the centerpiece of Pettigrew State Park, is an attractive enigma, a body of shallow water and deep history (page 47).

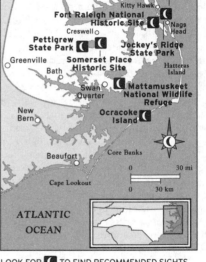

LOOK FOR ◖ TO FIND RECOMMENDED SIGHTS, ACTIVITIES, DINING, AND LODGING.

◖ **Mattamuskeet National Wildlife Refuge:** The landmark lodge on Lake Mattamuskeet towers over a dramatic waterscape that attracts migratory birds by the tens of thousands (page 49).

a great multitude of life for eons. Here is where North Carolina's oldest towns—Bath, New Bern, and Edenton—set down roots, from which the rest of the state grew and bloomed. In Washington County, 4,000-year-old canoes pulled out of Lake Phelps testify to the region's unplumbed depths of history.

PLANNING YOUR TIME

The reasons for visiting the coast in spring and summer are obvious: the beach, the restaurants and attractions that are only open in-season,

and the warm-weather festivals. But coastal North Carolina is beautiful four seasons of the year, and for many people fall and winter are favorite times to visit.

Around the time that the beach-bound traffic starts to thin out a little, towards the end of summer, eastern North Carolina's other busy season begins. Slow-moving trucks carry loads of loose tobacco leaves, bound from the field to the barn for curing. Stray yellow-green, wilted leaves litter the roadsides, blown off the trucks. On Saturdays in the early autumn,

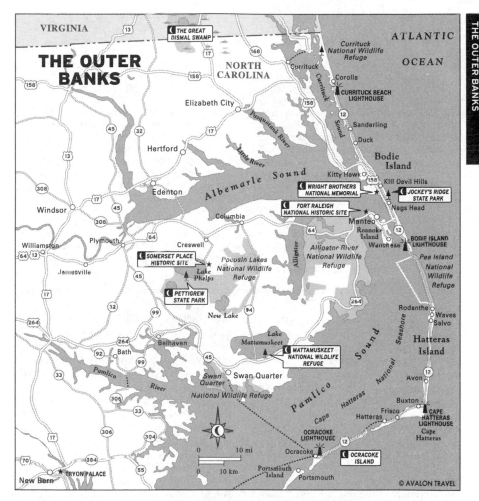

THE OUTER BANKS

the air is heavy in pockets with the smoke of yard fires, as folks clear out their summer gardens and the hot-weather overgrowth on their properties, and prepare for the cool-weather planting season. Collard patches are put in, often right alongside houses. At their sweetest after being touched by frost, collards are a favorite among fanciers of greens who prefer that musty mildness to the acrid twang of mustard greens. Cotton comes ripe late in the year. As the bolls begin to ripen, farm workers strip off the plants' leaves, until only the

flowering bolls remain atop the stalks. The stark beauty of a field of ripe cotton is a mesmerizing sight.

Fall and winter are wonderful times for canoeing and kayaking on eastern North Carolina's rivers, creeks, and swamps. The weather is often more than mild enough for comfort, and the landscape and wildlife are not so obscured by tropical verdancy as they are in the spring and summer. A word of caution: Don't assume that you won't encounter alligators or snakes in the winter. They're

PRONUNCIATION PRIMER

North Carolina is full of oddly pronounced place names, and this farthest northeast corner is a good place to pause for our first lesson in talking like a native. The Outer Banks are a garland of peculiar names, as well as names that look straightforward but are in fact pronounced in unexpectedly quirky ways. If you make reference publicly to the town of Corolla, and pronounce it like the Toyota model, you'll be recognized right away as someone "from off." It's pronounced "Ker-AH-luh." Similarly, Bodie Island, site of the stripy lighthouse, is pronounced "Body," as in one's earthly shell. That same pattern of pronouncing Os as Ahs, as in "stick out your tongue and say 'ah,'" is repeated farther down the coast at Chicamacomico, which comes out "Chick-uh-muh-CAH-muh-co." But

just to keep you on your toes, the rule doesn't apply to Ocracoke, which is pronounced like the Southern vegetable and Southern drink: "Okra-coke."

Farther south along the banks is the town of Rodanthe, which has an elongated last syllable, "Ro-DANTH-ee." On Roanoke Island, Manteo calls out for a Spanish emphasis, but is in fact front-loaded, like so many Carolina words and names. It's pronounced "MAN-tee-oh," or "MANNY-oh." Next door is the town of Wanchese. This sounds like a pallid dairy product, "WAN-cheese." Inland, the Cashie River is pronounced "Cuh-SHY," Bertie County is "Ber-TEE," and Chowan County is "Chuh-WON." Think the names around here are singular? Just wait 'til you get to the mountains.

never far away, and even a brief warm spell can have them out of their dens and looking for trouble. Wear snake boots if you have them, don't wade or swim in fresh water, and keep a lookout for gators' snouts along the surface of the water. Oftentimes all that's visible of an alligator are his nostrils and the little bony ridges of his brow. Spend enough time around gators, and you'll become accustomed to scanning the water before putting in.

Autumn, of course, is peak hurricane season. Dazzlingly beautiful in their ferocity, hurricanes are an unforgettable experience for anyone who has lived through one. For all the thrill, though, one should go to great pains to avoid them. Evacuation orders must always be obeyed, because hurricanes really are deadly, and highly unpredictable.

GETTING THERE AND AROUND

The closest major airport to this region is the **Norfolk International Airport** (2200 Norview Ave., 757/857-3351, www.norfolk airport.com), approximately an hour from the northern Outer Banks. **Raleigh-Durham**

International Airport (2600 W. Terminal Blvd., 919/840-2123, www.rdu.com) is 3–5 hours from most Outer Banks destinations.

Only two bridges exist between the mainland and the northern Outer Banks. U.S. 64/264 crosses over Roanoke Island to Whalebone, just south of Nags Head. Not too far north of there, Highway 158 crosses from Point Harbor to Southern Shores. Highway 12 is the main road all along the northern Outer Banks.

If you look at a map, Highway 12 is shown crossing from Ocracoke to Cedar Island, as if there's an impossibly long bridge over Pamlico Sound. In fact, that stretch of Highway 12 is a ferry route. The **Cedar Island-Ocracoke Ferry** (800/856-0343, www.ncdot.org/transit/ferry), which is a 2.25-hour ride, costs $15 per regular-sized vehicle, one-way. The other ferries (all with information at www.ncdot.org/transit/ferry), from north to south, are: **Currituck-Knotts Island** (877/287-7488, free, 45 min.); **Hatteras-Ocracoke** (800/368-8949, free, 40 min.); and **Ocracoke-Swan Quarter** (800/345-1665, $15/ regular-sized vehicle, one-way, 2.5 hours). There is also an inland ferry between **Bayview and Aurora** (252/964-4521, free, 30 min.).

Nags Head and Vicinity

The Outer Banks of North Carolina, unlike many barrier islands elsewhere in the world, are not attached to anchoring coral reefs. Instead, the Banks are a long sandbar, constantly eroding and amassing, slip-sliding into new configurations with every storm. The wind is the invisible player in this process, the man behind the curtain giving orders to the water and the sand. The enormous dune known as Jockey's Ridge was a landmark to early mariners, visible from miles out to sea.

According to legend, Nags Head was a place of sinister peril to those seafaring men. Islanders, it's said, would walk a nag or mule, carrying a lantern around its neck, slowly back and forth along the beach, trying to lure ships into the shallows where they might founder or wreck, making their cargo easy pickings for the land pirates.

It was the relentless wind at Kill Devil Hill that attracted the Wright brothers to North Carolina. It also brought the Rogallos, pioneer hang-glider inventors. Today, it brings thousands of enthusiasts every year, hang-gliders and parasailers, kite-boarders and kite-flyers. Add to these pursuits sailing, surfing, kayaking, hiking, birding, and, of course, beach-going, and the northern Outer Banks are perhaps North Carolina's most promising region for outdoor adventurers. Several reserves encompass large swaths of the unique ecological environments of the Banks, though increasingly the shifting sands are given over to the gamble of human development.

SIGHTS
◖ Wright Brothers National Memorial

Though they are remembered for a 12-second flight on a December morning in 1903, Wilbur and Orville Wright actually spent more than three years coming and going between their home in Dayton, Ohio, and Kitty Hawk, North Carolina. As the Wright Brothers tested their gliders on Kill Devil Hill, the tallest sand dune on the Outer Banks, locals fed and housed them, built hangars, and assisted with countless

practicalities that helped make the brothers' experiment a success. That first powered flight, and three subsequent ones less commonly known, are honored at the Wright Brothers National Memorial (Milepost 7.5 of Hwy. 158, Kill Devil Hills, 252/473-2111, www.nps.gov/wrbr, park open daily year-round, visitors center 9 A.M.–6 P.M. daily June–Aug., 9 A.M.–5 P.M.

THE OUTER BANKS

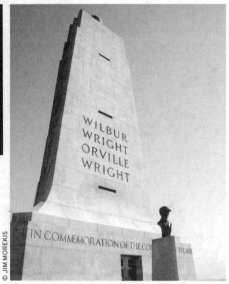

© JIM MOREKIS

the Wright Brothers National Memorial

NAGS HEAD
IN 1849

My first impressions of Nag's Head were very favorable...when we hove in sight of the harbor, in the gray of the morning, and saw the sun rise over Nag's Head, making still more than the usual contrast between the white sand-hills and the dark, beautiful green of its clusters of oak, when we discerned the neat white cottages among the trees, the smoke curling lazily from the low chimneys, the fishing-boats and other small craft darting to and fro, the carts plying between the shore and the dwellings, the loiterers who were eager to know who and how many had arrived...

Gregory Seaworthy, *Nags Head, or, Two Months Among "the Bankers"*
(1849)

daily Sept.–May, $4 per person). At the visitors center, replica gliders are on display, along with artifacts from the original gliders and changing displays sponsored by NASA. Occasional ranger programs are very educational, and you should try and catch one if you can.

You can also tour the reconstructed living quarters and flight hangar, and, of course, climb Kill Devil Hill to get a glimpse of what that first aviator saw. The elegant memorial at the top of Kill Devil Hill is a stirring monument to the brothers' work. At the base of the hill, you'll see markers at the end points of each of the powered flights that took place here.

◖ Jockey's Ridge State Park

Jockey's Ridge State Park (Carolista Dr. off Milepost 12 of Hwy. 158, Nags Head, 252/441-7132, www.jockeysridge statepark.com, 8 A.M.–6 P.M. daily Nov.–Feb., 8 A.M.–8 P.M. daily Mar. and Oct., 8 A.M.–8 P.M. daily Apr., May, and Sept., 8 A.M.–9 P.M. daily June–Aug., free) contains 420 acres of a strange and amazing environment, the largest active sand dune system in the eastern United States.

No one should miss this when they're in the area, especially considering it's free.

Ever-changing, this ocean-side desert is maintained by the constant action of the northeast and southwest winds. Visitors can walk on and among the dunes. It's a famously great place to fly kites, go sand-boarding, and hang-glide. (Hang-gliding requires a valid USHGA rating and a permit supplied by the park office.)

Kids especially will love running free across these seemingly limitless sands, and adults will enjoy the views from the top of the ridge. Keep in mind: It's easy to get lost and lose your way back to the parking lot—there's a lot of sand here!

Nags Head Woods Ecological Preserve

Bordering Jockey's Ridge is another unique natural area, the Nature Conservancy's Nags Head Woods Ecological Preserve (701 W. Ocean Acres Dr., about 1 mile from Milepost

THE OUTER BANKS

© JIM MOREKIS

on top of the dune at Jockey's Ridge State Park

9.5 of Hwy. 158, 252/441-2525, dawn–dusk daily year-round). Nags Head Woods is over 1,000 acres of deciduous maritime forest, dunes, wetlands, and inter-dune ponds. More than 50 species of birds nest here in season, including ruby-throated hummingbirds, green herons, and red-shouldered hawks, and it is also home to a host of other animals and unusual plants. Maps to the public trails are available at the visitors center.

Kitty Hawk Woods

Slightly smaller but no less important is the Nature Conservancy's Kitty Hawk Woods (south of Hwy. 158 at Kitty Hawk, trail access from Woods Rd. and Birch Ln., off Treasure St., 252/261-8891, dawn–dusk daily year-round). These maritime forests harbor the unusual species of flora and fauna of the maritime swale ecosystem, a swampy forest sheltered between coastal ridges. Kitty Hawk Woods is open to the public for hiking and birding, and can be explored from the water as well. A canoe and kayak put-in is next to the parking lot of **Kitty Hawk Kayaks** (6150

N. Croatan Rd./Hwy. 158, 252/261-0145, www.khkss.com).

Currituck Heritage Park

The shore of Currituck Sound is an unexpected place to find the art deco home of a 1920s industrial magnate. The **Whalehead Club** (1100 Club Rd., off of Milepost 11 from Route 12, 252/452-9040, www.whaleheadclub.com, visitors center open 11 A.M.–5 P.M. daily, standard tours 9 A.M.–4 P.M. daily, specialty tours require 24 hours advance notice, $5–15) was built as a summer cottage by Edward Collings Knight, Jr., an industrialist whose fortune was in railroads and sugar. This beautifully simple yellow house—only a "cottage" by the standards of someone like Knight—sits on a peaceful spit of land that catches the breeze off the sound. It's the centerpiece of Currituck Heritage Park (dawn–dusk daily, free), where visitors can picnic, wade, or launch from the boat ramp, in addition to touring the house.

Next to the Whalehead Club is the **Outer Banks Center for Wildlife Education** (Currituck Heritage Park, Corolla, 252/453-

INNOCENCE EXCEPTED

In 1728, William Byrd of Westover, a Virginia planter and man of letters, took part in an expedition to mark the dividing line between his home state and North Carolina. In his *Histories of the Dividing Line*, he detailed his adventures in the marshy wilds of Carolina, including a March 1728 encounter with a pair of castaways at Currituck Inlet.

While we continued here, we were told that on the south shore, not far from the inlet, dwelt a marooner, that modestly called himself a hermit, though he forfeited that name by suffering a wanton female to cohabit with him.

His habitation was a bower, covered with bark after the Indian fashion, which in that mild situation protected him pretty well from the weather. Like the ravens, he neither plowed nor sowed, but subsisted chiefly upon oysters, which his handmaid made a shift to gather from the adjacent rocks. Sometimes, too, for change of diet, he sent her to drive up the neighbor's cows, to moisten their mouths with a little milk. But as for raiment, he depended mostly upon his length of beard, and she upon her length of hair, part of which she brought decently forward, and the rest dangled behind quite down to her rump, like one of Herodotus's East Indian pygmies.

Thus did these wretches live in a dirty state of nature, and were mere Adamites, innocence only excepted.

0221, www.ncwildlife.org, 9 A.M.–5 P.M. daily, free). With exhibits focusing on the native birds, fish, and other creatures of Currituck Sound, the Center also has a huge collection of antique decoys—an important folk tradition of the Carolina coast—and offers many special nature and art programs throughout the year. (Check the website for a program calendar.)

The 1875 **Currituck Beach Lighthouse** (Currituck Heritage Park, 252/453-4939, www.currituckbeachlight.com, 9 A.M.–8 P.M. daily Easter–October, 10 A.M.–5 P.M. daily in November, closed December–Easter, closed in very rough weather, $7, children under 7 free) stands on the other side of the Center for Wildlife Education. It is one of the few historic lighthouses that visitors can climb. The 214-step spiral staircase leads to the huge Fresnel lens, and a panoramic view of Currituck Sound.

Corolla Wild Horse Museum

In the town of Corolla, the circa-1900 Corolla Schoolhouse has been transformed into a museum honoring the wild horses of the Outer Banks. The Corolla Wild Horse Museum (1126 Schoolhouse Ln., Corolla, 252/453-8002, www.corollawildhorses.com, 10 A.M.–4 P.M. Mon.–Sat. in the summer, off-season hours vary, free) tells of the history of the herd, which once roamed all over Corolla, but now live in a preserve north of the town.

ENTERTAINMENT AND EVENTS

Chip's Wine and Beer Market (Milepost 6, Croatan Hwy./Route 158, Kill Devil Hills, 252/449-8229, www.chipswinemarket.com) is, in addition to what the name suggests, the home of **Outer Banks Wine University.** In at least two classes a week, Chip himself and other instructors host wine and beer tastings with an educational as well as gustatory bent.

Nightlife

The **Outer Banks Brewing Station** (Milepost 8.5, Croatan Hwy./Hwy.

158, Kill Devil Hills, 252/449-2739, www.obbrewing.com, 11:30 A.M.–3 P.M. and 5–10 P.M. Sat. and Sun., 3–10 P.M. Mon. and Wed.–Fri., closed Tues.) was founded in the early 1990s by a group of friends who met in the Peace Corps. The brewery/restaurant they built here was designed and constructed by Outer Bankers, modeled on the design of the old life-saving stations so important in the region's history. The pub serves several very gourmet homebrews at $4.50 for a pint, and $6 for four five-ounce samplers. They've also got a nice lunch and supper menu, with elaborate entrées as well as the requisite pub fare.

Bacu Grill (Outer Banks Mall, Milepost 14 on Hwy. 158, Nags Head, 252/480-1892), a Cuban-fusion restaurant, features live jazz and blues music, and serves good beer, wine, and snacks into the wee hours of the morning. **Kelly's Outer Banks Restaurant and Tavern** (Milepost 10.5 on Hwy. 158, Nags Head, 252/441-4116, www.kellysrestaurant.com, 4:30 P.M.–midnight Sun.–Thurs., 4:30 P.M.–2 A.M. Fri.–Sat.) is also a good bet for live music, and has a long wine list with some lovely vintages. **Lucky 12 Tavern** (3308 S. Virginia Dare Tr., Nags Head, 252/255-5825, www.lucky12tavern.com, 11:30 A.M.–2 A.M. daily) is a traditional sports bar with TVs, foosball, and New York–style pizza.

SPORTS AND RECREATION
Hiking and Touring
The **Currituck Banks National Estuarine Research Reserve** (Hwy. 12, 252/261-8891, www.nccoastalreserve.net) protects nearly 1,000 acres of woods and water extending into Currituck Sound. A third-of-a-mile boardwalk runs from the parking lot to the sound, and a primitive trail runs from the parking lot 1.5 miles through the maritime forest.

Back Country Outfitters and Guides (107-C Corolla Light Town Center, Corolla, 252/453-0877, http://outerbankstours.com) leads a variety of tours in the Corolla region, including Segway beach tours, wild horse–watching trips, kayaking, and other off-road tours.

Surfing
The North Carolina coast has a strong surfing culture—not to mention strong waves—making this a top destination for experienced surfers and those who would like to learn.

Island Revolution Surf Co. and Skate Park (252/453-9484, www.islandrevolution.com, group lessons $60/person, private $75, must be older than 8 and a good swimmer) offers private and one-on-one surfing lessons as well as board rentals. So do **Ocean Atlantic Rentals** (Corolla Light Town Center, 252/453-2440, www.oceanatlanticrentals.com, $50/person group lessons, $75 private, $120 couples, must know how to swim, locations also in Duck, Nags Head, and Avon), and **Corolla Surf Shop** (several locations, 252/453-9283, www.corollasurfshop.com, 9 years old and up).

Online resources for Outer Banks surfing include the website of the Outer Banks District of the Eastern Surfing Association (http://outerbanks.surfesa.org), www.wrightcoastsurf.com, www.obxsurfinfo.com, and www.surfkdh.com.

Kayaking
The Outer Banks combines two very different possible kayaking experiences—the challenge of ocean kayaking, and the leisurely drifting zones of the salt marshes and back creeks. **Kitty Hawk Sports** (798 Sunset Blvd., 252/453-6900, www.kittyhawksports.com) is an old and established outdoors outfitter that leads kayaking and other expeditions. Another good bet is **Kitty Hawk Kayaks** (6150 N. Croatan Hwy., Kitty Hawk, 866/702-5061, www.khkss.com), which teaches kayaking and canoeing, rents equipment for paddling and surfing, and leads tours (including overnight expeditions) through gorgeous waterways in pristine habitats, in cooperation with the Nature Conservancy.

Kitty Hawk Kites (877/359-8447, www.kittyhawk.com), which *National Geographic Adventure* magazine calls one of the "Best Adventure Travel Companies on Earth," has

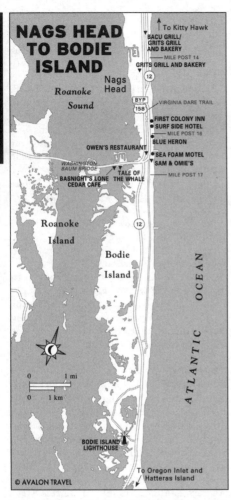

NAGS HEAD TO BODIE ISLAND

To Kitty Hawk
BACU GRILL/
GRITS GRILL
AND BAKERY
MILE POST 14
GRITS GRILL AND BAKERY

Roanoke
Sound

Nags
Head

BYP
158
VIRGINIA DARE TRAIL

FIRST COLONY INN
SURF SIDE HOTEL
MILE POST 16
BLUE HERON

OWEN'S RESTAURANT

SEA FOAM MOTEL
SAM & OMIE'S

WASHINGTON
BAUM BRIDGE
TALE OF
THE WHALE
MILE POST 17

BASNIGHT'S LONE
CEDAR CAFE

Roanoke
Island

Bodie
Island

ATLANTIC OCEAN

0   1 mi
0   1 km

BODIE ISLAND
LIGHTHOUSE

To Oregon Inlet and
Hatteras Island

© AVALON TRAVEL

locations throughout the Outer Banks, including at Corolla. They too teach and lead hang-gliding, parasailing, Jet Skiing, kiteboarding, kayaking, and lots more ways to ride the wind and water.

ACCOMMODATIONS
Under $150

In Kitty Hawk and Nags Head, you'll find an abundance of motels, from chains to classic 1950s mom-and-pops. The **Surf Side Hotel** (6701 Virginia Dare Tr., Nags Head, 800/552-7873, www. surfsideobx.com, from $55 out of season, from $165 in-season) is a favorite for simple and comfortable accommodations, with standard rooms and efficiencies in a location right on the dunes.

All rooms at the **Blue Heron** (6811 Virginia Dare Tr., Nags Head, 252/441-7447, www. blueheronnc.com, from $50 out of season, from $130 in-season) face the ocean. The Blue Heron has a heated indoor pool as a consolation on rainy days.

Super-affordable is the **Sea Foam Motel** (7111 Virginia Dare Tr., Nags Head, 252/441-7320, www.seafoam.com, from $62 out of season, from $140 in-season), an old-timer with a lot of retro appeal.

Other good choices in the area include the **Colony IV By The Sea** (405 S. Virginia Tr., Kill Devil Hills, 252/441-5581, from $70 out of season, from $85 in-season) and **Beach Haven Motel** (Ocean Rd. Milepost 4, Kitty Hawk, 252/261-4785, from $65 out of season, from $105 in-season).

$150–300

The ◖ **First Colony Inn** (6720 Virginia Dare Trail, Nags Head, 800-368/9390, www.first colonyinn.com, $79–329/night depending on season) is a wonderful 1932 beachfront hotel. This regional landmark has won historic preservation and landscaping awards for its 1988 renovation, which involved moving the entire building, in three pieces, three miles south of its original location. The pretty and luxurious rooms are surprisingly affordable.

The **Sanderling Resort and Spa** (1461 Duck Rd., near Duck, 877/650-4812, www .thesanderling.com, $130–450) is a full-sized, conventional resort, with three lodges, a spa, three restaurants (on- and off-site) including the **Lifesaving Station,** housed in an 1899 maritime rescue station, and various sports and recreational rental options.

Bed-and-breakfasts include the sound-front **Cypress Moon Inn** (1206 Harbor Ct., Kitty Hawk, 877/905-5060, www.cypressmoon inn.com, no guests under 18, $210), with three pretty guest rooms.

The **Baldview B&B** (3805 Elijah Baum Rd., Kitty Hawk, 252/255-2829, www.baldview.com, $150–200, no children or pets) is a modern residence located on a beautiful property along the sound, with four nicely appointed guestrooms and a carriage house.

The three guest rooms at the **Duck Inn** (1158 Duck Rd., Duck, 252/261-2300, www.theduckinnbnb.com, $125–250/night, depending on season) are also on the sound, with a nice dock and gazebo for guests to use. The **Colington Creek Inn** (1293 Colington Rd., Kill Devil Hills, 252/449-4124, www.colingtoncreekinn.com, $198, no children or pets) is a large outfit with a great view of the sound and the creek it's named for.

The **Cypress House Inn** (Milepost 8, Beach Rd., Kill Devil Hills 800/554-2764, www.cypresshouseinn.com, $120–200, depending on season) is a very traditional coastal Carolina-style house, built in the 1940s, with an easy walk to the beach. Its hurricane shutters and cypress-paneled rooms will give you a taste of Outer Banks life in the days before the motels and resorts.

FOOD

Sam & Omie's (7728 S. Virginia Dare Trail, Nags Head, 252/441-7366, www.samandomies.net, 7 A.M.–10 P.M. March–mid-Dec., $11–20) was opened during the summer of 1937, a place for charter fishing customers and guides to catch a spot of breakfast before setting sail. It still serves breakfast, with lots of options in the eggs and hotcakes department, including a few specialties like crab and eggs Benedict. It also has a dinner menu starring seasonal steamed and fried oyster, Delmonico steaks, and barbecue.

Tale of the Whale (7575 S. Virginia Dare Tr., Nags Head, 252/441-7332, www.taleofthewhalenagshead.com, dinner entrées $15–50) sits at a beautiful location, at the very edge of the water with a pier jutting into Roanoke Sound. There's outdoor music from a pier-side gazebo and a dining room with such a great view of the water that it feels like the inside of a ship—but the real draw is the incredibly

extensive menu of seafood, steak, and pasta specials. They also have an imaginative cocktail menu.

Grits Grill and Bakery (5000 S. Croatan Hwy., Nags Head, 252/449-2888, 6 A.M.–3 P.M.) is a favorite for breakfast, famous for its biscuits, Krispy Kreme donuts, eggs, and, of course, grits.

The **Blue Point** (1240 Duck Rd., Duck, 252/261-8090, www.goodfoodgoodwine.com, $20–35) has a nouveau Southern menu, with staples like catfish and trout done up in the most creative ways. Among the specialties, fresh Carolina shrimp is presented on "barley risotto," with broccolini, wine-soaked raisins, and lemon arugula pesto. Try the key lime pie with raspberry sauce, Kentucky bourbon pecan pie, or seasonal fruit cobblers. After-dinner drinks (among them espresso martinis and special dessert wines) complement an amazing wine list, which is, if anything, even more impressive than the menu. There are at least a dozen vintages in almost every category (prices ranging from $7/glass to $250/bottle), and several top-notch single-malts and small-batch bourbons. The Blue Point also occupies an amazing building, a custom-built waterside home with diner-style seating, an open kitchen with a counter and bar stools running its length, checkered floors, and a big screen porch. Reservations can be made online as well as by phone up to a month in advance, and are very necessary: Peak hours in season are booked two and three weeks in advance, while even winter weekends are usually booked solid several days before.

Owens' Restaurant (Milepost 16.5 on Beach Rd., Nags Head, 252/441-7309, www.owensrestaurant.com) has been in operation at Nags Head for more than 60 years, and in addition to their good seafood menu, visitors enjoy looking over the owners' collection of historical artifacts from Outer Banks maritime life.

Tortuga's Lie (Milepost 11.5 on Hwy. 158 on Beach Rd., 252/441-7299, www.tortugaslie.com, $7.50–17) has a good and varied menu specializing in seafood (some of it local) cooked in Caribbean-inspired dishes, with some good vegetarian options.

For casual and on-the-go chow options at Nags Head, try **Maxximuss Pizza** (5205 S. Croatan Hwy., Nags Head, 252/441-2377), which specializes in calzones, subs, and panini, in addition to pizza; **Yellow Submarine** (Milepost 14, Hwy. 158 Bypass, Nags Head, 252/441-3511), a super-casual subs and pizza shop; **Majik Beanz** (4104 S. Virginia Dare Tr., Nags Head, 252/255-2700) for coffee and shakes; or **New York Bagels** (Milepost 14 on Hwy. 158, 252/480-0106).

INFORMATION AND SERVICES

The **Aycock Brown Welcome Center** (U.S. 158, MP 1.5, 252/261-464, www.outerbanks.org, 9 A.M.–5 P.M. daily Dec.–Feb., 9 A.M.–5:30 P.M. daily Mar.–May and Sept.–Nov., 9 A.M.–6 P.M. daily June–Aug.) is located in Kitty Hawk and provides regional travel information, There is a major hospital in Nags Head.

Roanoke Island

Roanoke Island was the site of the Lost Colony, one of the strangest mysteries in all of American history. Its sheltered location—nestled between the Albemarle, Roanoke, and Croatan Sounds, and protected from the ocean by Bodie Island—made Roanoke Island a welcoming spot for that party of ocean-weary Englishmen in the 1580s. Unhappily, they lacked the foresight to use one of the bed-and-breakfast inns in Manteo or Wanchese as their home base, so that after a hard day of fort-building they could relax with a hot bath and free Wi-Fi. Instead they cast their lots in the wilderness, and what befell them may never be known.

At the northern end of Roanoke Island is the town of Manteo and the Fort Raleigh National Historic Site. This is where most of the tourist

Fort Raleigh on Roanoke Island

© JIM MOREKIS

attractions and visitor services are concentrated. At the southern end is Wanchese, where some of Dare County's oldest families carry on their ancestral trades of fishing and boatbuilding.

🄲 FORT RALEIGH NATIONAL HISTORIC SITE

Fort Raleigh National Historic Site (1401 National Park Dr., Manteo, 252/473-5772, www.nps.gov/fora, park open sunup–sundown daily year-round except Christmas Day, visitors center 9 A.M.–5 P.M. daily Sept.–May, 9 A.M.–6 P.M. daily June–Aug., admission to park free, admission charged to Elizabethan Gardens and "The Lost Colony") comprises much of the original site of this first English settlement in the New World. Some of the earthworks associated with the original 1580s fort remain and have been preserved. The visitors center displays some of the artifacts discovered during this restoration effort. Two nature trails in the park explore the island's natural landscape and the location of a Civil War battle.

Within the National Historic Site, two of Manteo's most famous attractions operate autonomously. About 60 years ago, Manteo's **Elizabethan Gardens** (Fort Raleigh National Historic Site, 252/473-3234, www.elizabethangardens.org, hours vary by season and day of the week, $8 adult, $5 ages 5–17) was conceived by the Garden Club of North Carolina as a memorial to the settlers of Roanoke Island. Much of the beautifully landscaped park recreates the horticulture of the colonists' native England in the 16th century. Many special nooks throughout the gardens hold treasures, such as: an ancient live oak believed to have been standing in the colonists' time; a Shakespearean herb garden; and a 19th-century statue of Virginia Dare that lay underwater off the coast of Spain for two years, was salvaged from a fire in Massachusetts, and upon her arrival in North Carolina in the 1920s was considered so racy that for decades she was tossed back and forth like a hot potato all across the state.

Also within the park boundaries is

© AVALON TRAVEL

THE LOST COLONY

On July 4, 1584, an expedition of Englishmen commissioned by Sir Walter Raleigh dropped anchor near Hatteras Island. Within a couple of days, local Native Americans were coming and going from the English ships, scoping out trade goods and making proffers of Southern hospitality. They got on famously, and when the Englishmen crossed the ocean again to bring tidings of the land they had found to Raleigh and the Queen, two Indian men, Manteo and Wanchese, came along as guests. It seems that Wanchese was somewhat taciturn and found London to be no great shakes, but Manteo got a kick out of everything he saw, and decided that Englishmen were all right.

In 1585, a new expedition set out for Roanoke, this time intending to settle in earnest. When they reached the Pamlico Sound, their bad luck began. Most of their store of food was

the amphitheatre where *The Lost Colony* drama is performed

© JIM MOREKIS

soaked and ruined when seawater breached the ship, so from the moment they arrived on shore they were dependent on the mercy of the Indians. Manteo and Wanchese went to Roanoke chief Wingina to discuss the Englishmen's plight. Wanchese, who was, it would turn out, a man of superior insight, tried to convince Wingina to withhold help. But Manteo pled the colonists' case convincingly, and the Englishmen were made welcome. Winter rolled around, and the colonists, having grown fat and happy on the Indians' food, and were doing precious little to attain self-sufficiency. Then a silver cup disappeared from the Englishmen's compound. It was posited that the thief came from a nearby village, which was promptly burned to the ground. Worried about his own people, Wingina shuttered the soup kitchen, hoping the English would either starve or go away. Instead, they killed him. Three weeks later, an English supply ship arrived with reinforcements of men and materiel, but they found the colony deserted.

Yet another attempt was made, this time with whole families rather than gangs of rowdy single men. A young couple named Eleanor and Ananais Dare were expecting a child when they landed at Roanoke, and soon Virginia Dare was born, the first English child

born in America. The Native American situation grew worse, though, and the Roanoke tribe, now under the leadership of Wanchese, were unwilling to aid a new wave of colonists. Manteo, still a friend, tried to enlist the help of his kinfolks, but they were facing lean times as well. John White, leader of the expedition and grandfather of Virginia Dare, lit out on what he planned would be a fast voyage back to England for supplies and food. Through no fault of his own, it was three years before he was able to come back. When he did, he found no sign of the settlers, except "CRO" carved on a tree, and "CROATOAN" on a rail.

Thus began 400 years of wonderment and speculation that will probably never be resolved. Some believe that the English were killed, some that they were captured and sold into slavery among tribes farther inland. Several communities in the South of uncertain or mixed racial heritage believe themselves to be descendants of the lost colonists (and some evidence suggests that this might in fact be possible). The answers may never be found, and for the foreseeable future the mystery will still hang heavily over Roanoke Island and its two towns: Manteo and Wanchese.

the Waterside Theater. North Carolina has a long history of outdoor drama celebrating regional heritage, and the best known of the many productions across the state is Roanoke Island's *The Lost Colony* (Fort Raleigh National Historic Site, Roanoke, 252/473-3414, www.thelostcolony.org, $18 adults, $17 seniors, $10 children 11 and under, $22 "producer's circle" seats). Chapel Hill playwright Paul Green was commissioned to write the drama in 1937, to celebrate the 350th anniversary of Virginia Dare's birth. What was expected to be a single-season production has returned almost every year for more than 70 years, interrupted only occasionally for emergencies such as prowling German U-boats. The annual season of *The Lost Colony* typically runs from late May to the end of August.

SIGHTS

The wonderful **North Carolina Maritime Museum,** whose mother ship is located in Beaufort, operates a branch here on Roanoke Island (104 Fernando St., Manteo, 252/475-1750, 9 A.M.–5 P.M. Tues.–Sat., free). In addition to the many traditional Outer Banks working watercraft on display, the museum holds boat-building and -handling courses at its George Washington Creef Boathouse. Visitors not enrolled in classes can still come in and watch traditional boat builders at work in the shop.

The **North Carolina Aquarium on Roanoke Island** (374 Airport Rd., 3 miles north of Manteo, 866-332-3475, www.ncaquariums.com/ri/riindex.htm, 9 A.M.–5 P.M. daily, $8 adults, $7 seniors, $6 ages 6–17, under 5 free) is one of three state aquariums here on the North Carolina coast. It's a great place to visit and see all sorts of marine fauna: sharks and other, less ferocious, fish, crustaceans, octopuses, turtles, and more. Like its sister aquariums, it's also a research station where marine biologists track and work to conserve the native creatures of the coast.

Roanoke Island Festival Park (1 Festival Park, Manteo, 252/475-1500, www.roanoke

island.com, 9 A.M.–5 P.M. daily Feb. 19–Apr. 1, 9 A.M.–6 P.M. daily Apr. 1–Nov. 1, 9 A.M.–5 P.M. daily Nov. 1–Dec. 31, closed Jan. 1–Feb. 19, $8 adults, $5 ages 6–17, under 5 free) is a state-operated living history site. The highlight is the *Elizabeth II,* a reconstruction of a 16th-century ship like the ones that brought Sir Walter Raleigh's men to the New World. There are also a museum, a reconstructed settlement site, and several other places where costumed interpreters will tell you about daily life in the Roanoke colony.

ENTERTAINMENT AND EVENTS

Outer Banks Epicurean Tours (252/305-0952, www.outerbanksepicurean.com) are a wonderful way to dine royally, while learning about the rich culinary traditions of this region and how the Banks' natural history creates this unique cuisine. The four-hour tours, which start at $95/person (not including the price of any alcohol you wish to order), give a teeth-on introduction to the native fish and shellfish of the area and the heritage of the people who harvest them, to bees and beekeeping, local wineries and microbreweries, coastal barbecue, indigenous and colonial cuisines, and many other topics.

SHOPPING

Manteo Booksellers (105 Sir Walter Raleigh St., 252/473-1221, www.manteobooksellers.com, 10 A.M.–6 P.M. daily) is a great independent bookstore, specializing in Outer Banks history and nature, but with a wide selection for all tastes.

Endless Possibilities (105 Budleigh St., 252/475-1575, www.ragweavers.com, 10 A.M.–5 P.M. Mon.–Sat.) is an unusual sort of a shop. Here you can buy cool purses, boas, rugs, and other adornments of home and body, made from recycled second-hand clothes. All the profits go to support the Outer Banks Hotline Crisis Intervention and Prevention Center, a regional help line for victims of rape and domestic violence, and an HIV/AIDS information center. And if you happen to be in

Manteo for long enough, you can even take lessons here to learn how to weave.

ACCOMMODATIONS
Under $150

The **Island Guesthouse** (706 Hwy. 64, 252/473-2434, www.theislandmotel.com, rooms from $60 out of season, from $85 in-season, cottages from $125 out of season, from $200 in-season, pets welcome with fee) offers simple and comfortable accommodations in its guest house, with two double beds, air conditioning, and cable TV in each room. They also rent out three tiny, cute cottages.

Another affordable option is the **Duke of Dare Motor Lodge** (100 S. US 64, 252/473-2175, www.ego.net, from $42 in-season). It's a 1960s motel, not at all fancy, but a fine choice when you need an inexpensive place to lay your head.

Over in Wanchese, the **Wanchese Inn** (85 Jovers Ln., Wanchese, 252/475-1166, from $69 out of season, from $129 in-season) is a simple and inexpensive bed-and-breakfast. It's a nice Victorian house (with modern rooms), and there is a boat slip and available on-site parking for a boat and trailer. The **Island House** (104 Old Wharf Rd., 252/473-5619, www.islandhouse-bb.com, $85–175) was built in the early 1900s for a local Coast Guardsman, with wood cut from the property and nails forged on-site. It's very comfortable and quiet, and a big country breakfast is served every day.

The **Scarborough Inn** (524 Hwy. 64, 252/473-3979, www.scarborough-inn.com, $45–75 off-season, $85–125 in-season) is a small hotel with 14 rooms and great rates. It's the sort of old-time hotel that's hard to find these days.

$150-300

The **Roanoke Island Inn** (305 Fernando St., 877/473-5511, www.roanokeislandinn.com, $150–200) has been in the present owner's family since the 1860s. It's a beautiful old place, with a big porch that overlooks the marsh. They also rent a single cottage on a

private island, five minutes away by boat, and a nice cypress-shingled bungalow in town.

Another top hotel in Manteo is the **Tranquil House Inn** (405 Queen Elizabeth Ave., 800/458-7069, www.1587.com, $99–239). It's in a beautiful location (hard not to be, on this island), and downstairs is one of the best restaurants in town, 1587.

The **Cameron House Inn** (300 Budleigh St., Manteo, 800/279-8178, http://cameronhouseinn.com, $120–195) is a cozy 1919 Arts and Crafts–style bungalow. All of the indoor rooms are furnished in a lovely and understated Craftsman style, but the nicest room in the house is the porch, which has an outdoor fireplace, fans, and flowery trellises.

Over $300

The **《 White Doe Inn** (319 Sir Walter Raleigh St., 800/473-6091, www.whitedoeinn.com, from $175 out of season, from approx. $350 in-season) is one of North Carolina's premier inns. The 1910 Queen Anne is the largest house on the island, and is on the National Register of Historic Places. Rooms are exquisitely furnished in turn-of-the-century finery. Guests enjoy a four-course breakfast, evening sherry, espresso and cappuccino any time, and a 24-hour wine cellar. Spa services are available on-site, and you need only step out to the lawn to play croquet or bocce.

FOOD

《 Basnight's Lone Cedar Cafe (Nags Head–Manteo Causeway, 252/441-5405, www.lonecedarcafe.com, 5 P.M.–closing Mon.–Wed., 11:30 A.M.–3 P.M. and 5 P.M.–closing Thurs.–Sat., 11 A.M.–closing Sun., closed in winter, lunch entrées $7–27, dinner entrées $12–33) is a water-view bistro that specializes in local food—oysters from Hyde and Dare Counties, fresh-caught local fish, and North Carolina chicken, pork, and vegetables. It's one of the most popular restaurants on the Outer Banks, and they don't take reservations, so be sure to arrive early. The full bar is open until midnight.

The **Full Moon Cafe** (208 Queen Elizabeth

St., 252/473-6666, www.thefullmooncafe .com, 11:30 A.M.–9 P.M. daily in season, call for off-season hours, $10–30) is simple and affordable, specializing in quesadillas and enchiladas, wraps, sandwiches, a variety of seafood and chicken bakes, and quiches. Despite the seemingly conventional selection, the food here is so good that the Full Moon has received glowing reviews from the *Washington Post* and the *New York Post*—quite a feat for a little café in Manteo.

The **Magnolia Grille** (408 Queen Elizabeth St., 252/475-9877, www.roanokeisland.net/lp/ magnoliagrille, 7 A.M.–4 P.M. Sun. and Mon., 7 A.M.–8 P.M. Tues.–Sat.) is a super-inexpensive place for all three meals of the day, and snacks in between. They've got a great selection of breakfast omelets, burgers, salads, soups, and deli sandwiches, with nothing costing more than $7.

INFORMATION AND SERVICES

The **Outer Banks Welcome Center** is located in Manteo.

Cape Hatteras National Seashore

To many Americans, Cape Hatteras is probably familiar as a name often repeated during hurricane season. Protruding far out on the Atlantic Ocean, it's a landmark to centuries of mariners, and a prime target for storms.

Cape Hatteras, the "Graveyard of the Atlantic," lies near Diamond Shoals, a treacherous zone of shifting sandbars that lies between the beach and the Gulf Stream. Two channels, Diamond Slough and Hatteras Slough, cross the shoals in deep enough water for a ship to navigate safely, but countless ships have missed their mark and gone down off of Cape Hatteras. The 1837 wreck of the steamboat *Home* on the Shoals, which killed 90 passengers, led Congress to pass the Steamboat Act, which established the requirement of one life vest per passenger in all vessels.

Hurricane Isabel in 2003 inflicted tremendous damage, and even opened a new channel right across Hatteras Island, a 2,000-foot-wide swash that was called Isabel Inlet. It separated the towns of Hatteras and Frisco, washing out a large portion of the highway that links the Outer Banks. For some weeks afterwards, Hatteras residents had to live as their forebears had, riding ferries to school and to the mainland. The inlet has since been filled in and Highway 12 reconnected, but Isabel Inlet's brief reign of terror and inconvenience highlighted the vulnerability of life on the Outer Banks.

BODIE ISLAND

The 156-foot **Bodie Island Lighthouse** (6 mi. south of Whalebone Junction), whose huge Fresnel lens first beamed in 1872, was the third to guard this stretch of coast. The first light was built in the 1830s, but leaned like the Tower of Pisa. The next stood straight, but promised to be such a tempting target for the Yankee Navy during the Civil War that the Confederates blew it up themselves. (An unfortunate flock of geese nearly put the third lighthouse out of commission soon after its first lighting, when they collided with and damaged the lens.) The lighthouse is not open to the public, but the keeper's house has been converted into a visitors center (252/441-5711, call for seasonal hours). This is also the starting point for self-guided nature trails to Roanoke Sound through the beautiful marshy landscape of Bodie Island.

The **Oregon Inlet Campground** (Hwy. 12, 877/444-6777, $20/night), operated by the National Park Service, offers camping behind the sand dunes, with cold showers, potable water, and restrooms.

HATTERAS ISLAND

Cape Hatteras makes a dramatic arch along the North Carolina coast, sheltering the Pamlico Sound from the ocean as if in a giant cradling arm. The cape itself is the point of the elbow,

COURTESY OF WWW.OUTERBANKS.ORG

Chicamocomico Life-Saving Station

a totally exposed, vulnerable spit of land that's irresistible to hurricanes because it juts so far to the southeast. Along the Cape Hatteras National Seashore, Hatteras Island is just barely wide enough to support a series of small towns—Rodanthe, Waves, Salvo, Avon, Buxton, Frisco, and the village of Hatteras—and a great deal of dramatic scenery on all sides.

Sights

Lifesaving operations are an important part of North Carolina's maritime heritage. Corps of brave men occupied remote stations along the coast, ready at a moment's notice to risk—and sometimes to give—their lives to save foundering sailors in the relentlessly dangerous waters off the Outer Banks. In Rodanthe, the **Chicamocomico Life-Saving Station** (Milepost 39.5 on Hwy. 12, Rodanthe, 252/987-1552, www.chicamacomico.net, noon–5 P.M. Mon.–Fri. mid-Apr.–Nov., $6, $4 under 17 and over 62 years old) preserves the original station building, a handsome, gray-shingled 1874 building, the 1911 building that replaced it—and which now houses a museum

of fascinating artifacts from maritime rescue operations—and a complex of other buildings and exhibits depicting the lives of lifesavers and their families.

Cape Hatteras Lighthouse (near Buxton, 252/473-2111, www.nps.gov/caha/planyour visit, $7, $3.50 children and seniors, children smaller than 3'5" not permitted), at 208 feet tall, is the tallest brick lighthouse in the United States. It was built in 1870 to protect ships at sea from coming upon the Shoals unaware. It still stands on the cape, and it is open for climbing during the warm months. If you have a healthy heart, lungs, and knees, and are not claustrophobic, get your ticket and start climbing. The lighthouse is open daily from the third Friday in April–Columbus Day: 9 A.M.–4:30 P.M. in the spring and fall; 9 A.M.–5:30 P.M. early June–Labor Day. Tickets are required and are sold on the premises beginning at 8:15 A.M. Climbing tours run every ten minutes starting at 9 A.M.

Sports and Recreation

Pea Island National Wildlife Refuge (Hwy.

COURTESY OF WWW.OUTERBANKS.ORG

Cape Hatteras Lighthouse

12, 10 mi. south of Nags Head, 252/473-1131, www.fws.gov/peaisland) occupies the northern reach of Hatteras Island. Much of the island is covered by ponds, making this an exceptional place for watching migratory waterfowl. Two nature trails link some of the best bird-watching spots, and one, the half-mile North Pond Wildlife Trail, is fully wheelchair-accessible. Viewing and photography blinds are scattered along the trails for extended observation.

The Outer Banks owe their existence to the volatile action of the tides. The same forces that created this habitable sandbar also make this an incredible place for water sports. **Canadian Hole,** a spot in the sound between Avon and Buxton, is one of the most famous windsurfing and sail-boarding places in the world. (It goes without saying that it's also perfect for kite-flying.) The island is extraordinarily narrow here, so it's easy to tote your board from the sound side over to the ocean for a change of scene.

As with any sport, it's important to know your own skill level and choose activities accordingly. Beginners and experts alike, though, can benefit from the guidance of serious water sports instructors. **Real Kiteboarding** (Cape Hatteras, 866-732-5548, www.realkiteboarding.com) is the largest kiteboarding school in the world. They offer kiteboarding camps and classes in many aspects of the sport for all levels. **Outer Banks Kiting** (Avon, 252/305-6838, www.outerbankskiting.com) also teaches lessons and two-day camps, and carries boarders out on charter excursions to find the best spots.

There are all manner of exotic ways to tour Hatteras. **Equine Adventures** (252/995-4897, www.equineadventures.com) leads two-hour horseback tours through the maritime forests and along the beaches of Cape Hatteras. With **Hatteras Parasail** (Hatteras, 252/986-2627, www.hatterasparasail.com, $60 parasail ride, $35 kayak tour) you can ride 400 feet in the air near the coast, or even higher with **Burrus Flightseeing Tours** (Frisco, 252/986-2679, www.hatterasislandflightseeing.com, $50–70/person depending on flight and number of riders in party).

Accommodations
Among the lodging choices on Hatteras Island is the very fine **Inn on Pamlico Sound** (49684 Hwy. 12, Buxton, 252/995-7030, www.innonpamlicosound.com, $120–295 depending on season). The inn is right on the sound, with a private dock and easy waterfront access. The dozen suites are sumptuous and relaxing, many with their own decks or private porches. Another good choice is the **Cape Hatteras Bed and Breakfast** (46223 Old Lighthouse Rd./Cape Point Way, Buxton, 800/252-3316, $79–139), which is only a few hundred feet from the ocean. Guests rave about the breakfasts.

Simpler motel accommodations include the clean, comfortable, and pet-friendly **Cape Pines Motel** (47497 Hwy. 12, Buxton, 866/456-9983, www.capepinesmotel.com, $49–149 depending on season, $20/pet); the **Outer Banks Motel** (47000 Hwy.

12, Buxton, 252/995-5601, www.outer banksmotel.com, $49–300 depending on season and style of accommodation), with both motel rooms and cottages; and the **Avon Motel** (Avon, 252/995-5774, www.avonmotel .com, $43–131 depending on season and style of accommodation, $10/pet), a pet-friendly motel that has been in business for more than 50 years.

CAMPING

Rodanthe Watersports and Campground (24170 Hwy. 12, 252/987-1431, www.water sportsandcampground.com) has a sound-front campground for tents and RVs under 25 feet, with water and electrical hookups and hot-water showers. Rates are $24 per night for two people, $4.75 for each additional adult, $5 for children and dogs, and an extra $4.75 per night for electrical hookup.

The Park Service operates two campgrounds in this stretch of the National Seashore. The **Frisco Campground** opens in early April, and **Cape Point Campground** at Buxton opens in late May (46700 Lighthouse Rd., Buxton, and 53415 Billy Mitchell Rd., Frisco, 877/444-6777, $20/night). At Frisco, one actually camps in the dunes, whereas at Cape Point, like the other NPS campgrounds here, the campsites are level and located behind the dunes. All have cold showers, bathrooms, and potable water. **Frisco Woods Campground** (Hwy. 12, Frisco, 800/948-3942, www.outer-banks.com/friscowoods, $30–90/night depending on accommodations and season) has a full spectrum of camping options, from no-utilities tent sites and RV sites with partial or full hookup to one- and two-bedroom cabins. The campground has wireless Internet access, hot showers, and a coin laundry.

Food

Though the **Restaurant at the Inn on Pamlico Sound** (Hwy. 12, Buxton, 252 /995-7030, www.innonpamlicosound.com) is primarily for guests of the inn, if you call in advance you might be able to get a reservation

for dinner even if you're staying elsewhere. The chef likes to use fresh-caught seafood, sometimes caught by the guests themselves earlier in the day. Vegetarian dishes and other special requests are gladly served.

For breakfast, try the **Gingerbread House** (52715 Hwy. 12, Frisco, 252/995-5204), which serves great baked goods made on the premises.

◖ OCRACOKE ISLAND

Sixteen miles long, Ocracoke Island comprises the southernmost reach of the Cape Hatteras National Seashore. The history of Ocracoke Island is, frankly, a little bit eerie. There's the remoteness, first of all. One of the most geographically isolated places in North Carolina, it's only accessible today by water and air. Regular ferry service didn't start until 1960, and it was only three years before that that Ocracokers had their first paved highway. In 1585, it was one of the first places in North America seen by Europeans, when the future Lost Colonists ran aground here. It may have been during the time they were waylaid at Ocracoke ("Wococon," they called it) that the ancestors of today's wild ponies first set hoof on the Outer Banks. Theirs was not the last shipwreck at Ocracoke, and in fact, flotsam and goods that would wash up from offshore wrecks was one of the sources of sustenance for generations of Ocracokers.

In the early 18th century, Ocracoke was a favorite haunt of Edward Teach, better known as the pirate Blackbeard. He lived here at times, married his 14th wife here, and died here. Teach's Hole, a spot just off the island, is where a force hired by Virginia's Governor Spottswood finally cornered and killed him, dumping his decapitated body overboard (it's said to have swum around the ship seven times before going under), and sailing away with the trophy of his head on the bowsprit.

All of **Ocracoke Village,** near the southern end of the island, is on the National Register of Historic Places. While the historical sites of the island are highly distinctive, the most unique thing about the island and its people is the culture that has developed here over

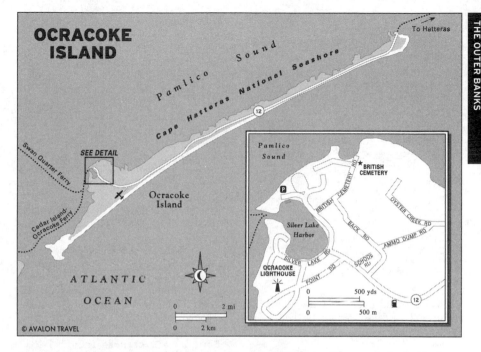

the centuries. Ocracokers have a "brogue" all their own, similar to those of other Outer Banks communities, but so distinctive that, in the unlikely event that there were two native Ocracokers who didn't know each other already, and they happened to cross paths somewhere out in the world, they would recognize each other right away as neighbors (and probably cousins) by the cadences of their speech.

Ocracoke Lighthouse

A lighthouse has stood on Ocracoke since at least 1798, but due to constantly shifting sands, the inlet that it protected kept sneaking away. Barely 20 years after that first tower was built, almost a mile stretched between it and the water. The current Ocracoke Light (village of Ocracoke, 888/493-3826) was built in 1823, originally burning whale oil to power the beam. It is still in operation—the oldest operating light in North Carolina, and the second oldest in the nation. Because it's on active duty, the public is not able to tour the inside, but a boardwalk nearby gives nice views.

British Cemetery

The British Cemetery (British Cemetery Rd.) is not, as one might suppose, a colonial burial, but rather a vestige of World War II. During the war, the Carolina coast was lousy with German U-boats. Many old-timers today remember catching a glimpse of a furtive German sub casing the beach. Defending the Outer Banks became a pressing concern, and on May 11, 1942, the HMS *Bedfordshire*, a British trawler sent to aid the U.S. Navy, was torpedoed by a German U-558. The *Bedfordshire* sank, and all 37 men aboard died. Over the course of the next week, four bodies washed up on Ocracoke—those of Lieutenant Thomas Cunningham, Ordinary Telegraphist Stanley Craig, and two unidentified men. An island family donated a burial plot, and there the four men lie today, memorialized with a plaque that bears a lovely verse by Rupert

THE OUTER BANKS

COURTESY OF
WWW.OUTERBANKS.ORG

the ferry to Ocracoke Island

Brooke, the young poet of World War I and member of the British Navy, who died of disease on his way to the battle of Gallipoli.

Sports and Recreation

Ride the Wind Surf Shop (www.surfocracoke.com) gives individual and group surfing lessons, for adults and children, covering ocean safety and surfing etiquette in addition to board handling. A three-day surf camp for kids ages 9–17 ($200, or $75/day) gives an even more in-depth tutorial. Ride the Wind also leads sunrise, sunset, and full-moon kayak tours around the marshes of Ocracoke ($35).

The **Schooner *Windfall*** (departs from Community Store Dock, Ocracoke, 252/928-7245, www.schoonerwindfall.com, daily May–Oct., $20–25), a beautiful 57-foot, old fashioned–looking schooner, sails on three one-hour tours a day around Pamlico Sound. Passengers are allowed, and even encouraged, to try their hand at the wheel or trimming the sails.

Accommodations

The **Captain's Landing** (324 Hwy. 12, 252/928-1999, www.thecaptainslanding.com, from $200 in-season, from $150 out of season), with a perch right on Silver Lake (the harbor) looking towards the lighthouse, is a modern hotel owned by a descendant of Ocracoke's oldest families. Suites have 1.5 baths, full kitchens, comfortable sleeper sofas for extra guests, and decks with beautiful views. They also have a bright, airy penthouse with two bedrooms, an office, a gourmet kitchen, and even a laundry room. The Captain's Cottage is a private two-bedroom house, also smack on the water, with great decks and its own courtyard.

The **Pony Island Motel and Cottages** (785 Irvin Garrish Hwy., 866/928-4411, www.ponyislandmotel.com, from $105 in-season, from $60 out of season) has been in operation since the late 1950s, and run by the same family for more than 40 years. It has regular and efficiency motel rooms, and four cottages on the grounds. Clean rooms, a good location, and year-round good prices make this a top choice on the island.

Edwards of Ocracoke (800/254-1359, www.edwardsofocracoke.com, from $43 spring and fall, from $90 summer) has several cozy bungalows typical of coastal Carolina, referred to here as "vintage accommodations." The mid-20th century vacation ambiance is very pleasant, the cabins are very clean and well kept, and the prices are great.

The **Island Inn** (25 Lighthouse Rd., 252/928-4351, www.ocracokeislandinn.com, from $60 out of season, from $100 in-season, children in villas only) is on the National Register of Historic Places, and bills itself as the oldest operating business on the Outer Banks. It was built in 1901, first used as an Odd Fellows Hall, later as a barracks during World War II. The building is made of salvaged shipwreck wood, which everyone knows brings strange juju; add that fact to the 1950s murder of a caretaker, and the discovery of colonial bones under the lobby, and it's a given that the place is haunted. The resident wraith is believed to be a lady ghost, because she seems to enjoy checking out female guests' cosmetics and clothes, which will sometimes turn up in the morning in places other than where they were left the night before. No one's ever seen her, but her footsteps are sometimes heard in empty rooms, and she causes odd things to happen—most notably, unraveling an entire roll of toilet paper in the presence of a terrified guest. Like many hotel ghosts, she is most active during the inn's less crowded seasons.

CAMPING

At **Ocracoke Campground** (4352 Irvin Garrish Hwy., Ocracoke, 877/444-6777, $23/night), campsites are right by the beach, behind the dunes. Remember to bring extra-long stakes to anchor your tent in the sand.

Food

Ocracoke's **Café Atlantic** (1129 Irvin Garris Hwy., 252/928-4681, $14–21) has a large and eclectic menu, with tastes venturing into Italian, Nuevo Latino, and local fare. Lunch and dinner choices can be as simple as a BLT or a crab cake (with Pamlico Sound crabmeat), to *caciucco,* an Italian seafood stew. While many restaurants will accommodate vegetarians with a single pasta dish at the end of the entrée list, Café Atlantic has tons of non-meat-or-seafood options. They've also got an extensive wine list.

INFORMATION AND SERVICES

The **Cape Hatteras National Seashore Visitors Center** is located on Ocracoke and provides regional travel information.

On Ocracoke, only accessible by air or water, non-emergency medical situations can be addressed by **Ocracoke Health Center** (305 Back Rd., 252/928-1511, after hours 252/928-7425). (Note that 911 works on Ocracoke, as everywhere else.)

Across the Sounds

Referred to historically as the Albemarle, and sometimes today as the Inner Banks, the mainland portion of northeastern North Carolina is the hearth of the state's colonial history, the site of its first European towns and earliest plantation and maritime economies.

The Great Dismal Swamp is here, a region thought of by early Carolinians and Virginians as a diseased and haunted wasteland, the sooner drained the better. They succeeded to some extent in beating back the swamp waters and vapors, but left enough for modern generations to recognize as one of the state's crown jewels, a natural feature as valuable to humans as to the bears and wolves who hide within.

Early cities like Edenton and Bath were influential centers of government and commerce, and today preserve some of the best colonial and early federal architecture in the Southeast. The vast network of rivers and creeks include some of the state's best canoeing and kayaking waters, and along the

Albemarle Regional Canoe/Kayak Trail, there are a growing number of camping platforms on which to spend an unforgettable night listening to owls hoot and otters splash. Country kitchens are found throughout the small towns here, and there are even a few old-fashioned fish shacks in which to sample the inland seafood traditions. Water is the soul of this region, with the Sounds and the rivers and swamps guiding life on the land as surely as if it were touched by the ocean.

◖ THE GREAT DISMAL SWAMP

Viewed for centuries as an impediment to progress, the Great Dismal Swamp is now recognized for the national treasure that it is, and tens of thousands of acres are protected. There are several points from which to gain access to the interior of the Dismal Swamp. A few miles south of the Carolina/Virginia line, on Highway 17, is the **Dismal Swamp**

Welcome Center (2356 Hwy. 17 N., South Mills, 877/771-8333, www.dismalswamp.com, 9 A.M.–5 P.M. daily Memorial Day–Halloween, 9 A.M.–5 P.M. Tues.–Sat. the rest of the year). Should you be arriving by water, you'll find the Welcome Center at Mile 28 on the Intracoastal Waterway. You can tie up to the dock here and spend the night, if you wish, or wait for one of the four daily lock openings (8:30 A.M., 11 A.M., 1:30 P.M., and 3:30 P.M.) to proceed. There are also picnic tables and grills here, and restrooms open day and night.

Another area of the swamp to explore is the **Great Dismal Swamp National Wildlife Refuge** (Suffolk, VA, 757/986-3705, www.fws.gov/northeast/greatdismalswamp, open daylight hours), which straddles the state line. Two main entrances are outside of Suffolk, Virginia, off of the White Marsh Road/Route 642. These entrances, Washington Ditch and Jericho Lane, are open 6:30 A.M.–8 P.M. daily between April 1–September 30, and 6:30 A.M.–5 P.M. October 1–March 31. In the middle of the refuge is Lake Drummond, an eerie 3,100-acre natural lake that's a wonderful place for canoeing. (Contact Refuge headquarters for directions on navigating the feeder ditch that lets out into Lake Drummond.) You may see all sorts of wildlife in the swamp—including poisonous cottonmouths, canebrake rattlers, and copperheads, and possibly even black bears. One more word of caution: Controlled hunting is permitted on certain days in October, November, and December, so if visiting in the fall, wear bright clothing, and contact refuge staff in advance of your visit to find out about closures.

ELIZABETH CITY

The **Museum of the Albemarle** (501 S. Water St., 252/335-1453, www.museumofthe albemarle.com, 9 A.M.–5 P.M. Tues.–Sat., 2–5 P.M. Sun.) is a relatively new, and growing, museum. It explores the four centuries of history in northeastern North Carolina since the first English settlers arrived at Roanoke. Come here to learn about the Lost Colonists, the pirates who swarmed in this region, the folkways of the Sound country, and more.

EDENTON

Incorporated in 1722 but inhabited long before that, Edenton was one of North Carolina's most important colonial towns, and remains one of its most beautiful.

Historic District

The whole town is lined with historic buildings, and several especially important sites are clustered within a few blocks of each other near the waterfront. The easiest starting point for a walking tour (guided or on your own) is the headquarters of the **Edenton State Historic Site** (108 Broad St., 252/482-2637, www.edenton.nchistoricsites.org, 9 A.M.–5 P.M. Mon.–Sat. and 1–5 P.M. Sun. Apr.–Oct., 10 A.M.–4 P.M. Mon.–Sat. and 1–4 P.M. Sun. Nov.–Mar.), also referred to as the Edenton Visitors Center. The 1782 **Barker House** (505 S. Broad St., 252/482-7800, www.edenton historicalcommission.org, 10 A.M.–4 P.M. Mon.–Sat., 1–4 P.M. Sun.), a stunning Lowcountry palazzo, was the home of Penelope Barker, an early revolutionary and organizer of the Edenton Tea Party. It's now the headquarters of the Edenton Historical Commission, and the location of their bookstore. The 1758 **Cupola House** (408 Broad St., 252/482-2637, www.cupolahouse.org, 9 A.M.–4:30 P.M. daily, tickets available at Edenton Visitors Center) is a National Historical Landmark, a home of great architectural significance. Although much of the original interior woodwork was removed in 1918 and sold to the Brooklyn Museum, where it remains, the Cupola House has been restored meticulously inside and out, and its colonial gardens re-created. Also a designated National Historical Landmark is the **Chowan County Courthouse** (111 E. King St., 252/482-2637, www.edenton.nchistoricsites.org, hours vary by season), a superb 1767 brick building in the Georgian style. It's the best-preserved colonial courthouse in the United States.

Accommodations and Food

The **◖ Lords Proprietors' Inn** (300 N. Broad St., 888/394-6622, www.edentoninn .com, from $155) occupies not one but four exceptional historic buildings: the 1901 main White-Bond House, the 1801 Satterfield House, a 1915 tobacco storage barn remodeled with beautiful guestrooms, and the 1870 Tillie Bond House cottage. Each one of these is artfully restored, with soft and restful furnishings. Breakfast cook Janie Granby prepares wonderful specialties like lemon soufflé pancakes, and North Carolina native and star chef Kevin Yokley prepares four-course dinners that are dazzling. Entrées include grilled swordfish with artichoke vinaigrette, lamb porterhouse chops with dried cherry sauce, and breast of Muscovy duck with red currant sauce. The other courses are no less impressive.

The **Granville Queen Inn** (108 S. Granville St., 866/482-8534, www.granvillequeen .com, $95–135) is a rather splendid early-1900s mansion decorated in a variety of early 20th-century styles. Breakfasts are as ornate and elegant as the house itself, featuring poached pears, potato tortillas, crepes, and much more.

⦗ Holladay's Island Camping Platforms (315 Cannon's Ferry Rd., Tyner, 252/482-8595, www.visitedenton.com, price varies depending on number of campers, $20/night one person, privy at campsite) are part of the Albemarle Regional Canoe/Kayak Paddling Trail. The five 16- by 24-foot raised platforms sit in the middle of the Chowan River about 20 miles from Edenton, and about one mile from the nearest boat ramp.

WINDSOR

A small, historic town on the Cashie River, Windsor is the county seat of Bertie County. Historic architecture, good food, and wetlands exploration are equally compelling reasons to visit this lesser-known treasure of the Albemarle region. Pronunciation is a little perverse here: The county name is pronounced "Ber-TEE," and the river is the "Cuh-SHY."

Sights

Hope Plantation (132 Hope House Rd., 252/794-3140, www.hopeplantation.org,

10 A.M.–5 P.M. Mon.–Sat. and 2–5 P.M. Sun. Apr.–Oct., 10 A.M.–4 P.M. Mon.–Sat. and 2–5 P.M. Sun. Nov.–Mar., $8, $7 seniors, $3 under 18) was built in 1803 for the former Governor David Stone. Stone did not live to see his 50th birthday, but by the time of his death he had been the governor of North Carolina, a U.S. senator and congressman, a state senator, a Superior Court judge, and a seven-times-elected member of the State House. He graduated from Princeton and passed the bar when he was 20; he was the father of 11 children, and one of the founders of the University of North Carolina. High among his most impressive accomplishments was the construction of this wonderful house. Characterized by a mixture of Georgian and Federal styles with significant twists of regional and individual aesthetics, Hope House is on the National Register of Historic Places. Also on the National Register, and now on the grounds of the plantation, is the brick-end, gambrel roof King-Bazemore House. The King-Bazemore House was built in 1763, and is also a highly significant example of its form.

The **Roanoke-Cashie River Center** (112 W. Water St., Windsor, 252/794-2001, www.partnershipforthesounds.org/Roanoke CashieRiverCenter.aspx, 10 A.M.–4 P.M. Tues.– Sat., $2, $1 children) has interpretive exhibits about this region's history and ecology. There is a canoe ramp outside where you can get out into the Cashie River, and canoe rentals are available ($10/hour, $20 for a half-day, and $35 for a whole day).

Southeast of Windsor on the Cashie River, the **San Souci Ferry** (Woodard and San Souci Rds., 252/794-4277, 6:30 A.M.–6 P.M. Mar. 16–Sept. 16, 6:45 A.M.–5 P.M. Sept. 17–March 15) operates, as it has for generations, by a cable and a honk of the horn. To cross the river, pull up to the bank, honk your horn, and wait. Directly the ferryman will emerge and pull you across.

Food

Bunn's Bar-B-Q (127 King St., 252/794-

2274, from $5) is a barbeque and Brunswick stew joint of renown, an early gas station converted in 1938 to its present state. Super-finely chopped barbeque is the specialty, with coleslaw, cornbread, and plenty of sauce from those little red bottles you see on every surface.

WILLIAMSTON AND VICINITY

Williamston is at the junction of U.S. 17 and U.S. 64. If you're passing through town, Williamston is a great place to stop for barbecue or a fresh seafood meal.

Sights

A little ways west of Williamston on U.S. 13/64 Alt., you'll find the town of Robersonville and the **St. James Place Museum** (U.S. 64 Alt. and Outerbridge Rd., open year-round by appointment, call Robersonville Public Library at 252/795-3591). A Primitive Baptist church built in 1910 and restored by a local preservationist and folk art enthusiast, St. James Place is an unusual little museum that fans of Southern craft will not want to miss. A serious collection of traditional quilts is the main feature of the museum. Of the 100 on display, nearly half are African American quilts—examples of which are much less likely to survive and find their way into museum collections than are their counterpane counterparts made by white quilters. Getting a glimpse of the two traditions side by side is an education in these parallel Southern aesthetics.

On the same highway is **East Carolina Motor Speedway** (4918 U.S. 64 Alt., 252/795-3968, www.ecmsracing.com, pits open at 3 P.M., grandstands at 5 P.M., usually Apr.–Oct.), a 0.4-mile hard-surface track featuring several divisions, including late-model street stock, modified street-stock, super stock four-cylinder, and four-cylinder kids' class.

Food

Come to Williamston on an empty stomach. It has an assortment of old and very traditional eateries. The ◖ **Sunny Side Oyster Bar** (1102 Washington St., 252/792-3416, open from 5:30 P.M. Mon.–Sat. and from

5 P.M. Sun., Sept.–Apr., www.sunnyside oysterbarnc.com) is the best known, a seasonal oyster joint open in the months with the letter R—that is, oyster season. It's been in business since 1935, and is a historic as well as gastronomic landmark. Oysters are steamed behind the restaurant, and then hauled inside and shucked at the bar. Visit the restaurant's website to acquaint yourselves with the shuckers. In eastern North Carolina, a good oyster shucker is regarded as highly as a good artist or athlete, and rightly so. The Sunny Side doesn't take reservations, but it fills to capacity in no time flat, so come early.

Down the road a piece, **Martin Supply** (118 Washington St., 252/792-2123), an old general store, is a good place to buy local produce and preserves, honey, molasses, and hoop cheese. Also on Washington Street is the **R&C Restaurant** (211 Washington St., 252/792-3161), a country kitchen with a special aptitude for collard greens and crispy cornbread. **Griffin's Quick Lunch** (204 Washington St., 252/792-2873) is a popular old diner with good barbecue. Back on U.S. 64, **Shaw's Barbecue** (U.S. 64 Alt., 252/792-5339) serves eastern Carolina-style barbecue, as well as good greasy breakfasts.

East of Williamston at the intersection of U.S. 64 and Highway 171, the small Roanoke River town of Jamesville is home to a most unusual restaurant that draws attention from all over the country (it's even been featured in the *New York Times*). The ◖ **Cypress Grill** (1520 Stewart St. off U.S. 64, 252/792-4175) is an unprepossessing wooden shack right-smack on the river, a survivor of the days when Jamesville made its living in the herring industry, dragging the fish out of the water with horse-drawn seine nets. Herring—breaded and seriously deep-fried, not pickled or sweet—is the main dish here, though they also dress the herring up in other outfits, and serve bass, flounder, perch, oyster, catfish, and other fish too. The Cypress Grill is open for the three and a half months of the year (from the second Thurs. in Jan. through the end of Apr.), when the herrings run, and you could hardly have a more intensely authentic, small-town dining experience anywhere else. Be aware that due to conservation efforts on the Roanoke River, the Cypress Grill is "importing" its herring from South Carolina. They're just as delicious as ever, though.

EAST ON U.S. 64

The eastern stretch of U.S. 64 runs along the Albemarle Sound between Williamston and the Outer Banks, passing through the towns of Plymouth, Creswell, and Columbia before it crosses over to Roanoke Island. Here you'll encounter evidence of North Carolina's ancient past, old-growth forests; recent past, a plantation with a long and complex history of slavery; and the present, art galleries and abundant wildlife-watching and recreational opportunities.

(Somerset Place Historic Site

Somerset Place Historic Site (2572 Lake Shore Rd., Creswell, 252/797-4560, www.ah.dcr .state.nc.us/Sections/hs/somerset/somerset .htm, 9 A.M.–5 P.M. Mon.–Sat. and 1–5 P.M. Apr.–Oct., 10 A.M.–4 P.M. Tues.–Sat and 1–4 P.M. Sun. Nov.–Mar., free) was one of North Carolina's largest and most profitable plantations for the 80 years leading up to the Civil War. In the late 18th century and early 19th centuries, 80 Africa-born men, women, and children were brought to Somerset to labor in the fields. The grief and spiritual disorientation they experienced, and the subsequent trials of the slave community that grew to include more than 300 people, are told by the historian Dorothy Spruill Redford in the amazing book *Somerset Homecoming.* Somerset is a significant place from many historical standpoints, but the story of its African American community makes it one of this state's most important historic sites.

Somerset Place is an eerily lovely place to visit. The restored grounds and buildings, including the Collins family's house, slave quarters, and many dependencies, are deafeningly quiet, and the huge cypress trees growing right up to the quarters and the mansion make the place feel almost prehistoric. Visitors are permitted to walk around the estate at their leisure. A small

bookshop on the grounds is a good source for books about North Carolina history in general, and African American history in particular.

(Pettigrew State Park

On the banks of Lake Phelps, Pettigrew State Park (2252 Lakeshore Rd., Creswell, 252/797-4475, www.ncparks.gov/visit/parks /pett/main.php) preserves a weird ancient waterscape that's unlike anywhere else in the state. Archaeology reveals that there was a human presence here a staggering 10,000 years ago. The lake, which is five miles across, has yielded more than 30 ancient dugout canoes, some as much as 4,000 years old and measuring more than 30 feet. The natural surroundings are ancient too, encompassing some of eastern North Carolina's only remaining old-growth forests. Pungo Lake, a smaller body of water within the park, is visited by 50,000 migrating snow geese over the course of the year, an unforgettable sight for wildlife watchers.

Visitors to Pettigrew State Park can camp at the family campground ($15/day), which has drive-to sites and access to restrooms and hot showers, or at primitive group campsites (starting at $9/day).

Art Galleries

Pocosin Arts (corner of Main and Water Sts., Columbia, 252/796-2787, www.pocosin arts.org, 10 A.M.–5 P.M. Tues.–Sat.) has helped spur a renaissance of craft in eastern North Carolina, teaching community classes in ceramics, fiber arts, sculpture, jewelry making, metalwork, and many other arts. At the sales gallery, beautiful handmade items are available for purchase, and the main gallery displays many kinds of folk art from eastern North Carolina.

Sports and Recreation

Palmetto-Peartree Preserve (entrance is east of Columbia on Pot Licker Rd./Loop Rd./SR 1220, 252/796-0723, www.palmetto peartree.org) is a 10,000-acre natural area, wrapped in 14 miles of shoreline along the Albemarle Sound and Little Alligator Creek.

Originally established as a sanctuary for the red cockaded woodpecker, this is a great location for bird-watching and spotting other wildlife (which include, in addition to the birds, alligators, wolves, bears, and bobcats); hiking, biking, and horseback riding along the old logging trails through the forest; and canoeing and kayaking. The preserve's excellent paddle trail passes by Hidden Lake, a wonderfully secluded cypress-swamp blackwater lake. There is an overnight camping platform at the lake, which can be used in the daytime without a permit for bird-watching and picnicking. To stay overnight, arrange for a permit through the Roanoke River Partners (252/792-3790, www.roanokeriverpartners.org).

Once the southern edge of the Great Dismal Swamp, **Pocosin Lakes National Wildlife Refuge** (headquarters at Walter B. Jones, Sr., Center for the Sounds, U.S. 64, six miles south of Columbia, 252/796-3004, www.fws.gov /pocosinlakes) is an important haven for many species of animals, including migratory waterfowl, and re-introduced red wolves. Five important bodies of water lie within the Refuge: Pungo Lake, New Lake, the 16,600-acre Lake Phelps, and stretches of the Scuppernong and Alligator Rivers. All of these areas are good spots for observing migratory waterfowl, but Pungo Lake is particularly special in the fall and winter, when snow geese and tundra swans visit in massive numbers—approaching 100,000— on their round-trip Arctic journeys.

The landscape here was drastically altered by a tremendous wildfire that burned for days in the summer of 2008, blanketing towns as far away as Raleigh with thick smoke. Wildfire is an important part of the natural cycle here, however, and now is a unique opportunity to watch the regeneration of an ecosystem.

WASHINGTON, BATH, AND BELHAVEN

On the north side of the Pamlico River, as you head towards Mattamuskeet National Wildlife Refuge and the Outer Banks, the towns of Washington, Bath, and Belhaven offer short diversions into the nature and history of this region.

North Carolina Estuarium

The North Carolina Estuarium (223 E. Water St., Washington, 252/948-0000, www.partnership forthesounds.org/NorthCarolinaEstuarium .aspx, 10 A.M.–4 P.M. Tues.–Sat., $4 adults, $2 children) is a museum about both the natural and cultural history of the Tar-Pamlico River basin. In addition to the exhibits, which include live native animals, historic artifacts, and much more, the Estuarium operates pontoon boat tours on the Pamlico River. River roving is free, but reservations are required.

Turnage Theater

Washington has a great performing arts facility in the restored early 20th-century Turnage Theater (150 W. Main St., Washington, 252/975-1711, www.turnagetheater.com). All sorts of performances take place at the Turnage throughout the year, including by prominent artists from around the country. There are concerts of all kinds of music, productions by touring dance troupes and regional theater companies, and screenings of classic movies.

Historic Bath

North Carolina's oldest town, Bath was chartered in 1705. The town is so little changed that even today it is mostly contained within the original boundaries laid out by the explorer John Lawson. For its first 70 or so years, Bath enjoyed the spotlight as one of North Carolina's most important centers of trade and politics—home of governors, refuge from Indian wars, frequent host to and victim of Blackbeard. Much as Brunswick Town, to the south, was made redundant by the growth of Wilmington, Bath faded into obscurity as the town of Washington grew in the years after the Revolution. Today almost all of Bath is designated as Historic Bath (252/923-3971, www.bath.nchistoricsites.org, visitors center and tours 9 A.M.–5 P.M. Tues.–Sat. year-round, Palmer-Marsh House and Bonner House admission $2 adults, $1 students). Important sites on the tour of the village are the 1734 St. Thomas Church, the 1751 Palmer-Marsh House, 1790 Van Der Veer House, 1830 Bonner House, and, from time immemorial, a set of indelible hoofprints said to have been made by the devil's own horse.

Belhaven Memorial Museum

The name of Belhaven Memorial Museum (210 E. Main St., Belhaven, 252/943-6197, www.beaufort-county.com/belhavenmuseum, 1–5 P.M. Thurs.–Tues., free) gives no hint as to what a very strange little institution this is. The museum houses the collection of Miss Eva—Eva Blount Way, who died in 1962 at the age of 92—surely one of the most accomplished collectors of oddities ever. The local paper wrote of her in 1951 that, "housewife, snake killer, curator, trapper, dramatic actress, philosopher, and preserver of all the riches of mankind, inadequately describes the most fascinating person you can imagine." Miss Eva kept among her earthly treasures a collection of pickled tumors (one weighs 10 pounds), a pickled one-eyed pig, a pickled two-headed kitten, cataracts (pickled), and—deep breath—three pickled human babies. There's also a dress that belonged to a 700-pound woman, a flea couple dressed in wedding togs, 30,000 buttons, and assorted snakes that Miss Eva felt needed killing. It must haven taken a very long time to carry everything over here, but Miss Eva's collection is now on public display, the core of the Belhaven Memorial Museum's collection.

◖ MATTAMUSKEET NATIONAL WILDLIFE REFUGE

Near the tiny town of Swan Quarter, the Mattamuskeet National Wildlife Refuge (Hwy. 94, between Swan Quarter and Englehard, 252/926-4021, www.fws.gov/mattamuskeet) preserves one of North Carolina's most remarkable natural features, as well as one of its most famous buildings. Lake Mattamuskeet, 18 miles long by 6 miles wide, is the state's largest natural lake, and being an average of a foot and half deep—five feet at its deepest point—it is a most unusual environment. The hundreds of thousands of waterfowl who rest here on their seasonal rounds make this a world-famous location for bird-watching and wildlife photography.

Old-timers in the area have fond memories of dancing at the **Lodge at Lake Mattamuskeet,** one of eastern North Carolina's best known buildings. The huge old building was constructed in 1915, and was at the time the world's largest pumping station, moving over one million gallons of water per minute. In 1934, it was bought by the federal government along with the wildlife sanctuary, and the Civilian Conservation Corps transformed it into the lodge that was a favorite gathering place for the next 40 years. The lodge is closed at the time of this writing, but is undergoing restoration for future public use.

Hiking and biking trails thread through the refuge, but camping is not permitted. In season, beware of hunters and keep an eye out as well for copperheads, cottonmouths, two kinds of rattlesnakes, and alligators. Bears and red wolves abound as well. Within the administration of the Mattamuskeet Refuge is the **Swan Quarter National Wildlife Refuge** (252/926-4021, www.fws.gov/swan-quarter), located along the north shore of the Pamlico Sound, and mostly accessible only by water. This too is a gorgeous waterscape full of wildlife.

NORTH CAROLINA CENTRAL COAST

Coming east from Raleigh towards the beaches and sounds of Carteret County, you'll start to feel the ocean when you're still many miles away from its shore. Somewhere between Kinston and New Bern, a good hour's drive from the Atlantic, the sky begins to expand in a way that suggests reflected expanses of water, like a mirage felt rather than seen. Getting closer to the coast, the pine forests on either side of the highway are peppered with mistletoe bundles. New Bern and Beaufort, centers of colonial commerce, connected North Carolina to the greater Atlantic world. Both towns are wonderfully preserved, ideal places for self-guided strolls with lots of window-shopping.

Below the crooked elbow of the Neuse River, the Croatan National Forest surrounds hidden lakes and tiny towns. To the northeast,

Cedar Island National Wildlife Refuge is a vast plain of marshes, gradually dropping off into Pamlico Sound. Cape Lookout National Seashore shelters the mainland from the ocean, a chain of barrier islands where a remote port, once one of the busiest maritime towns in North Carolina, and a whaling village, nearly washed away by a series of storms, now stand empty but for seagulls and ghosts.

You may hear folks in North Carolina refer to any point on the coast, be it Wilmington or Nags Head, as "Down East." In the most authentic, local usage of the term, Down East really refers to northeastern Carteret County, to the islands and marsh towns in a highly confined region along the banks of Core Sound, north of Beaufort. Like seemingly every scenic spot in North Carolina, Down East communities are

© JIM MOREKIS

HIGHLIGHTS

(Tryon Palace: The splendid and, in its day, controversial seat of colonial government in North Carolina is reconstructed in New Bern's historic district, a significant destination worthy of a whole day's leisurely exploration (page 56).

(Kinston: Few small towns can boast of such architectural wealth as Kinston. From the variety of old-time storefronts along Queen Street to the Victorian wedding cakes and shotgun houses in the residential neighborhoods, Kinston is a living museum of Southern popular architecture (page 61).

(North Carolina Maritime Museum: North Carolina's seafaring heritage, in living traditions as well as history, is represented in fascinating exhibits and activities at this great museum (page 65).

(Beaufort's Old Burying Ground: Even if it weren't the final resting place of the "Little Girl Buried in a Bottle of Rum," this little church-

yard would still be one of the prettiest and most interesting cemeteries in the South (page 66).

(Core Sound Waterfowl Museum: Actually a museum about people rather than ducks, the Waterfowl Museum eloquently tells of the everyday lives of past generations of Down Easterners, while bringing their descendants together to re-forge community bonds (page 70).

(Cape Lookout National Seashore: The more than 50 miles of coastline along Core and Shackleford Banks, now home to only wild horses and turtle nests, were once also the home of Bankers who made their livings in the fishing, whaling, and shipping trades (page 72).

(North Carolina Aquarium: Sharks and jellyfish and their aquatic kindred show their true beauty in underwater habitats at the aquarium, and trails and boat tours lead to the watery world outdoors (page 74).

CENTRAL COAST

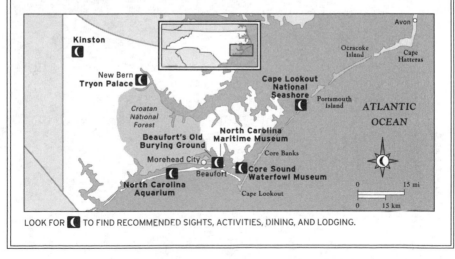

LOOK FOR **(** TO FIND RECOMMENDED SIGHTS, ACTIVITIES, DINING, AND LODGING.

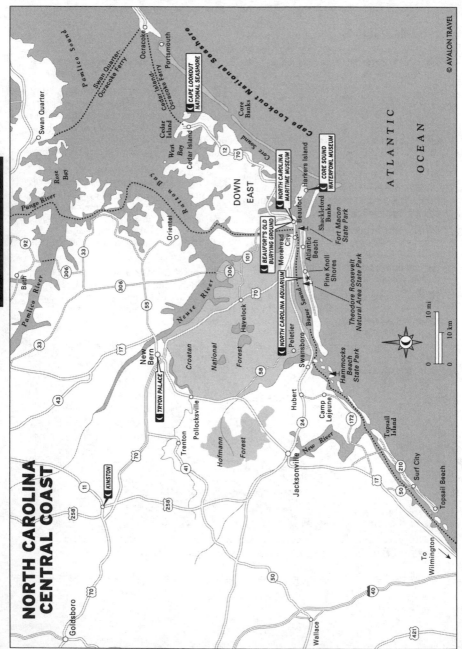

NORTH CAROLINA CENTRAL COAST

© AVALON TRAVEL

ATLANTIC OCEAN

Cape Lookout National Seashore

CAPE LOOKOUT NATIONAL SEASHORE

Pamlico Sound

Swan Quarter

Swan Quarter-Ocracoke Ferry

Ocracoke

Cedar Island-Ocracoke Ferry

Portsmouth

Core Banks

Cedar Island

West Bay

Cedar Island

Core Sound

CORE SOUND WATERFOWL MUSEUM

Harkers Island

NORTH CAROLINA MARITIME MUSEUM

Raton Bay

Rose Bay

Pungo River

Pamlico River

Bath

Oriental

DOWN EAST

Beaufort

Shackleford Banks

BEAUFORT'S OLD BURYING GROUND

Morehead City

Atlantic Beach

Fort Macon State Park

Pine Knoll Shores

Theodore Roosevelt Natural Area State Park

Neuse River

Havelock

NORTH CAROLINA AQUARIUM

Peletier

Bogue Sound

Swansboro

Hammocks Beach State Park

New Bern

TRYON PALACE

Croatan National Forest

Pollocksville

Trenton

Hofmann Forest

Hubert

Camp Lejeune

New River

Jacksonville

Topsail Island

KINSTON

Goldsboro

Wallace

Surf City

Topsail Beach

To Wilmington

10 mi

10 km

0

© JIM MOREKIS

along Morehead City's working waterfront

undergoing seismic cultural shifts as people "from off" move into the area, as young people leave home to make their lives and livings elsewhere, and as forces like global trade and environmental changes make the traditional maritime occupations of the region increasingly untenable. Nevertheless, Down Easterners fight to preserve the core treasures of Core Sound. Conservation and historic preservation efforts are underway, and they've already netted some victories. The best place to witness Down Easterners' passionate dedication to preserving their heritage is at the Core Sound Waterfowl Museum on Harkers Island. Members of the little communities along the sound have brought precious family objects to be displayed at the museum, and the quilts, family photos, baseball uniforms, oyster knives, net hooks, and other treasures eloquently tell of their love of the water, the land, and each other.

PLANNING YOUR TIME

The standard beach-season rules apply to the coastal areas covered in this chapter. Lodging prices go up dramatically between Memorial Day and Labor Day, and though you might score a rock-bottom price if you visit on a mild weekend out of season, you might also find that some of the destinations you'd like to visit are closed.

North Carolina Sea Grant (www.ncseagrant .org) provides wallet cards listing the seasons for different seafood caught and served in Carteret County. The cards can be ordered by mail, or downloaded and printed from the website.

Late summer and early autumn are hurricane season all through the Southeast. Hurricane paths are unpredictable, so if you're planning a week on the beach, and know that a hurricane is hovering over Cuba, it won't necessarily hit North Carolina, though the central Carolina coast is always an odds-on favorite for landfall. Chances are you'll have pretty fair warning if a storm is coming—you won't wake up one morning to find your motel room windows covered with plywood, and everybody else in town gone—but it's always a good idea to familiarize yourself with evacuation routes, and not take chances. A storm that's too far offshore to cause any weather problems can still mess up beach conditions, making waves and currents that are exciting for surfing but way too dangerous for swimming. (These caveats are relevant to the whole North Carolina coast, not just this region.)

Barring storms, the fall is a really beautiful time on the beaches here. The coastal weather is sometimes warm right into November, and though the water may be too chilly for swimming then, there's hardly a nicer time for walking tours of the old towns—except, of course, azalea season in the spring.

GETTING THERE AND AROUND
By Car

One of the state's main east–west routes, U.S. 70, gives easy access to almost all of the destinations in this chapter. From Raleigh to Beaufort is a distance of a little over 150 miles, but keep in mind that large stretches of the highway are in commercial areas with plenty of traffic and red lights. U.S. 70 continues past Beaufort, snaking up along Core Sound through little Down East towns like Otway and Davis, finally petering out in the town of Atlantic. At Sea Level, Highway 13 branches to the north, across the Cedar Island Wildlife Refuge and ending at the Cedar Island–Ocracoke Ferry.

Down south, to reach the Bogue Banks (Atlantic Beach, Emerald Isle, and neighboring beaches) by road, bridges cross Bogue Sound on Highway 58 at both Morehead City and Cedar Point (not to be confused with Cedar Island).

By Ferry

Except for the visitors center at Harkers Island, Cape Lookout National Seashore can only be reached by ferry. Most ferries operate between April and November, with some exceptions. Portsmouth, at the northern end of the park, is a short ferry ride from Ocracoke, but Ocracoke is a very long ferry ride from Cedar Island. The **Cedar Island-Ocracoke Ferry** (800/856-

0343) is part of the state ferry system, and costs $15 one-way for regular-sized vehicles (pets allowed). It takes 2.25 hours to cross Pamlico Sound, but the ride is fun, and embarking from Cedar Island feels like sailing off the edge of the earth. The **Ocracoke-Portsmouth ferry** is a passenger-only commercial route, licensed to Captain Rudy Austin. Call 252/928-4361 to ensure a seat. There's also a vehicle and passenger ferry, Morris Marina Kabin Kamps and Ferry Service (877/956-6568), **from Atlantic to Long Point** on the North Core Banks, leashed or in-vehicle pets are allowed.

Commercial ferries cross every day **from mainland Carteret County** to the southern parts of the National Seashore. There is generally a ferry route between Davis and Great Island, but service can be variable; check the Cape Lookout National Seashore website (www.nps.gov/calo) for updates.

From Harkers Island, passenger ferries to Cape Lookout Lighthouse and Shackleford Banks include Calico Jacks (252/728-3575), Harkers Island Fishing Center (252/728-3907), Local Yokel (252/728-2759), and Island Ferry Adventures at Barbour's Marina (252/728-6181).

From Beaufort, passenger ferries include Outer Banks Ferry Service (252/728-4129), which goes to both Shackleford Banks and to Cape Lookout Lighthouse; Island Ferry Adventures (252/728-7555) and Mystery Tours (252/728-7827) run to Shackleford Banks. Morehead City's passenger-only Waterfront Ferry Service (252/726-7678) goes to Shackleford Banks as well. On-leash pets are generally allowed, but call ahead to confirm for Local Yokel, Island Ferry Adventures, and Waterfront Ferry Service.

Back on the mainland, a 20-minute free passenger ferry **crosses the Neuse River** between Cherry Branch (near Cherry Point) and Minesott Beach in Pamlico County every half-hour (vehicles and passengers, pets allowed, 800/339-9156).

New Bern

New Bern's history is understandably a great draw, and that, coupled with its beautiful natural setting at the confluence of the Neuse and Trent Rivers, makes it one of North Carolina's prime spots for tourism and retirement living. Despite the considerable traffic it draws, it is still a small and enormously pleasant city.

One all-important note: how to say it. It's your choice of "NYEW-bern" or "NOO-bern"—and in some folks' accents it sounds almost like "Neighbor"—but never "New-BERN."

HISTORY

New Bern's early days were marked by tragedy. It was settled in 1710 by a community of Swiss and German colonists under the leadership of English surveyor John Lawson (author of the wonderful 1709 *A New Voyage to Carolina,* available today in reprint from the University of North Carolina Press), and Swiss entrepreneur Christoph von Graffenried (from Bern, of course). More than half of the settlers died en route to America, and those who made it across alive suffered tremendous

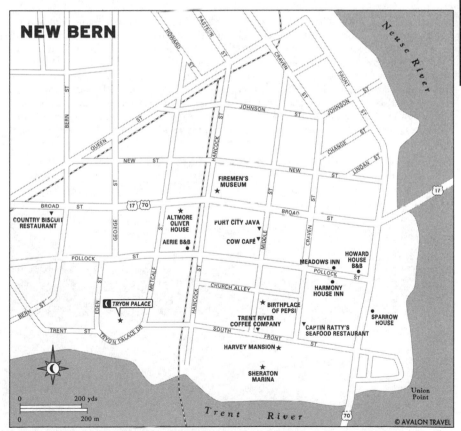

hardship in their first months and years. Lawson and Graffenried were both captured in 1711 by the Tuscarora tribe, in one of the opening sallies of the Tuscarora War. Graffenried was released—according to some accounts, because he wore such fancy clothes that the Tuscarora feared killing the governor. Lawson was burned at the stake, the first casualty of the Tuscarora War.

Despite early disaster, New Bern was on its feet again by the mid-18th century, at which time it was home to the colony's first newspaper, and its first chartered academy. It also became North Carolina's capital, an era symbolized by the splendor of Tryon Palace, one of the most recognizable architectural landmarks in North Carolina.

During the Civil War, New Bern was captured early by Ambrose Burnside's forces, and despite multiple Confederate attempts to retake the city, it remained a Union stronghold for the balance of the war. It became a center for African American resistance and political organization through the Reconstruction years, a story grippingly told in historian David Cecelski's *The Waterman's Song* (also UNC Press).

SIGHTS
◖ Tryon Palace

Tryon Palace (610 Pollock St., 252/514-4956, www.tryonpalace.org, 9 A.M.–5 P.M. Mon.–Sat., 1–5 P.M. Sun., last guided tour begins at 4 P.M., gardens open in the summer until 7 P.M., museum shop 9:30 A.M.–5:30 P.M. Mon.–Sat., 1 P.M.–5:30 P.M. Sun.; $15 adults admission to all buildings and gardens, $6 grades 1–12; $8 adults admission just to gardens, kitchen office, blacksmith shop, and stables, $3 grades 1–12) is a rather remarkable feat of historic re-creation, a from-the-ground-up reconstruction of the 1770 colonial capitol and governor's mansion. Tryon Palace was a magnificent project the first time around too. Governor William Tryon bucked the preferences of Piedmont Carolinians, and had his and the colonial government's new home built here in the coastal plain. He hired English architect John Hawks to design the complex, what would become a Georgian house upon an estate laid out in the Palladian style. The Palace's first incarnation was a fairly short one. It stood for a scant quarter-century before burning in 1798, and as the by-now state of

Tryon Palace

© JIM MOREKIS

CENTRAL COAST

North Carolina had relocated its governmental operations to Raleigh, there was no need to rebuild the New Bern estate.

It continued, however, to live on in Carolinians' imaginations for a century. In the early 20th century, a movement was afoot to rebuild Tryon Palace. By the 1950s, both the funds and, incredibly, John Hawks' original drawings and plans had been secured, and over a period of seven years the Palace was rebuilt. Today it's once again one of the most striking and recognizable buildings in North Carolina.

Tryon Palace is open for tours year-round, and it hosts many lectures and living history events throughout the year. One of the best times to visit is during the Christmas season, when not only is the estate decorated beautifully for the season, but they celebrate **Jonkonnu,** a colonial African American celebration that was once found throughout the Caribbean and Southeastern United States. For many generations it was celebrated in eastern North Carolina, and here at Tryon Palace the tradition is recreated. At Jonkonnu—also called Junkanoo, John Canoe, and several other variations—African and African American slaves would put on a Mardi Gras–like frolic with deep African roots, parading through the plantation to music and wearing outlandish costumes, some representing folk characters associated with the celebration. It was a sort of upside-down day, when the social order was momentarily inverted, and the slaves could boldly walk right up onto the master's porch and demand gifts or money. Some whites got into the spirit of the celebration, and played along with this remarkable pantomime. It was a tradition fraught with both joy and sorrow, tapping into deeply volatile issues. Tryon Palace puts on a great recreation of Jonkonnu, one that's both lively and enlightening.

When you visit Tryon Palace, allow yourself plenty of time—a whole afternoon or even a full day. There are several buildings on the property where tours and activities are going on, the gardens are well worth seeing, and the surrounding neighborhood contains some wonderful old houses.

In the year 2010, in honor of New Bern's 300th anniversary, Tryon Palace plans to open the doors of its North Carolina History Education Center, an enormous new complex along the Trent River, next to the Tryon Palace gardens, with galleries, a performance hall, outdoor interpretive areas, and a great deal more.

New Bern Firemen's Museum

The New Bern Firemen's Museum (408 Hancock St., 252/636-4087, www.newbern museums.com, 10 a.m.–4 p.m. Mon.–Sat., $5 adults, $2.50 children) is a fun little museum—an idyll for the gearhead with an antiquarian bent. The museum houses a collection of 19th- and early 20th-century fire wagons and trucks, and chronicles the lively and contentious history of firefighting in New Bern. The city was the first in North Carolina, and one of the first in the country, to charter a fire department. After the Civil War, three fire companies operated here, one of which was founded before the War, and one founded during the Yankee occupation. (The third was a boys' bucket brigade, a sort of training program for junior firefighters.) During Reconstruction, every fire was occasion for a competition, as residents would gather around to see which company got to a blaze first—the good old boys or the carpetbaggers.

Attmore-Oliver House

The beautiful 1790 Attmore-Oliver House (510 Pollock St., 252/638-8558, www.newbern historical.org, hours and tour schedule vary, call for specifics, $4 adults, free for students) is a nice historic house museum, with exhibits about New Bern's very significant Civil War history. It's also the headquarters of the New Bern Historical Society.

Birthplace of Pepsi

We often think of Coca-Cola as the quintessential Southern drink, but it was here in New Bern that Caleb Bradham, a drugstore owner, put together what he called Brad's Drink—later Pepsi-Cola. Pepsi-Cola Bottling Company operates a soda fountain

© JIM MOREKIS

the Birthplace of Pepsi in downtown New Bern

and gift shop at the location of Bradham's pharmacy, called the Birthplace of Pepsi (256 Middle St., 252/636-5898, www.pepsistore.com, 10 A.M.–6 P.M. Mon.–Sat., free).

ENTERTAINMENT AND EVENTS

New Bern's historic Harvey Mansion has a cozy old-fashioned pub in its cellar, the **1797 Steamer Bar** (221 S. Front St., 252/635-3232). As one would gather from its name, the pub serves steamed seafood and other light fare. **Captain Ratty's Seafood Restaurant** (202–206 Middle St., 800/633-5292, www .captanrattys.com) also has a bar that's a popular gathering spot for locals and tourists alike.

SHOPPING

New Bern is a great place for antique shopping. The majority of the shops are within the 220–240 blocks of Middle Street. There are also periodic antique shows (and even a salvaged antique architectural hardware show) at the New Bern Convention Center. See www.visitnewbern.com for details.

Tryon Palace is a fun shopping spot for history buffs and home-and-garden fanciers. The historical site's **Museum Shop** (Jones House at Eden and Pollock Sts., 252/514-4932, 9:30 A.M.–5:30 P.M. Mon.–Sat., 1–5:30 P.M. Sun.) has a nice variety of books about history and architecture, as well as handcrafts and children's toy and games. The **Garden Shop** (610 Pollock St., 252/514-4932, 10 A.M.–5 P.M. Mon.–Sat., 1–5 P.M. Sun.) sells special bulbs and plants, when in season, grown in Tryon Palace's own greenhouse. Out of season you can still find a nice variety of gardening tools and accessories. A Shop Pass is available at the Museum Shop; this allows you to visit the shops at Tryon Palace without paying the entrance fee.

SPORTS AND RECREATION

At New Bern's Sheraton Marina, **Barnacle Bob's Boat and Jet Ski Rentals** (100 Middle St., Dock F, 252/634-4100, www.boatandjetskinewbern.com, 9 A.M.–7 P.M. daily) rents one- and two-person Jet Skis ($65/hour, $45/half-hour) and

6–8-person pontoon boats ($65/hour, $220/4 hours, $420/8 hours).

ACCOMMODATIONS

Under $150

The (Aerie Bed and Breakfast (509 Pollock St., 800/849-5553, www.aerieinn.com, $119–169) is the current incarnation of the 1880s Street-Ward residence. Its seven luxurious guest rooms are done up in Victorian furniture and earth-tone fabrics reflecting the house's earliest era. There is a lovely courtyard for guests to enjoy, and the inn is only one short block from Tryon Palace.

Also on Pollock Street, a few blocks away, are the **Harmony House Inn** (215 Pollock St., 800/636-3113, www.harmonyhouseinn.com, $99–175), the **Howard House Bed and Breakfast** (207 Pollock St., 252/514-6709, www.howardhousebnb.com, $129–149), and the **Meadows Inn** (212 Pollock St., 877/551-1776, www.meadowsinn-nc.com, $112–166). All three are appealing 19th-century houses decorated in the classic bed-and-breakfast style, and easy walking distance to Tryon Palace and to downtown.

Over $300

There are plenty of weekend/vacation rental houses in eastern North Carolina, but New Bern's **Sparrow House** (220 E. Front St., 252/349-2441, www.thesparrowhouse.com) is one of a kind. It's a four-story antebellum brick city house, built in 1843 by a shipbuilder. The Sparrow House sleeps up to 12 people in its four bedrooms, and at $395/night on weekends ($289/weeknight), it's actually a very reasonable way to spend vacation bucks for families likely to rent two or more hotel rooms.

Camping

New Bern's **KOA Campground** (1565 B St., 800/562-3341, www.newbernkoa.com) is just on the other side of the Neuse River from town, located right on the riverbank. Choices include 20-, 30-, 40-amp RV sites, "kamping kabins and lodges," and tent sites. Pets are allowed, and there is a dog park on-site. The campground is set up with free wireless access,

so you can check your email from a rental paddleboat, if you've a mind to. Stop by the New Bern Convention Center's tourist information center before checking in, and pick up a KOA brochure for some major coupons.

FOOD

The Italian restaurant (**Nikola's** (1503-A S. Glenburnie Rd., 252/638-6061, www.nikolasrestaurant.com, 5–10 P.M. Tues.–Sat., $15–25) is both very small and very popular, so reservations are recommended. Specialties include flounder stuffed with crabmeat, scallops, and shrimp, and Flounder Nikola's, filleted and laced with ham in white sauce; veal or chicken Romani sautéed in wine with mushrooms and artichoke hearts; and veal or chicken Fiorentina, with meat sauce, creamed spinach, and mozzarella served over pasta. Vegetarian entrées are all in the pasta category, but offer plenty of great options.

Down-home food choices include the **Country Biscuit Restaurant** (809 Broad St., 252/638-5151), which is open for breakfast, and is popular for, not surprisingly, its biscuits. **Moore's Olde Tyme Barbeque** (3711 Hwy. 17 S./Martin Luther King, Jr., Blvd., 252/638-3937) is a family business, in operation (at a series of different locations) since 1945. They roast and smoke their own barbeque in a pit on-site, burning wood that you'll see piled up by the shop. The menu is short and simple—featuring pork barbeque, chicken, shrimp, fish, hush puppies, fries, and slaw—and their prices are lower than many fast-food joints.

There are lots of good snack stops in New Bern, places to grab a bite or a cup of coffee before a day of touring on foot or on the water. The **Trent River Coffee Company** (208 Craven St., 252/514-2030, www.trentrivercoffee.com) is a casual coffee shop in a cool old downtown storefront, and the coffee is good. It's sometimes patronized by well-behaved local dogs, who lie under the tables patiently while their owners read the newspaper. This is a nice meeting place, and a dark oasis in the summer heat. **Port City Java**

(323 Middle St., 252/633-7900, www.portci-tyjava.com) is an international chain, but it started in Wilmington, and has many locations on the North Carolina coast. The punch packed by Port City coffee is reliably good. One often stumbles upon cafés in communities where you wouldn't expect to be able to buy strong coffee, and it's at those times that a cup of espresso or a coffee shake is most appreciated. The **Cow Café** (319 Middle St., 252/672-9269) is a pleasant downtown creamery and snack shop with some homemade ice cream flavors you can't find anywhere else.

SERVICES

Craven Regional Medical Center (2000 Neuse Blvd., 252/633-8111, www.uhseast.com) is located in New Bern,

Croatan National Forest and Vicinity

A huge swath of swampy wilderness, the Croatan National Forest covers all the ground between the Neuse, Trent, and White Oak Rivers, and Bogue Sound, from New Bern to Morehead City and almost all the way to Jacksonville. Despite its size, Croatan is one of the lesser-known and less developed federal preserves in the state. The nearby towns (all three of them) of Jones County, population just over 10,000, enjoy a similar atmosphere of otherworldly sequestration, where barely traveled roads lead to dark expanses of forest and swamp, and old, narrow village streets.

CROATAN NATIONAL FOREST

Headquartered just off U.S. 70, south of New Bern, the Croatan National Forest (141 E. Fisher Ave., New Bern, 252/638-5628, www.cs.unca.edu/nfsnc) has few established amenities for visitors, but plenty of land and water trails to explore.

Hiking

The main hiking route is the **Neusiok Trail,** which begins at the Newport River Parking area and ends at the Pinecliff Recreation Area on the Neuse, crossing 20 miles of beach, salt marsh, swamp, pocosin, and pinewoods. The 1.4-mile **Cedar Point Tideland Trail** covers estuary marshes and woods, starting at the Cedar Point boat ramp near Cape Carteret. The half-mile **Island Creek Forest Walk** passes through virgin hardwood forests and marl (compacted shell) outcroppings.

Boating

The park has designated the spectacular **Saltwater Adventure Trail.** This water route (roughly 100 miles in length) starts at Brice's Creek south of New Bern, winds along north to the Neuse River, then follows the Neuse all the way to the crook at Harlowe, where it threads through the Harlowe Canal. The route then heads down to Beaufort and all the way through Bogue Sound, turning back inland on the White Oak River, and ending at Haywood Landing north of Swansboro. If you're up for the challenge, it's an incredible trip. For boat rentals, try **Brice's Creek Canoe Trails** (141 East Fisher Ave., New Bern, 252/636-6606).

Camping

Three campsites in the Croatan Forest are developed. **Neuse River** (also called Flanners Beach, $12–17) has 25 sites with showers and flush toilets. **Cedar Point** ($17), has 40 campsites with electricity, showers, and flush toilets. **Fisher's Landing** (free) has nine sites, but no facilities other than vault toilets. Primitive camping areas are at Great Lake, Catfish Lake, and Long Point.

TRENTON

A little ways outside of the Croatan National Forest is the impossibly pretty village of Trenton. The Jones County seat's tiny, historic business district is an appropriate focal point for this bucolic area. A Revolutionary-

JOHN LAWSON ON ALLIGATORS

Explorer John Lawson, in his *A New Voyage to Carolina*, describes a 1709 encounter with an alligator on the Neuse River.

The Allegator is the same, as the Crocodile, and differs only in Name. They frequent the sides of Rivers, in the Banks of which they make their Dwellings a great way under Ground...Here it is, that this amphibious Monster dwells all the Winter, sleeping away his time till the Spring appears, when he comes from his Cave, and daily swims up and down the Streams... This Animal, in these Parts, sometimes exceeds seventeen Foot long. It is impossible to kill them with a Gun, unless you chance to hit them about the Eyes, which is a much softer Place, than the rest of their impenetrable Armour. They roar, and make a hideous Noise against bad Weather, and before they come out of their Dens in the Spring. I was pretty much frightened with one of these once, which happened thus: I had built a House about half a Mile from an Indian Town, on the Fork of the Neus-River, where I dwelt by my self, excepting a young Indian Fellow, and a Bull-Dog, that I had along with me. I had not then been so long a So-journer in America, as to be thoroughly acquainted with this Creature. One of them had got his Nest directly under my House, which stood on pretty high Land, and by a Creek-side, in whose Banks his Entring-place was, his Den reaching the Ground directly on which my House stood. I was sitting alone by the Fire-side (about nine a Clock at Night, some time in March) the Indian Fellow being gone to Town, to see his Relations; so that there was no body in the House but my self and my Dog; when, all of a sudden, this ill-favour'd Neighbour of mine, set up such a Roaring, that he made the House shake about my Ears, and so continued, like a Bittern (but a hundred times louder, if possible), for four or five times. The Dog stared, as if he was frightened out of his Senses; nor indeed, could I imagine what it was, having never heard one of them before. Immediately I had another Lesson; and so a third. Being at that time amongst none but Savages, I began to suspect, that they were working some Piece of Conjuration under my House, to get away with my Goods...At last, my Man came in, to whom when I had told the Story, he laugh'd at me, and presently undeceiv'd me, by telling me what it was that made that Noise.

era millpond, presided over by a large wooden mill, is a good picnic spot. It also makes for a nice destination for a short stroll after a meal at **Pop Tucci's** (141 W. Jones St., 252/448-1101) or the **Old Plant Diner** (346 W. Jones St., 252/448-1600). The 1880s board-and-batten Grace Episcopal Church sits next to a cemetery full of Victorian stones showing earthly chains rent asunder and heavenward-pointing hands.

KINSTON

The town of Kinston does not appear on many tourist maps, but those who overlook it are missing out. It's been through some rough years recently, especially due to the economic vacuum left by the vanishing tobacco industry, which for generations made Kinston quite a prosperous place. The town is very much alive, though, and interesting things are happening here, particularly in the arts and in historic preservation.

Sights

Like a lot of towns that were prosperous for many years and suddenly experienced a drying-up of funds, Kinston is an architectural time capsule. Driving (or better yet,

KINSTON'S MUSIC LEGACY

Music has always been a big deal here, and African American Kinstonians have made immeasurable contributions to American music, from jazz to R&B to gospel. James Brown discovered what Kinston had to offer when, in Greensboro in 1964, he met and hired a talented young drummer and college student named Melvin Parker, a native of Kinston. Melvin accepted the job on the condition that Brown also hire his little brother – a saxophonist named Maceo. Melvin and Maceo Parker were not the only Kinstonians to tour with Brown's band. Band leader Nat Jones, trombonist Levi Raspberry, trumpeter Dick Knight, and quite a few other young men from this area made names for themselves and helped create the groundbreaking sound of funk. Plans are in the works to celebrate Kinston's African American musical history (and future). To find out if an event is planned for when you'll be in town, contact the **Kinston Community Council for the Arts** (400 N. Queen St., 252/527-2517, www.kinstoncca.com).

in threadbare glory, and on the other side of town, shotgun houses, that icon of Southern folk housing, line the alleys of the old working-class neighborhood.

The remains of the Confederate ironclad gunboat **CSS Neuse** are on display in Kinston, near the spot where she was scuttled in 1865 to keep her out of the hands of the advancing Union Army. All that remains is the core of the 158-foot-by-34-foot hull, but even in such deteriorated condition the *Neuse* is a striking feat of boatbuilding.

Entertainment and Events

Kinston is blessed with a great local arts engine, the **Kinston Community Council for the Arts** (400 N. Queen St., 252/527-2517, www.kinstoncca.com, 10 A.M.–6 P.M. Tues.–Fri., 10 A.M.–2 P.M. Sat.), which has the kind of energy and artistic vision one would expect to find in a much larger city. It occupies an old storefront on Queen Street, remodeled into a gorgeous gallery and studio space. In addition to the many community events that are hosted here, KCCA has consistently innovative exhibits in the main gallery. From avant-garde photography and collage to a recent exhibition of dozens of custom motorcycles, the Kinston Arts Council is a significant and provocative art space.

Sports and Recreation

The **Kinston Indians,** an old baseball team who are nowadays a Class-A affiliate of the Cleveland Indians, play their home games at historic **Grainger Stadium.** Grainger is a homey 1949 field, the second-oldest in the Carolina League. There's nothing like a baseball game in a small town that really, really cares, and baseball ranks nearly as high as music on the list of Kinstonians' favorite things. At a memorable weekday afternoon Indians game in the 2007 season, the opening pitch was delayed when the stadium's PA system malfunctioned and failed to play the recording of the national anthem. After a few impatient moments, a loud-voiced man in the crowd began singing. The rest of the crowd joined him at " . . .can you see . . ."

walking) the several downtown blocks of **Queen Street,** the town's main artery, is an education in early 20th-century commercial architecture. The Hotel Kinston is the town's tallest building, an 11-story hotel with a ground level that's a crazy blend of Art Deco and Moorish motifs. The 1914 post office is a big, heavy beaux arts beauty, and the Queen Street Methodist Church is turreted within an inch of its life. The People's Bank building testifies to the heyday of early 20th-century African American commerce. With its many strange and daring experiments in building styles, Queen Street looks like a crazy quilt, but the buildings are beautifully complementary in their diversity. In the Herritage Street neighborhood, near the bend of the river, block upon block of grand old houses stand

EARLY MENTAL INSTITUTIONS

Two of the state's most remarkable museums, both tiny and little-known, are located in Goldsboro and Kinston, about half an hour apart and an easy drive from Raleigh. They both display artifacts from the history of early mental institutions, from Cherry Hospital – formerly the state Asylum for the Colored Insane – in Goldsboro, and the Caswell Center, a residential home for the developmentally disabled in Kinston. These museums are not for the faint of heart; amid lists of accomplishments and milestones of medicine are hints and intimations of a tragic past, of suffering on an overwhelming scale and misguided early-20th-century attempts at progressive mental healthcare. Emblematic of these institutions' shared past is the fact that each museum has on display a cage, an early solution for controlling unruly patients.

Cherry Hospital is still a state-operated inpatient psychiatric hospital, located on the same grim, industrial-looking campus where the first patient was admitted in 1880. It was a segregated hospital, housing only African American patients, until 1965. The strikingly unselfconscious **Cherry Museum** focuses mainly on the history of the staff and the evolution of medical treatment at the facility, but among the displays one catches fleeting glimpses of what life may have been like here for the early patients. A framed page in one display case lists "Some Supposed Causes of Insanity in the Early Years," and among them are "religion," "jealousy," "hard study," "business trouble," "love affair," "pregnancy," "masturbation," "la grippe," "blow on head," and, most curious, simply "trouble." In a day when the definition of insanity was so all-encompassing, and, compounding the terror, African Americans had little or no legal recourse to protect themselves from false charges or incarceration, one can only imagine how many of the "insane" here were in fact healthy, lucid people who had fallen on hard times or committed some infraction of racial etiquette. In the earliest days, "therapy" consisted of work – picking crops in the fields, laboring in the laundry, or making bricks by the ton in the brickyard (which were then sold by the state for a profit). Clearly, such horrors as these are long behind us. They weren't confined to Cherry Hospital at the time,

and certainly don't occur here today (or any time in recent generations), but the grief of the tens of thousands of people who lived here in the early 1900s hangs heavy in the air.

To visit Cherry Museum, you must enter the campus of Cherry Hospital (201 Stevens Mill Rd., Goldsboro, 919/731-3417, www.cherryhospital.org), on Highway 581, near I-70 and U.S. 117, outside of Goldsboro. (You'll see a sign on I-70.) Once on campus, follow the signs to the museum. Once there, you must ring the doorbell and wait to be admitted. The public is admitted 8 A.M.–5 P.M. Monday–Friday.

Down the road in Kinston, about half an hour east, you'll find the **Caswell Center Museum and Visitors Center.** The Caswell Center admitted its first patients in 1914 as the Caswell School for the Feeble Minded. Like Cherry Hospital, the Caswell Center is still an active inpatient facility, and also like Cherry Hospital, it is nothing like the bleak place documented in the museum's displays about the first years here. But this too is an eye-opening education in early attitudes towards mental healthcare. The Caswell Center's museum is more blunt in its presentation than the delicate Cherry Museum, confronting directly the sad facts of its history by exhibiting objects like the combination straightjacket-rompers that the earliest patients had to wear, and addressing the Depression-era overcrowding and lack of food. Though the Caswell Center's patients were all white until the era of integration, they were like the residents of the Asylum for the Colored Insane in that among their ranks were mentally healthy people – unwed mothers, people with physical handicaps, juvenile delinquents – who were crowded into dormitories with the patients who did suffer from retardation. An articulate love letter written from one patient, clearly not retarded, to another hints at the bizarre contradictions of life in an early mental institution.

The Caswell Center Museum and Visitors Center (2415 W. Vernon Ave., Kinston, 252/208-3780, www.caswellcenter.org) is open 8 A.M.–5 P.M. Monday–Friday and other times by appointment.

Both museums are free, but please make a donation to help ensure that their amazing stories will continue to be told.

and sang the anthem all the way through (staying on pitch right through the high note—this is a musical town). When the singing was over, the players turned their backs to the flag just long enough to applaud the crowd, before they took the field and played ball.

Accommodations and Food

Several chain motels are located just outside of the downtown area. The **Hampton Inn** (1382 U.S. 258 S., 252/523-1400, www.hampton inn.com, around $108) is convenient and comfortable, and the staff are especially nice.

There are quite a few good places to eat in Kinston. The best bet for a quick and tasty sandwich is the **Peach House** (412 W. Vernon Ave., 252/522-2526). For Carolina barbecue,

King's BBQ (405 E. New Bern Rd., 800/332-6465, www.kingsbbq.com) has been a local favorite for more than 60 years. You'll see billboards throughout the area for their "Famous Pig in a Puppy," pork barbecue baked into a hush puppy sandwich. They also hit the nail on the head with their Brunswick stew, fried chicken, fried sea trout, and "banana pudding in an edible waffle bowl." King's also does a mail-order business in hand-chopped pork barbecue for $8 a pound.

Services

For medical services, **Lenoir Memorial Hospital** (100 Airport Rd., 252/522-7000, www.lenoirmemorial.org) is located in Kinston.

Beaufort and Vicinity

It's an oft-cited case of the perversity of Southern speech that Beaufort, North Carolina, receives the French treatment of "eau"—so it's pronounced "BO-furt"—whereas Beaufort, South Carolina, a rather similar Lowcountry port town south of Charleston, is pronounced "Byew-furt."

The third-oldest town in North Carolina, Beaufort holds its own with its elders, Bath and New Bern, in the pretty department. The little port was once North Carolina's window on the world, a rather cosmopolitan place that sometimes received news from London or Barbados sooner than from Raleigh. The streets are crowded with extremely beautiful old houses, many built in a double-porch, steep-roofed style that shows off the early citizenry's cultural ties to the wider Caribbean and Atlantic world.

In the late 1990s, a shipwreck was found in Beaufort Inlet that is believed to be that of the *Queen Anne's Revenge,* a French slaver captured by the pirate Blackbeard in 1717 to be the flagship of his unsavory fleet. He increased its arsenal to 40 cannons, but it was nevertheless sunk in the summer of 1718. Blackbeard himself was

Beaufort boasts many fine old homes.

killed at Ocracoke Inlet a few months later, and it took five musketballs and 40 sword wounds to finish him off. His body was dumped overboard, but his head carried on its master's

BLACKBEARD AND BONNET: THE BOYS OF 1718

In the 18th century, the Carolina coast was positively verminous with pirates. For the most part they hung out around Charleston Harbor, like a bunch of rowdies on a frat house balcony, causing headaches for passers-by. Some liked to venture up the coast, however, into the inlets and sounds of North Carolina. Our most famous pirate guests were Blackbeard, whose real name was Edward Teach, and Stede Bonnet. They did most of their misbehaving in our waters during the year 1718.

Blackbeard is said never to have killed a man except in self-defense, but clearly he was so bad he didn't need to kill to make his badness known. He was a huge man with a beard that covered most of his face, and his hair is usually depicted twisted up into ferocious dreadlocks. He wore a bright red coat and festooned himself with every weapon small enough to carry; and as if all that didn't make him scary enough, he liked to wear burning cannon fuses tucked under the brim of his hat. He caused trouble from the Bahamas to Virginia, taking ships, treasure, and child brides as fancy led him.

Poor Stede Bonnet. With a name like that, he should have known better than to try to make a living intimidating people. He is said to have been something of a fancy-pants, a man with wealth, education, and a nagging wife. To get away from his better half, he bought a ship, hired a crew, and set sail for a life of crime. Though never quite as tough as Blackbeard,

with whom he was briefly partners, Bonnet caused enough trouble along the Southern coast that the gentlemen of Charleston saw to it that he was captured and hanged. Meanwhile, the Virginia nabobs had also had it with Blackbeard's interference in coastal commerce, and Governor Spottswood dispatched his men to kill him. This they did at Ocracoke, but it wasn't easy; even after they shot, stabbed, and beheaded Blackbeard, his body taunted them by swimming laps around the ship before finally giving up the ghost.

Blackbeard has in effect surfaced again. In 1996, a ship was found off the North Carolina coast that was identified as Blackbeard's flagship, the *Queen Anne's Revenge*. All manner of intriguing artifacts have been brought up from the ocean floor: cannons and blunderbuss parts, early hand grenades, even a penis syringe supposed to have been used by the syphilitic pirates to inject themselves with mercury. (During one standoff in Charleston Harbor, Blackbeard and his men took hostages to ransom for medical supplies. Perhaps this explains why they were so desperate.) To view artifacts and learn more about Blackbeard, Stede Bonnet, and their lowdown ways, visit the North Carolina Maritime Museum in Beaufort and in Southport, as well as the websites of the *Queen Anne's Revenge* (www.qaronline.com) and the Office of State Archaeology (www.arch.dcr.state.nc.us).

CENTRAL COAST

infamous career a little longer, scaring folks from atop a pike in Virginia. Incredibly cool artifacts from the *QAR* keep emerging from the waters of the inlet. Beaufort had been a favorite haunt of Blackbeard's, and you can find out all about him at the North Carolina Maritime Museum.

From the Maritime Museum, it's just a few steps to Beaufort's cafés, antique shops, and docks, clustered along Front Street. From the docks you can see Carrot Island, with its herd of wild horses, one of the last in eastern North Carolina, and you can catch a ride on a ferry or tour boat to cross the sound to the Cape

Lookout National Seashore, or get a close-up glimpse of wildlife in the surrounding salt marshes.

SIGHTS
North Carolina Maritime Museum

The North Carolina Maritime Museum (315 Front St., 252/728-7317, www.ncmaritime.org, 9 A.M.–5 P.M. Mon.–Fri., 10 A.M.–5 P.M. Sat., 1–5 P.M. Sun., free) is among the best museums in the state. Even if you don't think you're interested in boatbuilding or maritime history, you'll get caught up in the exhibits here. Historic

CENTRAL COAST

© JIM MOREKIS

the North Carolina Maritime Museum

watercraft and reconstructions and models of boats are on display here, well presented in rich historical and cultural context. There's also a lot to learn about the state's fishing history—not only pertaining to the fisheries themselves, but also to related occupations, such as the highly complex skill of net-hanging. Far from being limited to the few species of catches of today's fisheries, early North Carolina seamen also carried on a big business hunting sea turtles, porpoises, and even whales.

Across the street from the museum's main building, perched on the dock, is the **Harvey W. Smith Watercraft Center.** North Carolina mariners had for many generations an international reputation as expert shipbuilders, and even today, some builders continue to construct large, seaworthy vessels in their own backyards. This has always been done "by the rack of the eye," as they say here, which means that the builders use traditional knowledge handed down over the generations, rather than modern industrial methods. Their exceptional expertise is beautifully demonstrated by the craft in the museum

and by boats still working the waters today. Here at the Watercraft Center, the Maritime Museum provides workspace for builders of full-size and model boats, and it teaches a vast array of classes in boatbuilding skills, both traditional and mechanized methods.

◖ Old Burying Ground
One of the most beautiful places in all of North Carolina, Beaufort's Old Burying Ground (Anne St., open daylight hours daily) is as picturesque a cemetery as you'd ever want to be buried in. It's quite small by the standards of some old Carolina towns, and crowded with 18th- and 19th-century stones. Huge old live oaks, Spanish moss, wisteria, and resurrection ferns, which unfurl and turn green after a rainstorm, give the Burying Ground an irresistibly gothic feel. Many of the headstones reflect the maritime heritage of this town, such as that of a sea captain whose epitaph reads, "The form that fills this silent grave/once tossed on ocean's rolling wave/but in a port securely fast/he's dropped his anchor here at last."

Captain Otway Burns, an early privateer who spent much time in Beaufort, is buried here; his grave is easy to spot, as it is topped by a canon from his ship, the *Snap Dragon*. Nearby is another of the graveyard's famous burials, that of the "Little Girl Buried in a Barrel of Rum." This unfortunate waif is said to have died at sea and been placed in a cask of rum, to preserve her body for burial on land. Visitors often bring toys and trinkets to leave on her grave, which is marked by a simple wooden plank. Though hers is the most gaudily festooned, you'll see evidence of this old tradition of funerary gifts on other graves here as well—most often, in this cemetery, coins and shells. This is a tradition found throughout the coastal South and the Caribbean, with roots tracing back to Africa. Feel free to add to her haul of goodies, but it's not karmically advisable to tamper with those already there.

Beaufort Historic Site

The Beaufort Historic Site (130 Turner St., 252/728-5225, www.beauforthistoricsite.org, $8 adults, $4 children) recreates life in late 18th- and early 19th-century Beaufort in several restored historic buildings. The 1770s "jump-and-a-half" (1.5-story) Leffers Cottage reflects middle-class life in its day, as a merchant, whaler, or—in this case—schoolmaster would have lived it. The Josiah Bell and John Manson Houses, both from the 1820s, reflect the graceful Caribbean-influenced architecture so prevalent in the early days of the coastal South. A restored apothecary shop, 1790s wooden courthouse, and a haunted 1820s jail that was used into the 1950s, are among the other important structures here. There are tours led by costumed interpreters, as well as driving tours of the old town in double-decker buses. Hours vary by season: 9:30 A.M.–5 P.M. Monday–Saturday March 1–November 31, plus 1–4 P.M. Sundays in June–August; 10 A.M.–4 P.M. Monday–Saturday December 1–February 28.

SPORTS AND RECREATION
Diving

North Carolina's coast is a surprisingly good place for diving. The **Discovery Diving Company** (414 Orange St., 252/728-2265, www.discoverydiving.com, $65–105/excursion) leads half- and full-day diving trips to explore the reefs and dozens of fascinating shipwrecks that lie at the bottom of the sounds and ocean near Beaufort.

Cruises and Wildlife Tours

Coastal Ecology Tours (252/247-3860, www.goodfortunesails.com, prices vary) runs very special tours on the *Good Fortune* of the Cape Lookout National Seashore and other island locations in the area, as well as a variety of half-day, day-long, overnight, and short trips, to snorkel, shell, kayak, and watch birds, and cruises to Morehead City restaurants, and other educational and fun trips. Prices range from $40 per person for a 2.5-hour dolphin-watching tour to $600 a night plus meals for an off-season overnight boat rental.

Lookout Cruises (600 Front St., 252/504-7245, www.lookoutcruises.com) carries sightseers on lovely catamaran rides in the Beaufort and Core Sound region, out to Cape Lookout, and on morning dolphin-watching trips.

Island Ferry Adventures (610 Front St., 252/728-7555, www.islandferryadventures.com, $10–15 adults, $5–8 children) runs dolphin-watching tours, trips to collect shells at Cape Lookout, and trips to see the wild ponies of Shackleford Banks.

Mystery Tours (600 Front St., 252/728-7827 or 866/230-2628, www.mysteryboattours.com, $10–50 adults, $15–30 children, some cruises for grown-ups only) offers harbor tours and dolphin-watching trips, as well as a variety of brunch, lunch, and dinner cruises, and trips to wild islands where children can hunt for treasure.

ACCOMMODATIONS
Under $150

The **Inlet Inn** (601 Front St., 800/554-5466, www.inlet-inn.com, $125–165) has one of the best locations in town, right on the water, near the docks where many of the ferry and tour boats land. If planning to go dolphin-watching or hop the ferry to Cape Lookout, you can get ready at a leisurely pace, and just step outside to the docks. Even in the high season, prices are quite reasonable. The **Beaufort Inn** (101 Ann St., 252/728-2600, www.beaufort-inn.com) is a large hotel on Gallants Channel, along one side of the colonial district. It's an easy walk to the main downtown attractions, and the hotel's outdoor hot tub and balconies with great views make it tempting to stay in as well.

The **Pecan Tree Inn** (116 Queen St., 800/728-7871, www.pecantree.com, $100–180) is such a grand establishment that the town threw a parade in honor of the laying of its cornerstone in 1866. The house is still splendid, as are the 5,000-square-foot gardens.

Catty-corner to the Old Burying Grounds is the **Langdon House Bed and Breakfast** (135 Craven St., 252/728-5499, www.langdonhouse.com, $115–200). One of the oldest buildings in town, this gorgeous house was built in the 1730s on a foundation of English ballast stones.

Over $300

⟨ Outer Banks Houseboats (324 Front St., 252/728-4129, www.outerbankshouseboats.com) will rent you your own floating vacation home, drive it for you to a scenic spot, anchor it, and then come and check in on you every day during your stay. You'll have a skiff for your own use, but you may just want to lie on the deck all day and soak up the peacefulness. Rates run from $700 per weekend for the smaller houseboat, to $3,000 per week for the luxury boat, with plenty of rental options in between.

FOOD

Among the Beaufort eateries certified by Carteret Catch as serving local seafood are the **Blue Moon Bistro** (119 Queen St., 252/728-5800, www.bluemoonbistro.biz, 5:30–10 P.M. Tues.–Sat.), **Sharpie's Grill and Bar** (521 Front St., 252/838-0101, www.sharpiesgrill.com, 5:30–10 P.M. Mon.–Sat.), and **Aqua Restaurant** (114 Middle Ln.

"behind Clawsons," 252/728-7777, www.aquaexperience.com, 5:30–10 P.M. Tues.–Sat.).

If you're traveling with a cooler and want to buy some local seafood to take home, try the **Fishtowne Seafood Center** (100 Wellons Dr., 252/728-6644) or **Tripps Seafood** (1224 Harkers Island Rd., 252/447-7700).

⟨ Beaufort Grocery (117 Queen St., 252/728-3899, www.beaufortgrocery.com, open for lunch and dinner every day but Tues., brunch on Sun., $20–36) is, despite its humble name, a sophisticated little eatery. At lunch it serves salads and crusty sandwiches, along with "Damn Good Gumbo" and specialty soups. In the evening the café atmosphere gives way to that of a more formal gourmet dining room. Some of the best entrées include boneless chicken breast sautéed with pecans in a hazelnut cream sauce; Thai-rubbed roast half duckling; and whole baby rack of lamb, served with garlic mashed potatoes, tortillas, and a margarita-chipotle sauce. Try the cheesecake for dessert.

The waterfront **Front Street Grill** (300 Front St., 252/728-4956, www.frontstreetgrillatstillwater.com, 11:30 A.M.–2 P.M. and 5:30–9:30 P.M. daily, 11:30 A.M.–2 P.M. Sunday brunch) is popular with boaters drifting through the area, as well as diners who arrive by land. The emphasis is on seafood and fresh regional ingredients. Front Street Grill's wine list is extensive, and they have repeatedly won *Wine Spectator* magazine's Award of Excellence.

MOREHEAD CITY

Giovanni da Verrazano may have been the first European to set foot in present-day Morehead City when he sailed into Bogue Inlet. It wasn't until the mid-19th century that the town actually came into being, built as the terminus of the North Carolina Railroad to connect the state's overland commerce to the sea. Despite its late start, Morehead City has been a busy place. During the Civil War it was the site of major encampments by both armies. A series of horrible hurricanes in the 1890s, culminating in 1899's San Ciriaco Hurricane, brought hundreds of refugees from the towns along what is now the Cape Lookout National Seashore. They settled in a neighborhood that they called Promise Land, and many of their descendants are still here.

The Atlantic and North Carolina Railroad operated a large hotel here in the 1880s, ushering in Morehead's role as a tourist spot, and the bridge to the Bogue Banks a few decades later increased holiday traffic considerably.

Morehead is also an official state port, one of the best deepwater harbors on the Atlantic Coast. This admixture of tourism and gritty commerce gives Morehead City a likeable, real-life feel missing in many coastal towns today.

Sights

Morehead City's history is on display at **The History Place** (1008 Arendell St., 252/247-7533, www.thehistoryplace.org, 10 A.M.–4 P.M. Tues.–Sat.). There are many interesting and eye-catching historical artifacts on display, but the most striking exhibit is that of a carriage, clothes, and other items pertaining to Emeline Pigott, Morehead City's Confederate heroine. She was a busy girl all through the Civil War, working as a nurse, a spy, and a smuggler. The day she was captured, she was carrying 30 pounds of contraband hidden in her skirts, including Union troop movement plans, a collection of gloves, several dozen skeins of silk, needles, toothbrushes, a pair of boots, and five pounds of candy.

Entertainment and Events

Seafood is a serious art here. North Carolina's second-largest festival takes place in Morehead City every October, the enormous **North Carolina Seafood Festival** (252/726-6273, www.ncseafoodfestival.org). The city's streets shut down and over 150,000 visitors descend on the waterfront. Festivities kick off with a blessing of the fleet, followed with music, fireworks, competitions (like the flounder-toss), and, of course, lots and lots of food.

If you're in the area on the right weekend in November, you'll not want to deprive yourself of the gluttonous splendor of the **Mill Creek Oyster Festival** (Mill Creek Volunteer Fire Department, 2370 Mill Creek Rd., Mill Creek, 252/247-4777). Food, and lots of it, is the focus of this event. It's a small-town fete, a benefit for the local volunteer fire department, and the meals are cooked by local experts. You'll be able to choose from all-you-can-eat roasted oysters, fried shrimp, fried spot (a local fish), and more, all in mass quantities. The oysters may not be local these days (and few served on this coast are), but the cooking is very local—an authentic taste of one of North Carolina's best culinary traditions. Mill Creek is northwest of Morehead City on the Newport River.

Sports and Recreation

Many of this region's most important historic and natural sites are underwater. From Morehead City's **Olympus Dive Center** (713 Shepard St., 252/726-9432, www.olympusdiving.com), divers of all levels of experience can take charter trips to dozens of natural and artificial reefs that teem with fish, including the ferocious-looking but not terribly dangerous eight-foot-long sand tiger shark. There are at least as many amazing shipwrecks to choose from, including an 18th-century schooner, a luxury liner, a German U-boat, and many Allied commercial and military ships that fell victim to the U-boats that infested this coast during World War II.

Food

The **Sanitary Fish Market** (501 Evans St., 252/247-3111, www.sanitaryfishmarket.com, $12–20) is probably Morehead City's best-known institution. The rather odd name reflects its 1930s origins as a seafood market that was bound by its lease and its fastidious landlord to be kept as clean as possible. Today it's a huge family seafood restaurant. Long lines in season and on weekends demonstrate its popularity. Of particular note are its famous hush puppies, which have a well-deserved reputation as some of the best in the state. Be sure to buy a Sanitary t-shirt on the way out; it'll help you blend in everywhere else in the state.

Captain Bill's (701 Evans St., 252/726-

2166, www.captbills.com) is Morehead City's oldest restaurant, founded in 1938. Try the conch stew, and be sure to visit the otters that live at the dock outside.

Another famous eating joint in Morehead City is **El's Drive-In** (3706 Arendell St., 252/726-3002), a tiny place across from Carteret Community College. El's has been around almost as many forevers as the Sanitary. It's most famous for its shrimp burgers, but serves all sorts of fried delights.

Mrs. Willis' Restaurant (3114 Bridges St., 252/726-3741) is a popular home-style lunch and dinner spot. It's a sit-down restaurant, certainly not as casual as El's, but plenty laid-back just the same. Charcoal-grilled steaks are the specialty.

Cox's Restaurant (4109 Arendell St., 252/726-6961) also has served down-home cooking for many years, and is known for its friendly staff and coterie of local regulars.

For an old fashioned ladies' luncheon or afternoon tea, visit the tiny, five-table tearoom at the **Tea Clipper** (The History Place, 1012 Arendell St., 252/240-2800, www.theteaclipper.com, 11 A.M.–5 P.M. Tues.–Sat.). In addition to the many teas, you can order scones and desserts, and dainty quiche and sandwiches. The Tea Clipper shop, the mother ship of the little tearoom, has more than 120 teas of all kinds sold by the scoop.

INFORMATION AND SERVICES

Extensive travel information is available from the **Crystal Coast Tourism Authority** (3409 Arendell St., 877/206-0929, www.crystalcoastnc.org).

Carteret General Hospital (3500 Arendell St., 252/808-6000, www.ccgh.org) is located in Morehead City.

HARKERS ISLAND

The Core Sound region, which stretches to the east-northeast of Beaufort many miles up to the Pamlico Sound, is a region of birds and boats. Like much of the Carolina coast, the marshes and pocosins here are visited by countless flocks of migratory birds on their ways to and from their winter quarters, as well as the many birds that live here year-round. Consequently, hunting has always been a way of life here, almost as much as fishing. In earlier generations (and to a much lesser extent today), men who fished most of the year did a sideline business in bird hunting; not only would they eat the birds they shot, but they made money selling feathers for ladies' hats, they trained bird dogs for their own and other hunters' use, and they served as guides to visiting hunters. Many Down Easterners also became expert decoy carvers. This art survives today, partly as art for art's sake, and also for its original purpose. Woodworking on a much grander scale has also defined the culture of this section, as it has bred generations of great boat-builders. Keep an eye out as you drive through Harkers Island, because you may see boats under construction in folks' backyards—not canoes or dinghies, but full-sized fishing boats.

To get to Harkers Island, follow U.S. 70 east from Beaufort, around the dogleg that skirts the North River. A little east of the town of Otway you'll see Harkers Island Road. Take a right on Harkers Island Road, and head south towards Straits. Straits Road will take you through the town by the same name, and then across a bridge over the Straits themselves, finally ending up on Harkers Island.

◖ Core Sound Waterfowl Museum

The Core Sound Waterfowl Museum (1785 Island Rd., Harkers Island, 252/728-1500, www.coresound.com, 10 A.M.–5 P.M. Mon.–Sat., 2–5 P.M. Sun., free), which occupies a beautiful modern building on Shell Point, next to the Cape Lookout National Seashore headquarters, is a community labor of love. The museum is home to exhibits crafted by members of the communities represented, depicting the Down East maritime life through decoys, nets, and other tools of the trades, everyday household objects, beautiful quilts and other utilitarian folk arts, and lots of other things held dear by the people who live and lived here. This is a sophisticated, modern institution, but its community roots are evident in touching details like the index-card labels, written in the careful script of elderly ladies, explaining what certain objects are, what they were used for, and who made them. For instance, just as Piedmont textile workers made and treasured their loom hooks, folks down here took pride in the hooks that they made to assist in the perennial off-season work of hanging nets. Baseball uniforms on display represent an era when one town's team might have to travel by ferry to its opponent's field. The museum hosts monthly get-togethers for members of communities Down East, a different town every month, which are like old home days. Families and long-lost friends reunite over home-cooked food, to reminisce about community history and talk about their hopes and concerns for the future.

The museum's gift shop has a nice selection of books and other items related to Down East culture. Be sure to pick up a copy of *The Harkers Island Cookbook* by the Harkers Island United Methodist Women. This cookbook has become a regional classic for its wonderful blend of authentic family recipes and community stories. You might also be able to find a Core Sound Christmas Tree, made by Harvey and Sons in nearby Davis. This old family fishery has made a hit in recent years manufacturing small Christmas trees out of recycled crab pots. It's a whimsical item, but it carries deep messages about the past and future of the Core Sound region.

Core Sound Decoy Carvers Guild

Twenty years ago, some decoy-carving friends Down East decided over a pot of stewed clams to found the Core Sound Decoy Carvers Guild (1575 Harkers Island Rd., 252/838-8818, www.decoyguild.com, call for hours). The Guild, which is open to the public, gives demonstrations, competitions, and classes for grown-ups and children, and has a museum shop that's a nice place to browse.

Events

The Core Sound Decoy Carvers Guild also hosts the **Core Sound Decoy Festival,** usually held in the early winter. Several thousand people come to this annual event—more than the number of permanent residents on Harkers Island—to buy, swap, and teach the art of making decoys.

Food

Captain's Choice Restaurant (977 Island Rd., 252/728-7122) is a great place to try traditional Down East chowder. Usually made of clams, but sometimes with other shellfish or fish, chowder in Carteret County is a point of pride. The point is the flavor of the seafood itself, which must be extremely fresh, and not hidden behind lots of milk and spices. Captain's Choice serves chowder in the old-time way—with dumplings.

VILLAGE OF CEDAR ISLAND

For a beautiful afternoon's drive, head back to the mainland, and follow U.S. 70 north. You'll go through some tiny communities— Williston, Davis, Stacy—and, if you keep bearing north on Highway 12 when U.S. 70 heads south to the town of Atlantic, you'll eventually reach the tip of the peninsula, and the fishing village of Cedar Island. This little fishing town has the amazing ambience of being at the end of the earth. From the peninsula's shore you can barely see land across the sounds. The ferry to Ocracoke departs from Cedar Island, and it's an unbelievable two-hours-plus ride across the Pamlico Sound to get there. The beach here is absolutely gorgeous, and horses roam. They're not the famous wild horses of the Outer Banks, but they move about freely as if they were.

A spectacular location for bird-watching is the **Cedar Island National Wildlife Refuge** (on U.S. 70, east of the town Atlantic, 252/926-4021, www.fws.gov/cedarisland). Nearly all of its 14,500 acres are brackish marshland, and it's often visited in season by redhead ducks, buffleheads, surf scoters, and many other species. While there are trails for hiking and biking, this refuge is primarily intended as a safe haven for the birds.

Accommodations and Food

(**The Driftwood Motel** (3575 Cedar Island Rd., 252/225-4861, www.clis.com/deg/drift2.htm) is a simple motel in an incredible location, and since the ferry leaves from its parking lot, it's the place to stay if you're coming from or going to Ocracoke. There's also camping here, for $16 per tent and $18–20 for RV, with electricity, water, and sewer.

The Driftwood's **Pirate's Chest Restaurant** is the only restaurant on Cedar Island, so it's a good thing that it's a good one. Local seafood is the specialty, and dishes can be adapted for vegetarians.

Lower Outer Banks

The southern reaches of the Outer Banks of North Carolina comprise some of the region's most diverse destinations. Core and Shackleford Banks lie within the Cape Lookout National Seashore, a wild maritime environment populated by plenty of wild ponies but not a single human. On the other hand, the towns of Bogue Banks—Atlantic Beach, Salter Path, Pine Knoll Shores, Indian Beach, and Emerald Isle—are classic beach towns, with clusters of motels and restaurants, and even a few towel shops and miniature golf courses. Both areas are great fun, though, Cape Lookout especially so for eco-tourists and history buffs, and Bogue Banks for those looking for a day on the beach followed by an evening chowing down on good fried seafood.

(CAPE LOOKOUT NATIONAL SEASHORE

Cape Lookout National Seashore (Headquarters 131 Charles St., Harkers Island, 252/728-2250, www.nps.gov/calo) is an otherworldly place, 56 miles of beach on four barrier islands, a long tape of sand so seemingly vulnerable to nature that it's hard to believe there were once several busy towns on its banks. Settled in the early 1700s, the towns of the south Core Banks made their living in fisheries that might seem brutal to today's seafood eaters—whaling, and catching dolphins and sea turtles, among the more mundane species. Portsmouth, at the north end of the park across the water from Ocracoke, was a busy port of great importance to the early economy of North Carolina. Portsmouth declined slowly, but catastrophe rained down all at once on the people of the

southerly Shackleford Banks, who were driven out of their own long-established communities to start new lives on the mainland when a series of terrible hurricanes hit in the 1890s.

Islands often support unique ecosystems. Among the dunes, small patches of maritime forest fight for each drop of fresh water, while ghost forests of trees that were defeated by advancing saltwater look on resignedly. Along the endless beach, loggerhead turtles come ashore to lay their eggs, and in the waters just off the strand, three other species of sea turtles are sometimes seen. Wild horses roam the beaches and dunes and dolphins frequent both the ocean and Sound sides of the islands. Other mammals, though, are all of the small and scrappy variety: raccoons, rodents, otters, and rabbits. Like all of coastal North Carolina, it's a great place for bird-watching, as it's located in a heavily traveled migratory flyway. (Pets are allowed, with leashes. The wild ponies on Shackleford Banks can pose a threat to dogs who get among them, and the dogs of course can frighten the horses, so be careful not to let them mingle should you and your dog find yourselves near the herd.)

Portsmouth Village

Portsmouth Village, at the northern tip of the Cape Lookout National Seashore, is a peaceful but eerie place. The village looks much as it did 100 years ago, the handsome houses and churches all tidy and in good repair, but with the exception of caretakers and summer volunteers, no one has lived here in nearly 40 years. In 1970, the last two residents moved away from what had once been a town of 700 people and one of the most important shipping ports in North Carolina. Founded before the Revolution, Portsmouth was a lightering station, a port where huge seagoing ships that had traveled across the ocean would stop, and have their cargo removed for transport across the shallow sounds in smaller boats. There is a visitors center located at Portsmouth, open varying hours April–October, where you can learn about the village before embarking on a stroll to explore the quiet streets.

In its busy history, Portsmouth was captured by the British during the War of 1812 and by the Yankees in the Civil War, underscoring its strategic importance. By the time of the Civil War, though, its utility as a waystation was already declining. An 1846 hurricane opened a new inlet at Hatteras, which quickly became a busy shipping channel. Then after abolition, the town's lightering trade was no longer profitable without slaves to perform much of the labor. The fishing and lifesaving businesses kept the town afloat for a couple more generations, but Portsmouth was never the same.

Once a year, an amazing thing happens. Boatloads of people arrive on shore, and the church bell rings, and the sound of hymn singing comes through the open church doors. At the Portsmouth Homecoming, descendants of the people who lived here come from all over the state and country to pay tribute to their ancestral home. They have an old-time dinner on the grounds with much socializing and catching up, and then tour the little village together. It's like a family reunion, with the town itself the family's matriarch. On the other 364 days of the year, Portsmouth receives its share of tourists and Park Service caretakers, but one senses that it's already looking forward to the next spring, when its children will come home again.

Shackleford Banks

The once-busy villages of Diamond City and Shackleford Banks are like Portsmouth in that, though they have not been occupied for many years, the descendants of the people who lived here retain a profound attachment to their ancestors' homes. Diamond City and nearby

communities met a spectacular end. The hurricane season of 1899 culminated in the San Ciriaco Hurricane, a disastrous storm that destroyed homes and forests, killed livestock, flooded gardens with saltwater, and washed the Shackleford dead out of their graves. The Bankers saw the writing on the wall, and moved to the mainland en masse, carrying as much of their property as would fit on boats. Some actually floated their houses across Core Sound. Harkers Island absorbed most of the refugee population (many also went to Morehead City), and their traditions are still an important part of Down East culture. Daily and weekly programs held at the Light Station Pavilion and the porch of the Keepers' Quarters during the summer months teach visitors about the natural and human history of Cape Lookout, including what day-to-day life was like for the keeper of the lighthouse and his family.

Descendants of the Bankers feel a deep spiritual bond to their ancestors' home, and for many years they would return frequently, occupying fish camps that they constructed along the beach. When the federal government bought the Banks, it was made known that the fish camps would soon be off-limits to their deedless owners. The outcry and bitterness that ensued testified to the depth of the Core Sounders' love of their ancestral grounds. The Park Service may have thought that the fish camps were of no more importance than duck blinds or tents— ephemeral and purely recreational structures. But to the fish camps' owners, the Banks was still home, even if they themselves had been born on the mainland and never lived there for longer than a fishing season—the camps were their homes every bit as much as their actual residences on the mainland. Retaining their pride of spiritual, if not legal, ownership, many burned down their own fish camps rather than allow the Park Service to destroy them.

Cape Lookout Lighthouse

By the time you arrive at the 1859 Cape Lookout Lighthouse (visitors center, 252/728-2250), you'll probably already have seen it portrayed on dozens of brochures, menus, business signs, and souvenirs. With its striking diamond pattern, it looks like a rattlesnake standing at attention. In years past, visitors were allowed into this working lighthouse only four dates each year. However, a negative safety report has caused the public visits to be suspended. The Visitor Center and Museum (9 A.M.–5 P.M. daily, Apr.–Nov.) remains open for part of the year. Visit Cape Lookout National Seashore's website (www.nps.gov/calo) for more information.

Camping

Camping is permitted within Cape Lookout National Seashore, though there are no designated campsites or camping amenities. Everything you bring must be carried back out when you leave. Campers can stay for up to 14 days.

Getting There and Around

There is only one small part of Cape Lookout National Seashore that is accessible by car, the tip of Harkers Island, where the visitors center is located next to the Core Sound Waterfowl Museum. To get to the other side of the Sound, you'll have to catch one of several ferries that run to and from the Banks. Some carry vehicles, but others are passenger-only; fees vary, and some require reservations; most operate only from mid-March to early December; some will allow your pets, and others won't. Plan ahead, and be sure to leave time for unexpected changes in schedule.

The passenger ferry to Portsmouth departs from Ocracoke, and it's a relatively short hop across Ocracoke Inlet (Capt. Rudy Austin, 252/928-4361, passengers); but if you're trying to get to Portsmouth from mainland Carteret County, you'll first have to take the Cedar Island–Ocracoke ferry (NC Dept. of Transportation, 800/856-0343, www.ncdot .org/transit/ferry/routes, vehicles and passengers) across Pamlico Sound, a trip of more than two hours. One ferry goes to North Core Banks, departing from Atlantic (Morris Marina Kabin Kamps and Ferry Service,

877/956-6568, www.nps.gov/calo/playnyour-visit/ferry.htm, vehicles and passengers), and from Davis to Great Island on the South Core Banks (Great Island Cabins and Ferry Service, 877/956-6568, vehicles and passengers).

Four passenger ferries travel between Harkers Island and Cape Lookout Lighthouse and Shackleford Banks (Captain Jack's Ferry, 252/728-3575; Harkers Island Fishing Center, 252/728-3907; Island Ferry Adventures at Barbour Marina, 252/728-6181; and Local Yokel, 252/728-2759), and one Beaufort ferry goes to both the lighthouse and Shackleford Banks (Outer Banks Ferry Service, 252/728-2759). Other options for getting to Shackleford Banks are Morehead City's Waterfront Ferry Service (252/726-7678), and Beaufort's Island Ferry Adventures (252/728-7555) and Mystery Tours (252/728-7827).

Morris Marina and Ferry Service (877/956-6568) is Cape Lookout's main transportation concessionaire. In addition to ferries, they operate some vehicle shuttles on the Banks. Call with inquiries about specific routes. Some of the other ferries also run four-wheel-drive taxis from point to point within the National Seashore.

BOGUE BANKS

The beaches of Bogue Banks are popular tourist spots, but they have a typically North Carolinian, laid-back feel, a quieter atmosphere than the fun-fun-fun neon jungles of other states' beaches. The major attractions here, Fort Macon State Park and the North Carolina Aquarium at Pine Knoll Shores, are a bit more cerebral than, say, amusement parks and bikini contests. In the surfing and boating, bars and restaurants, and the beach itself, there's also a bustle of activity to keep things hopping. Bogue, by the way, rhymes with "rogue."

◖ North Carolina Aquarium

The North Carolina Aquarium at Pine Knoll Shores (1 Roosevelt Blvd., Pine Knoll Shores, 866/294-3477, www.ncaquariums.com, 9 A.M.–5 P.M. daily, until 9 P.M. every Thurs.

in July, $8 adults, $7 seniors, $6 children 17 and younger) is one of the state's three great coastal aquariums. Here at Pine Knoll Shores, exhibit highlights include: a 300,000-gallon aquarium in which sharks and other aquatic beasts go about their business in and around a replica German U-Boat (plenty of originals lie right off the coast and form homes for reef creatures); a "jellyfish gallery" (they really can be beautiful); a pair of river otters; and many other wonderful animals and habitats.

Trails from the parking lot lead into the maritime forests of the 568-acre **Theodore Roosevelt Natural Area** (1 Roosevelt Dr., Atlantic Beach, 252/726-3775).

Fort Macon State Park

At the eastern tip of Atlantic Beach is Fort Macon State Park (2300 E. Fort Macon Rd., 252/726-3775, www.ncsparks.net/foma.html, 9 A.M.–5:30 P.M. daily, fort open 8 A.M.–6 P.M. Oct.–Mar., 8 A.M.–7 P.M. Apr., May, and Sept., and 8 A.M.–8 P.M. June–Aug., bathhouse area 8 A.M.–5:30 P.M. Nov.–Feb., 8 A.M.–7 P.M. Mar.–Oct., 8 A.M.–8 P.M. Apr., May, and Sept., and 8 A.M.–9 P.M. June–Aug., bathhouse $4/day, $3 child). The central feature of the park is Fort Macon itself, an 1820s Federal fort that was a Confederate garrison for one year during the Civil War. Guided tours are offered, and there are exhibits inside the casemates. For such a stern, martial building, some of the interior spaces are surprisingly pretty.

Sports and Recreation

The ocean side of Bogue Banks offers plenty of public beach access. In each of the towns, from the northeast end of the island to the southwest end—Atlantic Beach, Pine Knoll Shores, Salter Path, Indian Beach, and Emerald Isle—there are parking lots, both municipal and private, free and for-fee.

Aside from the fort itself, the other big attraction at **Fort Macon** is the beach, which is bounded by the ocean, Bogue Sound, and Beaufort Inlet. Because there's a Coast Guard station on the Sound side, and a jetty along the Inlet, swimming is permitted only along one stretch of the ocean beach. A concession stand and bathhouse are located at the swimming beach.

Atlantic Beach Surf Shop (515 W. Fort Macon Rd., Atlantic Beach, 252/646-4944, www.absurfshop.com) gives individual ($50/hour) and group ($40/hour) surfing lessons on the beach at Pine Knoll Shores. Lessons are in the morning and early afternoon. Call for reservations.

Accommodations

The **Atlantis Lodge** (123 Salter Path Rd., Atlantic Beach, 800/682-7057, www.atlantislodge.com, $72–235) is an old, established, family-run motel. It has simple and reasonably priced efficiencies in a great beachfront location. Well-behaved pets are welcome for a per-pet-per-night fee. The **Clamdigger** (511 Salter Path Rd., Atlantic Beach, 800/338-1533, www.clamdiggerinn.com, $49–205) is another reliable choice, with all oceanfront rooms. Pets are not allowed. The **Windjammer** (103 Salter Path Rd., Atlantic Beach, 800/233-6466, www.windjammerinn.com, $50–200) is another simple, comfortable motel, with decent rates through the high season.

Food

The **Channel Marker** (718 Atlantic Beach Causeway, Atlantic Beach, 252/247-2344) is an haute-er alternative to some of the old-timey fried seafood joints on Bogue Banks (which are also great—read on). Try the crab cakes with mango chutney, or the Greek shrimp salad. The extensive wine list stars wines from the opposite side of North Carolina, from the Biltmore Estate in Asheville.

White Swan Bar-B-Q and Chicken (2500-A W. Fort Macon Rd., Atlantic Beach, 252/726-9607) has been serving the Carolina trinity of barbecue, coleslaw, and hush puppies since 1960. They also flip a mean egg for breakfast.

The ◖ **Big Oak Drive-In and Bar-B-Q** (1167 Salter Path Rd., 252/247-2588, www.bigoakdrivein.com) is a classic beach drive-in, a

CENTRAL COAST

THE DECLINE OF THE FISHING INDUSTRY

It's ironic that along the coast of North Carolina, where for centuries fishing has been more than a business – it's been an entire culture – relatively little of the seafood served in restaurants or sold in markets nowadays is actually caught by local fishermen. Sitting in a dockside restaurant, looking out at fishermen unloading their day's haul, you may be eating shrimp that were flown in from Thailand, or fish from Chile, or oysters from France. Like the textile industry, North Carolina's commercial fisheries have suffered tremendously from global trade. There is, however, a growing concern for promoting the interests of local fisheries before it's too late – if it's not already. **Carteret Catch** is an organization dedicated to the promotion of the fishing industry here in Carteret County. At their website (www.carteretcatch .org), you can find out which local restaurants and fish markets are buying seafood from the fishermen who live and work in this community, rather than from international wholesalers.

As recently as 10 years ago, the shores and riverbanks of eastern North Carolina were covered with fish houses. Often small, family-run operations, fish houses were the best places

in the world for seafood lovers, who could buy their favorite fish and shellfish as soon as the boats were unloaded. Today, things are very different. For reasons both environmental and economic, the old-time seafood house is nearly extinct. Declines in popular species of fish and shellfish have hit North Carolina's fishermen, like others around the world, painfully hard. Concurrently, the skyrocketing value of land along the coast – and up the rivers and along the back creeks and marshes – often renders such a business unsustainable. Owners of fish houses are either run out of business by the exponential rise of their property taxes, or give in to the temptation to sell their waterfront lots for more money than they might have made in years of fishing.

This book will help you find some of the last remaining fish houses and seafood restaurants that still serve catches right off the docks. Though they have become so few and far between, the effort in finding traditional seafood houses is certainly worthwhile. You'll taste some of the freshest, best seafood in the world, and you'll be helping give a critically threatened traditional way of life a fighting chance.

little red-white-and-blue-striped building with a walk-up counter and drive-up spaces. They're best known for their shrimpburgers ($4.95 large), a fried affair slathered with Big Oak's signature red sauce, coleslaw, and tartar sauce. Then there are the scallopburgers, oysterburgers, clamburgers, hamburgers, and barbecue, all cheap, and made for snacking on the beach.

Frost Seafood House (1300 Salter Path Rd., Salter Path, 252/247-3202) began in 1954 as a gas station and quickly became the restaurant that it is today. The Frost family catch their own shrimp and buy much of their other

seafood locally. Be sure to request a taste of the "ching-a-ling sauce." Yet another community institution is the **Crab Shack** (140 Shore Dr., Salter Path, 252/247-3444). You'll find it behind the Methodist church in Salter Path. Operated by the Guthries (a family name that dates back to the dawn of time in this area, long before anyone thought of calling their home the "Crystal Coast"), the restaurant was wiped out in 2005 by Hurricane Ophelia, but they have since rebuilt, rolled up their sleeves, and plunged their hands back into the cornmeal.

WILMINGTON AND THE CAPE FEAR REGION

The Cape Fear region was and is very much a part of the Caribbean-basin culture that stretches up through the south Atlantic coast of North America—a world that reflects English, Spanish, and French adaptation to the tropics and, above all, to the profoundly transformative influence of the African cultures brought to the New World by captive slaves. Wilmington is part of the sorority that includes Havana, Caracas, Port au Prince, Santo Domingo, New Orleans, Savannah, and Charleston. Savannah, Charleston, and Wilmington are the main points of the Carolina Lowcountry, and like its closest sisters, Wilmington and the surrounding Cape Fear coast exhibits the richness of Afro-Caribbean culture in its architecture, cuisine, folklore, and speech.

Robeson County, along the South Carolina state line, is the geographic home of the Lumbee tribe, who are historically and spiritually tied to the beautiful blackwater Lumber River. The Lumbees are the largest tribe east of the Mississippi, yet many Americans have never heard of them. This is due in part to the fact that the government denies them federal recognition, a complex and highly contentious issue that casts a long shadow over much of the politics, economics, and history of this part of the state. A "non-reservated" tribe, the Lumbees have for centuries lived much as their white and African American neighbors have—a mostly rural existence, anchored in a profound devotion to the Christian faith. Their history is fascinating and often surprising, and can be explored by the traveler in and around the town of Pembroke.

COURTESY OF WWW.CAPEFEARCOAST.ORG

HIGHLIGHTS

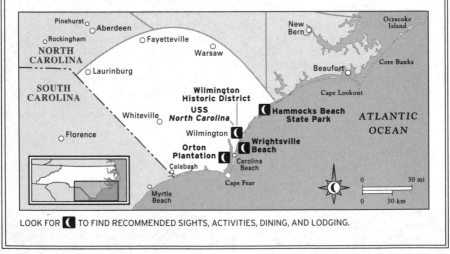

Wilmington Historic District: Wilmington's downtown reflects its glory days of commerce and high society. This is North Carolina's largest 19th-century historic district, a gorgeous collection of antebellum and late Victorian townhouses and commercial buildings, including many beautiful Southern iterations of the Italianate craze that preceded the Civil War (page 83).

Wrightsville Beach: North Carolina has many wonderful beaches, but few can compare with Wrightsville for its pretty strand, easy public access, clear waters, and overall beauty (page 86).

USS *North Carolina:* A state-of-the-art weapon in its time, this veteran World War II warship is a floating monument to the nearly 10,000 North Carolinians who died in World War II and a museum of what life was like onboard (page 87).

Hammocks Beach State Park: Accessible only by boat, one of the wildest and least disturbed Atlantic coast beaches, Bear Island is a popular stopover for migrating waterfowl and turtles (page 96).

Orton Plantation: Orton's formal gardens embody the aesthetic of "Southern Gothic," juxtaposing the romantic and largely imaginary idyll of the Old South with the mournful spookiness of moss-draped swamps, honking alligators, and the plantation's often tragic history. It's picturesque in the extreme (page 101).

LOOK FOR **C** TO FIND RECOMMENDED SIGHTS, ACTIVITIES, DINING, AND LODGING.

The area between Wilmington and Lumberton in the state's southeast corner is a strange, exotic waterscape (more so than a landscape) of seductively eerie swamps and backwaters. People from the Piedmont will turn up their noses at the swamps, claiming that they reek like rotten eggs and that the farmland's no good. But to those of us who are native to this corner of the Carolinas,

our cypress knees and tannic creeks and nests of snakes and alligators make this a region of sinister but incomparable beauty—and swamp air the best aromatherapy there is. In this little band of coastal counties straddling the state line, within a 100-mile radius of Wilmington, we share the native habitat—the only one in the world—of the Venus flytrap, a ferocious little plant of rather ghastly beauty. It somehow seems like an appropriate mascot for these weird backwaters.

The greatest draw to this region, even more than colonial cobblestones and carnivorous plants, are the beaches of Brunswick, New Hanover, and Onslow Counties. Some of them, like Wrightsville and Topsail, are well known, and others remain comparatively secluded barrier island strands. In some ways the "Brunswick Islands," as visitors bureaus designate them, can be thought of as the northern edge of the famous Grand Strand area around Myrtle Beach, South Carolina. No square mile of this region could be mistaken for Myrtle Beach, though; even the beaches that are most liberally peppered with towel shops and miniature golf courses will seem positively bucolic in comparison. But those with an appreciation for Myrtle Beach's inimitable style, our own chaotically commercial, in-your-face Paris of the Pee Dee (one of the rivers that flows through the border region of the Carolinas), will be glad to know that it's only a few short miles away.

PLANNING YOUR TIME

Depending on which part of the Cape Fear area you're planning to explore, you have a range of good choices for your home base. Wilmington is an easy drive from pretty much anywhere in this region, giving ready access to the beaches to the north and south. It's so full of sights and activities that you'll probably want to stay here anyway and give yourself a day or more just to explore the city itself. If you're planning on visiting the beaches south of Wilmington, you might also want to consider staying in Myrtle Beach, South Carolina, which is about a 20 minutes' drive on U.S. 17 (with no traffic—in high season it's a very different story) from the state line. Farther inland, you'll find plenty of motels around Fayetteville and Lumberton, which are also a reasonable distance from Raleigh to make day trips.

HISTORY

The Cape Fear River, deep and wide, caught the attention of European explorers as early as 1524, when Giovanni de Verrazano drifted by, and two years later, when Lucas Vásquez de Ayllón and his men (including, possibly, the first African slaves within the present-day United States) had a walk-about before proceeding to their appointment for shipwreck near Winyah Bay in South Carolina. Almost a century and a half later, William Hilton and explorers from the Massachusetts Bay Colony had a look for themselves. They were either disgusted with what they saw or knew they'd found a really good thing and wanted to psych out anyone with thoughts of a rival claim, because they left right away, and on their way out posted a sign at the tip of the Cape to the effect of, "Don't bother, the land's no good."

The next summer, John Vassall and a group of fellow Barbadians attempted settlement, but within a few years they abandoned the area. It wasn't until 1726, when Maurice Moore made the banks of the river his own on behalf of a group of allied families holding a patent to the area, that European settlement took. Moore lay out Brunswick Town, and his brother Roger established his own personal domain at Orton. (Today, only the ballast-stone foundations of houses and walls of the Anglican church remain at Brunswick, but Roger's home at Orton still stands.) The machinations of the Moore brothers led to the demise, or at least disintegration, of the Cape Fear tribe, who had been clinging to their land with varying success since the first Europeans arrived. Maurice Moore, with the aid of Tuscaroras, drove away many of the tribe, and then the few who remained at a settlement within present-day Carolina Beach State Park were slaughtered by Roger Moore in 1725. He claimed, whether truthfully or not, that a band of Cape Fear had attacked Orton.

Brunswick was briefly an important port, but it was soon eclipsed by Wilmington, a new settlement up the river established by an upstart group of non-Moores. By the time of the Revolution, it was Wilmington that dominated trade along the river. Meanwhile, a large population of Scottish immigrants had since the 1730s been farming and making a living from the pine forests (manufacturing naval stores—tar, pitch, and turpentine) in the area around present-day Fayetteville.

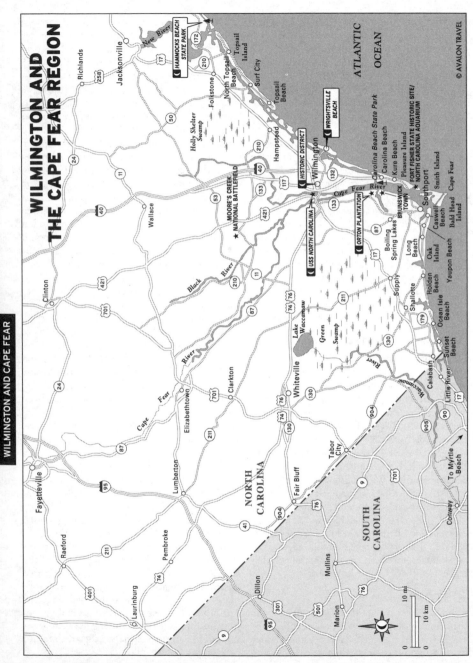

WILMINGTON AND CAPE FEAR

© JIM MOREKIS

USS *North Carolina* battleship on the Cape Fear River

The Lower Cape Fear region, particularly present-day Brunswick, New Hanover, Duplin, Bladen, and Onslow Counties, had a significantly larger slave population than most parts of North Carolina. The naval stores industry demanded a large workforce, and the plantations south of the river were to a large extent a continuation of the South Carolina Lowcountry economy, growing rice and indigo, crops that also led to the amassing of large populations of human chattel. All along the South Carolina and Georgia coasts, and into parts of Florida, these large communities of African-born and first-generation African American people established the culture now known as Gullah. Today the Gullah language and other aspects of the cultural heritage are most prominent around Charleston and on the islands just off the coast, and to a lesser extent in Savannah and points south, where a handful of communities still speak the Gullah language, a patois of English mixed with recognizably African vocabulary and grammar. The Gullah (sometimes called Geechee) accent, which has a heavy Caribbean resonance, can still be heard around Wilmington and the Brunswick Coast, in people who have never spoken any language but standard English. Aspects of Gullah traditions in cooking (gumbo, goobers/peanuts,

okra), folklore (houses with steps, shutters, window panes, and roof-lines painted bright blue to keep bad luck away), and folk medicine (root doctoring) are still in evidence throughout the Lowcountry.

Another major cultural group in the Cape Fear region is that of the Lumbee tribe. Their origins have long been mysterious. While the federal government denies Lumbees the recognition necessary to receive the federal benefits due Native American tribes in the United States, and while they are sometimes identified by ethnologists as a "tri-racial isolate" (grouped with other Southern communities of unknown origins, like the Melungeons of Appalachia), there's no question that the tribe is of Native American heritage. It also seems that their ancestry includes European and African Americans, leading to a variety of theories about their origin, including the especially persistent (though improbable) idea that they are descendants of the lost colonists of Roanoke. They've been variously called the Croatan Indians, Pembroke Indians, and Indians of Robeson County. In the days of slavery they were identified as Free People of Color, and the ever-evolving laws of the state concerning their civil rights long denied them the rights to vote or bear arms. Well into the 20th century the Lumbee were victims of segregation, and racism, both overt and vestigial, still places obstacles in the way of Lumbee advancement. Despite such hardships, a passionate devotion to the cause of education has produced a great many accomplished doctors, nurses, scholars, and other professionals who have in turn dedicated their careers and expertise to the well-being of their tribe.

The Lumbee also have a long history of resistance, and to the protection of their own land and rights. Most famously, the Lowry/Lowrie Band, outlaw heroes of the 19th century, defined the Lumbee cause for future generations. Another transformative moment in Lumbee history was the 1958 armed conflict near Maxton. Ku Klux Klan Grand Wizard "Catfish" Cole and about 40 other armed Klansmen held a rally here, at Hayes Pond. Local Lumbee, fed up with a recent wave of especially vicious intimidation at the hands of the Klan, showed up at the rally en masse—1,500 of them, all armed. The Lumbee shot out the one electric light and opened fire on the rally, causing the Klansmen to run like hell. The battle (which was won, incredibly, without a single death) was reported around the country, an energizing story for the cause of Native American rights, and a humiliation for the Ku Klux Klan.

In the late 20th and early 21st century, southeastern North Carolina's most prominent role is probably a military one. Fort Bragg, located in Fayetteville, is one of the country's largest Army installations, and the home base of thousands of the soldiers stationed in Iraq and Afghanistan. Nearby Pope Air Force Base is the home of the 43rd Airlift Wing, and at Jacksonville, the US Marine Corps' II Expeditionary Force, among other major divisions, are stationed at Camp Lejeune. Numerous museums in Fayetteville and Jacksonville tell the world-changing history of the military men and women of southeastern North Carolina.

GETTING THERE AND AROUND

Wilmington is the eastern terminus of I-40, more than 300 miles east of Asheville, approximately 120 miles east of Raleigh. The Cape Fear region is also crossed by a major north–south route, U.S. 17, the old Kings Highway of colonial times. Wilmington is roughly equidistant along U.S. 17 between Jacksonville to the north and Myrtle Beach, South Carolina, to the south; both cities are about an hour away. Wilmington International Airport serves the region with flights to and from East Coast cities. For a wider selection of routes, it may be worthwhile to consider flying into Myrtle Beach or Raleigh, and renting a car. If driving to Wilmington from the Myrtle Beach airport, add another half-hour or hour to get through Myrtle Beach traffic (particularly in the summer), as the airport there is on the southern edge of town. If driving from Raleigh-Durham International Airport, figure on the trip taking at least 2.5 hours. There is no passenger train service to Wilmington.

Topsail and Jacksonville are an easy drive on U.S. 17, as are the southerly Brunswick County beaches like Holden, Ocean Isle, and Sunset. The beaches and islands along the Cape itself, due south of Wilmington, are not as close to U.S. 17. They can be reached by taking U.S. 76 south from the city, or by ferry from Southport. The **Southport-Fort Fisher Ferry** (800/293-3779 or 800/368-8969) is popular as a sightseeing jaunt as well as a means simply to get across the river. It's a 30-minute crossing; most departures are 45 minutes apart, 5:30 A.M.–7:45 P.M. from Southport (until 6:15 P.M. in the winter), and 6:15 A.M.–8:30 P.M. leaving Fort Fisher (until 7 P.M. in the winter). For most vehicles, the fare is $5, but if you're driving a rig that's more than 20 feet long, boat trailers and the like included, the price can be as high as $15. It's $1 for pedestrians, $2 for bicycle riders, and $3 for folks on motorcycle. Pets are permitted if leashed or in a vehicle, and there are bathrooms on all ferries.

Wave Transit (910/343-0106, www.wave transit.com), Wilmington's public transportation system, operates buses throughout the metropolitan area and trolleys in the historic district. Fares are very low—$1 max, one-way. If you're planning on exploring outside the city, though, your best bet is to go by car.

Wilmington

In many cities, economic slumps have an unexpected benefit: historic preservation. With Wilmington's growth at a standstill in much of the 20th century, there was no need to replace the old buildings and neighborhoods. As a result, downtown Wilmington has remained a vast museum of beautiful architecture from its early days, and that historic appeal accounts for much of its popularity today as a tourist destination.

The city is once again ascendant, an ever more desirable place to live as well as to vacation. Hollywood noticed the little city a couple of decades ago, and Wilmington has become one of the largest film and TV production sites east of Los Angeles. *Dawson's Creek, Matlock,* and *One Tree Hill* are just some of the well-known series filmed here, and noteworthy movies filmed at least partly in Wilmington include *Forrest Gump, Sleeping with the Enemy, I Know What You Did Last Summer,* and many more (though not, ironically, either version of *Cape Fear*). It's not unlikely that, strolling through city, you'll happen on a film crew at work.

HISTORY

Incorporated in 1739, Wilmington was strategically situated for maritime commerce. Its deepwater port made it a bustling shipping center for the export of lumber, rice, and naval stores (turpentine and tar tapped from the now nearly vanished longleaf pine forests). Businessmen came to Wilmington from around the world, especially from Barbados, Scotland and northern Europe, and from the American colonies to the north. A fair number of New Englanders settled here, Nantucketers and other seafaring Yankees. In 1840, Wilmington became the eastern terminus of the 161-mile Wilmington and Weldon Railroad, which was at that time the longest railroad in the world. Now linking the commerce of land and sea with unprecedented efficiency, Wilmington's population exploded to almost 10,000 by 1860, making it the largest city in North Carolina.

During the War Between the States, the Wilmington and Weldon line was one of the crucial Confederate arteries for trade and transport, and Wilmington's port was a swarming hive of blockade runners. Its fall to the Union at the late date of January 1865 was a severe blow to the sinking Confederacy. Commerce allowed the city to weather the Civil War and Reconstruction, and it continued to grow and flourish. By 1890, the population had grown to 20,000. This was not an easy era socially, though, and tensions between white and black and Democrat and Republican Wilmingtonians exploded in the 1898 Wilmington Race Riot, one of the uglier incidents in the state's history. During the riot, a mob of white Democrats overthrew the city's Republican government, destroyed the black newspaper, the *Daily Record,* and murdered at least 22 African American citizens, leading to a radically accelerated revocation of the civil rights gained by African Americans in North Carolina during Reconstruction.

In the early 20th century, North Carolina's economic pulse was increasingly to be found in the Piedmont, with its textile and manufacturing boom. In 1910, Charlotte surpassed Wilmington in population. Economically, the darkest hour came in 1960, with the relocation of the Atlantic Coast Line headquarters to Florida. The old port city experienced a slow decline in vitality throughout the 20th century. Today Wilmington is a city of about 100,000 people, with ever-increasing cachet and economic vitality as a retirement and vacation destination.

SIGHTS
◖ Historic District

Wilmington is to 19th-century architecture what Asheville is to that of the early 20th century. Having been the state's most populous city until around 1910, when Charlotte and its Piedmont neighbors left the old port city in their wake, Wilmington's downtown reflects

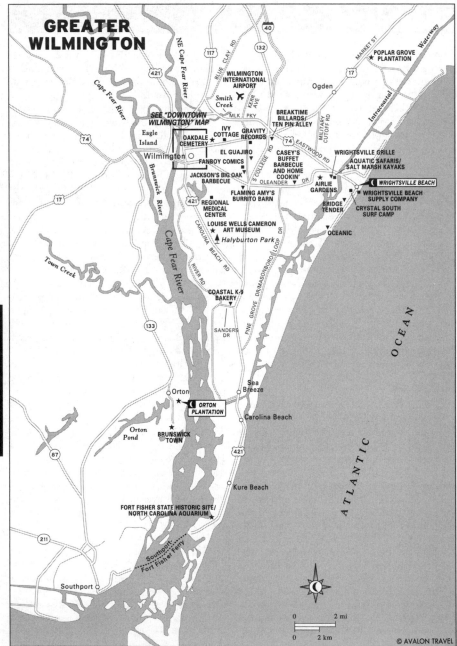

GREATER WILMINGTON

POPLAR GROVE
PLANTATION

WILMINGTON
INTERNATIONAL
AIRPORT

Smith
Creek

Ogden

SEE "DOWNTOWN
WILMINGTON" MAP

BREAKTIME
BILLARDS/
TEN PIN ALLEY

Eagle
Island

IVY
COTTAGE

GRAVITY
RECORDS

OAKDALE
CEMETERY

WRIGHTSVILLE GRILLE

EL GUAJIRO

CASEY'S
BUFFET
BARBECUE
AND HOME
COOKIN'

AQUATIC SAFARIS/
SALT MARSH KAYAKS

Wilmington

FANBOY COMICS

JACKSON'S BIG OAK
BARBECUE

WRIGHTSVILLE BEACH

AIRLIE
GARDENS

WRIGHTSVILLE BEACH
SUPPLY COMPANY

FLAMING AMY'S
BURRITO BARN

REGIONAL
MEDICAL
CENTER

BRIDGE
TENDER

CRYSTAL SOUTH
SURF CAMP

LOUISE WELLS CAMERON
ART MUSEUM

OCEANIC

Halyburton Park

COASTAL K-9
BAKERY

SANDERS
DR

Sea
Breeze

OCEAN

Orton

ORTON
PLANTATION

Carolina Beach

Orton
Pond

BRUNSWICK
TOWN

Kure Beach

ATLANTIC

FORT FISHER STATE HISTORIC SITE/
NORTH CAROLINA AQUARIUM

Southport-
Fort Fisher Ferry

Southport

0   2 mi

0   2 km

© AVALON TRAVEL

WILMINGTON AND CAPE FEAR

Bellamy Mansion

COURTESY OF WWW.CAPEFEARCOAST.ORG

its glory days of commerce and high society. This is North Carolina's largest 19th-century historic district, a gorgeous collection of antebellum and late Victorian townhouses and commercial buildings, including many beautiful Southern iterations of the Italianate craze that preceded the Civil War.

The **Bellamy Mansion** (503 Market St., 910/251-3700, www.bellamymansion .org, hourly tours 10 A.M.–5 P.M. Tues.–Sat., 1–5 P.M. Sun., $10 adults, $4 children under 12) is a spectacular example of Wilmington's late-antebellum Italianate mansions. This enormous white porticoed house ranks among the loveliest Southern city houses of its era. Built by planter Dr. John Bellamy just before the outbreak of the Civil War, the house was commandeered by the Yankees after the fall of Fort Fisher, and a trip to Washington and a pardon granted personally by President Andrew Johnson, a fellow North Carolinian, were required before Dr. Bellamy could pry his home out of Federal hands. In addition to the mansion, another highly significant building stands

on the property: the slave quarters. This confined but rather handsome two-story brick building is one of the few surviving examples in this country of urban slave dwellings. Extensive renovations are underway to restore the quarters to its early appearance.

The **Burgwin-Wright House** (224 Market St., 910/762-0570, www.burgwinwrighthouse .com, tours 10 A.M.–4 P.M. Tues.–Sat., closed in January, $6 adults, $3 children under 12) has an oddly similar history to that of the Bellamy Mansion, despite being nearly a century older. John Burgwin (the emphasis is on the second syllable), a planter and the treasurer of the North Carolina colony, built the house in 1770 on top of the city's early jail. Soon thereafter, Wilmington became a theater of war, and the enemy, as was so often the case, took over the finest dwelling in town as its headquarters. In this case the occupier, who had a particularly fine eye for rebel digs, was Lord Cornwallis, then on the last leg of his campaign before falling into George Washington's trap. The Burgwin-Wright House is, like the Bellamy Mansion, a vision of white-columned porticoes shaded by ancient magnolias, but the architectural style here is a less ostentatious, though no less beautiful, 18th-century form, the mark of the wealthy merchant and planter class in the colonial South Atlantic/Caribbean world. Seven terraced sections of garden surround the house; they are filled with native plants and many original landscape features, and make an intoxicating setting for an early spring stroll.

Yet another beautiful home in the historic district is the **Zebulon Latimer House** (126 S. Third St., 910/762-0492, www.latimerhouse .org, 10 A.M.–4 P.M. Mon.–Fri., noon–5 P.M. Sat., $10 adults, $5 if touring with a docent). The Latimer House is several years older than the Bellamy Mansion, but in its day was a little more fashion-forward, architecturally speaking. Mr. Latimer, a merchant from Connecticut, preferred a more urban expression of the Italianate style, a blocky, flat-roofed design with cast-iron cornices and other details that hint at the coming decades of Victorian aesthetics. Also located on the grounds is a

WILMINGTON AND CAPE FEAR

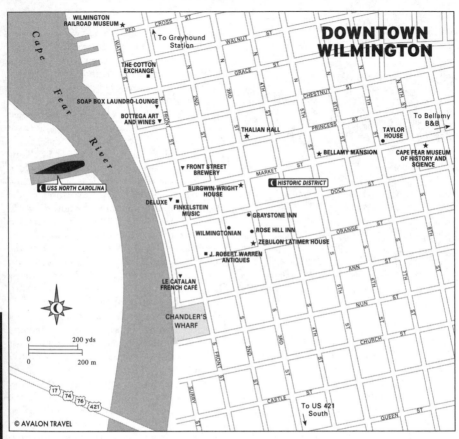

DOWNTOWN WILMINGTON

WILMINGTON RAILROAD MUSEUM

To Greyhound Station

THE COTTON EXCHANGE

SOAP BOX LAUNDRO-LOUNGE

BOTTEGA ART AND WINES

THALIAN HALL

To Bellamy B&B

TAYLOR HOUSE

BELLAMY MANSION

CAPE FEAR MUSEUM OF HISTORY AND SCIENCE

FRONT STREET BREWERY

USS NORTH CAROLINA

BURGWIN-WRIGHT HOUSE

HISTORIC DISTRICT

DELUXE

FINKELSTEIN MUSIC

GRAYSTONE INN

WILMINGTONIAN

ROSE HILL INN

ZEBULON LATIMER HOUSE

J. ROBERT WARREN ANTIQUES

LE CATALAN FRENCH CAFÉ

CHANDLER'S WHARF

0   200 yds
0   200 m

17 74 76 421

To US 421 South

© AVALON TRAVEL

very interesting two-story brick slave dwelling. The Latimer House is the headquarters of the Lower Cape Fear Historical Society, whose archive of regional history is important to genealogists and historic preservationists.

If you'd like to visit the Bellamy Mansion, Latimer House, and Burgwin-Wright House, be sure to buy a **three-house ticket** at the first house you visit. At $24, it will save you several bucks over what you'd pay were you to buy a ticket at each stop.

Wrightsville Beach

Wrightsville Beach, just outside of Wilmington, is easily one of the nicest beaches in the Carolinas, which is a linear kingdom of

beautiful strands. The beach is wide and easily accessible, visitor- and family-friendly, and simply beautiful. The water at Wrightsville often seems to be a brighter blue than one is accustomed to seeing this far north on the Atlantic coast, lending the feeling of a tropical coast. Wrightsville enjoys warm summertime water temperatures, a very large strand, and lots of lodging and rental choices along the beach. Numerous public beach access points (searchable at www.townofwrightsville beach.com/accesspoints.htm), some wheelchair-accessible and some with showers and/or bathrooms, line Lumina Avenue. The largest public parking lot, with 99 spaces, is at Beach Access #4, 2398 Lumina Avenue; #36 at 650

Lumina Avenue also has a large lot. They all fill up on busy days, but if you press on from one access point to the next, you'll eventually find a spot.

Historic Sights Around Wilmington

POPLAR GROVE PLANTATION

North of the city, about halfway between Wilmington and Topsail, is Poplar Grove Plantation (10200 U.S. 17 N., 910/686-9518, www.poplargrove.com, 9 A.M.–5 P.M. Mon.–Sat., noon–5 P.M. Sun, $10 adults, $9 seniors, $5 children ages 6–15). This antebellum peanut plantation features a beautiful 1850 big house, a restored tenant farmer's cabin, and other dependencies, as well as an extensive network of hiking trails through coastal forests and wetlands. In May, the plantation fills up with antique dealers and shoppers for the **Down Home Antique Fair.**

MOORE'S CREEK NATIONAL BATTLEFIELD

Not surprisingly, given its importance as a maritime center, the environs of Wilmington have seen much military action over the last 300 years. About 20 miles northwest, outside the town of Currie near Burgaw, is the Moore's Creek National Battlefield (40 Patriots Hall Dr., Currie, 910/283-5591, www.nps.gov/mocr, 9 A.M.–5 P.M. daily except Thanksgiving, Christmas, and New Year's Day). The site commemorates the brief and bloody skirmish of February 1776 in which a Loyalist band of Scottish highlanders, kilted and piping, clashed with Patriot colonists. The revolutionaries fired on the Scotsmen with cannons as they crossed a bridge over Moore's Creek, which they'd previously booby-trapped, greasing it and removing planks. About 30 of the Crown's soldiers died, some drowning after they were blown off the bridge. Important as a moment in the American Revolution, this was also a noteworthy occasion in Scottish military history as well: it was the last major broadsword charge in Scottish history, led by the last Scottish clan army.

◀ USS *NORTH CAROLINA*

Docked in the Cape Fear River, across from the Wilmington waterfront at Eagles Island, is the startling gray colossus of the battleship USS *North Carolina* (Eagles Island, 910/251-5797, www.battleshipnc.com, 8 A.M.–8 P.M. daily Memorial Day–Labor Day, 8 A.M.–5 P.M. daily Labor Day–Memorial Day, $12 adults, $6 ages 6–11, free ages 5 and under). This decommissioned World War II warship, which saw service at Guadalcanal, Iwo Jima, and many other important events in the Pacific theater, is a floating monument to the nearly 10,000 North Carolinians who died in WWII, and a museum of what life was like in a floating metal city.

Tours are self-guided, and include nine decks, the gun turrets and bridge, crew quarters, the sick deck, and the Roll of Honor display of the names of North Carolina's wartime dead. Allow yourself at least two hours to see it all. Visitors prone to claustrophobia might wish to stay above deck. The passageways and quarters below are close, dark, and very, very deep; from the heart of the ship it can take quite a while to get back out, and on a busy day the crowds can make the space seem even more constricted. (Just imagine how it would have felt to be in this ship in the middle of the Pacific, with nearly 2,000 other sailors aboard.)

The battleship is also one of North Carolina's most famous haunted houses, as it were—home to several ghosts who have been seen and heard on many occasions. The ship has been featured on the Sci-Fi Channel and on the ghost hunting show *TAPS,* and is the subject of extensive writing and paranormal investigation. Visit www.hauntednc.com to hear some chilling unexplained voices caught on tape.

OAKDALE CEMETERY

In the mid-19th century, as Wilmington was bursting at the seams with new residents, the city's old cemeteries were becoming overcrowded with former residents. Oakdale Cemetery (520 N. 15th St., 910/762-5682, www.oakdalecemetery.org, 8 A.M.–5 P.M. daily year-round) was founded a ways from downtown to ease the subterranean traffic jam. It was designed in the park-like style of graveyards that was popular at that time, and soon filled up with splendid funerary art—weeping angels, obelisks, willows—to set off the natural beauty of the place. (Oakdale's website has a primer of Victorian grave art symbolism.) Separate sections were reserved for Jewish burials and for victims of the 1862 yellow fever epidemic. It's a fascinating place for a quiet stroll.

Museums
CAPE FEAR MUSEUM OF HISTORY AND SCIENCE
The Cape Fear Museum of History and Science (814 Market St., 910/798-4370, www.capefearmuseum.com, 9 A.M.–5 P.M. Tues.–Sat., 1–5 P.M. Sun., closed Mon. Labor Day–Memorial Day, $6 adults, $5 students and seniors, $3 children 3–17) has exhibits about the ecology of the Cape Fear and its human history. Special treats are exhibits about giant native life forms, including the prehistoric ground sloth and Michael Jordan.

LOUISE WELLS CAMERON ART MUSEUM
The Louise Wells Cameron Art Museum (3201 S. 17th St., 910/395-5999, www.cameronartmuseum.com, 11 A.M.–2 P.M. Tues.–Fri., 11 A.M.–5 P.M. Sat. and Sun., $8 adults, $5 students and members, $3 children 2–12) is one of the major art museums in North Carolina, a very modern gallery with a good permanent collection of art of many media, with a special emphasis on North Carolina artists. Masters represented include Mary Cassatt and Utagawa Hiroshige. Special exhibits change throughout the year.

WILMINGTON RAILROAD MUSEUM
The Wilmington Railroad Museum (505 Nutt St., 910/763-2634, www.wilmingtonrailroadmuseum.org, 10 A.M.–5 P.M. Mon.–Sat., 1–5 P.M. Sun. Apr. 1–Sept. 30, closed Sun. Oct.–Mar., $7 adults, $6 seniors and military, $3 ages 2–12) explores a crucial but now largely forgotten part of this city's history: its

role as a railroad town. In 1840, Wilmington became the terminus for the world's longest continuous rail line, the Wilmington and Weldon. The Atlantic Coast Line Railroad (into which the W&W had merged around 1900) kept its headquarters at Wilmington until the 1960s, when it moved its offices, employees, and a devastatingly large portion of the city's economy, to Florida. All manner of railroad artifacts are on display in this great little museum, from timetables to locomotives. A classic iron horse, steam engine #250, sits on the track outside and has been restored beautifully.

Gardens and Parks
AIRLIE GARDENS
Airlie Gardens (300 Airlie Rd., 910/798-7700, www.airliegardens.org, 9 A.M.–5 P.M. Mon.–Sat. Jan. 2–Mar. 19, 9 A.M.–5 P.M. daily Mar. 20–Dec. 31, longer hours in Apr. and May, $5 adults, $3 children 6–12, no pets) is most famous for its countless azaleas, but this 100-year-old formal garden park has many remarkable features, including an oak tree believed to be nearly 500 years old, and the Minnie Evans Sculpture Garden and Bottle Chapel. Evans, a visionary African American artist whose mystical work is among the most prized of all "outsider art," was the gatekeeper here for 25 of her 95 years. Golf cart tours are available with 48 hours notice for visitors who are not mobile enough to walk the gardens. On second Saturdays, New Hanover County residents can get in free.

HALYBURTON PARK
A more natural landscape for hiking and biking is Halyburton Park (4099 S. 17th St., 910/341-7855, www.halyburtonpark.com, park open dawn–dusk daily, nature center 9 A.M.–5 P.M. Mon.–Sat.). The 58 acres of parkland, encircled by a 1.3-mile wheelchair-accessible trail and crisscrossed by interior trails, gives a beautiful glimpse of the environment of sandhills, Carolina bays (elliptical, often boggy depressions), and longleaf pine and oak forest that used to comprise so much of the natural landscape of this area.

ANOLES OF CAROLINA

During your visit to the Wilmington area, you'll almost certainly see anoles. These are the tiny green lizards that skitter up and down trees and along railings – impossibly fast, beady-eyed little emerald beasts. Sometimes called "chameleons" by the locals, anoles can change color to camouflage themselves against their backgrounds. They also like to puff out their crescent-shaped dewlaps, the little scarlet pouches under their chins, when they're courting, fighting, or otherwise advertising their importance.

Explorer John Lawson was quite taken with them, as he describes in his 1709 *A New Voyage to Carolina.*

Green lizards are very harmless and beautiful, having a little Bladder under their Throat, which they fill with Wind, and evacuate the same at Pleasure. They are of a most glorious Green, and very tame. They resort to the Walls of Houses in the Summer Season, and stand gazing on a Man, without any Concern or Fear. There are several other Colours of these Lizards, but none so beautiful as the green ones are.

NEW HANOVER COUNTY ARBORETUM

The New Hanover County Arboretum (6206 Oleander Dr., 910/452-6393), also a popular walking spot, is a Cooperative Extension horticulture laboratory that showcases native plants and horticultural techniques in a varied five-acre garden setting.

ENTERTAINMENT AND EVENTS
Performing Arts

Thalian Hall (310 Chestnut St., 800/523-2820, www.thalianhall.com) was built in the mid-1850s and today is the last standing theater designed by the prominent architect John Montague Trimble. At the time of Thalian Hall's opening, fully one-tenth of the population of Wilmington could fit into the Thalian opera house, and the combination of the grand facility and Wilmington's longstanding love of the arts made this an important stop for many artists and productions touring the country in those days. It is still a major arts venue in the region, hosting performances of classical, jazz, bluegrass, and all sorts of other music, as well as ballet, children's theater, and more. Its resident theater company is the **Thalian Association** (910/251-1788, www.thalian.org), which traces its roots back to 1788 and has been named the official community theater company of North Carolina.

Also making its home at Thalian Hall is **Big Dawg Productions** (http://bigdawgproductions.org). They put on a variety of plays and musicals throughout the year, of all genres, and host the wonderful **New Play Festival**, a festival of first-time productions of work by authors under the age of 18. In the more than a dozen years of this festival, many works have premiered here that have gone on to much wider audiences and acclaim. Another Thalian company for nearly 25 years, the **Opera House Theatre Company** (910/762-4234, www.operahousetheatrecompany.net) has produced one varied season after another of big-name musicals and dramas, as well as the work of North Carolinian and Southern playwrights. Rounding out the companies who perform at Thalian Hall is **Stageworks Youth Theater,** a community company of 10- to 17-year-old actors. Their productions "are not 'kiddie theater,'" as they write, "but substantial dramas, comedies, and musicals."

Festivals

Wilmington's best-known annual event is the **Azalea Festival** (910/794-4650, www.ncazaleafestival.com), which takes place in early April at venues throughout the city. It centers around the home and garden tours of Wilmington's most beautiful—and, at this time of year, azalea-festooned—historic sites. There is a dizzying slate of events, including a parade, circus, gospel concerts, shag and step competitions, even boxing matches. And like any self-respecting Southern town, it crowns royalty—in this case, the North Carolina Azalea Festival Queen, as well as its Princess, and the Queen's court, and a slate of cadets to escort all the Queen's ladies in waiting, and a phalanx of over 100 Azalea Belles. The Azalea Festival draws over 300,000 visitors, so book your accommodations well in advance; and if you're traveling through the area in early April but aren't coming to the festival, be forewarned, this will be one crowded town.

For all that Wilmington has become such a magnet for Hollywood, there's also a passion here for independent films. November's **Cucalorus Film Festival** (910/343-5995, www.cucalorus.org) has, over the course of a dozen years, become an important festival that draws viewers and filmmakers from around the world. Roughly 100 films are screened during each year's festival, which takes place at Thalian Hall and at the small Jengo's Playhouse (815 Princess St.) where the Cucalorus Foundation gives regular screenings throughout the year.

North of Wilmington, towards Topsail, the town of Hampstead has held its annual **North Carolina Spot Festival** (www.ncspotfestival.com) for nearly 50 years. The spot is a small fish that's a traditional favorite food on this coast, and in the fourth weekend of September hundreds of people gather here to deep-fry and gobble them up. There are bands and a pageant, but the fun centers around eating. It's a great little down-home festival.

Nightlife
The **Soap Box Laundro-Lounge** (255 N. Front St., 910/251-8500, www.soapboxlaundrolounge.com) has 11 washing machines, four dryers, and a good, long folding table. So what's it doing in the "Nightlife" section? It's also an important indie music venue (great bands, all kinds of music), a bar, a pool hall, and the setting of Monday-night Heavy Metal Bingo. ("No perfume scent down here, just the smell of PBR and ink.")

Bottega Art and Wines (208 N. Front St.,

910/763-3737, www.bottegagallery.com) is an innovative, energetic gallery/venue/art space/wine bar. It's a gallery of contemporary art, to a large extent but not exclusively abstract, with frequently changing exhibitions. It's a serious wine bar, with a list a mile long of mainly American, Italian, and organic wines and beers, and a selection of nice hors d'oeuvres. It's also a venue for a rich slate of music performances and poetry readings, and hosts arts gatherings like writers' forums and art discussion groups. At the time of this writing, Bottega has announced that they're planning a spelling bee. It's bound to be unique and well worth checking out.

Breaktime Billiards/Ten Pin Alley (127 S. College Rd., 910/452-5455, www.breaktimetenpin.com, billiards and bowling 11 A.M.–2 A.M. daily, lounge 6 P.M.–2 A.M. Mon.–Fri., 11 A.M.–2 A.M. Sat. and Sun.) is a 30,000-square-foot entertainment palace. It consists of Breaktime Billiards, with 24 billiard tables and one regulation-size snooker table; Ten Pin Alley, with 24 bowling lanes and skee-ball; and in between them, the Lucky Strike Lounge, a full bar and snack shop with all manner of video games, and which hosts soft-tip dart and foosball tournaments. Put in an order for a meal and a beer or cocktail, and the staff will bring it to you if you're in the middle of a game.

Front Street Brewery (9 N. Front St., 910/251-1935, www.thefrontstreetbrewery.com, 11:30 A.M.–midnight Mon.–Wed., 11:30 A.M.–2 A.M. Thurs.–Sat., 11:30 A.M.– 10 P.M. Sun., late-night menu starts at 10:30 P.M.) serves lunch and dinner, but what is most special is their menu of beers brewed on-site. They serve their own pilsner, IPA, and lager, Scottish and Belgian ales, and their specialty River City Raspberry Wheat ale. The space has an attractive dark-paneled saloon decor, and plenty of seating areas to choose from, depending on whether you're looking for a sit-down meal or simply to gab over beer with friends.

SHOPPING
Shopping Centers
The buildings of **The Cotton Exchange** (Front and Grace Sts., 910/343-9896,

www.shopcottonexchange.com) have housed all manner of businesses in over a century and a half of continuous occupation: a flour and hominy mill, a Chinese laundry, a peanut cleaning operation (really), a "mariner's saloon" (we'll say no more about that), and, of course, a cotton exchange. Today they're home to dozens of boutiques and restaurants, and lovely little specialty shops selling kites, beads, and spices.

Antiques and Consignment Stores

An especially intriguing shop is **J. Robert Warren Antiques** (110 Orange St., 910/762-6077, www.jrobertwarrenantiques.com), which occupies an 1810 townhouse downtown. Warren specializes in fine and rare antiques from North Carolina, like furniture from the early masters, the work of colonial silversmiths, prints and paintings of early Carolinians and Carolina scenes, nautical hardware from old ships, and much more.

The **Ivy Cottage** (3020/3030/3100 Market St., 910/815-0150, www.twocottages.com, 10 A.M.–6 P.M. Mon.–Sat., 1–5 P.M. Sun., hours vary in the winter) is generally described as a "consignment store," but that title doesn't begin to do justice to the strange, overwhelmingly varied nature of this wonderful store. Its four buildings and two gardens are overflowing, from folk pottery and antique ephemera to $40,000 antique diamond bracelets. Their website takes a stab at summing it all up: "classic furniture and home accessories, antiques, china, crystal, silver, fine jewelry, oriental carpets, art work and yard and garden items"—but really to understand, you'll have to see for yourself. Allow yourself plenty of time.

Books and Comics

Wilmington has quite a few nice bookstores, both retail and used. **McAllister & Solomon** (4402-1 Wrightsville Ave., 910/350-0189, www.mcallisterandsolomon.com) stocks over 20,000 used and rare books, a great treat for collectors to explore. **Two Sisters Bookery** (318 Nutt St., Cotton Exchange, 910/762-4444, www.twosisters

booksense.com, 10 A.M.–6 P.M. Mon.–Sat., noon–6 P.M. Sun.) is a nice little independent bookseller at the Cotton Exchange, with an inventory covering all genres and subject matters, and a calendar full of readings by favorite authors. Also excellent is **Pomegranate Books** (4418 Park Ave., 910/452-1107, www.pombooks.net, 10 A.M.–6 P.M. Mon.–Sat.), which has a progressive bent and a wide selection of good reads.

Fanboy Comics (3901-A Wrightsville Ave., 910/452-7828, www.fanboycomics.biz, 11 A.M.–9 P.M. Mon.–Wed., 11 A.M.–11 P.M. Thurs.–Sat., noon–9 P.M. Sun.) specializes in buying and selling Silver and Bronze Age superhero comics, a period beginning in the 1950s, and ending, at least in terms of Fanboy's stock, around 1977. The Silver and Bronze Ages have many defining characteristics, among which are graphic and technical innovations, the gradual transformation of two-dimensional superheroes into more fully developed characters with human problems and cares, the introduction of science fiction and, eventually, '70s noir storylines. Fanboy carries an amazing stock, and they also host frequent gaming events and tournaments.

Galleries and Art Studios

An unusual retail art gallery is found between Wilmington and Wrightsville, the 23,000-square-foot **Racine Center for the Arts** (203 Racine Dr., 910/452-2073, www.racinecenter.com). In addition to the sales gallery, it has art space for classes in pottery, stained glass, and other crafts, and operates the Firebird Paint Your Pottery and Art Studio. Visitors can show up at the Firebird without reservations, and go right to work on their own pottery and mosaics with the help of staff.

Music

Finkelstein Music (6 South Front St., 910/762-5662) is a family business that has been at this site, a great old commercial building on a busy downtown corner, for over 100 years. It began as a dry good store, but gradually evolved into today's music store, which carries a great selection of guitars, electric basses, and percussion.

WILMINGTON AND CAPE FEAR

Gravity Records (125-1 S. Kerr Ave., 910 /392-2414, www.gravity-records.com) is a record store with a wide selection of all sorts of music. They sell CDs and DVDs, but the focus is on LP records. They've got a huge stock of vinyl, and they also sell and service turntables. Another good choice is **Yellow Dog Discs** (341-12 S. College Rd., 910/792-0082, www.myspace.com/yellowdogdiscs), a buy/sell/trade store for CDs, DVDs, LPs, games, and posters. Their motto is "Skip free, guaranteed."

For Dogs
Coastal K-9 Bakery (5905 #9 Carolina Beach Rd., 866/794-4014, www.coastalk9 bakery.com, 10 A.M.–6 P.M. Mon.–Sat., 1–5 P.M. Sun.) sells fresh-baked gourmet dog treats, including various organic and hypoallergenic goodies, Carolina barbecue biscuits, liver brownies, and even vegetarian bacon bits.

SPORTS AND RECREATION
Surfing
Wrightsville Beach is a very popular destination for East Coast surfers and is home to several surfing schools. **Surf Camp** (530 Causeway Dr., 866/844-7873, www.wb surfcamp.com) is probably the area's largest surfing instruction provider. They teach a staggering number of multi-day camps; one-day courses; kids-only, teenagers-only, women-only, and whole-family offerings; and classes in safety as well as technique. **Wrightsville Beach Supply Company** (1 N. Lumina Ave., 910/256-8821, www.wbsupplyco.com) has a retail store, and offers surf classes in the summertime (8–10 A.M. daily, $45 including board rental) and private lessons ($60) arranged according to the customer's schedule. **Crystal South Surf Camp** (Public access #39 on the beach, 910/395-4431, www.crystal southsurfcamp.com) is a family-run operation that gives group and individual five-day instruction for all ages.

Other Water Sports
Salt Marsh Kayaks (Shop 222 Old Causeway Dr., rental facility 275 Waynick Blvd., 866

/655-2925, http://saltmarshkayakcompany .com), rents kayaks (sit-insides and sit-on-tops, singles and tandems) and sailboats, gives classes in sailing and kayaking, and guides tours through some of the area's most interesting waterscapes. **II Dolphins Sailing School** (222 Old Causeway Dr., 910/619-1646, www .iidolphins.com), which operates out of the Salt Marsh Kayaks storefront, teaches courses from Keelboat Sailing 101 to more advanced classes in navigation. They also run evening ocean cruises ($50 individuals, $95 couples, $45 children under 13) departing from the Blockade Runner docks.

Aquatic Safaris (6800-1A Wrightsville Ave., 910/392-4386, www.aquaticsafaris .com, in-season 9 A.M.–6 P.M. Mon.–Thurs., 9 A.M.–7 P.M. Fri., 6:30 A.M.–6 P.M. Sat., 6:30 A.M.–5 P.M. Sun., out of season 10 A.M.–6 P.M. Mon.–Fri., 10 A.M.–5 P.M. Sat., noon–4 P.M. Sun.) runs charter diving trips to shipwrecks (some sunken for artificial reefs, some scuttled during WWII when U-boats were a frequent sight here) and other underwater environments. They also teach dive classes and rent equipment.

ACCOMMODATIONS
Wilmington overflows with historic bed-and-breakfasts. These listed are by no means the only excellent bed-and-breakfast inns in Wilmington; the city is full of them. Check in with the **Cape Fear Convention and Visitors Bureau** (www.cape fear.nc.us) for a comprehensive listing. For those who prefer the privacy of a non-B&B setting, there are many chain motels, as well as small, family-run establishments, ranging from the most basic to luxurious accommodations.

$150-300
The **Rosehill Inn** (114 S. Third St., 800/815-0250, www.rosehill.com, $90–200) occupies a pretty 1848 residence three blocks from the river. The flowery high-B&B-style decor suits the house well, making for elegant but comfy quarters.

© JIM MOREKIS

Rosehill Inn

The **Taylor House** (14 N. Seventh St., 800/382-9982, www.taylor housebb.com, $125–140) is an absolutely lovely 1905 home—rather subdued in design when compared to some of the architectural manifestos nearby, but in a very attractive way. The pretty, sunny rooms promise relaxation.

Over $300

The ◖ **Wilmingtonian** (101 S. Second St., 910/343-1800, www.thewilming tonian.com, $87–325/night) is a complex of five buildings, four of which are renovated historic structures, from the 1841 de Rosset House to a 1950s convent. The de Rosset House is an utterly fabulous Italianate mansion, one of the most recognizable buildings in Wilmington. For $325 ($250 out of season), you can stay in the Cupola Suite, a spectacular aerie with a panoramic view of the port.

The famous ◖ **Graystone Inn** (100 S. Third St., 888/763-4773, www.graystone inn.com, $159–379) was built in the same year as the Taylor House, but its builder, the widow Elizabeth Bridgers, had a very different aesthetic. The splendor of the palace first known as the Bridger House reflects the fortune of Mrs. Bridgers' late husband, a former Confederate congressman and one of the most influential figures in Wilmington's days as a railroad center.

FOOD

Continental

Le Catalan French Café (224 S. Water St., 910/815-0200, www.lecatalan.com, from 11:30 A.M. for lunch and dinner Tues.–Sat., and Sun. in the summer), couldn't have a nicer location, on the Riverwalk in the old downtown. They serve wonderful classic French food—quiches and *feuilletés,* beef bourguignonne on winter Fridays, and a chocolate mousse for which they are famous. Their greatest draw, though, is the wine list (and attached wine store). The proprietor, Pierre Penegre, is a Cordon Bleu–certified oenologist, and is frequently on hand to make recommendations.

Seafood

Wrightsville Beach's **Bridge Tender** (1414 Airlie

Rd., Wilmington, 910/256-4519, www.the bridgetender.com, lunch 11:30 A.M.–2 P.M. daily, dinner from 5 P.M. daily, bar open all day, $20–35) has been in business for over 30 years and is an icon of the local restaurant scene. The atmosphere is simple and elegant, with a dockside view. Entrées focus on seafood and angus beef, with an extensive à la carte menu from which you can create delicious combinations of your favorite seafood and the Bridge Tender's special sauces. A sushi menu rounds out the appetizers, and a long wine list complements everything.

When you see a restaurant set in a really beautiful location, you dearly hope the food is as good as the view. Such is the case at Wrightsville's **Oceanic** (703 S. Lumina, Wrightsville Beach, 910/256-5551, www.oceanicrestaurant.com). The Wilmington *Star-News* has repeatedly voted it the Best Seafood Restaurant in Wilmington, and it receives similar word-of-mouth accolades right and left. It occupies a big old house right on the beach, with a wraparound porch and a pier. For an extra-special experience, ask for a table on the pier.

The relatively new **Wrightsville Grille** (6766 Wrightsville Ave., Suite J at Galleria Shopping Center, Wrightsville Beach, 910/509-9839) is roundly praised for its crab cakes ($20 for two), known for being super-hefty and having a high crab-to-breading ratio. The menu has a lot of casual café favorites, burgers and sandwiches, as well as extensive seafood and meat selections, and a daily "Chocoholic Special."

Southern and Barbecue

In business since 1984, **Jackson's Big Oak Barbecue,** (920 S. Kerr Ave., 910/799-1581, all dishes under $8) is an old favorite. Their motto is, "We ain't fancy, but we sure are good." Good old vinegary, Eastern North Carolina–style pork barbeque is the main item, though you can pick from Brunswick stew, fried chicken, and a mess of country vegetables. You'll get hush puppies and cornsticks at the table, but it will be worth your while not

to fill up too fast—the cobblers and banana pudding are great.

Another star of Southern cooking is **Casey's Buffet Barbecue and Home Cookin'** (5559 Oleander Dr., 910/798-2913, lunch Tues.–Sat., dinner Wed.–Sun.). Here you can feast on barbecue and Brunswick stew, fried chicken and catfish, okra and collard greens. Adventurous Yankees might want to venture into the Southern culinary backwoods and try chitterlings (pronounced "chitlins," of course) and chicken gizzards. The folks at the next table are enjoying them, so why not you?

Eclectic American

Keith Rhodes, a Wilmington native and chef of **Deluxe** (114 Market St., 910/251-0333, www.deluxenc.com, $16–35) beat out 69 other top chefs to win first place in the Goodness Grows championship, a statewide title. The menu at Deluxe features stunning high-gourmet creations that pay homage to down-home Southern cooking, including confit of bobwhite quail on apple corn-cake and a bed of braised collards, buttermilk-fried crispy calamari, and white soy-molasses grilled lamb chops. Deluxe deserves additional gold stars for two special features: excellent vegetarian selections and menu descriptions that identify locally caught and grown ingredients.

Flaming Amy's Burrito Barn (4002 Oleander Dr., 910/799-2919, www.flaming amysburritobarn.com, 11 A.M.–10 P.M. daily) is, in their own words, "Hot, fast, cheap, and easy." They've got a long menu with 20 specialty burritos (Greek, Philly steak, Thai), eight fresh salsas, and bottled and on-tap beers. It's very inexpensive—you can eat well for under $10, drinks included. Frequent special promotions include Tattoo Tuesdays; if you show the cashier your tattoo (come on, we all know you've got one), you can take 10 percent off your meal.

Latin American

There are certain elements that every good Cuban restaurant must possess, and if any one of them isn't just right, you should question the whole menu. It must have good, authentic Cuban coffee, Cuban bread (sort of like French bread, but ineffably different), *maduros* (fried sweet plantains), and flan. Even though none of these is a main dish, every good Cuban cook worth his or her salt knows the secrets to these all-important details. **El Guajiro** (1015-A S. Kerr Ave., 910/397-9253, 10 A.M.–7:30 P.M. Mon.–Sat., $5–10) gets them all right. You won't go wrong with the *ropa vieja* and classic Cuban sandwiches, but anything you order from Guajiro's menu is bound to be good.

El Sombrero Azul (127 S. College Rd., 910/791-4250) serves down-home Salvadoran food, a savory cuisine that shares a lot of elements with Mexican food, but with many subtle and delicious differences. They make their own tortillas at Sombrero Azul, which demonstrates their commitment to authenticity and flavor. Onion-festooned pork chops, tamales, and *pastelitos* are all great choices. The restaurant used to be called Cocina de Carmen, and you might still hear it recommended by that name.

Asian

C Double Happiness (4403 Wrightsville Ave., 910/313-1088, lunch and dinner) is a very popular Chinese and Malaysian restaurant, known for serving traditional dishes that are a refreshing departure from the standard canon of American Chinese restaurants. The setting is original too, without, as one local food critic wrote, "a buffet or glamour food photos over a hospital-white take-out counter." You can choose between regular booths and traditional floor seating. If you're lucky, you might be present when the chef decides to send around rice balls, a sweet dessert snack, for everyone on the house.

INFORMATION AND SERVICES

Extensive tourism and travel information is available from the **Wilmington/Cape Fear Coast CVB** (23 N. 3rd St., Wilmington, 877/406-2356, www.cape-fear.nc.us, 8:30 A.M.–5 P.M. Mon.–Fri., 9 A.M.–4 P.M. Sat., and 1–4 P.M. Sun.).

Wilmington has two hospitals: **Cape Fear Hospital** (5301 Wrightsville Ave., 910/452-8100, www.nhhn.org) and the **New Hanover Regional Medical Center** (2132 S. 17th St., 910/343-7000, www.nhhn.org).

NORTH OF WILMINGTON
Topsail Island

In the manner of an old salt, Topsail is pronounced "Tops'l." The three towns on Topsail Island—Topsail Beach, North Topsail Beach, and Surf City—are popular beach communities; they're less commercial than some of their counterparts elsewhere along the coast, but still destinations for throngs of visitors in the summer months. A swing bridge gives access to the island at Surf City (the bridge opens around the beginning of each hour, so expect backups) and a high bridge between Sneads Ferry and North Topsail.

Among Topsail's claims to fame is its importance in the conservation of sea turtle populations. The **Karen Beasley Sea Turtle Rescue and Rehabilitation Center** (822 Carolina Ave., Topsail Beach, www.seaturtlehospital .org, visiting hours 2–4 P.M. Mon., Tues., and Thurs.–Sat. in June, July, and Aug.) treats sea turtles that have been injured by sharks or boats, or are ill or stranded. Its 24 enormous tubs, which look something like the vats at a beer brewery, provide safe places for the animals to recover from their injuries and recoup their strength before being released back into the ocean. Guardian angels from the hospital also patrol the full shoreline of Topsail Island every morning in the summertime, before the crowds arrive, to identify and protect any new clutches of eggs that were laid overnight. Founder Jean Beasley has been featured as a Hero of the Year on the Animal Planet channel. Unlike most wildlife rehabilitation centers, this hospital allows the public to tour the facilities (during limited summer hours) and catch a glimpse of the patients.

Also at Topsail Beach is the **Missiles and More Museum** (720 Channel Ave., 910/328-8663, www.topsailmissilesmuseum .org, 2–4 P.M. Mon.–Fri. Apr.–mid-May and early Sept.–mid-Oct., 2–4 P.M. Mon.–Sat. mid-May–early Sept., closed late Oct.–Mar., free). This little museum commemorates a rather peculiar chapter in the island's history: when it was used by the U.S. government for a project called Operation Bumblebee. During Operation Bumblebee, Topsail was a proving ground for missiles, and the work done here led to major advancements in missile technology and the development of a precursor of the ram jet engine used later in supersonic jet design. Exhibits include real warheads left over from the tests, and even one that washed up on the beach 50 years after being fired out to sea. Especially interesting to lovers of projectiles will be the 1940s color film of missile firings here at Topsail.

Jacksonville

Jacksonville is best known as the home of **Camp Lejeune,** a massive Marine installation that dates to 1941. Lejeune is the home base of the II Marine Expeditionary Force, and of MARSOC, the Marine Corps division of U.S. Special Operations Command. The nearly 250 square miles that comprise the base include extensive beaches, where servicemen and women receive training in amphibious assault skills.

Construction has begun for the Museum of the Marine (www.museumofthemarine.org), a major commemorative museum that will explore the history of this branch of the military, with particular focus on the contributions of Marines from and trained in North Carolina.

Camp Johnson, a satellite installation of Camp Lejeune, used to be known as Montford Point, and was the home of the famous African American Montford Point Marines. Their history, a crucial chapter in the integration of the United States Armed Forces, is paid tribute to at the **Montford Point Marine Museum** (Building 101, East Wing, Camp Gilbert Johnson, 910/450-1340, www.montfordpoint marines.com, 11 A.M.–2 P.M. and 4–7 P.M., Tues. and Thurs., and 11 A.M.–4 P.M. Sat.).

Hammocks Beach State Park

At the very appealing little fishing town of Swansboro you'll find the mainland side of Hammocks Beach State Park (1572 Hammocks Beach Rd., 910/326-4881, http://ncparks.gov/ Visit/parks/habe, 8 A.M.–6 P.M. daily Sept.–May, 8 A.M.–7 P.M. daily June–Aug.). Most of the park lies on the other side of a maze of marshes, on Bear and Huggins Islands. These wild, totally undeveloped beaches are important havens for migratory waterfowl and nesting loggerhead sea turtles. Camping is permitted on Bear Island, in reserved and first-come sites ($9), with restrooms and showers available nearby. A private boat or **passenger ferry** (910/326-4881, $5 adults, $3 seniors and children) are the only ways to reach the islands. The ferry's schedule varies by days of the week and season: Wed.–Sat. May and Sept. and Fri.–Sat. Apr. and Oct., departs from the mainland every hour on the half-hour 9:30 A.M.–4:30 P.M., departs from the island every hour 10 A.M.–5 P.M.; Mon.–Tues. Memorial Day–Labor Day departs from the mainland every hour 9:30 A.M.–5:30 P.M., departs from the island every hour 10 A.M.–6 P.M.; Wed.–Sun. Memorial Day–Labor Day departs from the mainland every half-hour 9:30 A.M.–5:30 P.M., departs from the island every half-hour 10 A.M.–6 P.M.

The Southern Coast

From the beaches of Brunswick and New Hanover County to the swampy, subtropical fringes of land behind the dunes, this little corner of the state is incredibly special—and is one of the most beautiful parts of North Carolina.

There are a string of beaches here, starting with Carolina Beach and Kure, just south of Wilmington, and descending through the "Brunswick Islands," as they are designated in tourist literature. Most of these beaches are low-key, quiet family beaches, largely lined with residential and rental properties. They're crowded in the summertime, of course, but are still much more laid-back than Myrtle Beach, over the state line to the south, and even Wrightsville and some of the "Crystal Coast" beaches.

You'll see some distinctive wildlife here, too. The first you'll notice, more likely than not, is the ubiquitous green anole (called "chameleons" by many locals). These tiny lizards, normally a bright lime green, but able to fade to brown when invisibility is called for, are everywhere—skittering up porch columns and along balcony railings, peering at you around corners, hiding between the fronds of palmetto trees. The males put on a big show by puffing out their strawberry-colored dewlaps. Generations of Lowcountry children have spent thousands of frustrated hours trying to catch them, usually with next to no success. If you catch them from the front, they'll bite (albeit rather harmlessly), and if you catch them from behind, they'll be only too happy to cede to you their writhing tails, while the rest of them keeps running. But from a respectful distance, they're amusing companions all along one's outdoor sojourns in this region.

This is also the part of the state where the greatest populations of alligators live. Unlike anoles, who threaten but can't back it up,

WILMINGTON AND CAPE FEAR

COURTESY OF WWW.CAPEFEARCOAST.ORG

a boardwalk at Carolina Beach

alligators are nonchalant creatures who rarely appear better than comatose, but they are genuinely deadly if crossed. All along river and creek banks, bays, and swamps, you'll see their scaly hulks basking motionless in the sun. While canoeing or kayaking, you might only be able to see the little arcs of their eyes and nostrils poking out from underwater, and maybe the scaly ridges of their backs and tails. They may just as easily be totally submerged, floating underwater and thinking sinister thoughts. Be careful where you step, and avoid wading or swimming in fresh water. Above all, keep small children and pets well clear of anywhere a gator might lurk. That said, alligators are some of the most thrillingly strange animals to be found anywhere in the United States, and the herp-fancier, against better judgment, is bound to find them brutishly lovable.

In certain, highly specialized environments—mainly in and around Carolina bays that offer both moistness and nutrient-poor soil—the Venus flytrap and other carnivorous plants thrive. To the average fly, these are more threatening than an alligator any day. The flytrap and some of its cousins are endangered, but in this region—and nowhere else in the world—you'll have plenty of opportunities to see them growing and gorging.

Information and Services

Extensive tourism and travel information is available from the **Brunswick County Chamber of Commerce** in Shallotte (4948 Main St., 800/426-6644, www.brunswickcountychamber.org, 8:30 A.M.–5 P.M. Mon.–Fri.).

For medical services, **Brunswick Community Hospital** (1 Medical Center Dr., 910/755-8121, www.brunswickcommunityhospital.com) is located in Supply, and **Dosher Memorial Hospital** (924 N. Howe St., 910/457-3800, www.dosher.org) is located in in Southport.

KURE BEACH

Kure is a two-syllable name: pronounced "Kyur-ee," (as in Madame, but not "curry"). This is a small beach community, not an extravaganza of neon lights and shark-doored

towel shops. Most of the buildings on the island are houses, both rental houses for vacationers and the homes of Kure Beach's year-round residents. The beach itself, like all North Carolina ocean beaches, is public.

Carolina Beach State Park

Just to the north of Kure is Carolina Beach State Park (1010 State Park Rd. off of 421, Carolina Beach, 910/458-8206, www.ncparks.gov/Visit/parks/cabe/main.php). Of all the state parks in the coastal region, this may be the one with the greatest ecological diversity. Within its boundaries are coastal pine and oak forests, pocosins between the dunes, saltwater marshes, a 50-foot sand dune, and limesink ponds; of the limesink ponds, one is a deep cypress swamp, one is a natural garden of water lilies, and one an ephemeral pond that dries into a swampy field every year, an ideal home for the many carnivorous plants that live here. You'll see Venus flytraps and their ferocious cousins here, but please resist the urge to dig or pick them, or to tempt them with your fingertips. Sort of like stinging insects that die after delivering their payload, the flytraps' traps can wither and fall off once they're sprung.

The park has 83 drive-to/walk-in campsites, each with a grill and picnic table. Two are wheelchair-accessible. Restrooms and hot showers are nearby. Camping is $15 per night, $10 per night for campers over the age of 62.

Fort Fisher State Historic Site

At the southern end of Kure Beach is Fort Fisher State Historic Site (1000 Loggerhead Rd. off of U.S. 421, 910-458-5798, www.ncparks.gov/Visit/parks/fofi/main.php, 8 A.M.–9 P.M. June–Aug., 8 A.M.–8 P.M. Mar.–May and Sept.–Oct., 8 A.M.–6 P.M. Nov.–Feb.). Fort Fisher was a Civil War earthwork stronghold designed to withstand massive assault. Modeled in part upon the Crimean War's Tower of Malakhoff, Fort Fisher's construction was an epic saga in itself, as hundreds of Confederate soldiers, African American slaves, and conscripted Lumbee Indians were brought in to build what became the Confederacy's largest fort.

After the fall of Norfolk in 1862, Wilmington became the most important open port in the South, a vital harbor for blockade-runners and military vessels. Fisher held until nearly the end of the War. On Christmas Eve of 1864, U.S. General Benjamin "The Beast" Butler attacked the fort with 1,000 men, but was repulsed—a retreat that led to his being relieved of his command. A few of weeks later, in January 1865, Fort Fisher was finally taken, but it required a Yankee force of 9,000 men and 56 ships in what was to be the largest amphibious assault until World War II. Without its defenses at Fort Fisher, Wilmington soon fell, hastening the end of the war, which came only three months later. Thanks to the final assault by the Union forces, and a century and a half of subsequent winds, tides, and hurricanes, not a great deal of the massive earthworks survives. But the remains of this vitally important Civil War site are preserved in an oddly peaceful and pretty seaside park, which contains a restored gun emplacement and a visitors center with interpretive exhibits.

Also at Fort Fisher is a branch of the **North Carolina Aquarium** (910/458-8257, 9 A.M.–5 P.M. daily year-round, $8 adults, $7 seniors, $6 under 17). Like its sisters at Roanoke and Pine Knoll Shores, this is a beautiful aquarium that specializes in the native marine life of the North Carolina waters. It's also a center for marine biology and conservation efforts, assisting in the rescue and rehabilitation of sea turtles, marine mammals, freshwater reptiles, and other creatures of the coast.

Accommodations

The beaches of the Carolinas used to be lined with boarding houses, the old-time choice in lodging for generations of middle-class tourists. They were sort of a precursor to today's bed-and-breakfasts, cozy family homes where visitors dined together with the hosts and were treated not so much like customers as houseguests—which is just what they were. Hurricane Hazel razed countless guesthouses when it pummeled the coast in 1954, ushering in the next epoch, that of the family motel. The

Beacon House (715 Carolina Beach Ave. N., 877/232-2666, www.beaconhouseinnb-b.com, breakfast not included, some pets permitted in cottages with an extra fee) at Carolina Beach, just north of Kure, is a rare survival from that era. The early-1950s boarding house has the typical upstairs and downstairs porches, and dark wood paneling indoors. (Nearby cottages are also rented by the Beacon House.) The price is much higher than it was in those days (now $150 and up in the high season, much less in the off-season), but you'll be treated to a lodging experience from a long-gone era.

BALD HEAD ISLAND

Bald Head Island, an exclusive community where golf carts are the only traffic, is a two-mile, 20-minute ferry ride from Southport. More than eighty percent of the island is designated as a nature preserve, and at the southern tip stands "Old Baldy," the oldest lighthouse in North Carolina.

Sights

The **Bald Head Island Lighthouse** (910/457-7481, www.oldbaldy.org, 10 A.M.–4 P.M. Tues.–Sat., 11 A.M.–4 P.M. Sun., call for winter hours, $5 to climb) was built in 1818, replacing an even earlier tower that was completed in 1795. Despite being the newcomer at Bald Head, the 109-foot lighthouse is the oldest such structure surviving in North Carolina. A visit to the lighthouse includes a stop next door at the **Smith Island Museum** housed in the lighthouse keeper's home. The development of Smith Island (of which Bald Head is the terminus) allowed almost 17,000 acres to be set aside as an ecological preserve. The Old Baldy Foundation leads **historic tours** (910/457-5003, 10:30 A.M. Tues.–Sat., $40, $30 guests of island establishments) of Bald Head, departing from Island Ferry Landing, a short walk from the lighthouse.

Food

A popular eatery on Bald Head is **Eb and Flo's Steam Bar** (910/457-7217, closed Wed. and in the winter, $10–20). It's on the waterfront, with the lighthouse behind it and a dining room/deck view over Long Bay to Fort Caswell. The seafood steamer pot is the specialty, and there is also a selection of burgers and sandwiches.

SOUTHPORT

Without a doubt one of North Carolina's prettiest towns, Southport is an 18th-century river town whose port was overtaken by Wilmington in importance—and hence it has remained small and quiet. It was the Brunswick County seat until the late 1970s, when that job was outsourced to Bolivia. (Bolivia, North Carolina, that is.) There have been plans in the works for the construction of an enormous international port here, and should that ever come to pass, this peaceful riverbank will be irrevocably changed. Given Southport's history—which has included several eras when the town seemed just on the brink of large-scale growth and importance in the world of international trade—it may be that the North Carolina International Port will go the way of Southport's other pipe dreams. In the meantime, it's a wonderfully charming place, with block upon block of beautiful historic houses and public buildings. The old cemetery is a gorgeous spot, and in it you'll find many tombstones that bear witness to the town's seafaring history—epitaphs for sea captains who died while visiting Smithville (Southport's original name), and stones carved with pictures of ships on rolling waves.

Sights

The **North Carolina Maritime Museum at Southport** (116 N. Howe St., 910/457-0003, www.ncmaritime.org, 9 A.M.–5 P.M. Tues.–Sat., free) is a smaller, storefront branch of the Maritime Museum at Beaufort, where you can learn about the seafaring history of the Carolina coast. Among the many topics of interest here is the life of pirate Stede Bonnet, whose girly surname belies his infamous life of crime. Bonnet, who spent much time in the Southport area, was by turns the pillaging buddy and bitter rival of Blackbeard. Other cool displays in the museum include a section

of a 2,000-year-old, 54-inch Indian canoe, and an 8-foot jawbone of a whale.

Events

Southport hosts the state's best-known **Fourth of July celebration** (910/457-6964, www.nc4thofjuly.com), attended each year by up to 50,000 people. (That's approximately 20 times the normal population of the town.) In addition to the requisite fireworks, food, and music, the festival features a special tribute to veterans, a flag retirement ceremony (that is, folks bring their old and worn-out flags), and a naturalization ceremony for new Americans.

Shopping

There are two irresistible pet boutiques in Southport, where you can pick up treats for your canine traveling companion or presents to bring back to your pets at home. **Zeetlegoo's Pet and People Store** (1635 N. Howe St., 910/457-5663, www.zeetlegoo.com, 10 A.M.–6 P.M. Mon.–Fri., 10 A.M.–4 P.M. Sat.) sells toys and treats for cats, dogs, and exotics, as well as leashes, cat furniture, and health products. Timber, a golden retriever mix, and Sammy, a cream-colored cat, are the resident product testers. **Cool Dogs & Crazy Cats** (310 N. Howe St., 910/457-0115, www.cooldogscrazycats.com) has a selection of fresh-baked biscuit delicacies, organic catnip, supplies and toys for cats and dogs, and jewelry and other items for their human customers.

Accommodations

Lois Jane's Riverview Inn (106 W. Bay St., 800/457-1152, www.loisjanes.com, $100–160 depending on season) is a Victorian waterfront home built by the innkeeper's grandfather. The rooms are comfortably furnished, bright and not frou-frou, and the Queen Deluxe Street, a cottage behind the inn, has its own kitchen and separate entrance. The front porch of the inn gives a wonderful view of the harbor.

At the same location is the **Riverside Motel** (106 W. Bay St., 910/457-6986, www.riverside-motelinc.com, $75–90), which also has a front porch with a fantastic panorama of the shipping channel.

Another affordable option is the **Inn at River Oaks** (512 N. Howe St., 910/457-1100, www.theinnatriveroaks.com, $65–135), a motel-style inn with very simple suites.

The **Inn at South Harbour Village** (South Harbour Village, 800/454-0815, www.south harbourvillageinn.com, $120–370, two-night minimum in high season) is a waterfront hotel in a development between Southport and Oak Island. The nine condo-style luxury suites have efficiency kitchens and dining rooms, inviting extended stays. The property overlooks the Intracoastal Waterway and South Harbour marina.

At Oak Island, west of Southport, **Captain's Cove Motel** (6401 E. Oak Island Dr., Oak Island, 910/278-6026, www.realpages.com/ captainscove, avg. $65) is a long-established family motel one block from the beach. The **Island Resort and Inn** (500 Ocean Dr., Oak Island, 910/278-5644, www.islandresortand-inn.com, $75–190 depending on season) is a beachfront property with standard motel rooms and one- and two-bedroom apartment suites. The **Ocean Crest Motel** (1417 East Beach Dr., Oak Island, 910/278-3333, www.ocean crest-motel.com, $65–155 depending on season) is a large condo-style motel, also right on the beach.

Food

The 《 **Yacht Basin Provision Company** (130 Yacht Basin St., 910/457-0654, $10–20) is a popular Southport seafood joint with a super-casual atmosphere. Customers place their orders at the counter and serve themselves drinks (on an honor system), then seat themselves dockside to await the arrival of their chow. Most popular here are the conch fritters and grouper salad sandwich, but anything you order will be good.

OCEAN ISLE

Ocean Isle is the next-to-most-southerly beach in North Carolina, separated from South Carolina only by Bird Island and the town of Calabash. In October, Ocean Isle is the site of the **North Carolina Oyster Festival** (www.brunswickcountychamber.org/OF-nc-oyster-festival.cfm), a huge event that's been happening for nearly 30 years. In addition to an oyster stew cook-off, surfing competition, and entertainment, this event features the North Carolina Oyster Shucking Competition. Oyster shucking is not so picayune a skill as it might sound. In the not-that-long-ago days when North Carolina's seafood industry was ascendant, workers—most often African American women—lined up on either side of long work tables in countless oyster houses along the coast and the creeks, and opened and cut out thousands of oysters a day. A complex occupational culture was at work in those rooms, one that had its own vocabulary, stories, and songs. The speed at which these women worked was a source of collective and individual pride, and the fastest shuckers enjoyed quite a bit of prestige among their colleagues. High-speed shucking is a skill that's well remembered by many Carolinians who might now be working at Wal-Mart, rather than in the old dockside shacks and warehouses. The state shucking championship is the time when some of the best shuckers prove that although North Carolina may have changed around them, they haven't missed a beat.

SOUTH ALONG U.S. 17

U.S. 17 is an old colonial road—in fact, its original name, still used in some stretches, is the King's Highway. George Washington passed this way on his 1791 Southern tour, staying with the prominent planters of this area and leaving in his wake the proverbial legends about where he lay his head of an evening. Today, the King's Highway, following roughly its original course, is still the main thoroughfare through Brunswick County into South Carolina.

《 Orton Plantation

Gardens adorn the relentlessly beautiful grounds of an early 18th-century rice plantation (9149 Orton Rd. SE, Winnabow, 910/371-

6851, www.ortongardens.com, 8 A.M.–6 P.M. spring and summer, 10 A.M.–5 P.M. fall and winter, closed Dec.–Feb., $9 adults, $8 seniors, $3 children). The centerpiece of the estate is the 1735 house, with circa-1840 additions; it's a quintessential white-columned antebellum palace, and a dead-ringer for *Gone with the Wind*'s Twelve Oaks. (The house is still a home, and is not open to the public.) A tragic history underlies the plantation's beauty, beginning with the extermination of the local native tribe that tried to repulse white encroachment by destroying the first house on this site. The Lowcountry rice plantation was one of the most complex, labor-intensive kinds of antebellum industry, and Orton, no exception, was home to a large slave community. Yankees occupied it during the Civil War and used the house as a hospital. This was a blessing in disguise, as it probably saved the house from being burned, the fate of many of the other great plantations along and near the King's Highway.

It was in the early 20th century that the formal gardens came into being, the project of Mrs. Luola Sprunt. Many of the massive live oaks, which look like they've been here for centuries, were actually planted in this era. Orton is perhaps the state's most famous azalea garden, an amazing spectacle of color in the gentle Lowcountry springtime. Swamps and river marshes sidle up to the gardens, and are home to many species of water birds, and— mind where you walk along the water's edge— a population of fat and happy alligators.

Brunswick Town and Fort Anderson

Nearby to Orton is the Brunswick Town/ Fort Anderson State Historic Site (8884 St. Philip's Rd. SE, Winnabow, 910/371-6613, www.ah.dcr.state.nc.us/sections/hs/brunswic/brunswic.htm, 9 A.M.–5 P.M. Mon.–Sat.), the site of what was a bustling little port town in the early and mid-1700s. In its brief life, Brunswick saw quite a bit of action. It was attacked in 1748 by a Spanish ship, which, to residents' delight, blew up in the river. (One of that ship's cannons was dragged out of the

river about 20 years ago and is on display here.) In 1765, the town's refusal to observe royal tax stamps was a successful precursor to the Boston Tea Party eight years later. But by the end of the Revolutionary War, Brunswick Town was solid gone, burned by the British but having been made obsolete anyway by the growth of Wilmington. Today nothing remains of the colonial port except for the lovely ruins of the 1754 St. Philip's Anglican Church and some building foundations uncovered by archaeologists. During the Civil War, Fort Anderson was built upon this site, sand earthworks that were part of the crucial defenses of the Cape Fear, protecting the blockade-runners who came and went from Wilmington. Some of the walls of that fort also survive. A visitors center at the historic site tells the story of this surprisingly significant stretch of riverbank, and the grounds, with the town's foundations exposed and interpreted, are an intriguing vestige of a forgotten community.

Nature Preserves

The Nature Conservancy's **Green Swamp Preserve** (NC 211, 5.5 miles north of Supply, Nature Conservancy regional office 910/395-5000, www.nature.org/wherewework/northamerica/states/northcarolina/preserves/art5606.html) contains nearly 16,000 acres of some of North Carolina's most precious coastal ecosystems, the longleaf pine savanna and evergreen shrub pocosin. Hiking is allowed in the preserve, but the paths are primitive. It's important to stay on the trails and not explore in the wilds because this is an intensely fragile ecosystem. In this preserve are communities of rare carnivorous plants, including the monstrous little pink-mawed Venus flytrap, four kinds of pitcher plant, and sticky-fingered sundew. It's also a habitat for the rare red-cockaded woodpecker, which is partial to diseased, old-growth longleaf pines as a place to call home.

The Nature Conservancy maintains another nature preserve nearby, the **Boiling Spring Lakes Preserve** (off of NC 87, Boiling Spring Lakes, trail begins at Community

Center, Nature Conservancy regional office 910/395-5000, www.nature.org/wherewework/northamerica/states/northcarolina/preserves/art12787.html). Brunswick County contains the state's greatest concentration of rare plant species, and the most diverse plant communities anywhere on the East Coast north of Florida. This preserve is owned by the Plant Conservation Program, and includes over half the acreage of the town of Boiling Spring Lakes. The ecosystem here is made up of Carolina bays, pocosins, and longleaf pine forests. Like the Green Swamp Preserve, many of the species here are dependent on periodic fires in order to propagate and survive. The Nature Conservancy does controlled burning at both sites to maintain this rare habitat.

Calabash and Vicinity

The once tiny fishing village of Calabash, just above the South Carolina line, was founded in the early 18th century as Pea Landing, a shipping point for the bounteous local peanut crop. Calabashes, a kind of gourd, were used as dippers in the town supply of drinking water, and when the settlement was renamed in 1873, it was supposedly for that reason that it became Calabash. In the early 1940s, a style of restaurant seafood was developed here that involves deep-frying lightly battered fish and shellfish. As the style caught on and more restaurants were built here, the term "Calabash-style seafood" was born. Jimmy Durante was fond of dining in Calabash, and some will claim that it was in tribute to food here that he signed off on his shows saying, "Good night, Mrs. Calabash, wherever you are." Though Calabash seafood is advertised at restaurants all over the country now, this little town has more than enough restaurants of its own to handle the yearly onslaught of tourists in search of an authentic Calabash meal.

Indigo Farms (1542 Hickman Rd. NW, Calabash, 910/287-6794, 8 A.M.–5 P.M. Mon.–Sat., longer in the warm months), three miles above the South Carolina line in Calabash, is a superb farm market, selling all manner of produce, preserves, and baked goods. They also have corn mazes and farm activities in the fall, and are a training site for porcine contestants in the prestigious local NASPIG races.

Sunset Beach, the southernmost of the Brunswick County beaches, is a wonderfully small-time place, a cozy town that until 2008 could only be reached via a one-lane pontoon bridge. One of the area's most popular restaurants is located just on the inland side of the bridge to Sunset Beach. **Twin Lakes Seafood Restaurant** (102 Sunset Blvd., 910/579-6373, http://twinlakesseafood.com) was built almost 40 years ago by Clarice and Ronnie Holden, both natives of the area. Clarice was born into a cooking family, the daughter of one of the founders of the Calabash restaurant tradition. Twin Lakes serves fresh, locally caught seafood, a rarity in this time and place. In-season and on weekends, expect long lines.

In the nearby town of Shallotte (pronounced "Shuh-LOTE"), **Holden Brothers Farm Market** (5600 Ocean Hwy. W., 910/579-4500) is a popular source for local produce. The peaches in season are wonderful, and the variety of homemade canned goods and pickles are worth the trip.

Points Inland from Wilmington

Moving inland from the Wilmington area, you will pass first through a lush world of wetlands distinguished by the peculiar Carolina bays. Not necessarily bodies of water, as the name would suggest, the bays are actually ovoid depressions in the earth, of unknown and much-debated origin. They are often water-filled, but by definition are fed by rainwater rather than creeks or groundwater. They create unique environments, and are often surrounded by bay laurels (hence the name), and guarded by a variety of carnivorous plants.

The next zone, bounded by the Waccamaw and Lumber Rivers, is largely made up of farmland and small towns. This was for generations prime tobacco country, and that heritage is still very much evident in towns like Whiteville, where old tobacco warehouses line the railroad tracks. Culturally, this area—mostly in Columbus County, extending a little ways into Robeson to the west and Brunswick to the east—is of a piece with the three counties in South Carolina with which it shares a border—Horry, Marion, and Dillon. Many of the same family names are still to be found on either side of the state line.

The area around the Lumber River, especially in Robeson County, is the home of the Lumbee, native peoples with an amazing heritage of devotion to faith and family, and steadfast resistance to oppression. If you turn on the radio while driving through this area, you'll likely find Lumbee gospel programming, and get a sense of the cadences of Lumbee English. The characteristics that make it different from the speech of local whites and African Americans are very subtle, but certain hallmarks of pronunciation and grammar (which include the sub-variations of different families and towns within the community) distinguish the tribe's speech as one of the state's most distinctive dialects.

At the edge of the region covered in this chapter is Fayetteville. From its early days as the center of Cape Fear Scottish settlement to its current role as one of the most important military communities in the United States, Fayetteville has always been one of the most significant of North Carolina's cities.

ALONG HIGHWAY 74

A little ways inland from Calabash, the countryside is threaded by the Waccamaw River, a gorgeous, dark channel full of cypress knees and dangerous reptiles. (The name is pronounced "WAW-cuh-MAW," with slightly more emphasis on the first syllable than the third.) It winds its way down from Lake Waccamaw through a swampy little portion of North Carolina, crossing Horry County, South Carolina (unofficial motto: "The H is silent"), before joining its fellow North Carolina natives, the Pee Dee and Lumber Rivers, to let out in Winyah Bay at the colonial port of Georgetown. Through the little toenail of North Carolina that the Waccamaw crosses, it parallels the much longer Lumber River, surrounding the very rural Columbus County and part of Robeson County in an environment of deep, subtropical wetlands.

Sights

Pembroke is the town around which much of the Lumbee community revolves, and at the center of life here is the University of North Carolina at Pembroke. Founded in 1887 as the Indian Normal School, UNCP's population is now only about one-quarter Native American, but it's still an important site in North Carolina's native history. The **Museum of the Native American Resource Center** (Old Main, UNCP, 910/521-6282, www.uncp .edu/nativemuseum, 8 A.M.–noon and 1–5 P.M. Mon.–Sat., free) is on campus, occupying Old Main, a 1923 building that's a source of pride for the Pembroke community. The Resource Center has a small but very good collection of old artifacts and contemporary art by members of Native American tribes across the country. Laurinburg's **John Blue House** (13040

HENRY BERRY LOWRY

In some places, the Civil War didn't end the day Lee surrendered, but smoldered on in terrible local violence. One such place was the Lumbee community of Robeson County, in the days of the famous Lowry Band.

Then as now, Lowry (also spelled Lowrie) was a prominent name in the tribe. During the Civil War, Allen Lowry led a band of men who hid out in the swamps, eluding conscription into the backbreaking corps of semi-slave labor that was forced to build earthenworks to defend Wilmington. When the war ended, violence against the Lumbees continued, and the Lowry Band retaliated, attacking the plantations of their wartime pursuers. Allen Lowry and his oldest son were captured in 1865 and executed. Henry Berry Lowry, the youngest son, inherited the mantle of leadership.

For the next several years, long after the end of the Civil War, the Lowry Band was pursued relentlessly. Arrested and imprisoned, Lowry and his band escaped from prison in Lumberton and Wilmington. Between 1868 and 1872, the state and federal governments tried everything – putting a bounty on Lowry's head, even sending in a federal artillery battalion. After an 11-month campaign of unsuccessful pursuit, the federal soldiers gave up. Soon afterwards, the Lowry Band emerged from the swamps, raided Lumberton, and made off with a large amount of money. This was the end of the road for the Lowry Band, though, and one by one its members were all killed in 1872 – except, perhaps, Henry Berry. It's unknown whether he died, went back into hiding, or left the area altogether. As befits a legend, he seems simply to have disappeared.

Henry Berry Lowry is a source of fierce pride to modern Lumbees, a symbol of the tribe's resistance and resilience. Every summer, members of the tribe perform in the long-running outdoor drama *Strike at the Wind,* which tells the story of the Lowry Band. Another vivid retelling of the story is the 2001 novel *Nowhere Else on Earth,* by Josephine Humphreys.

X-way Rd., 910/276-2495, www.johnblue cottonfestival.com) is a spectacle of Victorian design, a polygonal house built entirely of heart pine harvested from the surrounding property, and done up like a wedding cake with endless decorative devices. John Blue, the builder and original owner, was an inventor of machinery used in the processing of cotton. A pre–Civil War cotton gin stands on the property, and is used for educational demonstrations throughout the year. This is the site of the **John Blue Cotton Festival,** an October event that showcases not only the ingenuity of the home's famous resident, and the process of ginning cotton, but also lots of local and regional musicians and other artists.

Strike at the Wind

For more than 30 years, the Lumbee tribe has put on a production of the play *Strike at the Wind* (North Carolina Indian Cultural Center, 638 Terry Sanford Rd., Pembroke, www.strikeatthewind.com), which takes place in the outdoor Adolph Dial Amphitheater on the banks of the Lumber River. (Adolph Dial was one of the greatest scholars of Lumbee history.) The play, which tells the story of Henry Berry Lowry and his gang, is acted by members of the Lumbee tribe, as well as white and African American cast members, and while a few of the cast are professional actors, most are people from the surrounding area who are simply passionate about their history and want to be part of its most famous public portrait. The music for the play was composed by songwriter Willie French Lowery, himself an important artistic ambassador of the Lumbee tribe.

While the performance occasionally takes a hiatus because of funding difficulties, it's worth seeing if it's being put on.

Entertainment and Events

Several of the state's big agricultural festivals

are held in this area. If you're in the little town of Fair Bluff in late July, you might be lucky enough to witness the coronation of the newest Watermelon Queen. The **North Carolina Watermelon Festival** (910/212-0013, www.ncwatermelonfestival.com) began as an annual competition between two friends, local farmers whose watermelons grew to over 100 pounds. The two-man competition expanded into this festival that celebrates watermelon-growing throughout the state, and in which a new court of watermelon royalty is crowned every year.

In Tabor City, there's a famous **Yam Festival** (www.discovercolumbuscounty.org) in October, during which the tiny town's population sometimes quadruples. Yam partisans crown their own royal court during this festival. Then when spring rolls back around, Chadbourn holds its annual **Strawberry Festival** (http://ncstrawberryfestival.com), at which the coronation of the Strawberry Queen takes place. If this seems a strange sort of royalty, bear in mind that across the South Carolina line, they have a Little Miss Hell Hole Swamp competition.

All of North Carolina, and in particular the Cape Fear region in the southeast, has a great deal of Scottish ancestry and heritage. In the small town of Red Springs in Robeson County, a small Presbyterian school, Flora Macdonald College, operated for many years. Though it's now been closed for a generation, its grounds and lovely gardens are listed in the National Register of Historic Places and are the setting of the annual **Flora Macdonald Highland Games** (200 South College St., Red Springs, 910/843-5000, www.capefearscots.com). Like its counterpart to the west at Grandfather Mountain, these Highland Games are a fun celebration of Celtic culture. The festival includes piping competitions, sheepdog competitions, food, dancing, and of course the traditional feats of highland athleticism like tossing the caber.

Sports and Recreation

Several beautiful state parks line the Waccamaw and Lumber Rivers. **Lake Waccamaw State Park** (1866 State Park Dr., Lake Waccamaw,

910/646-4748, http://ncparks.gov/Visit/parks/lawa/main.php) encompasses the 9,000-acre lake of that name. The lake is technically a Carolina bay, a mysterious geological feature of this region. Carolina bays are large, oval depressions in the ground, many of which are boggy and filled with water, but which are actually so-named because of the bay trees that typically grow in and around them. Lake Waccamaw has geological and hydrological characteristics that make it unique even within the odd enough category of Carolina bays. Because of its proximity to a large limestone deposit, the water is more neutral than its usually very acidic cousins, and so it supports a greater diversity of life. There are several aquatic creatures that live only here, with great names like the Waccamaw fatmucket and silverside (a mollusk and a fish, respectively). The park draws many boaters and paddlers, naturally, though the only available launches are outside the property. Primitive campsites are available in the park for $9/night.

Singletary Lake State Park (6707 Hwy. 53 E., Kelly, 910/669-2928, www.ncparks.gov/Visit/parks/sila/main.php), north of Lake Waccamaw in Kelly, centers around one of the largest of the Carolina bays, the 572-acre Singletary Lake, which lies within the Bladen Lakes State Forest. There is no individual camping here, though there are facilities for large groups—including the entrancingly named Camp Ipecac—which date from the Civilian Conservation Corps era. There is a nice one-mile hiking trail, the CCC-Carolina Bay Loop Trail, and a 500-foot pier extending over the bay. Some of the cypress trees here are estimated to have been saplings when the first Englishmen set foot on Roanoke Island.

Lumber River State Park (2819 Princess Ann Rd., Orrum, 910/628-4564, http://ncparks.gov/Visit/parks/luri/main.php) has 115 miles of waterways, with numerous put-ins for canoes and kayaks. The river, referred to as the Lumber or Lumbee River, or, in areas farther upstream, as Drowning Creek, traverses both the coastal plain region and the eastern edge of the Sandhills. Camping is available here for

$9 per night at unimproved walk-in and ca-noe-in sites.

Yogi Bear's Jellystone Park (626 Richard Wright Rd., 877/668-8586, www.taborcity jellystone.com), formerly known as Daddy Joe's, is a popular campground with RV and tent spaces, rental cabins, and yurts. The facilities are clean and well maintained, and there are tons of children's activities on-site. Some of the camping is in wooded areas, but for the most part expect direct sun and plan accordingly.

In Fair Bluff is **River Bend Outfitters** (1206 Main St., 910/649-5998, www.whiteville .nc/rbo), a canoe and kayak company that specializes in paddling and camping trips along the beautiful blackwater Lumber River.

Food

If you pass through Tabor City, don't neglect to have a meal at the **Todd House** (102 Live Oak St., 910/653-3778), which has been serving fine country cooking since 1923. The Todds are one of the oldest families in the area along the state line, and the first in the restaurant business was Mrs. Mary Todd, who took to cooking meals for visiting tobacco buyers. (This area lived and died by tobacco for generations.) Through her daughter's time, and a couple of subsequent owners, the Todd House has continued to serve famously good barbecue, fried chicken, and other down-home specialties. Their wonderful pies are available for purchase, so pick one up for the road.

FAYETTEVILLE

Fayetteville is North Carolina's sixth-largest city, and in its own quiet way has always been one of the state's most powerful engines of growth and change. In the early 1700s, it became a hub for settlement by Scottish immigrants, who helped build it into a major commercial center. From the 1818 initiation of steamboat travel between Fayetteville and Wilmington along the Cape Fear—initially a voyage of six days!—to the building of the Plank Road, a huge boon to intrastate commerce, Fayetteville was well connected to commercial resources all through the Carolinas.

At a national level, Fayetteville serves as the location of two high-level military installations. Fort Bragg is the home of the XVIII Airborne Corps, the 82nd Airborne, the Delta Force, and the John F. Kennedy Special Warfare Center and School. As such, it's also the home of many widows and children of soldiers who have died in Iraq and Afghanistan. Pope Air Force Base is nearby, the home of the 43rd Airlift Wing, and its Maintenance, Support, and Operations Groups.

Sights

The **Fayetteville Museum of Art** (839 Stamper Rd., 910/485-5121, www.fayetteville museumart.org, 10 A.M.–5 P.M. Mon.–Fri., 1–5 P.M. Sat. and Sun., closed state holidays) is one of North Carolina's major galleries. Featuring art from a variety of media, and an expansive view of the nature of art, the museum provides a valuable resource for art education and inspiration in the region.

The **Museum of the Cape Fear Regional Complex** (801 Arsenal Ave., 910/486-1330, www.museumofthecapefear.ncdcr.gov, 10 A.M.–5 P.M. Tues.–Sat., 1 P.M.–5 P.M. Sun.) has three components, each telling different stories of Fayetteville's history. The museum itself has exhibits on the history and prehistory of the region, including its vital role in developing transportation in the state, as well as its centrality as a military center. There is an 1897 house museum, the Poe House, which belonged to a Mr. Edgar Allen Poe—not Edgar Allan the writer, but Edgar Allen, a brickyard owner. The third section is the 4.5-acre Arsenal Park, the site of a federal arms magazine built in 1836, claimed by the Confederacy in 1861, and destroyed by General Sherman in 1865.

The **Airborne and Special Operations Museum** (100 Bragg Blvd., 910/643-2766, www.asomf.org, 10 A.M.–5 P.M. Tues.–Sat., noon–5 P.M. Sun., closed Mon. except for federal holidays, free admission, $4 for theater and motion simulator) is an impressive facility that presents the history of Special Ops paratroopers, from the first jump in 1940 to the divisions' present-day roles abroad in peacekeeping missions and war. In the museum's theater you can watch an amazing film of what it looks like when a paratrooper makes the jump, and the 24-seat Pitch, Roll, and Yaw Vista-Dome Motion Simulator makes the experience even more exciting.

The **JFK Special Warfare Museum** (Building D-2502, Ardennes and Marion Sts., Fort Bragg, 910/432-4272, www.jfkwebstore.com/index.php, 11 A.M.–4 P.M. Tues.–Sun., ID required to get onto the base) tells the story of further amazing facets of the U.S. military, including Special Ops and Psychological Ops. The museum focuses on the Vietnam War era, but chronicles unconventional warfare from colonial times to the present.

Going back a good bit further in time, the **Fayetteville Independent Light Infantry Armory and Museum** (210 Burgess St., 910/433-1612, open by appointment, free) displays artifacts from the history of the Light Infantry. The FILI is still active, dedicated as North Carolina's official historic military command, a ceremonial duty. But in its active-duty days, which began in 1793, FILI had some exciting times, particularly during the Civil War. In addition to the military artifacts, this museum also exhibits a carriage in which the Marquis de Lafayette was shown around Fayetteville—the only one of the towns bearing his name that he actually visited.

The 79-acre **Cape Fear Botanical Garden** (536 N. Eastern Blvd., 910/486-0221, www.capefearbg.org, 10 A.M.–5 P.M. Mon.–Sat., noon–5 P.M. Sun., closed Sun. mid-Dec.–Feb., $5 adults, $4 military and AAA, free under 12, everyone free first Sat. of every month and entire month of April) is one of the loveliest horticultural sites in North Carolina. The camellia and azalea gardens are spectacular sights in the early spring, but the variety of plantings and environments represented makes the whole park a delight. Along the banks of the Paw Paw River and Cross Creek, visitors will find dozens of garden environments, from lily gardens and hosta gardens, to woods and a bog, and an 1880s farmhouse garden. Without a doubt, this is the prettiest place in Fayetteville.

Cross Creek Cemetery (North Cool Spring and Grove Sts., 800/255-8217, dawn–dusk daily) is an attractively sad spot, the resting place of many Scots men and women who crossed the ocean to settle the Cape Fear. Though people of all kinds and times are buried here, it is the oldest section that is most poignant, where one stone after another commemorates Mr. or Mrs. Mac-So-and-So, Late of Glasgow or Perth, Merchant in this Town. One can feel the invisible ties of kith and kin that led these early immigrants to band together for comfort in the New World. (While strolling this cemetery, and especially when pausing to read a stone, beware of extraordinarily fast-moving fire ants.)

Entertainment and Events

The **Cameo Theatre** (225 Hay St., 910/486-6633, www.cameoarthouse.com) is a cool old early-20th-century movie house, originally known as the New Dixie. Today it is "Fayetteville's alternative cinematic experience," a place for independent and art house movies.

The **Cape Fear Regional Theatre** (1209 Hay St., 910/323-4233, www.cfrt.org) began in 1962 as a tiny company with a bunch of borrowed equipment. Today it is a major regional theater with a wide reputation. Putting on several major productions each season, with a specialty of popular musicals, it draws actors and directors from around the country, but maintains its heart here in the Fayetteville arts community. The **Gilbert Theater** (116 Green St., entrance on Bow St., above Fascinate-U Museum, 910/678-7186, www.gilberttheater.com) is a small company that puts on a variety of productions throughout the year, with special emphasis on classic drama and multicultural offerings. Tickets are $10 and seating is on a first-come basis.

Fayetteville's late-April **Dogwood Festival** features rock, pop, and beach music bands; a dog show; a recycled art show; a "hogs and rags spring rally"; and the selection and coronation of Miss, Teen Miss, Young Miss, and Junior Miss Dogwood Festival.

Accommodations and Food

Fayetteville's lodging options are by and large chain motels, a multitude of which can be found at the Fayetteville exits off of I-95. You'll generally find a pretty reasonable deal at the old standards, but if you'd like to stay somewhere with more personality, Wilmington and Raleigh are both easily accessible.

Likewise, the city's dining choices tend towards the highway chains. There are some exceptions, though. The 【 **Hilltop House** (1240 Fort Bragg Rd., 910/484-6699, www.hilltophousenc.com, lunch 11 A.M.–2 P.M. Mon.–Sat., supper 5 P.M.–9 P.M. Mon.–Thurs. and 5 P.M.–10 P.M. Fri. and Sat., Sun. brunch 10:30 A.M.–2:30 P.M., complimentary wine tasting every Tues. night, $15–25) serves hearty fare in an elegant setting, and was recognized in 2007 with a Wine Spectator Award for Excellence—not surprising, given that the Hilltop House has a 74-page wine list. More casual is the **Mash House** (4150 Sycamore Dairy Rd., 910/867-9223, www.themashhouse.com, $8–16), which has a good variety of pizzas and sandwiches, as well as heavier entrées and a selection of good homemade brews.

Information and Services

Cape Fear Valley Health Services (1638 Owen Dr., 910/609-4000, www.capefearvalley.com) is a large hospital complex with acute care services, a major cardiac care program, and everything else one would expect from an important regional hospital.

The website of the **Fayetteville Area Convention and Visitors Bureau** (www.visitfayettevillenc.com) is an excellent source of tourist information for this city. There you'll find not only the basics about what, where, and how much, but detailed driving tours, extensive historical information, and much more.

Getting There and Around

Fayetteville Regional Airport (400 Airport Rd., 910/433-1160, flyfay.ci.fayetteville.nc.us) has daily flights to and from Charlotte (US Airways Express) and Atlanta (ASA, Delta Connections). The city is served by **Amtrak** (472 Hay St., 800/872-7245, www.amtrak.com, 10 A.M.–5:45 P.M. and 10 P.M.–5:45 A.M. daily) via the Palmetto and Silver Service lines. It's also a short hop off of I-95.

WILMINGTON AND CAPE FEAR

MYRTLE BEACH AND THE GRAND STRAND

The West has Las Vegas, Florida has Orlando, and South Carolina has Myrtle Beach. There's no Bellagio Resort nor Magic Kingdom here, but Myrtle Beach remains the number one travel destination in the state, with more tourists than even Charleston.

Unlike Charleston, you'll find precious little history here. With several theme parks, 100 golf courses, 50 miniature golf courses, over 2,000 restaurants—not to mention miles of beautiful shoreline—Myrtle Beach is built for all-out vacation enjoyment. The hot, hazy height of the summer also marks the busy season on the Strand. Its long main drag, Kings Highway (a.k.a. Business U.S. 17), is packed full of families on the go eager for more swimming, more shopping, more eating, and just plain *more*.

While to many people simply uttering the words "Myrtle Beach" conjures an image of tacky, downscale people doing tacky, downscale things, that's becoming a more outmoded stereotype by the day. Certainly tacky is still very much in vogue here, but an influx of higher-quality development, both in accommodations and in entertainment value, has lifted the bar significantly.

Rather than slumming in a beat-up motel, quaffing PBR on the beach, and loading up on $2 T-shirts like in the "good old days," a typical Myrtle Beach vacation now involves a stay in a large condo apartment with flat screens, a full kitchen, and a sumptuous, palmetto-lined pool, dining at the House of Blues, having drinks at the Hard Rock Café, stops at high-profile attractions like Ripley's

© JIM MOREKIS

HIGHLIGHTS

◖ Broadway at the Beach: You'll find good cheesy fun here along with tons of interesting shops, theme restaurants, and of course, miniature golf (page 114).

◖ Barefoot Landing: This is North Myrtle Beach's answer to Broadway at the Beach, with the Alabama Theatre and the House of Blues nearby (page 117).

◖ Ocean Drive Beach: The still-beating, still-shuffling heart of the Grand Strand is also the center of shag dancing culture (page 119).

◖ Carolina Opry: This popular show offers corny, but quality, family entertainment in an intimate, friendly setting (page 123).

◖ Brookgreen Gardens: Enjoy America's largest collection of outdoor sculptures, set amid a fine collection of formal gardens (page 146).

◖ Huntington Beach State Park: The scenic beach combines with one-of-a-kind Atalaya Castle to make for a unique getaway (page 147).

◖ Hampton Plantation: This historic Georgian mansion on the scenic Wambaw Creek inspired a state poet laureate to give it to the state for posterity (page 158).

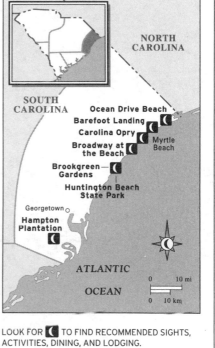

LOOK FOR ◖ TO FIND RECOMMENDED SIGHTS, ACTIVITIES, DINING, AND LODGING.

Aquarium, and shopping at trendy retailers like Anthropologie and Abercrombie & Fitch.

The Grand Strand on which Myrtle Beach sits—a long, sandy peninsula stretching 60 miles from Winyah Bay to the North Carolina border—has also been a vacation playground for generations of South Carolinians. Unlike Hilton Head to the south, where New York and New Jersey accents are more common than a Lowcountry drawl, Myrtle Beach and the Grand Strand remain largely home-grown passions, with many visitors living within a few hours' drive. Despite the steady increase of money and high-dollar development in the area, its strongly regional nature works to

your advantage in that prices here are generally lower than in Vegas or Orlando.

To the south of Myrtle proper lies the understated, affluent, and relaxing Pawleys Island, with nearby Murrells Inlet and its great seafood restaurants. Unique, eclectic Brookgreen Gardens hosts the largest collection of outdoor sculpture in America, with one-of-a-kind Huntington Beach State Park literally right across the street.

Even further south, in the northern quarter of the Lowcountry proper, you'll find a totally different scene: the remnants of the Carolina rice culture in quaint old Georgetown and the haunting antebellum mansions at Hampton Plantation and Hopsewee Plantation.

MYRTLE BEACH

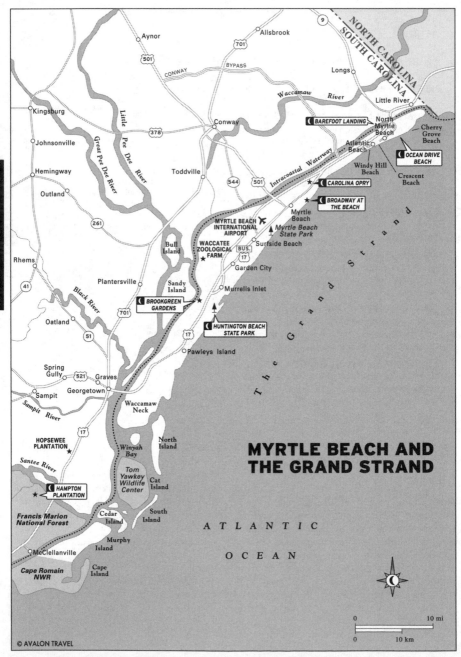

MYRTLE BEACH AND
THE GRAND STRAND

ATLANTIC

OCEAN

0   10 mi

0   10 km

© AVALON TRAVEL

HISTORY

The Grand Strand was once the happy hunting and shellfish-gathering grounds of the Waccamaw Indian people, whose legacy is still felt today in the name of the dominant river in the region and the Strand's main drag itself, Kings Highway, which is actually built on an old tribal trail.

The southern portion of the Strand, Georgetown and Pawleys Island in particular, rapidly became host to a number of rice plantations soon after the area was colonized. However, the area now known as Myrtle Beach didn't share in the wealth since its soil and topography weren't conducive to the plantation system. Indeed, the northern portion of the Grand Strand was largely uninhabited during colonial times, and hurricane damage prevented much development throughout the first half of the 19th century.

That changed after the Civil War with the boom of nearby Conway to the west, now the seat of Horry County (pronounced "OR-ee"). As Conway's lumber and export economy grew, a railroad spur was built to bring in lumber from the coast, much of which was owned by a single firm, the Conway Lumber Company. Lumber company employees began using the rail lines to take vacation time on the Strand, in effect becoming the first of millions of tourists to the area. At this time it was simply called "New Town," in contrast to Conway's "Old Town."

In the second half of the 19th century, Civil War veteran Franklin G. Burroughs of the Burroughs and Collins Company, which supplied lumber and turpentine to Conway business interests, sought to expand the tourism profitability of the coastal area. Though he died in 1897, his heirs continued his dream, inaugurated by the opening of the Seaside Inn in 1901. The first bona fide resort came in the 1920s with the building of the Arcady resort, which included the first golf course in the area.

In 1938 Burroughs's widow Adeline, known locally as "Miss Addie," was credited with giving the town its modern name, after the locally abundant wax myrtle shrub. During this time locals on the Strand originated the shagging subculture, built around the dance of the same name and celebrated at numerous pavilions and "beach clubs." The building of Myrtle Beach Air Force Base in 1940—now closed—brought further growth and jobs to the area.

Tourism, especially, grew apace here until Hurricane Hazel virtually wiped the slate clean in 1954. In typical Carolinian fashion, residents and landowners made lemonade out of lemons, using the hurricane's devastation as an excuse to build even bigger resort developments, including a plethora of golf courses.

Since then, the Strand has grown to encompass about a quarter-million permanent residents, with about ten million tourists on top of that each year. A huge influx of money in the 1990s led to a higher-dollar form of development on the coast leading to the sad demolition of many of the old beach pavilions in favor of new attractions and massive condo high-rises.

PLANNING YOUR TIME

The most important thing to remember is that the Grand Strand is *long*—60 miles from one end to the other. This has real-world effects that need to be taken into account. For example, while the separate municipality of North Myrtle Beach (actually a fairly recent aggregation of several small beachside communities) may sound like it's right next door to Myrtle Beach proper, getting from one to the other can take a half-hour even in light traffic.

Due to this geographical stretching, as well as to all the attractions here, it is impossible to cover this area in a single day, and even two days is a ridiculously short amount of time. That's probably the main reason many folks indulge in a weekly rental here. Not only does that give you enough time to see everything here, it enables you to relax, slow down, and enjoy the beaches and the general laid-back attitude.

In May, Memorial Day weekend and Bike Week have traditionally signaled the beginning of the tourist season in Myrtle Beach. The busy season here exactly corresponds with the hottest months of the year, July and August. This is when crowds are at their peak, restaurants are most crowded, and the two spurs of U.S. 17 are at their most gridlocked.

Springtime in Myrtle Beach is quite nice, but keep in mind that water temperatures are still chilly through April. There is almost always one last cold snap in March that augurs the spring.

Personally I recommend hitting Myrtle Beach just as the busy season wanes, right after Labor Day. Rooms are significantly cheaper, but most everything is still fully open and adequately staffed, with the added benefit of the biggest crush of tourists being absent.

Winter on the Grand Strand is very slow, as befitting this very seasonal locale. Many restaurants, especially down the Strand near Murrells Inlet, close entirely through February.

ORIENTATION

Don't get too hung up on place names around here. Though this part of the Strand comprises several different municipalities—from Surfside Beach to the south up to Little River near the North Carolina border—for all intents and purposes it's one big place all its own. As a general rule, development (read: money) is moving quicker to the North Myrtle Beach area rather than the older, sometimes seedy Myrtle Beach proper to the south. (North Myrtle is

actually a recent aggregation of several historic beachfront communities: Windy Hill, Crescent Beach, Cherry Grove, and Ocean Drive. You'll see numerous signs announcing the entrance or exit into or out of these communities, but keep in mind you're still technically in North Myrtle Beach.)

The Grand Strand grid is based on a system of east-west avenues beginning just north of Myrtle Beach State Park. Confusingly, these are separated into "North" and "South" avenues. Perhaps even more confusing, North Myrtle Beach also uses its own, distinct north/south avenue system (also for roads running east-west). Got it?

It goes like this: Myrtle Beach starts with 29th Avenue South at the Myrtle Beach International Airport and goes up to First Avenue South just past Family Kingdom Amusement Park. From there the avenues are labeled as "North" from 1st Avenue North up to 82nd Avenue North, which concludes Myrtle Beach proper.

North Myrtle Beach begins at 48th Avenue South near Barefoot Landing and goes up to Main Street (the center of the shag culture). It continues with 1st Avenue North, goes up to 24th Avenue North (Cherry Grove Beach), and finally concludes at 61st Avenue North, near the North Carolina state line.

Sights

◖ BROADWAY AT THE BEACH

Love it or hate it, Broadway at the Beach (1325 Celebrity Cir., 800/386-4662, www.broadway atthebeach.com) between 21st and 29th Avenues is one of Myrtle's biggest and flashiest attractions—which is saying a lot. First opened 14 years ago and added onto significantly since then, this collection of three hotels, over two dozen restaurants, about 50 shops, and a dozen kid-oriented activities, sprawls over 350 acres with several other major attractions, restaurants, and clubs (such as the Hard Rock Café and Planet Hollywood) on its periphery.

Just like the Magic Kingdom that many of Myrtle's attractions seek to emulate, Broadway at the Beach has at its center a large lagoon, around which everything else is situated. Needless to say there's also a massive parking lot, as at the Magic Kingdom.

Activity goes on here all day and well into the wee hours, with the weekly Tuesday night fireworks a big draw. While there's plenty to do, what with the greats shops, tasty treats, and fun, piped-in music following you everywhere, it's also fun to just walk around.

The main complaint about Broadway at the

Beach has to do with the price of the various attractions within the park, some of which are fairly small-scale. Indeed, the quality of the attractions within Broadway at the Beach varies, and much depends on what floats your boat, but you can still find plenty to enjoy as long as you know the scoop ahead of time. Here's a quick guide to the specific attractions.

Harry Potter fans will likely enjoy **MagiQuest** (1185 Celebrity Cir., 843/913-9460, www.magiquest.com, $25.95 first quest, subsequent quests vary), which takes you on a 90-minute journey to find clues that lead to hidden treasure. Folks of an older generation will find it a surprisingly high-tech experience for something dealing with the ancient arts of wizardry—including an orientation session and the programmable wands that are indispensable to the quest. But don't worry, the young ones will get it. However, don't be surprised to see adults getting into the game as much as any tyke—MagiQuest has a certain addictive quality, and many people opt to go back for more (additional quests are priced less) after their usually confusing, full-price first experience. Note that there's an intro game you can play online, which might help you get acquainted. Like many attractions at Myrtle Beach, this one can get very crowded, which is certain to impede the quality of your experience (Whose wand uncovered the clue? Who knows?). Try to go right when it opens.

Similarly medieval—and right nearby—is **Medieval Times** (2904 Fantasy Way, 843/236-4635, www.medievaltimes.com, $46.95 adults, $28.95 ages 12 and under), a combination dinner theatre and medieval tournament reenactment.

Now that almost all of the old-fashioned amusement parks at Myrtle Beach are gone, victims of "modernization," you can find a facsimile of sorts at **Pavilion Nostalgia Park** (843/913-9400, www.mbpavilion.com, 11 A.M.–11 P.M. during high season, other times vary, $3 admission, rides extra), which seeks to simulate the days of Myrtle gone by.

Of course nowhere in Myrtle is really complete without miniature golf, and Broadway at the

Beach's version is **Dragon's Lair Fantasy Golf** (1197 Celebrity Cir., 843/913-9301, $7.50 adults, $7 children), with two medieval-themed 18-hole courses boasting a fire-breathing dragon.

Ripley's Aquarium

If you've been to the New England Aquarium don't expect something similar at Ripley's Aquarium (1110 Celebrity Cir., 800/734-8888, www.ripleysaquarium.com, Sun.–Thurs. 9 A.M.–8 P.M., Fri.–Sat. 9 A.M.–9 P.M., $18.99 adults, $9.99 ages 6–11, $3.99 ages 2–5, under 2 free) at Broadway at the Beach. This is a smaller, but quite delightful, aquarium built primarily for entertainment purposes rather than educational ones.

Calming music plays throughout, and moving sidewalks take you around and under huge tanks filled with various marine creatures. There's even the requisite "stingray petting" touch tank.

You'll no doubt see the garish billboards for the Aquarium up and down U.S. 17, featuring massive sharks baring rows of scary teeth. But don't expect an over-the-top shark exhibit—the truth is that most of the sharks in the Aquarium are smaller and much more peaceful.

NASCAR SpeedPark

Just outside Broadway at the Beach you'll find the NASCAR SpeedPark (1820 21st Ave. N., 843/918-8725, www.nascarspeedpark.com, daily 10 A.M.–11 P.M. during high season, shorter hours during other times, ticket prices vary), where can you speed around at 50 miles per hour in a fairly decent replica of an actual NASCAR track. Because there are several different tracks to choose from, based on age and difficulty, there's something here for adults and kids alike.

The serious track, "Thunder Road," is only open to drivers 16 and over and allows them to get into half-size versions of Nextel Cup cars. Pint-size drivers 48, 40, and 36 inches tall can take part in racing on the "Champions," "Qualifier," and Kiddie Speedway courses, respectively. As if all that's not enough, there are water-based racing courses and, this being Myrtle Beach, NASCAR-themed miniature golf.

If you're worried about metal-shearing, flame-spewing, multiple car pileups like in a real NASCAR race, don't. Safety is a paramount concern at this national chain of parks, and the likelihood of an accident at the

Ripley's Aquarium

© JIM MOREKIS

SpeedPark is far less than on crowded U.S. 17, a stone's throw away. As for pricing, most choose the $32 all-day pass, but smaller packages ranging from $20–50 are also available.

Myrtle Waves Water Park

Billed as South Carolina's largest water park, Myrtle Waves Water Park (U.S. 17 Bypass and 10th Ave. N., 843/913-9260, www.myrtle waves.com, daily 10 A.M.–6 P.M. during high season, other times vary, $28 ages 7 and up, $22 ages 3–6, 2 and under free) is right across the street from Broadway at the Beach, covers 20 acres, and features all kinds of safe, fun "rides," such as the Ocean in Motion Wave Pool, the Layzee River, and the Saturation Station, wherein a huge water volcano absolutely soaks everybody in proximity every five minutes or so. That's just to name a few.

As you would expect, there are plenty of lifeguards on hand at all the rides. Food is plentiful if non-remarkable, and there are shaded areas for the less-adventurous to chill while the kids splash around. With one admission price covering you for all rides all day, this is one of the better deals in Myrtle Beach, which has more than its share of confusingly (and occasionally exorbitantly) priced attractions.

Hard Rock Park

The Hard Rock Park (211 George Bishop Pkwy., 843/236-7625, www.hardrockpark .com, daily 10 A.M.–11 P.M. during high season, other times vary, check website for prices) has been through some hard times itself, finding itself in bankruptcy and closed for much of 2008. As of this writing the park has been purchased by an investment group which plans to run it in a similar fashion as before, with the exception of lowering the high admission prices often cited for the park's original financial difficulties.

As for the park itself, it takes the nightclub/ restaurant chain's theme to the next level with a series of rock-themed rides. If it's hard to imagine what a nine-year-old's link to the Moody Blues' "Night in White Satin" might be, well, the attraction is for the parents, natch!

The clear standout among the rides is the Led Zeppelin rollercoaster, which like its namesake is grandiose, vaguely threatening, and larger-than-life. Many hardcore enthusiasts consider the Led Zep ride to be worth the price of admission alone, though that may be a stretch.

◖ BAREFOOT LANDING

Before the arrival of Broadway at the Beach was the Strand's original high-concept retail and dining complex, Barefoot Landing (4898 Hwy. 17 S., 843/272-8349, www.bflanding .com, hours vary). It's less flashy on the surface and certainly more tasteful, but trust me, it's just as commercial.

The centerpiece of the two-decade-old entertainment and shopping complex is **The Alabama Theatre** (4750 Hwy. 17 S., 843/272-5758, www.alabama-theatre.com, ticket prices vary), a project of the famed country/western band of the same name, who despite their eponymous roots actually got their start gigging in juke joints in the Grand Strand. A stone's throw away is the **House of Blues** (4640 Hwy. 17 S., 843/272-3000,

© JIM MOREKIS

MYRTLE BEACH

www.hob.com), bringing in name acts on an almost nightly basis (as well as diners to its excellent restaurant). And on some nights you can pose for a picture with a real live tiger cub on your lap at **T.I.G.E.R.S. Preservation Station** (843/361-4552, www.tigerfriends.com, hours vary). Shopping is mostly the name of the game here, though.

Alligator Adventure

One of the most popular attractions within Barefoot Landing is Alligator Adventure (www.alligatoradventure.com, $16.95 adults, $10.95 ages 4–12, 3 and under free). They have hundreds of alligators, yes, but also plenty of turtles, tortoises, snakes, and birds. The otters are a big hit as well. The highlight, though, comes during the daily alligator feedings, when you get a chance to see the real power and barely-controlled aggression of these magnificent indigenous beasts. Keep in mind that due to the cold-blooded reptiles' dormant winter nature, the feedings are not held in the colder months.

Alligator Adventure

CHILDREN'S MUSEUM OF SOUTH CAROLINA

A less expensive form of entertainment with an added educational component at Myrtle is the Children's Museum of South Carolina (2501 N. Kings Hwy., 843/946-9469, www.cmsckids .org, Mon.–Wed. and Fri.–Sat. 10 A.M.–4 P.M., Thurs. 10 A.M.–6 P.M., $7). This facility tries hard to compete with the splashier attractions in town, but still manages to keep a reasonably strong educational focus with programs like "Crime Lab Chemistry," "World of Art," and "Space Adventures."

FAMILY KINGDOM AMUSEMENT AND WATER PARK

For a taste of old-time beachfront amusement park fun, try the Family Kingdom (300 4th Ave. S., 843/626-3447l, www.family-kingdom .com, free admission, prices for rides vary) overlooking the Atlantic Ocean. It boasts several good, old-school rides, such as the Sling Shot, the Yo-Yo, and everyone's favorite, the wooden Swamp Fox rollercoaster with a crazy 110-foot free-fall in one section. The attached Water Park, though not a match to the one at Broadway at the Beach, is a lot of fun, with the requisite slides and a long, "lazy river" type floating ride.

As Family Kingdom's marketing is quick to point out, one of the big attractions here is the fact that you can look out over the beach itself. Personally, I think one of the best things is that there is no admission charge—you pay by the ride (though inclusive wristbands are available starting at about $22). This means parents and grandparents without the stomach for the rides don't have to pay through the nose just to chauffeur the little ones who do.

RIPLEY'S BELIEVE IT OR NOT!

Distinct in all but name from Ripley's Aquarium at Broadway at the Beach, this combo attraction down in the older area of Myrtle Beach features three separate, though more or less adjacent, offerings from the venerable Ripley's franchise.

© JIM MOREKIS

MYRTLE BEACH

The **Ripley's Believe it or Not! Odditorium** (901 N. Ocean Blvd., 843/448-2331, www .ripleys.com, Sun.–Thurs. 10 A.M.–10 P.M., Fri.–Sat. 10 A.M.–11 P.M., $13.99 adults, $7.99 ages 6–11, 5 and under free) is your typical Ripley's repository of strange artifacts from around the world, updated with video and computer graphics for the new generation. **Ripley's Haunted Adventure** (915 N. Ocean Blvd., 843/448-2331, www.ripleys .com, Sun.–Thurs. noon–10 P.M., Fri.–Sat. noon–11 P.M., $13.99 adults, $7.99 ages 6–11, 5 and under free) is a sort of scaled down version of Disney's famous Haunted House ride, with live actors scaring you through three floors. **Ripley's Moving Theater** (917 N. Ocean Blvd., 843/448-2331, www.ripleys.com, Sun.–Thurs. 10 A.M.–10 P.M., Fri.–Sat. 10 A.M.–11 P.M., $13.99 adults, $7.99 ages 6–11, 5 and under free) is a sort of combined ride and movie theater featuring two motion-oriented films screened in a self-contained human conveyor belt, sort of a kinetic IMAX effect.

WACCATEE ZOOLOGICAL FARM

The closest thing to a bona-fide zoo in Myrtle is Waccatee Zoological Farm (8500 Enterprise Rd., 843/650-8500, www.waccateezoo.com, daily 10 A.M.–5 P.M., $7 adults, $3.50 ages 1–12). A humble affair by comparison to the state's premier zoo in Columbia, Waccatee is a totally private venture on 500 acres of land about a 15-minute drive out of town. There are buffalo, zebras, kangaroos, and emu, many of which the kids will enjoy feeding for a few bucks per bag.

Animal activists be forewarned: Many of the animals are kept in enclosed spaces and there is a noticeable lack of professionally trained staff.

◖ OCEAN DRIVE BEACH

Less an actual place than a state of mind, the "OD" up in North Myrtle Beach is notable for its role in spawning one of America's great musical genres, beach music. Don't confuse beach music with the Beach Boys or Dick Dale—that's *surf* music. Beach music, simply put, is music to dance the shag to. Think The Drifters, The Platters, and The Swingin' Medallions.

To experience the OD, go to the intersection of Ocean Boulevard and Main Street and take in the vibe. There's still major shag action going on up here, specifically at several clubs specializing in the genre. If you don't want to shag, don't worry—this is still a charming, laidback area that's a lot of fun simply to stroll around and enjoy a hot dog or ice cream cone.

CHERRY GROVE PIER

One of the few grand old pavilions left on the Southeast Coast, North Myrtle's Cherry Grove Pier (3500 N. Ocean Blvd., 843/249-1625, www.cherrygrovepier.com, Sun.–Thurs. 6 A.M.–11 P.M., Fri.–Sat. 6 A.M.–midnight, $1.50) was built in the 1950s. Despite a remodeling in the late '90s, it still retains that nostalgic feel, with anglers casting into the waters and kids eating ice cream cones. There's a neat two-story observation deck, and on a clear day you can see North Carolina.

Unusually, this is a privately-owned pier (complete with its own website). It's particularly popular with anglers, who have their state licensing needs covered by the Pier. Get bait or rent a fishing rod ($20 a day with refundable $50 deposit) at the **Tackle and Gift Shop** (843/249-1625). They'll also sell you a crab net to cast off the pier for $6, with licenses and permits included.

LA BELLE AMIE VINEYARD

The only vineyard on the Strand, the peaceful and scenic La Belle Amie Vineyard (1120 St. Joseph Rd., 843/399-9463, www.labelle amie.com, Mon.–Sat. 10 A.M.–6 P.M.) in Little River is owned by two sisters, Vicki Weigle and June Bayman, who are descended from this old tobacco plantation's owners (though in French the vineyard's name means "beautiful friend," it's also a play on the family name, Bellamy). You can purchase wine for your own enjoyment or for gifts, or you can

MYRTLE BEACH

just visit the tasting room anytime Mon.–Sat. 10 A.M.–4:30 P.M., where a mere $5 per person gets you a sampling of any five wines. Coupons for discounted purchase are available at the tasting room.

TOURS

The number of tours offered in Myrtle Beach is nothing compared to Charleston, this being much more of a "doing" place than a "seeing"

place. The most fun and comprehensive tour in the area is **Coastal Safari Jeep Tours** (843/497-5330, www.carolinasafari.com, $38 adults, $20 children), which takes you on a guided tour in a super-sized jeep (holding 12–14 people). You'll go well off the commercial path to see such sights on the Waccamaw Neck as old plantations, Civil War sites, and slave cabins, as well as hear lots of ghost stories. They'll pick up at most area hotels.

Entertainment and Events

NIGHTLIFE

Any discussion of Myrtle Beach nightlife must begin with a nod to **The Bowery** (110 9th Ave. N., 843/626-3445, www.thebowery bar.com, 11 A.M.–2 A.M. daily), a country/ western and Southern rock spot right off the beach, which has survived several hurricanes since opening in 1944. Its roadhouse-style decor hasn't changed a whole lot since then, other than some cheesy marketing to play up

its role in history as the place where the country band Alabama got its start playing for tips in 1973, under the name Wildcountry. They were still playing gigs there when their first hit, "Tennessee River," hit the charts in 1980.

Bands usually crank up here around 9 P.M., with a nominal cover charge. There's only one type of draft beer served at The Bowery, at $2.50 a mug, and no real dance floor to speak

The Bowery, where country band Alabama got its start

© JIM MOREKIS

COURTESY OF THE MYRTLE BEACH AREA CONVENTION & VISITORS BUREAU

MYRTLE BEACH

Margaritaville at Broadway at the Beach is a must-stop location for Parrotheads everywhere.

of. If the proud display of Confederate flags doesn't bother you, it's usually a lot of fun.

Once overlooking the now razed, historic, Myrtle Beach Pavilion, as of this writing The Bowery is fronted by an empty lot, which will presumably be filled by a more modern attraction; if history is any guide, The Bowery will probably outlive it as well. Right next door is The Bowery's "sister bar," **Duffy's** (110 9th Ave. N.) owned by the same folks and with a similarly down-home vibe, except without the live music.

For a more upscale, if definitely less personal and unique experience, Broadway at the Beach hosts the high-profile (some say overrated) national clubs **Planet Hollywood** (2915 Hollywood Dr., 843/448-7827, www .planethollywood.com, seasonal hours) and the **Hard Rock Cafe** (1322 Celebrity Cir., 843/946-0007, www.hardrock.com, Mon.– Sun. 11 A.M.–midnight).

You don't have to be a Parrothead to enjoy **Jimmy Buffett's Margaritaville** (1114

Celebrity Cir., 843/448-5455, www.margarita ville.com, daily 11 A.M.–midnight) at Broadway at the Beach, actually a pretty enjoyable experience considering it's a national chain. The eponymous Margaritas are of course the beverage highlight, but they also serve Jimmy's signature LandShark Lager on tap for the beer-lovers.

Nearby is the techno and house music oriented **Club Kryptonite** (2925 Hollywood Dr., 843/839-9200, www.club-kryptonite.com), which is more of a full-on nightclub with DJs in both the main room and in the more intimate Cherry Martini Lounge. Their hours can be erratic during the off-season.

In addition to its attached live performance space, the **House of Blues** (4640 Hwy. 17, 843/272-3000, www.hob.com) at Barefoot Landing features a hoppin' bar in its dining area, situated amidst a plethora of folk art reminiscent of the Mississippi Delta. Most nights feature live entertainment on a small stage starting at about 10 P.M. or so.

UNDER THE BOARDWALK: THE STORY OF THE SHAG

In South Carolina, the shag is neither a type of rug nor what Austin Powers does in his spare time. It's a dance – a smooth, laidback, and happy dance done to that equally smooth, laidback, and happy kind of rhythm-and-blues called "beach music" (not to be confused with "surf music" such as The Beach Boys). The boys twirl the girls while the feet kick and slide around with a minimum of upper-body movement – the better to stay cool in the Carolina heat.

Descended from the Charleston, another indigenous Palmetto State dance, the shag originated on the Strand sometime in the 1930s, when the popular "Collegiate Shag" was slowed down to the subgenre now called the "Carolina Shag." While shag scholars differ as to the exact spawning ground, there's a consensus that North Myrtle Beach's Ocean Drive, or "OD" in local patois, became the home of the modern shag sometime in the mid-1940s.

Legend has it that the real shag was born when white teenagers, "jumping the Jim Crow rope" by watching dancers at black nightclubs in the segregated South, brought those moves back to the beach and added their own twists. Indeed, while the shag has always been primarily practiced by white people, many of the leading beach music bands were (and still are) African American.

By the mid-to-late 1950s the shag, often called simply "the Basic" or "the fas' dance," was all the rage with the Strand's young people, who gathered on beachfront pavilions and in local juke joints called "beach clubs," courting each other to the sounds of early beach music greats like The Drifters, The Clovers, and Maurice Williams and the Zodiacs. This is the time period most fondly remembered by today's shaggers, a time of penny loafers (no socks!), poodle skirts, and 45rpm records, when the sea breeze was the only air-conditioning.

The shag is practiced today by a graying but devoted cadre of older fans, with a vanguard of younger practitioners keeping the art form alive. A coterie of North Myrtle clubs specializes in the dance, while the area hosts several large-scale gatherings of shag aficionados each year.

To immerse yourself in shag culture, head on up to Ocean Drive Beach in North Myrtle at the intersection of Ocean Boulevard and Main, and look down at the platters in the sidewalk marking the **Shaggers Walk of Fame.** Walk a couple of blocks up to the corner of Main and Hillside Drive and visit the mecca of beach music stores, **Judy's House of Oldies** (300 Main St., 843/249-8649, www.judyshouseofoldies.com, Mon.-Sat. 9 A.M.-6 P.M.) They also sell instructional DVDs.

To get a taste of the dance itself, stop

SHAG DANCING

North Myrtle Beach is the nexus of that Carolina-based dance known as the shag. There are several clubs in town that have made a name for themselves as the unofficial "shag clubs" of South Carolina. The two main ones are **Duck's** (229 Main St., 843/249-3858, www.ducksatoceandrive.com) and **Fat Harold's** (210 Main St., 843/249-5779, www.fatharolds.com). There's also **The Pirate's Cove** (205 Main St., 843/249-8942).

Another fondly-regarded spot is the **OD Pavilion** (91 S. Ocean Blvd., 843/280-0715), a.k.a. the Sunset Grill or "Pam's Palace," on the same site as the old Roberts Pavilion that was destroyed in Hurricane Hazel. Legend has it this was where the shag was born. Also in North Myrtle, the **Ocean Drive Beach Club** (100 S. Ocean Blvd., 843/249-6460), a.k.a. "the OD Lounge," inside the Ocean Drive Beach and Golf Resort specializes in shag dancing after 4 P.M. most days. The resort is a focal point of local shag conventions, and is even home to the **Shaggers Hall of Fame.** Also inside the Ocean Drive Resort is another popular shag club, **The Spanish Galleon** (100 N. Ocean Blvd., 843/249-1047), a.k.a. "The Galleon."

There is one notable shag club in Myrtle

by the **OD Pavilion** (91 S. Ocean Blvd., 843/280-0715), **Duck's** (229 Main St., 843/249-3858, www.ducksatocean-drive.com) or **Fat Harolds** (210 Main St., 843-249-5779, www.fatharolds.com), or visit **The Spanish Galleon** (100 N. Ocean Blvd., 843/249-1047) inside the Ocean Drive Beach Resort. If you're interested, don't be shy. Shaggers are notoriously gregarious and eager to show off their stock in trade. It's easy to learn, it's family-friendly, and there will be no shortage of pleasant, young-at-heart shaggers around who will be happy to teach you the steps.

© JIM MOFEKIS

Judy's House of Oldies deals in rare shag music recordings.

MYRTLE BEACH

proper, **Studebakers** (2000 N. Kings Hwy., 843/626-3855, www.studebakersclub.com).

Key local shag events, which are quite well-attended, include the **National Shag Dance Championships,** the **Spring Safari,** and the **Fall Migration.**

THE ARTS
C Carolina Opry

Nothing can duplicate the experience of the Grand Old Opry in Nashville. But don't snicker at Myrtle's Carolina Opry (8901-A Business Hwy. 17, 800/843-6779, www.thecarolina opry.com, showtimes and ticket prices vary). Since 1986 this well-respected stage show, begun by legendary promoter Calvin Gilmore, has packed 'em in at the Grand Strand.

The main focus is the regular Opry show, done in the classic, free-wheeling variety format known to generations of old-school country fans from the original Opry itself. The Carolina Opry augments its regular music, comedy, and dance show with a seasonal Christmas special—which is highly popular and sells out even faster than the regular shows, often six or more months in advance—and generally one other bit of specialty programming, such as the recent "Good Vibrations" pop hits revue.

The 2200-seat Carolina Opry theater itself,

© JIM MOREKIS

Carolina Opry

while no match for Nashville's classic Ryman Theatre venue, is pretty classy for a venue only built in 1992. In all, the Carolina Opry is a professional, highly entertaining, and totally family-friendly experience, even for those not overly enamored of country music.

Legends in Concert

Way down in Surfside Beach, where the big buildup on the Strand begins, you'll find Legends in Concert (301 Business Hwy. 17, 843/238-7827, www.legendsinconcert.com, $35 adults, $15 children), a popular, rotating show of celebrity impersonators from Elvis to Barbra Streisand. As cheesy as that sounds, the resemblances can be quite uncanny and the shows quite entertaining.

House of Blues

Besides being a great place for dinner, on the other side of the restaurant is the stage for the House of Blues (4640 Hwy. 17 S., 843/272-3000, www.hob.com, prices vary) at Barefoot Landing in North Myrtle Beach.

They bring some pretty happening names in R&B, straight blues, and rock 'n' roll to this fun venue dedicated to preserving old-school music and live performance.

Medieval Times

Oh, come on—what's not to like about bountiful feasts, juggling jesters, skillful falconers, fetching maidens, and brave jousting knights? At Medieval Times (2904 Fantasy Way, 843/236-4635, www.medievaltimes .com, $46.95 adults, $28.95 ages 12 and under) you'll get all that and more. The kitsch quotient is high at this Renaissance Faire on steroids, a live-action story line featuring plenty of stage combat, music, and a steady stream of culinary items for your enjoyment (and yes, there's a full bar for those of drinking age). But there's an honest-to-goodness educational element as well. You'll be eating everything with your hands—no utensils in the 11th century—and most of the action and history is roughly authentic. The price may seem high at first glance, but keep in mind

COURTESY OF MYRTLE BEACH AREA CONVENTION & VISITORS BUREAU

MYRTLE BEACH

Dolly Parton's Dixie Stampede

you're getting a hearty, full dinner plus a two-hour stage show.

Dixie Stampede

Despite the attachment of the name of one of country music's best-known celebrities, Dolly Parton's Dixie Stampede (8901 Hwy. 17 N., 843/497-6615, www.dixiestampede .com, daily 6 P.M., $44–49) is really more of an old-fashioned Western road show than a country music performance—more Montana than Tennessee, and certainly more Buffalo Bill (or maybe P.T. Barnum?) than Dolly herself. After a certain amount of blatant hucksterism—a "pre-show" wherein various extra items are hawked—the crowds enter the main performance area and are treated to a decent dinner and a (much better) Western circus-type show, with horses and yippees galore. Cornball Americana at its finest, the Stampede is not for everyone, but fans of equestrian escapades and kitsch alike will probably find something to enjoy. (Warning: No alcoholic beverages are served.)

The Alabama Theatre

The Alabama Theatre (4750 Hwy. 17, 843/272-5758, www.alabama-theatre.com, tickets vary) at Barefoot Landing in North Myrtle Beach focuses on the long-running song-and-dance revue "One: The Show," as well as big-name acts who are past their prime but still able to fill seats, such as The Oakridge Boys, George Jones, Kenny Rogers, and of course the eponymous Troubadours, who got their big break while playing at Myrtle Beach. It's not all country, though—Motown and beach music acts like The Temptations and The Platters are often featured as well. As with the Carolina Opry, Barefoot has its own Christmas special, and as with the Opry's offering, this one sells out well in advance as well.

Palace Theatre

The Palace Theatre (1420 Celebrity Cir., 800/905-4228, www.palacetheatremyrtle beach.com, ticket prices vary) at Broadway at the Beach offers a variety of toned-down Vegas-style entertainment. The most recent

© JIM MOREKIS

IMAX theater at Broadway at the Beach

show was *Le Grande Cirque,* a family-friendly version of the kind of show made famous by *Cirque du Soleil.*

CINEMA

If you love IMAX, the **IMAX 3D Theatre** (1195 Celebrity Cir., 843/444-3333, www.imax 3dmyrtlebeach.com, daily 11 A.M.–10 P.M., $13 adults, $11 ages 4–12, 3 and under free) at Broadway at the Beach delivers the goods. It hosts a rotation of several generally-ocean-themed movies starting every hour on the hour. Save a couple of bucks by purchasing tickets online. Also at Broadway on the Beach, there's a regular multiplex, Carmike's **Broadway Cinema 16** (843/445-1600, www .carmike.com).

Other movie theaters include the **Cinemark** (2100 Coastal Grand Cir., 843/839-3221, www.cinemark.com) at the Coastal Grand Mall and the massive new **Grand 14 at The Market Common** (4002 Deville St., 843/282-0550) at the multi-use development of the same name, actually a repurposed Air Force base.

FESTIVALS AND EVENTS

Interestingly, most events here don't happen during the three-month tourist high season of June, July, and August—mostly because it's so darn hot and all anyone wants to do is get in the water.

Winter

The Grand Strand is the birthplace of the dance called the shag, and for the last quarter-century the **National Shag Dance Championships** (2000 North Kings Hwy., 843/497-7369, www.shagnationals.com, $70 weekend pass for finals) each winter have been the pinnacle of the art form. Beginning with preliminaries in January contestants in five age ranges compete for a variety of awards, culminating in the finals the first week in March. The level of professionalism might amaze you—for such a lazy-looking dance, these are serious competitors.

Spring

You might not automatically associate our colder neighbor to the north with Myrtle

Beach, but **Canadian American Days** (various venues, www.myrtlebeachinfo.com, free), or "Can Am," brings tens of thousands of visitors of both nationalities to sites all over the Strand to enjoy a variety of musical and cultural events. Always on top of marketing opportunities, the Myrtle Beach Chamber of Commerce makes sure this happens during Ontario's spring holidays to ensure maximum north-of-the-border attendance. While most of the events have little or nothing to do with Canada itself, this is basically a great excuse for Canucks to get some Carolina sunshine.

The **Spring Games and Kite Flying Contest** (843/448-7881, free) brings an exciting array of airborne craft to the Strand in front of Broadway on the Beach on an April weekend as the springtime winds peak.

Also in April comes the area's second-largest shag event, the **Society of Stranders Spring**

Safari (www.shagdance.com). Several clubs in North Myrtle Beach participate in hosting shag dancers from all over for a week of, well, shagging.

The biggest single event in Myrtle Beach happens in May with the **Spring Bike Rally** (various venues, www.myrtlebeachbikeweek.com, free), always known simply as "Bike Week." In this nearly 70-year-old event, over a quarter million Harley-Davidson riders and their entourages gather to cruise around the place, admire each other's custom rides, and generally party their patooties off. While the typical Harley dude these days is getting on in years and probably a mild-mannered store manager in regular life, young or old they all do their best to let their hair down at this festive event. Dozens of sub-events go on throughout the week at venues all over the Strand, from tough-man contests to "foxy boxing" matches to wet T-shirt contests.

MYRTLE BEACH

BIKE WEEK: RIP?

Growling engines...spinning tires...patriotic colors...polished chrome...erotic bull-riding contests? That is the spectacle known as Myrtle Beach Bike Week, one of the largest gatherings of Harley-Davidson enthusiasts on the East Coast, and one of the oldest at about 65 years.

The event generally happens each May on the weekend before Memorial Day weekend, bringing over a quarter million motorcyclists and their entourages to town for ten days of riding, bragging, and carousing. South Carolina's absence of a helmet law is a particular draw to these freedom-cherishing motorcyclists.

A few days later, on Memorial Day weekend proper, there's another bike rally, this one simply called Black Bike Week. Nearly as large as the regular Bike Week, the focus is on African American riders and their machines.

While contrary to stereotype, there's not much of an increase in crime during either Bike Week. Regardless, they are widely known as a particularly bad time to bring young children to the area. And therein lies the controversy.

As of this writing the complexion of both Bike Weeks has changed, perhaps irrevocably.

Joining other municipalities around the nation in discouraging motorcycle rallies, the city of Myrtle Beach recently enacted tough – some say draconian and possibly unconstitutional – measures to force the bike rallies to leave town and make the area more family-friendly during that time. Most controversial among the measures is a municipal helmet law, enforceable only within Myrtle Beach city limits. Other measures include stringent noise ordinances designed to include the roaring, rattling tailpipes of pretty much every Harley ever made.

The separate municipality of North Myrtle Beach, however, has made it clear that bikers are welcome there even if they're persona non grata a few miles to the south. As of now it remains to be seen if that will be enough to keep the rallies on the Strand, or if they will simply gun their collective throttle and head elsewhere.

The upshot for the non-motorcyclist visitor? With the decidedly adult proclivities of the bikers being much less of a factor, the time around Memorial Day is likely to be much more family-friendly than in the past – though probably still nearly as crowded as ever.

You get the picture. It's not for the politically correct—or for young children.

Summer

Right after the Spring Bike Rally, on Memorial Day weekend, comes the **Atlantic Beach Bikefest** (various venues, www.blackbeach week.com, free), much more commonly referred to as "Black Bike Week." This event started in the 1980s and is spiritually based in Atlantic Beach, formerly the area's "black beach" during the days of segregation. It sees over 200,000 African American motorcycle enthusiasts gather in Myrtle Beach for a similar menu of partying, bikini contests, cruising, and the like. While the existence of separate events often reminds some people of the state's unfortunate history of segregation, supporters of both Bike Week and Black Bike Week insist it's not a big deal, and that bikers of either race are welcome at either event.

Kicking off with a festive parade, the half-century-old **Sun Fun Festival** (various venues, www.sunfunfestival.com), generally held the weekend after Memorial Day weekend, signals the real beginning of the tourist season here with bikini contests, Jet Ski races, parades, air shows, and concerts galore.

The **City of Myrtle Beach Independence Day Celebration** (www.cityofmyrtlebeach .com, free) each July 4th weekend is when the largest total number of visitors is in Myrtle Beach. It's fun, it's hot, it's fireworks-a-plenty, and boy is it crowded.

Fall

For a week in mid-September, North Myrtle Beach hosts one of the world's largest shag dancing celebrations, the **Society of Stranders Fall Migration** (www.shag dance.com, free). Head up to the intersection of Ocean Drive and Main Street to hear the sounds of this unique genre, and party with the shaggers at various local clubs. If you don't know the steps, don't worry—instructors are usually on hand.

There's another, much smaller Harley riders' rally the first week in October, the **Fall Motorcycle Rally** (various venues, www .myrtlebeachbikeweek.com, free).

Thanksgiving Day weekend, when the beaches are much less crowded and the hotels much cheaper, is the **South Carolina Bluegrass Festival** (2101 N. Oak St., 706/864-7203, www.aandabluegrass.com, $30 adults, $20 ages 6–13, under 6 free), a delightful and well-attended event at the Myrtle Beach Convention Center celebrating the Appalachian music tradition in a coastal setting, with some of the biggest names in the genre.

Shopping

Shopping on the Grand Strand is strongly destination-oriented. You tend to find shops of similar price points and merchandise types clustered together in convenient locations, i.e., upscale shops are in one place and discount and outlet stores in another. Here's a rundown of the main retail areas on the Strand with some of the standout shops.

BROADWAY AT THE BEACH

The sprawling Broadway at the Beach complex (U.S. 17 Bypass and 21st Ave. N., www.broad wayatthebeach.com, hours vary) has scads of stores, some of which are quite interesting and rise well beyond tourist schlock. There are maps and directories of the site available at various kiosks around the area.

One of my favorites is **Retroactive** (843/916-1218, www.shopretroactive.com), a shop specializing in '70s and '80s styles and kitsch, with some of the best (and wittiest) pop culture T-shirts I've seen. The owners are frank about their continuing obsession with '80s hair bands. Another specialty shop is **Witness Wear** (843/448-0902), which deals in Christian pop culture items and clothing lines.

© JIM MOREKIS

a typical storefront at Broadway at the Beach

The kids—and those with a sweet tooth—will go crazy in the aptly-named **It'SUGAR** (843/916-1300, www.itsugar.com), a store dedicated to just about any kind of candy and candy themed merchandise you can think of, from modern brands to retro favorites. If the packaged or bulk varieties don't float your boat, you can design your own massive chocolate bar.

The **Foxworthy Store** (843/839-1652, www.thefoxworthystore.com) is actually less of an homage to the Southern comedian Jeff Foxworthy than a clearinghouse for just about any kind of down-home–chic merchandise and clothing. Look for the huge stuffed bear out front.

Dedicated Parrotheads will find yet more tropical merchandise, though with a Jimmy Buffett theme, at **The Smuggler's Hold** (843/448-5455) inside Broadway at the Beach's Margaritaville location.

And of course, this being Myrtle Beach, there's a **Harley Davidson** (843/293-5555) gift store with Hog-oriented merch galore.

The bottom line on Broadway at the Beach, though, is that it's made for walking around and browsing. Just bring your walking shoes—the place is huge—and keep in mind that there's not a lot of shade.

BAREFOOT LANDING

There are over 100 shops at Barefoot Landing (4898 Hwy. 17 S., 843/272-8349, www.bflanding.com, hours vary) in North Myrtle Beach—as well as one cool, old-fashioned carousel—but perhaps the most unique spot is **T.I.G.E.R.S. Preservation Station** (843/361-4552, www.tigerfriends.com, hours vary), where you get the opportunity to have your picture taken with a live tiger or lion cub. This is the fundraising arm of a local conservation organization for the big cats (and for gorillas and monkeys as well), so the service isn't cheap. Portraits begin at about $60 to pose with a single critter, and go up from there depending on the number of animals you want to pose with. However, you don't pay per person, so the whole family can get in the shot for the same price as a child. It may sound like a lot of money, but this is truly a once-in-a-lifetime

MYRTLE BEACH

© JIM MOREKIS

Meet a tiger cub at Barefoot Landing.

experience. An attendant takes the animal of your choice out of a spacious holding area, places it on your lap, and a photographer takes the shot. Sometimes you can hold a milk bottle to the cub's mouth. If you don't want to spring for a photo, you can just watch the frolicking (or more often, slumbering) cubs up close from behind a transparent wall. They're unbelievably cute, as you can imagine.

Just relocated to the Strand from their grape yards in Chester, South Carolina, is **Carolina Vineyards Winery** (843/361-9181, www .carolinavineyards.com). Buy wine as a gift, or taste any seven of their labels for only $2.

Animal lovers—and especially their pets—will enjoy **Bone Appetit Pet Bakery** (843/361-4477, http://mbboneappetit.com), who bake these often ridiculously elaborate pet treats from scratch on the premises, with all-natural ingredients. You'll want to chow down on these treats yourself, but down, boy—they're just for Fido or Fluffy.

There are magic shops, and then there are *magic shops*. **Conley's House of Magic**

(843/272-4227, http://conleyshouseofmagic. com) is definitely the latter. Packed in this relatively small space is just about every legendary trick (and trick deck) known to the magician's art, along with a cool variety of magic books teaching you, in a deadly serious fashion, the innermost secrets of the trade. **Toys & Co.** (843/663-0748, www.toysandco.com) carries a wide range of toys and games, with an emphasis on way-cool European-style brands you won't see at the local Wal-Mart.

My favorite place at Barefoot Landing is **Dr. Root Beer's Hall of Foam** (843/663-5628, www.drrootbeer.com), the labor of love of Jerome Gundrum and his wife Linda. Together they craft an amazingly tangy and refreshing home-brewed root beer on the premises. They have sandwiches and treats as well, but the attraction here is that unbelievably delicious sassafras concoction, especially delightful on a blazing hot South Carolina day. Particularly fun is the Gundrums' collection of vintage root beer advertising signs, a fun look at a slice of old Americana sadly gone by.

THE MARKET COMMON

One of the most hotly anticipated and cutting-edge things to hit Myrtle Beach in years, The Market Common (4017 Deville St., www.market commonmb.com, hours vary) is an ambitious residential/retail mixed-use development recently opened for business on the site of the decommissioned Myrtle Beach Air Force Base. While its location near to the Myrtle Beach International Airport means it's not exactly amid the sun-and-fun action (possibly a good thing depending on the season), the green-friendly development style and tasteful shops might prove a refreshing change of pace.

There are three dozen (and counting) stores here, including Anthropologie, Williams-Sonoma, Copper Penny, Chico's, Brooks Brothers, Banana Republic, Barnes and Noble, and Jake and Company ("Life is Good").

MALLS

The premier mall in the area is **Coastal Grand Mall** (2000 Coastal Grand Cir., 843/839-9100, www.coastalgrand.com, Mon.–Sat. 10 A.M.–9 P.M., Sun. noon–6 P.M.) at the U.S.

17 Bypass and Highway 501. It's anchored by Belk, J.C. Penney, Sears, Dillard's, and Dick's Sporting Goods.

Your basic meat-and-potatoes mall, **Myrtle Beach Mall** (10177 N. Kings Hwy., 843/272-4040, shopmyrtlebeachmall.com, Mon.–Sat. 10 A.M.–9 P.M., Sun. noon–6 P.M.) is anchored by Belk, J.C. Penney, and Bass Pro Shops.

DISCOUNT BEACHWEAR

Literally dozens of big, tacky, deep-discount T-shirt-and-towel type places are spread out up and down Kings Highway like mushrooms after a rain. The vast majority belong to one of these three well-established chains: **Eagles Beachwear** (www.eaglesbeachwear.net), **Wing's Beachwear** (www.wingsbeachwear .com), and **Bargain Beachwear.** These are the kinds of places to get assorted cheap bric-a-brac and items for your beach visit, nothing more.

OUTLET MALLS

There are two massive **Tanger Outlets** (www .tangeroutlet.com/myrtlebeach) at Myrtle

© JIM MOREKIS

Dr. Root Beer's Hall of Foam is a refreshing stop at Barefoot Landing.

Beach, Tanger Outlet North (10835 Kings Rd., 843/449-0491) off Kings Road/U.S. 17, and Tanger Outlet South (4635 Factory Stores Blvd., 843/236-5100) off Highway 501. Both offer over 100 factory outlet stores of almost every imaginable segment, from Fossil to Disney, from OshKosh to Timberland. Full food courts are available, and many folks spend an entire day here with no problem.

For years, busloads of hardcore shoppers from throughout the South have taken organized trips to the Grand Strand specifically to shop at **Waccamaw Factory Shoppes.** Their passion hasn't abated, as new generations of shopaholics get the fever to come here and browse the often deeply-discounted offerings at row after row of outlet stores. There are actually two locations, the Factory Shoppes themselves (3071 Waccamaw Blvd., 843/236-8200) and the nearby Waccamaw Pottery (3200 Pottery Dr., 843/236-6152). Bring your walking shoes (or buy some new ones at one of the many shoe stores), but don't worry about getting from one mall to the other—there's a free shuttle.

Sports and Recreation

Myrtle Beach's middle name may as well be recreation. While some of the local variety tends towards overkill—I personally loathe Jet Skis, for example—there's no denying that if it involves outside activity, it's probably offered here. For general info, go to www.myrtle beach.info. For municipal recreation info, go to www.cityofmyrtlebeach.com.

ON THE WATER
Beaches
The center of activity here is on the Strand itself: miles of user-friendly beaches. They're not the most beautiful in the world, but they're nice enough, and access is certainly no problem. In Myrtle Beach and North Myrtle Beach, you'll find clearly designated public access points off Ocean Boulevard, some with parking and some without. Both municipalities run well-marked public parking lots at various points, some of which are free during the off-season.

Dog owners will be pleased to know that from May 15–September 15, dogs are allowed on the beach before 9 A.M. and after 5 P.M. From September 15–May 15, dogs are allowed on the beach at any time of day.

Confine your swimming to 150 feet or closer to shore. Surfside Beach to the south is a "no-smoking" beach with access points at 16th Avenue North, Sixth Avenue North, Third Avenue North, Surfside Pier, Third Avenue South, Fourth Avenue South, 13th Avenue South, and Melody Lane.

Surfing
There's a steady, if low-key, surf scene in Myrtle Beach despite the fact that the surfing is not really that good and the sport is restricted to certain areas of the beach during the busy season of the summer. The rules are a little complicated. In Myrtle Beach proper, surfing is allowed *only* from 10 A.M.–5 P.M. in the following zones from April 15–September 15:

• 29th Avenue South to the southern city limits

• 37th Avenue North to 47th Avenue North

• 62nd Avenue North to 68th Avenue North

• 82nd Avenue North to northern city limits

Up in North Myrtle Beach, surfers must stay in the following zones between 9 A.M.–4 P.M. from May 15–September 15:

• Cherry Grove Pier

• 6th Avenue North

• 13th Avenue South

• 28th Avenue South

• 38th Avenue South

Down at Surfside Beach, surfing is restricted

to the following zones, 10 A.M.–5 P.M. year-round:

• 12th Avenue North to 14th Avenue North

• Melody Lane to 13th Avenue South

The oldest surf shop in the area, south of Myrtle in Garden City Beach, is the **Village Surf Shoppe** (500 Atlantic Ave., 843/651-6396, www.villagesurf.com), which since 1969 has catered to the Strand's growing surf scene. Nearly as old is the **Surf City Surf Shop** (www.surf citysurfshop.com) franchise in Myrtle proper, with a location in North Myrtle at 1758 Hwy. 17 South (843/272-1090) and a location at 3001 N. Kings Hwy. (843/626-5412).

Diving

Diving is popular on the Strand. As with fishing, many trips depart from Little River just above North Myrtle Beach. Offshore features include many historic wrecks, including the post-Civil War wreck of the USS *Sherman* offshore of Little River, and artificial reefs such as the famed "Barracuda Alley," teeming with marine life, off Myrtle Beach.

Coastal Scuba (1901 Hwy. 17 S., 843/361-3323, www.coastalscuba.com) in North Myrtle is a large operator, offering several different dive tours.

Parasailing, Windsurfing, and Jet Skis

Ocean Watersports (405 S. Ocean Blvd., 843/445-7777, www.parasailmyrtlebeach .com) takes groups up to six on well-supervised, well-equipped parasailing adventures ($50 per person), with tandem and triple flights available. Observers can go out on the boat for $20. They rent Jet Skis as well and offer "banana boat" rides ($15) in which a long—yes, banana-shaped—raft, on which several people straddle, is towed by a boat up and down the beach.

Downwind Watersports (2915 S. Ocean Blvd., 843/448-7245, www.downwindsails myrtlebeach.com) offers a similar menu of offerings, with the addition of good old-fashioned sailboat lessons and rentals ($16). Parasailing is about $65 per person single ride, banana boats

$16 for 20 minutes, and Jet Ski rentals about $100 an hour.

Farther up the Strand in North Myrtle, between Cherry Grove Beach and Little River, you'll find **Thomas Outdoors Watersports** (2200 Little River Neck Rd., 843/280-2448, www.mbjetski.com), which rents kayaks in addition to Jet Skis and pontoon boats. They offer several Jet Ski tours—including a dolphin-watch trip—from $75–125, and an all-day kayak rental is $45 per person.

Fishing

Most fishing on the Strand is saltwater, with charters, most based in Little River, taking anglers well into Atlantic waters. Tuna, wahoo, mackerel, and dolphin (not the mammal!) are big in the hot months, while snapper and grouper are caught year-round but best in the colder months.

A good operator up in Little River is **Longway Fishing Charters** (843/249-7813, www.longwaycharters.com), who specializes in offshore fishing. Another out of the same area is **Capt. Smiley's Inshore Fishing** (843/361-7445, www.captainsmileyfishing charters.com). **Fish Hook Charters** (2200 Little River Neck Rd., 843/283-7692, www .fishhookcharters.com) takes a 34-foot boat out from North Myrtle Beach.

For surf fishing on the beach, you do not need a license of any type. All other types of fishing require a valid South Carolina fishing license, available for a nominal fee online at dnr.sc.gov or at any tackle shop and most grocery stores.

Cruises

Outside of the winter months, there are plenty of places to cruise in the Strand, from Little River down to Murrells Inlet, from the Waccamaw River to the Intracoastal Waterway. The **Great American Riverboat Company** (8496 Enterprise Rd., 843/650-6600, www .mbriverboat.com) offers sightseeing and dinner cruises along the Intracoastal Waterway. **Island Song Charters** (4374 Landing Rd., 843/467-7088, www.islandsongcharters.com)

out of Little River takes you on sailboat sunset and dolphin cruises on the 32-foot *Island Song.*

Up in North Myrtle, **Getaway Adventures** (843/663-1100, www.myrtlebeachboatcruises.com) specializes in dolphin tours. Also in North Myrtle, **Thomas Outdoors Watersports** (2200 Little River Neck Rd., 843/280-2448, www.mbjetski.com) runs dolphin cruises.

ON LAND
Golf
The Grand Strand in general, and Myrtle Beach in particular, is world golf central. There are over 120 courses in this comparatively small area, and if golfers can't find something they like here then they need to sell their clubs. While the number of truly great courses is slim—the best courses are further down the Strand near Pawleys Island—the quality overall is still quite high.

A great bonus is affordability. Partially because of dramatically increased competition due to the glut of courses, and partially because of savvy regional marketing, green fees here are significantly lower than you might expect, in most cases under $100. For even more savings, finding a golf/lodging package deal in Myrtle Beach is like finding sand on the beach—almost too easy. Check with your hotel to see if they offer any golf packages.

While the golf high season here is early fall, don't discount the idea of winter golf. The courses are less crowded and the deals are rife. At any time of year, some good one-stop shops on the Internet are at www.mbn.com and www.myrtlebeachgolf.com.

Some highlights of area golf include The Davis Love III-designed course at **Barefoot Resort** (4980 Barefoot Resort Ridge Rd., 843/390-3200, www.barefootgolf.com, $125 green fees) in North Myrtle, maybe the best in the Strand outside of Pawleys Island. Or would that be the Greg Norman course, or the Tom Fazio course, or the Pete Dye course (soon to go private), all also at Barefoot? You get the picture.

Also up near North Myrtle is a favorite with visitors and locals alike, **Glen Dornoch Golf Club** (4840 Glen Dornoch Way, 800/717-8784, www.glensgolfgroup.com, $100 green fees), on 260 beautiful (and challenging) acres. Affiliated with Glen Dornoch are the 27 holes at Little River's **Heather Glen** (4650 Heather Glen Way, 800/868-4536, www.glensgolfgroup.com, $85 green fees), which are divided into Red, White, and Blue courses. They combine for what's consistently rated one of the best public courses in the U.S.

While it sounds gimmicky to some, you might want to try **World Tour Golf Links** (2000 World Tour Blvd., 843/236-2000, www.worldtourmb.com, $135 green fees), whose 27 holes are specifically designed to mimic legendary holes from St. Andrews to Augusta National. And no list of area golf is complete without a nod to **Myrtle Beach National** (4900 National Dr., 843/347-4298, www.mbn.com, $60 green fees). With three distinct courses—King's North, West, and South Creek with its South Carolina-shaped sand trap at hole 3—the National is one of the state's legendary courses, not to mention a heck of a deal.

Miniature Golf
Don't scoff—miniature golf, or "putt-putt" to an older generation, is a big deal in Myrtle Beach. If you thought there were a lot of regular golf courses here, the 50 miniature golf courses will also blow your mind. Sadly, almost all of the classic, old-school miniature golf courses are no more, victims of the demand for increased production values and modernized gimmick holes. But here are some of the standouts, including the best of the North Myrtle courses as well (prices listed are for 18 holes).

The most garishly wonderful course is the completely over-the-top **Mount Atlanticus Minotaur Goff** (707 N. Kings Hwy., 843/444-1008, Mon.–Thurs. 10 A.M.–9 P.M., Fri.–Sun. 10 A.M.–10 P.M., $8) down near the older section of Myrtle. And yes, that's how it's spelled—get it? Legend has it that this one course cost $3 million to build. Literally the

© JIM MOREKIS

Mount Atlanticus Minotaur Goff

MYRTLE BEACH

stuff of dreams—or maybe hallucinations—this sprawling course mixes the mythological with the nautical to wonderful effect. You don't actually encounter the Minotaur until the bonus 19th hole, a fiendish water trap. If you get a hole in one you get free golf there for life.

Hawaiian Rumble (3210 Hwy. 17, 843/458-2585, www.prominigolf.com, daily 9 A.M.–midnight, $8, $5.37 ages 3–4) in North Myrtle is not only a heck of a fun, attractive course, it's also the headquarters of the official training center for the U.S. Professional Miniature Golf Association (the folks who generally get a hole in one on every hole). The Rumble's sister course is **Hawaiian Village** (4205 Hwy. 17, 843/361-9629, www.promini golf.com, seasonal hours Apr.–Oct., $8–10) in North Myrtle, which is also the home of serious professional miniature golf competitions.

For a bit of retro action, try **Rainbow Falls** (9550 Kings Hwy., 843/497-2557, daily 9 A.M.–11 P.M. Mar.–Dec., $8 for 18 holes, 4 and under free, $12 all day pass). It's not as garish as some of the newer courses, but fans of old-school putt-putt will love it.

While at Broadway at the Beach you might want to try the popular, medieval-themed **Dragon's Lair** (1197 Celebrity Cir., 843/913-9301, seasonal hours, $7.50 adults, $7 children). Yep, it has a 30-foot fire-breathing dragon, Sir Alfred, that you have to make your way around. While the dinosaur craze has cooled somewhat, the golf at **Jurassic Golf** (445 29th Ave., 843/448-2116, daily 10 A.M.–11 P.M., $8 adults, $7.50 ages 3–6, $12 all day pass), festooned with dozens of velociraptors and the like, certainly has stayed hot. A similarly-themed site is in North Myrtle, the new **Dinosaur Adventure** (700 7th Ave., 843/272-8041).

Tennis

There are over 200 tennis courts in the Myrtle Beach area. The main municipal site is the **Myrtle Beach Tennis Center** (3302 Robert Grissom Pkwy., 843/918-2440, www.myrtlebeachtennis.com, $2 per hour per person), which has ten courts, eight of them lighted. The city also runs six lighted courts at Midway Park at U.S. 17 and 19th Avenue South. The privately-owned **Kingston Plantation** (843/497-2444, www.kingstonplantation.com) specializes in tennis vacations, and you don't even have to be a guest. They have a pro on staff and offer lessons. Down in Pawleys Island, the **Litchfield Beach and Golf Resort** (14276 Ocean Hwy., 866/538-0187, www.litchfield beach.com) has two dozen nice courts.

Biking

In Myrtle Beach when they say "biker" they mean a Harley dude. Bicycling here—or safe bicycling, anyway—is largely limited to fat-tire riding along the beach and easy pedaling through the quiet residential neighborhoods near Little River. There is a bike lane on North Ocean Boulevard from about 29th Avenue North to about 82nd Avenue North. Riding on the sidewalk is strictly prohibited.

As for bike rentals, a good operator is **Beach Bike Shop** (711 Broadway St., 843/448-5335, www.beachbikeshop.com), or try **Bicycles 'N' Gear Rentals** (Highway 501, www.bikesngear .com). In North Myrtle, try **Wheel Fun Rentals** (91 S. Ocean Blvd., 843/280-7900, www.wheelfunrentals.com).

Horseback Riding

A horse ride along the surf is a nearly iconic image of South Carolina, combining two of the state's chief pursuits: equestrian sports and hanging out on the beach. A great way to enjoy a horseback ride along the Grand Strand without having to bring your own equine is to check out **Horseback Riding of Myrtle Beach** (843/294-1712, www.myrtlebeachhorserides .com). They offer a variety of group rides, each

with a guide, going to nature preserve and/or beach locales. While they'll take you out any day of the week, advance reservations are required. Ninety minutes on a nature preserve cost $50 a person, while a 90-minute ride on the beach is $75.

You can go horseback riding on Myrtle Beach from the third Saturday in November until the end of February, with these conditions: You must access the beach from Myrtle Beach State Park, you cannot ride over sand dunes in any way, and you must clean up after your horse.

SPECTATOR SPORTS

Playing April through early September in a large, new stadium near Broadway at the Beach are the **Myrtle Beach Pelicans** (1251 21st Ave. N., 843/918-6000, www.myrtlebeachpelicans .com, $7–11), a single-A affiliate of the Atlanta Braves playing in the Carolina League.

NASCAR fans already know of the **Myrtle Beach Speedway** (455 Hospitality Lane, www.myrtlebeachspeedway.com, $12, under 10 free) off Highway 501, one of the more vintage tracks in the country dating back to 1958 (it was actually a dirt track well into the 1970s). Currently the main draw here are the NASCAR Whelen All-America series races, happening each Saturday night from April–November at 7:30 P.M.

Other spectator sports in the area tend to revolve around the Chanticleers of **Coastal Carolina University** (132 Chanticleer Dr. W., 843/347-8499, www.goccusports.edu) just inland from Myrtle Beach in Conway. They play football in the Big South Conference. By the way, a chanticleer is an old name for a rooster, and in this case, is a self-conscious derivative of the mascot of the University of South Carolina, the gamecock.

Accommodations

There is no dearth of lodging in the Myrtle Beach area, from the typical high-rise "resorts" (think condos on steroids) to chain hotels to vacation villas to house rentals to camping. Because of the plethora of options, prices are generally quite reasonable, and competition to provide more and more on-site amenities—free breakfasts, "lazy river" pools, washer/dryers, hot tubs, poolside grills, etc.—has only increased. You are the beneficiary, so you might as well take advantage of it.

Please note that the stated price range here may be very broad because so many Myrtle Beach lodgings offer several sizes of rooms, from one bed to full three-bedroom suites. Here are a few general tips to consider when booking a room:

- The larger suites are generally "condo apartments," meaning they're privately owned. While they're usually immaculately clean for your arrival, this also means that housekeeping is minimal and you won't get lots of complimentary goodies whenever you call the front desk.

- The entire Myrtle Beach area is undergoing growth, and that includes the accommodations. This means that many properties have older sections and newer ones. Ask beforehand about which section you're being booked in.

- Check www.myrtlebeachhotels.com for last-minute deals and specials at 11 well-run local resorts.

- By the end of September prices drop dramatically.

- Though almost all area lodgings, especially the high-rises, feature on-site pools galore, lounge chairs and tables are at a premium and go very quickly in the day.

- And always, *always* keep in mind that summer is the high season here—unlike the rest of South Carolina—and rooms, especially at beachfront places, get snapped up very early.

UNDER $150

For 75 years **((** **Driftwood on the Oceanfront** (1600 N. Ocean Blvd., 843/448-1544, www.driftwoodlodge.com, $100–120) has been a favorite place to stay here. Today, it continues to be an almost extinct creature: Tasteful beachfront lodging at Myrtle Beach. Upgraded since, but not *too* upgraded, this low, five-story, 90-room complex is family-owned and takes pride in delivering personalized service that is simply impossible to attain in the larger high-rises nearby. As you'd expect, the rooms and suites are a bit on the small side by modern Myrtle Beach standards—with none of the increasingly popular three-bedroom suites available—but most everyone is impressed by the value.

Probably the best-regarded bed and breakfast in Myrtle Beach (yes, there are a precious few) is the **((** **Serendipity Inn** (407 71st Ave. N., 843/449-5268, www.serendipityinn.com, $90–150). A short walk from the beach but sometimes seeming light years away from the typical Myrtle sprawl, this 15-room gem features a simple but elegant pool, an attractive courtyard, and sumptuous rooms. The full breakfast is simple but hearty. There's free Wi-Fi all over the property.

If you're looking for a basic, inexpensive, one-bed hotel experience on the beach, ask for a room at the new oceanfront section of the **Best Western Grand Strand Inn and Suites** (1804 S. Ocean Blvd., 843/448-1461, $80–140), a smallish but clean and attentively-run chain hotel. The property's other buildings are significantly older and located across busy Ocean Boulevard, and the walk across the street to the beach can be difficult, especially if you have small kids. That said, this is a great value and a quality property.

$150-300

Consistently one of the best-regarded properties in Myrtle proper, the **Hampton Inn & Suites Oceanfront** (1803 S. Ocean Blvd., 843/946-6400, www.hamptoninnocean

front.com, $169–259) has been made even better by a recent and thorough upgrade. This is a classic beachfront high-rise (not to be confused with the Hampton Inn at Broadway at the Beach), clean inside and out, with elegant, tasteful rooms in various sizes (yes, flat screens were part of the makeover). Rooms range from typical one bed, one bath hotel-style rooms to larger condo-style suites with a fridge.

Situated more toward North Myrtle and hence closer to those attractions, the **Sea Watch Resort** (161 Sea Watch Blvd., $171–395) is a good choice for those who want the full-on condo high-rise Myrtle Beach experience but not necessarily the crowds that usually go with it. The rooms are clean and well-equipped, and by edging north a little on the beach you can actually spread out and enjoy some breathing room.

An oldie but a goodie, the beachfront **Carolina Winds** (200 76th Ave. N., 843/497-5648, www.carolinawinds.com, $150–300) remains one of the best overall condo-style vacation spots in Myrtle. Unlike many of the newer, monolithic high-rises, Carolina Winds almost has a retro Miami Beach feel to it, both in architecture and attitude, and is one of the few beachfront properties here that you can almost see on a postcard. A two-night minimum stay is required during the high season.

One of the better-quality stays for the price in Myrtle is the **Roxanne Towers** (1604 N. Ocean Blvd., 843/839-1016, www.theroxanne .com, $150–250). Known for attentive service, this is a busy property in a busy area. Parking is historically somewhat of a problem. Keep in mind that room size is capped at two bedrooms, so there are none of the sprawling three-bedroom suites that many other local places have.

If water park-style entertainment is your thing try **Dunes Village Resort** (5200 N. Ocean Blvd., 877/828-2237, www.dunes village.com, $140–300), which is also one of the better values in Myrtle for the quality of the stay. Its huge indoor water park has copious water slides, including several for adults, and various other aquatic diversions. The buildings themselves—the property comprises two high-rise towers—are new and well-equipped, though since this is a timeshare-style property housekeeping is minimal.

For a quality stay in the heart of Myrtle's beach bustle, go for the **Sandy Beach Resort** (201 S. Ocean Blvd., 800/844-6534, www .beachtrips.com, $200–300). The rooms are top-notch and the service professional. As is the case with many local properties, there is a newer section, the Palmetto Tower, and an "old" section, the venerable Magnolia Tower. There are one-, two-, and three-bedroom units available, with the latter being a particularly good value.

Considered one of the major remaining centers of the shag subculture on the Strand, the **Ocean Drive Beach and Golf Resort** (98 N. Ocean Blvd., $200–350) up in North Myrtle Beach hosts many events surrounding the notable regional dance, including the Shaggers Hall of Fame. Its on-site lounge, The Spanish Galleon, specializes in beach music. It's also just a great place to stay with all the amenities from a "lazy river" to a whirlpool to full, galley-style kitchens and, of course, to extreme proximity to the beach. A remodel in 2007 has made it even more plush inside and out.

Also up in North Myrtle is the brand-spanking-new (**Tilghman Beach and Golf Resort** (1819 Ocean Blvd., 843/280-0913, www .tilghmanresort.com, $200–350), owned by the same company as the Ocean Drive Beach Resort. It's not directly on the beach, but since the buildings in front of it are pretty low you can still get awesome ocean views. Even the views from the back of the building aren't bad since they overlook a golf course. But you don't have to be a duffer to enjoy the Tilghman—the pool scene is great, the balconies roomy, and the suites are huge and well-equipped enough (a flat screen in every room) to make you feel right at home.

VACATION RENTALS

There are hundreds, probably thousands, of privately-rented condo-style lodgings at Myrtle

Beach, in all shapes and forms. Most, however, do a great job of catering to what vacationers here seem to really want: space, convenience, and a working kitchen. All rental agencies basically work off the same listings, so looking for and finding a rental is easier than you might think.

Some of the key brokers are **Myrtle Beach Vacation Rentals** (800/845-0833, www.mb-vacationrentals.com), **Beach Vacations** (866/453-4818, www.beachvacationsmb.com), **Barefoot Vacations** (800/845-0837, www.barefootvacations.info), **Elliott Realty and Beach Rentals** (www.elliottrealty.com), and **Atlantic Dunes Vacation Rentals** (866/544-2568, www.atlanticdunesvacations.com).

CAMPING

Let's start off with what should be obvious by now: Myrtle Beach is not where you go for a pristine, quiet, camping experience. For that, I suggest Huntington State Park down near Murrells Inlet. However, there is plenty of camping, almost all of it heavily RV-oriented, if you want it. For more info go to www.campmyrtlebeach.com.

The closest thing to a real live campground is good old **Myrtle Beach State Park** (4401 S. Kings Hwy., 843/238-5325, www.southcarolinaparks.com, daily 6 A.M.–10 P.M., $4 adults, $1.50 ages 6–15, under 6 free), which

despite being only a short drive from the rest of the beachfront sprawl is still a fairly relaxing place to stay, complete with its own scenic fishing pier (daily fishing fee $4.50). There's even a nature center with a little aquarium and exhibits. The charming and educational atmosphere is largely due to the fact that this is one of the 17 Civilian Conservation Corps parks, built during the Depression and still lovingly maintained by the state of South Carolina. There are four cabins available ($54–125), all fully furnished and about 200 yards from the beach. The main campground is about 300 yards from the beach and comprises 300 sites with electricity and water ($23–25) and a 45-site tent and overflow campground ($17–19), which is only open during the summer high season.

The **Myrtle Beach KOA** (613 6th Ave. S., 800/562-7790, www.myrtlebeachkoa.com), though not at all cheap at $40–50 a night even for tenters, offers the usual safe, dependable amenities of that well-known chain, including rental "kabins" and kids activities.

Willow Tree RV Resort and Campground (520 Southern Sights Dr., 843/756-4334, www.willowtreervr.com) is set inland on a well-wooded 300-acre tract with large sites well away from the sprawl and offers lakeside fishing and bike trails. Basic sites are $50–82 and the one- and two-bedroom cabins range from $120–190 (all prices during high season).

Food

There are about 2,000 restaurants in the Myrtle Beach area, not counting hotel room service and buffets. You can find any dining option that floats your boat, at most any price level. Seafood, of course, is big here, and heartily recommended. But there are steakhouses, rib joints, pizza places, and vegetarian restaurants galore as well. We can only explore a small fraction of that here, but following is a breakdown of some of the more unique and tasty experiences on this bustling part of the Grand Strand.

ASIAN

For upscale Pac Rim fusion cuisine, go directly to **◖UMI Pacific Grille** (959 Lake Arrowhead Rd., 843/497-6016, www.umipacificgrille.com, Sun.–Thurs. 5–10 P.M., Fri.–Sat. 5–10:30 P.M., $15–30), easily the hippest restaurant in Myrtle Beach and one of the best. While the specialty of the house is the mouthwatering Japanese Wagyu Kobe beef—offered on salads as well as in filet mignon form—they also offer some daring takes on seafood, such as Wok Monkfish Medallions and Green Tea

Crusted Butterfish. As you might expect, shellfish are big here as well, from the King Crab Pad Thai to the Sesame Dusted Scallops in a sweet chili *beurre-blanc* with shiitakes. Not a cheap meal, but a memorable one.

BREAKFAST

Pancakes are big on the Strand, with many flapjack places open 24 hours to accommodate partiers and night owls. If you've got a hankering, just drive up and down Kings Highway/U.S. 17 long enough and you're bound to find a place. A prime purveyor of pancakes is **Harry's Breakfast Pancakes** (2306 N. Kings Hwy., 843/448-8013). They're not open all day, but from the crack of dawn to 2 P.M. is a big enough window to enjoy their fluffy stacks and rich omelettes.

BURGERS AND HOT DOGS

I normally shy away from mentioning chain-type places because of the cheese factor, but I'll make an exception for Myrtle Beach, where you expect things to be a little cheesy. **Jimmy Buffett's Margaritaville** (1114 Celebrity Cir., 843/448-5455, www.margaritaville myrtlebeach.com, Mon.–Thurs. and Sun. 11 A.M.–10 P.M., Fri.–Sat. 11 A.M.–midnight, $13–22) at Broadway at the Beach is widely regarded as the best single location of the national chain. The signature Cheeseburger in Paradise is the obvious big hit. You get a lot of entertainment for your money as well, with balloon-twisting performers coming to your table and a bizarre whirling "hurricane" that acts up in the main dining area every now and then. As you'd expect, the margaritas are good, if expensive.

Many locals insist the better burger is at another Buffett-owned chain, the succinctly titled **Cheeseburger in Paradise** (7211 N. Kings Hwy., 843/497-3891, www.cheeseburgerin paradise.com, Sun.–Thurs. 11:30 A.M.–11 P.M., Fri.–Sat. 11:30 A.M.–midnight, $10–15), which offers a range of burgers on the menu with sweet potato chips on the side, all served up in a less flashy (but still very boisterous) atmosphere than the flagship restaurant. For a change of pace, try the El Cubano. In any

© JIM MOREKIS

Hot Diggety Dogz in Ocean Drive Beach

event, save room for the chocolate nachos (fried tortillas covered in chocolate and served with ice cream, though that prosaic description hardly does it justice).

For a quick, cheap meal up in North Myrtle, go to old Ocean Drive Beach and load up at **Hot Diggety Dogz** (206 N. Main St., 843/280-3300, http://papaspizzawingsandth ings.com, $2.50–8). Try a Sabrett hot dog with the works, or pizza by the slice, and finish with an Italian ice.

CLASSIC SOUTHERN

If you've got a hankering for some spicy Cajun/Creole food, go no further than **The House of Blues** (4640 Hwy. 17 S., 843/272-3000, www.hob.com, Mon.–Fri. 4–9 P.M., Sat. 8 A.M.–9 P.M., Sun. 9 A.M.–2 P.M., 3–9 P.M., $10–25) at Barefoot Landing in North Myrtle Beach. With 17 similarly-themed locations throughout North America, this particular venue deals in the same kind of retro Delta vibe, with specially-commissioned folk art festooning the walls and live music cranking up at about 9 P.M. At your table, a gregarious server will walk you through the limited but intense

MYRTLE BEACH

menu, which includes such tasty bits as Buffalo Tenders (actually boneless chicken wings in a perfectly spicy sauce) and a couple of excellent jambalaya-type dishes. All portions are enormous and richly spiced. It's a loud, clangy room, so keep in mind that this is less a romantic experience than an exuberant, earthy one.

A special experience here is the weekly Gospel Brunch ($19.95 adults, $9.95 ages 6–12) on Sundays, an opportunity not only to enjoy some tasty Southern-style brunch treats like cheese grits, jambalaya, and catfish tenders, but to enjoy some really rather outstanding gospel entertainment at the same time. The Gospel Brunch is served in seatings from 9 A.M.–2 P.M. each Sunday, and I do suggest reservations.

CONTINENTAL

In Myrtle Beach it can be difficult to find a good meal that's not fried or smothered, or both. For a highbrow change of pace, try **The Library** (1212 N. Kings Hwy., 843/448-4527, www.thelibraryrestaurantsc.com, Mon.–Sat. 5–10 P.M., $20–50), which is hands-down the most romantic dining experience in Myrtle proper. It's not cheap, but then again nothing about this place is pedestrian, from the hyper-attentive European-style service to the savvy wine list to the signature dishes (many of them prepared tableside), like she-crab soup, Caesar salads, Steak Diane, and the ultimate splurge—steak and lobster.

Like art? Like food? Try the **Collector's Café** (7726 N. Kings Hwy., 843/449-9370, www.collectorscafeandgallery.com), which as the name implies is a combined gallery and dining space. Don't be daunted by the strip mall setting—inside it is a totally different ball game with a trendy open kitchen and plush, eclectic furniture awaiting you amidst the original artwork. As for the menu, you may as well go for what's widely regarded as its best single dish, the scallop cakes. However, make sure you save room for dessert.

ITALIAN

The best-regarded Italian place in Myrtle Beach—though it could just as easily go in the Steaks category since that's their specialty—is

Angelo's (2011 S. Kings Hwy., 843/626-2800, www.angelosteakandpasta.com, Sun.–Thurs. 4–8:30 P.M., Fri.–Sat. 4–9 P.M., $12–25). Their signature dishes are intriguingly spiced cuts of steak (request beforehand if you don't want them seasoned), cooked medium and under for an exquisite tenderness. You can get spaghetti as a side with the steaks, or just go with the classic baked potato. Don't forget to check out the Italian buffet, including lasagna, Italian sausage, chicken cacciatore, ravioli, and of course pizza.

A particularly well-run franchise of a national chain, **Ultimate California Pizza** (2500 N. Kings Hwy., 843/626-8900, www.ultimatecaliforniapizza.com, Mon.–Sat. 11 A.M.–11 P.M., Sun. 5 A.M.–11 P.M., $7–18) delivers the goods in Barefoot Landing in North Myrtle. They offer an almost bewildering variety of specialty pizzas, from a surf & turf pizza to one topped with filet mignon to various interesting veggie styles. Many folks simply opt to build their own pie, however, with toppings from apples to goat cheese and an incredible diversity of sauces.

SEAFOOD

The grandest old Calabash seafood joint in town, **Original Benjamin's** (9593 N. Kings Hwy., 843/449-0821, daily 3:30–10 P.M., buffet $25 adults, $12 children) on the old Restaurant Row is one of the more unique dining experiences in Myrtle Beach. With themed rooms overlooking the Intracoastal Waterway, including the concisely-named "Bus Room"—yes, it has an old school bus in it—you'll find yourself in the mood to devour copious amounts of fresh seafood at its humongous 170-item buffet line. That's not a misprint—170 items, from mounds of shrimp prepared in every style, to all kinds of tuna and salmon and catfish, to a variety of crabmeat dishes, to non-seafood stuff like chicken and barbecue.

From old reliables like crab cakes and sea scallops to signature house dishes like the pecan-encrusted grouper or stuffed flounder, you can't go wrong at **The Sea Captain's House** (3002 N. Ocean Blvd., 843/448-8082,

MYRTLE BEACH

WHAT'S A CALABASH?

In Myrtle Beach you'll no doubt see garish restaurant signs boasting of "Calabash Cooking" or a "Calabash Buffet." Named for a seaside shrimping and fishing village just over the border in North Carolina, Calabash cooking basically means fresh seafood, fried in spiced corn meal soon after it's caught.

In usual practice, Calabash seafood is served in huge buffets, and to most people on the Strand the phrase really just refers to the sheer volume of food. Shrimp is the dominant motif, though flounder is big, too.

By all means enjoy Calabash cooking while you're on the Strand, but don't expect the catch to be fresh. Connoisseurs insist you need to go to Calabash, North Carolina, itself for that.

daily 6–10:30 A.M., 11:30 A.M.–2:30 P.M., 5–10 P.M., $10–20), one of Myrtle Beach's better seafood restaurants. This opinion is widely held, however, so prepare to wait—often up to two hours. Luckily, you can sip a cocktail and gaze out over the Atlantic Ocean as you do so. Old hands will tell you it's not as good as back in the day, but it's still a cut above.

When you're at Ocean Drive Beach up in North Myrtle, check out another venerable old name, the **Duffy Street Seafood Shack** (202 Main St., 843/281-9840, daily noon–10 P.M., $5). This is a humble, unkempt, roadside affair dealing in the kind of down-home treats Myrtle Beach seems to love ("pigskin" shrimp, fried pickles, and the like). Overall, it's a good place to get a tasty bite and soak in the flavor of this Cherry Grove neighborhood at the heart of the old shag culture.

STEAKS, BARBECUE, AND RIBS

The best barbecue in town—and a delightfully low-key experience in this often too-flashy area—is at **Little Pigs Barbecue** (6102 Frontage Rd., 843/692-9774, Mon.–Sat.

11 A.M.–8 P.M., $8–12). This is a local-heavy place dealing in no-frills pulled pork, piled high at the counter and reasonably priced with a selection of sauces. Here, the lack of atmosphere *is* the atmosphere, and they prefer to let the barbecue (and the hushpuppies and onion rings) do the talking.

Since opening 20 years ago, **Thoroughbreds** (9706 N. Kings Hwy, 843/497-2636, www.thoroughbredsrestaurant.com, Mon.–Thurs. and Sun. 5–10 P.M., Fri.–Sat. 5–11 P.M., $20) on the old Restaurant Row has been considered the premier fine-dining place in Myrtle Beach, dealing in the kind of wood-heavy, clubby, Old-World-meets-New World ambience you'd more expect to see in Palm Beach, Florida. That said, the prices are definitely more Myrtle Beach; you can easily have a romantic dinner for two for under $100. The menu is a carnivore's delight: Beef includes their signature prime rib, a great Steak Au Pivre, and their nod to cowboy machismo, the 22-ounce bone-in rib eye, while the veal, pork chops, and rack of lamb are also topflight. A special treat is the exquisite Chateaubriand for two, a steal at $75. However, seafood lovers shouldn't entirely skip Thoroughbreds as the crab cakes and the shrimp and grits stack up to most any you'll find in the Carolinas.

The new darling of the steak-loving set here is **Rioz Brazilian Steakhouse** (2920 Hollywood Dr., 843/839-0777, www.rioz.com, daily 4 P.M.–10 P.M., $20–40). It's not cheap—the recommended 15-item meat sampler is $35 per person—but then again an experience this awesome shouldn't be (though a big plus is that kids six and under eat for free). The meats are fresh and vibrant, slow-cooked over a wood fire in the simple but succulent style typical of the gaucho *churrascaria* tradition. The service is widely considered to be the best in the area. But the biggest surprise may turn out to be the salad and seafood bar ($19.95 buffet), which even has sushi.

There is no dearth of places to nosh at Barefoot Landing, but meat-lovers (not to mention golfers) will probably enjoy **Greg Norman's Australian Grill** (4930 Kings Hwy. S., 843/361-

0000, www.shark.com, daily 5–10 P.M., $20–30), which despite the chain-sounding name is the only restaurant of its kind. With the dark, clubby ambience you'd expect at a place named for a golf pro, this is not necessarily where you want to take the kids. Instead, it's the place to enjoy a cocktail by the lake and a premium entrée like the lobster-crusted swordfish, the rack of lamb, or the prime rib.

You wouldn't expect a place with the name **Carolina Roadhouse** (4617 N. Kings Hwy., 843/497-9911, Sun.–Thurs. 11 A.M.–10 P.M., Fri.–Sat. 11 A.M.–11 P.M., $10–28) to have excellent croissant appetizers, but that kind of twist is what makes this a cut above the usual steak-and-ribs joint. Virtually anything on the menu is very good, but since you're likely to be waiting on a table, you may as well go for the incredible ribs.

Information and Services

The main visitors center for Myrtle Beach is the **Myrtle Beach Area Chamber of Commerce and Visitor Center** (1200 N. Oak St., 843/626-7444, www.visitmybeach.com, Mon.–Fri. 8:30 A.M.–5 P.M., Sat. 10 A.M.–2 P.M.). There's an **airport welcome center** (1180 Jetport Rd., 843/626-7444) as well. There's also a visitors center in North Myrtle Beach, the **North Myrtle Beach Chamber of Commerce and Convention & Visitors Bureau** (270 Hwy. 17 North, 843/281-2662, www.north myrtlebeachchamber.com).

The main healthcare facility in the Myrtle Beach area is **Grand Strand Regional Medical Center** (809 82nd Pkwy., 843/692-1000, www.grandstrandmed.com).

Myrtle Beach is served by the **Myrtle Beach Police Department** (1101 N. Oak St., 843/918-1382, www.cityofmyrtlebeach.com). The separate municipality of North Myrtle

Beach is served by the **North Myrtle Beach Police Department** (843/280-5555, www.nmb.us).

The newspaper of record for Myrtle Beach is *The Sun News* (www.myrtlebeachonline.com). For a look at the grittier side of Myrtle Beach music and nightlife, look for a copy of *The Weekly Surge* (www.weeklysurge.com).

In Myrtle Beach, you can choose between the main **U.S. Post Office** (505 N. Kings Hwy., 800/275-8777, Mon.–Fri. 8:30 A.M.–5 P.M., Sat. 9 A.M.–1 P.M.) or its other convenient location (820 67th Ave. N., 800/275-8777, Mon.–Fri. 9 A.M.–4:30 P.M., Sat. 11 A.M.–1 P.M.).

In North Myrtle beach try the main post office (621 6th Ave. S., 800/275-8777, Mon.–Fri. 8:30 A.M.–5 P.M., Sat. 9 A.M.–noon) or its other convenient location in Cherry Grove Beach (227 Sea Mountain Hwy., 800/275-8777, Mon.–Fri. 8:30 A.M.–5 P.M.).

Getting There and Around

GETTING THERE
The Myrtle Beach area is served by the fast-growing **Myrtle Beach International Airport** (1100 Jetport Rd., 843/448-1589, www.fly myrtlebeach.com, airport code MYR), which hosts Continental, Delta, Northwest, Southern Skyways, Spirit, U.S. Airways, and United.

Unusually for South Carolina, a state which is exceptionally well-served by the U.S. Interstate

Highway system, the main route into this area is the smaller U.S. 17, which runs north-south—with a parallel business spur—from Georgetown on up to the North Carolina border. The approach from the west is by U.S. 501, called Black Skimmer Trail as it approaches Myrtle Beach.

The local **Greyhound Bus Lines** (511 7th Ave. N., 843/231-2222) terminal is in "downtown" Myrtle Beach.

GETTING AROUND

In practice the Myrtle Beach municipalities blend and blur into each other in one long sprawl parallel to the main north-south route, U.S. 17. However, always keep this in mind: Just south of Murrells Inlet U.S. 17 divides into two distinct portions. There's U.S. 17 Bypass, which continues to the west of much of the coastal growth, and there's Business 17, also known as Kings Highway, which is the main drag along which most key attractions and places of interest are located.

The other key north-south route, Ocean Boulevard, runs along the beach. This is a two-lane road that can get pretty stacked up in the summer, especially when it's used for cruising by younger visitors or during one of several motorcycle rallies throughout the year.

Thankfully, area planners have provided a great safety valve for some of this often-horrendous traffic. Highway 31, the Carolina Bays Parkway, begins inland from Myrtle Beach at about 16th Avenue. This new, wide highway roughly parallels the Intracoastal Waterway and takes you on a straight shot, with a 65 mph speed limit, all the way to Highway 22 (the Conway Bypass) and/or clear on up to Highway 9 at Cherry Grove Beach, the farthest extent of North Myrtle Beach. The bottom line is that if time is of the essence, I strongly urge you to make use of Highway 31 whenever possible.

Rental Car, Taxi, and Bus

You will really need a vehicle to make the most of this area. Rental cars are available at the airport. Rental options outside of the airport include **Enterprise** (1377 Hwy. 501, 843/626-4277 or 3401 Hwy. 17 S., 843/361-4410, www.enterprise.com); **Hertz** (851 Jason Blvd., 843/839-9530, www.hertz

.com); and the unique **Rent-a-Wreck** (901 3rd Ave. S., 843/626-9393).

Taxi service on the Strand is plentiful but fairly expensive. Look in the local Yellow Pages for full listings, but a couple of good services are **Yellow Cab** (917 Oak St., 843/448-5555) and **Beach Checker Cab** (843/272-6212) in North Myrtle.

The area is served by the **Coastal Rapid Public Transit Authority** (1418 Third Ave., 843/248-7277), which runs several routes up and down the Strand. Go by a visitors center or call for a schedule.

By Bike

Bicyclists in Myrtle Beach can take advantage of some completed segments of the South Carolina portion of the **East Coast Greenway** (www.greenway.org), which generally speaking is Ocean Boulevard. In Myrtle Beach there's a bike lane on North Ocean Boulevard from about 82nd Avenue North down to 29th Avenue North. You can actually ride Ocean Boulevard all the way from 82nd Avenue North down to the southern city limit if you like. Inland, a portion of the Greenway is on Grissom Parkway, which takes you by Broadway at the Beach.

In North Myrtle Beach, from Sea Mountain Highway in Cherry Grove you can bike Ocean Boulevard clear down to 46th Avenue South with a detour from 28th–33rd Avenues. A right on 46th takes you to Barefoot Landing. And of course for a scenic ride you can pedal on the beach itself for miles. But remember: Bicycling on the sidewalk is strictly prohibited.

As for bike rentals, try **Beach Bike Shop** (711 Broadway St., 843/448-5335, www .beachbikeshop.com). In North Myrtle, try **Wheel Fun Rentals** (91 S. Ocean Blvd., 843/280-7900, www.wheelfunrentals.com).

Points Inland

CONWAY

A nice day trip west of Myrtle Beach—and a nice change from that area's hyper-development—is to the charming town of Conway, just northwest of Myrtle Beach on U.S. 501 on the Waccamaw River. Founded in 1733 under the name Kingston, it originally marked the frontier of the colony. It was later renamed Conwayborough (soon shortened to Conway) in honor of local leader Robert Conway, and now serves as the seat of Horry County.

Conway's heyday was during Reconstruction when it became a major trade center for timber products and naval stores from the interior. The railroad came through town in 1887 (later being extended to Myrtle Beach itself), and most remaining buildings date from this period or later.

The most notable Conway native is perhaps an unexpected name. William Gibson, originator of the "cyberpunk" genre of science fiction, was born here in 1948.

Conway is small and easily explored. Make your first stop at the **Conway Visitors Center** (903 Third Ave., 843/248-1700, www.cityof conway.com, Mon.–Fri. 9 A.M.–5 P.M.), where you can pick up maps. They also offer guided tours ($2 per person), which depart at City Hall at the corner of Third Avenue and Main Street. Call for a schedule. You can also visit the **Conway Chamber of Commerce** (203 Main St.) for maps and information.

Sights

Conway's chief attraction is the 850-foot **Riverwalk** (843/248-2273, www.conwaysc chamber.com, daily dawn–dusk) along the blackwater Waccamaw, a calming location with shops and restaurants nearby. Waterborne tours on the *Kingston Lady* leave from the Conway Marina at the end of the Riverwalk.

Another key stop is the **Horry County Museum** (428 Main St., 843/248-1542, www.horrycountymuseum.org, Mon.–Sat. 9 A.M.–5 P.M., free), which tells the story of this rather large South Carolina county, from prehistory to the present. They hold an annual Quilt Gala in February, which features some great regional examples of that art.

Across from the campus of Coastal Carolina University is the circa 1972 Traveler's Chapel, a.k.a. **"The Littlest Church in South Carolina"** (intersection of U.S. 501 and Cox Ferry Road). At 12-by-24 feet, it seats no more than a dozen people. Weddings are held here throughout the year. While they say it's never locked, I would just stick to visiting it during daylight hours. Admission is free of course, but donations are accepted.

Accommodations

The best stay in town is at the four-star **Cypress Inn** (16 Elm St., 843/248-8199, www.acypressinn.com, $165), a beautiful and well-appointed 12-room B&B right on the Waccamaw River.

LEWIS OCEAN BAY HERITAGE PRESERVE

The humongous (over 9000 acres) Lewis Ocean Bay Heritage Preserve (803/734-3886, www.dnr.sc.gov, daily dawn–dusk, free) is one of the more impressive phenomena in the Palmetto State from a naturalist's viewpoint, all the more special because of its location a short drive from heavily-developed Myrtle Beach. Managed by the state, it contains an amazing 23—yes, 23—Carolina Bays, by far the largest concentration in South Carolina. (The nearby Highway 31 is named the Carolina Bays Parkway in a nod to its neighbors.)

As if that weren't enough, it boasts other unique aspects as well. The largest concentration of Venus flytraps in the state is here, and the preserve is also said to be the only place in eastern South Carolina where black bears still live in the wild. (Clemson University is conducting a study on their habits, and so far, has concluded that they go back and forth between here and North Carolina.)

The bird-watching is extra-special here too, with a goodly number of bald eagles and endangered red-cockaded woodpeckers in the area. Several miles of trails take you through a variety of habitats.

When you're here, keep in mind that despite its great natural beauty it is not pristine. As with most of Horry County, heavy logging and turpentine operations took place throughout the preserve's acreage during the 1800s and early 1900s. As with most all South Carolina heritage preserves, hunting does take place here and there are no facilities.

To get here from Myrtle Beach, take U.S. 501 north to Highway 90 and head east. After about seven miles turn east on the unpaved International Road across from the Wild Horse subdivision. After about a mile and a half on International Road, veer left onto Old Kingston Road. The preserve is shortly ahead on both sides of the road; park along the shoulder.

The Rest of the Grand Strand

Pawleys Island, Murrells Inlet, and the rest of the so-called "Waccamaw Neck" comprise the lower portion of the Grand Strand. While a certain amount of Myrtle Beach-style development is encroaching southward, this area is still far away in spirit and generally much more relaxed.

Tiny Pawleys Island—year-round population about 200—likes to call itself "America's first resort" because of its early role in the late 1700s as a place for planters to go with their families to escape the mosquito-infested rice and cotton fields. (George Washington himself visited in 1791.) It's still a vacation getaway, and still has a certain elite understatement, an attitude the locals call "arrogantly shabby."

Beach access is correspondingly more difficult than further up the Strand near Myrtle Beach. While you can visit casually, most people who enjoy the famous Pawleys Island beaches do so from one of the many vacation rental properties there.

Shabby arrogance does have its upside, however—there is a ban on further commercial development in the community, allowing Pawleys to remain slow and peaceful indefinitely. The maximum speed limit throughout town is a suitably lazy 25 miles per hour.

For generations Pawleys was famous for its cypress cottages, many on stilts. Sadly, Hurricane Hugo in 1989 destroyed a great many of these iconic structures—27 out of 29 on the south end alone, most of which have been replaced by far less aesthetically pleasing homes.

Directly adjacent to Pawleys, Litchfield Beach offers similar low-key enjoyment along with a world-class golf resort.

While several key attractions in the Grand Strand are technically in Murrells Inlet, that's more for post office convenience than anything else. Murrells Inlet itself is chiefly known for a single block of seafood restaurants on its eponymous waterway.

SIGHTS
(Brookgreen Gardens
One of the most unique—and unlikely—sights in the sometimes-overdeveloped Grand Strand area is bucolic Brookgreen Gardens (1931 Brookgreen Drive, 843/235-6000, www.brookgreen.org, daily 9:30 A.M.–5 P.M., 9:30 A.M.–8 P.M. in April, $12 adults, $5 ages 6–12, under 6 free) directly across U.S. 17 from Huntington Beach State Park. An eclectic compilation of sorts, Brookgreen combines scenic, manicured gardens, copious amounts of outdoor sculpture by a host of artists, and a low-key but worthwhile nature center with live animals.

Once one of several massive, contiguous plantations in the Pawleys Island area, the modern Brookgreen is a result of the charity and passion of Archer Milton Huntington and

Brookgreen Gardens

whimsical and even downright charming, such as the one near the visitors center with several kids pledging allegiance to the flag. To learn more, visit the **Carroll A. Campbell Jr. Center for American Sculpture** on-site, which offers seminars and workshops throughout the year.

Botanists and green thumbs will find plenty to enjoy as well. At least 2,000 species of plants have been planted at Brookgreen, with something always guaranteed to be in bloom regardless of the season of your visit. A special treat is the stunning "Oak Allee" section, with some of the live oaks 250 years old. One huge and ancient specimen, the "Constitution Oak," has been designated a "living witness" to the signing of the U.S. Constitution.

On the other end of the grounds opposite the gardens is the **E. Craig Wall Jr. Lowcountry Nature Center,** including a small, enclosed cypress swamp with a boardwalk, herons and egrets, and an absolutely delightful river otter exhibit where you can see the playful critters swim and frolic. Other animals include alligators and several species of raptors. Almost all the wildlife here have been treated for injuries which render them unfit for living in the wild again.

To add an extra layer of enjoyment to your visit, you can explore much deeper into this massive preserve by taking one of several tours offered on Brookgreen's pontoon boat. Most of the boat rides are $7 adults, $4 children on top of regular admission; check the website for a schedule.

his wife, Anna Hyatt Huntington. Seeking to preserve the area's flora and fauna and celebrate American sculpture at the same time, the couple turned the entire place into a nonprofit in 1931. Quite the sculptor in her own right, Mrs. Huntington saw to it that Brookgreen's 9,000 acres would host the largest single collection of outdoor sculpture in America by far.

Designed and added onto over the past century, the sculpture gardens themselves are a sprawling collection of tastefully-themed, colorfully planted gardens that are generally built around a key sculpture or two. As you're walking, don't forget to examine the various nooks, crannies, and corners inside and outside the walls, where you'll find hundreds of smaller sculptures, generally along natural or mythological themes. The sculptures don't stop there—you'll see plenty of them out in fields, overlooking lakes, and tucked into bushes all around the site. In all, there are over 1,200 works by over 300 artists.

While most sculptures here tend towards a certain style—thick, robust, and often depicting some form of struggle—some are more

Huntington Beach State Park

Right across the street from Brookgreen is Huntington Beach State Park (16148 Ocean Hwy., 843/237-4440, www.southcarolina parks.com, daily 6 A.M.–10 P.M., $5 adults, $3 ages 6–15, under 6 free), probably the best of South Carolina's non-CCC state parks. Once a part of the same vast parcel of land owned by Archer Huntington and Anna Hunter, the state has leased from the trustees of their estate since the 1960s.

You can tour their "castle" on the beach, Atalaya, former home of the Huntingtons

© SOPHIA MOREKIS

MYRTLE BEACH

and now the yearly site of the Atalaya Arts and Crafts Festival. This evocative, Moorish-style National Historic Landmark is open to the public by free guided tour from Memorial Day through the end of October daily from noon–1 P.M. Extra tours happen at 2 P.M. Tues.–Sat. from October 1–31.

Today a walk through the park is a delightful and convenient way to enjoy the Grand Strand's natural legacy. A great variety of birds use Huntington Beach as a migratory stopover. You can stroll three miles of beach; view birds and wildlife from several boardwalks into the marsh; hike several nature trails; and visit the well-done **Environmental Education Center** (843/235-8755, Tues.–Sun. 10 A.M.–5 P.M.), which features a saltwater touch tank and a baby alligator. In all it's a great experience for the whole family, or a very romantic one for a couple.

Pawleys Island Historic District

Though many of the island's homes were leveled by Hurricane Hugo, the Pawleys Island Historic District (843/237-1698, www.townof pawleysisland.com) in the central portion of the island still has a dozen contributing structures, almost all on Myrtle Avenue. Among them

© JIM MOREKIS

historic Weston House on Pawleys Island

are the **Weston House** (506 Myrtle Ave.), or Pelican Inn, and the **Ward House** (520 Myrtle Ave.), or Liberty Lodge. As you view the structures, many with their own historic markers, note the architecture. Because these were intended to be lived in from May–November, they resemble open and airy Caribbean homes, with extensive porches and plenty of windows.

EVENTS

The highlight of the lower Grand Strand calendar is the annual **Atalaya Arts and Crafts Festival** ($6 adults, ages 15 and under free), which takes place on the grounds of Huntington Beach State Park each September. Like the park itself the festival, now nearing its 40th year, is a philanthropic legacy of Archer Huntington and his wife Anna Hunter. There's music, food, and about 100 vendors who show their art and wares within the exotic Atalaya home itself. Admission to the park is free during the festival.

Also in September is the **Pawleys Island Festival of Music and Art** (www.pawleys music.com, prices vary), which happens across U.S. 17 outside under the stars in Brookgreen Gardens, with a few performances at nearby Litchfield Plantation.

A main event in Murrells Inlet is the annual **Fourth of July Boat Parade** (843/651-0900, free), which celebrates American independence with a patriotically-themed procession of all kinds of streamer-and-flag-bedecked watercraft down the inlet. It begins at about 6 P.M. and ends, of course, with a big fireworks display. Another big deal in Murrells Inlet is the annual **Blessing of the Inlet** (843/651-5099, www .belinumc.org), always held the first Saturday in May and sponsored by a local Methodist church. Enjoy food vendors, baked good from local ladies, and a great family atmosphere.

SHOPPING

The shopping scene here revolves around the famous Pawleys Island hammock, a beautiful and practical bit of local handiwork sold primarily at the **Hammock Shops Village** (10880 Ocean Hwy., 843/237-8448, Mon.–Sat. 10 A.M.–6 P.M.,

Sun., 1–5 P.M.). This is actually a collection of 25 shops and restaurants, the closest thing to a mall environment you'll find here.

To actually purchase a Pawleys Island hammock, go to **The Original Hammock Shop** (843/237-9122, www.thehammockshop.com), housed in a century-old cottage. Next door is the affiliated **Hammock Shop General Store,** which as the name implies, sells a number of other goods such as beachwear, books, and a notable style of local fudge. In the shed next door the actual hammocks are hand-crafted, the way they've been since 1889.

SPORTS AND RECREATION
Beaches

First, the good news: The beaches here are pristine and beautiful. The bad news: Public access is very limited. Simply put, that means the best way to enjoy the beach here is to rent one of the many private beach homes for a week or so. Though only a short distance from Myrtle Beach, the strands at Pawleys and vicinity are infinitely more peaceful and easy-going.

Beach access with parking at Pawleys Island includes a fairly large lot at the south end of the island and parking areas off Atlantic Avenue at Hazard, First, Pearce, Second and Third streets, and Shell Road.

Kayaking and Canoeing

The Waccamaw River and associated inlets and creeks are peaceful and scenic places to kayak, with plenty of bird-watching opportunities to boot. For a two-hour guided tour of the area salt marsh, reserve a spot on the kayak trips sponsored by the **Environmental Education Center** (Huntington Beach State Park, 843/235-8755, Tues.–Sun. 10 A.M.–5 P.M., $30 per person). Call for the times and days of trips. Or you can put in yourself at Oyster Landing, about a mile from the entrance to the state park.

Ecotours

The most popular and extensive dolphin tour in the area is the **Blue Wave Adventures Dolphin Watch** (843/651-3676, www.blue waveadventures.com, $29 adults, $19 ages 12

and under) on the waterfront in Murrells Inlet. The basic 90-minute tour leaves every day and takes you to the waters where the area pods, as well-known as any local resident, tend to congregate. Call for times; morning tours are the best for finding dolphin.

Fishing

A good all-around charter operator in Murrells Inlet, **Capt. Dicks** (4123 Bus. Hwy. 17, 843/651-3676, www.captdicks.com, prices vary), runs a variety of trips from deep-sea sportfishing to more casual inshore adventures. Dick also offers non-fishing trips, such as a dolphin tour and a popular marsh ecotour. They're in the same building as Spuds restaurant.

Leaving out of Pawleys Island is **Heidenseek Fishing Charters** (69 Pinehurst Lane, 843/685-4640, www.heidenseek.com). (Get it? Hide and seek? It's the name of their 26-foot Mako.)

Golf

Home to some of the best links in the Carolinas, the lower part of the Grand Strand recently organized its courses under the umbrella moniker **Waccamaw Golf Trail** (www .waccamawgolftrail.com), chiefly for marketing purposes. No matter, the courses are still as superb as ever, if generally pricer than their colleagues up the coast.

The best course, hands-down, in the area—and one of the best in the country—is the **Caledonia Golf and Fish Club** (369 Caledonia Dr., 843/237-3675, www.fishclub.com, $195). While the course itself is almost ridiculously young—it opened in 1995—this masterpiece is built, as so many area courses are, on the grounds of a former rice plantation. The clubhouse, in fact, dates from before the Civil War. Besides its signature 18th hole, other hallmarks of Caledonia are its copious amount of very old live oaks and its refusal to allow homes or condos to be built on the grounds. Packages are available at 800/449-4005 or www.myrtlebeach-condorentals.com. Affiliated with Caledonia is the fine **True Blue Golf Club** (900 Blue Stem Dr., 843/235-0900, www.fishclub.com,

$100), considered perhaps the most challenging single course on the Strand.

Another excellent Pawleys course, and one with a significantly longer pedigree, is the **Litchfield Country Club** (U.S. 17 and Magnolia Dr., 843/237-3411, www.litchcc.com, $60), one of the Grand Strand's oldest links and the first in Pawleys Island. The facilities are self-consciously dated—this is a country club, after all—setting it apart from the flashier, newer links sprouting like mushrooms further up the Strand. It's a deceptive course that's short on yards but heavy on doglegs.

The Jack Nicklaus-designed **Pawleys Plantation Golf and Country Club** (70 Tanglewood Dr., 843/237-6100, www.pawleys plantation.com, $150) has set a tough example for the last 20 years. Beautiful but challenging, it has a Jekyll/Hyde nature. The front nine is a traditional layout, while the back nine melts into the marsh.

ACCOMMODATIONS
$150-300

The premier bed-and-breakfast-style accommodation on the entire Grand Strand is (**Litchfield Plantation** (Kings River Rd., 843/237-9121, www.litchfieldplantation.com, $230–275) on Pawleys Island, built, as you've probably come to expect by now, on an old plantation. There is a host of lodging choices here, all of them absolutely splendid. The Plantation House has four sumptuous suites to choose from, all impeccably decorated. The humbly-named Guest House—actually an old mansion in and of itself—has six bedrooms, with the entire second floor being an executive suite. Lastly, the newer outparcel Villas contain an assortment of two- and three-bedroom suites. Amenities include a full, complimentary Plantation breakfast each morning and a three-story beach club for use only by guests. If you visit in the winter you can get a room for as little as $150, a heck of a deal regardless of the temperature outside.

Similarly named but definitely *not* to be confused with Litchfield Plantation is the nearby **Litchfield Beach and Golf Resort** (14276 Ocean Hwy., 866/538-0187, www

.litchfieldbeach.com, $100–170). In typical Grand Strand fashion, this property delivers a lot of service for a surprisingly low price. Also typical for the area, it offers a wide range of lodging choices, from your basic room at the Seaside Inn on the low end, to four-bedroom villas running $230 a night (still a great deal). Though not all units are right on the beach, a regular, free shuttle takes you to the sand pretty much whenever you want. There are also lots of water activities right on the premises, including a ubiquitous "lazy river" tube course.

Vacation Rentals

Many who enjoy the Pawleys area do so using a vacation rental as a home base rather than a traditional hotel or B&B. **Pawleys Island Realty** (88 N. Causeway Rd., 800/937-7352, www .pawleysislandrealty.com) can hook you up.

Camping

For great camping in this area, go no further than **Huntington Beach State Park** (16148 Ocean Hwy., 843/237-4440, www.south carolinaparks.com, daily 6 A.M.–10 P.M., $5 adults, $3 ages 6–15, under 6 free). The beach is beautiful, there are trails and an education center, and the bird-watching is known as some of the best on the East Coast. While there are 131 RV-suitable sites ($23–28), tenters should go to one of the six walk-in tent sites ($17–19).

FOOD
Breakfast and Brunch

The high-end strip mall setting isn't the most romantic, but by broad consensus the best breakfast on the entire Strand is at **Applewood House of Pancakes** (14361 Ocean Hwy., 843/979-1022, daily 6 A.M.–2 P.M., $5–10) in Pawleys. Eggs Benedict, specialty omelets, crepes, waffles, and pancakes abound in this roomy, unpretentious dining room. Do it, you won't regret it.

Seafood

The Pawleys/Litchfield/Murrells Inlet area has some good seafood places, though the long lines during high season at some of the better-

© JIM MOREKIS

Murrells Inlet is known for its seafood restaurants.

known, more touristy places are not necessarily a sign of quality. A trip here in the fall or winter brings a culinary treat to help take the chill off—fresh local oysters! Do keep in mind that many restaurants keep substantially shorter hours in the winter, if not closing altogether.

Murrells Inlet has several good places clustered together along the marsh on U.S. 17. The best is **Lee's Inlet Kitchen** (4460 Business Hwy. 17, 843/651-2881, www.leesinletkitchen .com, $20–40), which is the only original Murrells Inlet joint still in the original family—in this case the Lee family, who started the place in the mid-1940s. The seafood here is simply but delectably prepared (your choice of fried or broiled), with particular pride taken in its freshness. Their sole drawback is that they close down from December–February.

Along similar lines and almost as recommendable is **Flo's Place Restaurant** (3797 Business Hwy. 17, 843/651-7222, www.flos place.com, daily 11 A.M.–10 P.M., $15–25). Flo is sadly no longer with us, but her place still eschews schlock for a more humble, down-home feel. Everything is fresh, hot,

and tasty, from the fried green tomatoes to the crab cakes to the alligator nuggets—yes, that's real alligator meat folks (they like to say it tastes like a cross between chicken and veal). But the signature dish is the legendary Dunkin' Pot—a big kettle filled with oysters, clams, shrimp, potatoes, sausage, and seasonal shellfish. As if that weren't enough, it's topped with snow crab legs. Do save room for some fried pickles!

On the other end of the spectrum style-wise is **Divine Fish House** (3993 Business Hwy. 17, 843/651-5800, www.divinefishhouse.com, daily 5–10 P.M., $20–33), which offers more adventurous high-end cuisine like the fine San Antonio Salmon (smothered with pepper jack cheese and bacon) and the Asian-flavored Banana Leaf Mangrove Grouper.

Fried lobster—yes, fried lobster—is the signature dish at **The Mayor's House** (13089 Ocean Hwy., 843/237-9082, www.themayors houserestaurant.com, daily 5–10 P.M., $17–30) on U.S. 17 at Litchfield Beach. But really any seafood dish, from the rich Coquilles St. Jacques (sea scallops, 'shrooms, and shallots baked in a white sauce) to the Mayor's Shrimp and Grits will do just fine.

Just down the road at Pawleys is **Hanser House** (14360 Ocean Hwy., 843/235-3021, www.hanserhouse.com, daily 4–10 P.M., $19), which offers succulent seafood dishes like its signature crabmeat-stuffed flounder or King Crab legs, but also offers some crackerjack steaks. October through February, check out their frequent oyster roasts.

INFORMATION AND SERVICES

On Pawleys Island is the **Georgetown County Visitors Bureau** (95-A Centermarsh Lane, 843/235-6595, www.visitgeorgetowncounty sc.com).

The **Myrtle Beach Area Chamber of Commerce** (3401 Hwy. 17, 843/651-1010, www.visitmybeach.com) and new **Waccamaw Community Hospital** (4070 Hwy. 17 Bypass, 843/652-1000, www.georgetownhospital system.org) are in Murrells Inlet.

Pawleys Island is served by the **Pawleys Island Police Department** (321 Myrtle Ave., 843/237-3008, www.townofpawleysisland .com)

Pawleys Island has a small newspaper, the *Coastal Observer* (www.coastalobserver.com). There's a **U.S. Postal Service office** in Pawleys Island (10993 Ocean Hwy., 800/275-8777, Mon.–Fri. 8 A.M.–4:30 P.M., Sat. 10 A.M.–noon) and in Murrells Inlet (654 Bellamy Ave., 800/275-8777, Mon.–Fri. 8:30 A.M.–5 P.M., Sat. 9 A.M.–noon).

Georgetown and Vicinity

Think of Georgetown as Beaufort's lesser-known cousin. Like Beaufort, it's an hour away from Charleston, except to the north rather than to the south. Like Beaufort, it boasts a tidy historic downtown that can be walked from end to end in an afternoon. And like Beaufort, it was once a major center of Lowcountry plantation culture.

However, Georgetown gets significantly less attention and less traffic. Unlike Beaufort, no movies are shot here, and no rambling Southern memoirs were penned here. Certainly the fact that the entrance into town is dominated by the sprawling, ominous-looking Georgetown Steel mill on one side of the road and the massive, smelly International Paper plant on the other has something to do with it. Make no mistake, industry is a way of life here. An important seaport for most of its history, Georgetown today boasts South Carolina's second busiest port next to Charleston itself.

But when you take a quick turn to the east and go down to the waterfront, you'll see the charm of old Georgetown: bright, attractive, historical homes, cute shops and cafés, and the peaceful Sampit River flowing by.

There are several enjoyable and educational places a short ways north on U.S. 17. Chief among them are Hobcaw Barony—former playground of the rich turned environmental education center—and Hampton Plantation, a well-preserved look back into antebellum elegance and rice-culture history.

Indeed, that coastal stretch from Georgetown down to the Charleston suburb of Mt. Pleasant is an inexplicably underrated microcosm of the Lowcountry, one that's easy to travel, relatively rustic, yet close enough to "civilization" so that you never really have to leave your comfort zone.

One particularly delightful aspect is the fact that the massive Francis Marion National Forest is your constant companion on the west side of U.S. 17—helping to keep at bay much of the egregious overdevelopment that is taking place elsewhere on the South Carolina coast. The forest also provides plenty of hiking, biking, and bird-watching opportunities.

HISTORY

The third-oldest city in South Carolina, behind Charleston and Beaufort, Georgetown

THE SPANISH AT WINYAH BAY

The Georgetown area is best known for its Anglophilic tendencies in history, character, and architecture. But before the English came the Spanish.

Beautiful Winyah Bay outside of Georgetown – estuary of the Sampit, Pee Dee, Black, and Waccamaw Rivers – was the site of one of the first landfalls by Europeans to America. It happened in 1526 when six Spanish ships, commanded by Lucas Vasquez de Ayllon, came in order to establish a colony in the area.

The wealthy heir to a sugar-planting fortune on Hispaniola in the Caribbean, Ayllon was also a master of PR. On a previous scouting trip, Ayllon had captured an Indian and brought him back to Spain. Upon hearing the captive's proud descriptions of his homeland, King Charles V of Spain promptly gave permission to Ayllon to settle the area, just as Ayllon hoped. (The king was pretty crafty himself; he insisted that Ayllon mount the expedition at his own expense.)

Upon arrival with his 500 colonists, Ayllon's reluctant Indian passengers – including his only interpreter, the same man he'd brought before the king – vanished into the maritime forest, never to be found. Even worse for the Spanish, one of Ayllon's ships, the *Capitana*, sank in Winyah Bay with most of the expedition's supplies. It remains there to this day, though no one knows quite where it is or what is left of it.

Ayllon would finally get his colony, though not in South Carolina. Finding the local soil too acid for crops and the local tribes too scarce in number to provide dependable slave labor, he decamped and headed down the coast to the area of St. Catherine's Sound in modern-day Georgia. His settlement there, San Miguel de Gualdalpe, lasted only a few months until falling victim to disease, poor nutrition, and Indian attack. But it was indeed the first European colony in what would become the United States – preceding the Spanish settlement at St. Augustine, Florida, by nearly 40 years and the first English colony at Jamestown, Virginia, by almost a century.

MYRTLE BEACH

was founded in 1729 on a four-by-eight-block grid, most of which still exists today, complete with original street names.

Georgetown's influence was acute during the American Revolution, with the father-son team of Palmetto State signers of the Declaration of Independence Thomas Lynch and Thomas Lynch, Jr. both hailing from here. The Revolutionary hero Francis Marion, the "Swamp Fox," was born in nearby Berkeley County and conducted operations in and around the area during the entire war, including an unsuccessful assault on British forces holding Georgetown itself.

The biggest boom was still ahead for Georgetown. While Charleston-area plantations get most of the glory, the truth is that by 1840 about 150 rice plantations on the Sampit and Little Pee Dee rivers were producing half of the entire national output of the staple crop. Indeed, Georgetown held fast to rice even as most Southern planters switched to growing cotton after the invention of the cotton gin.

After the Civil War, the collapse of the slave-based economy (at its height 90 percent of Georgetown's population was slaves) meant the relative collapse of the rice economy as well. Though the plantations stayed in operation, their output was much smaller, and the coming of the boll weevil infestation in the early 1900s merely brought it to a merciful end.

In 1905 Bernard Baruch—native South Carolinian, Wall Street mover and shaker, and advisor to presidents—came to town, purchasing Hobcaw Barony, a former plantation. It became his winter residence and hunting ground, and his legacy of conservation lives on there today in an education center on the site.

The Depression was particularly hard on Georgetown, with virtually the entire city being unemployed at one point. But in 1936, the opening of a massive paper mill turned things around, with economic effects you can see (and olfactory effects you can smell, unfortunately) to this day.

Today, Georgetown is a quiet place where most people either make their living working at the port, the steel mill, or the paper plant, with a good smattering of tourist-related businesses in the historic district. On the national level it's perhaps best known for being the hometown of comedian Chris Rock (though Chris himself moved away long ago, many members of his family continue to live here and he usually pays a visit at Christmas).

SIGHTS
Kaminski House

The city of Georgetown owns and operates the historic Kaminski House (1003 Front St., 843/546-7706, www.cityofgeorgetownsc.com, Mon.–Sat. 9 A.M.–5 P.M., Sun. 1–4 P.M., $7 adults, $3 ages 6–12, 5 and under free). Built in 1769, it was home to several city mayors,

including the eponymous Harold Kaminski who ran the city from 1931 to 1935.

"Stately" pretty much describes the elegant exterior of this two-story masterpiece, but the real goods are inside. It's furnished with a particularly exquisite and copious selection of 18th- and 19th-century antiques. The grounds are beautiful as well, overlooking the Sampit River and lined with Spanish moss-lined oaks.

The catch is that the only way to see the inside of the house is to take the free, 45-minute guided tour. Fortunately, they're quite frequent, departing every hour on the hour Mon.–Sat. 10 A.M.–4 P.M. and Sun. 1–4 P.M.

Rice Museum

The succinctly-named Rice Museum (633 Front St., 843/546-7423, www.ricemuseum .org, Mon.–Sat. 10 A.M.–4:30 P.M., $7 adults, $3 ages 6–21, 5 and under free) is just that: A

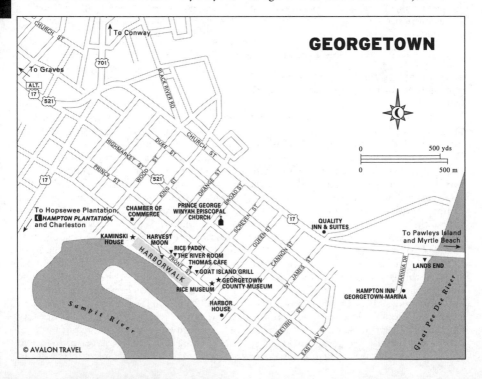

© JIM MOREKIS

Rice Museum

look back at the all-important staple crop and its massive effects on Georgetown, which at one point accounted for half of America's rice production.

There are actually two components. The Old Market building, often simply called "The Town Clock" because of its 1842 timepiece, hosts the bulk of the archival information on the impact of rice-growing on the region's history and economy. The adjacent Kaminski Hardware building includes a 17-minute video on the rice industry, a good Gullah/Geechee cultural exhibit, and a gift shop. However, its main claim to fame is its collection of regional maritime history, including the remains of the oldest colonial boat in North America, the 50-foot *Brown's Ferry Vessel,* built in 1710.

Several key exhibits in the Rice Museum trace the fundamental but generally reluctant role of African Americans in the rice industry, almost all of whom were slaves and comprised nearly 90 percent of the local population during rice's height. You'll learn the story of Joseph Rainey, the first African American elected to the House of Representatives, who once worked in the fields around Georgetown. You'll learn about Miss Ruby Forsythe, who spent her life teaching African American children in a one-room school on Pawleys Island.

Most visitors to the Rice Museum take a one-hour guided tour, included in the price of admission.

Georgetown County Museum

For a more complete look at all aspects of local history, check out the Georgetown County Museum (632 Prince St., 843/545-7020, Tues.–Sat. 10 A.M.–5 P.M., $4 adults, $2 ages 6–18, under 6 free). The highlight is a recently discovered letter written by Francis Marion himself.

Prince George Winyah Episcopal Church

It's seen better days—the British partially burned it during the Revolution—but Prince George Winyah Episcopal Church (301 Broad St., 843/546-4358, www.pgwinyah.org,

THE SWAMP FOX AND THE COMING OF GUERRILLA WARFARE

I have it from good authority, that this great soldier, at his birth, was not larger than a New England lobster, and might easily enough have been put into a quart pot.

Peter Horry,
who fought with Francis Marion

Short, bowlegged, and moody, Francis Marion was as far away from the template of the dashing war hero as his tactics were from the storybook exploits of military literature. The father of modern guerrilla warfare was born an unimpressively small and sickly baby, the youngest of seven, somewhere in Berkeley County, South Carolina in 1732 to hardworking French Huguenot parents. Soon his family would move near Georgetown on the coast, and the teenage Marion became enamored with the sea. While his infatuation with maritime life lasted exactly one voyage – a whale rammed and sank his ship – a taste for adventure remained.

During the French and Indian War, Marion fought local Cherokees, and revisionist historians would later revile the enthusiasm he showed in this venture. But Marion's own words show a more conflicted character, as shown by his reaction to an order to burn Cherokees out of their homes.

"Some of our men seemed to enjoy this cruel work, laughing very heartily at the curling flames, as they mounted loud crackling over the tops of the huts. But to me it appeared a shocking sight. Poor creatures! thought I, we

surely need not grudge you such miserable habitations."

While the irregular tactics Marion learned fighting the Cherokee would come in handy during the Revolution, his first experience in that conflict was in more textbook engagements, such as the defenses of Fort Moultrie and Fort Sullivan and the siege of Savannah. But with the fall of Charleston in 1780, a vengeful Marion and his ragged band of volunteer fighters – who unusually for the time included African Americans – vanished into the bogs of the Pee Dee and took up a different way of warfare: ambush and retreat, harass and vanish. In a foreshadowing of the revolutionary movements of the 20th century, "Marion's Men" provisioned themselves with food and supplies from a sympathetic local populace, offering receipts for reimbursement after the war.

Astride small, agile mounts called "Marsh Tackies," descendants of horses originally left by the Spanish, the Patriots rode where bigger British cavalry horses balked. Marion's nocturnal cunning and his superior intelligence network frustrated the British army and their Loyalist supporters to no end, leading to his nickname the "Swamp Fox."

British Col. Banastre Tarleton, himself known as "The Butcher" for atrocities toward civilians, was dispatched to neutralize Marion. The savage cat-and-mouse game between the two formed the basis for the storyline of Mel

---

Mon.–Fri. 11:30 A.M.–4:30 P.M., services Sun. 8 A.M., 9 A.M., 11 A.M.) is still a fine example of the Anglican tradition of the Lowcountry rice culture. First built in 1750 out of ballastones (the parish itself dates from substantially earlier, in 1721) the sanctuary features classic box pews, expert stained glass, and ornate woodwork on the inside. The bell tower dates from 1824.

One of the oldest churches in continuous use in North America, Prince George is certainly worth preserving. The parish has formed

its own nonprofit, The Preservation Trust for Historic Prince George Winyah Church (843/546-4358), to raise funds and direct conservation efforts.

Hopsewee Plantation

Beautiful in an understated way, Hopsewee Plantation (494 Hopsewee Rd., 843/546-7891, www.hopsewee.com, Mon.–Fri. 10 A.M.–4 P.M. Feb.–Nov., appointment only Nov.–Jan., $15 adults, $7.50 ages 5–17, under 5 free) on the

Gibson's 2000 film *The Patriot* (Gibson's character was reportedly a composite of Marion and several other South Carolina irregulars). Filmed entirely in South Carolina – including at Middleton Plantation, Cypress Gardens, and Historic Brattonsville – *The Patriot* is far from an exact chronicle. But it does accurately portray the nature of the war in the Southern theater, in which quarter was rarely asked or given, and little distinction was made between combatant and civilian.

While certainly the most famous, the Swamp Fox was merely first among equals in a veritable menagerie of hit-and-run fighters. Thomas Sumter, a Virginian by birth, became known as "The Carolina Gamecock" for his ferocity on the battlefield. Andrew Pickens, "The Wizard Owl," and his militiamen played a key role in the Battle of Cowpens in the Upstate.

After the war, Marion served in elective office, married, and settled down at his Pine Bluff Plantation, now submerged under the lake which bears his name. He died in 1795 at the age of 63, peaceful at last.

© JIM MOREKIS

Francis Marion monument at the State House

MYRTLE BEACH

Santee River 12 miles south of Georgetown was the birthplace of Thomas Lynch, Jr., one of South Carolina's signers of the Declaration of Independence. Some key archaeological work is going on at the former slave village on this old indigo plantation; you can visit two of the original slave cabins on your tour.

While not as grand as many other Lowcountry plantation homes, the 1740 main house is a masterpiece of colonial architecture and all the more impressive because it's very nearly original, the black cypress exterior largely intact. The focus here is on preservation, not restoration.

The home and its surrounding plantation were owned by the wealthy planter Thomas Lynch, one of South Carolina's original delegates to the First Continental Congress. While deliberating in Philadelphia in 1776, Lynch suffered a severe stroke. His son, Thomas Jr., asked for leave from the South Carolina militia in order to tend to his ailing father. The request was denied, but the state legislature intervened and named the 26-year-old son as a delegate to the Continental Congress so he could join his father in Philly. And that's how the Lynches became the only father-son team of signers of the Declaration of Independence. (Or in spirit, anyway. There's an empty signature line on the original Declaration between South Carolina's Edward Rutledge and the younger Lynch; the elder Lynch, who would die shortly afterward, was physically unable to sign his name.)

Unusually, this home remains in private hands, and as such has a more lived-in feel than other house museums of its type. There's a fairly active calendar of events throughout the year, including sweetgrass basket-weaving classes in the basement. Check the website for more specific info.

(Hampton Plantation

Tucked away three miles off U.S. 17 on the South Santee River is Hampton Plantation State Historic Site (1950 Rutledge Rd., 843/546-9361, www.southcarolinaparks.com,

house hours Tues.–Sun. noon–4 P.M. Mar.–Oct., Thurs.–Sun. noon–4 P.M. Nov.–Feb., $4 ages 16 and over, $3 ages 6–15, under 6 free). This Georgian gem, one of the grandest of antebellum Lowcountry homes, hosted George Washington in 1791. It was also the home of South Carolina poet laureate Archibald Rutledge, who sold it to the state in 1971. Because it's now a state-run project, admission fees are significantly lower than for most of the private plantation homes in the area.

Hampton's pedigree is a virtual who's-who of great South Carolina family names. In addition to the aforementioned Rutledges, the Pinckneys and the Horries also called this home at one time or another.

The imposing antebellum main house, circa 1735, is magnificent both inside and out, with some of the rooms remaining unfurnished to better explain the architecture. The grounds are gorgeous as well, overflowing with live oaks, azaleas, and camellias. If you want to skip the house tour, your visit is free (the grounds are open daily 9 A.M.–6 P.M.). A two-mile nature

© JIM MOREKIS

Hampton Plantation

© JIM MOREKIS

According to legend, George Washington saved this oak tree from being cut down at Hampton Plantation.

MYRTLE BEACH

trail takes you around one of the original rice fields on Wambaw Creek.

Hobcaw Barony

Once a plantation, then a winter home for a Wall Street investor, and now an environmental education center, Hobcaw Barony (22 Hobcaw Rd., 843/546-4623, www.hobcaw barony.org, hours and prices vary) is one of the more unusual stories of the Lowcountry. Its name comes from a Native American word meaning "between the waters," an allusion to its location on the Waccamaw Neck, the beginnings of the Grand Strand itself. By 1718 the surrounding land comprised various rice plantations, among South Carolina's earliest, staying in operation through the end of the 1800s.

Hobcaw entered its modern period when 11 of the former plantations were purchased *en masse* in 1905 by Wall Street investor Bernard Baruch, a South Carolina native who wanted a winter residence to escape the brutal

Manhattan winters. Presidents and prime ministers came to hunt and relax on its nearly 18,000 acres.

Fifty years later Baruch died, and his progressive-minded daughter Belle took over, immediately wanting to open the grounds for university and scientific research. Still privately-owned by the Belle W. Baruch Foundation, much of Hobcaw Barony is open only to researchers, but the **Hobcaw Barony Discovery Center** (843/546-4623, www.hobcawbarony .org, Mon.–Fri. 9 A.M.–5 P.M., free) has various exhibits on local history and culture, including Native American artifacts and a modest but fun aquarium with a touch tank.

To experience the rest of Hobcaw Barony, you must take one of the various themed, guided tours (call for times and days). The basic Hobcaw tour ($20) takes you on a three-hour van ride all around the grounds, including the main Hobcaw House, historic stables, and the old slave quarters, with an emphasis on the natural as well as human history of the area. Other special tours include "Birding on the Barony" ($30), "Christmas in the Quarters" ($20), and a catch-and-release fly-fishing tour ($250) of local waters.

Georgetown Lighthouse

While you can't access the state-owned Georgetown Lighthouse, you can indeed take a trip to the beach on North Island on which the lighthouse stands. The 1811 structure, repaired after heavy damage in the Civil War, is still an active beacon, though entirely automated.

North Island was part of lands bequeathed to the state by former Boston Red Sox owner Tom Yawkey. North Island is now part of a wildlife preserve bearing Yawkey's name. In 2001, the Georgetown Lighthouse was added to the preserve, and it's also on the National Register of Historic Places.

Tours and Cruises

One of the most sought-after tour tickets in the Georgetown area is for the annual **Plantation Home Tour** (843/545-8291). Sponsored by the Episcopal Church Women of Prince George

MYRTLE BEACH

BROAD STREET TO WALL STREET: THE STORY OF BERNARD BARUCH

He became one of America's most influential men and a world-famous advisor to presidents during both world wars, but Bernard Baruch never strayed far in spirit from his South Carolina home.

Born to German-Jewish parents in the town of Camden, near Columbia, Baruch was born a mere five years after the end of the Civil War. Ironically, his father emigrated from Prussia to avoid the draft, but soon after arrival in America, found himself a surgeon on Robert E. Lee's staff.

Educated in New York City, Baruch there gained a love of finance and a taste for the high life. By age 30 he had become so wealthy playing the market that he was able to buy a seat on the New York Stock Exchange. It was during this phase of his life that he purchased the 18,000-acre Hobcaw Barony near Georgetown, a conglomeration of several former rice plantations, which became his hunting retreat, a hallowed place of solitude where no phones were allowed.

Baruch's prowess in the realm of high finance led him to a post as advisor to President Woodrow Wilson (perhaps influencing the selection was the whopping $50,000 contribution Baruch gave to Wilson's 1914 campaign, an enormous – and now quite illegal – sum for that time). Required to divest his funds

and give up his stock exchange seat, Baruch turned his aggressive financier's mind to a larger playing field. A sort of economic czar for the Wilson administration, he would play a key role in mobilizing American industry for the war effort, turning what had been a largely agrarian, rural society into a modern manufacturing juggernaut.

Under President Franklin D. Roosevelt, Baruch was a key member of the New Deal's National Recovery Administration and favored a centralized (some said heavy-handed) approach to organizing the national economy. While this served him well during the New Deal and World War II, his often-idealistic approach – which envisioned a key role of the United States as an enforcer of nuclear nonproliferation – fell out of favor with the Truman administration's *realpolitik*. Still, Baruch would leave his mark on the post-war era as well: he was the first to coin the phrase "Cold War," in a speech in 1947.

Indeed, Baruch was always a colorful and succinct communicator, no doubt a legacy of his Southern boyhood. He is said to have originated the witticism "If all you have is a hammer, everything looks like a nail." Other great one-liners of his include "Millions saw the apple fall, but only Newton asked why," and "Old age is always 15 years older than I am."

Baruch died in New York City in June 1965,

Winyah Parish, this event, generally happening the first week in April, brings visitors onto many local private antebellum estates that are not open to the public at any other time. Each ticket is for either the Friday or Saturday tour, both of which feature a different set of homes. Tickets include a tea at the Winyah Indigo Society Hall each afternoon.

For a standard downtown tour, get on one of the blue and white trams of **Swamp Fox Historic District Tours** (1001 Front St., 843/527-6469), which leave daily on the hour starting at 10 A.M. near the Harborwalk.

The best walking tour of Georgetown is

Miss Nell's Tours (843/546-3975, Tues. and Thurs. 10:30 A.M. and 2:30 P.M., other times by appointment). Leaving from the Harborwalk Bookstore (723 Front St.), Miss Nell, who's been doing this for over 20 years, takes you on a delightful trek through Georgetown's charming downtown waterfront.

Water dominates life in this region, and that may just be the best way to enjoy it. One of the more interesting local water-borne tours is on board the *Jolly Rover* and *Carolina Rover* (735 Front St., 843/546-8822, www.rovertours.com, Mon.–Sat., times and prices vary). The former is an honest-to-goodness

but he spent all that May down in South Carolina at Hobcaw Barony. By that time his daughter Belle had purchased most of Hobcaw and would eventually deed it to a foundation in her name, administered by the University of South Carolina and Clemson University.

Baruch's boyhood home in Camden is no more, but is commemorated with a marker on Broad Street. You can also enjoy the beauty and tranquility of **Hobcaw Barony** (22 Hobcaw Rd., 843/546-4623, www.hobcawbarony.org, hours and prices vary) for yourself.

Bernard Baruch grew up in Camden before purchasing Hobcaw Barony.

tall ship which takes you on a two-hour tour of beautiful Winyah Bay and the Intracoastal Waterway, all courtesy of a crew in period dress. The latter takes you on a three-hour ecotour to nearby North Island, site of the historic Georgetown Lighthouse. You can't tour the Lighthouse itself, but you can get pretty darn close to it on this tour. The always-entertaining **Cap'n Sandy's Tours** (343 Ida Dr., 843/527-4106) also takes you to North Island in the shadow of the Lighthouse; call for times and rates.

For a more intense maritime ecotourism experience, contact **Black River Outdoors Center and**

Expeditions (21 Garden Ave., 843/546-4840, www.blackriveroutdoors.com). Their stock-in-trade is a nice half-day tour by kayak ($55 adults, $35 ages 12 and under), generally including creeks in and around Huntington Beach and through the fascinating matrix of blackwater/cypress swamps that once comprised the rice kingdom of Georgetown and vicinity. They also offer a harbor tour for $35 per person.

For a much simpler, less nature-oriented water tour, try **Cap'n Rod's Lowcountry Tours** (843/477-0287, www.lowcountrytours .com). Rod's pontoon boat is on the Harborwalk just behind the Rice Museum. A three-hour

"Plantation River Tour," leaving Mon.–Sat. at 10 A.M., runs $25 for adults and $20 children.

ENTERTAINMENT AND EVENTS

The **Winyah Bay Heritage Festival** (632 Prince St., 843/833-9919, www.winyahbay .org, free) happens each January in various venues and benefits the local historical society. The focus is on wooden decoys and waterfowl paintings, similar to Charleston's well-known Southeast Wildlife Exposition.

Each October brings the delightful **Wooden Boat Show** (843/545-0015, www.woodenboat show.com, free) to the waterfront, a 20-year-old celebration of, you guessed it, wooden boats. These aren't toys but the real thing—sleek, classic, and beautiful in the water. There are kid's activities, canoe-making demonstrations, a boat contest, and the highlight, a boatbuilding challenge involving two teams working to build a skiff in four hours.

SHOPPING

As you might expect, the bulk of shopping opportunities in Georgetown are down on the waterfront, chiefly at **The Shoppes on Front Street** (717-A Front St., 843/527-0066), the umbrella name for an association of downtown merchants. Highlights include **Harborwalk Books** (723 Front St., 843/546-8212, www.harborwalkbooks.com) and the children's boutique **Doodlebugs** (721 Front St., 843/546-6858).

SPORTS AND RECREATION
Kayaking and Canoeing

Kayakers and canoeists will find a lot to do in the Georgetown area, being the confluence of five rivers and the Atlantic Ocean.

A good trip for more advanced paddlers is to go out **Winyah Bay** to undeveloped North Island. With advance permission from the state Department of Natural Resources (803/734-3888), you can camp there. Any paddling in Winyah Bay is nice, though.

Another long trip is on the nine-mile, blackwater **Wambaw Creek Wilderness Canoe Trail** in the Francis Marion National Forest,

which takes you through some beautiful cypress and tupelo habitats. Launch sites are at the Wambaw Creek Boat Ramp and a bridge landing. Other good trips in the national forest are on the Santee River and Echaw Creek.

For rentals and guided tours, contact **Nature Adventures Outfitters** (800/673-0679), which runs daylong paddles at about $85 per person, and **Black River Outdoors Center and Expeditions** (21 Garden Ave., 843/546-4840, www.blackriveroutdoors.com), which runs a good half-day tour ($55 adults, $35 ages 12 and under). For those who want to explore the intricate matrix of creeks and tidal canals that made up the Georgetown rice plantation empire, a guided tour is essential.

Occasional kayak ecotours leave from the Hobcaw Barony Discovery Center (843/546-4623, www.hobcawbarony.org, Mon.–Fri. 9 A.M.–5 P.M., $50) under the auspices of the **North Inlet Winyah Bay National Estuarine Research Reserve** (843/546-6219, www.northinlet.sc.edu).

Fishing

Inshore saltwater fishing is big here, mostly red drum and sea trout. For the full-on Georgetown fishing experience, contact **Delta Guide Service** (843/546-3645, www.delta guideservice.com), which charges about $350 a day for a fishing charter along the coast.

Hiking

The Francis Marion National Forest (www .fs.fed.us) hosts a number of great hiking opportunities, chief among them the Swamp Fox passage of the **Palmetto Trail** (www.palmetto conservation.org). This 47-mile route winds through longleaf pine forests, cypress swamps, bottomland hardwood swamps, and various bogs much of the way along an old logging rail bed. The main entrance to the trail is near Steed Creek Road off U.S. 17. The entrance is clearly marked on the west side of the highway.

Another way to access the Swamp Fox passage is at **Buck Hall Recreation Area** (843/887-3257) on the Intracoastal Waterway.

This actually marks the trailhead of the "Awendaw Connector" of that part of the Palmetto Trail, a more maritime environment. Another trailhead from which to explore Francis Marion hiking trails is further down U.S. 17 at the **Sewee Visitor Center** (5821 U.S. 17, 843/928-3368, www.fws.gov/sewee center, Tues.–Sat. 9 A.M.–5 P.M.).

Golf
The closest really good links to Georgetown are the courses of the **Waccamaw Golf Trail** (www.waccamawgolftrail.com) a short drive north on U.S. 17. The best public course close to Georgetown is the **Wedgefield Plantation Golf Club** (129 Clubhouse Lane, 843/546-8587, www.wedgefield.com, green fees $69), on the grounds of an old rice plantation on the Black River about four miles west of town. A famous local ghost story revolves around Wedgefield; allegedly the ghost of a British soldier, beheaded with a single slash from one of Francis Marion's men, still wanders the grounds.

ACCOMMODATIONS
Under $150
Close to the historic district is **Quality Inn & Suites** (210 Church St., 843/546-5656, www .qualityinn.com, $90–140), which has an outdoor pool and free breakfast.

On the north side of town on U.S. 17 you'll find the **Hampton Inn Georgetown-Marina** (420 Marina Dr., 843/545-5000, www.hampton inn.com, $140–170), which also offers a pool and complimentary breakfast.

$150-300
By far the most impressive lodging near Georgetown—and indeed among the most impressive in the Southeast—is **Mansfield Plantation** (1776 Mansfield Rd., 843/546-6961, www.mansfieldplantation .com, $150–200), a bona fide antebellum estate dating from a king's grant in 1718. It's so evocative and so authentic that Mel Gibson shot part of his film *The Patriot* there, and renovation was recently completed on a historic slave chapel and cabin.

As is typical of the Georgetown area, you will find the prices almost ridiculously low for this unique experience on this historic 1,000-acre tract, with gardens, trails, and free bicycle use. Pets can even stay for an extra $20 a day. As for you, you can stay in one of nine rooms, situated in three guest houses on the grounds, each one within easy walking distance of the public areas in the main house, such as the 16-seat dining room.

With the recent closing of the longtime favorite B&B, the Dupre House, it's left to another B&B, the **Harbor House** (15 Cannon St., 843/546-6532, www.harborhousebb.com, $159–189), to carry on the tradition. Its four riverfront suites are maybe a little more modernized than you'd expect in this Georgian home, with eight fireplaces and heart-of-pine floors. But step into either the living room or the dining room, where you'll eat their sumptuous breakfasts, and it's like it's 1850 again.

FOOD
Don't be fooled by Georgetown's small size—there's often a wait for a table at the better restaurants.

Breakfast and Brunch
The *Southern Living*–recommended **Thomas Cafe** (703-A Front St., 843/546-7776, www .thomascafe.com, Mon.–Sat. 7 A.M.–2 P.M., $10–20) offers some awesome omelettes and pancakes, in addition to more Lowcountry-flavored dishes such as crawfish cake sandwiches and fried green tomatoes.

Classic Southern
Georgetown's most well-known fine-dining establishment is **The Rice Paddy** (732 Front St., 843/546-2021, www.ricepaddyrestaurant.com, Mon.–Sat. 11:30 A.M.–2 P.M. lunch, 6–10 P.M. dinner, $20–30), with the name implying not an Asian menu but rather a nod to the town's Lowcountry culture. Set inside a former bank building, the interior is a bit more modern than you might expect. Seafood is strong here, but they do a mean Veal Scallopini and rack of lamb as well. Reservations are highly recommended.

The **Goat Island Grill** (719 Front St., 843/527-3500, www.goatislandgrill.com, Mon.–Thurs. 11 A.M.–9 P.M., Fri.–Sat. 11 A.M.–10 P.M., Sun. noon–8 P.M., $14–21) is another of those great Georgetown spots that combines an upscale interior with a casual attitude. The signature dish here is a sampler of sorts, the Big G.I.G., including flounder, shrimp, scallops and a crab cake ($21). But they have some intriguing sandwiches as well, including a flounder hoagie and an oyster po'boy. A big advantage of the Goat Island Grill is that it's open on Sundays, when many local spots are closed.

Coffee, Tea, and Sweets
The **Harvest Moon** (801 Front St., 843/527-4110, Mon.–Thurs. 10 A.M.–7 P.M., Fri.–Sat. 10 A.M.–10 P.M., Sun. 11 A.M.–7 P.M.) is a fun place to stop for a cup of joe, in addition to offering sweet treats such as ice cream and yogurt.

Seafood
Find the best shrimp and grits in town at **The River Room** (801 Front St., 843/527-4110, www.riverroomgeorgetown.com, Mon.–Sat. 11:30 A.M.–2:30 P.M., 5–10 P.M., $15–25), which combines a gourmet attitude in the kitchen with a casual attitude on the floor. However, dishes like the herb-encrusted grouper or their signature crab cakes taste like fine dining all the way. No reservations are accepted, and dress is casual. Literally right on the waterfront, the dining room in this former hardware store extends 50 feet over the Sampit River, adjacent to a public dock where many diners arrive by boat. There's even a large aquarium inside to complete the atmosphere.

Over at the Georgetown Marina with great views of the river is **Lands End** (444 Marina Dr., 843/527-1376, Mon.–Fri. 11 A.M.–2:30 P.M., 5–9:30 P.M., Sat. 5–9:30 P.M., Sun. 11 A.M.–2:30 P.M., $15–25), which serves good Southern-style seafood and prime rib in a relaxing atmosphere.

INFORMATION AND SERVICES
In the historic waterfront area you'll find the **Georgetown County Chamber of Commerce and Visitor Center** (531 Front St., 843/546-8436, www.georgetown chamber.com).

The **Georgetown Memorial Hospital** (606 Black River Rd., 843/527-7000, www .georgetownhospitalsystem.org) is the main medical center in the area, and this 131-bed institution is in the midst of a proposed expansion and relocation.

If you need law enforcement help, call the **Georgetown Police** (2222 Highmarket St., 843/545-4300, www.cityofgeorgetownsc.com). In emergencies call 911.

The newspaper of record in Georgetown is the *Georgetown Times* (www.gtowntimes .com). An "unofficial visitor's guide" to the town is *Harborwalk* (www.theharborwalk.com), a monthly newsletter geared towards tourists.

For your postal needs, visit the main branch of the **U.S. Postal Service** (1101 Charlotte St., 800/275-8777, Mon.–Fri. 9 A.M.–5 P.M., Sat. 10 A.M.–noon) in Georgetown.

GETTING THERE AND AROUND
Georgetown is at the extreme southern tip of the Grand Strand, accessible by U.S. 17 from the east and south and U.S. 521 (Highmarket Street in town) from the west. Very centrally located for a tour of the coast, it's about an hour north of Charleston and slightly less than that from Myrtle Beach.

Though there's no public transportation to speak of in Georgetown, its small size makes touring fairly simple. Metered parking is available downtown.

CHARLESTON

Charleston boasts so many American "firsts" that it's almost a cliché to point them out: first museum, first theater, first public library, first municipal college, first golf club, first historic preservation ordinance, and the list goes on and on.

But for the majority of visitors, the most important Charleston first is its perennial ranking at the top of the late Marjabelle Young Stewart's annual list for "Most Mannerly City in America." (Charleston has won the award so many times that Stewart's successor at the Charleston School of Protocol and Etiquette, Cindy Grosso, has retired the city from the competition.) This is a city that takes civic harmony so seriously that it boasts the country's only "Livability Court," a binding legal proceeding that meets regularly to enforce local quality-of-life ordinances.

Everyone who spends time in Charleston comes away with a story to tell about the locals' courtesy and hospitality, and I'm sure you'll be no exception. Mine came while walking through the French Quarter admiring a handsome old single house on Church Street, one of the few that survived the fire of 1775. To my surprise, the lady chatting with a friend nearby turned out to be the homeowner. Noticing my interest in her house, she invited me in, a total stranger, to check out the progress of her renovation.

To some eyes, Charleston's hospitable nature has bordered on licentiousness. From its earliest days the city gained a reputation for

© JIM MOREKIS

HIGHLIGHTS

The Battery: Tranquil surroundings combine with beautiful views of Charleston Harbor, key historical points in the Civil War, and amazing mansions (page 176).

Rainbow Row: Painted in warm pastels, these old merchant homes near the cobblestoned waterfront take you on a journey to Charleston's antebellum heyday (page 179).

Fort Sumter: Take the ferry to this historic place where the Civil War began and take in the gorgeous views along the way (page 186).

St. Philip's Episcopal Church: A sublimely beautiful sanctuary and two historic graveyards await you in the heart of the evocative French Quarter (page 187).

Aiken-Rhett House: There are certainly more ostentatious house museums in Charleston, but none that provide such a

virtually intact glimpse into real antebellum life (page 198).

Drayton Hall: Don't miss Charleston's oldest surviving plantation home and one of America's best examples of professional historic preservation (page 202).

Middleton Place: Wander in and marvel at one of the world's most beautifully landscaped gardens – and the first in North America (page 205).

CSS *Hunley*: Newly ensconced for public viewing in its special preservation tank, the first submarine to sink a ship in battle is a moving example of bravery and sacrifice (page 208).

Edisto Beach State Park: Relax at this quiet, friendly, and relatively undeveloped Sea Island, a mecca for shell collectors. (page 264).

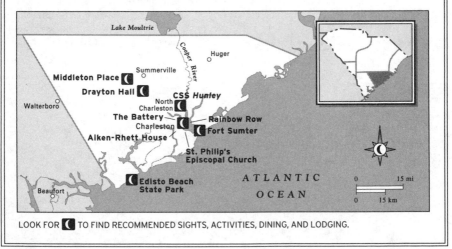

LOOK FOR 【 TO FIND RECOMMENDED SIGHTS, ACTIVITIES, DINING, AND LODGING.

indulging in all kinds of vice. (The city's nickname, "The Holy City," derives from the skyline's abundance of church steeples rather than any excess of piety among its citizens.) The old drinking clubs are gone, and the yearly bacchanal of Race Week—in which personal fortunes were won or lost in seconds—is but a distant memory. But that hedonistic legacy is alive and well today in Charleston; the city is full of lovers of strong drink and serious foodies, with every weekend night finding downtown packed with partiers, diners, and show-goers.

Don't mistake the Holy City's charm and *joie de vivre* for weakness, however. That would be a serious mistake, for within Charleston's velvet glove has always been an iron fist. This is where the colonists scored their first clear victory over the British during the Revolution (yet another Charleston first). This is the place where the Civil War began, and which stoically endured one of the longest sieges in modern warfare during that conflict. This is the city that survived the East Coast's

worst earthquake in 1886 and one of its worst hurricanes a century later.

Despite its fun-loving reputation, a martial spirit is never far from the surface in Charleston, from the Citadel military college along the Ashley River, to the aircraft carrier *Yorktown* moored at Patriots Point across the harbor, to the cannonballs and mortars that children climb on at the Battery, and even to the occasional tour guide in Confederate garb.

Some of the nation's most progressive urban activity is going on in Charleston despite its often-deserved reputation for conservatism, from the renovation of the old Navy Yard in North Charleston (one of the nation's largest urban redevelopment projects), to impressive green start-ups, to any number of cutting-edge, sustainable residential developments. Charleston's a leader in conservation as well, with groups like the Lowcountry Open Land Trust and the Coastal Conservation League setting an example for the entire Southeast in how to bring environmental organizations and

© JIM MOREKIS

a typically grand home on Charleston's Battery

CHARLESTON

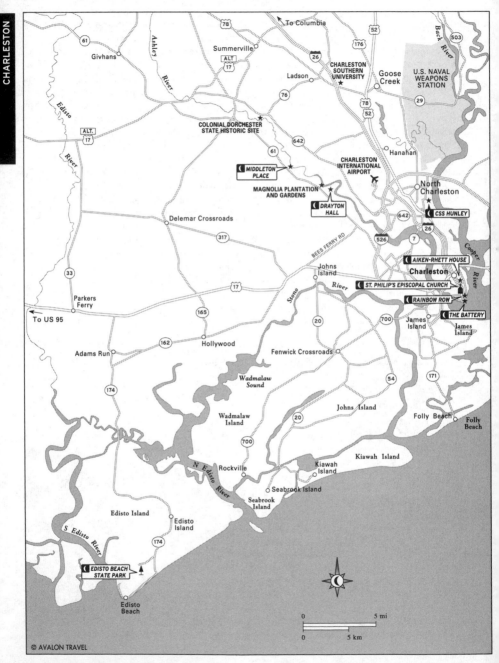

© AVALON TRAVEL

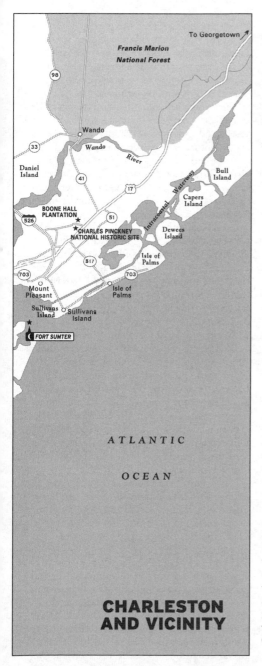

Francis Marion
National Forest

To Georgetown

98

Wando

33

Wando

River

Daniel
Island

41

17

Bull
Island

Capers
Island

BOONE HALL
PLANTATION

526

51

★CHARLES PINCKNEY
NATIONAL HISTORIC SITE

Dewees
Island

Intracoastal Waterway

Isle of
Palms

51?

703

703

Mount
Pleasant

Isle of
Palms

Sullivans
Island

Sullivans
Island

★
◖ FORT SUMTER

ATLANTIC

OCEAN

**CHARLESTON
AND VICINITY**

the business community together to preserve the area's beauty and ecosystem.

While many visitors come to see the Charleston of Rhett Butler and Pat Conroy—finding it and then some, of course—they leave impressed by the diversity of Charlestonian life. It's a surprisingly cosmopolitan mix of students, professionals, and longtime inhabitants—who discuss the finer points of Civil War history as if it were last year, party on Saturday night like there's no tomorrow, and go to church on Sunday morning dressed in their finest.

But don't be deceived by these history-minded people. Under the carefully honed tradition and the ever-present ancestor worship, Charleston possesses a vitality of vision that is irrepressibly practical and forward-looking.

HISTORY

Unlike so many of England's colonies in America that were based on freedom from religious persecution, Carolina was strictly a commercial venture from the beginning. The tenure of the Lords Proprietors—the eight English aristocrats who literally owned the colony—began in 1670 when the aptly named *Carolina* finished its journey to Albemarle Creek on the west bank of the Ashley River.

Those first colonists would set up a small fortification called Charles Town, named for Charles II, the first monarch of the Restoration. In a year they'd be joined by the first colonists from the prosperous but overcrowded British colony of Barbados, who brought a unique Caribbean sensibility that exists in Charleston to this day.

Finding the first Charles Town unhealthy, not very fertile, and vulnerable to attack from Native Americans and Spanish, they moved to the peninsula and down to "Oyster Point," what Charlestonians now call White Point Gardens. Just above Oyster Point they set up a walled town, bounded by modern-day Water Street to the south (then a marshy creek, as the name indicates), Meeting Street to the west, Cumberland Street to the north, and the Cooper River on the east.

Growing prosperous as a trading center for

deerskin from the great American interior, Charles Town came into its own after two nearly concurrent events in the early 1700s: the decisive victory of a combined force of Carolinians and Native American allies against the fierce Yamasee tribe, and the final eradication of the ominous pirate threat in the deaths of Blackbeard and Stede Bonnet.

Flushed with a new spirit of independence, Charles Town threw off the control of the anemic, disengaged Lords Proprietors, tore down the old defensive walls, and was reborn as simply Charleston—outward-looking, expansive, and increasingly cosmopolitan. With safety from hostile incursion came the time of the great rice and indigo plantations. Springing up all along the Ashley River soon after the introduction of the crops, they turned the labor and expertise of imported Africans into enormous profit for their owners. However, the planters preferred the pleasures and sea breezes of Charleston, and gradually summer homes became year-round residences.

It was during this Colonial era that the indelible marks of Charlestonian character were stamped: a hedonistic aristocracy combining a love of carousing with a love of the arts; a code of chivalry meant both to reflect a genteel spirit and reinforce the social order; and, ominously, an ever-increasing reliance on slave labor.

As the storm clouds of civil war gathered in the early 1800s, the majority of Charleston's population was of African descent, and the city was the main importation point for the transatlantic slave trade to the United States. The worst fears of white Charlestonians seemed confirmed during the alleged plot by slave leader Denmark Vesey in the early 1820s to start a rebellion. The Lowcountry's reliance on slave labor put it front and center in the coming national confrontation over abolition, which came to a head literally and figuratively in the bombardment of Fort Sumter in Charleston Harbor in April 1861.

By war's end, not only did the city lay in ruins—mostly from a disastrous fire in 1861, as well as from a 545-day Union siege—so did its way of life. Pillaged and burned by northern troops and freed slaves, the great plantations along the Ashley became the sites of the first strip mining in America, as poverty-stricken owners scraped away the layer of phosphate under the topsoil to sell—perhaps with a certain poetic justice—as fertilizer.

The Holy City didn't really wake up until the great "Charleston Renaissance" of the 1920s and '30s, when the city rediscovered art, literature, and music in the form of jazz and the world-famous Charleston dance. This also was the time that the world rediscovered Charleston. In the 1920s, George Gershwin read local author Dubose Heyward's novel *Porgy* and decided to write a score around the story. Along with lyrics by Ira Gershwin, the three men's collaboration became the first American opera, *Porgy and Bess,* which debuted in New York in 1935. It was also during this time that a new appreciation for Charleston's history sprang up, as the local Preservation Society spearheaded the nation's first historic preservation ordinance.

World War II brought the same economic boom that came to much of the South in those times, most notably with an expansion of the Navy Yard and the addition of an Air Force base. By the 1950s, the automobile suburb and a thirst for "progress" claimed so many historic buildings that the inevitable backlash came with the formation of the Historic Charleston Foundation, which continues to lead the fight to keep intact the Holy City's architectural legacy.

Civil rights began coming to Charleston in earnest with a landmark suit to integrate the Charleston Municipal Golf Course, an effort which concluded in 1960 when Mayor Palmer Gaillard chose not to fight with what was clearly a losing legal hand. The mostly nonviolent resolution of years of Jim Crow continued, as a series of lunch counter sit-ins and lawsuits went on peacefully. The biggest battle, however, would be the 100-day strike in 1969 against the Medical University of South Carolina, then, as now, a large employer of African Americans. The strike brought national attention to Charleston's civil rights

CHARLESTON

struggle and ensured that the sacrifices of previous generations would not be in vain.

Charleston's next great renaissance—still ongoing today—came with the redevelopment of downtown and the fostering of the tourism industry under the 30-year-plus tenure of Mayor Joe Riley, during which so much of the current, visitor-friendly infrastructure became part of daily life here. Today, Charleston is completing the transition away from a military and manufacturing base and attracting professionals and artists to town.

PLANNING YOUR TIME

Even if you're just going to confine yourself to the peninsula, I can't imagine spending less than two nights there. You'll want at least half a day for shopping on King Street and a full day for seeing various attractions and museums. Keep in mind that one of Charleston's key sights, Fort Sumter, will take almost half a day to see once you factor in ticketing and boarding time for the ferry out to the fort and back; plan accordingly.

If you have a rental car, there are several great places to visit off the peninsula—especially the plantations along the Ashley. None are very far away and navigation in Charleston is a snap. The farthest site from downtown should take no more than 30 minutes, and because the plantations are roughly adjacent, you can visit all of them in a single day if you get an early start.

While a good time is never far away in Charleston, keep in mind that this is the South and Sundays can get pretty slow. While the finely honed tourist infrastructure here means that there will always be something to do, the selection of open shops and restaurants dwindles on Sundays, though most other attractions keep working hours. But for those of us who love the old city, there's nothing like a Sunday morning in Charleston—church bells ringing, families on their way to worship, a beguiling slowness in the air, perhaps spiced with the anticipation of a particular Charleston specialty—a hearty and delicious Sunday brunch.

Technically speaking, there are two high seasons in Charleston: mid-March through the

COURTESY OF CHARLESTON AREA CVB, WWW.EXPLORECHARLESTON.COM

A carriage ride is a great way to enjoy downtown Charleston.

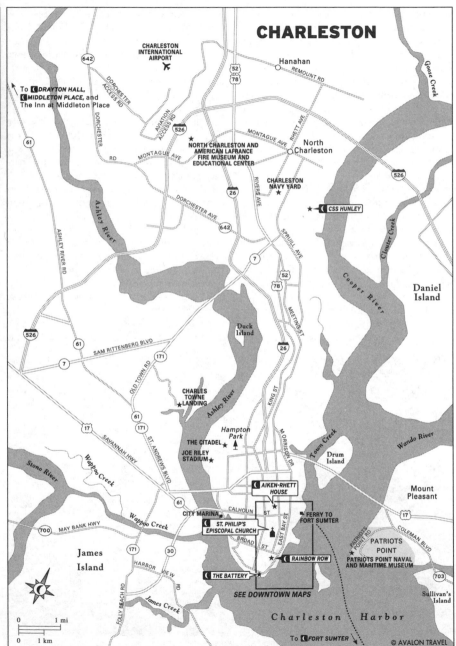

CHARLESTON

CHARLESTON
INTERNATIONAL
AIRPORT

Hanahan

REMOUNT RD

Goose Creek

To ❰DRAYTON HALL,
❰MIDDLETON PLACE, and
The Inn at Middleton Place

DORCHESTER ACCESS RD

AVIATION ACCESS RD

MONTAGUE AVE

RHETT AVE

NORTH CHARLESTON AND
AMERICAN LAFRANCE
FIRE MUSEUM AND
EDUCATIONAL CENTER

North
Charleston

DORCHESTER RD

MONTAGUE AVE

DORCHESTER AVE

RIVERS AVE

CHARLESTON
NAVY YARD

Ashley River

ASHLEY RIVER RD

★ ❰ CSS HUNLEY

SPRUILL AVE

Clouter Creek

Cooper River

Daniel
Island

MEETING ST

Duck
Island

SAM RITTENBERG BLVD

OLD TOWN RD

KING ST

Ashley River

CHARLES
TOWNE
★ LANDING

Hampton
Park

Wando River

SAVANNAH HWY

ST. ANDREWS BLVD

THE CITADEL ★
JOE RILEY
STADIUM ★

M MORRISON DR

Town Creek

Drum
Island

Stono River

Wappoo Creek

Mount
Pleasant

MAY BANK HWY

Wappoo Creek

CITY MARINA

CALHOUN ST

❰ AIKEN-RHETT
HOUSE
★

EAST BAY ST

■ FERRY TO
FORT SUMTER

PATRIOTS
POINT RD

PATRIOTS
POINT

James
Island

HARBOR VIEW RD

❰ ST. PHILIP'S
EPISCOPAL CHURCH

BROAD ST

★ ❰ RAINBOW ROW

PATRIOTS POINT NAVAL
AND MARITIME MUSEUM

COLEMAN BLVD

FOLLY BEACH RD

❰ THE BATTERY

James Creek

SEE DOWNTOWN MAPS

Sullivan's
Island

Charleston Harbor

0   1 mi

0   1 km

To ❰ FORT SUMTER

© AVALON TRAVEL

first half of June, which of course includes the Spoleto Festival; and mid-September through mid-November.

The real issue for most visitors boils down to two questions: How much do you want to spend on accommodations, and in which part of town do you want to stay? Lodging is generally not cheap in Charleston, but because the price differential is not that much between staying on the peninsula and staying on the outskirts, I recommend the peninsula. You'll pay more, but not *that* much more, with the bonus of probably being able to walk to most places you want to see—which, after all, is the best way to enjoy the city.

ORIENTATION

Charleston occupies a peninsula bordered by the Ashley River to the west and the Cooper River to the east, which "come together to form the Atlantic Ocean," according to the haughty phrase once taught to generations of Charleston schoolchildren.

Though the lower tip of the peninsula actually points closer to southeast, that direction is regarded locally as due south, and anything towards the top of the peninsula is considered due north. It's technically incorrect, but there's no use fighting it.

The peninsula is ringed by islands, many of which have become heavily-populated suburbs. Clockwise from the top of the peninsula they are: Daniel Island, Mount Pleasant, Isle of Palms, Sullivan's Island, Morris Island, Folly Island, and James Island. The resort island of Kiawah and the much less-developed Edisto Island are farther south down the coast.

North Charleston is not only a separate municipality, it's also a different state of mind. A sprawling combination of malls, light industry, and lower-income housing, it's known as an area of high crime and poverty, though that's gradually changing.

While Charlestonians would scoff, the truth is that Charleston proper, the "Holy City" itself, has a surprising amount in common with Manhattan. Both are on long spits of land situated roughly north-south. Both were settled originally at the lower end in walled fortifications—Charleston's walls came down in 1718, while Manhattan still has its Wall Street as a reminder. Both cityscapes rely on age-old north-south streets that run nearly the whole length—Charleston's King and Meeting Streets, with only a block between them, and Manhattan's Broadway and Fifth Avenue. And like Manhattan, Charleston also has its own "Museum Mile" just off of a major greenspace, in Charleston's case up near Marion Square—though certainly its offerings are not as expansive as those a short walk from New York's Central Park.

Unfortunately, also like Manhattan, parking is at a premium in downtown Charleston. Luckily the city has many reasonably priced parking garages, which I heartily recommend that you use. But cars should only be used when you have to. Charleston is best enjoyed on foot, both because of its small size and the cozy, meandering nature of its old streets, designed not for cars and tour buses but for boots, horseshoes, and carriage wheels.

Charleston performs a kind of magic with time and space, its compact, walkable scale paradoxically making the city a world unto itself. A new surprise awaits you around every corner. A few short blocks from Meeting Street and its constant bustle of hotel staff preparing for the evening's banquets, you follow narrow streets curling through the old French Quarter until you find yourself at an old cemetery. In a flash you go from new to old as you read the names and dates on the worn tombstones, imagining what life was like in former days. Then you catch a whiff of fresh bread from a nearby artisan bakery, drawing you back into the new again. That's the magic of Charleston.

Charleston is made up of many small neighborhoods, many of them quite old. The boundaries between them are confusing, so your best bet is to simply look at the street signs (signage in general is excellent in Charleston). If you're in a historic neighborhood, such as the French Quarter or Ansonborough, a smaller sign above the street name will indicate that.

Other key terms you'll hear are "the

KNOW YOUR CHARLESTON HOUSES

As architects and historic preservationists have long known, Charleston's homes boast not only a long pedigree, but quite an interesting and unique one as well. Here are some key terms you should be familiar with.

Single House: A direct legacy of the early Barbadian planters among the very first settlers here, the Charleston single house is named for the fact that it's a single room wide – the better to fit deep, narrow downtown lots. The phrase refers to layout, not style, which can range from Georgian to Federal to Greek Revival, or even a combination. Furnished with full-length piazzas on the south side to take advantage of southerly breezes, the single house is perhaps America's first sustainable house design. The house sits lengthwise on the lot, with the main entrance on the side of the house. This of course means that the "backyard" is actually the side yard.

Entry from the street is by a gate on one end of the lower piazza. A typical single house has three floors: a ground floor for business; a main floor for entertaining, living, and dining; and a top floor for sleeping. You can find them everywhere, but Church Street has some great examples, including 90, 92, and 94 Church Street, and the oldest single house in town, the 1730 Robert Brewton House (71 Church St.).

Double House: This layout is two rooms wide with a central hallway and a porched facade facing the street. Double houses often had separate carriage houses, the top floor of which was often reserved for servants' quarters. The Aiken-Rhett and Heyward-Washington houses are good examples of this more affluent, ostentatious design.

Piazza: The long porch or veranda of a single house. There is usually one piazza for

a fine example of a Charleston single house in the French Quarter

© JIM MOREKIS

each floor and with southern exposure so that prevailing winds can sweep the length of the house. The roof of the piazza shades the windows on that side of the house. Room doors are also on the piazza side so that they can be left open if need be. The typical dearth of windows on the north side exemplifies the so-called "northside manner," protecting the privacy of the house next door. Another Caribbean trait via Barbados, piazzas sometimes feature balconies on top.

Charleston Green: This distinctively Charlestonian color – an extremely dark green that looks pitch black in low light or at a casual glance – has its roots in the penurious aftermath of the Civil War. The federal government distributed thousands of gallons of surplus black paint to contribute to reconstruction of the shell-and-fire ravaged peninsula, but Charlestonians were too proud (not to mention too tasteful) to use it as is. So they added the tiniest bit of yellow to each gallon, producing the distinctive, historic color we now know as Charleston Green.

Earthquake Bolt: Structural damage after the 1886 earthquake was so extensive that many buildings were retrofitted with one or more long iron rods from wall to wall to keep the house stable. After installation the rod was then capped at both ends by a "gib plate," which was often disguised with a decorative element such as a lion's head, an S or X shape, or other design. Opinion among preservationists and engineers differs as to the efficacy of the bolts. Earthquake bolts can be seen all over town, but notable examples are at 235 Meeting Street, 198 East Bay Street, 407 King Street, 51 East Battery (rare star design), and 190 East Bay Street is unusual for having both an X and an S plate on the same building.

Joggling Board: This long (10–15 ft.), flexible plank of cypress, palm, or pine with a handle at each end served various recreational purposes for early Charlestonians depending on their age. As babies, they might be gently bounced to sleep. As small children, they might use it as a trampoline. Later, it was a method of courtship, whereby a couple would start out at opposite ends and bounce up and down until they met in the middle. Painted black or Charleston Green, joggling boards have made quite a comeback as decorative furnishings at many local homes.

Carolopolis Award: For over 50 years, the Preservation Society of Charleston has handed out these little black badges, to be mounted near the doorway of the winning home, to local homeowners who have renovated historic properties downtown. On the award you'll see "Carolopolis," the Latinized name of the city; "Condita A.D. 1670," the Latin word for founding with the date of Charleston's inception; and another date referring to when the award was given. Don't try counting them; well over 1,000 Carolopolis Awards have been given out since the Preservation Society came up with the idea in 1953.

Ironwork: Before the mid-19th century, wrought iron was a widely used ornament in Charleston, with the oldest surviving examples going back to the Revolutionary War period. Charleston's best-known blacksmith, Philip Simmons, has made a life's work of continuing the ancient craft of working in wrought iron, and his masterpieces are visible throughout the city, most notably at the Philip Simmons Garden (91 Anson St.), a specially commissioned gate for the Visitors Center (375 Meeting St.), and the Philip Simmons Children's Garden at Josiah Smith Tennent House (corner of Blake and East Bay Sts.). Mass-produced cast iron became more common after the mid 1800s. *Chevaux-de-frise,* an early security device of sorts, comprises an iron bar on top of a wall, through which project some particularly menacing iron spikes. *Chevaux-de-frise* became popular after the Denmark Vesey slave revolt conspiracy of 1822. The best existing example is on the perimeter wall of the Miles Brewton House (27 King St).

Crosstown," the portion of U.S. 17 that goes across the peninsula; "Savannah Highway," the portion of U.S. 17 that traverses "West Ashley," which is the suburb across the Ashley River; "East Cooper," the area across the Cooper River including Mount Pleasant, Isle of Palms, and Daniel and Sullivan's Islands; and "the Neck," up where the peninsula narrows. These are the terms that locals use, and hence what you'll see in this book.

Sights

Though most key sights in Charleston do indeed have some tie to the city's rich history, house museums are only a subset of the attractions here. Charleston's sights are excellently integrated into its built environment, and often the enjoyment of nearby gardens or a lapping river is part of the fun.

SOUTH OF BROAD

As one of the oldest streets in Charleston, the east-west thoroughfare of Broad Street is not only a physical landmark, it's a mental one as well. The first area of the Charleston peninsula to be settled, the area south of Broad Street—often shortened to the mischievous acronym "SOB" by local wags—features older homes, meandering streets (much of them built on "made land" filling in former wharfs), and a distinctly genteel, laid-back feel.

As you'd expect, it also features more affluent residents, sometimes irreverently referred to as "SOB Snobs." This heavily residential area has no nightlife to speak of and gets almost eerily quiet after hours, but rest assured that plenty of people live here.

While I highly recommend just wandering among these narrow streets and marveling at the lovingly restored old homes, keep in mind that almost everything down here is in private hands. Don't wander into a garden or take photos inside a window unless you're invited to do so (and given Charleston's legendary hospitality, that can happen).

◖ The Battery

For many, the Battery (E. Battery St. and Murray Blvd., 843/724-7321, 24 hrs., free) is the single most iconic Charleston spot, drenched in history and boasting dramatic views in all directions. A look to the south gives you the sweeping expanse of the Cooper River, with views of Fort Sumter, Castle Pinckney, Sullivan's Island, and off to the north the old carrier *Yorktown* moored at Mount Pleasant. A landward look gives you a view of the adjoining, peaceful **White Point Gardens,** the sumptuous mansions of the Battery, and a beguiling peek behind them into some of the oldest neighborhoods in Charleston.

But if you had been one of the first European visitors to this tip of the peninsula about 400 years ago, you'd have seen how it got its first name, Oyster Point: This entire area was once home to an enormous outcropping of oysters. Their shells glistened bright white in the harsh Southern sun as a ship approached from seaward, hence its subsequent name, White Point. Though the oysters are long gone and much of the area you're walking on is actually reclaimed marsh, the Battery and White Point Gardens are still a balm for the soul.

Once the bustling (and sometimes seedy) heart of Charleston's maritime activity, the Battery was where pirate Stede Bonnet and 21 of his men were hanged in 1718. As you might imagine, the area got its name for hosting cannon during the War of 1812, with the current distinctive seawall structure built in the 1850s.

Contrary to popular opinion, no guns fired from here on Fort Sumter at the beginning of the Civil War, as they would have been out of range. However, many thankfully inoperable cannon, mortars, and piles of shot still reside here, much to the delight of boys of all ages. This is where Charlestonians gathered

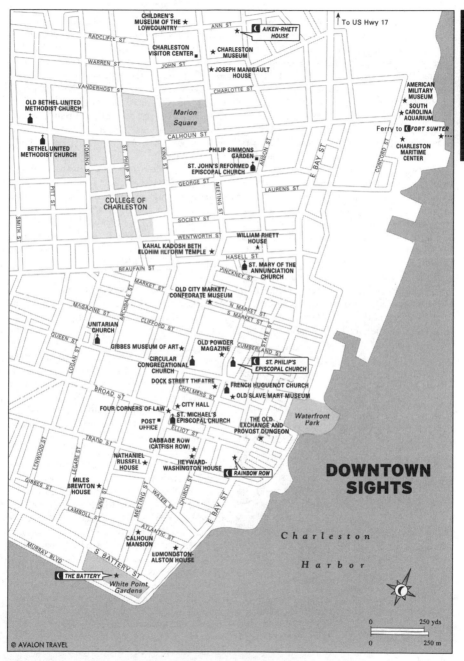

CHARLESTON

CHILDREN'S MUSEUM OF THE LOWCOUNTRY ★
ANN ST
AIKEN-RHETT HOUSE ★
RADCLIFFE ST
↑ To US Hwy 17
CHARLESTON VISITOR CENTER ■
CHARLESTON MUSEUM ★
WARREN ST
JOHN ST
★ JOSEPH MANIGAULT HOUSE
VANDERHOST ST
CHARLOTTE ST
AMERICAN MILITARY MUSEUM ★
OLD BETHEL UNITED METHODIST CHURCH ■
SOUTH CAROLINA AQUARIUM ★
Marion Square
Ferry to ◖FORT SUMTER ★
CALHOUN ST
CHARLESTON MARITIME CENTER ★
BETHEL UNITED METHODIST CHURCH ♦
COMING ST
ST. PHILIP ST
KING ST
PHILIP SIMMONS GARDEN ★
ANSON ST
E BAY ST
ST. JOHN'S REFORMED EPISCOPAL CHURCH ♦
PITT ST
GEORGE ST
MEETING ST
LAURENS ST
COLLEGE OF CHARLESTON
SOCIETY ST
SMITH ST
WENTWORTH ST
WILLIAM RHETT HOUSE ▲
KAHAL KADOSH BETH ELOHIM REFORM TEMPLE ★
HASELL ST
BEAUFAIN ST
ST. MARY OF THE ANNUNCIATION CHURCH ♦
PINCKNEY ST
MARKET ST
OLD CITY MARKET/ CONFEDERATE MUSEUM ★
ARCHDALE ST
N MARKET ST
S MARKET ST
MAGAZINE ST
CLIFFORD ST
UNITARIAN CHURCH ♦
STATE ST
QUEEN ST
GIBBES MUSEUM OF ART ★
OLD POWDER MAGAZINE ★
CUMBERLAND ST
LOGAN ST
CIRCULAR CONGREGATIONAL CHURCH ♦
ST. PHILIP'S EPISCOPAL CHURCH ◖
DOCK STREET THEATRE ★
BROAD ST
CHALMERS ST
★ FRENCH HUGUENOT CHURCH
★ OLD SLAVE MART MUSEUM
FOUR CORNERS OF LAW ★
CITY HALL ★
POST OFFICE ■
ST. MICHAEL'S EPISCOPAL CHURCH ♦
THE OLD EXCHANGE AND PROVOST DUNGEON ★
Waterfront Park
TRADD ST
ELLIOT ST
LENWOOD ST
LEGARE ST
CABBAGE ROW (CATFISH ROW) ★
NATHANIEL RUSSELL HOUSE ★
HEYWARD-WASHINGTON HOUSE ★
RAINBOW ROW ◖
DOWNTOWN SIGHTS
GIBBES ST
MILES BREWTON HOUSE ★
KING ST
MEETING ST
WATER ST
CHURCH ST
E BAY ST
LAMBOLL ST
ATLANTIC ST
Charleston
CALHOUN MANSION ★
EDMONDSTON-ALSTON HOUSE ★
MURRAY BLVD
S BATTERY ST
Harbor
◖THE BATTERY ★
White Point Gardens
0   250 yds
0   250 m

© AVALON TRAVEL

in a giddy, party-like atmosphere to watch the shelling of Fort Sumter in 1861, blissfully ignorant of the horrors to come. A short time later the North would return the favor, as the Battery and all of Charleston up to Broad Street would bear the brunt of shelling during the long siege of the city (the rest was out of reach of Union guns).

But now, the Battery is a place to relax, not fight. The relaxation starts with the fact that there's usually plenty of free parking all along Battery Street. A promenade all around the periphery is a great place to stroll or jog. Add the calming, almost constant sea breeze and the meditative influence of the wide, blue Cooper River, and you'll see why this land's end—once so martial in nature—is now a favorite place for after-church family gatherings, tourists, lovestruck couples, and weddings (about 200 a year at the gazebo in White Point Gardens).

Still, military history is never far away in Charleston, and one of the chief landmarks at the Battery is the USS *Hobson* Memorial, remembering the sacrifice of the men of that

© JIM MOREKIS
the Battery

vessel when it sank after a collision with the carrier USS *Wasp* in 1952. Another martial memorial includes a capstan from the USS *Maine,* part of an early PR effort in which pieces of the destroyed battleship were sent all over the United States to drum up support for the Spanish-American War. A less grim feature is the delightful "Little Dancer" fountain, just tall enough for small children to drink from (and pigeons as well, unfortunately).

Look for the three-story private residence where East Battery curves northward. You won't be taking any tours of it, but you should be aware that it's the **DeSaussure House** (1 E. Battery St.), best known in Charleston history for hosting rowdy, celebratory crowds on the roof and the piazzas to watch the 34-hour shelling of Fort Sumter in 1861.

Edmondston-Alston House

The most noteworthy single attraction on the Battery is the 1825 Edmondston-Alston House (21 E. Battery St., 843/722-7171, www.middle tonplace.org, Tues.–Sat. 10 A.M.–4:30 P.M., Sun.–Mon. 1:30–4:30 P.M., $10 adults, $8 students), the only Battery home open to the public for tours. This is one of the most unique and well-preserved such historic homes in the United States, thanks to the ongoing efforts of the Alston family, who acquired the house from shipping merchant Charles Edmondston for $15,500 after the Panic of 1837 and still live on the third floor (tours only go to the first two stories).

Over 90 percent of the home's furnishing are original items from the Alston era, a percentage that's almost unheard of in the world of house museums. (Currently the House is owned and administered by the Middleton Place Foundation, best known for its stewardship of Middleton Place along the Ashley River.)

You can still see the original paper bag used to store the house's deeds and mortgages. There's also a copy of the Ordinance of Secession and some interesting memorabilia from the golden days of Race Week, that time in February when all of Charleston society came out to bet on horses, carouse, and show off their finery.

The Edmondston-Alston House has withstood storm, fire, earthquake, and Yankee shelling, due in no small part to its sturdy construction; its masonry walls are two-bricks thick and it features both interior and exterior shutters. Originally built in the Federal style, second owner Charles Alston added several Greek Revival elements, notably the parapet, balcony, and piazza, where General Beauregard watched the attack on Fort Sumter.

【 Rainbow Row

From 79–107 East Bay between Tradd and Elliot Streets is one of the most photographed sights in the United States, colorful Rainbow Row. The reason for its name becomes obvious when you see the array of pastel-colored mansions, all facing the Cooper River. The bright, historically accurate colors—nine of them, to be exact—are one of the many vestiges you'll see around town of Charleston's Caribbean heritage, a legacy of the English settlers from the colony of Barbados who were among the city's first citizens.

The homes are unusually old for this fire-, hurricane-, and earthquake-ravaged city, with most dating from 1730–1750. As you admire Rainbow Row from across East Battery, keep in mind you're actually walking on what used to be water. These houses were originally right on the Cooper River, their lower stories serving as storefronts on the wharf. The street was created later on top of landfill, or "made land" as it's called locally.

Besides its grace and beauty, Rainbow Row is of vital importance to American historic preservation. These were the first Charleston homes to be renovated and brought back from early-20th-century seediness. The restoration projects on Rainbow Row directly inspired the creation of the Charleston Preservation Society, the first such group in the U.S.

Continue walking up the High Battery past Rainbow Row and find Water Street. This aptly named little avenue was in fact a creek in the early days, acting as the southern border of

COURTESY OF CHARLESTON AREA CVB, WWW.EXPLORECHARLESTON.COM

Historic Rainbow Row is located just south of Broad Street on East Bay Street.

the original walled city. The large brick building on the seaward side housing the Historic Charleston Foundation sits on the site of the old Granville bastion, a key defensive point in the wall.

Nathaniel Russell House

Considered one of Charleston's grandest homes despite being built by an outsider from Rhode Island, the Nathaniel Russell House (51 Meeting St., 843/724-8481, www.historic charleston.org, Mon.–Sat. 10 A.M.–5 P.M., Sun. 2–5 P.M., last tour begins 4:30 P.M., $10) is now a National Historic Landmark and one of America's best examples of neoclassicism. Built in 1808 for the then-princely sum of $80,000 by Nathaniel Russell, a.k.a., "King of the Yankees," the home is furnished as accurately as possible to represent not only the lifestyle of the Russell family, but the 18 African American servants who shared the premises. The house was eventually bought by the Allson family, who amid the poverty of Civil War and Reconstruction decided in 1870 to sell it to the Sisters of Charity of Our Lady of Mercy as a school for young Catholic women.

Restorationists have identified 22 layers of paint within the home, which barely survived a tornado in 1811, got away with only minimal damage in the 1886 earthquake, but was damaged extensively by Hurricane Hugo in 1989 (and since repaired). As with fine antebellum homes throughout coastal South Carolina and Georgia, the use of faux finishing is prevalent throughout, mimicking surfaces from marble to wood to lapis lazuli.

Visitors are often most impressed by the Nathaniel Russell House's magnificent "flying" spiral staircase, a work of such sublime carpentry and engineering that it needs no external support, twisting upwards of its own volition.

When you visit, keep in mind that you're in the epicenter of not only Charleston's historic preservation movement, but perhaps the nation's as well. In 1955, the Nathaniel Russell House was the first major project of the Historic Charleston Foundation, which

raised $65,000 to purchase it. Two years later, admission fees from the house would support Historic Charleston's groundbreaking revolving fund for preservation, the prototype for many successful programs throughout historic areas of the United States. For an extra $6, you can gain admission to the Aiken-Rhett House farther uptown, also administered by the Historic Charleston Foundation.

Calhoun Mansion

The single largest of Charleston's surviving grand homes, the 1876 Calhoun Mansion (16 Meeting St., 843/722-8205, www.calhoun mansion.net, tours daily 11 A.M.–5 P.M., $15) boasts 35 opulent rooms (with 23 fireplaces!) in a striking Italianate design taking up a whopping 24,000 square feet. The grounds feature some charming garden spaces. Though the interiors at this privately run house are packed with antiques and furnishings, be aware that not all of them are accurate or period.

Miles Brewton House

A short distance from the Nathaniel Russell House but much less viewed by tourists, the circa-1769 Miles Brewton House (27 King St.), now a private residence, is maybe the best example of Georgian-Palladian architecture in the world. The almost medieval wrought-iron fencing, or *cheveaux de frise,* was added in 1822 after rumors of a slave uprising spread through town.

This imposing double house was the site of not one but two headquarters of occupying armies, British General Clinton in the Revolution and the federal garrison after the end of the Civil War. The great Susan Pringle Frost, principal founder of the Charleston Preservation Society and a Brewton descendant, grew up here.

Heyward-Washington House

The Heyward-Washington House (87 Church St., 843/722-0354, www.charlestonmuseum .org, Mon.–Sat. 10 A.M.–5 P.M., Sun. 1–5 P.M., $10 adults, $5 children, combo tickets to Charleston Museum and Manigault House

© JIM MOREKIS

The Miles Brewton House hosted two occupation headquarters.

available) takes the regional practice of naming a historic home for the two most significant names in its pedigree to its logical extreme.

Built in 1772 by the father of Declaration of Independence signer Thomas Heyward Jr., the house also hosted George Washington himself during the president's visit to Charleston in 1791. It's now owned and operated by the Charleston Museum.

The main attraction at the Heyward-Washington House is its masterful woodwork, exemplified by the cabinetry of legendary Charleston carpenter Thomas Elfe. You'll see his work all over the house from the mantles to a Chippendale chair. Look for his signature of a figure eight with four diamonds.

Cabbage Row

You know these addresses from 89–91 Church Street better as "Catfish Row" of Gershwin's opera *Porgy and Bess* (itself based on the book *Porgy* by the great Charleston author Dubose Heyward, who lived at 76 Church St.). Today this complex—which once housed 10

families—next to the Heyward-Washington House is certainly upgraded from years past, but the row still has the humble appeal of the tenement housing it once was, primarily for freed African Americans after the Civil War. The house nearby at 94 Church Street was where John C. Calhoun and others drew up the infamous Nullification Acts that eventually led to the South's secession.

St. Michael's Episcopal Church

The oldest church in South Carolina, St. Michael's Episcopal Church (71 Broad St., 843/723-0603, mass Sun. 8 A.M. and 10:30 A.M., tours available after services) is actually the second sanctuary on this spot. The first church here was made out of black cypress and called St. Philip's, or "the English Church," which was later rebuilt on Church Street.

Though the designer is not known, we do know that work on this sanctuary in the style of Sir Christopher Wren began in 1752 as a response to the overflowing congregation at the rebuilt St. Philips, and it didn't finish

THE GREAT CHARLESTON EARTHQUAKE

The Charleston peninsula is bordered by three faults, almost like a picture frame: the Woodstock Fault above North Charleston, the Charleston Fault running along the east bank of the Cooper River, and the Ashley Fault to the west of the Ashley River. On August 31, 1886, one of them buckled, causing one of the most damaging earthquakes ever to hit the United States.

The earthquake of 1886 was actually signaled by several shocks earlier that week. Residents of the nearby town of Summerville, South Carolina, 20 miles up the Ashley River, felt a small earthquake after midnight on Friday, August 27. Most slept through it. But soon after dawn a larger shock came, complete with a loud bang, causing many to run outside their houses. That Saturday afternoon another tremor hit Summerville, breaking windows and throwing a bed against a wall in one home. Still, Charlestonians remained unconcerned.

Then that Tuesday at 9:50 P.M. came the big one. With an epicenter somewhere near the Middleton Place plantation, the Charleston earthquake is estimated to have measured about 7 on the Richter scale. Tremors were felt across half the country, with the ground shaking in Chicago and a church damaged in Indianapolis. A dam 120 miles away in Aiken, South Carolina, immediately gave way, washing a train right off the tracks. Cracks opened up parallel to the Ashley River, with part of the

riverbank falling into the water. Thousands of chimneys all over the state either fell or were rendered useless.

A Charleston minister at his summer home in Asheville, North Carolina, described a noise like the sound of wheels driving straight up the mountain, followed by the sound of many railroad cars going by. A moment later, one corner of his house lifted off the ground and slammed back down again. The quake brought a series of "sand blows," a particularly disturbing phenomenon whereby craters open up and spew sand and water up into the air like a small volcano. In Charleston's case, some of the craters were 20 feet wide, shooting debris another 20 feet into the air.

The whole event lasted less than a minute.

In crowded Charleston, the damage was horrific: over 2,000 buildings destroyed, a quarter of the city's value gone, 27 killed immediately and almost 100 more to die from injuries and disease. Because of the large numbers of newly homeless, tent cities sprang up in every available park and greenspace. The American Red Cross's first field mission soon brought some relief, but the scarcity of food, and especially fresh water, made life difficult for everyone.

Almost every surviving building had experienced structural damage, in some cases severe, so a way had to be found to stabilize them. This led to the widespread use of the

until 1761. Other than a small addition on the southeast corner in 1883 the St. Michael's you see today is virtually unchanged, including the massive pulpit, outsized in the style of the time.

Worship services here over the years hosted such luminaries as Marquis de Lafayette, George Washington, and Robert E. Lee, the latter two of whom are known to have sat in the "governor's pew." Two signers of the U.S. Constitution, John Rutledge and Charles Cotesworth Pinckney, are buried in the sanctuary.

The 186-foot steeple, painted black during

the Revolution in a futile effort to disguise it from British guns, actually sank eight inches after the earthquake of 1886. Inside the tower, the famous "bells of St. Michael's" have an interesting story to tell, having made seven transatlantic voyages for a variety of reasons. They were forged in London's Whitechapel Foundry and sent over in 1764, only to be brought back as a war prize during the Revolution, after which they were returned to the church. Damaged during the Civil War, they were sent back to the foundry of their birth to be recast and returned to Charleston. In 1989 they were damaged by Hurricane Hugo, sent back

"earthquake bolt" now seen throughout older Charleston homes. Essentially acting as very long screws with a washer on each end, the idea of the earthquake rod is simple: Poke a long iron rod through two walls that need stabilizing, and cap the ends. Charleston being Charleston, of course, the end caps were often decorated with a pattern or symbol.

The seismic activity of Charleston's earthquake was so intense that more than 300 aftershocks occurred in the 35 years after the event. In fact, geologists think that most seismic events measured in the region today – including a large event in December 2008, also centering near Summerville – are probably also aftershocks.

© JIM MOREKIS

Earthquake bolts are a common sight in downtown Charleston.

to Whitechapel yet again, and returned to St. Michael's in 1993. Throughout the lifespan of the bells, the clock tower has continued to tell time, though the minute hand wasn't added until 1849.

St. Michael's offers informal, free guided tours to visitors after Sunday worship services; contact the greeter for more information.

Four Corners of Law

No guidebook is complete without a mention of this famous intersection of Broad and Meeting Streets, so named for its confluence of federal law (the Post Office building), state law (the state courthouse), municipal law (City Hall), and God's law (St. Michael's Episcopal Church). That's all well and good, but no matter what the tour guides may tell you, the phrase "Four Corners of Law" was actually popularized by *Ripley's Believe It or Not!*

Still, there's no doubt that this intersection has been key to Charleston from the beginning. Meeting Street was laid out around 1672 and takes its name from the White Meeting House of early Dissenters, i.e., non-Anglicans. Broad Street was also referred to as Cooper Street in the early days. Right in the middle of the street once stood the very first statue in America, a figure of William Pitt erected in 1766. You can see it today in the Charleston Museum.

WATERFRONT

Charleston's waterfront is a place where tourism, history, and industry coexist in a largely seamless fashion. Yet another of the successful—if at one time controversial—developments spearheaded by Mayor Joe Riley, the centerpiece of the harbor area as far as tourists are concerned is Waterfront Park up toward the High Battery. Farther up the Cooper River is Aquarium Wharf, where you'll find the South Carolina Aquarium, the American Military Museum, the Fort Sumter Visitor Education Exhibit, and the dock where you take the various harbor ferries, whether to Fort Sumter or just a calming ride on the Cooper River.

The Old Exchange and Provost Dungeon

It's far from glamorous, but nonetheless The Old Exchange and Provost Dungeon (122 E. Bay St., 843/727-2165, www.oldexchange.com,

daily 9 A.M.–5 P.M., $7 adults, $3.50 children and students) at the intersection of East Bay and Meeting Streets is brimming with history. It's known as one of the three most historically significant colonial buildings in the United States (Philadelphia's Independence Hall and Boston's Faneuil Hall being the other two). This is actually the old Royal Exchange and Custom House, with the cellar serving as a British prison, all built over a portion of the old 1698 fortification wall, some of which you can see today.

Three of Charleston's four signers of the Declaration of Independence did time downstairs for sedition against the crown. Later, happier times were experienced upstairs in the Exchange, as it was here where the state selected its delegates to the Continental Congress and ratified the U.S. Constitution and where George Washington took a spin on the dance floor. Nearly a victim of early 20th-century shortsightedness—it was almost demolished for a gas station in 1913—the building now fittingly belongs to the Daughters of the American Revolution.

the Old Exchange and Provost Dungeon

© JIM MOREKIS

CHARLESTON

Fans of kitsch will get a hoot out of the animatronic, "Hall of the Presidents"–style figures. Kids might especially get a scary kick out of the basement dungeon, where the infamous pirate Stede Bonnet was imprisoned in 1718 before being hanged with his crew on the Battery.

Waterfront Park
Dubbing it "this generation's gift to the future," Mayor Joe Riley made this eight-acre project another part of his ambitious downtown renovation. Situated on Concord Street roughly between Exchange Street and Vendue Range, Waterfront Park (843/724-7327, daily dawn–dusk, free) was, like many waterfront locales in Charleston, built on what used to be marsh and water. This particularly massive chunk of "made land" juts about a football field's length farther out than the old waterline.

Visitors and locals alike enjoy the relaxing vista of Charleston Harbor, often from the many swinging benches arranged in an unusual front-to-back, single-file pattern all down the pier. On the end you can find viewing binoculars to see the various sights out on the Cooper River, chief among them the USS *Yorktown* at Patriot's Point and the big bridge to Mount Pleasant.

Children will enjoy the large "Vendue" wading fountain at the Park's entrance off Vendue Range, while a bit farther south is the large and quite artful Pineapple Fountain with its surrounding wading pool. Contemporary art lovers of all ages will appreciate the nearby **Waterfront Park City Gallery** (34 Prioleau St., Mon.–Fri. noon–5 P.M., free).

South Carolina Aquarium
Honestly, if you've been to any of the more expansive aquariums in Atlanta or Boston, you might be disappointed at the breadth of offerings at the South Carolina Aquarium (100 Aquarium Wharf, 843/720-1990, www.scaquarium.org, Mon.–Sat. 9 A.M.–6 P.M., Sun. noon–6 P.M., last ticket 5 P.M. Apr. 1–Aug. 15, Mon.–Sat. 9 A.M.–5 P.M., Sun. noon–5 P.M., last ticket 4 P.M. Aug. 16–Mar. 31,

© JIM MOREKIS
wading fountain at Waterfront Park

$16 adults, $8 students, combo tickets with Fort Sumter tour available). But nonetheless, it's clean and well done and is a great place for the whole family to have some fun while educating themselves on the rich aquatic life not only off the coast, but throughout this small but ecologically diverse state.

When you enter you're greeted with the 15,000-gallon Carolina Seas tank, with placid nurse sharks and vicious-looking moray eels. Other exhibits highlight the five key South Carolina ecosystems: beach, salt marsh, coastal plain, piedmont, and mountain forest. Another neat display is the Touch Tank, a hands-on collection of invertebrates found along the coast, such as sea urchins and horseshoe crabs. The *pièce de résistance,* however, is certainly the three-story Great Ocean Tank with literally hundreds of deeper-water marine creatures, including sharks, pufferfish, and sea turtles.

Speaking of sea turtles: A key part of the Aquarium's research and outreach efforts is the Turtle Hospital, which attempts to rehabilitate and save sick and injured specimens. The hospital has so far saved 20 sea turtles, the first one being a 270-pound female affectionately known as "Edisto Mama."

Keep in mind that on weekdays during the school year the place is often chockablock with local schoolchildren on field trips. During the summer, closing time is extended an hour until 6 P.M., with the last ticket sold at 5 P.M.

Note that you might run across some information about an IMAX movie theater near the Aquarium when researching your trip. No matter what you read or hear elsewhere, this IMAX location is now closed.

American Military Museum

Slightly out of place thematically with the Aquarium, the American Military Museum (360 Concord St., 843/577-7000, www.americanmilitarymuseum.org, Mon.–Sat. 10 A.M.–6 P.M., Sun. 1–5 P.M., $7 adults, $3 students) is one of those under-the-radar types of small, quaint museums that can be unexpectedly enriching. Certainly its location near the embarkation point for the Fort Sumter ferry hasn't hurt its profile. It's heavy on uniforms, with a wide range all the way from the Revolution to the modern day. My favorite is the 1907 naval uniform from the cruiser USS *Charleston,* part of Teddy Roosevelt's Great White Fleet. There's also a good collection of rare military miniatures.

Fort Sumter

This is it: the place that brought about the beginning of the Civil War, a Troy for modern times. Though many historians insist the war would have happened regardless of President Lincoln's decision to keep Fort Sumter (843/883-3123, www.nps.gov/fosu, hours seasonal) in federal hands, nonetheless the stated *causus belli* was Major Robert Anderson's refusal to surrender the fort when requested to do so in the early morning hours of April 12, 1861.

A few hours later came the first shot of the war, fired from Fort Johnson by Confederate Captain George James. That 10-inch mortar shell, a signal for the general bombardment to begin, exploded above Fort Sumter, and nothing in Charleston, or the South, or America, would ever be the same again.

Notorious secessionist Edmund Ruffin gets credit for firing the first shot in anger, only moments after James's signal shell, from a battery at Cummings Point. Ruffin's 64-pound projectile scored a direct hit, smashing into the fort's southwest corner.

The first return shot fired from Fort Sumter was fired by none other than Captain Abner Doubleday, the father of baseball. The first death of the Civil War also happened at Fort Sumter, not from the Confederate bombardment but on the day after. U.S. Army Private Daniel Hough died when the cannon he was loading, to be fired as part of a 100-gun surrender salute to the Stars and Stripes, exploded prematurely.

Today the battered but still-standing Fort Sumter remains astride the entrance to Charleston Harbor on a manmade, 70,000-ton sandbar. Sumter was part of the so-called Third System of fortifications ordered after the War of 1812. Interestingly, the fort was still not quite finished when the Confederate guns opened up on it 50 years later, and never enjoyed its intended full complement of 135 big guns.

As you might expect, you can only visit by boat, specifically the approved concessionaire **Fort Sumter Tours** (843/881-7337, www .fortsumtertours.com, $14 adults, $8 ages 6–11, $12.50 seniors). Once at the fort, there's no charge for admission. Ferries leave from Liberty Square at Aquarium Wharf on the peninsula three times a day during the high season; call or check the website for times. Make sure to arrive about a half-hour before the ferry departs. You can also get to Fort Sumter by ferry from Patriot's Point at Mount Pleasant through the same company.

Budget at least 2.5 hours for the whole trip, including an hour at Fort Sumter. At Liberty Square on the peninsula is the **Fort Sumter Visitor Education Center** (340 Concord St., daily 8:30 A.M.–5 P.M., free), so you can learn more about where you're about to go. Once there, you can be enlightened by the regular ranger's talks on the fort's history and construction (generally at 11:00 A.M. and 2:30 P.M.), take in the interpretive exhibits throughout the site, and enjoy the view of the spires of the Holy City from afar.

For many, though, the highlight is the boat trip itself, with beautiful views of Charleston Harbor and the islands of the Cooper River estuary. If you want to skip Sumter, you can still take an enjoyable 90-minute ferry ride around the harbor and past the fort on the affiliated **Spiritline Cruises** (800/789-3678, www.spirit linecruises.com, $14 adults, $8 ages 6–11).

Some visitors are disappointed to find many of the fort's gun embrasures bricked over. This was done during the Spanish-American War, when the old fort was turned into an earthwork and the newer Battery Huger (pronounced "Huge-E") was built on top of it.

FRENCH QUARTER

Unlike the New Orleans version, Charleston's French Quarter is strictly Protestant in origin

and flavor. Though not actually given the name until a preservation effort in the 1970s, historically this area was indeed the main place of commerce for the city's population of French Huguenots, primarily a merchant class who fled religious persecution in their native country.

Today the five-block area—roughly bounded by East Bay, Market Street, Meeting Street, and Broad Street—contains some of Charleston's most historic buildings, its most evocative old churches and graveyards, its most charming, narrow streets, and its most tasteful art galleries.

(St. Philip's Episcopal Church

With a pedigree dating back to the colony's fledgling years, St. Philip's Episcopal Church (142 Church St., 843/722-7734, www.stphilipschurchsc.org, sanctuary open weekdays 10 A.M.–noon and 2–4 P.M., mass Sun. 8:15 A.M.) is the oldest Anglican congregation south of Virginia. That pedigree gets a little complicated and downright tragic at

St. Philip's Episcopal Church

© JIM MOREKIS

times, but any connoisseur of Charleston history needs to be clear on the fine points, so here goes.

The first St. Philip's was built in 1680 at the corner of Meeting Street and Broad Street, the present site of St. Michael's Episcopal Church. That first St. Philip's was badly damaged by a hurricane in 1710, and the city fathers approved the building of a new sanctuary dedicated to the saint on Church Street. However, that building was nearly destroyed by yet another hurricane during construction. Sporadic fighting with local Native Americans further delayed rebuilding in 1721.

Alas, that St. Philip's burned to the ground in 1835—a distressingly common fate for so many old buildings in this area. Construction immediately began on a replacement, and it's that building you see today. Heavily damaged by Hurricane Hugo in 1989, a $4.5-million renovation kept the church usable.

So to recap: St. Philip's was originally on the site of the present St. Michael's. And while St. Philip's is the oldest congregation in South Carolina, St. Michael's has the oldest physical church building in the state. Are we clear?

South Carolina's great statesman John C. Calhoun—who ironically despised Charlestonians for what he saw as their loose morals—was originally buried across Church Street in the former "stranger's churchyard," or West Cemetery, after his death in 1850. (Charles Pinckney and Edward Rutledge are two other notable South Carolinians buried there.) But near the end of the Civil War, Calhoun's body was moved to an unmarked grave closer to the sanctuary in an attempt to hide its location from Union troops, who it was feared would go out of their way to wreak vengeance on the tomb of one of slavery's staunchest advocates and the man who invented the doctrine of nullification. In 1880, with Reconstruction in full swing, the state legislature directed and funded the building of the current large memorial in the West Cemetery.

French Huguenot Church

One of the oldest congregations in town, the French Huguenot Church (44 Queen St.,

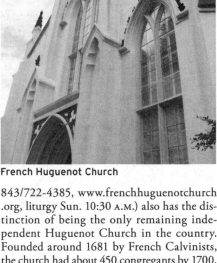

© JIM MOREKIS

French Huguenot Church

843/722-4385, www.frenchhuguenotchurch .org, liturgy Sun. 10:30 A.M.) also has the distinction of being the only remaining independent Huguenot Church in the country. Founded around 1681 by French Calvinists, the church had about 450 congregants by 1700. While refugees from religious persecution, they weren't destitute, as they had to pay for their passage to America.

As is the case with so many historic churches in the area, the building you see isn't the original sanctuary. The first church was built on this site in 1687, and became known as the "Church of Tides" because at that time the Cooper River lapped at its property line. This sanctuary was deliberately destroyed as a firebreak during the great conflagration of 1796.

The church was replaced in 1800, but that building was in turn demolished in favor of the picturesque, stucco-coated Gothic Revival sanctuary you see today, which was completed in 1845 and subsequently survived Union shelling and the 1886 earthquake.

Does the church look kind of Dutch to you? There's a good reason for that. In their diaspora, French Huguenots spent a lot of time in Holland and became influenced by the tidy sensibilities of the Dutch people.

The history of the circa-1845 organ is interesting as well. A rare "tracker" organ, so named for its ultra-fast linkage between the keys and the pipe valves, it was built by famed organ builder Henry Erben. After the fall of Charleston in 1865, Union troops had begun dismantling the instrument for shipment to New York when the church organist, T. P. O'Neale, successfully pleaded with them to let it stay.

Sunday services are conducted in English now, but a single annual service in French is still celebrated in April. The unique Huguenot Cross of Languedoc, which you'll occasionally see ornamenting the church, is essentially a Maltese Cross, its eight points representing the eight beatitudes. Between the four arms of the cross are four *fleurs-de-lis,* the age-old French symbol of purity.

Dock Street Theatre

Unfortunately for many visitors, the Dock

FRENCH HUGUENOTS

A visitor can't spend a few hours in Charleston without coming across the many French-sounding names so prevalent in the region. Some are common surnames, such as Ravenel, Manigault (pronounced "MAN-i-go"), Gaillard, Laurens, or Huger (pronounced "Huge-E"). Some are street or place names, such as Mazyck or Legare (pronounced "Legree").

Unlike the predominantly French Catholic presence in Louisiana and coastal Alabama, the Gallic influence in Charleston was strictly of the Calvinist Protestant variety. Known as Huguenots, these French immigrants – refugees of an increasingly intolerant Catholic regime in their mother country – were numerous enough in the settlement by the 1690s that they were granted full citizenship and property rights if they swore allegiance to the British crown.

The Huguenot's quick rise in Charleston was due to two factors. Unlike other colonies, Carolina never put much of a premium on religious conformity, a trait that exists to this day despite the area's overall conservatism. And unlike many who fled European monarchies to come to the New World, the French Huguenots were far from poverty-stricken. Most had to buy their own journeys across the Atlantic and arrived already well educated and skilled in one or more useful trades. In Charleston's early days, they were mostly wheat and barley farmers or tarburners. In later times their pragmatism and work ethic would lead them to higher positions in local society, such as lawyers, judges, and politicians.

One of the wealthiest Charlestonians of all, the merchant Gabriel Manigault, was by some accounts the richest person in America during the early 1700s. South Carolina's most famous French Huguenot of all was Francis Marion, the "Swamp Fox" of Revolutionary War fame. Born on the Santee River, Marion grew up in Georgetown and is now interred near Moncks Corner.

During that century a number of charitable aid organizations sprang up to serve various local groups, mostly along ethno-religious lines. The most wealthy and influential of them all was the South Carolina Society, founded in 1737 and first called "The Two Bit Club" because of the original weekly dues. The Society still meets today at its building at 72 Meeting Street, designed in 1804 by none other than Manigault's grandson, also named Gabriel, who was Charleston's most celebrated amateur architect. Another aid organization, the **Huguenot Society of Carolina** (138 Logan St., 843/723-3235, www.huguenotsociety. org, Mon.-Fri. 9 A.M.-2 P.M.), was established in 1885. Their library is a great research tool for anyone interested in French Protestant history and genealogy.

To this day, the spiritual home of Charleston's Huguenots is the same one as always: the French Huguenot Church on Church Street, one of the earliest congregations in the city. Though many of the old ways have gone, the church still holds one liturgy a year (in April) in French.

CHARLESTON

Dock Street Theatre, first such venue in North America

© JIM MOREKIS

Street Theatre (135 Church St., 843/720-3968) right down the street from the Huguenot Church will be closed for extensive (and long overdue) infrastructure repair and renovation through at least spring 2010. In any case, any thespian or lover of the stage must pay homage to this incarnation of the very first theater ever built in the Western Hemisphere.

In a distressingly familiar Charleston story, the original 1736 Dock Street Theatre burned down. A second theater opened on the same site in 1754. That building was in turn demolished for a grander edifice in 1773, which, you guessed it, also burned down.

The current building dates from 1809, when the Planter's Hotel was built near the site of the original Dock Street Theatre. To mark the theater's centennial, the hotel added a stage facility in 1835, and it's that building you see today.

For the theater's second centennial, the Works Progress Administration completely refurbished Dock Street back into a working theater in time to distract Charlestonians from the pains of the Great Depression. In addition to

a very active and well-regarded annual season from the resident Charleston Stage Company, the 464-seat venue has hosted umpteen events of the Spoleto Festival over the past three decades, which have been relocated until renovations are complete.

Old Powder Magazine

The Old Powder Magazine (79 Cumberland St., 843/722-9350, www.powdermag.org, Wed.–Sat. 10 A.M.–4 P.M., $2 adults, $1 children) may be small, but the building is quite historically significant. The 1713 edifice is the oldest public building in South Carolina and also the only one remaining of the days of the Lords Proprietors. As the name indicates, this was where the city's gunpowder was stored during the Revolution. The magazine is designed to implode rather than explode in the event of a direct hit.

This is another labor of love of the Historic Charleston Foundation, which has leased the building—which from a distance looks curiously like an ancient Byzantine church—from

The Colonial Dames since 1993. It was opened to the public as an attraction in 1997. Now directly across the street from a huge parking garage, the site has continued funding issues, so occasionally the hours for tours can be erratic.

Inside you'll see displays, a section of the original brick, and an exposed earthquake rod. Right next door is the privately owned, circa-1709 Trott's Cottage, the first brick dwelling in Charleston.

Old Slave Mart Museum

Slave auctions became a big business in the South after 1808, when the United States banned importation of slaves, thus increasing both price and demand. The auctions, with slaves forced to stand on display on long tables, generally took place in public buildings where everyone could watch the wrenching spectacle of families being torn apart and lives ruined.

But in the 1850s, public auctions in Charleston were put to a stop when city leaders discovered that visitors from European nations—all of which had banned slavery outright years before—were horrified at the practice. So the slave trade was moved indoors to "marts" near the Cooper River waterfront where the sales could be conducted out of the public eye.

The last remaining such structure is the Old Slave Mart Museum (6 Chalmers St., 843/958-6467, www.charlestoncity.info, Mon.–Sat. 9 A.M.–5 P.M., $7 adults, $5 children, 5 and under free). Built in 1859, and originally known as Ryan's Mart after the builder, it was only in service a short time before the outbreak of the Civil War. The last auction was held in November 1863.

After the war, the Slave Mart became a tenement, and then in 1938 an African American history museum. The city of Charleston acquired the building in the 1980s and reopened it as a museum in late 2007.

There are two main areas: the orientation area, where visitors learn about the transatlantic slave trade and the architectural history of the building itself; and the main exhibit area, where visitors can see documents, tools, and displays re-creating what happened inside during this sordid chapter in local history and celebrating the resilience of the area's African American community.

NORTH OF BROAD

This tourist-heavy part of town is sometimes called the Market area because of its proximity to the Old City Market. We'll start east at the border of the French Quarter on Meeting Street and work our way west and north toward Francis Marion Square.

Circular Congregational Church

The historic Circular Congregational Church (150 Meeting St., 843/577-6400, www.circular church.org, service Sun. 11 A.M., 10:15 A.M. during summer) has one of the most interesting pedigrees of any house of worship in Charleston, which is saying a lot. Originally held on the site of the "White Meeting House," for which Meeting Street is named, services were held here beginning in 1681 for a polyglot mix of Congregationalists, Presbyterians, and Huguenots. For that reason it was often called the Church of Dissenters ("Dissenters" being the common term at the time for anyone not an Anglican).

As with many structures in town, the 1886 earthquake necessitated a rebuilding, and the current edifice dates from 1891. Ironically, in this municipality called "the Holy City" for its many high spires, the Circular Church has no steeple, and instead stays low to the ground in an almost medieval fashion.

Look for the adjacent meeting house, which gave the street its name; a green-friendly addition houses the congregation's Christian outreach and has geothermal heating and cooling and boasts Charleston's only vegetative roof.

Gibbes Museum of Art

Directly across the street from the Circular Church, the Gibbes Museum of Art (135 Meeting St., 843/722-2706, www.gibbes museum.org, Tues.–Sat. 10 A.M.–5 P.M., Sun. 1–5 P.M., $9 adults, $7 students, $5 ages 6–12) is one of those rare Southern museums that manages a perfect blend of the modern and the traditional, the local and the international.

Beginning life in 1905 as the Gibbes Art Gallery—the final wish of James Shoolbred Gibbes, who willed $100,000 for its construction—the complex has grown through the years in size and influence. The key addition to the original Beaux Arts building came in 1978 with the addition of the modern wing in the rear, which effectively doubled the museum's display space. Shortly thereafter the permanent collection and temporary exhibit space was also expanded. Serendipitously, these renovations enabled the Gibbes to become the key visual arts venue for the Spoleto Festival, begun about the same time.

The influential Gibbes Art School in the early 20th century formed a close association with the Woodstock School in New York, bringing important ties and prestige to the fledgling institution. Georgia O'Keefe, who

© JIM MOREKIS

Gibbes Museum of Art

taught college for a time in Columbia, South Carolina, brought an exhibit here in 1955. The first solo show by an African American artist came here in 1974 with an exhibit of the work of William H. Johnson.

Don't miss the nice little garden and its centerpiece, the 1972 fountain and sculpture of Persephone by Marshall Fredericks. It's a perfect oasis to rest your feet before continuing on your personal art-appreciation journey.

Unitarian Church

In a town filled with cool old church cemeteries, the coolest belongs to the Unitarian Church (4 Archdale St., 843/723-4617, www.charleston uu.org, service Sun. 11 A.M., free tours Fri.–Sat. 10 A.M.–1 P.M.). As a nod to the beauty and power of nature, vegetation and shrubbery in the cemetery have been allowed to take their natural course (walkways excepted).

Virginia creeper wraps around 200-year-old-grave markers, honeybees feed on wildflowers, and tree roots threaten to engulf entire headstones. The whole effect is oddly relaxing, and one of my favorite places in Charleston.

The church itself—the second-oldest such edifice in Charleston and the oldest Unitarian sanctuary in the South—is pretty nice, too. Begun in 1776 because of overcrowding at the Circular Congregational Church, the brand-new building saw rough usage by British troops during the Revolution. In 1787 the church was repaired and formally dedicated, though it was not officially chartered as a Unitarian church until 1839.

An extensive modernization happened in 1852, during which the current English Perpendicular Gothic Revival walls were installed, along with the beautiful stained-glass windows. The church was spared in the horrible fire of 1861, which destroyed the old Circular Church itself but stopped right at the Unitarian Church's property line. Sadly, it was not so lucky during the 1886 earthquake, which toppled the original tower. The version you see today is a subsequent and less grand design.

Directly next door is **St. John's Lutheran**

© SONJA WALLEN

The Unitarian Universalist cemetery is intentionally left overgrown.

Church (5 Clifford St., 843/723-2426, www .stjohnscharleston.org, worship Sun. 8:30 and 11 A.M.), which had its origin in 1742 when Dr. Henry Melchior Muhlenberg stopped in town for a couple of days on his way to minister to the burgeoning Salzburger colony in Ebenezer, Georgia. He would later be known as the father of the Lutheran Church in America. To see the sanctuary at times other than Sunday mornings, go by the office next door 9 A.M.–2 P.M. Mon.–Fri. and they'll let you take a walk through the interior.

Old City Market

Part kitschy tourist trap, part glimpse into the old South, part community gathering place, Old City Market (Meeting and Market Sts., 843/973-7236, daily 6 A.M.–11:30 P.M.) remains Charleston's most reliable, if perhaps least flashy, attraction. It is certainly the practical center of the city's tourist trade, not least because so many tours originate nearby.

Originally built on Daniel's Creek—claimed

from the marsh in the early 1800s after the city's first marketplace at Broad and Meeting Streets burned in 1796—one of City Market's early features was a colony of vultures who hung around for scraps of meat from the many butcher stalls. Sensing that the carrion eaters would keep the area cleaner than any human could, city officials not only allowed the buzzards to hang around, they were protected by law, becoming known as "Charleston eagles" in tongue-in-cheek local jargon.

No matter what anyone tries to tell you, Charleston's City Market never hosted a single slave auction. Indeed, when the Pinckney family donated this land to the city for a "Publick Market," one stipulation was that no slaves were *ever* to be sold here—or else the property would immediately revert to the family's descendants. And judging by the prevalence of the Pinckney name in these parts to this day, there has never been a shortage of potential claimants should that stipulation have been violated.

Old City Market in downtown Charleston

And also no matter what anyone tells you, the old train tracks around this area weren't for trolleys. During World War II, a railroad ran from port facilities up the peninsula to warehouses down here.

Confederate Museum

Located on the second floor of City Market's main, iconic building, Market Hall on Meeting Street, the small but spirited Confederate Museum (188 Meeting St., 843/723-1541, Tues.–Sat. 11 A.M.–3:30 P.M., $5 adults, $3 children, cash only) hosts an interesting collection of Civil War memorabilia, with an emphasis on the military side, and is also the local headquarters of the United Daughters of the Confederacy. Perhaps its best contribution, however, is its research library.

William Rhett House

The oldest residence in Charleston is the circa 1713 William Rhett House (54 Hasell St.), which once belonged to the colonel who captured Stede Bonnet the pirate, bringing

him back for public execution at the Battery. It's now a private residence, but you can admire this excellent, prototypical example of a Charleston single house easily from the street and read the nearby historical marker.

St. Mary of the Annunciation Church

The oldest Roman Catholic church in the Carolinas and Georgia, St. Mary's of the Annunciation (89 Hasell St., 843/722-7696, www.catholic-doc.org/saintmarys) traces its roots to 1789, when the Irish priest Father Matthew Ryan was sent to begin the first Catholic parish in the colony.

The original church was destroyed in the great Charleston fire of 1838, and the present sanctuary dates from immediately thereafter. While it did receive a direct hit from a Union shell during the siege of Charleston in the Civil War—taking out the organ—the handsome Greek Revival edifice has survived the 1886 earthquake, the great hurricane of 1893, and Hurricane Hugo in fine form.

You can tour the interior most weekdays from 9:30 A.M.–3:30 P.M. Sunday Mass is at 9:30 A.M.

Kahal Kadosh Beth Elohim Reform Temple

The birthplace of Reform Judaism in the United States and the oldest continuously active synagogue in the nation is Kahal Kadosh Beth Elohim Reform Temple (90 Hasell St., 843/723-1090, www.kkbe.org, service Sat. 11 A.M., tours Mon., Tues., Fri. 10 A.M.–noon, Wed.–Thurs. 10 A.M.–noon and 1:30–3:30 P.M., Sun. 12:30–3:45 P.M.). The congregation—Kahal Kadosh means "holy community" in Hebrew—was founded in 1749, with the current temple dating from 1840 and built in the Greek Revival style so popular at the time.

The church's Reform roots came about indirectly because of the great fire of 1838. In rebuilding, some congregants wanted to introduce musical instruments into the temple—previously a no-no—in the form of an organ.

The Orthodox contingent lost the debate, and so the new building became the first home of Reform Judaism in the country, a fitting testament to Charleston's longstanding ecumenical spirit of religious tolerance and inclusiveness. Technically speaking, because the Holocaust destroyed all Reform temples in Europe, this is actually the oldest existing Reform synagogue in the world.

UPPER KING AREA

For many visitors, the area around King Street north of Calhoun Street is the most happening area of Charleston, and not only because its proximity to the Visitors Center makes it the first part of town many see up close. On some days—Saturdays when the Farmers Market is open, for instance—this bustling, active area of town seems a galaxy away from the quiet grace of the older South of Broad area.

Its closeness to the beautiful College of Charleston campus means there's never a shortage of young people around to patronize the area's restaurants and bars and to add a youthful feel to the whole place. And its closeness to the city's main shopping district, King Street, means there's never a shortage of happy shoppers toting bags of new merchandise.

Marion Square

While the Citadel moved lock, stock, and barrel almost a century ago, the college's old home, the South Carolina State Arsenal, still overlooks Francis Marion Square, a reminder of the former glory days when this was the institute's parade ground, the "Citadel Green" (the old Citadel is now a hotel). Interestingly, Marion Square (btwn. King and Meeting Sts. at Calhoun St., 843/965-4104) can still be used as a parade ground, under agreement with the Washington Light Infantry and the Sumter Guard, which lease the square to the city.

Seemingly refusing to give up on tradition—or perhaps just attracted by the many female College of Charleston students—uniformed cadets from the Citadel are still chockablock in Marion Square on any given weekend, a bit of local flavor that reminds you that you're definitely in Charleston.

Six-and-a-half acre Marion Square is named

© JIM MOREKIS

The Marion Square Farmers Market happens every Saturday.

for the "Swamp Fox" himself, Revolutionary War hero and father of modern guerrilla warfare Francis Marion, for whom the hotel at the square's southwest corner is also named. The newest feature of Marion Square is the Holocaust Memorial on Calhoun Street.

However, the dominant monument is the towering memorial to John C. Calhoun. Its 1858 cornerstone includes one of the more interesting time capsules you'll encounter: $100 in Continental money, a lock of John Calhoun's hair, and a cannonball from the Fort Moultrie battle.

Marion Square hosts many events, including the Farmers Market every Saturday from mid-April to late December, the Food and Wine Festival, and of course some Spoleto events.

College of Charleston

The oldest college in South Carolina and the first municipal college in America, the College of Charleston (66 George St., 843/805-5507, www.cofc.edu) boasts a fair share of history in addition to the way its 12,000-plus students bring a modern, youthful touch to so much of the city's public activities. While its services are no longer free, despite its historic moniker the College is now a full-blown, state-supported university in its own right.

Though the College has its share of new, modernistic buildings, a leisurely stroll around the campus will uncover some true gems of history. The oldest building on this gorgeous campus, the Bishop Robert Smith House, dates from the year of the College's founding in 1770 and is now the president's house. Find it on Glebe Street between Wentworth and George.

The large Greek Revival building dominating the College's old quad off George and St. Philip's Streets is the magnificent Randolph Hall (1828), the oldest functioning college classroom in the country and now host to the president's office. The huge circular feature directly in front of it is "The Cistern," a historic reservoir that's a popular place for students to sit in the grass and enjoy the sun filtering through the live oaks.

The cistern is also where then-candidate Barack Obama spoke at a packed rally in

the College of Charleston

January 2008. Movies that have shot scenes on campus include *Cold Mountain, The Patriot,* and *The Notebook.*

The College's main claims to academic fame are its outstanding Art History and Marine Biology departments and its performing arts program. The **Halsey Institute of Contemporary Art** (54 St. Philip St., 843/953-5680, www.halsey.cofc.edu, Mon.–Sat. 11 A.M.–4 P.M.) focuses on modern visual art and also offers film screenings and lectures. The groundbreaking **Avery Research Center for African American History and Culture** (843/953-7609, www.cofc.edu/avery, Mon.–Fri. 10 A.M.–5 P.M., Sat. noon–5 P.M.) features rotating exhibits from its permanent archive collection.

Charleston Museum

During its long history it's moved literally all over town. It's currently housed in a noticeably modern building, but make no mistake: The Charleston Museum (360 Meeting St., 843/722-2996, www.charlestonmuseum .org, Mon.–Sat. 9 A.M.–5 P.M., Sun. 1–5 P.M., $10 adults, $5 children, combo tickets to Heyward-Washington and/or Manigault Houses available) is the nation's oldest museum, founded in 1773. It still strives to stay as fresh and relevant as any new museum, with a rotating schedule of special exhibits in addition to its very eclectic permanent collection.

For a long time this was the only place to get a glimpse of the CSS *Hunley,* albeit just a fanciful replica in front of the main entrance. (Now you can see the real thing at its conservation site in North Charleston, and it's even smaller than the replica would indicate.)

Most of the Charleston Museum's collection focuses on the aspects of everyday life of Charlestonians from the aristocracy to the slaves, like utensils, clothing, and furniture. There are quirks as well, such as the Egyptian mummy and the fine lady's fan made out of turkey feathers. A particular and possibly surprising specialty includes work and research by noted regional naturalists like John James Audubon, André Michaux, and Mark Catesby. There are also numerous exhibits chronicling the local history of Native Americans and African Americans. There's something for children too, in the hands-on, interactive "Kidstory."

The location is particularly convenient, being close not only to the excellent Charleston Visitors Center and its equally excellent parking garage, but to the Joseph Manigault House (which the Museum runs), the Children's Museum of the Lowcountry, and the Gibbes Museum of Art.

Joseph Manigault House

Owned and operated by the nearby Charleston Museum, the Joseph Manigault House (350 Meeting St., 843/723-2926, www.charleston museum.org, Mon.–Sat. 10 A.M.–5 P.M., Sun., 1–5 P.M., last tour 4:30 P.M., $10 adults, $5 children, combo tickets to Charleston Museum and/or Heyward-Washington House available) is sometimes called the "Huguenot House." Its splendor is a good reminder of the fact that the French Protestants were far from poverty-stricken, unlike so many groups who came to America fleeing persecution.

This circa-1803 National Historic Landmark was designed by wealthy merchant and investor Gabriel Manigault for his brother, Joseph, a rice planter of local repute and fortune. (Gabriel, quite the crackerjack dilettante architect, also designed Charleston City Hall.) The three-story brick townhouse is a great example of Adams, or Federal, architecture.

The furnishings are top-notch examples of 19th-century handiwork, and the rooms have been restored as accurately as possible, down to the historically correct paint colors. Various outbuildings, including a privy and slaves' quarters, are clustered around the picturesque little Gate Temple to the rear of the main house in the large enclosed garden.

Each December, the Manigault House offers visitors a special treat, as the Garden Club of Charleston decorates it in period seasonal fashion, using only flowers that would have been used in the 19th century.

◖ Aiken-Rhett House

A comparatively recent acquisition of the Historic Charleston Foundation, the Aiken-Rhett House (48 Elizabeth St., 843/723-1159, www.historiccharleston.org, Mon.–Sat. 10 A.M.–5 P.M., Sun 2–5 P.M., last tour 4:15 P.M., $10) shows another side of that organization's mission. Whereas the Historic Charleston–run Nathaniel Russell House seeks to recreate and interpret a specific point in time, work at the Aiken-Rhett House, acquired in 1995, emphasizes stabilization, conservation, and research. Other than a limewash in 2006—work done under the auspices of a Save America's Treasures grant—comparatively little interpretive restoration is going on here.

And also unlike the Russell House, this is less of an ostentatious mansion than a working urban complex, a double house with a stable, a privy, and a particularly well-preserved slave quarters. Built in 1818 and expanded by South Carolina Governor William Aiken Jr., after whom we know the house today, parts of the house remained sealed from 1918 until 1975 when his family relinquished the property to the Charleston Museum, providing historians with a unique opportunity to study original documents from that period.

It was here that General Beauregard moved his headquarters during the Civil War to be out of range of the Union siege guns wreaking havoc in the lower part of the peninsula. As you enjoy your self-guided audio tour—unique in Charleston—you'd be forgiven for thinking the damaged state of some of the original wallpaper is due to the ravages of war, but it's actually water damage from Hurricane Hugo.

Archaeology continues at the site, specifically in the area of the old capped well, which is giving researchers some insight into 19th-century construction methods in this high water table area.

Simply put, while there are plenty of much more vivaciously restored homes in Charleston, the Aiken-Rhett House provides the single most realistic and educational glimpse into antebellum life in the Holy City.

Children's Museum of the Lowcountry

Yet another example of Charleston's savvy regarding the tourist industry is the Children's Museum of the Lowcountry (25 Ann St., 843/853-8962, www.explorecml.org, Tues.–Sat. 10 A.M.–5 P.M., Sun. 1–5 P.M., $7). Recognizing that historic homes and Civil War memorabilia aren't enough to keep a family with young children in town for very long, the city established this museum in 2005 specifically to give families with kids aged 3 months to 12 years a reason to spend more time (and money) downtown.

A wide variety of hands-on activities—such as a 30-foot shrimp boat replica and a medieval castle—stretch the definition of "museum" to its limit. In truth, this is just as much an indoor playground as a museum, but there's no need to quibble. The Children's Museum has been getting rave reviews since it opened, and visiting parents and their children seem very happy with the city's wise investment.

Philip Simmons Garden

Charleston's most beloved artisan is ironworker Philip Simmons, who died in 2009 at the age of 97. Born on nearby Daniel Island in 1919, Simmons went through apprenticeship to become one of the most creative and sought-after decorative ironworkers in America. In 1982, the National Endowment for the Arts awarded him its National Heritage Fellowship. His work is on display at the National Museum of American History, the Smithsonian Institution, and the Museum of International Folk Art in Santa Fe, among many other places.

In 1989, the congregation at Simmons's **St. John's Reformed Episcopal Church** (91 Anson St., 843/722-4241, www.stjohnsre. org) voted to make the church garden a commemoration of the life and work of the artisan. Completed in two phases, the Bell Garden and the Heart Garden, the project is a delightful blend of Simmons's signature graceful, sinuous style and fragrant flowers.

Old Bethel United Methodist Church

The history of the Old Bethel United Methodist Church (222 Calhoun St., 843/722-3470), third-oldest church building in Charleston, is a little confusing. Completed in 1807, the church once stood across Calhoun Street, until a schism formed in the black community over whether they should be limited to sitting in the galleries (in those days in the South, blacks and whites attended church together far more frequently than during the Jim Crow era).

The entire black congregation wanted out, so in 1852 it was moved aside for the construction of a new church for whites, and then entirely across the street in 1880. Look across the street and sure enough you'll see the circa-1853 **Bethel Methodist Church** (57 Pitt St., 843/723-4587, worship Sun. 9 A.M. and 11:15 A.M.).

HAMPTON PARK AREA

Expansive Hampton Park is a favorite recreation spot for Charlestonians. The surrounding area near the east bank of the Ashley River has some of the earliest suburbs of Charleston, now in various states of restoration and hosting a diverse range of residents. Hampton Park is bordered by streets all around, which can be fairly heavily trafficked because this is the only way to get to the Citadel. But the park streets are closed to traffic Saturday mornings in the spring 8 A.M.–noon so neighborhood people, especially those with young children, can enjoy themselves without worrying about the traffic. This is also where the Charleston Police stable their Horse Patrol steeds.

The Citadel

Though for many its spiritual and historic center will always be at the old state Arsenal in Marion Square, The Citadel (171 Moultrie St., 843/953-3294, www.citadel.edu, daily 8 A.M.–6 P.M.) has been at this 300-acre site farther up the peninsula along the Ashley River since 1922 and shows no signs of leaving. Getting there is a little tricky, in that the entrance to the college is situated behind

beautiful Hampton Park off Rutledge Avenue, probably the main north-south artery on the western portion of the peninsula.

The Citadel (technically its full name is The Citadel, The Military College of South Carolina) has entered popular consciousness through the works of graduate Pat Conroy, especially his novel *Lords of Discipline,* starring a thinly disguised "Carolina Military Institute." Other famous Bulldog alumni include construction magnate Charles Daniel (for whom the school library is named); Ernest "Fritz" Hollings, South Carolina governor and longtime U.S. senator; and current Charleston Mayor Joe Riley.

You'll see the Citadel's living legacy all over Charleston in the person of the ubiquitous cadet, whose gray-and-white uniforms, ramrod posture, and impeccable manners all hearken back to the days of the Confederacy. But to best experience the Citadel, you should go to the campus itself.

There's lots for visitors to see, including **The Citadel Museum** (843/953-6779, Sun.–Fri. 2–5 P.M., Sat. noon–5 P.M., free), on your right just as you enter campus; the "Citadel Murals" in the Daniel Library; "Indian Hill," highest point in Charleston and former site of an Indian trader's home; and the grave of U.S. General Mark Clark of World War II fame, who was Citadel president from 1954–1966.

Ringing vast Summerall Field—the huge open space as soon as you enter campus—are the many castle-looking cadet barracks. If you peek inside their gates, you'll see the distinctive checkerboard pattern on which the cadets line up. All around the field itself are various military items such as a Sherman tank and an F-4 Phantom jet.

The most interesting single experience for visitors to the Citadel, however, is the colorful Friday afternoon dress parade on Summerall Field, in which cadets pass for review in full dress uniform (the fabled "long gray line") accompanied by a marching band and pipers. Often called "the best free show in Charleston," the parade happens most every Friday at 3:45 P.M. during the school year; you might want to consult the website before your visit to confirm. Arrive well in advance to avoid parking problems.

The institute was born out of panic over the threat of a slave rebellion organized in 1822 by Denmark Vesey. The state legislature passed an act establishing the school to educate the strapping young men picked to protect Charleston from a slave revolt. Citadel folks will proudly tell you they actually fired the first shots of the Civil War, when on January 9, 1861, two cadets fired from a battery on Morris Island at the U.S. steamer *Star of the West* to keep it from supplying Fort Sumter. After slavery stopped—and hence the school's original *raison d'tre*—the Citadel continued, taking its current name in 1910 and moving to the Ashley River in 1922.

While the Citadel is rightly famous for its pomp and circumstance—as well as its now-defunct no-lock "honor system," done away with after the Virginia Tech shootings—the little-known truth is that to be one of the 2,000 or so currently enrolled Citadel Bulldogs you don't have to go through all that, or the infamous "Hell Week" either. You can just sign up

WOMEN AND THE CITADEL: THE ONGOING STRUGGLE

Though a lot has certainly changed at The Citadel over a decade after courts mandated that it open its doors to female cadets, many of the same issues and obstacles remain at Charleston's formerly male-only military academy.

The first attempt to crack the gender barrier, by Shannon Faulker in 1994, failed miserably when she dropped out after less than a week, to much open celebration on campus. During her efforts, she endured not only the usual physical stress any Citadel cadet must face, but was also the subject of assorted cruelties, like bumper stickers all over town saying things like "Save the Males," one of the more printable slogans. The star-crossed nature of Faulkner's effort was emphasized by the fact that her entrance came about because of a misunderstanding. School officials saw her first and middle names – Shannon Richey – and assumed she was a man!

The next episode came in 1996, when four female cadets were admitted, with two transferring out and filing suit against the school for sexual harassment. One of the two who remained, Nancy Mace, went on to become the first woman to graduate from The Citadel. While that accomplishment in 1999 was tempered somewhat by the fact that Mace's father was General James Emory Mace, Commandant of Cadets at the school at the time, it nonetheless marked a watershed moment in Citadel history.

In 2002, seven African American women cadets graduated from The Citadel, 32 years after Charles Foster first broke the racial barrier there in 1970 as the first African American graduate.

While the atmosphere has certainly gotten a lot more progressive at this conservative bastion – a "citadel" in more ways than one – not all is rosy. A 2006 survey found that 68 percent of women students (and 17 percent of male students) said they were victims of sexual harassment on campus. About one in five women reported a sexual assault on campus. General John Rosa, president of The Citadel and former president of the U.S. Air Force Academy, said that though those numbers are not far off national numbers, they were "not good enough for us."

Currently over 100 of The Citadel's cadets are female – or about six percent of the student body, as opposed to about 16 percent at the service academies. And freshmen women cadets routinely have not only higher SAT scores than male cadets, but higher grade point averages as well.

Interestingly, Lu Parker, crowned Miss USA in 1994, got her master's degree in education from The Citadel. But she wasn't a cadet – all grad courses at The Citadel are night classes. And they don't even make you wear a uniform or do push-ups.

© JIM MOREKIS

view inside the Citadel barracks

for one of their many evening graduate school programs.

Joseph P. Riley Jr. Ballpark

When you hear Charlestonians talk about "The Joe" (360 Fishburne St., 843/577-3647, www .riverdogs.com, general admission $5) they're referring to this charming minor league baseball stadium, home of the Charleston River Dogs, a New York Yankees affiliate playing April–August in the venerable South Atlantic League. It's also another part of the civic legacy of longtime Mayor Joe Riley, in this case in partnership with the adjacent Citadel. Inspired by the retro design of Baltimore's Camden Yards, The Joe opened in 1997 to rave reviews from locals and baseball connoisseurs all over the nation.

From downtown, get there by taking Broad Street west until it turns into Lockwood Drive. Follow that north until you get to Brittlebank Park and The Joe, right next to the Citadel.

WEST ASHLEY

Ironically, Charleston's first post-war automobile suburb also has roots back to the very first days of the colony's settlement and was the site of some of the antebellum era's grandest plantations. As the cost of housing on the peninsula continues to rise, this quiet residential area on the west bank of the Ashley River is experiencing a newfound cachet today for hipsters and young families alike, with restaurants and funky shops beginning to take their place along with churches, playgrounds, and big-box retail stores.

For most visitors, though, the biggest draws here are the ancient plantations and historic sites along the west bank of the river itself: Charles Towne Landing, Drayton Hall, Magnolia Plantation, and Middleton Place farthest north. Getting to this area from Charleston proper is easy. Take U.S. 17 ("the Crosstown") west across the Ashley River until the junction with Highway 61. Take a right north onto Highway 61; veer right to get on Highway 7 for Charles Towne Landing, or stay left on Highway 61 for the plantations.

Charles Towne Landing

Any look at West Ashley must begin where everything began, with the 600-acre historic site

Charles Towne Landing (1500 Old Towne Rd., 843/852-4200, www.charlestowne.org, daily 9 A.M.–5 P.M., $5 adults, $3 students, 5 and under free). This is where Charleston's original settlers first arrived from Barbados and camped in 1670, remaining only a few years before eventually moving to the more defensible peninsula where the Holy City now resides.

For many years the site was in disrepair and borderline neglect, useful only as a place to ship busloads of local schoolchildren on field trips. However, a recent, long-overdue upgrade came to fruition with a grand "reopening" of sorts in 2006, which has been very well received and has given the Landing a newfound sheen of respect. A new audio tour has been instituted, where you rent an mp3 player ($5).

A life-size replica of a settlers' ship is the main new highlight, but another feature is the long interpretive trail that takes you around the long reconstructed palisade wall and the remains of some of the original structures. A 12-room visitors center has many exhibits on the history and daily life of the early settlers.

Many traces of Native American habitation have been found on-site as well, and don't miss the exhibits chronicling the 6,000 years of human history here before the Europeans arrived, including an apparent ceremonial area. Ranger-guided programs are available Wed.–Fri. at 10 A.M.; call ahead for reservations.

Not just a historic site, this is also a great place to bring the family. It features Charleston's only zoo, the "Animal Forest," featuring otters, bears, cougars, and buffalo, and 80 acres of beautiful gardens to relax in, many featuring fabulously ancient live oaks and highlighting other indigenous flora the settlers would have been familiar with.

Archaeology and renovation are ongoing at Charles Towne Landing, with a key project being the excavation of the original western palisade wall. They've even found one of the settlers' tobacco pipes, marked with the maker's name, "Wil. Evans."

You can choose to participate vicariously through the "Digital Dig" interactive exhibit—or who knows, maybe you'll be inspired to join the park's archaeology volunteer program. It offers internships for college credit.

(Drayton Hall

A mecca for historic preservationists all over the country, Drayton Hall (3380 Ashley River Rd., 843/769-2600, www.draytonhall .org, daily 9:30 A.M.–4 P.M. Nov.–Feb., daily 8:30 A.M.–5 P.M. Mar.–Oct., $14 adults, $8 ages 12–18, $6 ages 6–11, $8 for grounds only) is remarkable not only for its pedigree but for the way in which it's been preserved. This stately redbrick Georgian-Palladian building, the oldest plantation home in America open to the public, has been *literally* historically preserved—as in no electricity, heat, or running water.

Since its construction in 1738 by John Drayton, son of Magnolia Plantation founder Thomas, Drayton Hall has amazingly survived almost completely intact through the ups and downs of Lowcountry history. Drayton died while fleeing the British army in 1779; subsequently his house served as the headquarters of British General Clinton and later General Cornwallis. By 1782, however, American General "Mad Anthony" Wayne had claimed the house as his own headquarters in the name of the new country.

During the Civil War, Drayton Hall escaped the depredations of the conquering Union Army, one of only three area plantation homes to survive. Three schools of thought have emerged to explain why it was spared the fate of so many other Lowcountry plantation homes: 1) a slave told the troops it was owned by "a Union Man," Drayton cousin Percival who served alongside Admiral David Farragut of "damn the torpedoes" fame; 2) General William Sherman was in love with one of the Drayton women; and 3) one of the Draytons, a doctor, craftily posted yellow smallpox warning flags at the outskirts of the property. Of the three scenarios, the last is considered the most likely, though we'll never know for sure.

Visitors expecting the more typical approach to house museums, i.e. subjective renovation with period furnishings that may or may not

© JIM MOREKIS

Drayton Hall

have any connection at all with the actual house, might be disappointed. But for others the experience at Drayton Hall is quietly exhilarating, almost in a Zen-like way.

Planes are routed around the house so that no rattles will endanger its structural integrity. There's no furniture here to speak of, only the bare rooms, decorated only with the original paint, no matter how little remains. It can be jarring at first, but after you get into it you might wonder why anyone does things any differently.

Another way the experience is different is in the almost military professionalism of the National Trust for Historic Preservation, which has owned and administered Drayton Hall since 1974. The guides are professionals and hold degrees in the field, and a tour of the house—offered punctually at the top of the hour, except for the last of the day which starts on the half-hour—takes every bit of 50 minutes, about twice as long as most house tours.

A separate 45-minute program is "Connections: From Africa to America," which chronicles the diaspora of the slaves who originally worked this plantation, from their capture to their eventual freedom. "Connections" is given at 11:15 A.M., 1:15 P.M., and 3:15 P.M.

The site comprises not only the main house but two self-guided walking trails, one along the peaceful Ashley River and another along the marsh. Note also the foundations of the two "flankers," or guest wings, at each side of the main house. They survived the Yankees only for one to fall victim to the 1886 earthquake and the other to the 1893 hurricane. Also on-site is an African American cemetery with at least 33 known graves. It's kept deliberately untended and unlandscaped to honor the final wish of Richmond Bowens (1908–1998), the seventh-generation descendant of some of Drayton Hall's original slaves.

Magnolia Plantation and Gardens

A different legacy of the Drayton family is Magnolia Plantation and Gardens (3550 Ashley Rd., 843/571-1266, www.magnoliaplantation .com, daily 8 A.M.–dusk Mar.–Oct., call for winter hours, $15 adults, $10 children, under 6 free). It claims not only the first garden in the United States, dating back to the 1680s, but also the first public garden, dating to 1872.

However, Magnolia's history spans back two full centuries before that, when Thomas Drayton Jr.—scion of Norman aristocracy,

The Maze at Magnolia Plantation

son of a wealthy Barbadian planter—came here from the Caribbean to build his own fortune. He immediately married the daughter of Stephen Fox, who began this plantation in 1676. Throughout wars, fevers, depressions, earthquakes, and hurricanes, Magnolia has stayed in the possession of an unbroken line of Drayton descendants to this very day.

As a privately run attraction, Magnolia has little of the academic veneer of other plantation sites in the area, most of which have long passed out of private hands. There's a slightly kitschy feel here, the opposite of the quiet dignity of Drayton Hall. And unlike Middleton Place a few miles down the road, the gardens here are anything but manicured, with a wild, almost playful feel.

All that said, Magnolia can claim fame to being one of the earliest bona fide tourist attractions in the United States and the beginning of Charleston's now-booming tourist industry. It happened after the Civil War, when John Grimke Drayton, reduced to near-poverty, sold off most of his property,

including the original Magnolia Plantation, just to stay afloat. (In a common practice at the time, as a condition of inheriting the plantation Mr. Grimke, who married into the family, was required to legally change his name to Drayton.) The original plantation home was burned during the war—either by Union troops or freed slaves—so Drayton barged a colonial-era summer house in Summerville, South Carolina, down the Ashley River to this site, and built the modern Magnolia Plantation around it specifically as an attraction. Before long, tourists regularly came here by crowded boat from Charleston (a wreck of one such ferry is still on-site). Magnolia's reputation became so exalted that at one point Baedecker's listed it as one of the three main attractions in America, alongside the Grand Canyon and Niagara Falls.

The family took things to the next level in the 1970s, when the family nursery business was no longer commercially viable. John Drayton Hastie bought out his brother and set about marketing Magnolia Plantation and

Gardens as a modern tourist destination, adding more varieties of flowers so that something would always be blooming nearly year-round. While spring remains the best time to come—and also the most crowded—a huge variety of camellias blooms in the early winter, a time marked by a yearly "Winter Camellia Festival" on-site.

Today the vision is fully a reality, and Magnolia is a place to bring the whole family, picnic under the massive old live oaks, and wander the lush, almost overgrown grounds. Children will enjoy finding their way through "The Maze" of manicured camellia and holly bushes, complete with a viewing stand to look within the giant puzzle. Plant lovers will enjoy the themed gardens such as the "Biblical Garden," the "Barbados Tropical Garden," and the "Audubon Swamp Garden," complete with alligators and named after John James Audubon, who visited here in 1851. Hundreds of varieties of camellias, clearly labeled, line the narrow walkways. House tours, the 45-minute Nature Train tour, the 45-minute Nature Boat tour, and a visit to the Audubon Swamp Garden run about $7 extra per person for each offering.

Of particular interest is the poignant old Drayton Tomb, along the Ashley River, which housed many members of the family until being heavily damaged in the 1886 earthquake. Look closely at the nose of one of the cherubs on the tomb; it was shot off by a vengeful Union soldier. Nearby you'll find a nice walking and biking trail along the Ashley among the old rice paddies.

🄲 Middleton Place

Not only the first formal, landscaped garden in America but still one of the most magnificent in the world, Middleton Place (4300 Ashley River Rd., 843/556-6020, www.middleton place.org, daily 9 A.M.–5 P.M., $25 adults, $5 ages 7–15, guided house tour additional $10) is a sublime, unforgettable combination of history and sheer natural beauty. Nestled along a quiet bend in the Ashley River, the grounds contain a historic restored home, working stables, and 60 acres of breathtaking gardens, all manicured to perfection. A stunning piece of modern architecture, the Inn at Middleton Place, completes the package in a surprisingly harmonic fashion.

First granted in 1675 a scant five years after the first English settlement here, Middleton Place is the culmination of the Lowcountry rice plantation aesthetic. That sensibility is most immediately seen in the graceful Butterfly Lakes at the foot of the green, landscaped terrace leading up to the Middleton Place House itself, the only surviving remnant of the vengeful Union occupation. The two wing-shaped lakes, 10 years in the construction, seem to echo the low rice paddies that once dotted this entire landscape.

In 1741 the plantation became the family seat of the Middletons, one of the most notable surnames in U.S. history. The first head of the household was Henry Middleton, president of the First Continental Congress, who began work on the meticulously planned and maintained gardens. The plantation passed to his son Arthur, a signer of the Declaration of Independence; then on to Arthur's son Henry, governor of South Carolina; and then down to Henry's son, Williams Middleton, signer of the Ordinance of Secession.

It was then that things turned sour, both for the family and for the grounds themselves. As the Civil War wound down, on February 22, 1865, the 56th New York Volunteers burned and looted the main house and destroyed the gardens, leaving only the circa-1755 guest wing, which today is the Middleton Place House Museum. The great earthquake of 1886 added insult to injury by wrecking the Butterfly Lakes.

It wasn't until 1916 that any renovation work began at all, when heir J. J. Pringle Smith took on the project as his own. No one can say he wasn't successful. At the garden's bicentennial in 1941, the Garden Club of America awarded its prestigious Bulkley Medal to Middleton Place. In 1971 Middleton Place was named a National Historic Landmark, and 20 years later the International Committee on Monuments and Sites named Middleton Place one of six U.S. gardens of international importance.

In 1974, Smith's heirs established the non-profit Middleton Place Foundation, which now owns and operates the entire site. As development has increased along the Ashley River, several developers and at least one nearby private landowner have donated easements to protect the irreplaceable view from the site.

All that's left of the great house are the broken remains of the foundation, still majestic even in ruin. But today visitors can tour the excellently restored **Middleton Place House Museum** (4300 Ashley River Rd., 843/556-6020, www.middletonplace.org, guided tours Tues.–Sun. 10 A.M.–4:30 P.M., Mon. 1:30–4:30 P.M., $10) and see furniture, silverware, china, and books belonging to the Middletons, as well as family portraits by Thomas Sully and Benjamin West. A short walk takes you to the Plantation Stableyards, where costumed craftspeople still work using historically authentic tools and methods, surrounded by a happy family of domestic animals.

The newest addition to the Stableyards is a pair of magnificent young male water buffalo. Henry Middleton originally brought a pair in to work the rice fields—the first in North America—but today they're just there to relax and add atmosphere. They bear the Turkish names of Adem (the brown one) and Berk (the white one), or "Earth" and "Solid." Meet the fellas daily 9 A.M.–5 P.M.

However, if you're like most folks you'll best enjoy simply wandering and marveling at the gardens. "Meandering" is not the right word to describe them, since they're very systematically laid out. "Intricate" is the word I prefer, and that seems to sum up the attention to detail that characterizes all the garden's various portions, each with a distinct personality and landscape design template of its own. A major floral focal point of the gardens is its vast repertoire of camellia, with hundreds of varieties present including the 1786 *Reine des Fleurs,* one of the first types planted in America. While the museum closes at 5 P.M., you can enjoy the gardens until dusk if you're already on the grounds.

To get a real feel for how things used to be here, for an extra $15 per person you can take a 45-minute carriage ride through the bamboo forest to an abandoned rice field. Rides start around 10 A.M. and run every hour or so, weather permitting.

The 53-room **Inn at Middleton Place,** besides being a wholly gratifying lodging experience, is also a quite self-conscious and largely successful experiment. Its bold, Wright-influenced modern design, comprising four units joined by walkways, is modern but both inside and outside manages to blend quite well with the surrounding fields, trees, and riverbanks. The Inn also offers kayak tours and instruction—a particularly nice way to enjoy the grounds from the waters of the Ashley—and features its own organic garden and labyrinth, intriguing modern counterpoints to the formal gardens of the plantation itself.

They still grow the exquisite Carolina Gold rice in a field at Middleton Place, harvested in the old style each September. You can sample some of it in many dishes at the **Middleton Place Restaurant** (843/556-6020, www.middletonplace.org, lunch daily 11 A.M.–3 P.M., dinner Tues.–Thurs. 6–8 P.M., Fri.–Sat. 6–9 P.M., Sun. 6–8 P.M., $15–25). Hint: You can tour the gardens for free if you arrive for a dinner reservation at 5:30 P.M. or later.

The Coburg Cow

The entire stretch of U.S. 17 (Savannah Highway) heading into Charleston from the west is redolent of a particularly Southern brand of retro Americana. The chief example is the famous Coburg Cow, a large, rotating dairy cow accompanied by a bottle of chocolate milk.

The current installation dates from 1959, though a version of it was on this site as far back as the early 1930s when this area was open countryside. During Hurricane Hugo the Coburg Cow was moved to a safe location.

In 2001 the attached dairy closed down, and the city threatened to have the cow moved or demolished. But community outcry preserved the delightful landmark, which is visible today on the south side of U.S. 17 in the 900 block. You can't miss it—it's a big cow on the side of the road!

NORTH CHARLESTON

For years synonymous with crime, blight, and sprawl, North Charleston—actually a separate municipality—was for the longest time considered a necessary evil by most Charlestonians, who generally ventured there only to shop at a huge mall or see a show at its concert venue, the Coliseum. But as the cost of real estate continues to rise on the peninsula in Charleston proper, more and more artists and young professionals are choosing to live here.

Make no mistake, North Charleston still has its share of crime and depressing squalor, but some of the most exciting things going on in the metro area are taking place right here. While many insisted that the closing of the U.S. Navy Yard here in the 1990s would be the economic death of the whole city, the free market stepped in and is transforming the former military facility into a hip, mixed-use shopping and residential area. This is also where to go if you want to see the raised submarine CSS *Hunley,* now in a research area on the grounds of the old Navy Yard.

In short, North Charleston offers a lot for the more adventurous traveler and will no doubt only become more and more important to the local tourist industry as the years go by. And as they're fond of pointing out up here, there aren't any parking meters.

Magnolia Cemetery

Though not technically in North Charleston, historic Magnolia Cemetery (70 Cunnington Ave., 843/722-8638, daily 8 A.M.–5 P.M. Sept.–May, daily 8 A.M.–6 P.M. Jun.–Aug.) is on the way, in the area well north of the general downtown tourist district called "The Neck." This historic burial ground, while not the equal of Savannah's Bonaventure, is still a stirring site for its natural beauty and ornate memorials as well as for its historic aspects. Here are buried the crewmen who died aboard the CSS *Hunley,* re-interred after their retrieval from Charleston

Harbor. In all, over 2,000 Civil War dead are buried here, including five Confederate generals and 84 rebels who fell at Gettysburg and were moved here.

Charleston Navy Yard

A vast post-industrial wasteland to some and a fascinating outdoor museum to others, the Charleston Navy Yard is in the baby steps of rehabilitation from one of the Cold War era's major military centers to the largest single urban redevelopment project in the United States.

The Navy's gone now, forced off the site during a phase of base realignment in the mid-1990s. But a 340-acre section, the **Navy Yard at Noisette** (1360 Truxtun Ave., 843/302-2100, www.navyyardsc.com, daily 24 hours), now hosts an intriguing mix of homes, green-friendly design firms, small nonprofits, and commercial maritime companies that was named America's sixth-greenest neighborhood by *Natural Home* magazine in 2008. It's even played host to some scenes of the Lifetime TV series *Army Wives.*

Enter on Spruill Avenue and shortly you'll find yourself on wide streets lined with huge, boarded-up warehouse facilities, old machine shops, and dormant power stations. A notable project is the restoration of **10 Storehouse Row** (2120 Noisette Blvd., 843/302-2100, Mon.–Fri. 9 A.M.–5 P.M.), which now hosts the American College of Building Arts, design firms, galleries, and a small café.

At the north end of the redevelopment lies the brand-new **Riverfront Park** (843/745-1087, daily dawn–dusk) in the old Chicora Gardens military residential area. The Park comprises a nifty little fishing pier going out into the scenic Cooper River, an excellent naval-themed bandshell, and many sleekly designed, modernist sculptures paying tribute to the sailors and ships that made history here.

From Charleston you get to the Navy Yard by taking I-26 north to exit 216-B (you can reach the I-26 junction by just going north on Meeting Street). After exiting take a left onto Spruill Avenue and a right onto McMillan, which takes you straight in.

(CSS *Hunley*

For the longest time the only glimpse of the ill-fated Confederate submarine was a not-quite-accurate replica outside the Charleston Museum. But after maritime novelist and adventurer Clive Cussler and his team finally found the *Hunley* in 1995 off Sullivan's Island, the tantalizing dream became a reality: we'd finally find out what it looked like, and perhaps even be lucky enough to bring it to the surface.

That moment came on August 8, 2000, when a team comprising the nonprofit **Friends of the Hunley** (Warren Lasch Conservation Center, 1250 Supply St., Building 255, 866/866-9938, www.hunley.org, Sat. 10 A.M.–5 P.M., Sun. noon–5 P.M., $12, children under 5 free), the

---

RAISING THE *HUNLEY*

The amazing, unlikely raising of the Confederate submarine CSS *Hunley* from the muck of Charleston harbor sounds like the plot of an adventure novel – which makes sense considering that the major player is an adventure novelist.

For 15 years, the undersea diver and best-selling author Clive Cussler looked for the final resting place of the *Hunley*. The sub was mysteriously lost at sea after sinking the USS *Housatonic* on February 17, 1864, with the high-explosive "torpedo" mounted on a long spar on its bow. It marked the first time a sub ever sank a ship in battle.

For over a century before Cussler, treasure-seekers had searched for the sub, with P. T. Barnum even offering $100,000 to the first person to find it. But on May 3, 1995, a magnetometer operated by Cussler and his group, the National Underwater Marine Agency, discovered the *Hunley*'s final resting place – in 30 feet of water and under three feet of sediment about four miles off Sullivan's Island at the mouth of the harbor.

Using a specially designed truss to lift the entire sub, a 19-person dive crew and a team of archaeologists began a process that would result in raising the vessel on August 8, 2000. But before the sub could be brought up, a dilemma had to be solved: For 136 years the saltwater of the Atlantic had permeated its metallic skin. Exposure to air would rapidly disintegrate the entire thing. So the conservation team, with input from the U.S. Navy, came up with a plan to keep the vessel submerged in a special solution indefinitely at the specially constructed **Warren Lasch Conservation Center** (1250 Supply St., Building 255, 866/866-9938, www.hunley.org,

Sat. 10 A.M.–5 P.M., Sun. noon–5 P.M., $12, 5 and under free) in the old Navy Yard while research and conservation was performed on it piece-by-piece.

And that's how you see the *Hunley* today, submerged in its special conservation tank, still largely covered in sediment. Upon seeing the almost unbelievably tiny, cramped vessel – much smaller than most experts imagined it would be – visitors are often visibly moved at the bravery and sacrifice of the nine-man Confederate crew, who no doubt would have known that the *Hunley*'s two previous crews had drowned at sea in training accidents. Theirs was, in effect, a suicide mission. That the crew surely realized this only makes the modern visitor's experience even more poignant and meaningful.

The Warren Lasch Center, operated under the auspices of Clemson University, is only open to the public on weekends. Archaeology continues apace during the week – inch by painstaking inch, muck and tiny artifacts removed millimeter by millimeter. The process is so thorough that archaeologists have even identified an individual eyelash from one of the crew. Other interesting artifacts include a three-fold wallet with a leather strap, owner unknown; seven canteens; and a wooden cask in one of the ballast tanks, maybe used to hold water or liquor or even used as a chamber pot.

The very first order of business once the sub was brought up, however, was properly burying those brave sailors. In 2004, Charleston came to a stop as a ceremonial funeral procession took the remains of the nine to historic Magnolia Cemetery, where they were buried with full military honors.

CHARLESTON

federal government, and private partners successfully implemented a plan to safely raise the vessel. It was recently moved to its new home in the old Navy Yard, named after Warren Lasch, chairman of the Friends of the Hunley.

You can now view the sub in a 90,000-gallon conservation tank on the grounds of the old Navy Yard, see the life-size model from the TNT movie *The Hunley,* and look at artifacts such as the "lucky" gold piece of the commander. You can even see facial reconstructions of some of the eight sailors who died onboard the sub that fateful February day in 1864, when it mysteriously sank right after successfully destroying the USS *Housatonic* with the torpedo attached to its bow.

So that research and conservation can be performed during the week, tours only happen on Saturdays and Sundays, so it's wise to reserve tickets ahead of time. The sub itself is completely submerged in an electrolyte formula to better preserve it, and photography is strictly forbidden. (The remains of the crew lie in Magnolia Cemetery, where they were buried in 2004 with full military honors.)

To get to the Warren Lasch Center from Charleston, take I-516 north to exit 216-B. Take a left onto Spruill Avenue and a right onto McMillan. Once in the Navy Yard, take a right on Hobson, and after about a mile take a left onto Supply Street. The Lasch Center is the low white building on your left.

Park Circle

The focus of restoration in North Charleston is the old Park Circle neighborhood (intersection of Rhett and Montague Aves., www.parkcircle .net). The adjacent **Olde North Charleston** development has a number of quality shops, bars, and restaurants.

Fire Museum

It's got a mouthful of a name, but the new **North Charleston and American LaFrance Fire Museum and Educational Center** (4975 Centre Pointe Dr., 843/740-5550, www.legacy ofheroes.org, Mon.–Sat. 10 A.M.–5 P.M., last ticket 4 P.M., $6 adults, 13 and under free) right next to the huge Tanger Outlet Mall does what it does with a lot of chutzpah—which is fitting

COURTESY OF CHARLESTON AREA CVB, WWW.EXPLORECHARLESTON.COM

North Charleston and American LaFrance Fire Museum and Educational Center considering that it pays tribute to firefighters and the tools of their dangerous trade.

The museum, which opened in 2007 and shares a huge 25,000-square-foot space with the North Charleston Convention and Visitors Bureau, is primarily dedicated to maintaining and increasing its collection of antique American LaFrance firefighting vehicles and equipment. The 18 fire engines here date from 1857 to 1969.

The museum's exhibits have taken on greater poignancy in the wake of the tragic loss of nine Charleston firefighters killed trying to extinguish a warehouse blaze on U.S. 17 in summer 2007—second only to the 9/11 attacks as the largest single loss of life for a U.S. firefighting department.

EAST COOPER

The main destination in this area on the east bank of the Cooper River is the island of Mount Pleasant, primarily known as a peaceful, fairly affluent suburb of Charleston—a role it's played for about 300 years now. Though few old-timers (called "hungry necks" in local

lingo) remain, Mount Pleasant does have several key attractions well worth visiting—the old words of former Charleston Mayor John Grace notwithstanding: "Mount Pleasant is neither a mount, nor is it pleasant." Through Mount Pleasant is also the only land route to access Sullivan's Island, Isle of Palms, and historic Fort Moultrie.

Shem Creek, which bisects Mount Pleasant, was once the center of the local shrimping industry, and while there aren't near as many shrimp boats as there once were, you can still see them docked or on their way to and from a trawling run. (Needless to say, there are a lot of good seafood restaurants around here as well.)

The most common route for visitors is by way of U.S. 17 over the massive Arthur Ravenel Jr. Bridge.

Patriots Point Naval and Maritime Museum

Directly across Charleston Harbor from the old city lies the Patriots Point Naval and Maritime Museum complex (40 Patriots Point Rd., 843/884-2727, www.patriotspoint.org, daily

Patriots Point and the USS *Yorktown*

COURTESY OF CHARLESTON AREA CVB, WWW.EXPLORECHARLESTON.COM

9 A.M.–6:30 P.M., $16 adults, $8 ages 6–11, free for active duty military), one of the first chapters in Charleston's great tourism renaissance. The project began in 1975 with what is still its main attraction, the World War II aircraft carrier **USS Yorktown,** named in honor of the carrier lost at the Battle of Midway. Much of "The Fighting Lady" is open to the public, and kids and nautical buffs will thrill to walk the decks and explore the many stations below deck on this massive 900-foot vessel, a veritable floating city. You can even have a full meal in the C.P.O. Mess Hall just like the crew once did (except you'll have to pay $6.99 a person). And if you really want to get up close and personal, try the Navy Flight Simulator for a small added fee.

Speaking of planes, aviation buffs will be overjoyed to see that the *Yorktown* flight deck (the top of the ship) and the hangar deck (right below) are packed with authentic warplanes, not only from World War II but from subsequent conflicts the ship participated in. You'll see an F6F Hellcat, an FG-1D Corsair, and an SBD Dauntless such as those that fought the Japanese, on up to an F4F Phantom and an F14 Tomcat from the jet era.

Patriots Point's newest exhibit is also on the *Yorktown:* the **Medal of Honor Memorial Museum,** which opened in 2007 by hosting a live broadcast of the *NBC Nightly News* with Brian Williams. Included in the cost of admission, the Medal of Honor museum is an interactive experience documenting the exploits of the medal's honorees from the Civil War through today. It's broken up into four segments: the Wall of Honor, the Combat Tunnel, "Freedom Isn't Free," and the Hall of Heroes.

Other ships moored beside the *Yorktown* and open for tours are the Coast Guard cutter USCG *Ingham,* the submarine USS *Clamagore,* and the amazing destroyer USS *Laffey,* which survived being hit by three Japanese bombs and five kamikaze attacks—all within an hour. The Vietnam era is represented by a replica of an entire Naval Support Base Camp, featuring a river patrol boat and several helicopters.

A big plus is the free 90-minute guided tour. If you really want to make a big family history day out of it, you can also hop on the ferry from Patriots Point to Fort Sumter and back.

Old Village

It won't blow you away if you've seen Charleston, Savannah, or Beaufort, but Mount Pleasant's old town has its share of fine colonial and antebellum homes and historic churches. Indeed, Mount Pleasant's history is almost as old as Charleston's. First settled for farming in 1680, it soon acquired cachet as a great place for planters to spend the hot summers away from the mosquitoes inland at the rice paddies.

The main drag is Pitt Street, where you can shop and meander among plenty of shops and restaurants (try an ice cream soda at the historic Pitt Street Pharmacy). The huge meeting hall on the waterfront, Alhambra Hall, was the old ferry terminal.

Boone Hall Plantation

Visitors who've also been to Savannah's Wormsloe Plantation will immediately see the similarity in the majestic, live oak–lined entrance avenue to Boone Hall Plantation (1235 Long Point Rd., 843/884-4371, www.boone hallplantation.com, $17.50 adults, $7.50 children). But this site is about half a century older, dating back to a grant to Major John Boone In the 1680s (the oaks of the entranceway were planted in 1743).

Unusually in this area, which made its fortune mostly on rice, Boone Hall's main claim to fame was as a cotton plantation as well as a noted brick-making plant. Boone Hall takes the phrase "living history" to its extreme, as it's not only an active agricultural facility but lets visitors go on "u-pick" walks through its fields, which boast succulent strawberries, peaches, tomatoes, and even pumpkins in October—as well as free hayrides.

Currently owned by the McRae family, which first opened it to the public in 1959, Boone Hall is called "the most photographed plantation in America." And photogenic it certainly is, with natural beauty to spare in its

© JIM MOREKIS

The nine humble brick slave cabins at Boone Hall Plantation date from the 1790s.

scenic location on the Wando River and its adorable Butterfly Garden. But as you're clicking away with your camera, do keep in mind that the plantation's "big house" is not original; it's a 1935 reconstruction.

While Boone Hall's most genuine historic buildings include the big Cotton Gin House (1853) and the 1750 Smokehouse, to me the most poignant and educational structures by far are the nine humble brick slave cabins from the 1790s, expertly restored and most fitted with interpretive displays. The cabins are the center of Boone Hall's educational programs, including an exploration of Gullah culture at the outdoor "Gullah Theatre" on the unfortunately named Slave Street. Summers see some serious Civil War reenacting going on.

In all, three different tours are available, a 30-minute house tour, a tour of Slave Street, and a garden tour. Boone Hall's seasonal hours are a little tricky: from Labor Day through March 31, Boone Hall is open Monday–Saturday 9 A.M.–5 P.M. and Sunday 1–4 P.M.; from April

through Labor Day, it's open Monday–Saturday 8:30 A.M.–6:30 P.M. and Sunday 1–5 P.M.

Charles Pinckney National Historic Site

This is one of my favorite sights in Charleston, for its uplifting, well-explored subject matter as well as its tastefully maintained house and grounds. Though "Constitution Charlie's" old Snee Farm is down to only 28 acres from its original magnificent 700, the Charles Pinckney National Historic Site (1240 Long Point Rd., 843/881-5516, www.nps.gov/chpi, daily 9 A.M.–5 P.M., free) that encompasses it is still an important repository of local and national history.

Sometimes called "the forgotten Founder," Charles Pinckney was not only a hero of the American Revolution and a notable early abolitionist, but one of the main authors of the U.S. Constitution. His great aunt Eliza Lucas Pinckney was the first woman agriculturalist in America, responsible for opening up the indigo trade. Her son Charles Cotesworth Pinckney was one of the signers of the Constitution.

© JIM MOREKIS

Charles Pinckney National Historic Site

The current main house, doubling as the visitors center, dates from 1828, 11 years after Pinckney sold Snee Farm to pay off debts. That said, it's still a great example of Lowcountry architecture, replacing Pinckney's original home, where President George Washington slept and had breakfast under a nearby oak tree in 1791 while touring the south. Another highlight at this National Parks Service-administered site is the half-mile, self-guided walk around the site, some of it on boardwalks over the marsh.

No matter what anyone tells you, no one is buried underneath the tombstone in the grove of oak trees bearing the name of Constitution Charlie's father, Colonel Charles Pinckney. The marker incorrectly states the elder Pinckney's age, so it was put here only as a monument. A memorial to the colonel is in the churchyard of the 1840s-era Christ Church about a mile down Long Point Road.

Isle of Palms

This primarily residential area of about 5,000 people received the state's first "Blue Wave"

designation from the Clean Beaches Council for its well-managed and preserved beaches. Like adjacent Sullivan's Island, there are pockets of great wealth here, but also a laidback, windswept beach town vibe. You get here from Mount Pleasant by taking the Isle of Palms Connector off U.S. 17 (Johnnie Dodds/Chuck Dawley Boulevard).

Aside from just enjoying the whole scene, the main self-contained attraction here is **Isle of Palms County Park** (14th Ave., 843/886-3863, www.ccprc.com, daily 9 A.M.–7 P.M. May–Labor Day, daily10 A.M.–6 P.M. Mar.–Apr. and Sept.–Oct., daily 10 A.M.–5 P.M. Nov.–Feb., $5 per vehicle, pedestrians/cyclists free), with its oceanfront beach, complete with umbrella rental, a volleyball court, a playground, and lifeguards. Get here by taking the Isle of Palms Connector/Highway 517 from Mount Pleasant, going through the light at Palm Boulevard and taking the next left at the gate.

The island's other claim to fame is the excellent (and surprisingly affordable) **Wild Dunes Resort** (5757 Palm Blvd., 888/778-1876, www.wilddunes.com), with its two Fazio golf courses and 17 clay tennis courts.

Breach Inlet, between Isle of Palms and Sullivan's Island, is where the Confederate sub *Hunley* sortied to do battle with the USS *Housatonic*. During Hurricane Hugo the entire island was submerged.

Sullivan's Island

Part funky beach town, part ritzy getaway, Sullivan's Island has a certain timeless quality. While much of this largely residential area was rebuilt after Hurricane Hugo's devastation, plenty of local character remains, as evidenced by some really cool little bars in its tiny "business district" on the main drag of Middle Street.

There's a ton of history on Sullivan's, but you can also just while the day away on the quiet, windswept beach on the Atlantic, or ride a bike all over the island and back. Unless you have a boat, you can only get here from Mount Pleasant.

From U.S. 17 follow the signs for Highway 703 and Sullivan's Island. Cross the Ben Sawyer Bridge and then turn right onto Middle Street; continue for about a mile and a half.

FORT MOULTRIE

While Fort Sumter gets the vast bulk of the press, the older Fort Moultrie (1214 Middle St., 843/883-3123, www.nps.gov/fosu, daily 9 A.M.–5 P.M., $3 adults, $5 per family, under 16 free) on Sullivan's Island actually has a much more sweeping history. Furthering the irony, Major Robert Anderson's detachment at Fort Sumter at the opening of the Civil War was actually the Fort Moultrie garrison, reassigned to Sumter because Moultrie was thought too vulnerable from the landward side.

Indeed, Moultrie's first incarnation, a perimeter of felled palm trees, didn't even have a name when it was unsuccessfully attacked by the British in the summer of 1776, the first victory by the colonists in the Revolution. The redcoat cannonballs bounced off those soft, flexible trunks, and thus was born South Carolina's nickname, "The Palmetto State." The hero of the battle, Sergeant William Jasper, would gain immortality for putting the blue and white regimental banner—forerunner to the modern blue and white state flag—on a makeshift staff after the first one was shot away.

Subsequently named for the commander at the time, William Moultrie, the fort was

Fort Moultrie

© JIM MOREKIS

captured by the British at a later engagement. That first fort fell into decay and a new one was built over it in 1798, which was soon destroyed by a hurricane.

In 1809 a brick fort was built here; it soon gained notoriety as the place where the great chief Osceola was detained soon after his capture, posing for the famous portrait by George Catlin. His captors got more than they bargained for when they jokingly asked the old guerrilla soldier for a rendition of the Seminole battle cry. According to accounts, Osceola's realistic performance scared some bystanders half to death. The chief died here in 1838 and his modest gravesite is still on-site, in front of the fort on the landward side.

Other famous people to have trod on Sullivan's Island include Edgar Allen Poe, who was inspired by Sullivan's lonely, evocative environment to write *The Gold Bug* and other works. There's a Gold Bug Avenue and a Poe Avenue here today, and the local library is named after him as well. A young Lieutenant William Tecumseh Sherman was also stationed here during his Charleston stint in the 1830s before his encounter with history in the Civil War.

Moultrie's main Civil War role was as a target for Union shot during the long siege of Charleston. It was pounded so hard and for so long that its walls fell below a nearby sand hill and were finally unable to be hit anymore.

A full military upgrade happened in the late 1800s, extending over most of Sullivan's Island (some private owners have even bought some of the old batteries and converted them into homes). It's the series of later forts that you'll visit on your trip to the Moultrie site, which is technically part of the Fort Sumter National Monument and administered by the National Park Service.

Most of the outdoor tours are self-guided, but ranger programs typically happen Memorial Day through Labor Day daily at 11 A.M. and 2:30 P.M. There's a bookstore and visitors center across the street that offers a 20-minute video on the hour and half-hour 9 A.M.–4:30 P.M. Keep in mind there's no regular ferry to Fort

Sumter from Fort Moultrie; the closest ferry to Sumter leaves from Patriots Point on Mount Pleasant.

BENCH BY THE ROAD

Scholars say that about half of all African Americans alive today had an ancestor who once set foot on Sullivan's Island. As the first point of entry for at least half of all slaves imported to America, the island's "pest houses" acted as quarantine areas so slaves could be checked for communicable diseases before going to auction in Charleston proper.

But few people seem to know this. In a 1989 magazine interview, African American author and Nobel laureate Toni Morrison said about historic sites concerning slavery, "There is no suitable memorial, or plaque, or wreath or wall, or park or skyscraper lobby. There's no 300-foot tower, there's no small bench by the road."

In 2008, that last item became a reality, as the first of several planned "benches by the road" was installed on Sullivan's Island to mark the sacrifice of enslaved African Americans. It's a simple black steel bench, with an attached marker and a nearby plaque. The Bench by the Road is just near Fort Moultrie, which has also recently expanded its African American–oriented interpretation at its visitors center.

FOLLY BEACH

Though a large percentage of the town of Folly Beach was destroyed in Hurricane Hugo, enough of its funky, cozy charm is left to make it worth visiting. Called "The Edge of America" during its heyday from the 1930s through the '50s as a swinging resort getaway, Folly Beach is now a slightly beat, but thoroughly enjoyable little getaway on this barrier island far from the crowds of greater Charleston. Though as with all areas of Charleston, the cost of living here is rapidly increasing, Folly Beach still reminds locals of a time that once was, a time of soda fountains, poodle skirts, stylish one-piece bathing suits, and growling hot rods.

Folly's main claim to larger historic fame is playing host to George Gershwin, who stayed

CHARLESTON

Folly Beach from the pier

at a cottage on West Arctic Avenue to write the score to *Porgy and Bess,* set in downtown Charleston across the harbor. (Ironically, Gershwin's opera couldn't be performed in its original setting until 1970 because of segregationist Jim Crow laws.) Original *Porgy* author Dubose Heyward stayed around the corner at a summer cottage on West Ashley Avenue that he dubbed "Follywood."

Called Folly Road until it gets to the beach, Center Street is the main drag here, dividing the beach into east and west. In this area you'll find the **Folly Beach Fishing Pier** (101 E. Arctic Ave., 843/588-3474, daily 6 A.M.–11 P.M. Apr.–Oct., daily 7 A.M.–7 P.M. Nov. and Mar., daily 8 A.M.–5 P.M. during winter, $5 parking, $8 fishing fee), which replaced the grand old wooden pier-and-pavilion structure that tragically burned down in 1960.

Back in the day, restaurants, bars, and amusement areas with rides lined the way up to the old pavilion. As the premier musical venue in the region, the pavilion hosted legends like Tommy and Jimmy Dorsey, Benny Goodman, and Count Basie. The new fishing pier, while not as grand as the old one, is very much worth visiting, a massive, well-built edifice jutting over 1,000 feet into the Atlantic with a large, diamond-shaped pavilion at the end. Fishing rod holders and cleaning stations line the entire thing.

Out on the "front beach," daytime activities once included regular boxing matches and extralegal drag races. Because of the fluctuating nature of the sand here, the narrow ramps from the boardwalk to the beach sometimes require a big jump at the bottom. (They were long ago replaced by more practical means of access, but Folly Beach remains subject to frequent erosion.)

In the old days, the "Washout" section on the far west end was where you went to go crabbing or fly-fishing or maybe even steal a kiss from your sweetie. Today though, the Washout is known as the prime surfing area in the Carolinas, with a dedicated group of diehards.

Another attraction, humble though it is, is **Folly Beach County Park** (1100 West Ashley Ave., 843/588-2426, www.ccprc.com, daily 9 A.M.–7 P.M. May–Labor Day, daily 10 A.M.–6 P.M. Mar., Apr., Sept., and Oct., daily 10 A.M.–5 P.M. Jan., Feb., Nov., and Dec., $7 per vehicle, free for pedestrians and cyclists) at the far west end of the island. Swim, tan, and relax, maybe under a rented beach umbrella.

To get to Folly Beach from Charleston, go west on Calhoun Street and take the James Island Connector. Take a left on Folly Road/Highway 171, which becomes Center Street on into Folly Beach.

At the far east end of Folly Island, about 300 yards offshore, you'll see the **Morris Island Lighthouse,** an 1876 beacon that was once surrounded by lush, green landscape, now completely surrounded by water as the land has eroded around it. Now privately owned, there's an extensive effort to save and preserve the lighthouse (www.savethelight.org). There's also an effort to keep high-dollar condo development off of beautiful, bird-friendly Morris Island itself (www.morrisisland.org).

To get there while there's still something left to enjoy, take East Ashley Street until it dead-ends. Park in the lot and take a quarter-mile walk to the beach.

TOURS

Because of the city's small, fairly centralized layout, the best way to experience Charleston is on foot—either yours or via hooves of equine nature. Thankfully, there's a wide variety of walking and carriage tours for you to choose from.

The sheer number and breadth of tour options in Charleston is beyond the scope of this section. For a full selection of available tours, visit the **Charleston Visitor Reception and Transportation Center** (375 Meeting St., 800/774-0006, www.charlestoncvb.com, Mon.–Fri. 8:30 A.M.–5 P.M.), where they have entire walls of brochures for all the latest tours, with local tourism experts on-site. Here are some notable highlights.

Walking Tours
If you find yourself walking around downtown

soon after dark, you'll almost invariably come across a walking tour in progress, with a small cluster of people gathered around a tour guide. There are too many walking tours to list them all, but here are the best.

For more than 10 years, **Ed Grimball's Walking Tours** (306 Yates Ave., 843/762-0056, www.edgrimballtours.com, $16 adults, $8 children) has run two-hour tours on Friday and Saturday mornings, courtesy of the knowledgeable and still-sprightly Ed himself, a native Charlestonian. All of Ed's walks start from the big Pineapple Fountain in Waterfront Park and reservations are a must.

Original Charleston Walks (45 Broad St., 800/729-3420, www.charlestonwalks.com, 8:30 A.M.–9:30 P.M., $18.50 adults, $10.50 children) has received much national TV exposure. They leave from the corner of Market and State Streets. They have a full slate of tours, including a popular adults-only pub crawl. **Charleston Strolls Walk with History** (843/766-2080, www.charlestonstrolls.com, $18 adults, $10 children) is another popular tour good for a historical overview and tidbits. They have three embarkation points: Charleston Place, the Mills House, and the Days Inn. **Architectural Walking Tours** (173 Meeting St., 800/931-7761, www.architecturalwalkingtoursofcharleston.com, $20) offers an 18th-century tour at 10 A.M. and a 19th-century tour at 2 P.M., except Tuesdays and Sundays, which are geared more toward historic preservation.

Ghost tours are very popular in Charleston. **Bulldog Tours** (40 N. Market St., 843/722-8687, www.bulldogtours.com, $18) has exclusive access to the Old City Jail, and runs several other well-received ghost tours, such as a Ghost & Dungeon Tour, a Ghost & Graveyard Tour, and the adults-only Dark Side of Charleston. **Tour Charleston** (184 E. Bay St., 843/723-1670, www.tourcharleston.com, $18) offers two paranormal tours, Ghosts of Charleston I, which leaves at 5 P.M., 7:30 P.M., and 9:30 P.M. from Waterfront Park, and Ghosts of Charleston II, which leaves at 7 P.M. and 9 P.M. from Marion Square.

Carriage Tours

The city strictly regulates the treatment of carriage horses and their upkeep, so there's not a heck of a lot of difference in service or price among the various tour companies. Typically rides take 1–1.5 hours. They sometimes book up early, so call ahead.

The oldest service in town is **Palmetto Carriage Works** (40 N. Market St., 843/723-8145, www.carriagetour.com), which offers free parking at its "red barn" base near City Market. Another popular tour is **Old South Carriage Company** (14 Anson St., 843/723-9712, www.oldsouthcarriage.com, $20 adults, $12 children) with its Confederate-clad drivers. **Carolina Polo & Carriage Company** (16 Hayne St., 843/577-6767, www.cpcc.com, $20 adults, $12 children) leaves from several spots, including the Doubletree Hotel, the Noisy Oyster, and at their Hayne Street stables.

Motorized Tours

Leaving from Charleston Visitor Reception and Transportation Center at 375 Meeting Street, **Adventure Sightseeing** (843/762-0088, www.touringcharleston.com) offers several comfortable 1.5–2 hour rides, including the only motorized tour to the Citadel area. You can make a day of it with **Charleston's Finest Historic Tours** (843/577-3311, www.historictoursofcharleston.com), which has a basic two-hour city tour each day at 10:30 A.M. plus offers some much longer tours to outlying plantations. They also offer free downtown pickup from most lodgings. The old faithful **Gray Line of Charleston** (843/722-4444, www.graylineofcharleston.com, $20 adults, $12 children) offers a 90-minute tour departing from the Visitors Center every half-hour 9:30 A.M.–3 P.M. during the high season (hotel pickup by reservation).

African American History Tours

Charleston is rich in African American history,

and a couple of operators specializing in this area are worth mentioning: Al Miller's **Sites & Insights Tours** (843/762-0051, www.sitesandinsightstours.com, $13–18) has several packages, including a Black History and Porgy & Bess Tour as well as a good combo city and island tour, all departing from the Visitors Center. Alphonso Brown's **Gullah Tours** (843/763-7551, www.gullahtours.com), featuring stories told in the Gullah dialect, all leave from Gallery Chuma at 43 John St. near the Visitors Center at 11 A.M. and 1 P.M. Mon.–Fri. and 11 A.M., 1 P.M., and 3 P.M. Saturdays.

Water Tours

The best all-around tour of Charleston Harbor is the 90-minute ride offered by **Spiritline Cruises** (800/789-3678, www.spiritlinecruises.com, $15 adults, $9 ages 6–11), which leaves from either Aquarium Wharf or Patriots Point. Allow about a half-hour for ticketing and boarding. They also have a three-hour dinner cruise in the evening leaving from Patriots Point (about $50 per person) and a cruise to Fort Sumter.

Sandlapper Water Tours (843/849-8687, www.sandlappertours.com) offers many types of evening and dolphin cruises on a 45-foot catamaran. They also offer Charleston's only water-borne ghost tour.

Ecotours

This aspect of Charleston's tourist scene is very well represented. The best operators include: **Barrier Island Eco Tours** (50 41st Ave., 843/886-5000, www.nature-tours.com), taking you up to the Cape Romain Refuge out of Isle of Palms; **Coastal Expeditions** (843/884-7684, www.coastalexpeditions.com), offering several different-length sea kayak adventures; and **PaddleFish Kayaking** (843/330-9777, www.paddlefishkayaking.com), offering several kinds of kayaking tours (no experience necessary) from downtown, Kiawah Island, and Seabrook Island.

Entertainment and Events

Charleston practically invented the idea of diversion and culture in America, so it's no surprise that there's plenty to do here, from museums to festivals to a brisk nightlife scene.

NIGHTLIFE

One of the unique things about Charleston is the inclusiveness of its active nightlife scene. Unlike the strict locals vs. tourist divide you find so often in other destination cities, in Charleston it's nothing for a couple of tourists to find themselves at a table next to four or five college students enjoying themselves in that particularly Charlestonian fashion, i.e., loudly and with lots of good food and strong drink nearby.

Indeed, the Holy City is downright ecumenical in its partying. The smokiest dives also have some of the best brunches. The toniest restaurants also have some of the most hopping bar scenes. Tourist hot spots written up in all the guidebooks also have their share of local regulars.

But through it all, one constant remains: Charleston's finely honed ability to seek out and enjoy the good life. It's a trait that comes naturally and traditionally, going back to the days of the earliest Charleston drinking and gambling clubs, like the Fancy Society, the Meddlers Laughing Club, and the Fort Jolly Volunteers.

Bars close in Charleston at 2 A.M. The old days of the "mini-bottle" are gone—in which no free pour was allowed and all drinks had to be made from the little airline bottles—and it seems that local bartenders have finally figured

DOIN' THE CHARLESTON

It's been called the biggest song and dance craze of the 20th century. Though it first entered the American public consciousness via New York City, in a 1923 Harlem musical called *Runnin' Wild*, the roots of the dance soon to be known as the Charleston were indeed in the Holy City.

Though no one is quite sure of the day and date, local lore assures us that members of Charleston's legendary Jenkins Orphanage Band were the first to start dancing that crazy "Geechie step," a development that soon became part of the band's act. The Jenkins Orphanage was started in 1891 by the African American Baptist minister Reverend D. J. Jenkins, and originally housed in the Old Marine Hospital at 20 Franklin Street (which you can see today, though it's not open to the public). To raise money, Reverend Jenkins acquired donated instruments and started a band comprising talented orphans from the house.

The orphans traveled as far away as London, where they were a hit with the locals but not with the constabulary, who unceremoniously

fined them for stopping traffic. A Charleston attorney who happened to be in London at the time, Augustine Smyth, paid their way back home, becoming a lifelong supporter of the Orphanage in the process.

From then on, playing in donated old Citadel uniforms, the Jenkins Orphanage Band frequently took its act on the road. They played at the St. Louis and Buffalo expositions, and even at President Taft's inauguration. They also frequently played in New York, and it was there that African American pianist and composer James P. Johnson heard the Charlestonians play and dance to their Gullah rhythms, considered exotic at the time. Johnson would incorporate what he heard into the tune "Charleston," one of many songs in the revue *Runnin' Wild*. The catchy song and its accompanying loose-limbed dance seemed tailor-made for the Roaring Twenties and its liberated, hedonistic spirit.

Before long the Charleston had swept the nation, becoming a staple of jazz clubs and speakeasies across America, and indeed, the world.

out how to pour a decent drink after an initial breaking-in period. At the retail level, all hard liquor sales stop at 7 P.M., with none at all on Sundays. You can buy beer and wine in grocery stores 24/7.

Pubs and Bars

In a nod to the city's perpetual focus on well-prepared food, it's difficult to find a Charleston watering hole that *doesn't* offer really good food in addition to a well-stocked bar.

One of Charleston's favorite neighborhood spots is **Moe's Crosstown Tavern** (714 Rutledge Ave., 843/722-3287, daily 11 A.M.–2 A.M.) at Rutledge and Francis in the Wagener Terrace/Hampton Square area. A new second location, **Moe's Downtown Tavern** (5 Cumberland St., 843/577-8500) offers a similar vibe and menu, but the original, and best, Moe's experience is at the Crosstown.

Nipping on Moe's heels for best pub food in town is **A.C.'s Bar and Grill** (467 King St., 843/577-6742, daily 11 A.M.–2 A.M.). Though this dark, quirky watering hole might seem out of place in the increasingly tony Upper King area, that only adds to its appeal. A.C.'s at its best is all things to all people: Charleston's favorite late-night bar, a great place to get a burger basket, and also one of the best (and certainly most unlikely) Sunday brunches in town, featuring chicken and waffles.

The action gets going late at **Social Wine Bar** (188 E. Bay St., 843/577-5665, daily 4 P.M.–2 A.M.), a hopping hangout near the French Quarter. While the hot and cold tapas are tasty—I like the special sashimi—the real action here, as you'd expect, is the wine. They offer at least 50 wines by the glass and literally hundreds of wines by the bottle. My favorite thing to do here is partake of the popular "flights," triple tastes of kindred spirits, as it were. If the pricing on the menu seems confusing—and it will—just ask a server to help you out with it.

Currently one of the most popular spots on Upper King for the college crowd, **Charleston Beer Works** (468 King St., 843/577-5885, daily 5 P.M.–2 A.M.) is particularly well regarded for its beer on tap, generally thought to be one of the best selections in town. The menu offers a wide range of appetizers and entrées, which while not particularly inventive are certainly tasty. **Johnson's Pub** (12 Cumberland St., 843/958-0662, daily noon–2 A.M.), a quirky but popular downtown spot, offers seven varieties of burger, all incredible, plus great pizza; it's also well known for its Caesar salad. Oh, yeah, and they keep the drinks coming, too.

The Guinness flows freely at **Tommy Condon's Irish Pub** (160 Church St., 843/577-3818, www.tommycondons.com, Sun.–Thurs. 11 A.M.–2 A.M., dinner served until 10 P.M., Fri.–Sat. 11 A.M.–2 A.M., dinner served until 11 P.M.)—after the obligatory and traditional slow-pour, that is—as do the patriotic Irish songs performed live most nights. You have three sections to choose from in this large, low building right near City Market: the big outdoor deck, the cozy pub itself, and the back dining room with classic wainscoting.

If it's a nice day out, a good place to relax and enjoy happy hour outside is **Vickery's Bar and Grill** (15 Beaufain St., 843/577-5300, www.vickerysbarandgrill.com, Mon.–Sat. 11:30 A.M.–2 A.M., Sun. 11 A.M.–1 A.M., kitchen closes 1 A.M.), actually part of a small regional chain based in Atlanta. Start with the oyster bisque, and maybe try the turkey and brie sandwich or crab cakes for your entrée.

Because of its commercial nature, Broad Street can get sparse when the sun goes down and the office workers disperse back to the 'burbs. But a warm little oasis can be found a few steps off Broad Street in the **Blind Tiger** (36–38 Broad St., 843/577-0088, daily 11:30–2 A.M., kitchen closes 10 P.M. Mon.–Thurs., 9 P.M. Fri.–Sun.), which takes its name from the local Prohibition-era nickname for a speakeasy. Wood panels, Guinness and Bass on tap, and some good bar-food items make this a good stop off the beaten path if you find yourself in the area. A patio out back often features live music.

Located not too far over the Ashley River on U.S. 17, Charleston institution **Gene's Haufbrau** (17 Savannah Hwy.,

Poe's Tavern on Sullivan's Island

843/225-4363, www.geneshaufbrau.com, daily 11:30 A.M.–2 A.M.) is worth making a special trip into West Ashley. Boasting the largest beer selection in Charleston—from the Butte Creek Organic Ale from California to a can of PBR—Gene's also claims to be the oldest bar in town, established in 1952.

If you find yourself thirsty and hungry in Mount Pleasant after dark, you might want to stop in the **Reddrum Gastropub** (803 Coleman Blvd., 843/849-0313, www.reddrum pub.com, Mon.–Tues. 5:30–9 P.M., Wed.–Sat. 5:30–10 P.M.), so named because here the food is just as important as the drink. While you're likely to need reservations for the dining room, where you can enjoy Lowcountry/Tex-Mex fusion-style cuisine with a typically Mount Pleasant–like emphasis on seafood, the bar scene is very hopping and fun, with live music every Wednesday and Thursday night.

Though Sullivan's Island has a lot of high-dollar homes, it still has friendly watering holes like **Dunleavy's Pub** (2213-B Middle St., 843/883-9646, Sun.–Thurs. 11:30 A.M.–1 A.M.,

Fri.–Sat. 11:30 A.M.–2 A.M.). Inside is a great bar festooned with memorabilia, or you can enjoy a patio table. The other Sullivan's watering hole of note is **Poe's Tavern** (2210 Middle St., 843/883-0083, daily 11 A.M.–2 A.M., kitchen closes 10 P.M.) across the street, a nod to Edgar Allan Poe and his service on the island as a clerk in the U.S. Army. It's a lively, mostly locals scene, set within a fun but suitably dark interior (though you might opt for one of the outdoor tables on the raised patio). Simply put, no trip to Sullivan's is complete without a stop at one (or possibly both) of these two local landmarks, each within a stone's throw of the other.

Next door to Sullivan's, Isle of Palms is less-known for its nightlife. But the **Acme Cantina** (31 JC Long Blvd., 843/886-0024) offers good company and good prices. Though not quite on the beach, the vibe is relaxed, beachy, and boozy.

The most notable watering hole in Folly Beach is the **Sand Dollar Social Club** (7 Center St., 843/588-9498, Sun.–Fri. noon–1 A.M., Sat.

noon–2 A.M.), the kind of cash-only, mostly local, and thoroughly enjoyable dive you often find in little beach towns. You have to pony up for a "membership" to this private club, but it's only a buck. There's a catch though: you can't get in until your 24-hour "waiting period" is over.

Live Music

Charleston's music scene is best described as hit-and-miss. There's no distinct "Charleston sound" to speak of (especially now that the heyday of Hootie and the Blowfish is long past) and there's no one place where you're assured of finding a great band any night of the week.

The scene is currently in even more of a state of flux because the city's best-regarded live rock club, Cumberland's on King Street, closed in late 2007 after 15 years in business. The best place to find up-to-date music listings is the local free weekly *Charleston City Paper* (www.charlestoncitypaper.com).

These days the hippest music spot in town is out on James Island at **The Pour House** (1977 Maybank Hwy., 843/571-4343, www.charlestonpourhouse.com, 9 P.M.–2 A.M. on nights with music scheduled, call for info), where sometimes the local characters are just as entertaining as the acts onstage.

In West Ashley, **The Map Room** (1650 Sam Rittenberg Blvd., 843/769-6336, www.themaproom.net, Mon.–Fri. 4 P.M.–2 A.M., Sat.–Sun. 6 P.M.–2 A.M.) is bringing in some of the best local and regional acts on a consistent basis. The range of acts is quite diverse, ranging from Athens, Georgia alt-rock to bluegrass to the occasional Middle Eastern dance troupe. A big plus is the full menu available until 1 A.M.

The venerable **Music Farm** (32 Ann St., 843/722-8904, www.musicfarm.com) on Upper King isn't much to look at from the outside, but inside, the cavernous space has played host to all sorts of bands over the past 15 years including Talking Heads, Ween, Widespread Panic, and De La Soul.

For jazz, check out **Mistral** (99 S. Market St., 843/722-5708, Sun.–Thurs. 11 A.M.–11 P.M.,

Fri.–Sat. 11 A.M.–midnight). There's a constant stream of great performers from a variety of traditions, including Dixieland, every night of the week—not to mention some awesome food. Another great jazz place—and, like Mistral, a very good restaurant to boot—is the relatively new **Mercato** (102 N. Market St., 843/722-6393, www.mercatocharleston.com, bar 4 P.M.–2 A.M., late night menu until 1 A.M.). Italian in menu and feel, the live jazz and R&B Wed.–Sat. at this establishment—owned by the same company that owns the five-star Peninsula Grill—is definitely all-American. The late kitchen hours are a great bonus.

Lounges and Tapas

Currently the undisputed queen of Upper King, the ultrachic tapas place **Raval** (453 King St., 843/853-8466, daily 5:30 P.M.–2 A.M.) always has a long line on weekend nights full of beautiful people waiting to sample the tasty bites and the vast wine selection at the oaken community tables. Try the *patatas bravas* and the Manchego cheese. For a take on Spain under the Moorish influence, go to the more exotic back bar for a trendy Euro cocktail, enjoyed in a deep comfy sofa.

Across the street from Gene's Haufbrau, the retro chic **Voodoo Lounge** (15 Magnolia Ln., 843/769-0228, Mon–Fri. 4 P.M.–2 A.M., Sat.–Sun. 5:30 P.M.–2 A.M., kitchen open until 1 A.M.) is another very popular West Ashley hangout. It has a wide selection of trendy cocktails and some killer gourmet tacos.

The aptly named **Rooftop Bar and Restaurant** (23 Vendue Range, 843/723-0485, Tues.–Sat. 6 P.M.–2 A.M.) at the Library Restaurant in the Vendue Inn is a very popular waterfront happy hour spot from which to enjoy the sunset over the Charleston skyline. It's also a hot late-night hangout with a respectable menu.

Located in a 200-year-old building and suitably right above a cigar store, **Club Habana** (177 Meeting St., 843/853-5900, Mon.–Sat. 5 P.M.–1 A.M., Sun. 6 P.M.–midnight) is the perfect place to sink down into a big couch, warm yourself by the fireplace, sip a martini (or port or single-malt scotch), and enjoy a good smoke in the dim light. Probably the last, best vestige of the cigar bar trend in Charleston, Club Habana remains popular. You get your cigars downstairs in Tinderbox Internationale, which features a range of rare "Legal Cuban" smokes, i.e., rolled from pre-embargo tobacco that's been warehoused for decades in Tampa, Florida.

If martinis are your game, head to **Cintra** (16 N. Market St., 843/377-1090, Tues.–Wed. 5:30–10 P.M., Thurs.–Sat. 5:30–11 P.M.), where they boast 40 different martini recipes at last count. While you're sipping one you might decide to stay for dinner, which is also superb. Try the butternut squash ravioli or the veal Marsala.

Dance Clubs
The **Trio Club** (139 Calhoun St., 843/965-5333, Thurs.–Sat. 9 P.M.–2 A.M.) right off Marion Square is a favorite place to make the scene. There's a relaxing outdoor area with piped-in music, an intimate, sofa-filled upstairs bar for dancing and chilling, and the dark, candelit downstairs with frequent live music.

Without a doubt Charleston's best dance club is **Club Pantheon** (28 Ann St., 843/577-2582, Thurs.–Sun. 10 P.M.–2 A.M.).

Gay and Lesbian
Charleston is very tolerant by typical Deep South standards, and this tolerance extends to the gay and lesbian community as well. Most gay- and lesbian-oriented nightlife centers in the Upper King area.

Charleston's hottest and hippest dance spot of any type, gay or straight, is **Club Pantheon** (28 Ann St., 843/577-2582, Thurs.–Sun. 10 P.M.–2 A.M.) on Upper King on the lower level of the parking garage across from the Visitors Center (375 Meeting St.). Pantheon's not cheap—cover charges are routinely well over $10—but it's worth it for the great DJs, the dancing, and the people-watching, not to mention the drag cabaret on Friday and Sunday nights.

Just down the street from Club Pantheon—and owned by the same people—is a totally different kind of gay bar, **Dudley's** (42 Ann St., 843/577-6779, daily 4 P.M.–2 A.M.). Mellower and more appropriate for conversation or a friendly game of pool, Dudley is a nice contrast to the thumping Pantheon a few doors down.

Though **Vickery's Bar and Grill** (15 Beaufain St., 843/577-5300, www.vickerys barandgrill.com, Mon.–Sat. 11:30 A.M.–2 A.M., Sun. 11 A.M.–1 A.M., kitchen closes 1 A.M.) does not market itself as a gay and lesbian establishment, it's nonetheless become quite popular with that population—not least because of the good reputation its parent tavern in Atlanta has with that city's large and influential gay community.

PERFORMING ARTS
Theater
Unlike the more puritanical (literally) colonies farther up the American coast, Charleston was from the beginning an arts-friendly settlement. The first theatrical production in the western hemisphere happened in Charleston in January 1735, when a nomadic troupe rented a space at Church and Broad Streets to perform Thomas Otway's *The Orphan.*

The play's success led to the building of the Dock Street Theatre on now-Queen Street, which held its first production on February 12, 1736, *The Recruiting Officer,* a popular play for actresses of the time because it calls for some female characters to wear tight-fitting British army uniforms. Live theater became a staple of Charleston social life, with notable thespians performing here including both Edwin and Junius Booth, brothers of Lincoln's assassin John Wilkes, and Edgar Allan Poe's mother Eliza.

Several high-quality troupes continue to keep that proud old tradition alive, chief among them being **Charleston Stage** (843/577-7183, www.charlestonstage.com), a professional company with 20 full-time staffers founded in 1978. Also the resident company of the Dock Street Theatre, they will perform at the American Theatre (446 King St.) and the Sottile Theatre (44 George St. just off King) until Dock Street's renovations are complete in 2010. In addition to its

NATIVE SONS:
STEPHEN COLBERT AND SHEPARD FAIREY

A purist would insist that Charlestonians are born, not made. While it's true that Comedy Central star Stephen Colbert was actually born in Washington, D.C., he did spend most of his young life in the Charleston suburb of James Island. And regardless of his literal birthplace, few would dispute that Colbert is the best-known Charlestonian in American pop culture today.

While it's commonly assumed that Colbert's surname is a link to Charleston's French Huguenot heritage, the truth is that it's really an Irish name. To further burst the bubble, Colbert's father adopted the current French pronunciation himself – historically his family pronounced the "t" at the end.

That said, Colbert returns often to Charleston, whether it's to throw out the first pitch at a River Dogs game or for a one-man performance, as he did in December 2007 at the Sottile Theater. In 2008 Colbert embarked on an ill-fated, tongue-in-cheek bid to get on the South Carolina presidential primary ballot. In a video message to the South Carolina Agricultural Summit he cried mock tears and said, "I wanted to be president of South Carolina so bad. I was going to be sworn in on a sack of pork ribs and I was going to institute the death penalty for eating Chinese shrimp."

Close behind Colbert is artist Shepard Fairey, most well-known for his now iconic *HOPE* portrait of Barack Obama, which *Time* magazine used on the cover of its 2008 "Person of the Year" issue. (A version is now in the Smithsonian's National Portrait Gallery in Washington, D.C.) Though based for quite some time in Los Angeles, Fairey is Charleston-born and bred. He first gained notoriety for a series of guerrilla art images involving the late pro wrestler Andre the Giant and the slogan *Obey*. Fairey remains a bit more aloof from his home state, though the Halsey Institute of Contemporary Art at the College of Charleston did host him for the opening of an exhibit featuring his work in 2007.

© JIM MOREKIS

iconic *Obey* graffitti of native Charlestonian Shepard Fairey

Other famous pop culture figures born in Charleston or closely associated with the city include:

- Author Alexandra Ripley (attended Ashley Hall)
- Singer Darius Rucker (Hootie and the Blowfish)
- Author/lyricist Dubose Heyward
- Author Josephine Humphreys
- Actress/model Lauren Hutton
- Author Nancy Friday (grew up in Charleston, born in Pittsburgh)
- Author Sue Monk Kidd (*The Secret Life of Bees*)
- Actor Thomas Gibson (*Dharma & Greg*)
- Actress Vanessa Minnillo (attended high school here)
- Actor Will Patton (*Remember the Titans*)

well-received regular season of classics and modern staples, Charleston Stage has debuted more than 30 original scripts over the years, most recently *Gershwin at Folly,* recounting the composer's time at Folly Beach working on *Porgy and Bess.*

The city's most unusual players are **The Have Nots!** (843/853-6687, www.thehavenots .com), with a total ensemble of 35 comedians who typically perform their brand of edgy improv every Friday night at Theatre 99 (280 Meeting St.). Perhaps unusually for such a dicey concept in this still-traditional arts town, The Have Nots! have managed to last 12 years, and are now partners with Piccolo Spoleto's Fringe series and a local comedy festival.

As of this writing, the players of **PURE Theatre** (843/723-4444, www.puretheatre .org) are performing at the Circular Congregation Church's Lance Hall (150 Meeting St.). Their shows emphasize compelling, mature drama, beautifully performed. This is where to catch less-glitzy, more-gritty productions like *Rabbit Hole, American Buffalo,* and *Cold Tectonics,* a hit at Piccolo Spoleto.

The Footlight Players (843/722-4487, www.footlightplayers.net) are the oldest continuously active company in town (since 1931). This community-based, amateur company performs a mix of crowd-pleasers *(The Full Monty)* and cutting-edge drama *(This War is Live)* at their space at 20 Queen Street.

Music

The forerunner to the **Charleston Symphony Orchestra** (843/554-6060, www.charleston symphony.com) performed for the first time on December 28, 1936, at the Hibernian Hall on Meeting Street. During that first season the CSO accompanied the inaugural show at the renovated Dock Street Theatre, *The Recruiting Officer.* Since then, the CSO has continued to provide world-class orchestral music, gaining "Metropolitan" status in the 1970s, when they accompanied the first-ever local performance of *Porgy and Bess,* which despite its downtown setting couldn't be performed locally before then due to segregation laws.

Under the baton of Maestro David Stahl, the CSO is the largest year-round performing arts entity in South Carolina. While as of this writing they are currently facing serious financial difficulties, they perform primarily at the Gaillard Municipal Auditorium (77 Calhoun St.), but a "blue jeans" contemporary chamber music series geared toward a younger fan base, "Backstage Pass at the Sottile," is held at the Sottile Theatre (44 George St. just off King).

Comprising mostly players with the CSO, the separate group **Chamber Music Charleston** (843/763-4941, www.chambermusiccharleston .org) is another excellent local ensemble, performing under the baton of Sandra Nikolajevs. They play a wide variety of picturesque historic venues, including the Old Exchange (120 E. Bay St.), the Calhoun Mansion (16 Meeting St.), and the Footlight Players Theatre (20 Queen St.). They can also be found at private house concerts, which sell out quickly.

The excellent music department at the College of Charleston sponsors the annual **Charleston Music Fest** (www.charleston musicfest.com), a series of chamber music concerts at various venues around the beautiful campus, featuring many faculty members of the College as well as visiting guest artists.

Other College musical offerings include: The **College of Charleston Concert Choir** (www .cofc.edu/music), which performs at various venues, usually churches, around town during the fall; the **College of Charleston Opera,** which performs at least one full-length production during the school year and often performs at Piccolo Spoleto; and the popular **Yuletide Madrigal Singers,** who sing in early December at a series of concerts in historic Randolph Hall.

Dance

The premier company in town is the 20-year-old **Charleston Ballet Theatre** (477 King St., 843/723-7334, www.charlestonballet.org). Its 18 full-time dancers perform a great mix of classics, modern pieces, and, of course, a yuletide *Nutcracker* at the Gaillard Municipal Auditorium. Most performances are at the Sottile Theatre (44 George St., just off King), but for the past few years Charleston Ballet Theatre has offered the "King Street Series" of selected, themed pieces (e.g., *pas de deux*, tango) geared toward a younger audience, danced at their home office on Upper King.

CINEMA

The most interesting art house and indie venue in town is currently **The Terrace** (1956 Maybank Hwy., 843/762-9494, www.terrace theater.com), and not only because they offer beer and wine, which you can enjoy at your seat. Shows before 5 P.M. are $6.50. It's west of Charleston on James Island. Get there by taking U.S. 17 west out of Charleston and go south on Highway 171, then take a right on Maybank Highway (Highway 700).

For a generic but good multiplex experience, go over to Mount Pleasant to the **Palmetto Grande** (1319 Theater Dr., 843/216-8696).

FESTIVALS AND EVENTS

Charleston is a festival-mad city, especially in the spring and early fall. And new festivals are being added every year, further enhancing the hedonistic flavor of this city that has also mastered the art of hospitality. Here's a look through the calendar at all the key festivals in the area.

January

Held on a Sunday in late January at historic Boone Hall Plantation on Mount Pleasant, the **Lowcountry Oyster Festival** (www.charleston lowcountry.com, 11 A.M.–5 P.M., $8, food additional) features literally truckloads of the sweet shellfish for your enjoyment. Gates open at 10:30 A.M. and there's plenty of parking. Oysters are sold by the bucket and served with crackers and cocktail sauce. Bring your own shucking knife and/or glove, or buy them on-site.

February

One of the more unique events in town is the **Southeastern Wildlife Exposition** (various venues, 843/723-1748, www.sewe.com, $12.50/day, $30/three days, 12 and under free). For the last quarter century, the Wildlife Expo has

brought together hundreds of artists and exhibitors to showcase just about any kind of naturally themed art you can think of, in over a dozen galleries and venues all over downtown. Kids will enjoy the live animals on hand as well.

March

Generally straddling late February and the first days of March, the four-day **Charleston Food & Wine Festival** (www.charlestonfood andwine.com, various venues and admission) is a glorious celebration of one of the Holy City's premier draws: its amazing culinary community. While the emphasis is on Lowcountry gurus like Donald Barickman of Magnolia's and Robert Carter of the Peninsula Grill, guest chefs from as far away as New York, New Orleans, and Los Angeles routinely come to show off their cooking skills. Oenophiles, especially of domestic wines, will be in heaven as well. Tickets aren't cheap—an all-event pass is over $500 per person—but then again, this is one of America's great food cities, so you might find it worth every penny.

Coming immediately before the Festival of Houses and Gardens is the **Charleston International Antiques Show** (40 E. Bay St., 843/722-3405, www.historiccharleston.org, varied admission), held at Historic Charleston's headquarters at the Missroon House on the High Battery. It features over 30 of the nation's best-regarded dealers and offers lectures and tours.

Running mid-March through April, the perennial favorite **Festival of Houses and Gardens** (843/722-3405, www.historic charleston.org, varied admission) is sponsored by the Historic Charleston Foundation and held at the very peak of the spring blooming season for maximum effect. In all, the Festival goes into a dozen historic neighborhoods to see about 150 homes. Each day sees a different three-hour tour of a different area, at about $45 per person. This is a fantastic opportunity to peek inside some amazing old privately owned properties that are inaccessible to visitors at all other times. A highlight is a big oyster roast and picnic at Drayton Hall.

Not to be confused with the above festival, the **Garden Club of Charleston House and Garden Tours** (843/530-5164, www.the gardenclubofcharleston.com, $35) are held over a weekend in late March. Highlights include the Heyward-Washington House and the private garden of the late great Charleston horticulturalist Emily Whaley.

One of Charleston's newest and most fun events, the five-night **Charleston Fashion Week** (www.fashionweek.charlestonmag.com, varied admission) is sponsored by *Charleston Magazine* and benefits a local women's charity. Mimicking New York's Fashion Week events under tenting in Bryant Park, Charleston's version features runway action under big tents in Marion Square—and, yes, past guests have included former contestants on *Project Runway*.

April

The annual **Cooper River Bridge Run** (www .bridgerun.com) happens the first Saturday in April (unless it's Easter weekend, in which case it runs the week before) and features a 10,000-meter jaunt across the massive new Arthur Ravenel Bridge over the Cooper River, the longest cable span in the western hemisphere. It's not for those with a fear of heights, but it's still one of Charleston's best-attended events—with well over 30,000 participants.

The whole crazy idea started when Dr. Marcus Newberry of the Medical University of South Carolina in Charleston was inspired by an office fitness trail in his native state of Ohio to do something similar in Charleston to promote fitness. Participants can walk the course if they choose, and many do.

Signaled with the traditional cannon shot, the race still begins in Mount Pleasant and ends downtown, but over the years the course has changed to accommodate growth—not only in the event itself but in the city. Auto traffic, of course, is rerouted from the night before the race. The Bridge Run remains the only elite-level track and field event in South Carolina, with runners from Kenya typically dominating year after year. Each participant in the Bridge Run now must wear a transponder

chip; new "Bones in Motion" technology allows you to track a favorite runner's exact position in real-time during the race. The 2006 Run had wheelchair participants for the first time. There's now a Kid's Run in Hampton Square the Friday before, which also allows strollers.

From 1973–2000—except for 1976 when it was in Florida—the **Family Circle Cup** (161 Seven Farms Dr., Daniel Island, 843/856-7900, www.familycirclecup.com, varied admission) was held at Sea Pines Plantation on Hilton Head Island. But the popular Tier 1 Women's tennis tournament in 2001 moved to Daniel Island's brand-new Family Circle Tennis Center, specifically built for the event through a partnership of the magazine and the city of Charleston. (The Tennis Center is also open to the public and hosts many community events as well.)

Mount Pleasant is the home of Charleston's shrimping fleet, and each April sees all the boats parade by the Alhambra Hall & Park for the **Blessing of the Fleet** (843/884-8517, www .townofmountpleasant.com). Family events and lots and lots of seafood are also on tap.

May

Free admission and free parking are not the only draws at the outdoor **North Charleston Arts Festival** (5000 Coliseum Dr., www .northcharleston.org), but let's face it, that's important. Held beside North Charleston's Performing Arts Center & Convention Center, the Festival features music, dance, theater, multicultural performers, and storytellers. There are a lot of kid's events as well.

Held over three days at the Holy Trinity Greek Orthodox Church up towards the Neck, the **Charleston Greek Festival** (30 Race St., 843/577-2063, www.greekorthodoxchs.org, $3) offers a plethora of live entertainment, dancing, Greek wares, and of course fantastic Greek cuisine cooked by the congregation. Parking is not a problem, and there's even a shuttle to the church from the lot.

One of Charleston's newest annual events is the **Charleston International Film Festival** (various venues and prices, 843/817-1617, www.charlestonIFF.com). Despite being a relative latecomer to the film festival circuit, the event is pulled off with Charleston's usual aplomb.

The free, weekend-long, outdoor **Charleston Harbor Fest** (www.charlestonharborfest.org, free) at the Maritime Center on the waterfront is without a doubt one of the coolest events in town for the whole family. You can see and tour working tall ships, and watch master boatwrights at work building new ones. There are free sailboat rides into the harbor and the U.S. Navy provides displays. As if all that weren't enough, you get to witness the start of the 777-mile annual Charleston-to-Bermuda race.

Indisputably Charleston's single biggest and most important event, **Spoleto Festival**

A MAN, A PLAN – SPOLETO!

Sadly, Gian Carlo Menotti is no longer with us, having died in 2007 at the age of 95. But the overwhelming success of the composer's brainchild and labor of love, **Spoleto Festival USA,** lives on, enriching the cultural and social life of Charleston and serving as the city's chief calling card to the world at large.

Menotti began writing music at age seven in his native Italy. As a young man he would move to Philadelphia to study music, where he shared classes – and lifelong connections – with Leonard Bernstein and Samuel Barber. His first full-length opera, *The Consul* would garner him the Pulitzer Prize, as would 1955's *The Saint of Bleecker Street.* But by far Menotti's best-known work is the beloved Christmas opera *Amahl and the Night Visitors,* composed especially for NBC television in 1951.

At the height of his fame in 1958, the charismatic and mercurial genius – fluent and witty in five languages – founded the "Festival of Two Worlds" in Spoleto, Italy, specifically as a forum for young American artists in Europe. But it wasn't until nearly two decades later, in 1977, that Menotti was able to make his long-imagined dream of an American counterpart a reality.

Attracted to Charleston because of its longstanding support of the arts, its undeniable good taste, and its small size – ensuring that his festival would always be the number-one activity in town while it was going on – Menotti worked closely with the man who was to become the other key part of the equation: Charleston Mayor Joe Riley, then in his first term in office. Since then, the city has built on Spoleto's success by founding its own local version, **Piccolo Spoleto** – literally, "little Spoleto" – which focuses exclusively on local and regional talent.

Things haven't always gone smoothly. Menotti and the stateside festival parted ways in 1993, when he took over the Rome Opera. Making matters more uneasy, the Italian festival – run by Menotti's longtime partner (and later adopted son) Chip – also became estranged from what was intended to be its soul mate in South Carolina. (Chip was later replaced by the Italian Culture Ministry). And though Mayor Riley and Spoleto Mayor Massimo Brunini have gone public with their desire for reconciliation between the two events, as of this writing that possibility remains sketchy at best.

But perhaps this kind of creative tension is what Menotti intended all along. Indeed, each spring brings a Spoleto USA that seems to thrive on the inherent conflict between the festival's often cutting-edge offerings and the very traditional city that hosts it. Unlike so many of the increasingly generic arts "festivals" across the nation, Spoleto still challenges its audiences, just as Menotti intended it to do. Depending on the critic and the audience member, that modern opera debut you see may be groundbreaking or gratuitous. The drama you check out may be exhilarating or tiresome.

Still, the crowds keep coming, attracted just as much for Charleston's many charms as for the art itself. Each year, a total of about half a million people attend both Spoleto and Piccolo Spoleto. (Despite a weak economy, the 2009 edition actually broke a five-day ticket sales record.) Nearly a third of attendees are Charleston residents – the final proof that when it comes to supporting the arts, Charleston puts its money where its mouth is.

USA (843/579-3100, www.spoletousa.org, varied admission) has come a long way since it was a sparkle in the eye of the late Gian Carlo Menotti three decades ago. Though Spoleto long ago broke ties with its founder, his vision remains indelibly stamped on the event from start to finish.

There's plenty of music, to be sure, in genres from orchestral to opera to jazz to avant-garde, but you'll find something in every other performing art here, from dance to drama to spoken word, in traditions from Western to African to Southeast Asian. For 17 days from Memorial Day weekend through early June, Charleston hops and hums nearly 24 hours a day to the energy of this vibrant, cutting-edge, yet accessible artistic celebration, which dominates everything and every conversation for those three weeks. Events happen in historic venues and churches all over downtown and as far afield as Middleton Place, which hosts the grand finale under the stars.

If you want to come to Charleston during Spoleto—and everyone should at least once—book your accommodations and your tickets far in advance. Tickets usually go on sale in early January for that summer's festival.

As if all the hubbub around Spoleto didn't give you enough to do, there's also **Piccolo Spoleto** (843/724-7305, www.piccolospoleto .com, various venues and admission), literally "little Spoleto," running concurrently. The intent of Piccolo Spoleto—begun just a couple of years after the larger festival came to town and run by the city's Office of Cultural Affairs—is to give local and regional performers a time to shine, sharing some of that larger spotlight on the national and international performers at the main event. Of particular interest to visiting families will be Piccolo's children's events, a good counter to some of the decidedly more adult fare at Spoleto USA.

June

Technically part of Piccolo Spoleto but gathering its own following, the **Sweetgrass Cultural Arts Festival** (www.sweetgrass festival.org) is held the first week in June in

sweetgrass baskets

COURTESY OF CHARLESTON AREA CVB, WWW.EXPLORECHARLESTON.COM

Mount Pleasant at the Laing Middle School (2213 Hwy. 17 N.). The event celebrates the traditional sweetgrass basketmaking skills of African Americans in the historical Christ Church Parish area of Mount Pleasant. If you want to buy some sweetgrass baskets made by the world's foremost experts in the field, this would be the time.

July

Each year, over 30,000 people come to see the **Patriots Point Fourth of July Blast** (866/831-1720), featuring a hefty barrage of fireworks shot off the deck of the USS *Yorktown* moored on the Cooper River in the Patriots Point complex. Food, live entertainment, and kids' activities are also featured.

September

From late September into the first week of October, the city-sponsored **MOJA Arts Festival** (843/724-7305, www.mojafestival .com, varied venues and admission), highlights the cultural contributions of African Americans and people from the Caribbean with dance, visual art, poetry, cuisine, crafts, and music in genres from gospel to jazz to reggae to classical. In existence since 1984, MOJA's name comes from the Swahili word for "one," and its incredibly diverse range of offerings in so many media have made it one of the Southeast's premier events. Highlights include a Reggae Block Party and the always-fun Caribbean Parade. Some events are ticketed, while others, such as the kids' activities and many of the dance and film events, are free.

For five weeks from the last week of September into October, the Preservation Society of Charleston hosts the much-anticipated **Fall Tours of Homes & Gardens** (843/722-4630, www.preservationsociety.org, $45). The tour takes you into over a dozen local residences and is the nearly 90-year-old organization's biggest fundraiser. Tickets typically go on sale the previous June, and they tend to sell out very quickly.

October

Another great food event in this great food city, the **Taste of Charleston** (1235 Long Point Rd., 843/577-4030, www.charlestonrestaurant association.com, 11 A.M.–5 P.M., $12) is held at Boone Hall Plantation in Mount Pleasant and sponsored by the Greater Charleston Restaurant Association. Over 50 area chefs and restaurants come together so you can sample their wares, including a wine and food pairing, with proceeds going to charity.

November

Plantation Days at Middleton Place (4300 Ashley River Rd., 843/556-6020, www .middletonplace.org, daily 9 A.M.–5 P.M., last tour 4:30 P.M., guided tour $10) happen each Saturday in November, giving visitors a chance to wander the grounds and see artisans at work practicing authentic crafts, as they would have done in antebellum days, on the grounds, with a special emphasis on the contributions of African Americans. A special treat comes on Thanksgiving, when a full meal is offered at the Middleton Place restaurant (843/556-6020, www.middletonplace.org) on the grounds (reservations highly recommended).

Though the **Battle of Secessionville** actually took place in June 1862 much further south, November is the time the battle is reenacted at Boone Plantation (1235 Long Point Rd., 843/884-4371, www.boonehallplantation .com, $17.50 adults, $7.50 children) on Mount Pleasant. Call for specific dates and times.

December

A yuletide in the Holy City is an experience you'll never forget, as the **Christmas in Charleston** (843/724-3705, www.charleston city.info) events clustered around the first week of the month prove. For some reason—whether it's the old architecture, the friendly people, the churches, the carriages, or all of the above—Charleston feels right at home during Christmas. The festivities begin with Mayor Joe Riley lighting the city's 60-foot Tree of Lights in Marion Square, followed by a parade of brightly lit boats from Mount Pleasant all the way around Charleston up the Ashley River. The key event is the Sunday Christmas Parade through downtown featuring bands, floats, and performers in the holiday spirit. The Saturday Farmer's Market in the square continues through the middle of the month with a focus on holiday items.

Shopping

For a relatively small city, Charleston has an impressive amount of big-name, big-city stores to go along with its charming, one-of-a-kind locally owned shops. I've never known anyone to leave Charleston without bundles of good stuff.

KING STREET

Without a doubt, King Street is by far the main shopping thoroughfare in the area. It's unique not only for the fact that so many national name stores are lined up so close to each other, but because there are so many great restaurants of so many different types scattered in and amongst all the retail outlets, ideally positioned for when you need to take a break to rest and refuel.

Though I don't necessarily recommend doing so—Charleston has so much more to offer—a visitor could easily spend an entire weekend doing nothing but shopping, eating,

and carousing up and down King Street from early morning to the wee hours of the following morning.

King Street has three distinct areas with three distinct types of merchandise: Lower King is primarily top-of-the-line antique stores (most are closed Sundays, so plan your trip accordingly); Middle King is where you'll find upscale name-brand outlets from traditional (Saks Fifth Avenue) to hip (American Apparel), as well as some excellent shoe stores; and Upper King north of Calhoun is where you'll find funky housewares shops, generally locally owned.

Antiques

On the 100 block of Lower King, **George C. Williams American Antiques** (155 King St., 843/377-0290, Mon.–Fri. 10 A.M.–5:30 P.M., Sat. 10 A.M.–5 P.M.) has some fine local and regional pieces. A relatively new addition to Lower King's cluster of antique shops,

© JIM MOREKIS

When in Charleston, don't forget to budget time to shop on King Street.

Alexandra AD (156 King St., 843/722-4897, Mon.–Sat. 10 A.M.–5 P.M.) features great chandeliers, lamps, and fabrics.

As the name implies, **English Patina** (179 King St., 843/853-0380, Mon.–Sat. 10 A.M.–5 P.M.) specializes in European furniture, brought to its big James Island warehouse three times a year in shipping containers. Since 1929, **George C. Birlant & Co.** (191 King St., 843/722-3842, Mon.–Sat. 9 A.M.–5:30 P.M.) has been importing 18th- and 19th-century furniture, silver, china, and crystal, and also deals in the famous "Charleston Battery Bench."

On the 200 block, **A'riga IV** (204 King St., 843/577-3075, Mon.–Sat. 10:30 A.M.–4:30 P.M.) deals in a quirky mix of 19th-century decorative arts, including rare apothecary items. **Carlton Daily Antiques** (208 King St., 843/853-2299, Mon.–Sat. 10 A.M.–5:30 P.M.) intrigues with its unusual focus on deco and modernist pieces and furnishings.

Art Galleries

Ever since native son Joseph Allen Smith began one of America's first art collections in Charleston in the late 1700s, the Holy City has been fertile ground for visual artists.

For most visitors, the center of visual arts activity is in the French Quarter between South Market and Tradd Streets. Thirty galleries reside there within short walking distance, including: **Charleston Renaissance Gallery** (103 Church St., 843/723-0025, www.fineart south.com, Mon.–Sat. 10 A.M.–5 P.M.) specializing in 19th- and 20th-century oils and sculpture featuring artists from the American South, including some splendid pieces from the Charleston Renaissance; the city-funded **City Gallery at Waterfront** (34 Prioleau St., 843/958-6484, Tues.–Fri. 11 A.M.–6 P.M., Sat.–Sun. noon–5 P.M.); the **Pink House Gallery** (17 Chalmers St., 843/723-3608, http://pinkhouse-gallery.tripod.com, Mon.–Sat. 10 A.M.–5 P.M.), in the oldest tavern building in the South, circa 1694; **Helena Fox Fine Art** (12 Queen St., 843/723-0073, www.fraserfoxfineart.com,

Mon.–Sat. 10 A.M.–5 P.M.), dealing in 20th-century representational art; and the **Anne Worsham Richardson Birds Eye View Gallery** (119-A Church St., 843/723-1276, Mon.–Sat. 10 A.M.–5 P.M.), home of South Carolina's official painter of the state flower and state bird.

The best way to experience the area is to go on one of the popular **French Quarter ArtWalks** (843/724-3424, www.frenchquarter arts.com), held the first Friday of March, May, October, and December between 5–8 P.M. and featuring lots of wine, food, and, of course, art. You can download a map at the website.

One of the most important single venues, the nonprofit **Redux Contemporary Art Center** (136 St. Philip St., 843/722-0697, www.redux studios.org, Wed.–Sat. noon–5 P.M.) features modernistic work in a variety of media, from illustration to video installation to blueprints to performance art to graffiti. Outreach is hugely important to this venture, including lecture series, classes, workshops, and internships.

Part art gallery, part artsy home goods store, **Plum Elements** (161 1/2 King St., 843/727-3747, Mon.–Tues. and Fri.–Sat. 10 A.M.–6 P.M., Wed. noon–6 P.M., Thurs. 10 A.M.–7 P.M.) is the labor of love of Andrea Schenck, who was inspired to open the shop from her time in Asia. The shop offers lots of absolutely unique gift items with an Eastern twist, plus there's a bona fide art gallery in the adjacent space.

For a more modern take from local artists, check out the **Sylvan Gallery** (171 King St., 843/722-2172, www.thesylvangallery.com, Mon.–Fri. 9 A.M.–5 P.M., Sat. 10 A.M.–5 P.M., Sun. 11 A.M.–4 P.M.), which specializes in 20th- and 21st-century art and sculpture.

Right up the street and incorporating works from the estate of Charleston legend Elizabeth O'Neill Verner is **Ann Long Fine Art** (177 King St., 843/577-0447, www.annlongfineart .com, Mon.–Sat. 11 A.M.–5 P.M.), which seeks to combine the painterly aesthetic of the Old World with the edgy vision of the New. Its Old Master–inspired Florentine gallery is nicely juxtaposed with a modern gallery, featuring works from the estate of German Expressionist Otto Neumann, among other modernists. You'll find the African American–themed portraiture of Mario Robinson here as well.

Farther up King and specializing in original Audubon prints and antique botanical prints is **The Audubon Gallery** (190 King St., 843/853-1100, www.audubonart.com, Mon.–Sat. 10 A.M.–5 P.M.), the sister store of the Joel Oppenheimer Gallery in Chicago.

In the Upper King area is **Gallery Chuma** (43 John St., 843/722-7568, www.gallery chuma.com, Mon–Sat. 10 A.M.–6 P.M.), which specializes in the art of the Gullah people of the South Carolina coast. They do lots of cultural and educational events about Gullah culture as well as displaying art on the subject.

By far Charleston's favorite art supply store is **Artist & Craftsman Supply** (434 King St., 843/579-0077, www.artistcraftsman.com, Mon.–Sat. 10 A.M.–7 P.M., Sun. noon–5 P.M.), part of a well-regarded Maine-based chain. They cater to the pro as well as the dabbler, and have a fun children's art section as well.

Books and Music

It's easy to overlook at the far southern end of retail development on King, but the excellent **Preservation Society of Charleston Book and Gift Shop** (147 King St., 843/722-4630, Mon.–Sat. 10 A.M.–5 P.M.) is perhaps the best place in town to pick up books on Charleston lore and history as well as locally themed gift items.

The charming **Pauline Books and Media** (243 King St., 843/577-0175, Mon.–Sat. 10 A.M.–6 P.M.) is run by the Daughters of St. Paul and has Christian books, Bibles, rosaries, and images from a Roman Catholic perspective.

Housed in an extremely long and narrow storefront on Upper King, Jonathan Sanchez's funky and friendly **Blue Bicycle Books** (420 King St., 843/722-2666, www.bluebicycle books.com, Mon.–Sat. 10 A.M.–6 P.M., Sun. 1–6 P.M.) deals primarily in used books and has a particularly nice stock of local and regional books, art books, and fiction.

The local bastion of indie music and the best place to find that rare vinyl is **52.5 Records** (561 King St., 843/722-3525, Mon.–Thurs. 11 A.M.–7 P.M., Fri.–Sat. 11 A.M.–9 P.M., Sun. 1–6 P.M.).

Clothes

Cynics may scoff at the proliferation of high-end national retail chains on Middle King, but rarely will a shopper find so many so conveniently located, and in such a pleasant environment. The biggies are: **Saks Fifth Avenue** (211 King St., 843/853-9888, Mon.–Wed. 10 A.M.–6 P.M., Thurs.–Sat. 10 A.M.–7 P.M., Sun. noon–5 P.M.); **Banana Republic** (247 King St., 843/722-6681, Mon.–Fri. 10 A.M.–7 P.M., Sat. 10 A.M.–8 P.M., Sun. noon–6 P.M.); **J. Crew** (264 King St., 843/534-1640, Mon.–Thurs. 10 A.M.–6 P.M., Fri.–Sat. 10 A.M.–8 P.M., Sun. noon–6 P.M.); and **American Apparel** (348 King St., 843/853-7220, Mon.–Sat. 10 A.M.–8 P.M., Sun. noon–7 P.M.).

As for locally owned clothing shops, try **Lula Kate** (231 King St. 843/723-5885, Mon.–Sat. 10 A.M.–6 P.M., Sun. noon–5 P.M.), which specializes in professional, business attire, or the innovative **Worthwhile** (268 King St., 843/723-4418, Mon.–Sat. 10 A.M.–6 P.M., Sun. noon–5 P.M.), which has lots of organic fashion.

On the next block, some way-cool indie stores include the upscale **Copper Penny** (311 King St. 843/723-2999, Mon.–Sat. 10 A.M.–7 P.M., Sun. noon–6 P.M.) and the all-around excellent **Luna** (334 King St., 843/853-5862, Mon.–Sat. 10:30 A.M.–7 P.M., Sun. noon–5 P.M.). After living for a time in L.A., native Charlestonian Guilds Bennett brought back a fun and flirty West Coast vibe to her boutique **Miostile** (346 King St., 843/722-7073, Mon.–Sat. 10 A.M.–7 P.M., Sun. noon–5 P.M.), which offers designer items in a beautifully restored setting.

Also in this area is one of the city's most unique locally owned shops: the nationally famous **Mary Norton** (318 King St., 843/724-1081, www.marynorton.com, Mon.–Sat. 10 A.M.–6 P.M.), formerly Moo Roo, where

MAYOR JOE'S LEGACY

Few cities anywhere have been as greatly influenced by one mayor as Charleston has by Joseph P. "Joe" Riley, re-elected in November 2007 to his ninth four-year term. Now mayor for over 30 years, "Mayor Joe," as he's called, is not only responsible for instigating the vast majority of redevelopment in the city, he continues to set the bar for its award-winning tourist industry – always a key component in his long-term plans.

Riley won his first mayoral race at the age of 32. He was the second Irish American mayor of the city, the first being the great John Grace, who was first elected in 1911 and eventually defeated by the allegedly anti-Catholic Thomas P. Stoney. Legend has it that soon after winning his first mayoral election in 1975, Riley was handed an old envelope written decades before by the Bishop of Charleston, addressed to "The Next Irish Mayor." Inside was a note with a simple message: "Get the Stoneys."

Though young, the well-regarded lawyer, Citadel grad, and former member of the state legislature had a clear vision for his administration: It would bring unprecedented numbers of women and minorities into city government, rejuvenate then-seedy King Street, and enlarge the city's tax base by annexing surrounding areas (during Riley's tenure the city has grown from 16.7 square miles to over 100).

But in order to make any of that happen, one thing had to happen first: Charleston's epidemic street crime had to be brought under control. Enter a vital and perhaps underrated partner in Riley's effort to remake Charleston – Chief of Police Reuben Greenberg. From 1982-2005, Greenberg – who intrigued locals and the national media not only for his dominant personality but because he was that comparative rarity, an African American Jew – turned old ideas of law enforcement in Charleston upside down through his introduction of "community policing." Charleston cops would have to have a college degree. Graffiti would not be tolerated. And for the first time

in recent memory, they would have to walk beats instead of stay in their cars. With Greenberg's help, Riley was able to keep together the unusual coalition of predominantly white business and corporate interests and African American voters that brought him into office in the first place.

It hasn't all been rosy. Riley was put on the spot in 2007 after the tragic deaths of the "Charleston 9" firefighters, an episode which seemed to expose serious policy and equipment flaws in the city's fire department. And he's often been accused of being too easily infatuated with high-dollar development projects instead of paying attention to the needs of regular Charlestonians. But while every four years there's talk around town that somebody might finally be able to beat Mayor Joe, every four years the naysayers are disappointed as he's reelected again.

Here's only a partial list of the major projects and events Mayor Joe has made happen in Charleston that visitors are likely to enjoy:

- Charleston Maritime Center

- Charleston Place

- Children's Museum of the Lowcountry

- Hampton Park rehabilitation

- King Street/Market Street retail district

- Mayor Joseph P. Riley Ballpark (named after the mayor at the insistence of city council over his objections)

- MOJA Arts Festival

- Piccolo Spoleto

- The South Carolina Aquarium

- Spoleto USA

- Waterfront Park

- West Ashley Bikeway & Greenway

native Charlestonian Mary Norton creates and sells her one-of-a-kind designer handbags.

Big companies' losses are your gain at **Oops!** (326 King St., 843/722-7768, Mon.–Fri. 10 A.M.–6 P.M., Sat. 10 A.M.–7 P.M., Sun. noon–6 P.M.), which buys factory mistakes and discontinued lines from major brands at a discount, passing along the savings to you. The range here tends towards colorful and preppy.

The fun and unique "lifestyle boutique" **b'zar** (541 King St., 843/579-2889, www.shopbzar.com, Mon.–Sat. 11 A.M.–6 P.M., Sun. noon–5 P.M.) on Upper King has cutting-edge women's and men's clothes, as well as accessories, great candles, books, and music.

If hats are your thing, make sure you visit **Magar Hatworks** (57 Cannon St., 843/577-7740, leighmagar@aol.com, www.magarhatworks.com), where Leigh Magar makes and sells her whimsical, all-natural hats, some of which she designs for Barneys New York.

Notable locally owned clothing stores on King Street include the classy **Berlins Men's and Women's** (114–120 King St., 843/722-1665, Mon.–Sat. 9:30 A.M.–6 P.M.), dating from 1883, and **Jos. A. Bank** (328 King St., 843/723-9770, Mon.–Sat. 9 A.M.–8 P.M., Sun. noon–6 P.M.), a mecca for reasonably priced preppy menswear.

Health and Beauty

The Euro-style window display of **Stella Nova** (292 King St., 843/722-9797, Mon.–Sat. 10 A.M.–7 P.M., Sun. 1–5 P.M.) beckons at the corner of King and Society. Inside this locally owned cosmetics store and studio, you'll find a wide selection of high-end makeup and beauty products. There's also a Stella Nova day spa (78 Society Street, 843/723-0909, Mon.–Sat. 9 A.M.–6 P.M., Sun. noon–5 P.M.).

Inside the Francis Marion Hotel near Marion Square is **Spa Adagio** (387 King St., 843/577-2444, Mon.–Sat. 10 A.M.–7 P.M., Sun. by appointment only), offering massage, waxing, and skin and nail care. On

Upper King you'll find **Allure Salon** (415 King St., 843/722-8689, Tues. and Thurs. 10 A.M.–7 P.M., Wed. and Fri. 9 A.M.–5 P.M., Sat. 10 A.M.–3 P.M.) for stylish haircuts.

Home, Garden, and Sporting Goods

With retail locations in Charleston and Savannah and a new cutting-edge, green-friendly warehouse in North Charleston, **Half Moon Outfitters** (280 King St., 843/853-0990, www.halfmoonoutfitters.com, Mon.–Sat. 10 A.M.–7 P.M., Sun. noon–6 P.M.) is something of a local legend. Here you can find not only top-of-the-line camping and outdoor gear and good tips on local recreation, but some really stylish, outdoorsy apparel as well.

Probably Charleston's best-regarded home goods store is the nationally recognized **ESD, Elizabeth Stuart Design** (314 King St., 843/577-6272, www.esdcharleston.com, Mon.–Sat. 10 A.M.–6 P.M.), with a wide range of antique and new furnishings, art, lighting, jewelry, and more.

Several great home and garden stores are worth mentioning on Upper King: **Global Awakening Market** (499 King St., 843/577-8579, www.globalawakeningmarket.com, Mon.–Sat. 11 A.M.–6 P.M.), which deals exclusively in fair trade clothing, crafts, and furnishings from all over the world; **Charleston Gardens** (650 King St., 843/723-0252, www.charlestongardens.com, Mon.–Sat. 9 A.M.–5 P.M.) for furniture and accessories; and **Haute Design Studio** (489 King St., 843/577-9886, Mon.–Fri. 9 A.M.–5:30 P.M.) for upper-end furnishings with an edgy feel.

Jewelry

Joint Venture Estate Jewelers (185 King St., 843/722-6730, www.jventure.com, Mon.–Sat. 10 A.M.–5:30 P.M.) specializes in antique, vintage, and modern estate jewelry as well as pre-owned watches, including Rolex, Patek Philippe, and Cartier. Since 1919, **Croghan's Jewel Box** (308 King St.,

843/723-3594, Mon.–Fri. 9:30 A.M.–5:30 P.M., Sat. 10 A.M.–5 P.M.) has offered amazing locally crafted diamonds, silver, and designer pieces to generations of Charlestonians. An expansion in the late 1990s tripled the size of the historic location. **Art Jewelry by Mikhail Smolkin** (312 King St., 843/722-3634, Mon.–Sat. 10 A.M.–5 P.M.) features one-of-a-kind pieces by this St. Petersburg, Russia native.

Shoes

Rangoni of Florence (270 King St., 843/577-9554, Mon.–Sat. 9:30 A.M.–6 P.M., Sun. 12:30–5:30 P.M.) imports the best women's shoes from Italy, with a few men's designs as well. **Copper Penny Shooz** (317 King St., 843/723-3838, Mon.–Sat. 10 A.M.–7 P.M., Sun. noon–6 P.M.) combines hip and upscale fashion. Funky and fun **Phillips Shoes** (320 King St., 843/965-5270, Mon.–Sat. 10 A.M.–6 P.M.) deals in Dansko for men, women, and kids (don't miss the awesome painting above the register of Elvis fitting a customer). **Mephisto** (322 King St., 843/722-4666, www.mepcomfort.com, Mon.–Sat. 10 A.M.–6 P.M.) deals in that incredibly comfortable, durable brand.

The most famous locally owed place for footwear is **Bob Ellis Shoe Store** (332 King St., 843/722-2515, Mon.–Sat. 9 A.M.–6 P.M.), which has served Charleston's elite with high-end shoes since 1950. Hip and popular **Pete Banis Shoes** (375 King St., 843/577-0950, Mon.–Sat. 10 A.M.–6 P.M., Sun. noon–5 P.M.) still does layaway. **Farushga** (377A King St., 843/722-3131, Mon.–Sat. 10:30 A.M.–6:30 P.M., Sun. 11:30 A.M.–5:30 P.M.) has provocative European styles for men and women.

CHARLESTON PLACE

Charleston Place (130 Market St., 843/722-4900, www.charlestonplaceshops.com, Mon.–Wed. 10 A.M.–6 P.M., Thurs.–Sat. 10 A.M.–8 P.M., Sun. noon–5 P.M.), a combined retail/hotel development begun to much controversy in the late 1970s, was the first big downtown redevelopment project of Mayor Riley's tenure. While naysayers said people would never come downtown to shop

for boutique items, Riley proved them wrong, and 30 years later The Shops at Charleston Place and the Riviera (the entire complex has itself been renovated through the years) remains a big shopping draw for locals and tourists alike.

Highlights inside the large, stylish space include Crabtree & Evelyn, Gucci, Talbot's Laura Ashley, VSOE Boutique, Everything But Water, and Godiva.

NORTH OF BROAD

In addition to the myriad of tourist-oriented shops in the Old City Market itself, there are a few gems in the surrounding area that also appeal to locals. A laid-back flea market vibe dominates at **Old City Market** (Meeting and Market Sts., 843/973-7236, daily 6 A.M.–11:30 P.M.), with the front, westward Market Hall featuring meandering halls lined with smallish, tourist-oriented shops and the subsequent, less-grand buildings purely for touristy flea market stalls. Pricier establishments, such as the famous Peninsula Grill, line the perimeter. Tip: If you must have one of the handcrafted sweetgrass baskets, try out your haggling skills—the prices have wiggle room built in.

Women come from throughout the region to shop at the incredible consignment store **The Trunk Show** (281 Meeting St., 843/722-0442, Mon.–Sat. 10 A.M.–6 P.M.). You can find one-of-a-kind vintage and designer wear and accessories. Some finds are bargains, some not so much, but there's no denying the quality and breadth of the offerings. For a more budget-conscious and counter-culture vintage shop, walk a few feet next door to **Factor Five** (283 Meeting St., 843/965-5559), which has retro clothes, rare CDs, and assorted paraphernalia.

Indigo (4 Vendue Range, 800/549-2513, Sun.–Thurs. 10 A.M.–6 P.M., Fri.–Sat. 10 A.M.–7 P.M.), a favorite home accessories store, has plenty of one-of-a-kind pieces, many of them by regional artists and rustic in flavor, almost like outsider art.

Affiliated with the hip local restaurant chain

vintage store on Meeting Street

Maverick Kitchens, **Charleston Cooks!** (194 East Bay St., 843/722-1212, www.charleston cooks.com, Mon.–Sat. 10 A.M.–9 P.M., Sun. 11 A.M.–6 P.M.) has an almost overwhelming array of gourmet items and kitchen ware, and even offers cooking classes.

OFF THE PENINSULA

Though the best shopping is in Charleston proper, there are some noteworthy independent stores in the surrounding areas.

One of the most famous area stores is in West Ashley, **Avondale Junk & Jive Retro Mart** (827 Savannah Hwy., 843/225-5483), a wild vintage shop on U.S. 17 right down from the Goodwill thrift shop.

Mount Pleasant boasts two fun antiques spots, **Linda Page's Thieves Mart** (1460 Ben Sawyer Blvd., 843/884-9672, Mon.– Fri., 9 A.M.–5:30 P.M., Sat. 9 A.M.–5 P.M.) and **Hungryneck Antique Mall** (401 Johnnie Dodds Blvd., 843/849-1744, Mon.–Sat. 10 A.M.–6 P.M., Sun. 1–5 P.M.) off U.S. 17.

The biggest music store in the region is **The Guitar Center** (7620 Rivers Ave., 843/572-9063, Mon.–Fri. 11 A.M.–7 P.M., Sat. 10 A.M.–7 P.M., Sun. noon–6 P.M.) in North Charleston across from Northwood Mall. With just about everything a musician might want or need, it's part of a chain that's been around since the late 1950s, but the Charleston location is relatively new.

SHOPPING CENTERS

The newest and most pleasant mall in the area is the retro-themed, pedestrian-friendly **Mount Pleasant Towne Center** (1600 Palmetto Grande Dr., 843/216-9900, www.mtpleasant townecentre.com, Mon.–Sat. 10 A.M.–9 P.M., Sun. noon–6 P.M.), which opened in 1999 to serve the growing population of East Cooper residents tired of having to cross a bridge to get to a big mall. In addition to national chains you'll find a few cool local stores in here, like Stella Nova spa and day salon, Shooz by Copper Penny, and the men's store Jos. A. Banks.

You'll find the **Northwoods Mall** (2150 Northwoods Blvd., North Charleston,

843/797-3060, www.shopnorthwoods mall.com, Mon.–Sat. 10 A.M.–9 P.M., Sun. noon–6 P.M.) up in North Charleston. Anchor stores include Dillard's, Belk, Sears, and J.C. Penney. North Charleston also hosts the **Tanger Outlet** (4840 Tanger Outlet Blvd., 843/529-3095, www.tangeroutlet.com, Mon.– Sat. 10 A.M.–9 P.M., Sun. 11 A.M.–6 P.M.). Get factory-priced bargains from stores such as Adidas, Banana Republic, Brooks Brothers, Corningware, Old Navy, Timberland, and more.

Citadel Mall (2070 Sam Rittenberg Blvd., 843/766-8511, www.shopcitadel-mall.com, Mon.–Sat. 10 A.M.–9 P.M., Sun. noon–6 P.M.) is in West Ashley (and not at all close to the real Citadel). Anchors here are Dillards, Parisian, Target, Belk, and Sears.

Sports and Recreation

Because of the generally gorgeous weather in the Charleston area, helped immensely by the steady, soft sea breeze, outdoor activities are always popular and available. Though it's not much of a spectator sports town, there are plenty of things to do on your own, such as golf, tennis, walking, hiking, boating, and fishing.

ON THE WATER
Beaches
Folly Beach is the area's most famous beach, if not necessarily its best. In addition to the charming town of Folly Beach itself, there's the modest, county-run **Folly Beach County Park** (1100 West Ashley Ave., 843/588-2426, www.ccprc.com, daily 10 A.M.–dark, open 9 A.M. Mar. and Apr., $7 per vehicle, free for pedestrians and cyclists) at the far west end of Folly Island. It has a picnic area, restrooms, outdoor showers, and beach chair and umbrella rentals. Get there by taking Highway 171/Folly Road until it turns into Center Street, and then take a right on West Ashley.

On Isle of Palms you'll find **Isle of Palms County Park** (14th Ave., 843/886-3863, www.ccprc.com, daily 10 A.M.–dark, open 9 A.M. summer, $5 per vehicle, free for pedestrians and cyclists), which has restrooms, showers, a picnic area, a beach volleyball area, and beach chair and umbrella rentals. Get there by taking the Isle of Palms Connector/Highway 517 to the island, go through the light at Palm Boulevard and take the next left at the park gate. There's good public beach access near

the Pavilion Shoppes on Ocean Boulevard, accessed via JC Long Boulevard.

On the west end of Kiawah Island to the south of Charleston is **Kiawah Island Beachwalker Park** (843/768-2395, www.ccprc.com, weekends only 10 A.M.–6 P.M. Mar.–Apr., 9 A.M.–7 P.M. during summer, 10 A.M.–6 P.M. Sept., weekends only 10 A.M.–6 P.M. Oct., closed Nov.–Feb., $7 per vehicle, free for pedestrians and cyclists), the only public facility on this mostly private resort island. It has restrooms, showers, a picnic area with grills, and beach chair and umbrella rentals. Get there from downtown by taking Lockwood Avenue onto the Highway 30 Connector bridge over the Ashley River. Turn right onto Folly Road, then take a left onto Maybank Highway. After about 20 minutes you'll take another left onto Bohicket Road, which leads you to Kiawah in 14 miles. Turn left from Bohicket onto the Kiawah Island Parkway. Just before the security gate, turn right on Beachwalker Drive and follow the signs to the park.

For a totally go-it-alone type of beach day, go to the three-mile beach on the Atlantic Ocean at **Sullivan's Island.** There are no facilities, no lifeguards, strong offshore currents, and no parking lots on this residential island (park on the side of the street). There's also a lot of dog-walking on this beach since no leash is required November–February. Get there from downtown by crossing the Ravenel Bridge over the Cooper River and bearing right onto Coleman Boulevard, which turns into

Ben Sawyer Boulevard. Take the Ben Sawyer Bridge onto Sullivan's Island. Beach access is plentiful and marked.

Kayaking

An excellent outfit for guided kayak tours is **Coastal Expeditions** (654 Serotina Ct., 843/881-4582, www.coastalexpeditions.com), which also runs the only approved ferry service to the Cape Romain National Wildlife Refuge. They'll rent a kayak for roughly $50 a day. Coastal Expeditions also sells an outstanding kayaking/boating/fishing map of the area for about $12.

Barrier Island Eco Tours (50 41st Ave., 843/886-5000, www.nature-tours.com) takes you up to the Cape Romain refuge out of Isle of Palms. **PaddleFish Kayaking** (843/330-9777, www.paddlefishkayaking .com) offers several kinds of kayaking tours (no experience necessary) and is quite accommodating in terms of scheduling them. Another good tour operator is **Nature Adventures Outfitters** (1900 Iron Swamp Rd., 800/673-0679) out of Awendaw Island.

COURTESY OF CHARLESTON AREA CVE, WWW.EXPLORECHARLESTON.COM

The Charleston area offers a variety of nature-based activities to visitors.

Closer to town, many kayakers put in at the **Shem Creek Marina** (526 Mill St., 843/884-3211, www.shemcreekmarina.com) or the public **Shem Creek Landing** in Mount Pleasant. From there it's a safe, easy paddle—sometimes with appearances by dolphins or manatee—to the Intracoastal Waterway. Some kayakers like to go from Shem Creek straight out into Charleston Harbor to **Crab Bank Heritage Preserve,** a prime birding island. Another good place to put in is at **Isle of Palms Marina** (50 41st Ave., 843/886-0209) on Morgan Creek behind the Wild Dunes Resort, emptying into the Intracoastal Waterway.

Local company **Half Moon Outfitters** (280 King St., 843/853-0990; 425 Coleman Blvd., 843/881-9472, www.halfmoonoutfitters.com, Mon.–Sat. 10 A.M.–7 P.M., Sun. noon–6 P.M.) sponsors an annual six-mile Giant Kayak Race at Isle of Palms Marina in late October, benefiting the Coastal Conservation League.

Behind Folly Beach is an extensive network of waterways, including lots of areas that are great for camping and fishing. The Folly River Landing is just over the bridge to the island. On Folly a good tour operator and rental house is **OceanAir Sea Kayak** (520 Folly Rd., 800/698-8718, www.seakayaksc.com).

Fishing and Boating

For casual fishing off a pier, try the well-equipped new **Folly Beach Fishing Pier** (101 E. Arctic Ave., 843/588-3474, $5 parking, $8 fishing fee, rod rentals available) on Folly Beach or the **North Charleston Riverfront Park** (843/745-1087, www.northcharleston .org, daily dawn–dusk) along the Cooper River on the grounds of the old Navy Yard. Get onto the Navy Yard grounds by taking I-26 north to exit 216-B. Take a left onto Spruill Avenue and a right onto McMillan Avenue.

Key local marinas include **Shem Creek Marina** (526 Mill St., 843/884-3211, www.shem creekmarina.com), **Charleston Harbor Marina** (24 Patriots Point Rd., 843/284-7062, www .charlestonharbormarina.com), **Charleston City Marina** (17 Lockwood Dr., 843/722-4968),

Charleston Maritime Center (10 Wharfside St., 843/853-3625, www.cmcevents.com), and the **Cooper River Marina** (1010 Juneau Ave., 843/554-0790, www.ccprc.com). Good fishing charter outfits include **Barrier Island Eco Tours** (50 41st Ave., 843/886-5000, www.nature-tours.com, about $80) out of Isle of Palms; **Bohicket Boat Adventure & Tour Co.** (2789 Cherry Point Rd., 843/559-3525, www.bohicketboat.com) out of the Edisto River; and **Reel Fish Finder Charters** (315 Yellow Jasmine Ct., Moncks Corner, 843/697-2081). Captain James picks clients up at many different marinas in the area.

For a list of all public landings in Charleston County, go to www. ccprc.com.

Diving

Diving here can be challenging because of the fast currents, and visibility can be low. But as you'd expect in this historic area, there are plenty of wrecks, fossils, and artifacts. In fact, there's an entire Cooper River Underwater Heritage Trail with the key sites marked for divers.

Offshore diving centers on the network of offshore artificial reefs (go to www.dnr .sc.gov for a list and locations), particularly the "Charleston 60" sunken barge and the new and very popular "Train Wreck," comprising 50 deliberately sunk New York City subway cars.

The longtime popular dive spot known as the "Anchor Wreck" was recently identified as the Norwegian steamer *Leif Erikkson,* which sank in 1905 after a collision with another vessel. In addition to being fun dive sites, these artificial reefs have proven to be important feeding and spawning grounds for marine life.

Probably Charleston's best-regarded outfitter and charter operator is **Charleston Scuba** (335 Savannah Hwy., 843/763-3483, www .charlestonscuba.com) in West Ashley. You also might want to check out **Cooper River Scuba** (843/572-0459, www.cooperriverdiving.com) and **Atlantic Coast Dive Center** (209 Scott St., 843/884-1500).

Surfing and Boarding

The surfing at the famous **Washout** area on

the eastside of Folly Beach isn't what it used to be due to storm activity and beach erosion. But the diehards still gather at this area when the swell hits—generally about 3–5 feet (occasionally with dolphins!). Check out the conditions yourself from the three views of the Folly Surfcam (www.follysurfcam.com).

The best local surf shop is undoubtedly the historic **McKevlin's Surf Shop** (8 Center St., 843/588-2247, www.mckevlins.com) on Folly Beach, one of the first surf shops on the entire East Coast, dating to 1965 (check out an employee's "No Pop-Outs" blog at http:// mckevlins.blogspot.com). Other shops include **Barrier Island Surf Shop** (2013 Folly Rd., 843/795-4545) on Folly Beach and **The Point Break** (369 King St., 843/722-4161) on the peninsula.

For lessons, **Folly Beach Shaka Surf School** (843/607-9911, www.shakasurfschool .com) offers private and group sessions at Folly; you might also try **Sol Surfers Surf Camp** (843/881-6700, www.solsurfers.net).

Kiteboarders might want to contact **Air** (843/388-9300, www.catchsomeair.us), which offers several levels of lessons, as well as **Whitecap Windsurfing** (706/833-9463, www .whitecapwindsurfing.com).

Water Parks

During the summer months, Charleston County operates three water parks, though none are on the peninsula: **Splash Island Waterpark** (444 Needlerush Pkwy., 843/884-0832) in Mount Pleasant; **Whirlin' Waters Adventure Waterpark** (University Blvd., 843/572-7275) in North Charleston; and **Splash Zone Waterpark at James Island County Park** (871 Riverland Dr., 843/795-7275) on James Island west of town. Admission runs about $10 per person. Go to www.ccprc.com for more information.

ON LAND
Golf

America's first golf course was constructed in Charleston in 1786. The term "green fee" is alleged to have evolved from the maintenance fees charged to members of the South Carolina Golf Club and Harleston Green in what's now downtown Charleston. So as you'd expect, there's some great golfing in the area, generally in the outlying islands. Here are some of the highlights (green fees are averages and subject to season and time).

The folks at the nonprofit **Charleston Golf, Inc.** (423 King St., 843/958-3629, www.charlestongolfguide.com) are your best one-stop resource for tee times and packages.

The main public course is the 18-hole **Charleston Municipal Golf Course** (2110 Maybank Hwy., 843/795-6517, www.charlestoncity.info, $40). To get there from the peninsula, take U.S. 17 south over the Ashley River, take Highway 171/Folly Road south, and then take a right onto Maybank Highway.

Probably the most renowned area facilities are at the acclaimed **Kiawah Island Golf Resort** (12 Kiawah Beach Dr., 800/654-2924, www.kiawahgolf.com) about 20 miles from Charleston. The Resort has five courses in all, the best known of which is the **Kiawah Island Ocean Course,** site of the famous "War by the Shore" 1991 Ryder Cup. This 2.5-mile course, which is walking-only until noon each day, hosted the Senior PGA Championship in 2007 and will host the 2012 PGA Championship. The Resort offers a golf academy and private lessons galore. These are public courses, but be aware that tee times are limited for golfers who aren't guests at the resort.

Two excellent resort-style public courses are at **Wild Dunes Resort Golf** (5757 Palm Blvd., 888/845-8932, www.wilddunes.com, $165) on Isle of Palms. The 18-hole **Patriots Point Links** (1 Patriots Point Rd., 843/881-0042, www.patriotspointlinks.com, $100) on the Charleston Harbor right over the Ravenel Bridge in Mount Pleasant is one of the most convenient courses in the area, and it boasts some phenomenal views.

Also on Mount Pleasant is perhaps the best course in the area for the money, the award-winning **Rivertowne Golf Course** (1700 Rivertowne Country Club Dr., 843/856-9808, www.rivertownecountryclub.com, $150) at the Rivertowne Country Club. This relatively

COURTESY OF CHARLESTON AREA CVB, WWW.EXPLORECHARLESTON.COM

Kiawah Island Ocean Course

new course, opened in 2002, was designed by Arnold Palmer.

Tennis

Tennis fans are in for a treat at the brand-new **Family Circle Tennis Center** (161 Seven Farms Dr., 800/677-2293, www.familycirclecup.com, Mon.–Thurs. 8 A.M.–8 P.M., Fri. 8 A.M.–7 P.M., Sat. 8 A.M.–5 P.M., Sun. 9 A.M.–5 P.M., $15/hr.) on Daniel Island. This multimillion-dollar facility is owned by the city of Charleston, and was built in 2001 specifically to host the annual Family Circle Cup women's competition, which was previously held in Hilton Head for many years. But it's also open to the public year-round (except when the Cup is on) with 17 courts.

The best resort tennis activity is at the **Kiawah Island Golf Resort** (12 Kiawah Beach Dr., 800/654-2924, www.kiawahgolf.com), with a total of 28 courts.

There are four free, public, city-funded facilities on the peninsula: **Moultrie Playground** (Broad St. and Ashley Ave., 843/769-8258, www.charlestoncity.info, six lighted hard courts), **Jack Adams Tennis Center** (290 Congress St., six lighted hard courts), **Hazel Parker Playground** (70 East Bay St. on the Cooper River, one hard court), and **Corrine Jones Playground** (Marlowe and Peachtree Sts., two hard courts). Over in West Ashley, the city also runs the public **Charleston Tennis Center** (19 Farmfield Rd., 843/769-8258, www.charlestoncity.info, 15 lighted courts).

Hiking and Biking

If you're like me, you'll walk your legs off just making your way around the sights on the peninsula. Early risers will especially enjoy the incredible beauty of a dawn breaking over the Cooper River as they walk or jog along the Battery or a little farther north at Waterfront Park.

Charleston-area beaches are perfect for a leisurely bike ride on the sand. Sullivan's Island is a particular favorite, and it's worth the drive just to enjoy a sunset after pedaling nearly the whole length of the island. Indeed, you might be surprised at how long you can ride in one direction on these beaches.

Those desiring a more demanding use of their legs can walk or ride their bike in the dedicated pedestrian/bike lane on the massive **Arthur Ravenel Jr. Bridge** over the Cooper River, the longest cable-stayed bridge in the western hemisphere. The extra lanes are a huge advantage over the old span on the same site, and a real example for other cities to follow in practical, sustainable transportation solutions. There's public parking on both sides of the bridge, on the Charleston side off of Meeting Street and on the Mount Pleasant side on the road to Patriots Point. **Bike the Bridge Rentals** (360 Concord St., 843/853-2453, www.bikethebridgerentals.com) offers self-guided tours over the Ravenel Bridge and back on a Raleigh Comfort bike, and also rents road bikes for lengthier excursions.

In West Ashley, there's a good urban walking/biking trail, the **West Ashley Greenway**, built on a former rail bed. The 10-mile trail runs parallel to U.S. 17 and passes parks, schools, and the Clemson Experimental Farm, ending near John Island. To get to the trailhead from downtown, drive west on U.S. 17. About a half-mile after you cross the bridge, turn left onto Folly Road (Highway 171). At the second light, turn right into South Windermere Shopping Center; the trail's behind the center on the right.

The most ambitious trail in South Carolina is the **Palmetto Trail** (www.palmettoconservation.org), begun in 1997 and eventually covering 425 miles from the Atlantic to the Appalachians. The coastal terminus near Charleston, the seven-mile Awendaw Passage through the Francis Marion National Forest, begins at the trailhead at the Buck Hall Recreational Area (843/887-3257, $5 vehicle fee), which has parking and bathroom facilities. Get there by taking U.S. 17 north about 20 miles out of Charleston and through the Francis Marion National Forest and then Awendaw. Take a right onto Buck Hall Landing Road.

Another good nature hike outside town is on the eight miles of scenic and educational trails at **Caw Caw Interpretive Center** (5200 Savannah Hwy., 843/889-8898, www.ccprc

.com, Wed.–Fri. 9 A.M.–3 P.M., Sat.–Sun. 9 A.M.–5 P.M., $1) in nearby Ravenel on an old rice plantation.

One of the best outfitters in town is **Half Moon Outfitters** (280 King St., 843/853-0990, www.halfmoonoutfitters.com, Mon.–Sat. 10 A.M.–7 P.M., Sun. noon–6 P.M.). They have a Mount Pleasant location (425 Coleman Blvd., 843/881-9472) as well (and it has better parking).

Bird-Watching

Right in Charleston Harbor is the little **Crab Bank Heritage Preserve,** (803/734-3886) where thousands of migratory birds can be seen depending on the season. You can either kayak there yourself or take a charter with **Nature Adventures Outfitters** (1900 Iron Swamp Rd., 800/673-0679) out of Awendaw Island.

On James Island southwest of Charleston is **Legare Farms** (2620 Hanscombe Point Rd., 843/559-0763, www.legarefarms.com), which holds migratory bird walks each Saturday in autumn at 8:30 A.M. ($6 adults, $3 children).

Ice Skating

Ice skating in South Carolina? Yep, 100,000 square feet of it, year-round at the two NHL-size rinks of the **Carolina Ice Palace** (7665 Northwoods Blvd., 843/572-2717, www.carolinaicepalace.com, $7 adults, $6 children) in North Charleston. This is also the practice facility for the local hockey team, the Stingrays, as well as where the Citadel hockey team plays.

SPECTATOR SPORTS
Charleston River Dogs

A New York Yankees farm team playing in the South Atlantic League, the Charleston River Dogs (360 Fishburne St., www.riverdogs.com, $5 general admission) play April–August at Joseph P. Riley Jr. Park, a.k.a., "The Joe." The park is great, and there are a lot of fun promotions to keep things interesting should the play on the field be less than stimulating (as minor league ball often can be). Because of the intimate, retro design of the park, there are no bad

seats, so you might as well save a few bucks and go for the general admission ticket.

From downtown, get to The Joe by taking Broad Street west until it turns into Lockwood Drive. Follow that north until you get to Brittlebank Park and The Joe, next to the Citadel. Expect to pay $3–5 for parking.

Family Circle Cup

Moved to Daniel Island in 2001 from its long-time home in Hilton Head, the prestigious Family Circle Cup women's tennis tournament is held each April at the **Family Circle Tennis Center** (161 Seven Farms Dr., Daniel Island, 843/856-7900, www.familycirclecup.com, varied admission). Almost 100,000 people attend the multi-week event. Individual session tickets go on sale the preceding January.

Charleston Battery

The professional, A-League soccer team Charleston Battery (1990 Daniel Island Dr., 843/971-4625, www.charlestonbattery.com, about $10) play April–July at Blackbaud Stadium on Daniel Island north of Charleston. To get there from downtown, take I-26 north and then I-526 to Mount Pleasant. Take exit 23A, Clements Ferry Road, and then a left on St. Thomas Island Drive. Blackbaud Stadium is about a mile on the left.

South Carolina Stingrays

The ECHL professional hockey team the South Carolina Stingrays (843/744-2248, www.stingrayshockey.com, $15) get a good crowd out to their rink at the North Charleston Coliseum, playing October–April.

Citadel Bulldogs

The Citadel (171 Moultrie St., 843/953-3294, www.citadelsports.com) plays Southern Conference football home games at Johnson-Hagood Stadium next to the campus on the Ashley River near Hampton Park. The basketball team plays home games at McAlister Field House on campus. The school's hockey team skates home games at the Carolina Ice Palace.

Accommodations

As one of America's key national and international destination cities, Charleston has a very well-developed infrastructure for housing visitors—a task made much easier by the city's longstanding tradition of hospitality. Because the bar is set so high, few visitors experience a truly bad stay in town. Hotels and bed-and-breakfasts are generally well maintained and have a high level of service, ranging from good to excellent. Note that there's a 12.5 percent tax on hotel rooms in Charleston.

SOUTH OF BROAD
Over $300

On the south side of Broad Street is a great old Charleston lodging, ◖ **Governor's House Inn** (117 Broad St., 843/720-2070, www .governorshouse.com, $285–585). This circa-1760 building, a National Historic Landmark, is associated with Edward Rutledge, signer of the Declaration of Independence. Though most of its 11 rooms—all with four-poster beds, period furnishings, and high ceilings—go for around $300, some of the smaller rooms here can be had for closer to $200 in the off-season. The Governer's House is highly recommended not only for its good value and location, but also for its service and romantic feel.

The nine rooms of the ◖ **Two Meeting Street Inn** (2 Meeting St., 843/723-7322, www.twomeetingstreet.com, $220–435) way down by the Battery are individually appointed, with themes like "The Music Room" and the "The Spell Room." The decor in this 1892 Queen Anne bed-and-breakfast is very traditional, with lots of floral patterns and hunt club–style pieces and artwork; it's considered by many to be the most romantic lodging in town, and you won't soon forget the experience of sitting on the veranda enjoying the sights, sounds, and breezes of the Battery South of Broad. Three of the rooms, the Canton, Granite, and Roberts, can be had for not much over $200.

WATERFRONT AND FRENCH QUARTER
$150-300

About as close to the Cooper River as a hotel gets, the **Harbourview Inn** (2 Vendue Range, 843/853-8439, www.harbourviewcharleston .com, $259) comprises a "historic wing" and a larger, newer, but still tastefully done main building. For the best of those eponymous harbor views, try to get a room on the third floor or you might have some obstructions. It's the little touches that keep guests happy here, with wine, cheese, coffee, tea, and cookies galore and an emphasis on smiling, personalized service. The rooms are quite spacious, with big bathrooms and 14-foot ceilings. You can take your complimentary breakfast—good but not great—in your room or eat it on the nice rooftop terrace.

Over $300

The rooms and the thoroughly hospitable service are the focus at the nearby ◖ **Vendue Inn** (19 Vendue Range, 843/577-7970, www .vendueinn.com, $359). With a range of decor from Colonial to French Provincial, all rooms are sumptuously appointed in that "boutique" style, with lots of warm, rich fabrics, unique pieces, and high-end bath amenities. That said, the public spaces are cool, too, with a cozy den area with chess and checkers and a nice area in which to enjoy your excellent, made-to-order hot breakfast (complimentary!). They have a row of bikes out front for guests to use, free of charge, to roam around the city. The Inn gets a lot of traffic in the evenings because of the popular Library restaurant and its hopping Rooftop Bar, which has amazing views of the city and the river.

Another great place in this part of town is the **French Quarter Inn** (166 Church St., 843/722-1900, www.fqicharleston.com, $359). And the decor in the 50 surprisingly spacious rooms is suitably high-period French, with low-style, non-canopied beds and crisp,

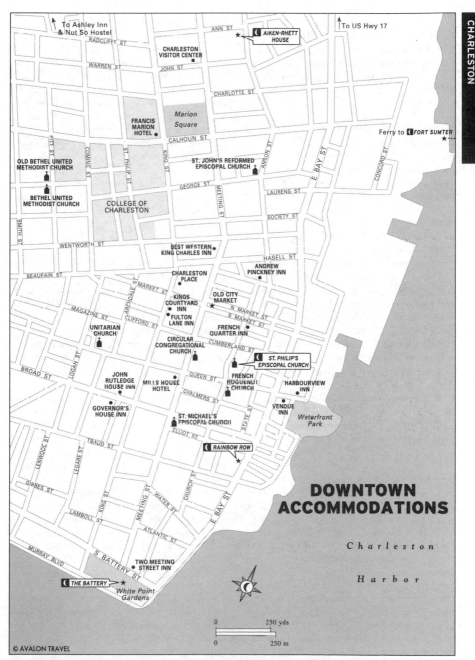

To Ashley Inn
& Nut So Hostel

RADCLIFFE ST

ANN ST

To US Hwy 17

AIKEN-RHETT
HOUSE

CHARLESTON
VISITOR CENTER

WARREN ST

JOHN ST

CHARLOTTE ST

FRANCIS
MARION
HOTEL

Marion
Square

Ferry to FORT SUMTER

CALHOUN ST

PITT ST

COMING ST

ST. PHILIP ST

KING ST

ST. JOHN'S REFORMED
EPISCOPAL CHURCH

ANSON ST

E BAY ST

CONCORD ST

OLD BETHEL UNITED
METHODIST CHURCH

GEORGE ST

MEETING ST

LAURENS ST

BETHEL UNITED
METHODIST CHURCH

COLLEGE OF
CHARLESTON

SOCIETY ST

SMITH ST

WENTWORTH ST

BEST WESTERN
KING CHARLES INN

HASELL ST

ANDREW
PINCKNEY INN

BEAUFAIN ST

MARKET ST

ARCHDALE ST

CHARLESTON
PLACE

OLD CITY
MARKET

MAGAZINE ST

CLIFFORD ST

KINGS
COURTYARD
INN

FULTON
LANE INN

N MARKET ST

S MARKET ST

UNITARIAN
CHURCH

FRENCH
QUARTER INN

CIRCULAR
CONGREGATIONAL
CHURCH

CUMBERLAND ST

ST. PHILIP'S
EPISCOPAL CHURCH

BROAD ST

LOGAN ST

JOHN
RUTLEDGE
HOUSE INN

MILLS HOUSE
HOTEL

QUEEN ST

FRENCH
HUGUENOT
CHURCH

HARBOURVIEW
INN

CHALMERS ST

STATE ST

VENDUE
INN

GOVERNOR'S
HOUSE INN

ST. MICHAEL'S
EPISCOPAL CHURCH

Waterfront
Park

ELLIOT ST

RAINBOW ROW

LENWOOD ST

LEGARE ST

TRADD ST

CHURCH ST

WATER ST

GIBBES ST

E BAY ST

**DOWNTOWN
ACCOMMODATIONS**

LAMBOLL ST

KING ST

MEETING ST

Charleston

MURRAY BLVD

S BATTERY ST

ATLANTIC ST

Harbor

TWO MEETING
STREET INN

THE BATTERY

White Point
Gardens

0   250 yds

0   250 m

© AVALON TRAVEL

fresh linens. Many rooms feature fireplaces, whirlpool baths, and private balconies. One of Charleston's hottest restaurants, Tristan, is on the ground floor. You're treated to champagne on your arrival, and goodies are available all day, with wine and cheese served every night at 5 P.M.

NORTH OF BROAD
$150-300

It calls itself a boutique hotel, perhaps because each room is totally different and sumptuously appointed. But the charming ((**Andrew Pinckney Inn** (199 Church St., 843/937-8800, www.andrewpinckneyinn.com, $170–260) is very nearly in a class by itself in Charleston not only for its great rates, but for its casual, West Indies–style decor, charming courtyard, gorgeous three-story atrium, and rooftop terrace on which you can enjoy your complimentary (and delicious) breakfast. With 37 rooms and four suites, it's larger than it looks, but the friendly staff—including a concierge—does a good job of making everyone feel special. For the money and the amenities, it's possibly the single best lodging package in town.

Free parking, a great location, friendly staff, and reasonable prices are the highlights of the **Best Western King Charles Inn** (237 Meeting St., 843/723-7451, www.kingcharlesinn.com, $200–250). It's not where you'd want to spend your honeymoon, but it's plenty nice enough and frequent visitors to town swear by it.

If you plan on some serious shopping, you might want to stay right on the city's main shopping thoroughfare at the **Kings Courtyard Inn** (198 King St., 866/720-2949, www.kingscourtyardinn.com, $245–285). This 1853 Greek Revival building houses a lot more rooms—more than 40—than meets the eye, and can get a little crowded at times. Still, its charming courtyard and awesome location on King Street are big bonuses, as is the convenient but cramped parking lot right next door (about $12 a day, a bargain for this part of town), with free in/out privileges.

Affiliated with the Kings Courtyard—and right next door, in fact—is the smaller, cozier

Fulton Lane Inn (202 King St., 866/720-2940, www.fultonlaneinn.com, $245), with its lobby entrance on tiny Fulton Lane between the two inns. Small, simple guest rooms—some with fireplaces—have comfortable beds and spacious bathrooms. This is the kind of place for active people who plan to spend most of their days out and about, but want a cozy place to come back to at night. You mark down your Continental breakfast order at night, leave it on your doorknob, and it shows up at the *exact* time you requested the next morning. Then when you're ready to shop and walk, just go down the stairs and take the exit right out onto busy King Street. Also nice is $12-a-day parking with free in/out privileges.

Over $300

Considered Charleston's premier hotel, ((**Charleston Place** (205 Meeting St., 843/722-4900, www.charlestonplace.com, $419–529) maintains a surprisingly high level of service and decor considering its massive, 440-room size. Now owned by the London-based Orient-Express Hotels, Charleston Place is routinely rated as one of the best hotels in North America by *Condé Nast Traveler* and other publications.

The rooms aren't especially large but they are well appointed, featuring Italian marble baths, high-speed Internet, and voice messaging—and, of course, there's a pool available. A series of suite offerings—Junior, Junior Executive, Parlor, and the 800-square-foot Senior—feature enlarged living areas and multiple TVs and phones. A Manager's Suite on the Private Club level up top comprises 1,200 square feet of total luxury that will set you back at least $1,600 a night.

It's the additional offerings that make Charleston Place closer to a lifestyle decision than a lodging decision. The on-site spa (843/937-8522) offers all kinds of massages, including couples and "mommy to be" sessions. Diners and tipplers have three fine options to choose from: the famous **Charleston Grill** (843/577-4522, dinner daily beginning at 6 P.M.) for fine dining;

the breakfast, lunch, and brunch hot spot **Palmetto Cafe** (843/722-4900, breakfast daily 6:30 A.M.–11 A.M., lunch daily 11:30 A.M.–3 P.M.); and the **Thoroughbred Club** (daily 11 A.M.–midnight) for cocktails and afternoon tea.

On the north side of Broad Street, the magnificent **(((John Rutledge House Inn** (116 Broad St., 843/723-7999, www.johnrutledge houseinn.com, $300–405) is very close to the old South of Broad neighborhood not only in geography, but in feel. Known as "America's most historic inn," the Rutledge House boasts a fine old pedigree indeed: Built for Constitution signer John Rutledge in 1763, it's one of only 15 homes belonging to the original signers to survive. George Washington breakfasted here with Mrs. Rutledge in 1791. The interior is stunning: Italian marble fireplaces, original plaster moldings, and masterful ironwork abound in the public spaces. The inn's 19 rooms are divided among the original mansion and two carriage houses. All have antique furnishings and canopy beds, and some suites have fireplaces and whirlpool baths. A friendly and knowledgeable concierge will give you all kinds of tips and make reservations for you.

Though this is a new building owned by Holiday Inn, the **Mills House Hotel** (115 Meeting St., 843/577-2400, www.ichotelsgroup .com, $309–359) boasts an important pedigree and still tries hard to maintain the old tradition of impeccable Southern service at this historic location. An extensive round of renovations completed in 2007 has been well-received, though it also means prices have gone up (even parking is up to $19 a day now). Centrally located and within walking distance of almost all key historic sites, the original Mills House was built in 1853 and immediately became one of the South's premier hotels, hosting luminaries like Robert E. Lee and President Theodore Roosevelt.

UPPER KING AREA
Under $150
Stretching the bounds of the "Upper King" definition, we come to the **Ashley Inn** (201 Ashley Ave., 843/723-1848, www.charleston-

sc-inns.com, $139) well northwest of Marion Square, almost in the Citadel area. Though it's too far to walk from here to most any historic attraction in Charleston, the Ashley Inn does provide free bikes to its guests, as well as free off-street parking, a particularly nice touch. It also deserves a special mention not only because of the romantic, well-appointed nature of its six guest rooms, suite, and carriage house, but for its outstanding breakfasts. You get to pick a main dish, such as Carolina sausage pie, stuffed waffles, or cheese blintzes.

$150–300
In a renovated 1924 building overlooking beautiful Marion Square, the **Francis Marion Hotel** (387 King St., 843/722-0600, www .francismarioncharleston.com, $189–329) offers quality accommodation in the hippest, most bustling area of the peninsula—though be aware that it's quite a walk down to the Battery from here. The rooms are plush and big, though the bathrooms, for some reason, are downright cramped. The hotel's parking garage costs $12 a day, with valet parking available until about 8 P.M. A Starbucks in the lobby pleases many a guest on their way out or in. Most rooms hover around $300, but some are a real steal.

HAMPTON PARK AREA
Under $150
Charleston's least-expensive lodging is also its most unique, the **(((Not So Hostel** (156 Spring St., 843/722-8383, www.notsohostel .com, $21 dorm, $60 private). The already-reasonable prices also include a great make-your-own breakfast, off-street parking, bikes, high-speed Internet access in the common room, and even an airport/train/bus shuttle. The inn actually comprises three 1840s Charleston single houses, all with the obligatory piazzas to catch the breeze. (However, unlike some hostels, there's air-conditioning in all the rooms.) Because the free bike usage makes up for its off-the-beaten-path location, a stay at the Not So Hostel is a fantastic way to enjoy the Holy City on a budget, while having a great time with some cool people to boot.

CHARLESTON

WEST ASHLEY
$150-300

Looking like Frank Lloyd Wright parachuted into a 300-year-old plantation and got to work, the ☾ **The Inn at Middleton Place** (4290 Ashley River Rd., 843/556-0500, www.theinn atmiddletonplace.com, $220) is one of Charleston's most unique lodgings—and not only because it's on the grounds of the historic and beautiful Middleton Place Plantation. The four connected buildings comprising over 50 guest rooms are modern, yet deliberately blend in with the forested, neutral-colored surroundings. The spacious rooms have that same woody minimalism, with excellent fireplaces, spacious Euro-style baths, and huge, floor-to-ceiling windows overlooking the grounds and the river. Guests also have full access to the rest of the gorgeous Middleton grounds. The only downside is that you're a lengthy drive from the peninsula and all its attractions, restaurants, and nightlife.

While those who need constant stimulation will be disappointed in the deep quietude here, nature-lovers and those in search of peace and quiet will find this almost paradise. And don't worry about food—the excellent Middleton Place Restaurant is open for lunch and dinner.

ISLE OF PALMS
$150-300

One of the more accessible and enjoyable resort-type stays in the Charleston area is on the Isle of Palms at **Wild Dunes Resort** (5757 Palm Blvd., 888/778-1876, www.wilddunes.com, $200). This is the place to go for relaxing, beach-oriented vacation fun, either in a traditional hotel room, a house, or a villa. Bustling Mount Pleasant is only a couple of minutes away and Charleston proper not much farther.

CAMPING

Charleston County runs a family-friendly, fairly boisterous campground at **James Island County Park** (871 Riverland Dr., 843/795-7275, www.ccprc.com, $31 tent site, $37 pull-thru site). A neat feature here is the $5 per person round-trip shuttle from the Visitors Center downtown, Folly Beach Pier, and Folly Beach County Park. The Park also has 10 furnished cottages for rental, sleeping up to eight people (843/795-4386, $138 a day). Reservations are recommended.

For more commercial camping in Mount Pleasant, try the **KOA of Mt. Pleasant** (3157 Hwy. 17 N., 843/849-5177, www.koa.com, $30+ tent sites, $50+ pull-thrus).

Food

If you count the premier food cities in the United States on one hand, Charleston has to be one of the fingers. Its long history of good taste and livability has combined with an affluent and sophisticated population to attract some of the brightest chefs and restaurateurs in the country today. Kitchens here eschew fickle trends and innovation for innovation's sake, instead emphasizing quality, professionalism, and most of all, freshness of ingredients. In a sort of Southern Zen, the typical Charleston chef seems to take pride in making a melt-in-your-mouth masterpiece out of the culinary commonplace—in not fixing

what ain't broke, as they say down here. (I've heard Charleston's cuisine described as "competent classics," which also isn't far off the mark.)

Unlike Savannah, its more drink-oriented neighbor to the south, even Charleston's bars have great food. So don't assume you have to make reservations at a formal restaurant to fully enjoy the cuisine here. Though an entire volume could easily be written about Charleston restaurants, here's a baseline from which to start your epicurean odyssey. You'll note a high percentage of ☾ icons in the list; there's a good reason for that.

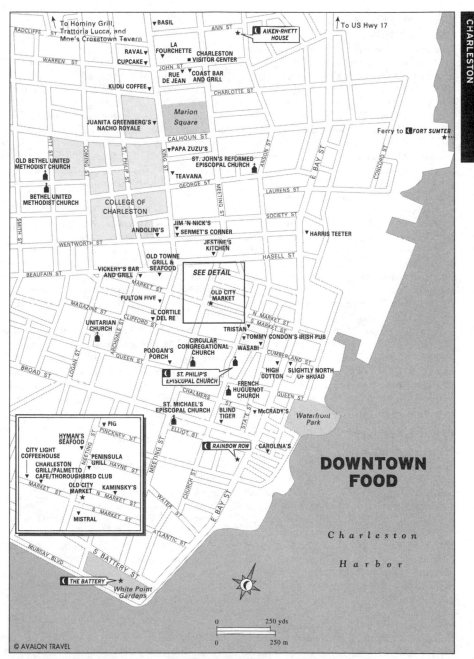

RADCLIFFE ST

To Hominy Grill,
Trattoria Lucca, and
Moe's Crosstown Tavern

▼BASIL

ANN ST

AIKEN-RHETT
HOUSE

↑To US Hwy 17

WARREN ST

RAVAL▼
CUPCAKE▼

LA
FOURCHETTE
▼

JOHN ST
RUE ▼ ▼COAST BAR
DE JEAN AND GRILL

CHARLESTON
■ VISITOR CENTER

KUDU COFFEE▼

CHARLOTTE ST

JUANITA GREENBERG'S▼
NACHO ROYALE

Marion
Square

Ferry to ◖FORT SUMTER
★┈

PITT ST
COMING ST
ST. PHILIP ST

CALHOUN ST

KING ST

ANSON ST

E BAY ST

CONCORD ST

OLD BETHEL UNITED
METHODIST CHURCH

▼PAPA ZUZU'S

ST. JOHN'S REFORMED
EPISCOPAL CHURCH ♰

▼TEAVANA

GEORGE ST

MEETING ST

LAURENS ST

BETHEL UNITED
METHODIST CHURCH

COLLEGE OF
CHARLESTON

SOCIETY ST

SMITH ST

ANDOLINI'S
▼

JIM 'N NICK'S
▼ SERMET'S CORNER
▼

▼HARRIS TEETER

WENTWORTH ST

JESTINE'S
KITCHEN
▼

BEAUFAIN ST

VICKERY'S BAR
AND GRILL ▽

OLD TOWNE
GRILL &
SEAFOOD ▽

HASELL ST

SEE DETAIL

MARKET ST

OLD CITY
MARKET
★

FULTON FIVE ▼

MAGAZINE ST

CLIFFORD ST

IL CORTILE
▼ DEL RE

N. MARKET ST

UNITARIAN
CHURCH

ARCHDALE ST

S. MARKET ST

TRISTAN▼

▼TOMMY CONDON'S IRISH PUB

CIRCULAR
CONGREGATIONAL
CHURCH
▼ WASABI

CUMBERLAND ST

POOGAN'S
PORCH ▼

BROAD ST

LOGAN ST

QUEEN ST

HIGH
COTTON

SLIGHTLY NORTH
OF BROAD

ST. PHILIP'S
EPISCOPAL CHURCH ♰

CHALMERS ST

FRENCH
HUGUENOT
CHURCH

QUEEN ST

ST. MICHAEL'S
EPISCOPAL CHURCH ♰

BLIND
TIGER ▼

STATE ST

▼McCRADY'S

Waterfront
Park

▼ FIG

PINCKNEY ST

ELLIOT ST

MEETING ST

◖ RAINBOW ROW

CAROLINA'S

HYMAN'S
SEAFOOD
▼

CITY LIGHT
COFFEEHOUSE

PENINSULA
GRILL ▼

HAYNE ST

CHURCH ST

E BAY ST

**DOWNTOWN
FOOD**

CHARLESTON
GRILL/PALMETTO
CAFE/THOROUGHBRED CLUB ▼

MEETING ST

OLD CITY
MARKET
★

KAMINSKY'S
▼

MARKET ST

N MARKET ST

MARKET ST

S MARKET ST

Charleston

MISTRAL
▼

ATLANTIC ST

Harbor

MURRAY BLVD

S BATTERY ST

WATER ST

◖ THE BATTERY ★

White Point
Gardens

S BATTERY ST

0   250 yds

0   250 m

© AVALON TRAVEL

SOUTH OF BROAD
Classic Southern

The only restaurant in the quiet old South of Broad area is also one of Charleston's best and oldest: **⟨ Carolina's** (10 Exchange St., 843/724-3800, Sun.–Thurs. 5–10 P.M., Fri.–Sat. 5–11 P.M., $18–30). There's a new chef in town, Jeremiah Bacon, a Charleston native who spent the last seven years honing his craft in New York City. His Lowcountry take on European classics includes grilled salmon with potato gnocchi, tagliatelle with Lowcountry prosciutto, and pan-roasted diver scallops, with as many fresh ingredients as possible from nearby Kensington Plantation.

A tried-and-true favorite that predates Bacon's tenure, however, is Perdita's fruit de mer—a recipe that goes back to the restaurant's 1950s predecessor, Perdita's, which is commonly regarded as Charleston's first fine-dining restaurant. If you can get the whole table to agree, try the $49-per-person Perdita's four-course tasting menu (wine flights extra).

A recent renovation of this Revolutionary War–era building—once the legendary Sailor's Tavern—hasn't negatively affected the romantic ambience of the three themed areas: Perdita's Room (the oldest dining area), the Sidewalk Room, and the Bar Room. Free valet parking is a nice plus.

WATERFRONT
New Southern

Few restaurants in Charleston inspire such impassioned, vocal advocates as **⟨ McCrady's** (2 Unity Alley, 843/577-0025, www.mccradys restaurant.com, Sun.–Thurs. 5:30–10 P.M., Fri.–Sat. 5:30–11 P.M., $25–34). Housed in Charleston's oldest tavern building (circa 1788), McCrady's is also known as Charleston's best-kept secret, since despite its high quality it's managed to avoid the siege of tourists common at many local fine-dining spots. But their loss can be your gain, as you enjoy the prodigious talents of young chef Sean Brock, whose *sous vide,* or vacuum cooking, is spoken of in hushed tones by his clientele. The restaurant's relatively low profile undoubtedly has to do with Brock's

daring choices, all based on his unending quest for fresh and adventurous local ingredients.

This is not the place to gorge on usual Lowcountry fare. Portions here are small and dynamic, and range from a yam soup with marshmallow and roasted chestnuts to seared foie gras with maple syrup to seared Hawaiian tuna in a saffron-vegetable juice emulsion. The menu changes seasonally according to the local market and the chef's whim. Many diners find the seven-course, $70 Chef's Tasting a near-religious experience. For an extra $60, master sommelier Clint Sloan provides paired wine selections.

FRENCH QUARTER
New Southern

With an Art Deco-style vibe that's a refreshing change from the usual Charleston restaurant decor, **⟨ Tristan** (55 Market St., 843/534-2155, www.tristandining.com, Mon.–Thurs. 11:30 A.M.–10 P.M., Fri.–Sat. 11:30 A.M.–11 P.M., Sun. 11 A.M.–10 P.M., $18–32) inside the French Quarter Inn draws raves for the globally influenced cuisine of Chef Aaron Deal.

At last count, the copious wine list boasted over 400 labels. The real scene here is for the à la carte Sunday brunch, with crab cake benedicts, corned beef hash, frittatas, live jazz, and Bloody Marys galore. Save room for the ridiculously good fried chocolate doughnut dessert.

NORTH OF BROAD
Asian

For whatever reason, the Asian influence is not prevalent in Charleston cuisine. But **Wasabi** (61 State St., 843/577-5222, Mon.–Thurs. 11 A.M.–9:30 P.M., Fri.–Sat. 11 A.M.–11 P.M., Sun. noon–9 P.M., $10–15) has made quite a name for itself as a great place for sushi downtown, though its hibachi work is impressive as well if you're more in the mood for the classic Japanese steakhouse experience. The bar gets hopping after dinner.

Barbecue

Charleston proper isn't the place to go for

great barbecue; you need to leave the peninsula for that. But **Jim 'n' Nick's** (288 King St., 843/577-0406, www.jimnnicks.com, Sun.–Thurs. 10:30 A.M.–9 P.M., Fri.–Sat. 10:30 A.M.–10 P.M., $10–30) offers some good tomato and vinegar barbecue—not to mention fresh collards and homemade cheese biscuits.

Classic Southern

Walk through the gaslit courtyard of the Planter's Inn at Market and Meeting Streets into the stately yet surprisingly intimate dining room of the (**Peninsula Grill** (112 N. Market St., 843/723-0700, www.peninsulagrill.com, nightly from 5:30 P.M., $28–35) and begin an epicurean journey you'll not soon forget. Known far and wide for impeccable service as well as the mastery of Chef Robert Carter, Peninsula Grill is perhaps Charleston's quintessential purveyor of high-style Lowcountry cuisine and the odds-on favorite as best restaurant in town.

From the lobster skillet cake and crab cake appetizer to the bourbon-grilled jumbo shrimp to the benne-crusted rack of lamb to sides like wild mushroom grits and hoppin' John, the menu reads like a "greatest hits" of regional cooking. You'll almost certainly want to start with the sampler trio of soups and finish with Carter's legendary coconut cake, a family recipe (only huge, whole cakes are served, so you'll definitely be leaving with some). Whatever you choose in between those bookends is almost guaranteed to be excellent.

To accompany your inevitably near-perfect meal, choose from 20 wines by the glass or from over 300 bottles. Four stars from the Mobil Travel Club, four diamonds from AAA, and countless other accolades have come this restaurant's way in its relatively brief (by Charleston standards) decade of existence. Needless to say, reservations are highly recommended.

Named for a now-deceased, beloved dog who once greeted guests, (**Poogan's Porch** (72 Queen St., 843/577-2337, www.poogansporch .com, lunch Mon.–Fri. 11:30 A.M.–2:30 P.M., dinner daily 5–9:30 P.M., $12–20) is the very prototype of a classic Charleston restaurant: Lovingly restored old home, professional but unpretentious service, great fried green tomatoes, and rich, calorie-laden Lowcountry classics to die for. I can't decide which entrée I like best, the crab cakes or the shrimp and grits, but either one could qualify as a finalist for best dish in Charleston. Some swear that even the biscuits at Poogan's—flaky, fresh-baked, and moist—are better than some meals around town, though that's a stretch. Brunch (Sat.–Sun. 9 A.M.–3 P.M.) is the big thing here, a bustling affair with big portions, Bloody Marys, mimosas, and soft sunlight bathing what were, after all, living and dining rooms where people once lived.

For many visitors to Charleston, there comes a point where they just get tired of stuffing themselves with seafood. If you find yourself in that situation, the perfect antidote is (**High Cotton** (199 E. Bay St., 843/724-3815, www .mavericksouthernkitchens.com, Mon.–Thurs. 5:30–10 P.M., Fri. 5:30–11 P.M., Sat. 11:30 A.M.–2:30 P.M. and 5:30–11 P.M., Sun. 10 A.M.–2 P.M. and 5:30–10 P.M., $20–44), a self-professed meat-lovers paradise offering some of the best steaks in town, as well as a creative menu of assorted lamb and pork dishes.

Chef Anthony Gray places heavy emphasis on using fresh local ingredients, whether they be veggies or game, and the rotating menu always reflects that. None of this comes particularly cheap, but splurges rarely do. In the woody (and very popular) bar area after 6 P.M. there is usually a solo live pianist or sax player to serenade the entire restaurant. I particularly enjoy the warm, tasteful dining room, an understated masterpiece of décor that never tries too hard to be either tony or trendy.

The long lines at Wentworth and Meeting Streets across from the fire station are waiting to follow Rachael Ray's lead and get into **Jestine's Kitchen** (251 Meeting St., 843/722-7224, Tues.–Thurs. 11 A.M.–9:30 P.M., Fri.–Sat. 11 A.M.–10 P.M., $8–15) and enjoy a simple, Southern take on such meat-and-three comfort food classics as meatloaf, pecan-fried fish, and fried green tomatoes. Instead of bread, you're greeted with a plate of cucumber pickles. Most of the recipes are handed down from the restaurant's namesake, Jestine Matthews, the African American woman who raised owner Dana Berlin. Mrs. Matthews passed away in 1997 at the age of 112, her longevity perhaps a testament to the healthy qualities of traditional Southern country cooking. Save room for her signature Coca-Cola cake.

Mediterranean

One of the most romantic restaurants in Charleston—which is saying a lot—**〖 II Cortile del Re** (193A King St., 843/853-1888, Mon.–Sat. 5–10:30 P.M., $18–30) stands out amidst the antique stores on Lower King. Thankfully the Italian owners don't overdo the old country sentimentality, either in atmosphere or in menu. Sure, the tablecloths are white and the interior is warm, dark, and decorated with opera prints. But the piped-in music is long on cool jazz and short on over-the-top tenors, and the skinny wine bar in the front room is a favorite destination all its own.

Il Cortile del Re on King Street

Portions here manage to be simultaneously large and light, as in the overtopped mussel plate in a delightfully thin and spicy tomato sauce, or the big spinach salad with goat cheese croutons sprinkled with a subtle vinaigrette. The entrées emphasize the Tuscan countryside, focusing both on slow-roasted meats and sublime takes on traditional pasta dishes, all somehow managing the same blend of heartiness and melt-in-your mouth lightness. My favorite is the simply perfect roasted lamb in a dark juniper and rosemary sauce, served on a bed of what are likely to be the best mashed potatoes in the world. Save room for the gelato dessert, served swimming in a pool of dark espresso.

Literally right around the corner from Il Cortile del Re is the other in Charleston's one-two Italian punch, **Fulton Five** (5 Fulton St., 843/853-5555, Mon.–Sat. from 5:30 P.M., $15–32). The cuisine of Northern Italy comes alive in this bustling, dimly lit room, from the *bresaola* salad of spinach and thin dried beef to the caper-encrusted tuna on a bed of sweet pea risotto. It's not cheap and the portions aren't

necessarily the largest, but with these tasty, non-tomato-based dishes and this romantic, gusto-filled atmosphere, you'll be satiated with life itself.

You'll find some of the best gyros this side of the Mediterranean at **Papa Zuzu's** (370 King St., 843/534-1666, daily 11 A.M.–9 P.M., $6–10), a long, narrow, funky eatery for which the phrase "hole in the wall" seems to have been invented. Look for the fresh tomatoes in the window, ripening in the sun. The cuts of lamb—generously but artfully sliced—are perfectly cooked and complimented by a tangy but light tzaziki sauce. The service is mellow and friendly, and they'll either call your name to come get your order or just bring it out to you if it's not too busy. If you're not a gyro fan, the Greek pizza's awesome, too. There's also a nice range of alternative beverages and juices for the health-conscious.

Commonly known as the oldest family-run restaurant in Charleston, **Old Towne Grill and Seafood** (229 King St., 843/723-8170, www.oldtownerestaurant.com, Sun.–Thurs. 11 A.M.–10 P.M., Fri.–Sat. 11 A.M.–11 P.M.,

$10–20), right next to the Riviera Theatre, also brings a little taste of Greece to King Street. It's the usual moussaka, avgolemono, and roasted chicken type of place in the usual taverna atmosphere, but in this city of foodies who sometimes take themselves a little too seriously, it's a nice place to take a break from the scene.

One of Charleston's original hip people-watching spots and still a personal favorite is **Sermet's Corner** (276 King St., 843/853-7775, lunch daily 11 A.M.–3 P.M., dinner Sun.–Thurs. 4–10 P.M., Fri.–Sat. 4–11 P.M., $9–16), on a bustling intersection of King and Wentworth. Charismatic chef and owner Sermet Aslan—who also painted most of the artwork on the walls of this charming, high-ceilinged space—dishes up large, inexpensive portions of Mediterranean-style goodies like panini, pastas, pestos, calamari, and inventive meat dishes.

The best "regular" pizza in Charleston can be found at the multiple locations of the local chain **Andolini's** (82 Wentworth St., 843/722-7437, daily 11 A.M.–11 P.M., $2–10). As if the great taste, long hours, and fun decor weren't enough, it's also cheap. One of the best deals in town at this quirky, college-friendly institution is the lunch special: six bucks even for a huge one-topping slice of their signature New York–style pies, a salad, and a soda. Or for the same money you can have two cheese slices and a Bud. Their best special, however, might be a massive 19-inch with one topping and a pitcher of beer for $20. In any event, know that all the sauce and dough is made and hand-tossed daily. There's a less funky but just as tasty incarnation in Mount Pleasant (414 W. Coleman Blvd., 843/849-7437) and a fun retro-style location in West Ashley (1117 Savannah Hwy., 843/225-4743), in addition to branches way out on James Island (967 Folly Rd., 843/576-7437) and up in North Charleston (6610 Rivers Ave., 843/266-7437).

Mexican

If you suddenly find yourself craving Mexican while shopping on King Street, duck about a block down Wentworth to

find the cavernous, delightful **Yo' Burrito** (86 Wentworth St., 843/853-3287, www.yoburrito.com, Sun.–Thurs. 11 A.M.–10 P.M., Fri.–Sat. 11 A.M.–11 P.M., $5–8), a local legend in its own right. Order from a variety of overstuffed specialty burritos, tasty quesadillas, and stacked nachos at the counter and take a seat at one of the large, communal-style tables, perhaps enjoying a freshly squeezed lemonade while you wait.

But the real kicker is the condiment bar of homemade salsas, including a smoky chipotle number that is the closest thing to real red salsa I've had this side of New Mexico. But I suggest trying them all. In typical Charleston tradition, there's a great little bar area in back of this large space, where $5 mason jar margaritas and other drink specials make happy hour (Mon.–Fri. 4–7 P.M.) very happy indeed.

New Southern

Don't be put off by the initials of **Slightly North of Broad** (192 East Bay St., 843/723-3424, www.mavericksouthernkitchens.com, lunch Mon.–Fri. 11:30 A.M.–3 P.M., dinner daily

Slightly North of Broad

© JIM MOREKIS

5:30–11 P.M., $15–35). Its acronym is an ironic play on the often-pejorative reference to the insular "South of Broad" neighborhood. This hot spot, routinely voted best restaurant in town in such contests, is anything but snobby. Hopping with happy foodies for lunch and dinner, the fun is enhanced by the long, open kitchen with its own counter area.

The dynamic but comforting menu here is practically a bible of the new wave of Lowcountry cuisine, with dishes like beef tenderloin, jumbo lump crab cakes, grilled BBQ tuna—and of course the sinful Wednesday night dinner special: deviled crab-stuffed flounder. An interesting twist at SNOB is the selection of "medium plates," i.e., dishes a little more generous than an app but with the same adventurous spirit. Examples include the sesame-encrusted tuna medallions, a charcuterie plate for the paté-lovers, and the to-die-for shrimp and grits. Lunch reservations only accepted for parties of five or more; reservations for dinner are highly recommended.

Just across the street from Hyman's Seafood is that establishment's diametrical opposite, the intimate bistro and stylish bar FIG (232 Meeting St., 843/805-5900, www.eatatfig .com, Mon.–Thurs. 6–11 P.M., Fri.–Sat. 6 P.M.–midnight, $20–25)—but the two do share one key thing: a passion for fresh, simple ingredients. While Hyman's packs in the tourists, who in turn pack in giant plates of seafood, FIG—short for "Food Is Good"—attracts young professional scenesters, as well as the diehard foodies. Chef Mike Lata was nominated in 2007 for James Beard's Best Chef of the Southeast. FIG is one of Charleston's great champions of the Sustainable Seafood Initiative, and the kitchen staff strives to work as closely as possible with local farmers and anglers in determining its seasonal menu.

Inside the plush Charleston Place Hotel you'll find ☙ Charleston Grill (224 King St., 843/577-4522, www.charlestongrill.com, dinner daily beginning at 6 P.M., $27–50), one of the city's favorite (and priciest) fine-dining spots for locals and tourists alike. Veteran Executive Chef Bob Waggoner was

recently replaced by his longtime *sous chef* Michelle Weaver, but the menu still specializes in French-influenced Lowcountry cuisine like a nicoise vegetable tart. There are a lot of great fusion dishes as well, such as the tuna and hamachi sashimi topped with pomegranate molasses and lemongrass oil. Reservations are a must.

The hard-to-define Mistral (99 S. Market St., 843/722-5708, Sun.–Thurs. 11 A.M.–11 P.M., Fri.–Sat. 11 A.M.–midnight, $10–25) is part seafood restaurant, part sexy French bistro, part Lowcountry living. With live, serious jazz blowing it hot Monday–Saturday nights and some of the best mussels and shrimp in the area served up fresh, all you really need to do is enjoy. If you're not a shellfish fan, try the sweetbreads or their excellent veal. This is a great place to relax and enjoy an evening of great music and great food in a dimly lit, unhurried environment.

Seafood
Routinely voted the best seafood restaurant in the South, Hyman's Seafood (215 Meeting St., 843/723-6000, www.hymanseafood .com, Mon.–Thurs. 11 A.M.–9 P.M., Fri.–Sun. 11 A.M.–11 P.M., $14–25) is thought by many locals to border on being a tourist trap. That said, this is a genuine tradition—rest assured that some member of the same family that began Hymans in 1890 will be on the premises any time it's open for business. To keep things manageable, Hymans offers the same menu and prices for both lunch and dinner. After asking for some complimentary fresh boiled peanuts in lieu of bread, start with the Carolina Delight, a delicious app (also available as an entrée) involving a lightly fried cake of grits topped with your choice of delectable seafood, or maybe a half-dozen oysters from the Half Shell oyster bar. In any case, definitely try the she-crab soup, some of the best you'll find anywhere. As for entrées, the ubiquitous Lowcountry crispy scored flounder is always a good bet, as is any fish special; but the real action at Hymans comes from anything that has a shell.

Alas, this establishment, popular with locals and tourists as well as the occasional movie star (Anthony Hopkins, Barbra Streisand, Mel Gibson), rock band (AC/DC, Metallica), and astronaut (Neil Armstrong) doesn't take reservations, so budget your time accordingly. Lunch crowds are generally lighter, though that's a relative term.

Perhaps only in Charleston would the best-known Irish pub also be one of its better seafood restaurants. But then again, **Tommy Condon's Irish Pub** (160 Church St., 843/577-3818, www.tommycondons.com, dinner Sun.–Thurs. until 10 P.M., Fri. and Sat. until 11 P.M., bar daily until 2 A.M., $13–20) is unusual in a lot of ways: Irish in a town that tends to celebrate all things English and French, and fairly expensive in a town where pub food is surprisingly reasonable for the high quality. The best picks are the shepherd's pie and the shrimp and grits. If you're feeling particularly adventurous and/or have had a few Guinnesses, try the Irish nachos, featuring the usual ingredients but on fried potatoes instead of tortilla chips.

UPPER KING AREA
Asian
There's usually a long wait to get a table at the great Thai place **Basil** (460 King St., 843/724-3490, www.basilthairestaurant.com, lunch Mon.–Thurs. 11:30 A.M.–2:30 P.M., dinner Mon.–Thurs. 5–10:30 P.M., Fri.–Sat. 5–11 P.M., Sun. 5–10 P.M., $15–23) on Upper King, since they don't take reservations. But Basil also has one of the hippest, most happening bar scenes in the area as well, so you won't necessarily mind. (Tip: Basil calls your cell phone when your table is ready, so a lot of people go across the street to Chai's to have a drink while they wait.)

Basil is a long, loud room, with big open windows to people-watch. But most of the action takes place inside, as revelers down cosmos and diners enjoy fresh, succulent takes on Thai classics like cashew chicken and pad thai, all cooked by Asian chefs. The signature dish, as you might imagine, is the basil duck.

French
A taste of the Left Bank on Upper King, the intimate bistro **La Fourchette** (432 King St., 843/722-6261, Mon.–Sat. from 6 P.M., $15–20) is regarded as the best French restaurant in town and, *naturalment,* one of the most romantic as well. You'll be pleasantly surprised at the reasonable prices as well. Cassoulet, the French national dish, is front and center among Chef Perig Goulet's concoctions, arriving in its own casserole dish on a trivet. Whatever you do, make sure you start with the *pommes frites* double-fried in duck fat. Your arteries may not thank you, but your taste buds will.

Mexican
The best quesadilla I've ever had was at **Juanita Greenberg's Nacho Royale** (439 King St., 843/723-6224, www.juanitagreenbergs.com, daily 11 A.M.–11 P.M., $6–8)— perfectly packed with Jack cheese but not overly so, full of spicy sausage, and finished with a delightful *pico de gallo.* This modest Mexican joint on Upper King—owned by Edie and Michael Rabin, the same folks that run the local Andolini's chain—caters primarily to a college crowd, as you can tell from the reasonable prices, the large patio out back, the extensive tequila list, and the bar that stays open 'til 2 A.M. on weekends. But don't let that give you pause. The service is quick and friendly, the margarita pitchers rock, and the food—from quesadillas to burritos to the eponymous nachos—constitutes one of the tastiest bargains in town.

Seafood
Many say the cashew-encrusted seared rare tuna on a bed of crabmeat and buckwheat noodles at **C COAST Bar and Grill** (39-D John St., 843/722-8838, www.coastbarandgrill.com, nightly from 5:30 P.M., $18–30) is the single best dish in Charleston. I wouldn't go that far, but it's certainly up there. (To be honest, the buttery, smoky, bacon-wrapped scallop appetizer is just about as good.) A new darling of local scenesters, COAST makes the most of its loud, hip former warehouse setting. Beautifully textured Lowcountry-themed paintings and kitschy faux-Polynesian items ring the walls,

as the clanging silverware competes with the boisterous conversation.

While the fun-loving decor in the dining room will suck you in, what keeps you happy is what goes on in the kitchen—specifically on its one-of-a-kind hickory-and-oak grill, which cooks up some of the freshest seafood in town. The raw bar is also satisfying, with a particularly nice take on and selection of ceviche. COAST is perhaps the strongest local advocate of the Sustainable Seafood Initiative, whereby restaurants work directly with local fishermen to make the most out of the area's stock while making sure it thrives for future generations. This forward focus extends to the wine list, which features plenty of organic selections.

Right next to and affiliated with the more Old World seafood stylings of Rue de Jean, COAST is one of the most happening places in the bustling Upper King scene. Getting there's a little tricky: find Rue de Jean on John Street and then duck about 100 feet down the alley beside it.

HAMPTON PARK AREA
Classic Southern
Moe's Crosstown Tavern (714 Rutledge Ave., 843/722-3287, Mon.–Sat. 11 A.M.–midnight, bar until 2 A.M., $10–15) is not only one of the classic Southern dives, but they've got one of the best kitchens on this side of town, known for hand-cut fries, great wings, and, most of all, excellent burgers. On Tuesdays, the burgers are half-price at happy hour—one of Charleston's best deals.

With a motto like "Grits are good for you," you know what you're in store for at **Hominy Grill** (207 Rutledge Ave., 912/937-0930, breakfast Mon.–Fri. 7:30–11:30 A.M., lunch and dinner 11:30 A.M.–8:30 P.M., brunch Sat.–Sun. 9 A.M.–3 P.M., $10–20), set in a renovated barbershop at Rutledge and Cannon near the Medical University of South Carolina. Primarily revered for his Sunday brunch, Chef Robert Stehling has fun, almost mischievously so, breathing new life into American and Southern classics. Because this is largely a locals' place, you can impress your friends back home by saying you

had the rare pleasure of the Hominy's sautéed shad roe with bacon and mushrooms—when the shad are running, that is.

Italian
The newest rave of Charleston foodies is the fare of Chef Ken Vedrinski at (**Trattoria Lucca** (41 Bogard St., 843/973-3323, www .trattorialuccadining.com, $20–30). Combining the freshest of ingredients with a modern yet true-to-form take on Tuscan cuisine, this is the kind of Stateside restaurant that can come close to competing with those of the old country. The specialty is a mouthwatering pork chop that is spoken of in hushed, reverential tones around town.

WEST ASHLEY
American
The kitchen at **Gene's Haufbrau** (17 Savannah Hwy., 843/225-4363, www.geneshaufbrau .com, daily 11:30 A.M.–1 A.M., $6–10) complements its fairly typical bar-food menu with some good wraps. Start with the "Drunken Trio" (beer-battered cheesesticks, mushrooms, and onion rings) and follow with a portobello wrap or a good old-fashioned crawfish po' boy. One of the best meals for the money in town is Gene's rotating, $6.95 blue plate special, offered Monday–Friday 11:30 A.M.–4:30 P.M. The late-night kitchen hours, 'til 1 A.M., are a big plus.

Barbecue
For connoisseurs, **Bessinger's** (1602 Savannah Hwy., 843/556-1354, www.bessingersbbq .com, prices and hours vary) is worth the trip over to West Ashley for its Carolina-style mustard-based wizardry—best exemplified by the legendary "Big Joe" sandwich, named for old family patriarch Joseph "Big Joe" Bessinger, founder of the legendary "Eat at Joe's" on the road to Orangeburg. It's eight ounces of hand-pulled pork and a one-way passport to nirvana. Smaller tummies might opt for the Little Joe, a five-ounce version of the same. You can always leave with a bottle or two of the "family secret" Gold Recipe sauce.

There are two scenes at Bessinger's, the sit-down Southern buffet (Thurs. 5–8 P.M., Fri.–Sat. 5–9 P.M., Sun. noon–8 P.M., $11.50 adults, $5.95 children)—Friday is fried catfish night—and the Sandwich Shop (Mon.–Sat. 10:30 A.M.–9:30 P.M., $6.35 for a "Big Joe" basket) for quick takeout. In old-school tradition, Bessinger's is a dry joint that doesn't sell alcohol.

And just to clarify, Bessinger's in Charleston was founded by the brother of Maurice Bessinger, who started the Columbia-based "Maurice's Gourmet BBQ" chain, famous for its ultra-right-wing, neo-Confederate sensibilities. You may safely patronize Bessinger's in Charleston without worrying that you are supporting anything you may have objections to.

Many local cognoscenti insist that another West Ashley joint, the new **Fiery Ron's Home Team** (1205 Ashley River Rd., 843/225-7427, www.hometeambbq.com, Mon.–Sat. 11 A.M.–9 P.M., Sun. 11:30 A.M.–9 P.M., $7–22) is even better than Bessinger's, though purists might object to the fact that Ron cooks without a sauce, instead letting you pick one: vinegar, mustard, or tomato-based. (Some fans insist you need no sauce at all on Ron's barbecue.) The Home Team offers sandwiches, but the best course of action is any of the platters, with a choice of two of Ron's already legendary sides, including perfect collards, awesome mashed potatoes, and tasty mac-and-cheese. As if that weren't enough, the owners' close ties to the regional jam-band community means there's great live blues and indie rock after 10 P.M. most nights (Thursday is bluegrass night) to spice up the bar action, which goes until 2 A.M.

Classic Southern

Tucked away on the grounds of the Middleton Place Plantation is the romantic **Middleton Place Restaurant** (843/556-6020, www.middletonplace.org, lunch daily 11 A.M.–3 P.M., dinner Tues.–Thurs. 6–8 P.M., Fri.–Sat. 6–9 P.M., Sun. 6–8 P.M., $15–25). Theirs is a respectful take on traditional plantation fare like hoppin' John, gumbo, she-crab soup, and collards. The special annual Thanksgiving buffet is a real treat.

Reservations are required for dinner. A nice plus is being able to wander the gorgeous landscaped gardens before dusk if you arrive at 5:30 P.M. or later with a dinner reservation.

Mediterranean

Anything on this Northern Italian–themed menu is good, but the risotto—legacy of original chef John Marshall—is the specialty dish at **Al Di La** (25 Magnolia Rd., 843/571-2321, Tues.–Sat. 6–10 P.M.), West Ashley's most popular fine dining spot. Reservations are recommended.

For pizza, chain **Andolini's** (1117 Savannah Hwy., 843/225-4743) has a location in West Ashley.

MOUNT PLEASANT

Most restaurant action in Mount Pleasant centers on the picturesque shrimping village of Shem Creek, which is dotted on both banks with bars and restaurants, most dealing in fresh local seafood. As with Murrells Inlet up the coast, some spots on Shem Creek border on tourist traps. Don't be afraid to go where the lines aren't.

Mediterranean

Tasty Greek cuisine is the order of the day at the relatively new **Samos Taverna** (819 Coleman Blvd., 843/856-5055, Mon.–Thurs. 5:30–10 P.M., Fri.–Sat. 5:30–11 P.M., $15), named after the Aegean island from whence one of the partners came. The décor is upscale, if the prices aren't. Best thing to do here is sample several of the *mezethes,* or small plates. Don't forget the octopus!

Seafood

A well-regarded spot on Shem Creek is **Water's Edge** (1407 Shrimp Boat Lane, 843/884-4074, daily 11 A.M.–11 P.M., $20–30), which consistently takes home a Wine Spectator Award of Excellence for its great selection of vintages. Native Charlestonian Jimmy Purcell concentrates

© JIM MOREKIS

Shem Creek

on fresh seafood with a slightly more upscale flair than many Shem Creek places.

Right down the road from Water's Edge is another popular spot, especially for a younger crowd: **Vickery's Shem Creek Bar and Grill** (1313 Shrimp Boat Lane, 843/884-4440, daily 11:30 A.M.–1 A.M., $11–16). With a similar menu to its partner location on the peninsula, this Vickery's has the pleasant added bonus of a beautiful view overlooking the Creek. You'll get more of the Vickery's Cuban flair here, with a great black bean soup and an awesome Cuban sandwich.

Vegetarian

For a vegetarian-friendly change of pace from seafood, go to the **Mustard Seed** (1026 Chuck Dawley Blvd., 843/849-0050, Mon.–Sat. 11 A.M.–2:30 P.M. and 5–9:30 P.M., $14–18). The pad thai is probably the best thing on New York–trained Chef Sal Parco's creative and dynamic menu, but you might also get a kick out of the sweet potato ravioli.

For a *real* change of pace, try **The Sprout Cafe** (629 Johnnie Dodds Blvd.,

843/849-8554, www.thehealthysprout.com, Mon.–Fri. 6 A.M.–8 P.M., Sat. 9 A.M.–3 P.M., Sun. 11 A.M.–3 P.M., $3–10) on U.S. 17. Dealing totally in raw foods, the obvious emphasis here is on health and freshness of ingredients. You might be surprised at the inventiveness of their breakfast-through-dinner, seasonal menu—memorably described as "grab and go" by the staff—which might include a tasty crepe topped with a pear-and-nut puree and topped with maple syrup, or a raw squash and zucchini "pasta" dish topped with walnut "meatballs." There's also an abundance of herbal and organic teas and beverages, good not only for vegans, but for those with severe food allergies as well.

SULLIVAN'S ISLAND

For a friendly bite and an adult beverage or two, go straight to **Poe's Tavern** (2210 Middle St., 843/883-0083, daily 11 A.M.–2 A.M., kitchen closes 10 P.M.), a nod to Edgar Allan Poe's stint at nearby Fort Moultrie.

Atlanticville (2063 Middle St., 843/883-9452, www.atlanticville.net, daily

5:30–10 P.M., Sunday brunch 10 A.M.–2 P.M., $25) is where to go for classic fine dining on Sullivan's.

If you just want to pick up some healthy goodies for picnicking on the beach, head to **Green Heron Grocery** (2019 Middle St., 843/883-0751).

FOLLY BEACH
Breakfast and Brunch
The closest thing to a taste of old Folly is the **Lost Dog Café** (106 W. Huron St., 843/588-9669, daily 6:30 A.M.–3 P.M., $5–7), so named for its bulletin board stacked with alerts about lost pets, pets for adoption, and newborns for sale or giveaway. They open early, the better to offer a tasty, healthy breakfast to the surfing crowd. It's a great place to pick up a quick, inexpensive, and tasty meal while you're near the beach.

Mexican
Owned by the same folks that run chic Raval on the peninsula, the new **Taco Boy** (15 Center St., 843/588-9761, Sun.–Thurs. 11 A.M.–10 P.M., Fri.–Sat. 11 A.M.–11 P.M., $5–15) is a fun place to get a fish taco, have a margarita, and take a walk on the nearby beach afterward. Though no one is under any illusions that this is an authentic Mexican restaurant, the fresh guacamole is particularly rave-worthy, and there's a good selection of tequilas and beers *hecho en Mexico*, with the bar staying open until 2 A.M. on weekends.

Seafood
Fans of the legendary **(Bowen's Island Restaurant** (1870 Bowens Island Rd., 843/795-2757, Tues.–Sat. 5–10 P.M., $5–15, cash only) on James Island off the main road to Folly nearly went into mourning when it burned to the ground in late 2006. But you can't keep a good oysterman down; owner Robert Barber rebuilt and regulars insist that this institution, which began in the 1940s as a fishing camp, is as old-school as ever.

A universe removed from the Lexus-and-khaki scene downtown, Bowen's Island isn't

the place for the hung-up, the uptight, or the well dressed. This is the place to go when you want shovels of oysters—literally thrown onto your table, freshly steamed and delicious and all-you-can-eat. The fried shrimp, flounder, and hush puppies are incredible, too.

The bizarre setting—a nondescript building, little to no signage—only adds to the authenticity of the whole experience. To get there from the peninsula, take Calhoun Street west onto the James Island Connector/Highway 30. Take exit 3 onto Highway 171 South and look for Bowens Island Road on your right. The restaurant will be on your left in a short while, after passing by several ritzy McMansions that in no way resemble the restaurant you're about to experience.

NORTH CHARLESTON
If you have a hankering for pizza in North Charleston, don't miss **EVO Pizzeria** (1075 E. Montague Ave., 843/225-1796, www.evopizza .com, lunch Tues.–Fri. 11 A.M.–2:30 P.M., dinner 5–10 P.M., Sat. 6–10 P.M., $10–15) in the Olde North Charleston area at Park Circle. They specialize in a small but rich menu of unusual gourmet pizza toppings, like pistachio pesto.

Vegans might also want to make a special trip up I-26 to find **Soul Vegetarian** (3225-A Rivers Ave., 843/744-1155, $5–10), the only all-vegan place in the state. Owned and operated by members of the African Hebrew Israelites of Jerusalem, they make their own soy "dairy" products. You'll find barbecue tofu, vegan lasagna, and even faux milkshakes. Hours are flexible, so call ahead.

COFFEE, TEA, AND SWEETS
By common consensus, the best java joint in Charleston is **Kudu Coffee** (4 Vanderhorst Ave., 843/853-7186, Mon.–Sat. 6:30 A.M.–7 P.M., Sun. 9 A.M.–6 P.M.) in the Upper King area. A kudu is an African antelope, and the Africa theme extends to the beans, which all have an African pedigree. Poetry readings and occasional live music add to the mix. A lot of green-friendly, left-of-center community activism

goes on here as well; a recent discussion group was titled "How to Survive the Bible Belt but Still Find God." The adjacent African art store shop is owned by the coffeehouse.

If you find yourself needing a quick pick-me-up while shopping on King Street, avoid the lines at the two Starbucks on the avenue and instead turn east on Market and duck inside **City Lights Coffeehouse** (141 Market St., 843/853-7067, Mon.–Thurs. 7 A.M.–9 P.M., Fri.–Sat. 7 A.M.–10 P.M., Sun. 8 A.M.–6 P.M.). The sweet goodies are delectable in this cozy little Euro style place, and the Counter Culture organic coffee is to die for. If you're really lucky they'll have some of their Ethiopian Sidamo brewed.

Though technically a retail location of a national chain rather than a traditional tea room per se, the truth is that you can get an outstanding fresh cup of herbal tea or maté at **Teavana** (340 King St., 843/723-0600, www.teavana.com, Mon.–Thurs. 10 A.M.–6 P.M., Fri.–Sat. 10 A.M.–9 P.M., Sun. noon–6 P.M.) and even take the time to enjoy it in the little courtyard out back. Stored in big cans along the back wall, all the tea here is loose, fresh, and of extremely high quality. The friendly and quite knowledgeable staff will let you do sniff tests until you find the aroma that appeals to you most.

A unique Charleston phenomenon on Upper King by Marion Square is the aptly named **Cupcake** (433 King St., 843/853-8181, www.freshcupcakes.com, Mon.–Sat. 10 A.M.–7 P.M.). Their eponymous specialty compels Charlestonians to form lines onto the sidewalk, waiting to enjoy one or more of the 30 flavors of little cakes.

Routinely voted as having the best desserts in the city, **Kaminsky's** (78 N. Market St., 843/853-8270, daily noon–2 A.M.) cakes alone are worth the trip to the City Market area. The fresh fruit torte, the red velvet, and the "Mountain of Chocolate" are the three best-

sellers. There's a Mount Pleasant location, too (1028 Johnnie Dodds Blvd., 843/971-7437).

Some key **Starbucks** locations in Charleston are 239 King Street, 387 King Street, 168 Calhoun Street, and 475 East Bay Street.

MARKETS AND GROCERIES

A fun and favorite local fixture from April through mid-December, the **Charleston Farmers Market** (843/724-7309, www.charlestoncity.info, 8 A.M.–2 P.M. each Saturday) rings beautiful Marion Square with stalls of local produce, street eats, local arts and crafts, and kids activities. Running April through October, East Cooper has its own version in the **Mount Pleasant Farmers Market** (843/884-8517, http://townofmountpleasant.com, 3 P.M. until dark each Tuesday) at the Moultrie Middle School on Coleman Boulevard.

For organic groceries and/or a quick, healthy bite while you're in Mount Pleasant, check out **Whole Foods** (923 Houston Northcutt Blvd., 843/971-7240, daily 8 A.M.–9 P.M.). The biggest and best supermarket near the downtown tourist area is the regional chain **Harris Teeter** (290 E. Bay St., 843/722-6821, 24 hours daily). There are other Harris Teeter stores in Mount Pleasant (920 Houston Northcutt Blvd. and 620 Long Point Rd., 843/881-4448) and Folly Beach (675 Folly Rd., 843/406-8977).

For a charming grocery shopping experience, try **King Street Grocery** (435 King St., 843/958-8004, daily 8 A.M.–midnight) on Upper King. If you're down closer to the Battery, go to the delightful and historic **Burbage's Self-Serv** (157 Broad St., 843/723-4054, 8 A.M.–6 P.M. Sun.–Fri., 8 A.M.–2 P.M. Sat.), serving the South of Broad neighborhood and nearby points since 1874.

Need groceries at 4 A.M. on Folly Beach? Go to **Bert's Market** (202 E. Ashley Ave., 843/588-9449), which is open 24 hours.

Information and Services

VISITORS CENTERS

I highly recommend a stop at the **Charleston Visitor Reception and Transportation Center** (375 Meeting St., 800/774-0006, Mon.–Fri. 8:30 A.M.–5 P.M., www.charleston cvb.com). Housed in a modern building with an inviting, open design, the Visitor Center has several high-tech, interactive exhibits, including an amazing model of the city under glass. Wall after wall of well-stocked, well-organized brochures will keep you informed on everything a tourist would ever want to know about or see in the city. A particularly welcoming touch is the inclusion of the work of local artists all around the Center.

I recommend using the attached parking garage not only for your stop at the Visitor Center but also anytime you want to see the many sights this part of town has to offer, such as the Charleston Museum, the Manigault and Aiken-Rhett Houses, and the Children's Museum. Most of all, the big selling point at the Visitor Center is the friendliness of the smiling and courteous staff, who welcome you in true Charleston fashion and are there to book rooms and tours, find tickets for shows and attractions, and to fill you in on every aspect of what to expect and look for while you're in the area.

If for no other reason, you should go to the Visitor Center to take advantage of the great deal offered by the **Charleston Heritage Passport** (www.heritagefederation.org), which gives you 40 percent off admission to all of Charleston's key historic homes, the Charleston Museum, and the two awesome plantation sites on the Ashley River: Drayton Hall and Middleton Place. You can get the Heritage Passport *only* at the Visitor Center on Meeting Street.

Other area visitors centers include the **Mt. Pleasant-Isle of Palms Visitor Center** (Johnnie Dodds Blvd., 843/853-8000, daily 9 A.M.–5 P.M.) and the new **North Charleston**

Visitor Center (4975-B Centre Pointe Dr., 843/853-8000, Mon.–Sat. 10 A.M.–5 P.M.).

HOSPITALS

If there's a silver lining in getting sick or injured in Charleston, it's that there are plenty of high-quality medical facilities available. The premier institution is the **Medical University of South Carolina** (171 Ashley Ave., 843/792-2300, www.muschealth.com) in the northwest part of the peninsula.

Two notable facilities are near each other downtown: **Roper Hospital** (316 Calhoun St., 843/402-2273, www.roperhospital.com) and **Charleston Memorial Hospital** (326 Calhoun St., 843/792-2300).

In Mount Pleasant there's **East Cooper Regional Medical Center** (1200 Johnnie Dodds Blvd., www.eastcoopermedctr.com). In West Ashley there's **Bon Secours St. Francis Hospital** (2095 Henry Tecklenburg Ave., 843/402-2273, www.ropersaintfrancis.com).

POLICE

For non-emergencies in Charleston, West Ashley, and James Island, contact the **Charleston Police Department** (843/577-7434, www.charlestoncity.info). You can also contact the police department in Mount Pleasant (843/884-4176). North Charleston is a separate municipality with its own police department (843/308-4718, www .northcharleston.org).

Of course, for emergencies always call **911.**

MEDIA

The daily newspaper of record is the *Post and Courier* (www.charleston.net). Its entertainment insert, *Preview,* comes out on Thursdays. The free alt-weekly is the decade-old *Charleston City Paper* (www.charlestoncitypaper.com), which comes out on Wednesdays and is the best place to find local music and arts listings.

A particularly well done and lively metro

glossy is *Charleston Magazine* (www.charleston mag.com), which comes out once a month.

LIBRARIES

The main branch of the **Charleston County Public Library** (68 Calhoun St., 843/805-6801, www.ccpl.org, Mon.–Thurs. 9 A.M.–9 P.M., Fri.– Sat. 9 A.M.–6 P.M., Sun. 2–5 P.M.) has been on its current site since 1998. Named for Sullivan's Island's most famous visitor, the **Edgar Allan Poe** (1921 I'On Ave., 843/883-3914, www. ccpl.org, Mon. and Fri. 2–6 P.M., Tues., Thurs., and Sat. 10 A.M.–2 P.M.) has been housed in Battery Gadsden, a former Spanish-American War gun emplacement, since 1977.

The College of Charleston's main library is the **Marlene and Nathan Addlestone Library** (205 Calhoun St., 843/953-5530, www.cofc .edu), home to special collections, the Center for Student Learning, the main computer lab, the media collection, and even a café. The college's **Avery Research Center for African American History and Culture** (125 Bull St., 843/953-7609, www.cofc.edu/avery, Mon.– Fri. 10 A.M.–5 P.M., Sat. noon–5 P.M.) houses documents relating to the history and culture of African Americans in the Lowcountry.

For other historical research on the area, check out the collections of the **South Carolina Historical Society** (100 Meeting St., 843/723-3225, www.southcarolinahistorical society.org, Mon.–Fri. 9 A.M.–4 P.M., Sat. 9 A.M.–2 P.M.). There's a $5 research fee for non-members.

GAY AND LESBIAN RESOURCES

Contrary to many media portrayals of the region, Charleston is quite open to gays and lesbians, who play a major role in arts, culture, and business. As with any other place in the South, however, it's generally expected that people—straights as well—will keep personal preferences and politics to themselves in public settings.

A key local advocacy group is the **Alliance for Full Acceptance** (29 Leinbach Dr., Ste. D-3, 843/883-0343, www.affa-sc.org). The **Lowcountry Gay and Lesbian Alliance** (843/720-8088) holds a potluck the last Sunday of each month. For the most up-to-date happenings, try the Gay Charleston blog (http:///gaycharleston.ccpblogs.com), part of the *Charleston City Paper.*

Getting There and Around

BY AIR

Way up in North Charleston is **Charleston International Airport** (5500 International Blvd., 843/767-1100, airport code CHS, www .chs-airport.com), served by AirTran (www.air tran.com), American Airlines (www.aa.com), Continental Airlines (www.continental.com), Delta (www.delta.com), Northwest Airlines (www.nwa.com), United Airlines (www.ual .com), and US Airways (www.usairways.com).

As in most cities, taxi service from the airport is regulated. The fare from the airport is $2.15 per mile, with $12 fee for each passenger over two (no additional charge up to two people). For example, this translates to about $27 for two people from the airport to Charleston

Place downtown. For the airport vicinity there's a fixed rate of $9 per person.

BY CAR

There are two main routes in to Charleston, I-26 from the west-northwest (which dead-ends downtown) and U.S. 17 from the west (called Savannah Highway when it gets close to Charleston proper), which continues on over the Ravenel Bridge into Mount Pleasant and beyond.

There's a fairly new perimeter highway, I-526 (Mark Clark Expressway), which loops around the city from West Ashley to North Charleston to Daniel Island and into Mount Pleasant. It's accessible both from I-26 and U.S. 17.

Keep in mind that I-95, while certainly a gateway to the region, is actually a good ways out of Charleston, about 30 miles west of the city.

Car Rentals

Charleston International Airport has rental kiosks for **Avis** (843/767-7031), **Budget** (843/767-7051), **Dollar** (843/767-1130), **Enterprise** (843/767-1109), **Hertz** (843/767-4550), **National** (843/767-3078), and **Thrifty** (843/647-4389).

There are a couple of rental locations downtown: **Budget** (390 Meeting St., 843/577-5195) and **Enterprise** (398 Meeting St., 843/723-6215). **Hertz** has a location in West Ashley (3025 Ashley Town Center Dr., 843/573-2147), as does **Enterprise** (2004 Savannah Hwy., 843/556-7889).

BY BUS

Public transportation by **Charleston Area Regional Transit Authority** (843/724-7420, www.ridecarta.com), or CARTA, is a fairly convenient and inexpensive way to enjoy Charleston without the more structured nature of an organized tour. There are a wide variety of routes all over the area, but most visitors will limit their acquaintance to the tidy, trolley-like **DASH** (Downtown Area Shuttle) buses run by CARTA throughout the peninsula, primarily for tourists. Each ride is $1.25 per person (seniors are $0.60). The best deal is the $4 one-day pass, which you get at the Charleston Visitor Center (375 Meeting St.). Keep in mind that DASH only stops at designated places.

DASH has three routes: the 210, which runs a northerly circuit from the Aquarium to the College of Charleston; the 211, running up and down the parallel Meeting and King Streets from Marion Square down to the Battery; and the 212 Market/Waterfront shuttle from Aquarium area down to Waterfront Park.

BY TAXI

The South is generally not big on taxis, and Charleston is no exception. The best bet is simply to call, rather than try to flag one down. Charleston's most fun service is **Charleston Black Cabs** (843/216-2627, www.charlestonblackcabcompany.com), using Americanized versions of the classic British taxi (at over $50,000 a pop, they're not a cheap investment). A one-way ride anywhere on the peninsula below the bridges is a flat $10 per person, and rates go up from there. They're very popular, so call as far ahead as you can or try to get one at their stand at Charleston Place. Two other good services are **Safety Cab** (843/722-4066) and **Yellow Cab** (843/577-6565).

You can also try a human-powered taxi service from **Charleston Rickshaw** (843/723-5685). A cheerful (and energetic) young cyclist will pull you and a friend to most points on the lower peninsula for about $10–15. Call 'em or find one by City Market. They work late on Friday and Saturday nights, too.

PARKING

As you will quickly see, parking is at a premium in downtown Charleston. An exception seems to be the large number of free spaces all along the Battery, but unless you're an exceptionally strong walker, that's too far south to use as a reliable base from which to explore the whole peninsula.

Most metered parking downtown is on and around Calhoun Street, Meeting Street, King Street, Market Street, and East Bay Street. That may not sound like a lot, but it constitutes the bulk of the area that most tourists visit. Most meters have three-hour limits but you'll come across some as short as 30 minutes. Technically you're not supposed to "feed the meter" in Charleston, as city personnel put little chalk marks on your tires to make sure people aren't overstaying their welcome. Metered parking is free 6 P.M.–6 A.M. and all day on Sunday. On Saturdays, expect to pay.

The city has several conveniently located and comparatively inexpensive parking garages. I strongly suggest that you make use of them. They're located at: The Aquarium, Camden and Exchange Streets, Charleston

Place, Concord and Cumberland Streets, East Bay and Prioleau Streets, Marion Square, Gaillard Auditorium, Liberty and St. Philip Streets, Majestic Square, the Charleston Visitor Reception and Transportation Center, and Wentworth Street. There are several private parking garages as well, primarily clustered in the City Market area. They're convenient, but many of them have parking spaces that are simply too small for some cars.

The city's website (www.charlestoncity.info) has a pretty good interactive map of parking possibilities on the peninsula.

Greater Charleston

Though one could easily spend a lifetime enjoying the history and attractions of Charleston itself, there are many unique experiences to be had in the less-developed areas surrounding the city. Generally there are two types of vibes: isolated close-knit communities with little overt development (though that's changing), or private, resort-style communities amid stunning natural beauty.

EDISTO ISLAND

One of the last unspoiled, down-home places in the Lowcountry, Edisto Island has been highly regarded as a getaway spot since the Edisto tribe first starting coming here for shellfish. (Proof of their patronage is in the huge shell midden, or debris pile, at the state park.) In fact, locals here swear that the island was settled by English-speaking colonists even before Charleston was settled in 1670.

In any case, we do know that the Spanish established a short-lived mission on St. Pierre's Creek. Then in 1674, the island was purchased from the Edistos for a few trinkets by the perhaps appropriately named Earl of Shaftesbury. For most of its modern history, cotton plantations specializing in the top-of-the-line Sea Island strain were Edisto Island's main claim to fame—it was called McConkey's Island for most of that time—though after the Civil War fishing became the primary occupation. Because of several hurricanes in the mid-20th century, little remains of previous eras.

Now this barrier island, for the moment unthreatened by the encroachment of planned communities and private resorts so endemic to the Carolina coast, is a nice getaway for area residents in addition to just plain being a great—if a little isolated—place to live for its 800 or so full-time residents. The beaches are quiet and beautiful, the shells are plentiful, the walks are romantic, the people are friendly, and the food is good but casual. The residents operate on "Edisto Time," with a *mañana* philosophy (i.e., it'll get done when it gets done) that results in a mellow pace of life out in these parts.

Orientation

There's basically one main land route here, south on Highway 174 off U.S. 17. It's a long way down to Edisto, but the 20–30 minute drive is scenic and enjoyable. Most activity on the island centers on the township of Edisto Beach, which voted to align itself with Colleton County for its lower taxes (the rest of Edisto Island is part of Charleston County).

Once in town, there are two main routes to keep in mind. Palmetto Boulevard runs parallel to the beach and is noteworthy for the almost total lack of high-rise style development so common in other beach areas of South Carolina. Jungle Road runs parallel to Palmetto Boulevard several blocks inland, and contains the tiny "business district."

(Edisto Beach State Park

Edisto Beach State Park (8377 State Cabin Rd., 843/869-2156, www.southcarolinaparks .com, daily 8 A.M.–6 P.M. Nov.–mid-Mar., 6 A.M.–10 P.M. mid-Mar.–Oct., $4 adult, $1.50 children, 5 and under free) is one of the world's foremost destinations for shell collectors.

CHARLESTON

© JIM MOREKIS

interpretive center at Edisto Beach State Park

Largely because of fresh loads of silt from the adjacent ACE Basin, there are always new specimens, many of them fossils, washing ashore.

The park stretches almost three miles and features the state's longest system of fully accessible hiking and biking trails, including one leading to the 4,000-year-old shell midden, now much eroded from past millennia. The new and particularly well-done **interpretive center** (Tues.–Sat. 9 A.M.–4 P.M.) has plenty of interesting exhibits about the nature and history of both the park as well as the surrounding ACE Basin. Don't let the kids miss it.

Like many state recreational facilities in the South, Edisto Beach State Park was developed by the Civilian Conservation Corps (CCC), one of President Franklin D. Roosevelt's New Deal programs during the Great Depression, which had the doubly beneficial effect of employing large numbers of people while establishing much of the conservation infrastructure we enjoy today.

Other Sights

The charming **Edisto Museum** (8123 Chisolm

Plantation Rd., 843/869-1954, www.edisto museum.org, Tues.–Sat. 1–4 P.M., adults $4, $2 children, under 10 free), a project of the Edisto Island Historic Preservation Society, is in the midst of plans for a major expansion that will incorporate a nearby slave cabin.

Opened in 1999 by local snake-hunters the Clamp brothers, the **Edisto Island Serpentarium** (1374 Hwy. 174, 843/869-1171, www.edistoserpentarium.com, seasonal hours vary, $12.95 adults, $9.95 ages 6–12, $5.95 ages 4–5, under 3 free) is educational and fun, taking you up-close and personal with a variety of reptilian creatures native to the area. The serpentarium is on the main route into Edisto before you get to the beach area. Keep in mind they usually close Labor Day through April 30.

Tours

Edisto has many beautiful plantation homes, relics of the island's longtime role as host to cotton plantations. While all are in private hands and therefore off limits to the public, an exception is offered through **Edisto Island Tours & T'ings** (843/869-9092, $20 adults, $10 ages 12 and under). You'll take a van tour around Edisto's beautiful churches and old plantations.

The only other way to see the homes is during the annual **Tour of Homes** (843/869-1954, www.edistomuseum.org) the second weekend in October, run by the Edisto Island Historic Preservation Society. Tickets sell out very early.

Shopping

Not only a convenient place to pick up odds and ends, the **Edistonian Gift Shop & Gallery** (406 Highway 174, 843/869-4466) is also an important landmark, as the main supplying point before you get into the main part of town. Think of a really nice convenience store with an attached gift shop and you'll get the picture.

For various ocean gear, try the **Edisto Surf Shop** (145 Jungle Rd., 843/869-9283, daily 9 A.M.–5 P.M.). For a new or used beach read, go right next door to the **Cozy Corner** (145 Jungle Rd., 843/869-1221), which also serves a mean espresso. You can find whimsical Lowcountry-themed art for enjoyment or purchase at **Fish or Cut Bait Gallery** (142 Jungle Rd., 843/869-2511, Tues.–Sat. 10 A.M.–5 P.M., www.fishorcutbaitgallery.com).

If you need some groceries, there's always the **Piggly Wiggly** (104 Jungle Rd., 843/869-0055, Sun.–Thurs. 7 A.M.–9 P.M., Fri.–Sat. 7 A.M.–10 P.M.) grocery store, a.k.a., "The Pig." For fresh seafood, try **Flowers Seafood Company** (1914 Hwy. 174, 843/869-0033, Mon.–Sat. 9 A.M.–7 P.M., Sun. 9 A.M.–5 P.M.).

Sports and Recreation

As the largest river of the ACE (Ashepoo, Combahee, Edisto) Basin complex, the Edisto River figures large in the lifestyle of residents and visitors. A good public landing is at Steamboat Creek off Highway 174 on the way down to the island. Take Steamboat Landing Road (Hwy. 968) off Highway 174 near the James Edwards School. Live Oak Landing is farther up Big Bay Creek near the Interpretive Center at the State Park. The **Edisto Marina** (3702 Docksite Rd., 843/869-3504) is on the far west side of the island.

Captain Ron Elliott of **Edisto Island**

Tours (843/869-1937) offers various ecotours and fishing trips, as well as canoe and kayak rentals for about $25 a day. A typical kayak tour runs about $35 per person for a one-and-a-half to two-hour trip, though he offers a "beachcombing" trip for $15 per person. **Ugly Ducklin'** (843/869-1580) offers creek and inshore fishing charters.

You can get gear as well as book boat and kayak tours of the entire area, including into the ACE Basin, at **Edisto Watersports & Tackle** (3731 Docksite Rd., 843/869-0663, www.edistowatersports.com). Their guided tours run about $30 per person, with a two-hour rental running about $20.

Riding a bike on Edisto Beach and all around the island is a great, relaxing way to get some exercise and enjoy its scenic, laid-back beauty. The best place to rent a bike—or a kayak or canoe, for that matter—is **Island Bikes and Outfitters** (140 Jungle Rd., 843/869-4444, Mon.–Sat. 9–4 P.M.). Bike rentals there run about $16 a day; single kayaks are about $60 a day.

There's one golf course on the island, the 18-hole **Plantation Course at Edisto** (21 Fairway Dr., 843/869-1111, $60), finished in 2006.

Accommodations

A great thing about Edisto Island is the total absence of ugly chain lodging or beachfront condo development. My recommended option is staying at the **Edisto Beach State Park** (843/869-2156,www.southcarolinaparks.com, $75–100 cabins, $25 tent sites) itself, either at a campsite on the Atlantic side or in a marsh-front cabin on the northern edge. During high season (Apr.–Nov.), there's a minimum week-long stay in the cabins; during the off-season, the minimum stay is two days. You can book cabins up to 11 months in advance, and I highly recommend doing so as they go very quickly.

If you want something a little more plush, there are rental homes galore on Edisto Island. Because of the aforementioned lack of hotels, this is the most popular option for most vacationers here—indeed, just about the only option. Contact **Edisto Sales and Rentals Realty** (1405 Palmetto Blvd., 800/868-5398, www.edistorealty.com).

Food

One of the all-time great barbecue places in South Carolina is on Edisto, **(Po Pigs Bo-B-Q** (2410 Hwy. 174, 843/869-9003, Wed.–Sat. 11:30 A.M.–9 P.M., $4–10) on the way into town. This is the real thing, the full pig cooked in all its many ways: white meat, dark meat, cracklin's, and hash, served in the local style of "all you care to eat." Unlike many BBQ spots, they do serve beer and wine.

Another popular joint on the island is **Whaley's** (2801 Myrtle St., 843/869-2161, Tues.–Sat. 11:30 A.M.–2 P.M. and 5–9 P.M., bar daily 5 P.M.–2 A.M., $5–15), a down-home place in an old gas station a few blocks off the beach. This is a good place for casual seafood like boiled shrimp, washed down with a lot of beer. The bar is open seven days a week.

McConkey's Jungle Shack (108 Jungle Rd., 843/869-0097, Mon.–Fri. 11 A.M.–8 P.M., Sat.–Sun. 8 A.M.–8 P.M., $4–10) on the eastern end of the beach is known for its fish-and-chips basket and great burgers.

As of this writing, the legendary Old Post Office restaurant, a fine dining Lowcountry-style spot, was closed down, but there's talk of it reopening. Ask a local for an update; Edisto's a very tight-knit little community and they're sure to know.

SUMMERVILLE

The Dorchester County town of Summerville, population 30,000, is gaining a reputation as a friendly, scenic, and upscale suburb north of Charleston. That's funny, since that's basically what Summerville has always been.

Founded as Pineland Village in 1785, Summerville made its reputation as a place for plantation owners and their families to escape the insects and heat of the swampier areas of the Lowcountry. While the plantation system disintegrated with the South's loss in the Civil War, Summerville got a second wind at the turn of the 20th century, when it was recommended by doctors all over the world as a great place to recover from tuberculosis (supposedly all the turpentine fumes in the air from the pine trees was a big help).

Summerville's about 30 minutes from downtown Charleston. Take I-26 north.

Sights

Due to its longstanding popularity as a getaway for wealthy planters and then as a spa town, Summerville boasts a whopping 700 buildings on the National Register of Historic Places. For a walking tour of the historic district, download the map at www.visitsummerville.com or pick up a hardcopy at the **Summerville Visitors Center** (402 N. Main St., 843/873-8535). (Alas, the grand old Pine Forest Inn, perhaps the greatest of all Summerville landmarks, Winter White House for presidents William Taft and Theodore Roosevelt, was torn down after World War II, a victim of the Florida vacation craze.)

Much visitor activity in Summerville centers on **Azalea Park** (South Main St. and W. 5th St. South, daily dusk-dawn, free), rather obviously named for its most scenic inhabitants. Several fun yearly events take place here, most notably the **Flowertown Festival** (www.flower townfestival.com, free) each April, a three-day affair heralding the coming of spring and the blooming of the flowers. One of the biggest festivals in South Carolina, a quarter-million people usually attend. Another event, **Sculpture in the South** (www.sculptureinthesouth.com) in May, takes advantage of the extensive public sculpture in the park.

To learn more about Summerville's interesting history, go just off Main Street to the **Summerville-Dorchester Museum** (100 E. Doty Ave., 843/875-9666, www.summerville dorchestermuseum.org, Mon.–Sat. 9 A.M.–2 P.M.). Located in the former town police station, the museum has a wealth of good exhibits and boasts a new curator, Chris Ohm, with wide local experience, including at Middleton Place and with the CSS *Hunley* project in North Charleston.

Just south of Summerville on the way

back to Charleston is **Colonial Dorchester State Historic Site** (300 State Park Rd., 843/873-1740, www.southcarolinaparks.com, daily 9 A.M.–6 P.M., $2 adults, 15 and under free), marking the remains of the dead town of Dorchester. With a pedigree going back to 1697, almost to the colony's founding, Dorchester was fortified by colonists during the Revolution, commanded briefly for a time by the Swamp Fox himself, Francis Marion. The encampment was reclaimed by the surrounding forest, with research not beginning until the 1960s. Today you can view the beautifully poignant remains of the 1719 church bell tower and a circa 1750 tabby fort from the French and Indian War, as well as enjoying interpretive trails.

Accommodations and Food

The renowned **Woodlands Resort & Inn** (125 Parsons Rd., 843/875-2600, $325–650) is one of a handful of inns in America with a five-star rating both for lodging and dining. Its 18 rooms within the 1906 great house are decorated in a mix of old-fashioned plantation high-style and contemporary designer aesthetics, with modern, luxurious baths. There's also a free-standing guest cottage ($850) which seeks to replicate a hunting-lodge type of vibe.

As you'd expect, there's a full day spa on premises; an hour massage, the most basic offering, will run you $110. The pool is outside, but heated for all-year enjoyment, at least theoretically. Woodlands is making a big play for the growing pet-friendly market, and eagerly pampers your dog or cat while you stay. You might not want to leave the grounds, but you should take advantage of their complimentary bikes to tour around historic Summerville.

Within Woodlands is its award-winning, world-class restaurant, simply called **The Dining Room** (Mon.–Sat. 11 A.M.–2 P.M., 6–9 P.M., brunch Sun. 11:30 A.M.–2 P.M., $25–40). New executive chef Nate Whiting, once the *sous chef* here, mixes the love of the fresh ingredients of his Italian heritage with the boldness of his French training. His signature dishes include a linguini with wild burgundy escargot and sweet chili threads. It will come as no surprise to find out that the 900-entry wine list and sommelier are collectively awesome, as well as the desserts of pastry chef Sheree McDowell. Jackets required, and reservations are highly advisable.

In Summerville proper, try **Mustard Seed** (101 N. Main St., 843/821-7101, lunch Mon.–Sat. 11 A.M.–2:30 P.M., dinner Mon.–Thurs. 5–9 P.M. and Fri.–Sat. 5–10 P.M., $8–10), a health food restaurant that doesn't skimp on the taste. For a more down-home style pancakes-and-sandwich place that's popular with the locals, try **Flowertown Restaurant** (120 E. 5th North St., 843/871-3202, $8).

Another popular local landmark is **Guerin's Pharmacy** (140 S. Main St., 843/873-2531, Mon.–Fri. 9 A.M.–6 P.M., Sat. 9 A.M.–5 P.M.), which claims to be the State's oldest pharmacy. Complete with old-fashioned soda fountain, they offer malted milkshakes and lemonade.

NORTH ALONG THE COAST
Sewee Visitor Center

Twenty miles north of Charleston you'll find the Sewee Visitor and Environmental Education Center (5821 Hwy. 17, 843/928-3368, www.fws.gov/seweecenter, Tues.–Sat. 9 A.M.–5 P.M., free). Besides being a gateway of sorts for the almost entirely aquatic Cape Romain National Wildlife Refuge, Sewee is primarily known for its population of rare red wolves, who were part of a unique release program on nearby Bull Island begun in the late 1970s.

Cape Romain NWR

One of the best natural experiences in the area is north of Charleston at **Cape Romain National Wildlife Refuge** (5801 Hwy. 17 N., 843/928-3264, www.fws.gov/caperomain, sunrise–sunset year-round). Essentially comprising four barrier islands, the 66,000-acre refuge—almost all of which is marsh—provides a lot of great paddling opportunities, chief among them **Bull Island** (no overnight camping). A fairly lengthy trek from where you put in lies famous Boneyard Beach, where hundreds of

CHARLESTON

downed trees lie on the sand, bleached by sun and salt.

Slightly to the south within the refuge, **Capers Island Heritage Preserve** (843/953-9300, www.dnr.sc.gov, daily dawn–dusk, free) is still a popular camping locale, despite heavy damage from Hurricane Hugo. Get permits in advance by calling the South Carolina Department of Natural Resources. You can kayak to the refuge yourself or take the only approved ferry service from **Coastal Expeditions** (654 Serotina Ct., 843/881-4582, www.coastalexpeditions.com). **Barrier Island Eco Tours** (50 41st Ave., 843/886-5000, www.nature-tours.com) on Isle of Palms also runs trips to the area.

I'on Swamp Trail

Once part of a rice plantation, the I'on Swamp Trail (843/928-3368, www.fs.fed.us, daily dawn–dusk, free) is one of the premier birdwatching sites in South Carolina, particularly during spring and fall migrations. The rare Bachman's warbler, commonly considered one of the most elusive birds in North America, has been seen here. To get here head about 15 miles north of Mount Pleasant and take a left onto I'on Swamp Road (Forest Service 228). The parking area is 2.5 miles ahead on the left.

POINTS WEST AND SOUTHWEST
Caw Caw Interpretive Center

Just west of town on U.S. 17, you'll find the unique Caw Caw Interpretive Center (5200 Savannah Hwy., Ravenel, 843/889-8898, www.ccprc.com, Wed.–Sun. 9 A.M.–5 P.M., $1), a treasure trove for history buffs and naturalists wanting to learn more about the old rice culture of the South. With a particular emphasis on the expertise of those who worked on the rice plantations using techniques they brought with them from Africa, the county-run facility comprises 650 acres of land (on an actual former rice plantation built on former cypress swamp), eight miles of interpretive trails, an educational center with exhibits, and a wildlife

sanctuary with seven different habitats. Most Wednesday and Saturday mornings, guided bird walks are held at 8:30 A.M. ($5 per person). You can put in your own canoe for $10 on Saturdays and Sundays October–April. Bikes and dogs aren't allowed on the grounds.

Johns Island

The outlying community of Johns Island is where you'll find **Angel Oak Park** (3688 Angel Oak Rd., Mon.–Sat. 9 A.M.–5 P.M., Sun. 1–5 P.M.) home of a massive live oak, 65 feet in circumference, that's well over 1,000 years old and commonly considered the oldest tree east of the Mississippi River. The tree and the park are owned by the city of Charleston, and the grounds are often used for weddings and special events. Get here from Charleston by taking U.S. 17 over the Ashley River, then Highway 171 to Maybank Highway. Take a left onto Bohicket Road near the Piggly Wiggly, and then look for signs on your right.

Here is also where you'll find **Legare Farms** (2620 Hanscombe Point Rd., 843/559-0763, www.legarefarms.com), open to the public for various activities, like its annual pumpkin patch in October, its "sweet corn" festival in June, and bird walks each Saturday morning in autumn (8:30 A.M., $6 adults, $3 children).

If you find your tummy growling on Johns Island, don't miss **(Fat Hen** (3140 Maybank Hwy., Johns Island, 843/559-9090, Tues.–Sat. 11:30 A.M.–3 P.M. and 5:30–10 P.M., Sun. 10 A.M.–3 P.M., $15–20), a self-styled "country French bistro" begun by a couple of old Charleston restaurant hands. The fried oysters are a particular specialty. There's also a bar menu for late-night hours (10 P.M.–2 A.M.).

If barbecue's more your thing, head straight to **(JB's Smokeshack** (3406 Maybank Hwy., 843/557-0426, www.jbssmokeshack.com, Wed.–Sat. 11 A.M.–8:30 P.M., $8), one of the best 'cue joints in the Lowcountry. They offer a buffet for $8.88 per person ($4.95 for kids 10 and under), or you can opt for a barbecue plate, including hash, rice, and two sides. In a nice twist, the plates include a three-meat option: pork, chicken, ribs, or brisket.

Wadmalaw Island

Like Johns Island, Wadmalaw Island is one of those lazy, scenic sea islands gradually becoming subsumed within Charleston's growth. That said, there's plenty of meandering, laidback beauty to enjoy, and a couple of interesting sights.

Currently owned by the R.C. Bigelow Tea corporation, the **Charleston Tea Plantation** (6617 Maybank Hwy., 843/559-0383, www .bigelowtea.com, Wed.–Sat. 10 A.M.–4 P.M., Sun. noon–4 P.M., free) is no cute living history exhibit: It's a big, working tea plantation, with acre after acre of *Camilla sinensis* being worked by modern farm machinery. Visitors get to see a sample of how the tea is made, "from the field to the cup," as they put it here, first by a trolley tour of the "Back 40" and then at a viewing gallery of the processing machines at work. And of course there's a gift shop where you can sample and buy all types of teas and tea-related products.

Unlike many agricultural sites in the area, the 127-acre Charleston Tea Plantation was never actually a plantation. It was first planted at the relatively late date of 1960, when the Lipton tea company moved some plants from Summerville, South Carolina, to its research facility on Wadmalaw Island. Lipton decided the climate and high labor costs of the American South weren't conducive to making money, so they sold the land to two employees, Mack Fleming and Bill Hall, in 1987. The two held onto the plantation until 2003, when R.C. Bigelow won it at auction for $1.28 million. Growing season is from April through October. The tea bushes, direct descendants of plants brought over in the 1800s from India and China, "flush up" 2–3 inches every few weeks during growing season.

To get here from Charleston, take the Ashley River Bridge, stay left to Folly Road (Highway 171), turn right onto Maybank Highway for 18 miles, and look for the sign on your left.

The muscadine grape is the only varietal that dependably grows in South Carolina. That said, the state has several good wineries, among them Wadmalaw's own **Irvin House Vineyard** (6775 Bears Bluff Rd., 843/559-6867, www.charlestonwine.com, Thurs.–Sat. 10 A.M.–5 P.M.), Charleston area's only vineyard. Jim Irvin, a Kentucky boy, and his wife Anne, a Johns Island native, make several varieties of muscadine wine here, with tastings and a gift shop. They also give free tours of the fifty-acre grounds every Saturday at 2 P.M. There's a Grape-Stomping Festival at the end of each August ($5 per car). To get here from town, go west on Maybank Highway about ten miles to Bears Bluff Road, veering right. The vineyard entrance is on your left after about eight miles.

Kiawah Island

Only one facility for the general public exists on beautiful Kiawah Island, the **Kiawah Island Beachwalker Park** (843/768-2395, www .ccprc.com, weekends only 10 A.M.–6 P.M. Mar., Apr., and Oct.; 9 A.M.–7 P.M. during summer; 10 A.M.–6 P.M. Sept.; closed Nov.–Feb., $7 per vehicle, free for pedestrians and cyclists). Get there from downtown by taking Lockwood Avenue onto the Highway 30 Connector bridge over the Ashley River. Turn right onto Folly Road, then a left onto Maybank Highway. After about 20 minutes you'll take a left onto Bohicket Road, which leads you to Kiawah in 14 miles. Turn left from Bohicket onto the Kiawah Island Parkway. Just before the security gate, turn right on Beachwalker Drive and follow the signs to the park.

The island's other main attraction is the **Kiawah Island Golf Resort** (12 Kiawah Beach Dr., 800/654-2924, www.kiawahgolf.com), which is a key location for PGA tournaments. Several smaller private, family-friendly resorts exist on Kiawah, with fully furnished homes and villas and every amenity you could ask for and then some, giving you full access to the island's 10 miles of beautiful beach. Go to www .explorekiawah.com for a full range of options or call 800/877-0837.

Through the efforts of the **Kiawah Island Conservancy** (23 Beachwalker Dr., 843/768-2029, www.kiawahconservancy.org), over 300 acres of the island have been kept as undeveloped nature preserve. The island's famous bobcat population has made quite a comeback, with somewhere between 24 and 36 animals currently active. The bobcats are vital to the island ecosystem, since as top predator they help cull what would otherwise become untenably large populations of deer and rabbit. As a side note, while you're enjoying the beautiful scenery of the islands on the Carolina coast, it's always important to remember that most, including Kiawah, were logged and/or farmed extensively in the past. While they're certainly gorgeous now, it would be incorrect to call them "pristine."

Seabrook Island

Like its neighbor Kiawah, Seabrook Island is also a private resort-dominated island. In addition to offering miles of beautiful beaches, on its 2,200 acres are a wide variety of golfing, tennis, equestrian, and swimming facilities, as well as extensive dining and shopping options. There are also a lot of kids' activities as well. For information on lodging options and packages, go to www.seabrook.com or call 866/249-9934.

SOUTH CAROLINA LOWCOUNTRY

For many people around the world, the Lowcountry is the first image that comes to mind when they think of the American South. For the people that live here the Lowcountry is altogether unique, but it does embody many of the region's most noteworthy qualities: an emphasis on manners, a constant look back into the past, and a slow and leisurely pace (embodied in the joking but largely accurate nickname "Slowcountry").

History hangs in the humid air where first the Spanish came to interrupt the native tribes' ancient reverie, then the French, followed by the English. Though time, erosion, and development have erased most traces of these multicultural occupants, you can almost hear their ghosts in the rustle of the branches in a sudden sea breeze, or in the piercing call of a heron over the marsh.

Artists and arts lovers the world over are drawn here to paint, photograph, or otherwise be inspired by some of the most gorgeous wetlands in the United States, so vast that human habitation appears fleeting and intermittent. Sprawling between Beaufort and Charleston is the huge ACE (Ashley, Combahee, Edisto) Basin, a beautiful and important estuary and a national model for good conservation practices.

In all, the defining characteristic of the Lowcountry is its liquid nature—not only literally, in the creeks and waterway that dominate every vista and the seafood cooked in all manner of ways, but figuratively, too, in the slow but deep quality of life here. Once outside what passes for urban areas here, you'll find yourself taking a look back through the decades to a time of roadside produce stands,

© JIM MOREKIS

HIGHLIGHTS

◖ **Henry C. Chambers Waterfront Park:** Walk the dog or while away the time on a porch swing at this clean and inviting gathering place on the serene Beaufort River (page 279).

◖ **St. Helena's Episcopal Church:** To walk through this Beaufort sanctuary and its walled graveyard is to walk through Lowcountry history (page 280).

◖ **Penn Center:** Not only the center of modern Gullah culture and education, this is a key site in civil rights history as well (page 293).

◖ **Hunting Island State Park:** This is one of the most peaceful natural getaways on the East Coast, but it's only minutes away from the more civilized temptations of Beaufort (page 298).

◖ **ACE Basin:** It can take a lifetime to learn your way around this massive, marshy estuary – or just a few hours soaking in its lush beauty (page 300).

◖ **Pinckney Island National Wildlife Refuge:** This excellently maintained sanctuary is a major birding location and a great little getaway from nearby Hilton Head (page 306).

◖ **Old Bluffton:** Gossipy and gorgeous by turns, this charming village on the May River centers on a thriving artist colony (page 321).

◖ **South Carolina Artisans Center:** From folk art to classic watercolors, this happening place is the center of artistic life in Walterboro (page 327).

LOOK FOR ◖ TO FIND RECOMMENDED SIGHTS, ACTIVITIES, DINING, AND LODGING.

shadetree mechanics, and men gathered along tidal creeks fishing and crabbing—not for sport but for the family dinner.

Indeed, not so very long ago, before the influx of resort development, retirement subdivisions, and tourism, much of the Lowcountry was like a flatter, more humid Appalachia—poverty-stricken and desperately underserved. While the archetypal South has been marketed in any number of ways to the rest of the world, here you get a sense that this is the real thing—timeless, endlessly alluring, but somehow very familiar.

South of Beaufort is the historically significant Port Royal area and the East Coast Marine Recruit Depot of Parris Island. East of Beaufort is the center of Gullah culture, St. Helena Island, and the scenic and unspoiled gem of Hunting Island.

To the south is the also scenic but entirely developed golf and tennis mecca, Hilton Head Island, and Hilton Head's close neighbor but diametrical opposite in every other way, Daufuskie Island, another important Gullah center. Nestled in between is the charming,

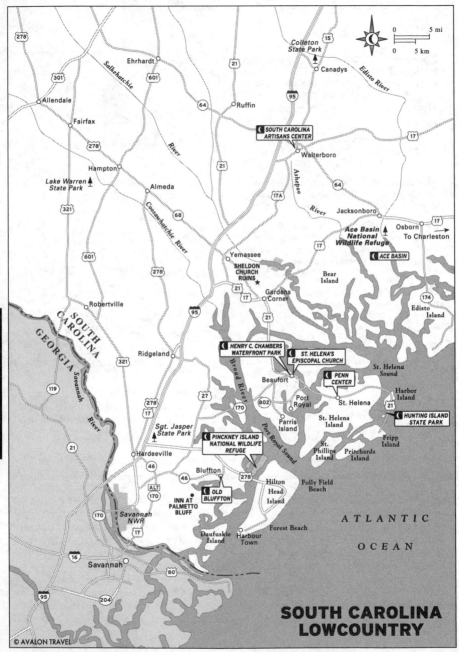

SOUTH CAROLINA
LOWCOUNTRY

© AVALON TRAVEL

close-knit, and gossipy little village of Bluffton on the gossamer May River.

PLANNING YOUR TIME

The small-scale and comparative lack of traffic in most of the Lowcountry are its more charming aspects. Don't let that fool you into thinking you can knock everything out in a day, though. That would defeat the purpose, which is not only to see the sights but to fully enjoy its laidback, slow, and leisurely pace. The common-sense game plan is to use the centrally located Beaufort as a home base. Not only is it easy to get from there to anywhere else in the area, but there's also a preponderance of affordable and charming lodging.

Take at least a half-day of leisure to walk all over Beaufort. There's no need to hurry; just do what the locals do and take everything in its own time. Another full day should go to St. Helena's Penn Center and on to Hunting Island. If you're in the mood for a road trip, dedicate a full day to tour the surrounding area to the north and northeast, with perhaps a jaunt to the ACE Basin National Wildlife Refuge, and a stop at the Old Sheldon Church Ruins in the late afternoon on your way back to Beaufort. If you have extra time, split it between Port Royal and a tour of the historic and military sites of interest on Parris Island.

While the New York accents fly fast and furious on Hilton Head Island, that's no reason for you to rush. Certainly a casual visitor can do Hilton Head in a day but its natural attractions beg for a more considered sort of enjoyment. Plan on at least a half-day just to enjoy the fine, broad beaches alone. I recommend another half-day to tour the island itself, maybe including a stop in Sea Pines for a late lunch or dinner.

While most of the marketing materials make scant mention of it, nature-lovers shouldn't miss the Pinckney Island National Wildlife Refuge, gorgeous enough to be a must-see, but small and convenient enough to fully enjoy in a few hours.

Beaufort

Sandwiched halfway between the prouder, louder cities of Charleston and Savannah, Beaufort is in many ways a more authentic slice of life from the past than either of those two. Long a staple of movie crews seeking to portray some archetypal aspect of the old South *(Prince of Tides, The Great Santini, Forrest Gump)* or just to film beautiful scenery for its own sake *(Jungle Book, Last Dance),* Beaufort—pronounced "Byoofert," by the way, not "Bo-fort"—features many well-preserved examples of Southern architecture, most all of them in idyllic, family-friendly neighborhoods.

The pace in Beaufort is languid, slower even than the waving Spanish moss in the massive old live oak trees. The line between business and pleasure is a blurry one here. As you can tell from the signs you see on storefront doors saying things like "Back in an hour or so," time is an entirely negotiable commodity.

The architecture combines the relaxed Caribbean flavor of Charleston with the Anglophilic dignity of Savannah. In fact, plenty of people prefer the well-kept, highly individualistic old homes of Beaufort, seemingly tailor-made for the exact spot on which they sit, to the historic districts of either Charleston or Savannah in terms of sheer architectural delight.

While you'll run into plenty of charming and gracious locals during your time here, you might be surprised at the amount of transplanted Northerners. That's due not only to the high volume of retirees who've moved to the area, but the active presence of three major U.S. Navy facilities, the Marine Corps Air Station Beaufort, the Marine Corps Recruit Depot on nearby Parris Island, and the Beaufort Naval Hospital. Many's the time a former sailor or Marine has decided to put down roots in the area after being stationed here, the most famous example being author Pat Conroy's father, a.k.a. "The Great Santini."

HISTORY

Though little known to most Americans, the Port Royal Sound area is not only one of the largest natural harbors on the East Coast, it's one of the nation's most historic places. It's a fact made all the more maddening in how little of that history remains.

This was the site of the second landing by the Spanish on the North American continent, the expedition of Captain Pedro de Salazar in 1514. (Ponce de Leon's more famous landing at St. Augustine was but a year earlier.) A Spanish slaver named Francisco Cordillo (sometimes spelled Gordillo) made a brief stop in 1521, long enough to name the area Santa Elena—one of the oldest European place names in America.

Port Royal Sound didn't get its modern name until the first serious attempt at a permanent settlement, Jean Ribault's exploration in 1562. Though ultimately disastrous, Ribault's historic expedition was the first French settlement in America, named Charlesfort. Ribault returned to France for reinforcements to find his country in an all-out religious civil war. He sought safety in England only to be clapped in the Tower of London.

Meanwhile his soldiers at Charlesfort became restive and essentially revolted against their absentee commander, with most moving to a subsequent French settlement, Fort Caroline, near present-day Jacksonville, Florida. In a twist straight out of Hollywood, in 1565 Fort Caroline bought food and a ship to return to France from a passing vessel, which turned out to be commanded by the infamous English privateer John Hawkins. While the French waited for a favorable wind for the trip home, who should arrive but none other than Jean Ribault himself, fresh out of prison and at the head of 600 French soldiers and settlers sent to rescue his colony!

In yet another unlikely development, a Spanish fleet soon appeared, intent on driving

PAT CONROY'S LOWCOUNTRY

I was always your best subject, son. Your career took a nose dive after The Great Santini *came out.*

Colonel Donald Conroy to his son Pat

Though born in Georgia, no other person is as closely associated with the South Carolina Lowcountry as author Pat Conroy. After moving around as a child in a military family, he began high school in Beaufort.

His painful teen years there formed the basis of his first novel, a brutal portrait of his domineering Marine pilot father, Colonel Donald Conroy, a.k.a., Colonel Bull Meecham of *The Great Santini* (1976). Many scenes from the 1979 film adaptation were filmed at the famous "Tidalholm," or Edgar Fripp House (1 Laurens St.) in Beaufort. (The house was also front and center in *The Big Chill.*)

Conroy's pattern of thinly veiled autobiography actually began with his first book, the self-published *The Boo,* a tribute to a teacher at The Citadel in Charleston while Conroy was still a student there.

His second work, *The Water is Wide* (1972), is a chronicle of his experiences teaching in a one-room African American school on Daufuskie Island. Though ostensibly a straightforward, first-person journalistic effort, Conroy changed the location to the fictional Yamacraw Island, supposedly to protect its fragile culture from curious outsiders. The 1974 film adaptation starring Jon Voight was titled *Conrack* after the way his students mispronounced his name. You can visit that same two-room school today on Daufuskie. Known as the Mary Field School, the building is now a local community center.

Conroy also wrote the forward to the cookbook *Gullah Home Cooking the Daufuskie Way: Smokin' Joe Butter Beans, Ol' 'Fuskie Fried Crab Rice, Sticky-Bush Blackberry Dumpling,*

the French out for good. Ribault went on the offensive, intending to mount a preemptive attack on the Spanish base at St. Augustine. However, a storm wrecked the French ships and Ribault was washed ashore near St. Augustine and killed by waiting Spanish troops. As if the whole story couldn't get any stranger, back at Charlesfort things had become so desperate for the 27 original colonists who stayed behind that they decided to build a ship to sail back home to France—technically the first ship built in America for a transatlantic crossing. The vessel made it across the Atlantic, but not without price; running out of food, the French soldiers began eating shoe leather before moving on, so the accounts say, to eating each other. Twenty survivors were rescued in the English Channel.

After the French faded from the scene, Spaniards came to garrison Santa Elena. But steady Indian attacks and Francis Drake's attack on St. Augustine forced the Spanish to abandon the area in 1587. Within the next

generation British indigo planters had established a firm presence in the Port Royal area, chief among them John "Tuscarora Jack" Barnwell of Port Royal Island and Thomas Nairn of St. Helena. These men would go on to found the town of Beaufort, named for Henry Somerset, Duke of Beaufort, and it was chartered in 1711 as part of the original Carolina colony.

In 1776, Beaufort planter Thomas Heyward Jr. signed the Declaration of Independence. After independence was gained, Lowcountry planters turned to cotton as the main cash crop, since England had been their prime customer for indigo. The gambit paid off, and Beaufort soon became one of the wealthiest and highest-regarded towns in the new nation. The so-called "Golden Age" of Sea Island cotton saw storm clouds gather on the horizon as the Lowcountry became the hotbed of secession, with the very first Ordinance of Secession being drawn up in Beaufort's Milton Maxey House. Only seven months after secessionists

and Other Sea Island Favorites, by Daufuskie native and current Savannah resident Sallie Ann Robinson.

Conroy would go on in 1980 to publish The Lords of Discipline, a reading of his real-life experience with the often-savage environment faced by cadets at The Citadel – though Conroy would change the name, calling it the Carolina Military Institute. Still, when it came time to make a film adaptation in 1983, The Citadel refused to allow it to be shot there. So the "Carolina Military Institute" was filmed in England instead!

For many of his fans, Conroy's The Prince of Tides is his ultimate homage to the Lowcountry. Surely, the 1991 film version starring Barbra Streisand and Nick Nolte – shot on location and awash in gorgeous shots of the Beaufort River marsh – did much to implant an idyllic image of the area to audiences around the world. According to local legend, Streisand

originally didn't intend to make the film in Beaufort, but a behind-the-scenes lobbying effort allegedly coordinated by Conroy himself, and including a stay at the Rhett House Inn, convinced her.

The Bay Street Inn (601 Bay St.) in Beaufort was seen in the film, as was the football field at the old Beaufort High School. The beach scenes were shot on nearby Fripp Island. Interestingly, some scenes set in a Manhattan apartment were actually shot within the old Beaufort Arsenal (713 Craven St.), now a museum. Similarly, the Beaufort Naval Hospital doubled as New York's Bellevue.

Despite the many personal tribulations he faced in the area, Conroy has never given up on the Lowcountry and still makes his home there with his family on Fripp Island. As for the "Great Santini" himself, you can visit the final resting place of Colonel Conroy in the Beaufort National Cemetery – Section 62, Grave 182.

fired on Fort Sumter in nearby Charleston in 1861, a huge Union fleet sailed into Port Royal and occupied Hilton Head, Beaufort, and the rest of the Lowcountry for the duration of the war—a relatively uneventful occupation that ensured that many of the classic homes would survive.

Gradually evolving their own distinct dialect and culture, much of it linked to their West African roots, isolated Lowcountry African Americans became known as the Gullah. Evolving from an effort by abolitionist missionaries early in the Civil War, in 1864 the Penn School was formed on St. Helena Island specifically to teach the children of the Gullah communities. Now known as the Penn Center, the facility has been a beacon for the study of this aspect of African American culture ever since.

The 20th century ushered in a time of increased dependence on military spending, with the opening of a training facility on Parris Island

in the 1880s (the Marines didn't begin training recruits there until 1915). The Lowcountry got a further boost from wartime spending in the '40s. Parris Island, already thriving as a Marine hub, was joined by the Marine Corps Naval Air Station in nearby Beaufort in 1942. In 1949, the Naval Hospital opened.

Today, the tourism industry has joined the military as a major economic driver in the Lowcountry. Hollywood discovered its charms as well, in a series of critical and box-office hits like *The Big Chill, The Prince of Tides,* and *Forrest Gump.*

ORIENTATION

Don't be discouraged by the big-box sprawl that assaults you on the approaches to Beaufort on Boundary Street, lined with the usual discount megastores, fast food outlets, and budget motels. This is a popular area for relocation as well as for tourists, and when you add to the

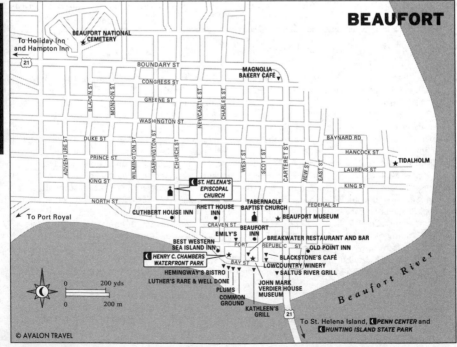

mix the presence of several bustling military facilities, you have a recipe for gridlock and architectural ugliness.

But after you make the big ninety-degree bend where Boundary turns into Carteret Street—known locally as the "Bellamy Curve"—it's like entering a whole new world of slow-paced, Spanish moss–lined avenues, friendly people, gentle breezes, and inviting storefronts. This is the Beaufort Historic District, often called simply the "Old Point" or even more simply, "the Point." Whatever you call it, it's surely one of the most beguiling little towns you'll ever visit.

While you can make your way to downtown by taking Carteret all the way to Bay Street—don't continue over the big bridge unless you want to go straight to Lady's Island and St. Helena Island—I suggest availing yourself of one of the "Downtown Access" signs before you get that far. Because Carteret Street is the only way to that bridge, it can get backed up at rush hour. By taking a quick right and then a left all the way to Bay Street, you can come into town from the other, quieter end, with your first glimpse of downtown proper being

its timelessly beguiling views of the Beaufort River.

Once there, try to park your car slightly outside the town center and simply walk everywhere you want to go. Conversely you can park in the long-term metered spaces at the marina. Unlike Charleston or Savannah, any visitor in reasonably good shape can walk the entire length and breadth of Beaufort's 300-acre downtown with little trouble. In fact, that's by far the best way to experience it.

SIGHTS
◖ Henry C. Chambers Waterfront Park

Before you get busy shopping and dining and admiring Beaufort's fine old homes, go straight to the town's pride and joy since 1980, the Henry C. Chambers Waterfront Park (843/525-7054, www.cityofbeaufort .org, daily 24 hours), stretching for hundreds of feet directly on the Beaufort River. A tastefully designed and user-friendly mix of walkways, bandstands, and patios, Waterfront Park is a favorite gathering place for locals and visitors alike, beckoning one and all with its open

LOWCOUNTRY

© JIM MOREKIS

Henry C. Chambers Waterfront Park on the Beaufort River

greenspace and wonderful marsh-front views. My favorite part is the long row of swinging benches on which to peacefully sit and while away the time looking out over the marsh.

Many of the popular restaurants on Bay Street have back entrances and outdoor seating facing Waterfront Park, but you may opt for a casual picnic. Kids will especially enjoy the park not only because there's so much room to run around, but for the charming playground at the east end near the bridge, complete with a jungle gym in the form of a Victorian home. The clean, well-appointed public restrooms are a particularly welcome feature here.

John Mark Verdier House Museum

A smallish but stately Federalist building on the busiest downtown corner, the Verdier House Museum (801 Bay St., 843/379-6335, www.historicbeaufort.org, Mon.–Sat. 11 A.M.–4 P.M., $6 adults, $4 students) is the only historic Beaufort home open to regular tours. Built in 1805 for the wealthy planter John Mark Verdier, its main claim to fame was acting as the Union headquarters during the long occupation of Beaufort during the Civil War.

However, perhaps its most intriguing link to history—a link it shares with Savannah's Owens-Thomas House—is its connection to the Revolutionary War hero the Marquis de Lafayette, who stayed at the Verdier House on the Beaufort leg of his 1825 U.S. tour. Despite the late hour of his arrival, a crowd gathered at the corner of Bay and Scott Streets, and Lafayette finally had to come to the entranceway to satisfy their desire for a speech.

When the Verdier House was faced with demolition in the 1940s, the Historic Beaufort Foundation purchased the house and renovated it to its current state, reflective of the early 1800s.

Beaufort Museum

Housed in the imposing yellow-gray tabby facade of the historic 1852 Beaufort Arsenal, the Beaufort Museum (713 Craven St., 843/379-3331, www.historicbeaufort.org,

Mon.–Sat. 11 A.M.–4 P.M., $3) capably tells the story of Beaufort from its early plantation days, through its key role in the secession movement, to the modern era. I suggest purchasing the discounted combo ticket to the Beaufort Museum and the Verdier House Museum ($8 adults, $4 students).

❰ St. Helena's Episcopal Church

Nestled within the confines of a low brick wall surrounding this historic church and cemetery, St. Helena's Episcopal Church (505 Church St., 843/522-1712, Tues.–Fri. 10 A.M.–4 P.M., Sat. 10 A.M.–1 P.M.) has witnessed some of Beaufort's most compelling tales. Built in 1724, this was the parish church of Thomas Heyward, one of South Carolina's signers of the Declaration of Independence. John "Tuscarora Jack" Barnwell, early Indian fighter and one of Beaufort's founders, is buried on the grounds.

The balcony upstairs in the sanctuary was intended for black parishioners; as was typical

St. Helena's Episcopal Church

© JIM MOREKIS

throughout the region before the Civil War, both races attended the same church services. After the entire congregation fled with the Union occupation, Federal troops decked over the second floor and used St. Helena's as a hospital—with surgeons using tombstones as operating tables. The wooden altar was carved by the crew of the USS *New Hampshire* while the warship was docked in the harbor during Reconstruction.

While the cemetery and sanctuary interior are likely to be your focus, take a close look at the church exterior—many of the bricks are actually ship ballastones. Also be aware that you're not looking at the church's original footprint; the building has been expanded several times since its construction (a hurricane in 1896 destroyed the entire cast end). A nearly $3 million restoration, mostly for structural repairs, was completed in 2000.

Tabernacle Baptist Church

Built in 1845, this handsome sanctuary (911 Craven St., 843/524-0376) had a congregation of over 3,000 before the Civil War. Slaves made up most of the congregation, though the vast majority of slaves generally worshipped separately on plantation ground. During the war, freed slaves purchased the church for their own use. A congregant was the war hero Robert Smalls, who kidnapped the Confederate steamer he was forced to serve on and delivered it to Union forces. He is buried in the church cemetery and has a nice memorial dedicated to him there, proudly facing the street.

Beaufort National Cemetery

It's not as poignantly ornate as Savannah's Victorian cemeteries, but Beaufort National Cemetery (1601 Boundary St., daily 8 A.M.–sunset) is worth a stop, as you enter or leave Beaufort, for its history. Begun by order of Abraham Lincoln in 1863, this is one of the few cemeteries containing the graves of both Union and Confederate troops, mostly the former. National Cemetery is where 19 soldiers of the all-black Massachusetts 54th and 55th Infantry were re-interred with full military

sculpture of Robert Smalls at the Tabernacle Baptist Church

© JIM MOREKIS

honors after being found on Folly Island near Charleston.

Sergeant Joseph Simmons, "Buffalo Soldier" and veteran of both World Wars, is buried here, as is none other than the "Great Santini" himself, novelist Pat Conroy's father, Donald.

Tours

Colorful character Jon Sharp runs the popular **Jon Sharp's Walking History Tour** (843/575-5775, www.jonswalkinghistory.com, Tues.–Sat. 11 A.M., Sun. 1 P.M., $20), taking a break during the summer months. The two-hour jaunt begins and ends at the Downtown Marina and takes you all through the downtown area.

The Spirit of Old Beaufort (103 West St. Extension, 843/525-0459, www.thespiritof oldbeaufort.com, Mon.–Sat. 10:30 A.M., 2 P.M., and 7 P.M., $13 adults, $8 children) runs a series of good, year-round walking tours, roughly two hours long, with guides usually in period dress. If you don't want to walk, you can hire one of their guides to join you in your own vehicle for a $50 minimum.

A WALKING TOUR OF BEAUFORT HOMES

One of the unique aspects of the Lowcountry is the large amount of historical homes in totally private hands. When buyers purchase one of these fine old homes, they generally know what's in store: a historical marker of some sort will be nearby, organized tours will periodically swing by their home, and production companies will sometimes approach them about using the home as a film set. It's a trade-off most homeowners are only too glad to accept.

Here's a walking tour of some of Beaufort's fine historic homes in private hands. You won't be taking any tours of the interior, but these homes are part of the legacy of the area and are locally valued as such. Be sure to respect the privacy of the inhabitants by keeping the noise level down and not trespassing on private property to take photos.

- **Thomas Fuller House:** Begin at the corner of Harrington and Bay, and view this 1796 home (1211 Bay St.), one of the oldest in existence in Beaufort and even more unique in that much of the building material is tabby (hence the home's other name, the Tabby Manse).

- **Milton Maxcy House:** Walk east on Bay Street one block and take a left on Church Street; walk up to the corner of Church and Craven Streets. Otherwise known as the Secession House (113 Craven St.), this 1813 home was built on a tabby foundation dating from 1743. In 1860, when it was the residence of attorney Edmund Rhett, the very first Ordinance of Secession was signed here and the rest, as they say, was history.

- **Lewis Reeve Sams House:** Pick up the walking tour on the other side of the historic district, at the foot of the bridge. This gorgeous house (602 Bay St.) at the corner of

Bay and New Streets, with its double-decker veranda, dates from 1852 and served as a Union hospital during the Civil War.

- **Berners Barnwell Sams House:** Continue up New Street where you'll find this 1818 home (310 New St.), which served as the African American hospital during the Union occupation. Harriet Tubman of Underground Railroad fame worked here for a time as a nurse.

- **Joseph Johnson House:** Continue up New Street and take a right on Craven Street. Cross East Street to find this 1850 home, nicknamed "The Castle" (411 Craven St.), with the massive live oak in the front yard. Legend has it that when the Yankees occupied Hilton Head, Mr. Johnson buried his valuables under an outhouse. After the war he returned to find his home for sale due to unpaid back taxes. He dug up his valuables, paid the taxes, and resumed living in the home. You might recognize the home from the film *Forces of Nature*.

- **Marshlands:** Backtrack to East Street and walk north to Federal Street. Then take a right and go to the end of the street. Built by James R. Verdier, Marshlands (501 Pinckney St.) was used as hospital during the Civil War, as many Beaufort homes were, and is now a National Historic Landmark. It was the setting of Francis Griswold's 1931 novel *A Sea Island Lady*.

- **The Oaks:** Walk up to King Street, take a right, and go to the corner of King and Short Streets. The Oaks (100 Laurens St.) at this intersection was owned by the Hamilton family, who lost a son who served with General Wade Hampton's cavalry in the Civil War. After the conflict, the family couldn't afford the back taxes, and neighbors paid the debts and returned the deed to the Hamiltons.

- **Edgar Fripp House:** Walk east on Laurens toward the water to find this handsome Lowcountry mansion, sometimes called Tidalholm (1 Laurens St.). Built in 1856 by the wealthy planter for whom nearby Fripp Island is named, this house was a key setting in *The Big Chill* and *The Great Santini*.

- **Francis Hext House:** Go back to Short Street, walk north to Hancock Street and take a left. This palatial estate, known as Riverview (207 Hancock St.), is one of the oldest structures in Beaufort; it was built in 1720.

- **Robert Smalls House:** Continue west on Hancock Street, take a short left on East Street, and a quick right on Prince Street. This 1834 home (511 Prince St.) was the birthplace of Robert Smalls, a former slave and Beaufort native who stole the Confederate ship *Planter* from Charleston Harbor while serving as its helmsman and delivered it to Union troops in Hilton Head. Smalls and a few compatriots commandeered the ship while the officers were at a party at Fort Sumter, taking it right past Confederate pickets. Smalls used the bounty he received for the act of bravery to buy his boyhood home for his own. After the war, Smalls was a longtime U.S. congressman.

© JIM MOREKIS

Lewis Reeve Sams House

LOWCOUNTRY

As you might expect, few things could be more Lowcountry than an easy-going carriage ride through the historic neighborhoods. **Southurn Rose Buggy Tours** (843/524-2900, www.southurnrose.com, 10 A.M.–5 P.M., $18 adults, $7 children)—yes, that's how they spell it—offers 50-minute narrated carriage rides of the entire Old Point, including movie locations, embarking and disembarking near the Downtown Marina. Another similarly priced carriage operator is **Carolina Buggy Tours** (901 Port Republic St., 843/525-1300).

An important specialty bus tour in the area is **Gullah-N-Geechie Man Tours** (843/838-7516, www.gullahngeechietours.net, $20 adults, $18 children), focusing on the rich Gullah history and culture of the St. Helena Island area, including the historic Penn Center. Call for pickup information.

ENTERTAINMENT AND EVENTS
Nightlife
Those looking for a rowdy time will be happier seeking it in the notorious party towns of Charleston or Savannah. However, a few notable places in downtown Beaufort do double duty as dining havens and neighborhood watering holes.

Sadly, the well-regarded restaurant within the Beaufort Inn on Port Republic Street closed for good in 2007. But several establishments tucked together on Bay Street, all with café seating out back facing the waterfront, can also show you a good time.

A charming little bar is **Hemingway's Bistro** (920 Bay St., 843/521-4480, daily 11 A.M.–2 A.M.), which is a great place to relax over a cocktail. There's live music on the weekend. The convivial **Kathleen's Grill** (822 Bay St., 843/524-2500, daily 11 A.M.–2 A.M.) features live music by a variety of regional artists. Weekend tunes crank up about 10 P.M.

Plum's (904 1/2 Bay St., 843/525-1946, daily 5 P.M.–2 A.M.) offers not only a tasty menu but some fun at 10 P.M. when the kitchen closes down and the focus turns to its great beer selection. Close by is **Luther's Rare & Well Done** (910 Bay St., 843/521-1888, 5 P.M.–midnight. $15),

which offers a late-night appetizer menu to go with its rock-oriented live music on weekends.

Performing Arts
Beaufort's fine arts scene is small but professional in outlook. Most performances are based in the nice new Performing Arts Center on the oak-lined campus of the University of South Carolina Beaufort (801 Carteret St., 843/521-4100).

A prime mover of the local performing arts scene is **Beaufort Performing Arts, Inc.** (www.uscb.edu), formed by a mayoral task force in 2003 specifically to encourage arts and cultural development within the area. The most recent season, with performances at USCB's Performing Arts Center, included performances by famed Celtic fiddler Natalie MacMaster, the Claremont Trio, and the Bee Gees. Ticket prices typically range $12–40.

Perhaps surprisingly for such a small place, Beaufort boasts its own full orchestra, the **Beaufort Orchestra** (1106 Carteret Street, 843/986-5400, www.beaufortorchestra.org), which plays in the Performing Arts Center. A recent season included Paganini's Violin Concerto in D, Tchaikovsky's "Pathetique" Symphony No. 6, and "Beaufort Goes to Broadway."

The closest place for quality live theatre is Hilton Head; however, just across the bridge from Beaufort on Lady's Island is the **Sea Island Dinner Theatre** in the little Sea Island Conference Center (178 Sam's Point Rd., 843/522-3924, www.seaislandconference center.com).

Cinema
One of only two functional drive-ins in the state, the **Highway 21 Drive In** (55 Parker Dr., 843/846-4500, www.hwy21drivein.com) has two screens, great sound, and awesome concessions including Angus beef hamburgers. All you need to provide is the car and the company. The best multiplex in the area is the cool **Sea Turtle Cinemas** (106 Buckwalter Pkwy., 843/706-2888, www.seaturtlecinemas.com) in the Berkeley Place shopping center.

Festivals and Events

Surprisingly for a town so prominent in so many films, Beaufort didn't have its own film festival until 2007. The **Beaufort Film Festival** (843/986-5400, www.beaufortfilm festival.com) is held in late winter. It's small in scale—the inaugural festival was only two days, at a now-defunct theater—but boasts a diverse range of high-quality, cutting-edge entries, including shorts and animation.

Technically the film festival is part of a larger event, **Kaleidoscope: Film, Food, and Fine Arts** (843/986-5400, www.beaufortkaleido scope.com), a celebration of Lowcountry culture in various venues around town. Highlights include an "arts walk" (basically a town-wide art gallery open house), an "Iron Chef Beaufort" chef competition, and Friday night wine dinners wherein some leading Southern chefs take over the kitchen at a number of local restaurants.

Foodies will also enjoy **A Taste of Beaufort** (www.downtownbeaufort.com), usually held the first Saturday in May, which features the offerings of two dozen or so local restaurants with live music, all along historic Bay Street.

Now over 20 years old, the **Gullah Festival of South Carolina** celebrates Gullah history and culture on Memorial Day weekend at various locations throughout town, mostly focusing on Waterfront Park.

By far the biggest single event on the local festival calendar is the over 50-year-old **Beaufort Water Festival** (www.bftwaterfestival .com), held over two weeks in June or July each year, centering on the Waterfront Park area. One of the most eclectic and idiosyncratic events of its kind in a region already known for quirky, hyper-local festivals, the Beaufort Water Festival features events as diverse as a raft race, badminton, bocce, billiards, croquet and golf tournaments, a children's toad fishing tournament, a ski show, a bed race, a street dance, and all sorts of live music and local art exhibits. The signature events are two galas, the Commodore's Ball and the Regatta Ball, and the Saturday morning two-hour Grand Parade, historically organized by the local Lions Club. A delightfully regional touch completes

the festival, with a blessing and parade of the shrimp fleet on the closing Sunday.

Fall in the Lowcountry means shrimping season, and early October brings the **Beaufort Shrimp Festival** (www.beaufortsc.org). Highlights include an evening concert with specially lighted shrimpboats docked along the river, a 5K run over the Woods Memorial Bridge, and a more laid-back 5K walk through the historic district. Various cooking competitions are held, obviously centering around the versatile crustaceans that are the *raison d' tre* of the shrimp fleet.

October also brings a relatively new event, the **Chalk on the Walk** (www.beaufortcounty arts.com). Based on European street festivals—and similar to Savannah's Sidewalk Arts Festival—Chalk on the Walk features a delightful blend of street painting and performing, live music, and an art market.

St. Helena Island hosts the three-day **Penn Center Heritage Days** (www.penncenter.com) each November, without a doubt the Beaufort area's second-biggest celebration after the Water Festival. Focusing on Gullah culture, history, and delicious food, Heritage Days does a great job of combining fun with education. The event culminates in a colorful Saturday morning parade, featuring lots of traditional Gullah garb, from St. Helena Elementary School to the Penn Center Historic District.

SHOPPING

The Beaufort area's shopping allure comes from the rich variety of independently owned shops, most of which keep a pretty high standard and don't deal too much in touristy schlock. As you might expect, the main drag in town, Bay Street, is also the shopping hub. Note that in Beaufort's shops as well as most everything else in town, hours of operation are loose guidelines and not rigidly observed.

My favorite shop in Beaufort is **The Bay Street Trading Company** (808 Bay St., 843/524-2000, www.baystreettrading .com, Mon.–Fri. 10 A.M.–5:30 P.M., Sat. 10 A.M.–5 P.M., Sun. noon–5 P.M.), sometimes known simply as "The Book Shop," which has a very friendly staff and the best collection of

LOWCOUNTRY

Lowcountry-themed books I've seen in one place.

Across the street, the recently renovated, so-bright-red-you-can't-miss-it Old Bay Marketplace houses a few very cute shops, most notably the **McIntosh Book Shoppe** (917 Bay St., 843/524-1119, Mon.–Sat. noon–5 P.M., Sun. 1–5 P.M.). Also in the Marketplace is the stylish **Lulu Burgess** (917 Bay St., 843/524-5858, Mon.–Sat. 10 A.M.–6 P.M., Sun. noon–5 P.M.), an eclectic store that brings a rich, quirky sense of humor to its otherwise tasteful assortment of gift items for the whole family.

A unique gift item, as well as something you can enjoy on your own travels, can be found at **Lowcountry Winery** (705 Bay St., 843/379-3010, Mon.–Sat. 10 A.M.–5 P.M.). Not only can you purchase bottles of their various red and white offerings, they host tastings daily in their tasting room (because of state law they must charge a fee for the tasting, but it's only a buck per person).

One of the more unusual shops in town is **Cravings by the Bay** (928 Bay St., 843/522-3000, Mon.–Sat. 10 A.M.–5 P.M., Sun. noon–4 P.M.), primarily known for its collection of gift baskets incorporating regional gourmet goodies like She-Crab Soup, Praline Mustard Glaze, and Benne Wafers, any of which you can purchase separately, of course.

Art Galleries

As you'd expect in such a visually stirring locale, there's a plethora of great art galleries in the Beaufort-St. Helena area. While most are clustered on Bay Street, there are gems scattered all over. Almost all are worth a look, but here are a few highlights.

My favorite gallery in town is the simply named **The Gallery** (802 Bay St., 843/470-9994, www.thegallery-beaufort.com, Mon.–Sat. 11 A.M.–5 P.M.). Deanna Bowdish brings in the most cutting-edge regional contemporary artists in a large, friendly, loft-like space.

The **Beaufort Art Association Gallery** (1001 Bay St., 843/379-2222, www.beaufort artassociation.com, Mon.–Sat. 10 A.M.–5 P.M.) hosts rotating exhibits by member artists in the stately and historic Elliott House.

Lovers of the Lowcountry will enjoy the aesthetic at the two-floor **Rhett Gallery** (901 Bay St., 843/524-3339, www.rhettgallery.com, Mon.–Sat. 9 A.M.–5:30 P.M., Sun. variable hours). Owner Nancy Rhett submitted one of the designs for the state's Friends of Hunting Island license plate. Close by in the Old Bay Marketplace is **Art and Soul** (917 Bay St., 843/379-9710, Mon.–Sat. 10 A.M.–5:30 P.M.), featuring over 50 regional artists.

A complete art experience blending the traditional with the cutting-edge is at the **I. Pinckney Simons Art Gallery** (711 Bay St., 843/379-4774, www.ipinckneysimonsgallery.com, Tues.–Fri. 11 A.M.–5 P.M., Sat. 11 A.M.–3 P.M.), which is pronounced "Simmons" despite the spelling. There you will find not only paintings, but compelling photography, sculpture, and jewelry as well, all by local and regional artists of renown.

There aren't many local artists featured at **Four Winds Gallery** (709 Bay St., 843/379-5660, www.fourwindstraders.com, Mon.–Wed. and Sat. 10:30 A.M.–5:30 P.M., Thurs. 10:30 A.M.–7 P.M., Sun. 11 A.M.–4 P.M.), but it's a great place to find religious folk art from around the world, from wooden African tribal votives to Orthodox icons from Greece.

A few blocks from Bay Street is a fun local favorite, the **Longo Gallery** (103 Charles St., 843/522-8933, Mon.–Sat. 11 A.M.–5 P.M.). Friendly owners Suzanne and Eric Longo provide a whimsical assortment of less traditional art than you might find in the more touristy waterfront area. Take Charles Street as it works its way toward the waterfront, and the gallery is right behind a storefront on the corner of Charles and Bay Streets.

You'll find perhaps the area's best-known gallery over the bridge on St. Helena Island. Known regionally as one of the best places to find Gullah folk art, **Red Piano Too** (870 Sea Island Parkway, 843/838-2241, www.redpiano too.com, Mon.–Sat. 10 A.M.–5 P.M.) is on the corner before you turn onto the road to the historic Penn Center. Over 150 artists from a diverse range of traditions and styles are represented in this charming little 1940 building with the red tin awning, historically significant

in its own right because it once hosted a produce cooperative that was the first store in the
area to pay African Americans with cash rather
than barter for goods.

SPORTS AND RECREATION

Beaufort County comprises over 60 islands, so
it's no surprise that nearly all recreation in the
area revolves around the water, which dominates so many aspects of life in the Lowcountry.
The closer to the ocean you get, the more it's
a salt marsh environment. But as you explore
more inland, in the sprawling ACE Basin,
you'll encounter primarily blackwater.

Kayaking

The Lowcountry is tailor-made for kayaking.
An option in downtown Beaufort is to put in
at the public ramp at the **Downtown Marina**
(1006 Bay St., 843/524-4422) and paddle along
the peaceful Intracoastal Waterway, either north
up the Beaufort River or south into the Sound.

A 10-minute drive away from Beaufort in little Port Royal is **The Sands** public boat ramp
into Battery Creek. You can also put in at the
ramp at the **Lady's Island Marina** (73 Sea
Island Pkwy., 843/522-0430) just across the
bridge from Beaufort. A good compendium of
Beaufort-area landings is at www.beaufortusa
.com/marinas.htm.

The catch here, as with all the Lowcountry,
is to know your way around if you choose to
leave the main waterways. It's easy to get lost
because of the sheer number of creeks, and they
all seem to look the same once you get into them
a good ways. If you don't feel comfortable with
your navigation skills, it's a good idea to contact Kim and David at **Beaufort Kayak Tours**
(843/525-0810, www.beaufortkayaktours.com),
who rent kayaks and can guide you on a number of excellent tours of all three key areas. They
charge about $40 for adults, $30 for children for
a two-hour trip. A tour with Beaufort Kayak
Tours is also the best (and nearly the only) way
to access the historically significant ruins of the
early British tabby Fort Frederick, now located
on the grounds of the Beaufort Naval Hospital
and inaccessible by car.

Hunting Island State Park (2555 Sea
Island Pkwy., 866/345-7275, www.hunting
island.com, daily 6 A.M.–6 P.M., until 9 P.M.
DST, $4 adults, $1.50 children) has a wonderful inlet that is very popular with kayakers.

North and northeast of Beaufort lies the
ACE Basin region, with about two dozen public ramps indicated by brown signs. Comprising
hundreds of miles of creeks and tributaries in
addition to its three eponymous rivers, the ACE
Basin also features a fun paddling bonus: canals
from the old rice plantations. A good service for
rental and knowledgeable guided tours of the
Basin is **Outpost Moe's** (843/844-2514, www
.geocities.com/outpostmoe), where the basic
2.5-hour tour costs $40 per person, and an
all-day extravaganza through the Basin is $80.
Moe's provides lunch for most of its tours.

Another premier local outfitter for ACE Basin
tours is **Carolina Heritage Outfitters** (Hwy.
15 in Canadys, 843/563-5051, www.canoe
sc.com), who focus on the Edisto River trail. In
addition to guided tours and rentals, you can
camp overnight in their cute treehouses along
the kayak routes ($125). They load you up with
your gear and drive you 22 miles upriver, then
you paddle downriver to the treehouse for the
evening. The next day you paddle yourself the
rest of the way downriver back to home base.

To have a more dry experience of the ACE
Basin from the deck of a larger vessel, try
ACE Basin Tours (One Coosaw River Dr.,
843/521-3099, www.acebasintours.com, Wed.
and Sat. 10 A.M. Mar.–Nov., $35 adults, $15
children), which will take you on a three-hour
tour in the 40-passenger *Dixie Lady*. To get to
their dock, take Carteret Street over the bridge
to St. Helena Island and then take a left on
Highway 802 east (Sam's Point Rd.). Continue
until you cross Lucy Point Creek, and the ACE
Basin Tours marina is on your immediate left
after you cross the bridge.

If you prefer self-guided paddling, keep in
mind that you can spend a lifetime learning
your way around the ACE Basin. But the state
of South Carolina has conveniently gathered
some of the best self-guided kayak trips at
www.acebasin.net/canoe.html.

LOWCOUNTRY

Fishing and Boating

Key public marinas in the area are the Downtown Marina in Beaufort, the **Lady's Island Marina** (73 Sea Island Pkwy., 843/522-0430), and the **Port Royal Landing Marina** (843/525-6664). Hunting Island has a popular thousand-foot fishing pier at the south end. A good local fishing charter service is Captain Josh Utsey's **Lowcountry Guide Service** (843/812-4919, www.beaufort scfishing.com). Captain Ed Hardee (843/441-6880) offers good inshore charters.

The ACE Basin is a very popular fishing, crabbing, and shrimping area. It has about two dozen public boat ramps, with colorful names like Cuckold's Creek and Steamboat Landing. There's a useful map of them all at www.ace basin.net, or look for the brown signs along the highway.

Hiking and Biking

Despite the Lowcountry's, well, lowness, biking opportunities abound. It might not get your heart rate up like a ride in the Rockies, but the area lends itself to laid-back two-wheeled enjoyment.

Many local B&Bs provide bikes free for guests, and you can rent your own just across the river from Beaufort in Lady's Island at **Lowcountry Bikes** (102 Sea Island Pkwy., 843/524-9585, Mon.–Tues. and Thurs.–Fri. 10 A.M.–6 P.M., Wed. 10 A.M.–1 P.M., Sat. 10 A.M.–3 P.M., about $5/hr). They can also hook you up with some good routes around the area.

Bicycling around Beaufort is a delight for its relative paucity of traffic as well as its picturesque beauty. Port Royal is close enough that you can easily make a circuit to that evenless trafficked little town. To get to Port Royal from Beaufort, take Bay Street west to Ribault Road (U.S. 21) and veer left onto Paris Avenue into downtown Port Royal, where the biking is easy, breezy, and fun.

For a visually delightful ride, the bridge over the Beaufort River also features a pedestrian/bike lane with some awesome views. You can either turn back at the base of the bridge and go back into Beaufort or push on to Lady's Island and St. Helena Island, though the traffic on U.S. 21 can get daunting.

An interesting, if long (about 20 miles round-trip) bike route on St. Helena Island begins at St. Helena Elementary School on U.S. 21. From there you take Land's End Road past the Penn Center, all the way to—you guessed it—land's end, whereupon you circle back on Seaside Road. Cut back to Land's End Road and the school via Club Bridge Road.

Some good, if marshy, hiking is at the large **Bear Island Wildlife Management Area** (843/844-8957, www.dnr.sc.gov, Mon.–Sat. dawn–dusk Feb.–Oct.). To get there, take U.S. 21 north out of Beaufort to U.S. 17 north. Take a right on Bennett's Point Road and continue south about 13 miles. The entrance is about a mile on your left after crossing the Ashepoo River.

Bird-Watching

Because of its abundance of both saltwater and freshwater environments and its relatively low human density, the Lowcountry offers a stunning glimpse into the diversity and majesty of the Southeast's bird population, both regional and migratory.

Serious birders swear by **Hunting Island State Park** (2555 Sea Island Pkwy., 866/345-7275, www.huntingisland.com, daily 6 A.M.–6 P.M., until 9 P.M. DST, $4 adults, $1.50 children), which thanks to its undeveloped state and its spot on key migratory routes makes it a great place to see brown pelicans, loons, herons, falcons, plovers, and egrets of all types. Park naturalists conduct frequent guided walks.

The tall observation tower at Port Royal's The Sands, where Battery Creek joins the Beaufort River, is a convenient vantage point from which to see any number of local bird species. The big, wild **ACE Basin** (8675 Willtown Rd., 843/889-3084, www.fws.gov/acebasin, grounds year-round daylight–dark, office Mon.–Fri. 7:30 A.M.–4 P.M.) hosts at least 19 species of waterfowl and 13 species of wading birds. At the northeast corner of the ACE Basin is the **Bear Island Wildlife Management Area** (843/844-8957, www.dnr.sc.gov, Mon.–Sat. dawn–dusk Feb.–Oct.), considered one of the best birding spots in South Carolina. To get there, take U.S. 21 north out of Beaufort to U.S. 17 north. Take a right on Bennett's Point Road and continue south about 13 miles. The entrance is about a mile on your left after crossing the Ashepoo River.

Golf

Golf is bigger in Hilton Head than in Beaufort, but here are some local highlights. The best-regarded public course in the area, and indeed one of the best military courses in the world, is **Legends at Parris Island** (Building 299, Parris Island, 843/228-2240, www.mccssc .com, $30). You need to call in advance for a tee time before you can come on Parris Island to golf.

Another popular public course is **South Carolina National Golf Club** (8 Waveland Ave., Cat Island, 843/524-0300, www.sc national.com, $70). Get to secluded Cat Island

by taking the Sea Island Parkway onto Lady's Island and taking it south as it turns into Lady's Island Drive. Take Island Causeway and continue.

ACCOMMODATIONS

Beaufort's historic district is blessed with an abundance of high-quality accommodations that blend well with their surroundings. There are plenty of budget-minded chain places, some of them acceptable, in the sprawl of Boundary Street outside of downtown, but here are some suggestions within bicycle distance of the Point. (That's not a hypothetical, as most inns offer free bicycles to use as you please during your stay.)

Under $150

The aptly named **Old Point Inn** (212 New St., 843/524-3177, www.oldpointinn.com, $115–175) is not only a great value, but also the only historic inn in Beaufort with full views of the river and marsh. Tucked between the historic Lewis Reeve Sams House and the

© JIM MOREKIS

Old Point Inn

circa-1717 Thomas Hepworth House, the oldest building in town, the Old Point Inn combines Southern style with a delightful lack of pretension. There's a hammock on the upstairs veranda and a small garden patio. Owners Paul and Julie Michau have furnished each themed suite with their own eclectic collection of international furniture and *objets d'art*.

The **Best Western Sea Island Inn** (1015 Bay St., 843/522-2090, www.bestwestern.com, $135–170) is a good value for those for whom the B&B experience is not paramount. Anchoring the southern end of the historic district in a low, tasteful brick building, the Best Western offers decent service, basic amenities, and surprisingly attractive rates for the location on Beaufort's busiest street.

$150-300

Any list of upscale Beaufort lodging must highlight the **(€ Beaufort Inn** (809 Port Republic St., 843/379-4667, www.beaufortinn.com, $152–425), consistently voted one of the best B&Bs in the nation. It's sort of a hybrid in that it comprises not only the 1897 historic central home, but a cluster of freestanding historical cottages, each with a charming little porch and rocking chairs. With everything connected by gardens and pathways, you could almost call it a campus. Still, for its sprawling nature-44 rooms in total—the Beaufort Inn experience is intimate, with attentive service and top-flight amenities such as wet bars, large baths, and sumptuous king beds. Within or without the main building, each suite has a character all its own, whether it's the 1,500-square-foot Loft Apartment (complete with guest bedroom and full kitchen) or one of the cozier (and more affordable) Choice Rooms with a queen-sized bed.

The 18-room, circa 1820 **Rhett House Inn** (1009 Craven St., 843/524-9030, www.rhetthouseinn.com, $175–320) is the local vacation getaway for the stars. Such arts and entertainment luminaries as Robert Redford, Julia Roberts, Ben Affleck, Barbra Streisand, Dennis Quaid, and Demi Moore have all stayed here at one time or another. Owner Steve Harrison is also a local realtor and no doubt has helped

many a guest relocate to town after they've fallen in love with it while staying at his inn. As if Beaufort's great restaurants weren't caloric enough, you can put on a few pounds just staying at the Rhett House. Of course you get the requisite full Southern breakfast, but you'll also be treated to afternoon tea and pastries, more munchies at cocktail hour, and homemade late-night desserts.

There's nothing like enjoying the view of the Beaufort River from the expansive porches of the **(€ Cuthbert House Inn** (1203 Bay St., 843/521-1315, www.cuthberthouseinn.com, $205–250), possibly the most romantic place to stay in Beaufort. This grand old circa-1790 Federal mansion was once the home of the wealthy Cuthbert family of rice and indigo planters and is now on the National Register of Historic Places. General Sherman himself spent a night here in 1865. Some of the king rooms have fireplaces and clawfoot tubs. Of course you get a full Southern breakfast, in addition to sunset *hors d'oeuvres* on the veranda.

Situated in a restored 1890 farmhouse smack in the heart of Port Royal's little downtown, the **Beaulieu Guest House at Port Royal** (1103 Paris Ave., Port Royal, 843/770-0303, www.beaulieuhouse.com, $155–225) has three suites to choose from. They claim to have the oldest live oaks in Port Royal on the grounds, which are right next to the historic Union Church.

Camping

Hunting Island State Park (2555 Sea Island Pkwy., 866/345-7275, www.huntingisland.com, daily 6 A.M.–6 P.M., until 9 P.M. DST, $4 adults, $1.50 children, $25 campsites, $87–172 cabins) has 200 campsites on the north end of the island, with individual water and electric hookups. Most are available by reservation only, but 20 are available on a first-come, first-served basis.

On the south end the park has 15 two- or three-bedroom cabins for rent, fully heated and air-conditioned and equipped with TVs and kitchens. The cabins sometimes fill up a full year in advance, so book as early as you can. There's a one-week minimum stay during the high season (Mar.–Nov.) and a two-night minimum at other times. Also be aware that checkout time at the cabins is a chipper 10 A.M., which is strictly enforced.

Another neat place to camp is **Tuck in De Wood** (22 Tuc In De Wood Lane, St. Helena, 843/838-2267, $25), a 74-site campground just past the Penn Center on St. Helena Island.

FOOD
Breakfast and Brunch
One of the best breakfasts I've had anywhere in the world was a humble two-egg plate for five bucks at Beaufort's most popular morning hangout, **Blackstone's Café** (205 Scott St., 843/524-4330, Mon.–Sat. 7:30 A.M.–2:30 P.M., Sun. 7:30 am.–2 P.M., under $10), complete with tasty hash browns, a comparative rarity in this part of the country where grits rule as the breakfast starch of choice. Many come from miles around just for Blackstone's large-portion shrimp and grits entrée and "shrimpburger" specials.

Tucked on a side street just off busy Bay Street, Blackstone's roomy but inviting interior—festooned with various collegiate, nautical, and military motifs and a checkerboard floor—has more than enough room for you to spread out and relax before continuing on with your travels (there's even free Wi-Fi). The friendly, chipper waitstaff are on a first-name basis with the many regulars, but don't worry—in true Lowcountry fashion, they'll treat you like a regular, too.

Coffeehouses
The charming and popular **Common Ground** (102 West St., 843/524-2326, daily 7:30 A.M.–10 P.M.) coffeehouse in the Waterfront Park area is not only a great place for a light sandwich or sweet treat: the java is a cut above most such places, featuring a wide selection of excellent fair trade "Dancing Goat" brews.

Burgers and Sandwiches
Another longtime lunch favorite is **Magnolia Bakery Café** (703 Congress St., 843/524-1961, Mon.–Sat. 9 A.M.–5 P.M., under $10). It's a little ways north of the usual tourist area, but well worth going out of your way for (Beaufort's pretty small, after all). Lump crab cakes are a particular specialty item, but you can't go wrong with any of the lunch sandwiches. They even offer a serviceable crepe. Veggie diners are particularly well taken care of with a large selection of black bean burger plates. As the name indicates, the range of desserts here is tantalizing, to say the least, with the added bonus of a serious espresso bar.

Seafood
Comfort food mecca **Kathleen's Grill** (822 Bay St., 843/524-2500, daily 11 A.M.–10 P.M., breakfast Sat.–Sun. 7–11 A.M., $7–20) is a longtime favorite of locals and tourists alike. Like most places on Bay Street, indoor dining as well as outdoor dining overlooking the water is available. Start with fried green tomatoes or peel-and-eat shrimp, then move on to one of the house specialties, a grouper or oyster sandwich piled high. Pricier seafood and steak entrées are also available, including a great softshell crab plate. Kathleen's is also a nightlife hub, with live music almost every night of the week starting up around 8 P.M. or so, later on Friday and Saturday nights.

The hottest table in town these days is at the **Saltus River Grill** (802 Bay St., 843/379-3474, Sun.–Thurs. 5–9 P.M., Fri.–Sat. 5–10 P.M., $10–39). Executive Chef Jim Spratling has made this fairly new restaurant, housed in a historic tabby building on the waterfront, famous throughout the state for its unbelievable raw bar menu featuring oysters from Nova Scotia to the Chesapeake Bay to Oregon and British Columbia. Sushi lovers can also get a fix here as well, whether it's a basic California roll or great sashimi. Other specialties include she-crab bisque, lump crab cakes, flounder fillet, and of course the ubiquitous shrimp and grits. The Saltus River Grill is definitely more upscale in feel and in price than most Lowcountry places, with a very see-and-be-seen type of attitude and a hopping bar. Reservations recommended.

LOWCOUNTRY BOIL

What we now know as "Lowcountry Boil" was originally called Frogmore Stew – not because of any amphibian presence, but for the tiny township on St. Helena Island, South Carolina where the first pot was made, supposedly by Mr. Richard Gay of the Gay Fish Company. Old-timers still call it Frogmore Stew, however.

As with any vernacular dish, dozens of local and family variants abound. The key ingredient that makes Lowcountry Boil what it is – a well-blended mélange with a character all its own rather than just a bunch of stuff thrown together in a pot of boiling water – is some type of crab boil seasoning. You'll find Zatarain's seasoning suggested on a lot of websites, but in my experience Old Bay is far more common in the eponymous Lowcountry where the dish originated.

In any case, here's a simple six-serving Lowcountry Boil recipe to get you started. The only downside to it is that it's pretty much impossible to make it for just a few people. The dish is intended for large gatherings, whether a football tailgating party on a Saturday or a family afternoon after church on Sunday. Note the typical ratio of one ear of corn per person and half a pound each of meat and shrimp.

- 6 ears fresh corn on the cob, cut into three-inch sections
- 3 pounds smoked pork sausage, cut into three-inch sections
- 3 pounds fresh shrimp, shells on
- 5 pounds new potatoes
- 6 ounces Old Bay Seasoning

Put the sausage and potato pieces, along with half of the Old Bay, in two gallons of boiling water. When the potatoes are about halfway done, about 15 minutes in, add the corn and boil for about half that time, seven minutes. Add the shrimp and boil for another three minutes, until they just turn pink. *Do not overcook the shrimp.* Take the pot off the heat and drain; serve immediately. If you cook the shrimp just right, the oil from the sausage will cause those shells to slip right off.

This is but one of countless recipes. Some cooks add some lemon juice and beer in the water as it's coming to a boil; others add onion, garlic, and/or green peppers.

Sharing an owner with the Saltus River Grill is **Plum's** (904 1/2 Bay St., 843/525-1946, lunch daily 11 A.M.–4 P.M., dinner daily 5–10 P.M., $15–25). The short and focused menu keys in on daringly prepared entrées highlighting local ingredients, such as the shrimp penne al'amatriciana and fresh black mussel pasta. Because of the outstanding microbrew selection, Plum's is a big nightlife hangout as well; be aware that after 10 P.M., when food service ends but the bar remains open until 2 P.M., it's no longer smoke-free, though there's a friendly porch where you can get some fresh air and feed the resident cat.

An up-and-comer downtown is **Breakwater Restaurant and Bar** (205 West St., 843/379-0052, www.breakwater-restaurant.com, dinner Thurs.–Sat. 6–9:30 P.M., bar until 2 A.M., $10–20). The concise menu makes up in good taste what it lacks in comprehensiveness, with an emphasis on seafood, of course. An especially enticing marine-oriented tapas plate is the diver scallops in a vanilla cognac sauce.

Steaks
Luther's Rare & Well Done (910 Bay St., 843/521-1888, daily 10 A.M.–midnight) on the waterfront is the kind of meat-lover's place where even the French onion soup has a morsel of rib eye in it. While the patented succulent, rubbed steaks are a no-brainer here, the hand-crafted specialty pizzas are also quite popular. Housed in a historic pharmacy building, Luther's is also a great place for late eats after many other places in this quiet town have rolled up the sidewalk. A limited menu of appetizers and bar food is available after 10 P.M.

Tapas

Right around the corner from Breakwater is **Emily's** (906 Port Republic St., 843/522-1866, www.emilysrestaurantandtapasbar.com, dinner Mon.–Sat. 4–10 P.M., bar until 2 A.M., $10–20), a very popular fine dining spot that specializes in a more traditional brand of rich, tasty tapas (available 4–5 P.M.) and is known for its active bar scene.

INFORMATION AND SERVICES

The nice, new, Chamber of Commerce–run **Beaufort Visitors Information Center** (1106 Carteret St., 843/986-5400, www.beaufortsc .org , daily 9 A.M.–5:30 P.M.) is easy to find as you enter the historic district.

The U.S. Postal Service has a **post office** (501 Charles St., 843/525-9085) in downtown Beaufort.

The daily newspaper of record in Beaufort is the *Beaufort Gazette* (www.beaufortgazette .com). An alternative weekly focusing mostly on the arts is *Lowcountry Weekly* (www .lcweekly.com), published every Wednesday.

GETTING THERE AND AROUND

While the Marines can fly their F-18s directly into Beaufort Naval Air Station, you won't have that luxury. The closest major airport to Beaufort is the **Savannah/Hilton Head International Airport** (400 Airways Ave., 912/964-0514, www.savannahairport.com, airport code SAV) off I-95 outside Savannah. If you're not going into Savannah for any reason, the easiest route to the Beaufort area from the airport is to take exit 8 off I-95, and from there to take U.S. 278 east to U.S. 170.

Conversely, you could fly into the **Charleston International Airport** (5500 International Blvd., www.chs-airport.com, airport code CHS), but because that facility is on the far north side of Charleston it actually might take you longer to get to Beaufort. From the Charleston Airport the best route south to Beaufort is U.S. 17 south, exiting at U.S. 21 at Gardens Corner and then into Beaufort.

If you're coming into the region by car, I-95 will be your likely primary route, with your main point of entry being exit 8 off I-95 connecting to U.S. 278.

There's no public transportation to speak of in Beaufort, but that's OK—the historic section is quite small and can be traversed in an afternoon. A favorite mode of transport is by bicycle, which is often provided complimentary to bed and breakfast guests. Rent one at **Lowcountry Bikes** (102 Sea Island Pkwy., 843/524-9585, Mon.–Tues. and Thurs.–Fri. 10 A.M.–6 P.M., Wed. 10 A.M.–1 P.M., Sat. 10 A.M.–3 P.M., about $5/hr) in Lady's Island just over the bridge.

OUTSIDE BEAUFORT

The areas outside tourist-traveled Beaufort can take you even further back into sepia-toned Americana, into a time of sharecropper homesteads, sturdy oystermen, and an altogether variable and subjective sense of time.

Penn Center

By leaving town and going over the long, low Richard V. Woods Memorial Bridge over the Beaufort River on the Sea Island Parkway (which eventually turns into U.S. 21), you'll pass through little Lady's Island and eventually reach St. Helena Island. Known to old-timers as Frogmore, the area took back its old, Spanish-derived place name in the 1980s.

Today St. Helena Island is most famous for the Penn Center (16 Martin Luther King Jr. Dr., 843/838-2474, www.penncenter.com, Mon.–Sat. 11 A.M.–4 P.M., $4 adults, $2 seniors and children), the spiritual home of Gullah culture and history. When you visit here among the live oaks and humble but well-preserved buildings, you'll instantly see why Dr. Martin Luther King Jr. chose this as one of his major retreat and planning sites during the civil rights era.

The dream began as early as 1862, when a group of abolitionist Quakers from Philadelphia came down during the Union occupation with the specific goal of teaching recently freed slave children. With a student body of about 50, they

Penn School on St. Helena Island

© JIM MOREKIS

LOWCOUNTRY

were soon joined by African American educator Charlotte Forten. After Reconstruction, the Penn School continued its mission by offering teaching and agricultural/industrial trade curricula.

The migration of blacks out of the South during World War II took a toll on the school, however, which became a community improvement center after classes ceased in 1948. In the late 1960s, the Southern Christian Leadership Conference used the school as a retreat and planning site, with both the Peace Corps and the Conscientious Objector Programs training here.

In addition to its role as an education and research hub for the study of Gullah culture, the Penn Center continues to serve in an important civil rights role by providing legal counsel to African American homeowners in St. Helena. Because clear title is extremely difficult to acquire in the area due to the fact that so much of the land has stayed in the families of former slaves, developers are constantly making shady offers so that ancestral land can be opened up to upscale development.

The beautiful 50-acre campus of the Penn Center is part of the Penn School Historic District, a National Historic Landmark comprising 19 buildings, most of key historical significance, including Darrah Hall, the oldest building on the campus; the old "Brick Church" right across MLK Jr. Drive; and Gantt Cottage, where Dr. King himself stayed periodically in the 1963–1967 period. Another building, the Retreat House, was intended for Dr. King to continue his yearly strategy meetings, but he was assassinated before being able to stay there. The museum and bookshop are housed in the Cope Building, now called the York W. Bailey Museum, situated right along MLK Jr. Drive. A self-guided nature trail takes you all around the campus.

The key public event here happens each November with the Penn Center Heritage Days, in which the entire St. Helena community comes together to celebrate and enjoy entertainment such as the world-famous, locally based Hallelujah Singers.

To get to the Penn Center from Beaufort, proceed over the bridge until you get to St.

Helena Island. Take a right onto MLK Jr. Drive when you see the Red Piano Too Art Gallery. The Penn Center is a few hundred yards on your right.

If you drive past the Penn Center and continue a few hundred yards down MLK Jr. Drive, look for the ancient tabby ruins on the left side of the road. This is the **Chapel of Ease,** the remnant of a 1740 church destroyed by forest fire in the late 1800s.

Old Sheldon Church Ruins

A short ways north of Beaufort are the poignantly desolate ruins of the once-magnificent Old Sheldon Church (Old Sheldon Church Rd. off U.S. 17 just past Gardens Corner, daily dawn–dusk). Set a couple of miles off the highway on a narrow road, the serene, oak-lined grounds containing this massive, empty edifice give little hint of the violence so intrinsic to its history.

One of the first Greek Revival structures in the United States, the house of worship held its first service in 1757 as Prince William's Parish Church. The sanctuary was first burned by the British in 1779, mainly because of reports that the Patriots were using it to store gunpowder captured from a British ship. After being rebuilt in 1826, the sanctuary survived until General Sherman's arrival in 1865, whereupon Union troops razed it once more. Nothing remains now but these towering walls and columns, made of red brick instead of the tabby often seen in similar ruins on the coast.

It's now owned by the nearby St. Helena's Episcopal Church in Beaufort, which holds outdoor services here the second Sunday after Easter. In all, it's an almost painfully compelling bit of history set amid stunning natural beauty, and well worth the short drive.

Oyotunji Village

By continuing north of the Sheldon Church a short ways, the more adventurous can find a quirky Lowcountry attraction, Oyotunji Village (56 Bryant Ln., 843/846-8900, hours vary). Built in 1970 by self-proclaimed "King" Ofuntola Oseijeman Adelabu Adefunmi I, former used car dealer with an interesting past, Oyotunji claims to be North America's only

© JIM MOREKIS

Old Sheldon Church ruins

LOWCOUNTRY

LOWCOUNTRY

THE LOST ART OF TABBY

Let's clear up a couple of misconceptions about tabby, that unique construction technique combining oyster shells, lime, water, and sand found all along the South Carolina and Georgia coast.

First, it did not originate with Native Americans. The confusion is due to the fact that the native population left behind many middens, or enormous trash heaps, of oyster shells. While these middens indeed provided the bulk of the shells for tabby buildings to come, Native Americans had little else to do with it.

Secondly, though the Spanish were responsible for the first use of tabby in the Americas, contrary to lore almost all remaining tabby in the area dates from later English settlement.

© JIM MOREKIS

Chapel of Ease on St. Helena Island

authentic African village, with 5–10 families residing on its 30 acres. It also claims to be a separate kingdom and not a part of the United States—though I'm sure the State Department begs to differ.

With a mission to preserve the religious and cultural aspects of the Yoruba Orisa culture of West Africa, each spring the village hosts an annual Warrior's Festival, celebrating traditional male rites of passage. Truth is, there's not much to see here but a few poorly built "monuments." But connoisseurs of roadside Americana will be pleased.

Yemassee

Going still further north on U.S. 17 you'll come to the small town of Yemassee. Its main claim to fame is nearby **Auldbrass,** designed by Frank Lloyd Wright in 1939. The home is privately owned by Hollywood producer Joel Silver, but rare, much-sought-after tours happen every other year in November through the auspices of the Beaufort County Open Land Trust. To find out about the next tour and to get on the list, email your mailing address to bcolt2@islc.net or call 843/521-2175 to receive ticket information the summer prior.

Port Royal

This sleepy little town of 4,000 between Beaufort and Parris Island touts itself as a leader in "small town New Urbanism." This is certainly true, with its manicured emphasis on livability, retro-themed shopping areas, and

The British first fell in love with tabby after the siege of Spanish-held St. Augustine, Florida and quickly began building with it in their colonies to the north.

Scholars are divided as to whether tabby was invented by West Africans, or its use spread to Africa from Spain and Portugal, circuitously coming to America through the knowledge of imported slaves. The origin of the word itself is also unclear, as similar words exist in Spanish, Portuguese, Gullah, and Arabic to describe various types of wall.

We do know for sure how tabby is made: The primary technique was to burn alternating layers of oyster shells and logs in a deep hole in the ground, thus creating lime. The lime was then mixed with oyster shells, sand, and freshwater and poured into wooden molds, or "forms," to dry and then be used as building blocks, much like large bricks. The walls were usually plastered with stucco. Tabby is remarkably strong and resilient, able to easily survive the hurricanes that often batter the area. It stays cool in the summer and is insect-resistant, two enormous plusses down here.

The following are the best examples of true tabby you can see today in South Carolina.

- Several younger tabby buildings still exist in downtown Beaufort: the **Barnwell-Gough House** (705 Washington St.); the magnificent Thomas Fuller House, or **"Tabby Manse"** (1211 Bay St.); and the **Saltus House** (on the 800 block of Bay St.), perhaps the tallest surviving tabby structure.

- The **Chapel of Ease** (off Land's End Rd.) on St. Helena Island dates from the 1740s. If someone tells you Sherman burned it down, don't believe them; the culprit was a forest fire long after the war.

- The **Stoney-Baynard Ruins** (Plantation Dr.) in Sea Pines Plantation on Hilton Head are all that's left of the home of the old Braddock's Point Plantation. Foundations of a slave quarters are nearby.

- The remains of the old Wilson home are within the **Palmetto Bluff Resort** (476 Mt. Pelia Rd.) in Bluffton.

- **Dorchester State Historic Site** (300 State Park Rd., Summerville) north of Charleston contains a well-preserved tabby fort.

relaxing walking trails. However, Port Royal is still pretty sleepy—but not without very real charms, not the least of which is the fact that everything in town is within easy walking distance of everything else.

The highlight of the year is the annual Soft Shell Crab Festival, held each April to mark the short-lived harvesting season for that favorite crustacean. Indeed, the rhythms of the sea mean everything to Port Royal, as indicated by the recent hubbub over a proposal to close the town's Port Authority dock. Though the controversy happened at the height of the season, anxious shrimp-boat captains refused to leave the dock for fear that demolition might begin in the middle of the night while they were offshore.

While much of the tiny historic district has a scrubbed, tidy feel, the main historic structure is the charming little **Union Church** (11th St., 843/524-4333, Mon.–Fri. 10 A.M.–4 P.M.), one of the oldest buildings in town, with guided docent tours.

Don't miss the new boardwalk and observation tower at **The Sands** municipal beach and boat ramp. The 50-foot-tall structure provides a commanding view of Battery Creek. To get to The Sands, go to 7th Street and then turn onto Sands Beach Road.

Another environmentally oriented point of pride is the new **Lowcountry Estuarium** (1402 Paris Ave., 843/524-6600, www.lowcountry estuarium.org, Fri. and Sat. 10 A.M.–5 P.M., feedings at 11:30 A.M. and 3 P.M., $4 adults,

$2 children). The point of the facility is to give hands-on opportunities to learn more about the flora and fauna of the various ecosystems of the Lowcountry, such as salt marshes, beaches, and estuaries.

Parris Island
Though more commonly known as the home of the legendary **Marine Corps Recruit Depot Parris Island** (283 Blvd. de France, 843/228-3650, www.mcrdpi.usmc.mil, free), the island is also of historic significance as the site of some of the earliest European presence in America. The U.S. Marine Corps began its association with Parris Island in 1891, though the island's naval roots actually go back to its use as a coaling station during the long Union occupation.

By the outbreak of World War I, a full-blown military town had sprung up, now with its own presence on the National Register of Historic Places. In November 1915, Parris Island officially went in business as a recruit depot, and today it's where all female Marine recruits and all male recruits east of the Mississippi River go through the grueling 13-week boot camp. Currently about 19,000 recruits are processed each year—2,000 of them women—with almost every Friday during the year marking the graduation of a company of newly minted Marines. That's why you might notice an influx of visitors to the area each Thursday, a.k.a. "Family Day," with the requisite amount of celebration on Fridays after that morning's ceremony. This begins a 10-day leave period, after which the recruits go to Camp Lejeune, North Carolina.

Unlike many military facilities in the post-9/11 era, Parris Island still hosts plenty of visitors, about 120,000 a year. While the vast majority come by invitation only to witness one of the weekly graduations, there are a few important facilities of interest to the history buff. But word to the wise: Thursdays and Fridays can get crowded.

The **Parris Island Museum** (Bldg. 111, 111 Panama St., 843/228-2951, daily 8:30 A.M.–4:30 P.M.) near the entrance not only lovingly details the entire U.S. military experience in the area, but also features many surprisingly good exhibits on the area's earliest colonial history. The Spanish built Santa Elena directly on top of the original French settlement, Charlesfort. They then built two other settlements, San Felipe and San Marcos. All are now on the circa-1950s depot golf course and available to the public for self-guided tours.

Archaeological exploration has continued since 1979, with intensive research on the long-lost Santa Elena/Charlesfort site (http://santaelena.us), now a National Historic Landmark, beginning in the late 1990s. Many artifacts are viewable at the nearby **clubhouse/interpretive center** (daily 7 A.M.–5 P.M.).

The **Douglas Visitor Center** (Bldg. 283, Blvd. de France, 843/228-3650, Mon. 7:30 A.M.–noon, Tues. and Wed. 7:30 A.M.–4:30 P.M., Thurs. 6:30 A.M.–7 P.M., Fri. 7:30 A.M.–3 P.M.) is a great place to find maps and touring information. All visitors to the Parris Island Recruit Depot must get a pass at the gate. You must have a valid driver's license, registration, and proof of insurance. Rental car drivers must show a copy of the rental agreement. *Do not* use your cell phone while driving. While Parris Island kindly welcomes visitors, be aware that all traffic rules within the camp are strictly enforced, and your vehicle is subject to inspection at any time.

◖ Hunting Island State Park
Rumored to be a hideaway for Blackbeard himself, the aptly named Hunting Island was indeed for many years a notable hunting preserve, and its abundance of wildlife holds true to this day. The island is one of the East Coast's best birding spots and also hosts dolphins, loggerheads, alligators, and deer. However, thanks to preservation efforts by President Franklin Roosevelt and the Civilian Conservation Corps, the island is no longer for hunting but for sheer enjoyment. And enjoy it people do, to the tune of a million visitors a year.

A true family-friendly outdoor adventure spot, Hunting Island State Park (2555 Sea Island Pkwy., 866/345-7275, www

view of Hunting Island from the top of the lighthouse

© JIM MOREKIS

.huntingisland.com, daily 6 A.M.–6 P.M., until 9 P.M. DST, $4 adults, $1.50 children) has something for everyone—kids, parents, and newlyweds. Yet it still retains a certain sense of lush wildness—so much so that it doubled as Vietnam in *Forrest Gump.*

At the north end past the campground is the island's main landmark, the historic **Hunting Island Light,** which dates from 1875. Though the lighthouse ceased operations in 1933, a rotating light—not strong enough to serve as an actual navigational aid—is turned on at night. While the 167-step trek to the top ($2 donation per person) is quite strenuous, the view from the little observation area at the top of the lighthouse is stunning, a complete panorama of Hunting Island and much of the Lowcountry coast.

At the south end of the island is a marsh walk, nature trail, and a fishing pier complete with a cute little nature center. Hunting Island's three miles of beautiful beaches also serve as a major center of loggerhead turtle nesting and hatching, a process that begins around June as the mothers lay their eggs and culminates in late summer and early fall, when the hatchlings make their daring dash to the sea. At all phases the turtles are strictly protected, and while there are organized events to witness the hatching of the eggs, it is strictly forbidden to touch or otherwise disturb the turtles or their nests. Contact the park ranger for more detailed information.

The tropical-looking inlet running through the park is a great place to kayak or canoe.

Getting to Hunting Island couldn't be easier—just take the Sea Island Parkway (U.S. 21) about 20 minutes beyond Beaufort and you'll run right into it.

Fripp Island

If you keep driving past Hunting Island you'll reach Fripp Island, one of South Carolina's private, developed barrier islands. Unlike its more egalitarian neighbor, Fripp only welcomes visitors who are guests of the **Fripp Island Golf and Beach Resort** (800/845-4100, www .frippislandresort.com), which offers a range of lodging from oceanfront homes to villas to golf cottages. Family-friendly recreation abounds, not only in 36 holes of high-caliber golf, but in over three miles of uncrowded beach. A major allure is Camp Fripp, providing activities for kids.

(ACE Basin

Occupying pretty much the entire area between Beaufort and Charleston, the ACE Basin—the acronym signifies its role as the collective estuary of the Ashepoo, Combahee, and Edisto Rivers—is one of the most enriching natural experiences America has to offer. The Basin's three core rivers, the Edisto being the largest, are the framework for a matrix of waterways criss-crossing its approximately 350,000 acres of salt marsh.

It's this intimate relationship with the tides that makes the area so enjoyable, and also what attracted so many plantations throughout its history (canals and dikes from the old rice paddies are still visible throughout). Other uses have included tobacco, corn, and lumbering.

While the ACE Basin can in no way be called "pristine," it's a testament to the power of nature that after 6,000 years of human presence and often intense cultivation the Basin manages to retain much of its untamed feel.

The ACE Basin is so big that it is actually broken up into several parts for management purposes under the umbrella of the ACE Basin Project (www.acebasin.net), a task force begun in 1988 by the state of South Carolina, the U.S. Fish and Wildlife Service, and various private firms and conservation groups. The Project is now considered a model for responsible watershed preservation techniques in a time of often rampant coastal development. A host of species, both common and endangered, thrive in the area, including wood storks, alligators, sturgeon, loggerheads, teals, and bald eagles.

About 12,000 acres of the ACE Basin Project comprise the **Ernest F. Hollings ACE Basin National Wildlife Refuge** (8675 Willtown Rd., 843/889-3084, www.fws.gov/acebasin, grounds open daylight–dark year-round, office open weekdays 7:30 A.M.–4 P.M.), run by

LOWCOUNTRY

© JIM MOREKIS

the Grove Plantation House in the ACE Basin National Wildlife Refuge

the U.S. Fish and Wildlife Service. The historic 1828 **Grove Plantation House** is in this portion of the Basin and in fact houses the refuge's headquarters. Sometimes featured on local tours of homes, it's one of only three antebellum homes left in the ACE Basin. Surrounded by lush, ancient oak trees, it's really a sight in and of itself.

This section of the Refuge, the Edisto Unit, is almost entirely composed of impounded rice paddies from the area's role as a plantation before the Civil War. Restored rice trunks—the tidal gates used to manage waterflow into the paddies—are still used to maintain the right amount of water in the impounded areas, which are now rife with birds since the refuge is along the Atlantic Flyway. You may not always see them, but you'll definitely hear their calls echoing over the miles of marsh. (Speaking of miles, there are literally miles of walking and biking trails throughout the Edisto Unit, through both wetland and forest.)

To get to the Edisto Unit of the Hollings/ ACE Basin NWR, take U.S. 17 to Highway 174 (going all the way down this route takes you to Edisto Island) and turn right onto Willtown Road. The unpaved entrance road is about two miles ahead on your left. There are restrooms and a few picnic tables, but no other facilities of note.

You can also visit the two parts of the Combahee Unit of the Refuge, which offers a similar scene of trails among impounded wetlands along the Combahee River, with parking. It's further west near Yemassee. Get there by taking a left off U.S. 17 onto Highway 33. The larger portion of the Combahee Unit is very soon after the turnoff, and the smaller, more northerly portion about five miles up the road.

About 135,000 acres of the entire ACE Basin falls under the protection of the South Carolina Department of Natural Resources as part of the **National Estuarine Research Reserve System** (www.nerrs.noaa.gov/ace basin). The South Carolina DNR also runs two Wildlife Management Areas, **Donnelly WMA** (843/844-8957, www.dnr.sc.gov,

Mon.–Sat. 8 A.M.–5 P.M. year-round) and **Bear Island WMA** (843/844-8957, www.dnr.sc.gov, Mon.–Sat. dawn–dusk Feb. 1–Oct. 14), both of which provide rich opportunities for birding and wildlife observation.

Over 128,000 acres of the ACE Basin Project are permanently protected through conservation easements, management agreements, and fee title purchases. While traditional uses such as farming, fishing, and hunting do indeed continue in the ACE Basin, the area is off-limits to the gated communities, which are sprouting like mildew all along the Carolina coast. Because it is so well defended, the ACE Basin also functions like a huge outdoor laboratory for the coastal scientific community, with constant research going on in botany, zoology, microbiology, and marine science.

Food

If you find yourself in charming little Port Royal, try the waterfront seafood haven **11th Street Dockside** (1699 11th St., 843/524-7433, daily 4:30–10 P.M., $17–27). The Dockside Dinner is a great sampler plate with lobster tail, scallops, crab legs, and shrimp. The views of the waterfront and the adjoining shrimp-boat docks are relaxing and beautiful.

For more upscale dining in Port Royal, try **Bateaux** (610 Paris Ave., 843/379-0777, www .bateauxrestaurant.net, Mon.–Sat. 5–9 P.M., $20–30). On Lady's Island for many years, Bateaux has moved a few miles away to a new Port Royal location in the historic Customs House downtown. It's highly regarded for its adventurous small-plate items such as *foie gras* and scallops, and its daring Lowcountry seafood creations such as the Bateaux seafood stew. Reservations are recommended.

A Lady's Island hot spot is the very casual **Steamer Oyster and Steak House** (168 Sea Island Pkwy., 843/522-0210, daily 11 A.M.–9:30 P.M., $15–20). The big hit here is the Frogmore stew, a.k.a. Lowcountry Boil.

For vegan/vegetarian soups, salads, and sandwiches on Lady's Island, jump across the Beaufort River Bridge a short ways and

LOWCOUNTRY

try **It's Only Natural** (45 Factory Creek Ct., 843/986-9595, Mon.–Fri. 8 A.M.–6 P.M., Sat. 9 A.M.–4:30 P.M., $5). It's visible right off the main road, the Sea Island Parkway (U.S. 21). They also offer a range of health food items and produce.

Right before you take a right to get to the Penn Center on St. Helena Island is **Gullah Grub** (877 Sea Island Pkwy., 843/838-3841, Mon.–Thurs. 11:30 A.M.–7 P.M., under $20), an unpretentious, one-room lunch spot focusing on down-home Southern specialties with a Lowcountry touch, such as hushpuppies, collard greens, and shrimp-'n'-shark.

Hilton Head Island

Literally the prototype of the modern planned resort community, Hilton Head Island is also a case study in how quickly and utterly a landscape can change when enough money is introduced. Once consisting almost entirely of African Americans with deep historic roots in the area, in the mid-1950s Hilton Head began its transformation into an almost all-white, upscale golf, tennis, and shopping mecca populated largely by northern transplants and retirees. As you can imagine, the flavor here is now quite different from surrounding areas of the Lowcountry, to say the least, with an emphasis on material excellence, top prices, get-it-done-yesterday punctuality, and the attendant aggressive traffic.

Giving credit where it's due, however, Hilton Head knows what its target audience is and delivers the goods in a thoroughly professional manner. While it's easy to dismiss it as a sort of Disney World for the elite—a disjointed collection of gated communities comprising 70 percent of its area—the truth is that millions of visitors, not all of them elite by any stretch, not only enjoy what Hilton Head has to offer, they swear by it, returning year after year. The attraction is quality, whether in the stunning beaches, outstanding cultural offerings, plush accommodations, attentive service, or copious merchandise. The intentional elimination of risk is also part of the island's appeal, both to the senior demographic as well as the family segment. You won't see any litter during your stay, and you're very unlikely to experience any crime.

Certainly that's to Hilton Head's credit and no small reason for its continued success.

One of the great unsung positive aspects of modern Hilton Head is its dedication to sustainable living. With the support of voters, the town routinely buys large tracts of land to preserve as open space. Seemingly every hundred yards or so, you'll come across a sign indicating how many acres have been preserved in the immediate area. Hilton Head was the first municipality in the country to mandate the burying of all power lines, and one of the first to regularly use covenants and deed restrictions. All new development must conform to rigid guidelines on setbacks and tree canopy. It has one of the most comprehensive signage ordinances in the country as well, which means no garish commercial displays will disrupt your views of the night sky. If those are "elite" values, then certainly we might do well in making them more mainstream.

Just outside Hilton Head are two of the Lowcountry's true gems, Bluffton and Daufuskie Island. While Bluffton's outskirts have been taken over by the same gated community sprawl spreading throughout the coast, at its core is a delightfully charming little community on the quiet May River, now called Old Bluffton, where you'd swear you just entered a time warp. Daufuskie Island, though home to a top-flight golf resort, still maintains much of its age-old isolated, timeless personality, and the island—still accessible by boat only—is still one of the spiritual centers of the Gullah culture and lifestyle.

© JIM MOREKIS

Golf and nature coexist peacefully on Hilton Head.

HISTORY

The second-largest barrier island on the East Coast, Hilton Head Island was inhabited by Native Americans at least 10,000 years ago. The first European to sight the island was Spain's Francisco Cordillo in 1521, but it didn't enter mainstream consciousness until the 1663 sighting by Sir William Hilton, who thoughtfully named the island—with its notable headland or "Head"—after himself. Hilton, who like many of Charleston's original settlers was from the British colony of Barbados, was purposely trying to drum up interest in the island as a commercial venture, famously describing his new namesake as having "sweet water" and "clear sweet air."

Though Hilton Head wasn't the first foothold of English colonization in Carolina, as Hilton wanted it to be, it did acquire commercial status first as the home of several rice and indigo plantations. Later it gained fame as the first location of the legendary "Sea Island Cotton," a long-grain variety which, following its introduction in 1790 by William Elliott II

of the Myrtle Bank Plantation, would soon be the dominant version of the cash crop.

Hilton Head planters were outspoken in the cause of American independence. The chief pattern in the Lowcountry during that conflict involved the British raiding Hilton Head and surrounding areas from their stronghold on Daufuskie, burning plantations and capturing slaves to be resold in Caribbean colonies. As a reminder of the savage guerrilla nature of the conflict in the South, British hit-and-run raids on Hilton Head continued for weeks after Cornwallis surrendered.

Nearby Bluffton was settled by planters from Hilton Head Island and the surrounding area in the early 1800s as a summer retreat. Though Charleston likes to claim the label today, Bluffton was actually the genuine "cradle of secession." Indeed, locals still joke that the town motto is "Divided We Stand."

Fort Walker, a Confederate installation on the site of the modern Port Royal Plantation development on Hilton Head, was the target of the largest fleet ever assembled in North

America at the time, when a massive Union force sailed into Port Royal Sound in October 1861. A month later, the Fort—and effectively the entire area—had fallen, though by that time most white residents had long since fled. During the Civil War, Bluffton was also evacuated and, like Hilton Head, escaped serious action. However, in June 1863, Union troops destroyed most of the town of Bluffton except for about a dozen homes and two churches.

Though it seems unlikely given the island's modern demographics, Hilton Head was almost entirely African American through much of the 20th century. Given its role as a plantation site, the population was always mostly African American, becoming even more so when Union troops occupied the island at the outbreak of the Civil War. Freed and escaped slaves flocked to the island, and most of the dwindling number of African Americans on the island today are descendants of this original Gullah population.

For the first half of the 20th century, logging was Hilton Head's main commercial pursuit. Things didn't take their modern shape until the 1950s, when the Fraser family bought 19,000 of the island's 25,000 acres with the intent to continue forestry on them. But in 1956—not at all coincidentally the same year the first bridge to the island was built—Charles Fraser convinced his father to sell him the southern tip of Hilton Head Island. Fraser's brainchild and decades-long love—some said his obsession—Sea Pines Plantation was the prototype of the golf-oriented resort community so common today on both U.S. coasts.

Though Fraser himself was killed in a boating accident in 2002, he survived to see Sea Pines encompass much of Hilton Head's economic activity, including Harbour Town, and to see the Town of Hilton Head incorporated in 1983. Fraser is buried under the famous Liberty Oak in Harbour Town, which he personally made sure wasn't harmed during the development of the area.

ORIENTATION

Hilton Head Islanders have long referred to their island as the "shoe" (and speak of driving to the toe, going to the heel, etc.). If you take a look at a map, you'll see why. Hilton Head bears an uncanny resemblance to a running shoe in action pointed toward the southeast, with the aptly named Broad Creek forming a near facsimile of the Nike "swoosh" symbol.

Running the length and circumference of the shoe is the undisputed main drag, U.S. 278 Business (William Hilton Parkway), which crosses onto Hilton Head right at the "tongue" of the shoe, a relatively undeveloped area where there are still a few old African American communities. The new Cross Island Parkway toll route (U.S. 278), beginning up toward the ankle as you first get on the island, is a quicker, much more convenient route straight to the toe near Sea Pines.

While it is technically the business spur, when locals say "278" they're talking about the William Hilton Parkway. It takes you the entire sole of the shoe, including the beaches, and on down to the toe, where you'll find a confusing, crazy British-style roundabout called Sea Pines Circle. It's also the site of the Harbour Town Marina and the island's oldest planned development, Sea Pines Plantation.

There's no "town center" per se, but activity here tends to revolve around just a few places: the Shelter Cove mall and residential development near the entrance to the island; Coligny Plaza, an older, more casual shopping center near the main beach entrance; Sea Pines Circle, a center of nightlife; and two spots within Sea Pines itself, Harbour Town and South Beach—the former a blend of upscale and family attractions, and the latter catering a bit more to the beach crowd.

While precious little history is left on Hilton Head, place names reverberate with the names of key figures long-gone: Cordillo Parkway, named for the first Spaniard to come to the area; Coligny Plaza, named for the admiral who sent the first French expedition to the area; and Ribault Road, named for the leader of that expedition. In any case, while making your way around the island always keep in mind that the bulk of it consists of private developments, and local law enforcement frowns

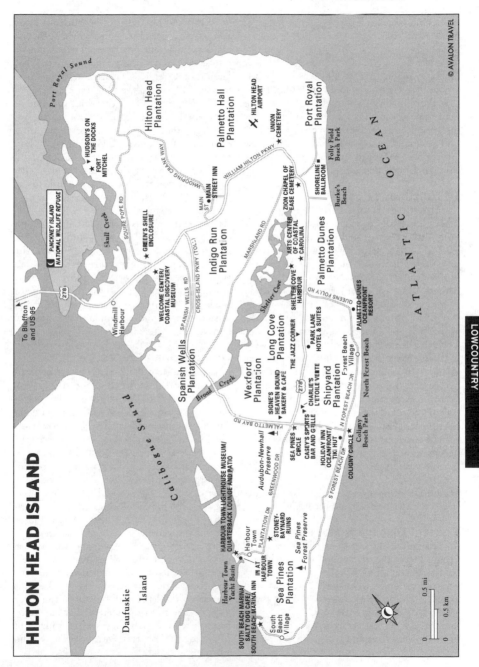

HILTON HEAD ISLAND

Port Royal Sound

Daufuskie Island

Calibogue Sound

Port Royal Sound

© AVALON TRAVEL

Hilton Head Plantation

Palmetto Hall Plantation

HILTON HEAD AIRPORT

Port Royal Plantation

UNION CEMETERY

Folly Field Beach Park

HUDSON'S ON THE DOCKS

FORT MITCHEL

WHOOPING CRANE WAY

SQUIRE POPE RD

Skull Creek

PINCKNEY ISLAND NATIONAL WILDLIFE REFUGE

GREEN'S SHELL ENCLOSURE

MAIN ST

MAIN STREET INN

WILLIAM HILTON PKWY

MARSH ISLAND RD

ZION CHAPEL OF EASE CEMETERY

ARTS CENTER OF COASTAL CAROLINA

SHORELINE BALLROOM

Burke's Beach

SHELTER COVE OF COASTAL HARBOUR

Palmetto Dunes Plantation

WELCOME CENTER/ COASTAL DISCOVERY MUSEUM

SPANISH WELLS RD

CROSS-ISLAND PKWY (TOLL)

Indigo Run Plantation

Shelter Cove

QUEENS FOLLY RD

PALMETTO DUNES OCEANFRONT RESORT

To Bluffton and US-95

276

Windmill Harbour

Spanish Wells Plantation

Wexford Plantation

Long Cove Plantation

THE JAZZ CORNER

PARK LANE HOTEL & SUITES

Forest Beach

North Forest Beach

ATLANTIC OCEAN

Brood Creek

SIGNE'S HEAVEN BOUND BAKERY & CAFÉ

CHARLIE'S L'ETOILE VERTE

Shipyard Plantation

N FOREST BEACH DR

Forest Beach Village

PALMETTO BAY RD

SEA PINES CIRCLE

CASEY'S SPORTS BAR AND GRILLE

HOLIDAY INN OCEANFRONT TIKI HUT

COLIGNY CIRCLE

Coligny Beach Park

Audubon-Newhall Preserve

GREENWOOD DR

HARBOUR TOWN LIGHTHOUSE MUSEUM/ QUARTERDECK LOUNGE AND PATIO

STONEY-BAYNARD RUINS

PLANTATION DR

Sea Pines Forest Preserve

S FOREST BEACH DR

Harbour Town Yacht Basin

Harbour Town

INN AT HARBOUR TOWN

SOUTH BEACH MARINA/ SALTY DOG CAFE/ SOUTH BEACH MARINA INN

South Beach Village

Sea Pines Plantation

0.5 mi

0.5 km

0

on people who aimlessly wander among the condos and villas.

SIGHTS

Contrary to what many think, there are actually quite a few things to do on Hilton Head that don't involve swinging a club at a little white ball or shopping for designer labels, but instead celebrate the area's rich history and natural setting. The following are some of those attractions, arranged in geographical order from where you first access the island.

【 Pinckney Island National Wildlife Refuge

Though actually consisting of many islands and hammocks, Pinckney Island NWR (912/652-4415, daily dawn–dusk, free) is the only part of this small but very well-managed 4,000-acre refuge that's open to the public. Almost 70 percent of the former rice plantation is salt marsh and tidal creeks, making it a perfect microcosm for the Lowcountry as a whole, as well as a great place to kayak or canoe.

Native Americans liked the area as well, with an approximately 10,000-year presence and over 100 archaeological sites being identified to date. Like many coastal refuges, it was a private game preserve for much of the 20th century. Some of the state's richest birding opportunities abound here, with observers able to spot gorgeous white ibis, rare wood storks, herons, egrets, eagles, and ospreys with little trouble from its miles of trails.

Getting there is easy: On U.S. 278 east to Hilton Head, the refuge entrance is right between the two bridges onto the island.

Coastal Discovery Museum

Surprisingly in an area as awash in money as Hilton Head, the island abounds with small, under-funded, but worthwhile endeavors such as the Coastal Discovery Museum (100 William Hilton Pkwy., 843/689-6767, www.coastaldiscovery.org, Mon.–Sat. 9 A.M.–5 P.M., Sun. 10 A.M.–2 P.M., free) just as you get onto Hilton Head. The exhibits here are small-scale but heartfelt, like the excellent little dioramas

of traditional island life. The Museum hosts a variety of specialty guided tours, such as a Native Americans on the Sea Islands tour, a Pinckney Island walking tour, and a Sea Pines Plantation Overview. The cost for most of the tours is $12 for adults and $7 for children.

The Museum is a partner with the state in a sea turtle protection program, which you can learn more about once there. Standing exhibits include a historical timeline of Hilton Head, a Butterfly Garden, and the Sea Island Biodiversity Room, intended for use with local schoolchildren but fully available to the public. The Museum also plays an important role locally as the steward of the 68-acre **Honey Horn** greenspace at the intersection of the Cross Island Parkway and U.S. 278. Purchased by the town in the late 1990s, the plan is for the Honey Horn parcel, which contains several historic structures, to be a cultural attraction preserving the heritage of the island. Currently many annual events are hosted here, including wine tastings and the annual Chili Cookoff.

Green's Shell Enclosure

Less-known than the larger Native American shell ring farther south at Sea Pines, the Green's Shell Enclosure (803/734-3886, daily dawn–dusk) is certainly easier to find and you don't have to pay five bucks to enter the area, as with Sea Pines. This three-acre Heritage Preserve dates back to at least the 1300s. The heart of the site comprises a low embankment, part of the original fortified village. Don't expect to be wowed—shell rings are a subtle pleasure. As is the case with most shell rings, the shells themselves are underneath a layer of dirt. Please don't disturb them.

To get here, take a left at the intersection of U.S. 278 and Squire Pope Road. Turn left into Greens Park, pass the office on the left, and park. The entrance to the shell enclosure is on the left behind a fence. You'll see a small community cemetery that has nothing to with the shell ring; veer to your right to get to the short trail entrance. There is no camping allowed.

grave of African American Civil War veteran

© JIM MOREKIS

Union Cemetery

A modest but key aspect of African American history on Hilton Head is at **Union Cemetery** (Union Cemetery Rd.), a small burial ground featuring several graves of black Union Army troops (you can tell by the designation "U.S.C.I." on the tombstone, or "United States Colored Infantry"). Also of interest are the charming, hand-carved cement tombstones of non-veterans.

To get here, turn north off of William Hilton Parkway onto Union Cemetery Road. The cemetery is a short ways ahead on your left. There is no signage or site interpretation.

Fort Mitchel and Mitchelville

There's not much left of the old Union encampment at Fort Mitchel, nor of the freedmen community, Mitchelville, which grew up alongside it. You can see the earthworks, a couple of cannon, and a historical marker on the grounds of the Hilton Head Plantation, a gated development. Tell the security guard you'd like to see Fort Mitchel. Once inside Hilton Head

Plantation, take a left onto Seabrook Drive and then a right onto Skull Creek Drive. Fort Mitchel is a short ways ahead on your left. It's not a well-maintained site, but It's an important part of local history.

At the intersection of Bay Gall and Beach City Roads is a marker for the site of Mitchelville, founded in 1862 as the first freedman settlement in the U.S. Also on Beach City Road is a fenced-in area with what's left of Fort Howell, a Union encampment built by African American troops.

Zion Chapel of Ease Cemetery

More like one of the gloriously desolate scenes common to the rest of the Lowcountry, this little cemetery in full view of the William Hilton Parkway at Folly Field Road is all that remains of one of the "Chapels of Ease," a string of chapels set up in the 1700s. The cemetery (daily dawn–dusk, free) is said to be haunted by the ghost of William Baynard, whose final resting place is in a mausoleum on-site (the remains of his ancestral home are farther south at Sea Pines Plantation).

Audubon-Newhall Preserve

Plant lovers shouldn't miss this small but very well-maintained 50-acre wooded tract in the south-central part of the island on Palmetto Bay Road between the Cross Island Parkway and Sea Pines circle. Almost all plant life, even that in the water, is helpfully marked and identified. But if all you want to do is just enjoy, that's fine too, because the preserve has two miles of nature trails. Unusually, there's a well-preserved bog environment (*pocosin* to the indigenous tribes here). The preserve (dawn–dusk year-round, free) is open to the public, but you can't camp here, though it sure is inviting. For more information, call the Hilton Head Audubon Society (843/842-9246).

Harbour Town

Okay, it's not that historic and not all that natural, but Harbour Town is still pretty cool. The dominant element is the squat, colorful **Harbour Town Lighthouse Museum** (149 Lighthouse Rd., 843/671-2810, www.harbour townlighthouse.com, 10 A.M.–dusk), which has never really helped a ship navigate its way to

the island. The 90-foot structure was built in 1970 purely to give the tourists a little atmosphere, and that it does, as kids especially love climbing the stairs to the top (at $2 per person, that is) and looking out over the island's expanse. This being Hilton Head, of course, there's a gift shop at the top, too.

The other attraction here is the boisterous café and shopping scene around the marina and the nearby park area. The public can access Sea Pines Plantation, which contains Harbour Town, but it'll cost you a $5 "road use fee." It's worth it especially if you also pay a visit to the following Sea Pines attractions.

Stoney-Baynard Ruins

These tabby ruins (Plantation Dr., dawn–dusk, free) in Sea Pines are what remains of the circa-1790 central building of the old Braddock's Point Plantation, first owned by Patriot and raconteur Captain "Saucy Jack" Stoney and then the Baynard family. Active during the island's heyday as a cotton center, the plantation was destroyed after the Civil War. Site interpretation here is barebones, but

© JIM MOREKIS

Harbour Town

suffice it to say that this is a great remaining example of colonial tabby architecture. Two other foundations are nearby, one for slave quarters and one whose use is still unknown. Note that there is that $5 fee to enter Sea Pines.

Sea Pines Forest Preserve
The Sea Pines Forest Preserve (175 Greenwood Dr., 843/363-4530, free) is set amid the Sea Pines Plantation golf resort development, but you don't need a bag of clubs to enjoy this 600-acre preserve, which is built on the site of an old rice plantation (dikes and logging trails are still visible). Here you can ride a horse, fish, or just take a walk on the eight miles of trails (open dawn–dusk) and enjoy the natural beauty around you. No bike riding is allowed on the trails, however.

As we've seen, Hilton Head has a Native American shell ring further north off Squire Pope Road. The Sea Pines Forest Preserve also boasts a shell ring set within a canopy of tall pines, forming a natural cathedral of sorts. A combination ceremonial area and communal common space, the shell ring today is actually a series of low rings made of discarded oyster shells covered with earth. As with Greens Shell Enclosure, the rewards here are contemplative in nature, since the actual oyster shells are beneath layers of soil. Scientists date the ring itself to about 1450 B.C., though human habitation on the island goes as far back as 8000 B.C.

Tours and Cruises
Almost all guided tours on Hilton Head focus on the water. **Harbour Town Cruises** (843/363-9023, www.vagabondcruise.com) offers several sightseeing tours, as well as excursions to Daufuskie and Savannah. They also offer a tour on a former America's Cup racing yacht.

"Dolphin tours" are extremely popular on Hilton Head and there is no shortage of proprietors. **Dolphin Watch Nature Cruises** (843/785-4558, $25 adults, $10 children) departs from Shelter Cove, as does **Lowcountry Nature Tours** (843/683-0187, $40 adult, $35 children, 2 and under free). **The Gypsy**

(843/363-2900, $12 adults, $6 children) sails out of South Beach Marina, taking you all around peaceful Calibogue Sound.

Two dolphin tours are based on Broad Creek, the large body of water which almost bisects the island through the middle. "Captain Jim" runs **Island Explorer Tours** (843/785-2100, $40 per person for two-hour tour) from a dock behind the old Oyster Factory on Marshland Road. Not to be outdone, "Captain Dave" leads tours at **Dolphin Discoveries** (843/681-1911 $40 adults, $30 ages 12 and under for two-hour tour), leaving out of Simmons Landing next to the Broad Creek Marina on Marshland Road.

Outside Hilton Head (843/686-6996, www.outsidehiltonhead.com) runs a variety of eco/dolphin waterborne tours as well as a guided day-trip excursion to Daufuskie, complete with golf cart rental. **Calibogue Cruises** (843/342-8687, thehiltonhead-daufuskieconnection.com) provides a similar service.

For an in-depth look at Hilton Head's rich Gullah history, you might want to call **Gullah Heritage Trail Tours** (843/681-7066, www.gullahheritage.com, Wed.–Sat. 10 A.M. and 2 P.M., Sun. 2 P.M., $22 adults, $11 children), which departs from the Coastal Discovery Museum.

ENTERTAINMENT AND EVENTS
Nightlife
The crowd is definitely on the older side, but without a doubt the most high-quality live entertainment on the island is at **The Jazz Corner** (1000 William Hilton Pkwy., 843/842-8620, www.thejazzcorner.com, dinner daily 6–9 P.M., late-night menu after 9 P.M.), which brings in the best names in the country—and outstanding regulars like Bob Masteller and Howard Paul—to perform in this space in the somewhat unlikely setting of a boutique mall, the Village at Wexford. The dinners are great, but the attraction here is definitely the music. Reservations are recommended. Live music starts around 7 P.M.

The premier live concert venue in Hilton

LOWCOUNTRY

WHO ARE THE GULLAH?

A language, a culture, and a people with a shared history, Gullah is more than that – it's also a state of mind.

Simply put, the Gullah are African Americans of the Sea Islands of South Carolina and Georgia. (In Georgia, the term "Geechee," from the nearby Ogeechee River, is more or less interchangeable.) Protected from outside influence by the isolation of this coastal region after the Civil War, Gullah culture is the closest living cousin to the West African traditions of their ancestors imported as slaves.

While you might hear that "Gullah" is a corruption of "Angola," some linguists think it simply means "people" in a West African language. In any case, the Gullah speak what's known as a "creole" language, i.e., one derived from several sources. Gullah combines elements of Elizabethan English, Jamaican patois, and several West African dialects; for example "goober" (peanut) comes from the Congo n'guba.

Another creole element is a word with multiple uses, for example Gullah's shum could mean "see them," "see him," "see her," or "see it," in either past or present tense, depending on context.

Though several white writers in the 1900s published collections of Gullah folk tales, for the most part the Gullah tongue was simply considered broken English. That changed with the publication of Lorenzo Dow Turner's groundbreaking Africanisms in the Gullah Dialect in 1949. Turner traced elements of the language to Sierra Leone in West Africa and more than 300 Gullah words directly to Africa.

Gullah is typically spoken very rapidly, which of course only adds to its impenetrability to the outsider. Gullah also relies on colorful turns of phrase. "E tru mout" ("He true mouth") means the speaker is referring to someone who doesn't lie. "Ie een crack muh teet" ("I didn't even crack my teeth") means "I kept quiet." A forgetful Gullah speaker might say, "Mah head leab me" ("My head left me").

Gullah music, as practiced by the world-famous Hallelujah Singers of St. Helena Island, also uses many distinctly African techniques, such as call and response (the folk hymn "Michael Row the Boat Ashore" is a good example).

The most famous Americans with Gullah roots are boxer Joe Frazier (Beaufort), hip-hop star Jazzy Jay (Beaufort), NFL great Jim Brown (St. Simons Island, Georgia), and Supreme Court Justice Clarence Thomas (Pin Point, Georgia, near Savannah).

Upscale development continues to claim more and more traditional Gullah areas, generally by pricing them out through rapidly increasing property values. Today, the major pockets of living Gullah culture in South

Head these days is the relatively new **Shoreline Ballroom** (40 Folly Field Rd., 843/842-0358, www.shorelineballroom.com), which has a very eclectic show calendar ranging from rapper Snoop Dogg to bluegrass legend Ralph Stanley.

For years islanders have jokingly referred to the "Barmuda Triangle," an area named for the preponderance of bars within walking distance of Sea Pines Circle. The longtime heart of the Barmuda Triangle is the **Tiki Hut** (1 S. Forest Beach Dr., 843/785-5126, Sun.–Thurs. 11 A.M.–8 P.M., Fri.–Sat. 11 A.M.–10 P.M., bar until 2 A.M.), actually part of the Holiday Inn Oceanfront Hotel at the entrance to Sea

Pines. This popular watering hole is the only beachfront bar on the island, which technically makes it the only place you can legally drink alcohol on a Hilton Head beach. Another Barmuda Triangle staple is **Casey's Sports Bar and Grille** (37 New Orleans Rd., 843/785-2255, daily 11 A.M.–2 A.M.), which despite its moniker and its 40 TVs is not just for sports fans—there's also a lively karaoke scene.

Inside Sea Pines is the **Quarterdeck Lounge and Patio** (843/842-1999, www.seapines.com, Sun.–Thurs. 5:30–10 P.M., Fri.–Sat. 5:30 P.M.–midnight) at the base of the Harbour Town Lighthouse. This is where the party's at after

Carolina are in Beaufort, St. Helena Island, Daufuskie Island, Edisto Island, and a northern section of Hilton Head Island.

The old ways are not as prevalent as they were, but two key educational and outreach institutions are keeping alive the spirit of Gullah: the **Penn Center** (16 Martin Luther King Dr.,

843/838-2474, www.penncenter.com, Mon.-Sat. 11 A.M.-4 P.M., $4 adults, $2 seniors and children) on St. Helena Island, near Beaufort, and the **Avery Research Center** (66 George St., 843/953-7609, www.cofc.edu/avery, Mon.-Fri. 10 A.M.-5 P.M., Sat. noon-5 P.M.) at the College of Charleston.

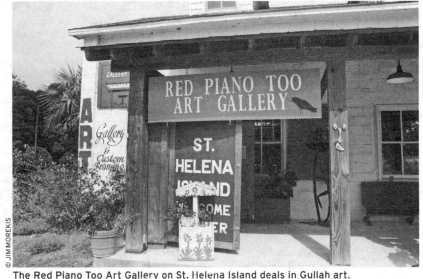

© JIMMOREKIS

The Red Piano Too Art Gallery on St. Helena Island deals in Gullah art.

a long day on the fairways during the Verizon Heritage golf tournament.

Within Sea Pines at the South Beach marina is also where you'll find **The Salty Dog Cafe** (232 S. Sea Pines Dr., 843/671-2233, www .saltydog.com, lunch daily 11 A.M.–3 P.M., dinner daily 5–10 P.M., bar daily until 2 A.M.), one of the area's most popular institutions (some might even call it a tourist trap) and something akin to an island empire, with popular T-shirts, a gift shop, books, and an ice cream shop, all overlooking the marina. It's a fun place at night, with live entertainment and a fun-loving, reasonably diverse crowd. Margaritas are great here, but skip the food; if

you're hungry, try the affiliated Wreck of the Salty Dog nearby.

Performing Arts

Because so many of its residents migrated here from art-savvy metropolitan areas in the northeast, Hilton Head maintains a very high standard of top-quality entertainment. Much of the activity centers on the multimillion-dollar **Arts Center of Coastal Carolina** (14 Shelter Cove Ln., 843/842-2787, www.artshhi.com), which hosts touring shows, resident companies, musical concerts, dance performances, and visual arts exhibits.

Now over a quarter-century old and under

the direction of maestro Mary Woodmansee Green, the **Hilton Head Symphony Orchestra** (843/842-2055, www.hhso.org) performs a year-round season of masterworks and pops programs, generally at the First Presbyterian Church (540 William Hilton Pkwy.). They also take their show on the road with several concerts in Bluffton, and even perform several "Symphony Under the Stars" programs at Shelter Cove.

Chamber Music Hilton Head (www.cmhh .org) performs throughout the year with selections ranging from Brahms to Smetana at All Saints Episcopal Church (3001 Meeting St.).

The **South Carolina Repertory Company** (136B Beach City Rd., Studio B, 843/342-2057, www.hiltonheadtheatre .com) performs an eclectic, challenging season, from musicals *(Tomfoolery)* to cutting-edge drama *(The Drawer Boy)* to the outright avant-garde *(Some Things you Need to Know Before the World Ends [A Final Evening with the Illuminati]).*

Cinema

There's an art house on Hilton Head, the charming little **Coligny Theatre** (843/686-3500, www.colignytheatre.com) in the Coligny Plaza shopping center before you get to Sea Pines. For years this was the only movie theatre for miles around, but it reincarnated as a primarily indie film venue in 2002. Look for the entertaining murals by local artist Ralph Sutton. Daily showtimes are 4 P.M. and 7 P.M. (no 7 P.M. show on Mondays) and Monday, Tuesday, and Friday at 11:30 A.M.

The main multiplex on Hilton Head is **Northridge Cinema 10** (Hwy. 278 and Mathews Dr., 843/342-3800, www.southeast cinemas.com) in the Northridge Plaza shopping center. Off the island is the way-cool new **Sea Turtle Cinemas** (106 Buckwalter Pkwy., 843/706-2888, www.seaturtlecinemas.com) in the Berkeley Place shopping center. To get there take the William Hilton Parkway/U.S. 278 west off Hilton Head about 10 miles. Turn left at Buckwalter Parkway. Sea Turtle Cinemas is a half-mile farther on the right.

Festivals and Events

Late February and early March brings the Hilton Head **WineFest** (www.hiltonheadhospitality .org), which culminates in what they call "The East Coast's Largest Outdoor Public Tasting and Auction" in Shelter Cove Community Park. Some events charge admission.

A small but delightful event is the **Hilton Head Quilt Festival** (www.palmettoquiltguild .org), sponsored each March by the Palmetto Quilt Guild and held at the St. Andrew by the Sea Methodist Church. A nominal fee gets you in to see a display of over 100 handcrafted quilts.

Hilton Head's premier event is the **Verizon Heritage Classic Golf Tournament** (843/671-2248, www.verizonheritage.com), held each April at the Harbour Town Golf Links on Sea Pines Plantation. Formerly known as the MCI Heritage Classic, the event is South Carolina's only PGA Tour event and brings thousands of visitors to town yearly.

September brings one of Hilton Head's most beloved events, the **Food Fest** (www .hiltonheadhospitality.org). Activity centers on the Shelter Cove shopping district and features diverse culinary entertainment such as a Drink Making Contest, a Tailgate Gourmet Challenge, and a Hospitable Waiters Race. Some events charge admission.

A fun and fondly anticipated yearly event is the **Kiwanis Club Chili Cookoff** (www.hilton headkiwanis.org), held each October at Honey Horn on the island's south end. A low admission price gets you all the chili you can eat plus free antacids. All funds go to charity, and all excess chili goes to a local food bank.

Every November brings Hilton Head's second-largest event, the world-famous **Hilton Head Concours d'Elegance & Motoring Festival** (www.hhiconcours.com), a multi-day event bringing together vintage car clubs from throughout the nation and culminating in a prestigious "Best of Show" competition.

SHOPPING

As you'd expect, Hilton Head is a shopper's delight, with an emphasis on upscale stores and prices to match. Keep in mind that hours may be shortened in the off season (Nov.–Mar.). Here's a rundown of the main island shopping areas in the order you'll encounter them as you enter the island.

Shelter Cove

Associated with the attached residential community, this shopping area on Broad Creek right off the William Hilton Parkway actually comprises three entities, the larger **Mall at Shelter Cove,** the smaller **Plaza at Shelter Cove,** and the dockside **Shelter Cove Harbour.**

The Mall opens at 10 A.M. Monday–Saturday and noon on Sunday and features the usual national stores you'd expect, but with a few typically Hilton Head upgrades like **Off 5th/ Saks Fifth Avenue Outlet** (843/341-2088) and **Williams-Sonoma** (843/785-2408). Other neat stores in the Mall are **DeGullah Creations** (843/686-5210), specializing in authentic Gullah wares, and **Blue Parrot** (800/252-6653), with gift lines such as Wee Forest Folk and Swarovski Crystal.

The most interesting store at the Plaza is no doubt the flagship location of **Outside Hilton Head** (843/686-6996, www.outsidehilton head.com, Mon.–Sat. 10 A.M.–5:30 P.M., Sun. 11 A.M.–5:30 P.M.), a complete outdoor outfitter with a thoroughly knowledgeable staff (they have a smaller satellite store in Sea Pines). Whatever outdoor gear you need and whatever tour you want to take, they can most likely hook you up.

Shelter Cove Harbour hosts a few cute shops hewing to its overall nautical/vacation theme, such as the clothing stores **Camp Hilton Head** (843/842-3666, Mon.–Sat. 10 A.M.–9 P.M., Sun. noon–5 P.M.) and the marine supplier **Ship's Store** (843/842-7001, Mon.–Sat. 7:30 A.M.–5 P.M., Sun. 7:30 A.M.–4 P.M.).

Village at Wexford

This well-shaded shopping center on William Hilton Parkway hosts the Lily Pulitzer signature women's store **S.M. Bradford Co.** (843/686-6161, Mon.–Sat. 10 A.M.–6 P.M.)

and the aromatic **Scents of Hilton Head** (843/842-7866, Mon.–Fri. 10 A.M.–6 P.M., Sat. 10 A.M.–5 P.M.).

Coligny Circle

This is the closest Hilton Head comes to funkier beach towns like Tybee Island or Folly Beach, though it's doesn't really come that close. You'll find some delightful and somewhat quirky stores here, many keeping long hours in the summer, like the self-explanatory **Coligny Kite & Flag Co.** (843/785-5483, Mon.–Sat. 10 A.M.–9 P.M., Sun. 11 A.M.–6 P.M.), the hippie-fashion **Loose Lucy's** (843/785-8093, Mon.–Sat. 10 A.M.–6 P.M., Sun. 11 A.M.–5 P.M.), and the Caribbean-flavored **Jamaican Me Crazy** (843/785-9006, daily 10 A.M.–10 P.M.). Kids will love both **The Shell Shop** (843/785-4900, Mon.–Sat. 10 A.M.–9 P.M., Sun. noon–9 P.M.) and **Black Stone Minerals** (843/785-7090, Mon. Sat. 10 A.M.–10 P.M., Sun. 11 A.M.–8 P.M.).

Harbour Town

The Shoppes at Harbour Town are a collection of 20 mostly boutique stores along Lighthouse Road. Probably the most interesting is **Match** (843/671-4653, www.match goods.com, daily 10 A.M.–9 P.M.), an upscale vintage store that acquires antiques, designer items, and home goods through a corporate partnership for resale, and also boasts its own walk-in humidor.

At **Planet Hilton Head** (843/363-5177, www.planethiltonhead.com) you'll find some cute, eclectic gifts and home goods. Other highlights include the clothier **Knickers Men's Store** (843/671-2291, daily 10 A.M.–9 P.M.), and the **Top of the Lighthouse Shoppe** (843/671-2810, www.harbourtownlight house.com, daily 10 A.M.–9 P.M.), where many a climbing tourist has been coaxed to part with some of their disposable income.

South Beach Marina

On South Sea Pines Drive at the Marina you'll find several worthwhile shops, including an "outpost" location of the great local outfitter

LOWCOUNTRY

Outside Hilton Head (800/686-6996, www.outsidehiltonhead.com) as well as a good ship's store and all-around grocery dealer **South Beach General Store** (843/671-6784, daily 8 A.M.–10 P.M.).

I like to stop in the **Blue Water Bait and Tackle** (843/671-3060) and check out the cool nautical stuff. They can also hook you up with a variety of kayak trips and fishing charters. And of course right on the water there's the ever-popular **Salty Dog Café** (843/671-2233, www.saltydog.com, lunch daily 11 A.M.–3 P.M., dinner daily 5–10 P.M.), whose ubiquitous T-shirts seem to adorn every other person on the island.

Thrift Shops

Don't scoff. Every thrift store connoisseur knows the best place to shop second-hand is in an affluent area like Hilton Head, where the locals try hard to stay in style and their castoffs are first-class. Key stops here are **The Bargain Box** (546 William Hilton Pkwy., 843/681-4305, Mon., Wed., and Fri. 1–4 P.M., Sat. 9:15 A.M.–12:15 P.M.) and **St. Francis Thrift Store** (2 Southwood Dr., 843/689-6563, Wed.–Sat. 10 A.M.–3 P.M.) right off the William Hilton Parkway.

Art Galleries

As with all the Lowcountry, visual artists are inexorably drawn to this area. Despite the wealth apparent in some quarters here, there's no free-standing art museum in the area, that role being filled by dozens of independent galleries.

My favorite gallery in the Hilton Head area would perhaps be more at home in Bluffton. The folk-art oriented **America. Oh Yes!** (1540 Fording Island Rd., 15 Bridge Center, 843/757-0088, Mon.–Sat. 11 A.M.–4 P.M.) has as its motto "art for people who don't care what their neighbors think." Fittingly for a gallery devoted to outsider art, America. Oh Yes! is actually just outside Hilton Head before you cross the bridge to the island.

For a more formal approach, go to **Morris & Whiteside Galleries & Sculpture Garden** (807

William Hilton Pkwy., 843/842-4433, www.morris-whiteside.com, daily 10 A.M.–5 P.M.), which features a variety of paintings and sculpture, heavy on landscapes but also showing some fine figurative work.

Not to be confused with the Red Piano Too on St. Helena Island, the **Red Piano Art Gallery** (220 Cordillo Pkwy., 843/785-2318, www.redpianoartgallery.com, daily 10 A.M.–5 P.M.) isn't devoted to Gullah art, but rather concentrates on natural landscapes with an often-whimsical touch.

The nonprofit **Art League of Hilton Head** (Pineland Station, Suite 207, Mon.–Sat. 10 A.M.–6 P.M.) displays work by member artists in all media.

SPORTS AND RECREATION
Beaches

First, the good news: Hilton Head Island has 12 miles of some of the most beautiful, safe beaches you'll find anywhere. The bad news is that there are only a few ways to gain access, generally at locations referred to as "beach parks." Don't just drive into a residential neighborhood and think you'll be able to park and find your way to the beach; for better or worse, Hilton Head is not set up for that kind of casual access.

Driessen Beach Park has 207 long-term parking spaces, costing $0.25 for 30 minutes. There's free parking but fewer spaces at the Coligny Beach Park entrance and at Fish Haul Creek Park. Also, there are 22 metered spaces at Alder Lane Beach Access, 51 at Folly Field Beach Park, and 13 at Burkes Beach Road. Most other beach parks are for permit parking only. Clean, well-maintained public restrooms are available at all the beach parks. You can find beach information at 843/342-4580 and www.hiltonheadislandsc.gov. Beach Park hours vary: Coligny Beach Park is open daily 24 hours. All other beach parks are open 6 A.M.–8 P.M. March–September and 6 A.M.–5 P.M. October–February.

Alcohol is strictly prohibited on Hilton Head's beaches. This may cut down on your vacation fun, but the plus side is the ban makes the beaches very friendly for families. There are lifeguards on all the beaches during the summer, but be aware that the worst undertow is on the northern stretches. Also please remember to leave the sand dollars where they are; their population is dwindling due to souvenir hunting.

Kayaking

Kayakers will enjoy Hilton Head Island, which offers several gorgeous routes, including Calibogue Sound to the south and west and Port Royal Sound to the north. For particularly good views of life on the salt marsh, try Broad Creek, which nearly bisects Hilton Head Island, and Skull Creek, which separates Hilton Head from the natural beauty of Pinckney Island. Broad Creek Marina is a good place to put in. There are also two public landings, Haigh Landing and Buckingham Landing, on Mackays Creek at the entrance to the island, one on either side of the bridge.

If you want a guided tour, there are plenty of great kayak tour outfits to choose from in the area. Chief among them is certainly **Outside Hilton Head** (32 Shelter Cove Ln., 800/686-6996, www.outsidehiltonhead.com). They offer a wide range of guided trips, including "The Outback," in which you're first boated to a private island and then taken on a tour of tidal creeks, and five- or seven-hour "Ultimate Lowcountry Day" trips to Daufuskie, Bluffton, or Bull Creek.

Other good places to book a tour or just rent a kayak are **Water-Dog Outfitters** (Broad Creek Marina, 843/686-3554) and **Kayak Hilton Head** (Broad Creek Marina, 843/684-1910). **Cool Breeze Kayaking** (Broad Creek Landing, 843/683-4040) offers two-hour dolphin kayak tours. Leaving out of the Harbour Town Yacht Basin is **H2O Sports** (843/671-4386, www.h2osports online.com), which offers 90-minute guided kayak tours ($30) and rents kayaks for about $20 per hour.

Within Palmetto Dunes Oceanfront Resort (4 Queens Folly Rd., 800/827-3006, www .palmettodunes.com) is **Palmetto Dunes**

Outfitters (843/785-2449, www.pdoutfitters .com, daily 9 A.M.–5 P.M.), which rents kayaks and canoes and offers lessons on the resort's 11-mile lagoon.

Fishing and Boating

As you'd expect, anglers and boaters love the Hilton Head/Bluffton area, which offers all kinds of saltwater, freshwater, and fly-fishing opportunities. Captain Brian Vaughn runs **Off the Hook Charters** (843/298-4376, www.offthehookcharters.com), which offers fully licensed trips at $400 for a half-day. **Carolina Sportfishing** offers deep-sea action on the 58-foot Viking yacht *Judith E* at about $200 per hour. Captain Dave Fleming of **Mighty Mako Sport Fishing Charters** (843/785-6028, www.mightymako.com) can take you saltwater fishing, both backwater and near-shore, on the 25-foot *Mighty Mako* for about $400 for a half-day.

If you're at the South Beach Marina area of Sea Pines Plantation head into **Blue Water Bait and Tackle** (843/671-3060) and see if they can hook you up with a trip.

Public landings in the Hilton Head area include the Marshland Road Boat Landing and the Broad Creek Boat Ramp under the Charles Fraser Bridge.

Hiking and Biking

Though the very flat terrain is not challenging, Hilton Head provides some scenic and relaxing biking opportunities. Thanks to wise planning and foresight, the island has an extensive 40-mile-plus network of biking trails that does a great job of keeping bikers out of traffic. A big plus is the long bike path paralleling the William Hilton Parkway, enabling cyclists to use that key artery without braving its traffic. There is even an underground bike path beneath the Parkway to facilitate crossing that busy road. In addition, there are also routes along Pope Avenue and North and South Forest Beach Drive.

Palmetto Dunes Oceanfront Resort (4 Queens Folly Rd., 800/827-3006, www .palmettodunes.com) has a particularly nice,

25-mile network of bike paths which all link up to the island's larger framework. Within the resort is **Palmetto Dunes Outfitters** (843/785-2449, www.pdoutfitters.com, daily 9 A.M.–5 P.M.), which will rent you any type of bike you might need. Sea Pines Plantation also has an extensive, 17-mile network of bike trails; you can pick up a map at most information kiosks within the plantation.

With the exception of Sea Pines, where five bucks gets you daily access, for biking purposes be aware that on the private residential developments, such as Palmetto Dunes, access technically is limited to residents and you may be challenged and asked where you're residing. Also, please pay attention to the miniature stop signs on the bike paths, ignorance of which can lead to some nasty scrapes or worse.

But the best bike path on Hilton Head is the simplest of all, where no one will ask you where you're staying that night: the beach. For a few hours before and after low tide the beach effectively becomes a 12-mile bike path around most of the island, and a pleasant morning or afternoon ride may well prove to be the highlight of your trip to the island.

There's a plethora of bike rental facilities on Hilton Head with competitive rates. Be sure and ask if they offer free pick-up and delivery. Try **Coconut Bike Rentals** (81 Pope Ave., 843/686-5055, daily 8 A.M.–5 P.M.) or **Hilton Head Bicycle Company** (112 Arrow Rd., 843/686-6888, Mon.–Sat. 9 A.M.–5 P.M., Sun. noon–5 P.M.).

Hikers will particularly enjoy Pinckney Island National Wildlife Refuge, which takes you through several key Lowcountry ecosystems, from maritime forest to salt marsh. Other peaceful, if non-challenging, trails are at the Audubon-Newhall Preserve on Hilton Head Island.

Horseback Riding

Within the Sea Pines Forest Preserve is **Lawton Stables** (190 Greenwood Dr., 843/671-2586, www.lawtonstableshhi.com), which features pony rides, a small animal farm, and guided horseback rides through the Preserve. You don't need any riding experience, but you do need reservations.

Bird-Watching

The premier birding locale in the area is the

Pinckney Island National Wildlife Refuge outside Hilton Head

© JIM MOREKIS

fabulous **Pinckney Island National Wildlife Refuge** (U.S. 278 East just before Hilton Head, 912/652-4415, www.fws.gov). You can see bald eagles, ibis, wood storks, painted buntings, and many more species. Birding is best in spring and fall. The refuge has several freshwater ponds that serve as wading bird rookeries. During migratory season, so many beautiful birds abound here making such a ruckus that you'll think you wandered onto an Animal Planet shoot.

Another good bird-watching locale is **Victoria Bluff Heritage Preserve** (803/734-3886, daily dawn–dusk, free), an 1100-acre pine-and-palmetto habitat. Get here from Hilton Head by taking U.S. 278 off the island. Take a right onto Sawmill Creek Road heading north. The parking area is shortly ahead on your right. Note that there are no facilities available here.

"Fore!"

Golf

Hilton Head is one of the world's great golf centers, with no less than 23 courses, and one could easily write a book about nothing but that. This, however, is not that book. Perhaps contrary to what you might think, most courses on the island are public and some are downright affordable. (All courses are 18 holes unless otherwise described; green fees are averages and vary with season and tee time.)

The best-regarded course, with prices to match, is **Harbour Town Golf Links** (Sea Pines Plantation, 843/363-4485, www.sea pines.com, $239). It's on the island's south end at Sea Pines and is the home of the annual Verizon Heritage Classic, far and away the island's number-one tourist draw.

There are two Arthur Hills–designed courses on the island, **Arthur Hills** at Palmetto Dunes Resort (843/785-1140, www.palmettodunes .com, $125) and **Arthur Hills at Palmetto Hall** (Palmetto Hall Plantation, 843/689-4100, www.palmettohallgolf.com, $130), both of which now offer the use of Segway vehicles on the fairways.

The reasonably priced **Barony Course** at Port Royal Plantation (843/686-8801, www

.portroyalgolfclub.com, $98) also boasts some of the toughest greens on the island. Another challenging and affordable course is the **George Fazio** at Palmetto Dunes Resort (843/785-1130, www.palmettodunes.com, $105).

Hilton Head National Golf Club (60 Hilton Head National Dr., 843/842-5900, www.golf hiltonheadnational.com), which is actually on the mainland just before you cross the bridge to Hilton Head, not only boasts a total of 27 challenging holes, but is consistently rated among the best golf locales in the world for both condition and service. *Golf Week* has named it one of America's best golf courses. All three courses here are public and green fees at each are below $100.

It's a good idea to book tee times through the **Golf Island Call Center** (888/465-3475, www.golfisland.com), which can also hook you up with good packages.

Tennis

One of the top tennis destinations in the country, Hilton Head has over 20 tennis clubs, some of which offer court time to the public

© CHERYL KUNDE/WWW.123RF.COM

(walk-on rates vary; call for information). They are: **Palmetto Dunes Tennis Center** (Palmetto Dunes Resort, 843/785-1152, www.palmetto dunes.com, $30/hr.), **Port Royal Racquet Club** (Port Royal Plantation, 843/686-8803, www.portroyalgolfclub.com, $25/hr.), **Sea Pines Racquet Club** (Sea Pines Plantation, 843/363-4495, www.seapines.com, $25/ hr.), **South Beach Racquet Club** (Sea Pines Plantation, 843/671-2215, www.seapines.com, $25/hr.), and **Shipyard Racquet Club** (Shipyard Plantation, 843/686-8804, $25/hr.).

Free, first-come-first-serve play is available at the following public courts maintained by the Island Recreation Association (www.island reccenter.org): **Chaplin Community Park** (Singleton Beach Rd., four courts, lighted), **Cordillo Courts** (Cordillo Pkwy., four courts, lighted), **Fairfield Square** (Adrianna Ln., two courts), **Hilton Head High School** (School Rd., six courts), and **Hilton Head Middle School** (Wilborn Rd., four courts).

ACCOMMODATIONS
Under $150

It won't blow you away, but you can't beat the price at **Park Lane Hotel and Suites** (12 Park Ln., 843/686-5700, www.hiltonheadparklane hotel.com, $120). This is your basic suite-type hotel (formerly a Residence Inn) with the basic free Continental breakfast. The allure here is the price, hard to find anywhere these days at a resort location. For a non-refundable $50 fee, you can bring your pet. The one drawback, probably reflected in the price, is that the beach is a good ways away. The hotel does offer a free shuttle, however, so it would be wise to take advantage of that and avoid the usual beach parking hassles.

$150-300

By Hilton Head standards, the **Main Street Inn** (2200 Main St., 800/471-3001, www.mainstreetinn.com, $229) can be considered a bargain stay, and with high quality to boot. With its Old World touches, sumptuous appointments, charming atmosphere, and attentive service, this 33-room inn on the grounds of Hilton Head Plantation seems like it would be more at home in Charleston than Hilton Head. They serve a great full breakfast—not Continental—daily 7:30–10:30 A.M. As a bonus, most of the less-expensive rooms have a great view of the formal garden, another part of that old Lowcountry appeal that's hard to come by on the island. If you want to upgrade, there are larger rooms with a fireplace and a smallish private courtyard for not much more. Overall, it's one of Hilton Head's best values.

Another good place for the price is the **South Beach Marina Inn** (232 S. Sea Pines Dr., 843/671-6498, www.sbinn.com, $186) in Sea Pines. Located near the famous Salty Dog Café and outfitted in a similar nautical theme, the inn not only has some pretty large rooms for the price, it offers a great view of the marina and has a very friendly feel, great for families with kids and romantic couples alike (especially with a beach on calm Calibogue Sound only a couple minutes' walk away). As with all Sea Pines accommodations, staying on the plantation means you don't have to wait in line with other visitors to pay the $5 a day "road fee." Sea Pines also offers a free trolley to get around the plantation.

One of Hilton Head's favorite hotels for true beach-lovers is the **Holiday Inn Oceanfront** (1 South Forest Beach Dr., 843/785-5126, www.hihiltonhead.com, $200), home of the famed Tiki Hut bar on the beach. Staff turnover is less frequent here than at other local accommodations, and while it's no Ritz-Carlton and occasionally shows signs of wear, it's a good value on a bustling area of the island. Parking has always been a problem here, but at least there's a free valet service.

One of the better resort-type places for those who prefer the putter and the racquet to the Frisbee and the surfboard is the **Inn at Harbour Town** (7 Lighthouse Ln., 843/363-8100, www.seapines.com, $199) in Sea Pines. The big draw here is the impeccable service, delivered by a staff of "butlers" in kilts, comprising mostly Europeans who take the venerable trade quite seriously. While it's not on the beach, you can take advantage of the free Sea Pines Trolley every 20 minutes.

Recently rated number-one family resort in the U.S. by *Travel & Leisure,* the well-run **⟨ Palmetto Dunes Oceanfront Resort** (4 Queens Folly Rd., 800/827-3006, www .palmettodunes.com, $150–300) offers something for everybody in terms of lodging. There are small, cozy condos by the beach, or larger villas overlooking the golf course, and pretty much everything in between. The prices are perhaps disarmingly affordable considering the relative luxury and copious recreational amenities, which include 25 miles of very well-done bike trails, 11 miles of kayak/canoe trails, and of course three signature links. As with most developments of this type on Hilton Head, most of the condos are privately owned and therefore each has its particular set of guidelines and cleaning schedules.

FOOD

You'll have no problem finding good restaurants in and around Hilton Head. Because of the fairly cosmopolitan nature of the population, with so many transplants from the northeastern United States and Europe, you might be surprised by the quality. Because of another demographic quirk of the area, its large percentage of senior citizens, you can also find some great deals by looking for some of the common "early bird" dinner specials, usually starting around 5 P.M.

Breakfast and Brunch

There are a couple of great diner-style places on the island. Though known more for its hamburgers and Philly cheesesteaks, **Harold's Diner** (641 William Hilton Pkwy., 843/842-9292, Mon.– Sat. 7 A.M.–3 P.M., $4–6) has great pancakes as well as its trademark brand of hilariously sarcastic service. Unpretentious and authentic in a place where those two adjectives are rarely used, Harold's is one of a few must-visit restaurants on Hilton Head. As one patron has said, "The lack of atmosphere *is* the atmosphere."

You'll find another great locally owned breakfast spot at **Skillets** (1 N. Forest Beach Dr., 843/785-3131, www.skilletscafe.com, breakfast daily 7 A.M.–5 P.M., dinner daily 5–10 P.M.,

$5–23) in Coligny Plaza in the Forest Beach area. Their eponymous stock in trade is a layered breakfast dish of sautéed ingredients served in a porcelain skillet, like the "Kitchen Sink" (pancakes ringed with potatoes, sausage, and bacon, topped with two poached eggs). The lunches are good too, including, believe it or not, an excellent meatloaf. Dinner is surprisingly upscale; try any of the excellent seafood dishes, like the blackened shrimp and scallops with tasso ham and blue cheese.

A great all-day breakfast place with a twist is **⟨ Signe's Heaven Bound Bakery & Café** (93 Arrow Rd., 843/785-9118, www.signes bakery.com, Mon.–Fri. 8 A.M.–4 P.M., Sat. 9 A.M.–2 P.M., $5–10). The breakfast comprises tasty dishes like frittatas and breakfast polenta, while the twist is the extensive artisan bakery, with delicious specialties like the signature key lime pound cake. You'll be surprised at the quality of the food for the low prices. Expect a wait in line at the counter during peak periods.

Mediterranean

For upscale Italian, try **Bistro Mezzaluna** (55 New Orleans Rd., 843/842-5011, daily 5–9:30 P.M.). Known far and wide for its osso bucco as well as its impeccable service, there's also a great little bar for cocktails before or after dinner.

Staying with that Southern European vibe, you might also like **Vassili's Mediterranean Tavern** (11 Lagoon Rd., 843/842-4033, www.vassilisofhiltonhead.com, lunch daily 11 A.M.–3 P.M., dinner daily 5–10 P.M., $15–40), owned by the locally revered restaurateurs of the Maniotis family. At this friendly place near Coligny Plaza you'll find all the high points of a typical Greek menu, including calamari, spanakopita, and of course a Greek salad. There are some great non-Greek items on the menu as well, including crab-stuffed grouper and a fine chicken piccata.

Mexican

Like many affluent areas in the United States, Hilton Head is almost entirely dependent on Mexican-American skilled labor, so it's no surprise that there are a couple of excellent and authentic Mexican restaurants on the island. Just off the William Hilton Parkway near the island's entrance, **(Mi Tierra** (160 Fairfield Square, 843/342-3409, lunch daily 11 A.M.–4 P.M., dinner Mon.–Fri. 4–9 P.M., Sat.–Sun. 4–10 P.M., $3–15) has a clientele about half-Gringo and half-Hispanic. (They also run a taco stand, **Baja Tacos,** closer to the road.) The tacos at both places are the real thing, nothing like what you'd find in a Taco Bell, as is the homemade and perfect guacamole. You'll find lots of traditional seafood dishes here, like ceviche, octopus, shrimp, and oysters. Mondays often host a real Mariachi band.

Another great Mexican place—also with a Bluffton location—is **Amigo's Café Y Cantina** (70 Pope Ave., 843/785-8226, Mon.–Sat. 11 A.M.–9 P.M., $8). While its strip-mall locale is not great, the food is fresh, simple, excellent, fast, and inexpensive.

Seafood

Not to be confused with Charley's Crab House next door to Hudson's, seafood lovers will enjoy the experience down near Sea Pines at **(Charlie's L'Etoile Verte** (8 New Orleans Rd., 843/785-9277, www.charliesofhiltonhead.com, lunch Tues.–Sat. 11:30 A.M.–2 P.M., dinner Mon.–Sat. 6–9:30 P.M., $25–40), which is considered by many connoisseurs to be Hilton Head's single best restaurant. The emphasis here is on "French country kitchen" cuisine—think Provence, not Paris. In keeping, each day's menu is concocted from scratch and handwritten. Listen to these recent entrées and feel your mouth water: flounder saute Meuniere, grilled wild coho salmon with a basil pesto, and breast of duck in a raspberry demi-glace. Get the picture? Of course you'll want to start with the escargot and leeks vol-au-vent, the house paté, or even some pan-roasted Bluffton oysters. As you'd expect the wine selection is celestial. Reservations are essential.

Perhaps the most unique restaurant on Hilton Head is **Red Fish** (8 Archer Rd., 843/686-3388, www.redfishofhiltonhead.com, lunch Mon.–Sat. 11:30 A.M.–2 P.M., dinner daily beginning with early-bird specials at 5 P.M., $20–37). Strongly Caribbean in decor as well as menu, with romanticism and panache to match, this is a great place for couples. The creative but accessible menu by Executive Chef Sean Walsh incorporates unique spices, fruits, and vegetables for a fresh, zesty palate. The recommended course of action is to pick your own wine from the truly vast, thousand-bottle-plus, award-winning selection in the attached wine shop and cellar to go with your dinner (there's a small corkage fee). You can't go wrong with any entrée here, but highlights include the grilled grouper with a mango avocado salsa, the horseradish-encrusted salmon, and the Dominican braised pork cooked in coconut milk with cilantro, chilies, fried bananas, jasmine rice, and Cuban black beans. Reservations are essential.

It's not cheap, but fresh seafood lovers will enjoy one of Hilton Head's staples, the huge **Hudson's on the Docks** (1 Hudson Rd., 843/681-2772, www.hudsononthedocks.com, lunch daily 11 A.M.–4 P.M., opens for dinner at 5 P.M., $14–23) on Skull Creek just off Squire Pope Road on the less-developed north side. Much of the catch—though not all of it by any means—comes directly off the boats you'll see dockside. Built on the old family oyster factory, Hudson's is now owned by transplants from, of all places, Long Island, New York. Still, its record of satisfied customers, heavy on the families, remains intact. Try the stuffed shrimp, filled with crabmeat, or just go for a combination platter. Leave room for one of the homemade desserts by Ms. Bessie, a 30-year Hudson's veteran employee.

INFORMATION AND SERVICES

The best place to get information on Hilton Head, book a room, or secure a tee time is just as you come onto the island at the **Hilton Head Island Chamber of Commerce Welcome Center** (100 William Hilton Pkwy., 843/785-3673, www.hiltonheadisland.org, daily 9 A.M.–6 P.M.). It's in the same building as the Coastal Discovery Museum.

Hilton Head's paper of record is the *Island Packet* (www.islandpacket.com).

Hilton Head's **post office** (13 William Hilton Pwy., 843/893-3490) is in an easy-to-find location.

GETTING THERE AND AROUND

A few years back, the Savannah International Airport added Hilton Head to its name specifically to identify itself with that lucrative market. It's been a success, and that facility remains the closest airport to Hilton Head Island and Bluffton. From the airport go north on I-95 into South Carolina, and take exit 8 onto U.S. 278 east.

If you're entering the area by car, the best route is also exit 8 off of I-95 onto U.S. 278, which takes you by Bluffton and right into Hilton Head. Near Bluffton, U.S. 278 is called Fording Island Road, and on Hilton Head proper it becomes the William Hilton Parkway business route. Technically, U.S. 278 turns into the new Cross Island Parkway, but when most locals say "278" they're almost always referring to the William Hilton Parkway.

Other than taxi services, there is no public transportation to speak of in the Lowcountry, unless you want to count the free shuttle around Sea Pines Plantation. Taxi services include **Yellow Cab** (843/686-6666), **Island Taxi** (843/683-6363), and **Ferguson Transportation** (843/842-8088).

BLUFFTON

Similar to Beaufort, except even quieter and smaller, Bluffton is an idyllic village on the banks of the wide, hypnotically serene, and well-preserved May River. Despite its friendly, open ways today, Bluffton was the original hotbed of secession, with Charleston diarist Mary Chesnut famously referring to the town as "the center spot of the fire eaters."

Old Bluffton

While its outskirts (so-called "Greater Bluffton") are now a haven for new planned communities hoping to mimic some aspect of Bluffton's historic patina, the town center itself remains an authentic and charmingly retro look at old South Carolina. Retro cuts both ways, however, and Bluffton has been a notorious speed trap for generations. Always obey the speed limit.

When General Sherman came through, he repaid the favor of those original Bluffton secessionists, which is why only nine homes in Bluffton are of antebellum vintage; the rest his troops torched. One of the survivors is the **Heyward House Historic Center** (70 Boundary St., 843/757-6293, www.heyward house.org, Mon.–Fri. 10 A.M.–3 P.M., Sat. 11 A.M.–2 P.M., $5 adults, $2 students), which is not only open to tours but serves as Bluffton's visitors center. Built in 1840 as a summer home for the owner of Moreland Plantation, John Cole, the house was later owned by George Cuthbert Heyward, grandson of Declaration of Independence signer Thomas Heyward. (Remarkably, it stayed in the family until the 1990s.) Of note are the intact slave quarters on the grounds.

The center of tourist activity focuses on the **Old Bluffton Historic District,** several blocks of 1800s buildings clustered between the parallel Boundary and Calhoun Streets (old-timers sometimes call this the "original square mile"). Many of the buildings are private residences, but most have been converted into art studios and antiques stores. The wares feature a whimsical, folk art quality very much in tune with Bluffton's whole Southern Shangri-la feel. While the artists and shopkeepers are serious about their work, they make a point to warmly invite everyone in, even when they're busy at work on the latest project.

Whatever you do, don't fail to go all the way to the end of Calhoun Street as it dead-ends on a high bluff on the May River at the Bluffton Public Dock. Overlooking this peaceful marsh-front vista is the sublimely photogenic **Church of the Cross** (110 Calhoun St., 843/757-2661, www.thechurchofthecross.net, tours Mon.–Sat. 10 A.M.–2 P.M.). Though the current sanctuary

LOWCOUNTRY

© JIM MOREKIS

Church of the Cross on the May River in Bluffton

was built in 1854 and is one of only two local churches not burned in the Civil War, the parish itself began in 1767, with the first services on this spot held in the late 1830s. Standing here on the bluff, with the steady south breeze blowing the bugs away and relieving you of the Lowcountry heat, you can see why affluent South Carolinians began building summer homes here in the 1800s.

You might want to get a gander at the state's last remaining working oyster house, the **Bluffton Oyster Company** (63 Wharf St., 843/757-4010, Mon.–Sat. 9 A.M.–5:30 P.M.), while you still can. The adjoining five acres were recently purchased by the Beaufort County Open Land Trust with the intention of evolving the area into a community greenspace celebrating a key aspect of local heritage, the celebrated May River oyster. Meanwhile Larry and Tina Toomer continue to oversee the oyster harvesting-and-shucking family enterprise, which has roots going back to the early 1900s.

While the oysters are growing scarce on the May River, get a close-up look at an interesting

state-funded seafood farm on the Colleton River estuary, the **Waddell Mariculture Center** (Sawmill Creek Rd., 843/837-3795). Free tours are available Monday, Tuesday, Wednesday, and Friday mornings. Shrimp, fish, and shellfish are some of the "product" raised and harvested here. Get to Waddell by taking U.S. 278 east out of Bluffton and then taking a left on Sawmill Creek Road.

Festivals and Events

A fairly new event happens each October in Bluffton, the **Arts & Seafood Festival** (www .blufftonartsandseafoodfestival.com). The emphasis is on locally harvested shrimp and oysters. A 5K run is featured on Saturday morning, with Sunday bringing a traditional Blessing of the Fleet ceremony on the river.

Shopping

Bluffton's eccentric little art studios, most clustered in a two-block stretch on Calhoun Street, are by far its main shopping draw. Named for the Lowcountry phenomenon you find in the

© JIM MOREKIS

the docks of the Bluffton Oyster Company

marsh at low tide amongst the fiddler crabs, Bluffton's **Pluff Mudd Art** (27 Calhoun St., 843/757-5551, Mon.–Sat. 10 A.M.–5:30 P.M.) is a cooperative of 16 great young painters and photographers from throughout the area.

The **Guild of Bluffton Artists** (20 Calhoun St., 843/757-5590, Mon.–Sat., 10 A.M.–4:30 P.M.) features works from many local artists, as does the outstanding **Society of Bluffton Artists** (48 Boundary St., 843/757-6586).

For cool, custom handcrafted pottery, try **Preston Pottery and Gallery** (10 Church St., 843/757-3084). Another great Bluffton place is the hard-to-define **eggs'n'tricities** (71 Calhoun St., 843/757-3446). The name pretty much says it all for this fun and eclectic vintage/junk/jewelry/folk art store.

While the most unique gift items in Bluffton are in its many local art galleries and studios, there are a couple of charming, non-art related shops that are very much worth checking out— and conveniently, they're right next to each other! The aptly named **The Store** (56 Calhoun St., 843/757-3855, Mon.–Sat. 10 A.M.–5 P.M.) is located, sure enough, in the historic 1904 Peeples Store building. Babby Guscio's place not only offers a lot of neat knick-knacks and gifts in addition to tasty comestibles, it's also a great place to meet locals and strike up a conversation. But no high heels, please! Literally right next door in an adjoining space is the tiny but thoroughly delightful **Scuppernongs** (56-A Calhoun St., 843/757-8463, Mon.–Sat. 11 A.M.–7 P.M.) wine shop.

If you want to score some fresh local seafood for your own culinary adventure, the no-brainer choice is the **Bluffton Oyster Company** (63 Wharf St., 843/757-4010), the state's only active oyster facility. They also have shrimp, crab, clams, and fish, nearly all of it from the nearly pristine May River on whose banks it sits.

For a much more commercially intense experience, head just outside of town on U.S. 278 on the way to Hilton Head to find the dual **Tanger Outlet Centers** (1414 Fording Island Rd., 843/837-4339, Mon.–Sat. 10 A.M.–9 P.M., Sun. 11 A.M.–6 P.M.), an outlet-shopper's

© JIM MOREKIS

Many fun shops, such as eggs'n'tricities, are on Calhoun Street in Old Bluffton.

paradise with virtually every major brand represented, from Nine West to Ralph Lauren to Abercrombie & Fitch and dozens more, including new additions Skechers and the Limited Too. A serious shopper can easily spend most of a day here between its two sprawling malls, Tanger I and Tanger II, so be forewarned!

Sports and Recreation

A key kayaking outfitter in Bluffton is **Native Guide Kayak Tours** (8 2nd St., 843/757-5411), which features tours of the May and New Rivers led by native Ben Turner. Another good outfit is **Swamp Girls Kayak Tours** (843/784-2249, www.swampgirls.com), the labor of love of Sue Chapman and Linda Etchells.

To put in your own kayak or canoe on the scenic, well-preserved May River, go to the **Alljoy Landing** at the eastern terminus of Alljoy Road along the river. Or try the dock at the end of Calhoun Street near the Church of the Holy Cross. There's also a rough put-in area at the Bluffton Oyster Company (63 Wharf St.), which has a public park adjacent

to it. For fishing, public landings include the dock on Calhoun Street, Alljoy Landing, and Bluffton Oyster Company.

You can find a great 12-mile tour of Old Town Bluffton at www.greaterblufftonpathways.org. It starts at the Piggly Wiggly grocery store in town, goes south on Thomas Heyward Street, east on Bridge Street, north on Calhoun Street, south on Bluffton Road, and east on Alljoy Road. The route includes spurs to the Church of the Cross, Myrtle Island, the marsh on the May River, and Pine Island.

For a much more wild hiking and bird-watching experience, go north of Bluffton to **Victoria Bluff Heritage Preserve** (803/734-3886, daily dawn–dusk, free), an 1100-acre flatwoods habitat notable for featuring all four native species of palmetto tree. There are no facilities, and a lot of hunting goes on in November and December. Get here from Bluffton by taking Burnt Church Road to U.S. 278. Take a right onto U.S. 278 and then a left onto Sawmill Creek Road heading north. The parking area is shortly ahead on your right.

The closest public golf courses to Bluffton are the Arnold Palmer–designed **Crescent Pointe Golf Club** (1 Crescent Pointe Dr., 888/292-7778, www.crescentpointegolf.com, $90) and the nine-hole **Old Carolina Golf Club** (89 Old Carolina Rd., 888/785-7274, www.oldcarolinagolf.com, $26), certainly one of the best golf deals in the region.

Accommodations
UNDER $150
A quality bargain stay right between Bluffton and Hilton Head is the **Holiday Inn Express Bluffton** (35 Bluffton Rd., 843/757-2002, www.ichotelsgroup.com, $120), on U.S. 278 as you make the run onto Hilton Head proper. It's not close to the beach or to Old Town Bluffton, so you'll definitely be using your car, but its central location will appeal to those who want to keep their options open.

OVER $300
For an ultra-upscale spa and golf resort environment near Bluffton, the clear pick is the **Inn at Palmetto Bluff** (476 Mt. Pelia Rd., 843/706-6500, www.palmettobluffresort.com, $650–900) just across the May River. This Auberge property was picked in 2006 as the number-two U.S. resort by *Condé Nast Traveler* magazine. Despite its glitzy pedigree and extremely upper-end prices, it's more Tara than Trump Tower. The main building is modeled after a Lowcountry plantation home, and the idyllic views of the May River are blissful. Lodging is dispersed among a series of cottages and "village home" rentals.

Needless to say, virtually your every need is provided for here, though the nearest off-site restaurant of any quality is quite a drive away. That will likely make little difference to you, however, since there are three top-flight dining options on the grounds: the fine dining **River House Restaurant** (843/706-6542, breakfast daily 7–11 A.M., lunch or "porch" menu daily 11 A.M.–10 P.M., dinner daily 6–10 P.M., $30–40); the **May River Grill** (Tues.–Sat. 11 A.M.–4 P.M., $9–13) at the golf clubhouse; and the casual **Buffalo's** (843/706-6630,

Sun.–Tues. 11:30 A.M.–5 P.M., Wed.–Sat. 11:30 A.M.–9 P.M., $10–15).

Food
BREAKFAST AND BRUNCH
No discussion of Bluffton cuisine is complete without the famous **Squat 'n' Gobble** (1231 May River Rd., 843/757-4242, Mon.–Fri. 7 A.M.–9 P.M., Sat.–Sun. 7 A.M.–3 P.M.), a wholly local phenomenon—and not to be confused with a similarly named chain of eateries in California. Long a site of gossiping and politicking as well as, um, squatting and gobbling, this humble diner on the May River Road in town is an indelible part of the local consciousness. Believe it or not, despite the totally unpretentious greasy-spoon ambience—or because of it—the food's actually quite good. They specialize in the usual "American" menu of eggs, bacon, hamburgers, hot dogs, and fries. There's a tie for best thing on the menu—I can't decide whether the Greek pizza is better or the barbecue, so I'll go with both.

CLASSIC SOUTHERN
Another beloved Bluffton institution (and believe me, Blufftonians love their institutions) is **Pepper's Porch** (1255 May River Rd., 843/757-2295, Tues.–Sun. 11:30 A.M.–9 P.M., $12–20). Housed in an old barn for drying a local herb called deer tongue, this is the kind of distinctly Southern place where they bring out a basket of little corn muffins instead of bread. Entrées include a great stuffed grouper and delicious, fresh-fried shrimp. Don't miss the fried strawberry dessert, which tastes a million times better than it sounds. Weekends see live music and karaoke in the aptly named Back Bar, a favorite local hangout.

Prime rib is the house specialty at **Myrtle's Bar & Grill** (32 Bruin Rd., 843/757-6300, lunch Tues.–Fri. 11:30 A.M.–2:30 P.M., dinner Tues.–Sat. 5–9:30 P.M., brunch Sun. 10 A.M.–2 P.M.), generally served on Tuesday nights. They also do a mean flounder. Housed in the old post office, Myrtle's is a favorite local hangout and has recently begun hosting an interactive murder-mystery dinner theatre show.

FRENCH

Most dining in Bluffton is pretty casual, but you'll get the white tablecloth treatment at **Claude & Uli's Signature Bistro** (1533 Fording Island Rd., 843/837-3336, lunch Mon.–Fri. 11:30 A.M.–2:30 P.M., dinner Mon.–Sat. starting at 5 P.M., $18–25) just outside of town in Moss Village. Chef Claude has brought his extensive European training and background (including Maxim's in Paris) to this romantic little spot. Claude does a great veal cordon bleu as well as a number of fine seafood entrées, such as an almond-crusted tilapia and an excellent seafood pasta. Don't miss their specialty soufflé for dessert, which you should order with dinner as it takes almost a half-hour to bake.

MEXICAN

My favorite restaurant in Bluffton is a near-copy of an equally fine Mexican restaurant in Hilton Head, **Mi Tierra** (101 Mellichamp Center, 843/757-7200, lunch daily 11 A.M.–4 P.M., dinner Mon.–Fri. 4–9 P.M. Sat.–Sun. 4–10 P.M., $3–15). They have very high-quality Tex-Mex style food in a fun atmosphere at great prices. Another highly-regarded Mexican place in Bluffton is **Amigo's Café Y Cantina** (133 Towne Dr., 843/815-8226, Mon.–Sat. 11 A.M.–9 P.M., $8).

Information and Services

You'll find Bluffton's visitors center in the **Heyward House Historic Center** (70 Boundary St., 843/757-6293, www.heyward house.org).

A good Bluffton publication is *Bluffton Today* (www.blufftontoday.com).

If you need postal services, Bluffton also has its own **post office** (32 Bruin Rd., 843/757-3588).

DAUFUSKIE ISLAND

Sitting right between Savannah and Hilton Head Island and accessible only by water, Daufuskie Island has about 500 full-time residents, most of whom ride around on golf carts or bikes (there's only one paved road, Haig Point Road, and cars are a rare sight). Once the home of rice and indigo plantations and rich oyster beds—the latter destroyed by pollution and overharvesting—the two upscale residential resort communities on the island, begun in the 1980s, give a clue as to where the future lies, though the recent global economic downturn has slowed development to a standstill.

The area of prime interest to tourists is the unincorporated western portion, or **Historic District,** the old stomping grounds of Pat Conroy during his stint as a teacher of resident African American children. His old two-room schoolhouse of *The Water is Wide* fame, the **Mary Field School,** is still there, as is the adjacent 140-year-old **Union Baptist Church,** but Daufuskie students now have a surprisingly modern new facility (middle school students are still ferried to mainland schools every day).

Farther north on Haig Point Road is the new **Billie Burn Museum,** housed in the old Mt. Carmel Church and named after the island's resident historian. On the southern end you'll find the **Bloody Point Lighthouse,** named for the vicious battle fought nearby during the Yamasee War of 1815 (the light was actually moved a half-mile inland in the early 1900s). Other areas of interest throughout the island include Native American sites, tabby ruins, the old Baptist Church, and a couple of cemeteries.

Otherwise there's really not much to do on Daufuskie. It's a place where you go to see a slice of Sea Island and Gullah history and relax, relax, relax. While at one time there was an operating resort and spa on the island, as of this writing it is deep in bankruptcy proceedings.

For the freshest island seafood, check out the **Old Daufuskie Crab Company** (Freeport Marina, 843/785-6652, daily 11:30 A.M.–9 P.M., $7–22).

A good public ferry to and from Daufuskie from Hilton Head is **Calibogue Cruises** (843/342-8687). It brings you in on the landward side of the island, and from there you can take shuttles or rent golf carts or bikes.

For overnight stays, you can rent a humble cabin at **Freeport Marina** (843/785-8242, rates vary).

Points Inland

WALTERBORO

The very picture of the slow, moss-drenched Lowcountry town—indeed, the municipal logo is the silhouette of a live oak tree—Walterboro is a delightful, artsy oasis. Right off I-95, Walterboro serves as a gateway of sorts to the Lowcountry, and the cheap commercial sprawl on the interstate shows it. But don't be put off by this ugliness—once you get into town it's as charming as they come, with roots back to 1783 and offering the added bonus of being one of the best antiquing locales in South Carolina. Convenient and eminently walkable, the two-block Arts and Antiques District on Washington Street centers on a dozen antiques stores on the town's main drag, interspersed with gift shops and eateries.

Sights

◖ SOUTH CAROLINA ARTISANS CENTER

Don't miss the South Carolina Artisans Center (334 Wichman St., 843/549-0011, Mon.–Sat. 10 A.M.–6 P.M., Sun. 1–6 P.M., free), an expansive and vibrant collection of the best work of local and regional painters, sculptors, jewelers, and other craftspeople, for sale and for enjoyment. Imagine a big-city folk art gallery, except without the pretension, and you get the idea. It's not on the main drag, but it's only about a block around the corner, so there's no excuse not to drop in.

You can find most any genre represented here, from jewelry to watercolors to shawls to photography to sweetgrass baskets. The Artisans Center hosts numerous receptions, and every third Saturday of the month they hold live artist demonstrations from 11 A.M.–3 P.M.

MUSEUMS

Walterboro and Colleton County boast three museums. The **Colleton Museum** (239 N. Jefferies Blvd., 843/549-2303, Tues.–Fri. 10 A.M.–5 P.M., Sat. noon–4 P.M., free) is in the 1855 "Old Jail" downtown, and houses exhibits exploring area history and culture from

LOWCOUNTRY

the South Carolina Artisans Center in Walterboro

dinosaurs to the present day. This is also where you can pick up a good self-guided walking tour of the whole town.

The **Bedon-Lucas House Museum** (205 Church St., 843/549-9633, Thurs.–Sat. 1–4 P.M., $3 adults, 7 and under free) was built by a local planter in 1820. An example of the local style of "high house," built off the ground to escape mosquitoes and catch the breeze, the house today is a nice mix of period furnishings and unadorned simplicity.

The **Slave Relic Museum** (208 Carn St., 843/549-9130, Tues.–Fri. 9:30 A.M.–5:30 P.M., Sat. 10 A.M.–3 P.M., $6 adults, $5 children) houses the area Center for Research and Preservation of the African American Culture. It features artifacts, photos, and documents detailing the Atlantic passage, slave life, and the Underground Railroad.

TUSKEGEE AIRMEN MEMORIAL
Yes, the Tuskegee Airmen of World War II fame were from Alabama, not South Carolina. But a contingent trained in Walterboro, at the site of the present-day Lowcountry Regional Airport (537 Aviation Way, 843/549-2549) a short ways south of downtown on U.S. 17. Today, on a publicly accessible, low-security area of the airport, stands the Tuskegee Airmen Memorial, an outdoor monument to these brave flyers. There's a bronze statue and several interpretive exhibits.

GREAT SWAMP SANCTUARY
A short ways out of town in the other direction is the Great Swamp Sanctuary (www.thegreatswamp.org, daily dawn–dusk, free), a still-developing ecotourism project focusing on the Lowcountry environment. Located in one of the few braided-creek habitats accessible to the public, the 842-acre Sanctuary has three miles of walking and biking trails, some along the path of the old Charleston-Savannah stagecoach route. Kayakers and canoeists can paddle along over two miles of winding creeks. A 10,000 square-foot interpretive center is in the works.

There are three entry points to the Great Swamp Sanctuary, all off Jefferies Boulevard. Here they are in west-to-east order from I-95: north onto Beach Road, north onto Detreville Street (this is considered the main entrance), and west onto Washington Street.

Accommodations and Food
If you're looking for big-box lodging, the section of Walterboro close to I-95 is absolutely chock-a-block with it. The quality is surprisingly good, perhaps because they tend to cater to northerners on their way to and from Florida.

A good choice is **Holiday Inn Express & Suites** (1834 Sniders Hwy., 843/538-2700, www.hiexpress.com, $85), or try the **Comfort Inn & Suites** (97 Downs Lane, 843/538-5911, www.choicehotels.com, $95).

If you'd like something with a bit more character, there are two B&Bs on Hampton Street downtown. **Old Academy Bed & Breakfast** (904 Hampton St., 843/549-3232, www.oldacademybandb.com, $80–115) has four rooms housed in Walterboro's first school building. They offer a full Continental breakfast. Note that credit cards are not accepted! Though built recently by local standards, the 1912 **Hampton House Bed and Breakfast** (500 Hampton St., 843/542-9498, www.hamptonhousebandb.com, $125–145) has three well-appointed rooms and offers a full country breakfast. By appointment only, you can see the Forde Doll and Dollhouse Collection, with over 50 dollhouses and oodles of antique dolls.

The story of food in Walterboro revolves around **Duke's Barbecue** (949 Robertson Blvd., 843/549-1446, $7), one of the best-regarded barbecue spots in the Lowcountry and one of the top two joints named "Duke's" in the state (the other, by common consensus, is in Orangeburg). The pulled pork is delectable, cooked with the indigenous South Carolina mustard-based sauce. Unlike most area barbecue restaurants, some attention is devoted to the veggies, such as collard greens, green beans, and black-eyed peas with rice.

TUSKEGEE AIRMEN IN WALTERBORO

In a state where all too often African American history is studied in the context of slavery, a refreshing change is the tale of the Tuskegee Airmen, one of the most-lauded American military units of World War II. Though named for their origins at Alabama's Tuskegee Institute, the pilots of the famed 332nd Fighter Group actually completed final training in South Carolina at Walterboro Army Airfield, where the regional airport now sits.

The U.S. military was segregated during World War II, with African Americans mostly relegated to support roles. An interesting exception was the case of the 332nd, formed in 1941 as the 99th Pursuit Squadron by an act of Congress and the only all-black flying unit in the American military at the time. For the most part flying P-47 Thunderbolts and P-51 Mustangs, the pilots of the 332nd had one of the toughest missions of the war: escorting bombers over the skies of Germany and protecting them from Luftwaffe fighters. Though initially viewed with skepticism, the Tuskegee Airmen wasted no time in proving their mettle.

In fact, it wasn't long before U.S. bomber crews – who were, needless to say, all white – specifically requested that they be escorted by the Airmen, who were given the nickname "Red-Tail Angels" because of the distinctive markings of their aircraft. (While legend has it that the 332nd never lost a bomber, this claim has been debunked. But as Tuskegee Airman Bill Holloman said: "The Tuskegee story is about pilots who rose above adversity and discrimination and opened a door once closed to black America, not about whether their record is perfect.") The 332nd's reputation for aggressiveness in air combat was so widely-known that the Germans also had a nickname for them – *Schwartze Vogelmenschen*, or "Black Bird Men."

Today Walterboro honors the Airmen with a monument on the grounds of the Lowcountry Regional Airport, on U.S. 17 just northeast of town. In an easily accessible part of the airport grounds, the monument features a bronze statue and several interpretive exhibits. Another place to catch up on Tuskegee Airmen history is at the **Colleton Museum** (239 N. Jefferies Blvd., 843/549-2303, Tues.-Fri. 10 A.M.-5 P.M., Sat. noon-4 P.M., free), which has a permanent exhibit on the pilots and their history in the Walterboro area.

Walterboro Army Airfield's contribution to the war effort was not limited to the Tuskegee Airmen, however. Seven of the famed Doolittle Raiders were trained here, there was a compound for holding German prisoners of war, and it was also the site of the U.S. military's largest camouflage school.

Tuskegee Airmen monument at the Walterboro Airport

© JIM MOREKIS

HARDEEVILLE

For most travelers, Hardeeville is known for its plethora of low-budget lodging and garish fireworks stores at the intersection of I-95 and U.S. 17. Truth be told, that's about all that's there.

However train buffs will enjoy getting a gander at the rare and excellently-restored **Narrow Gauge Locomotive** near the intersection of U.S. 17 and Highway 46. Donated by the Argent Lumber Company in 1960, Engine #7 memorializes the role of the timber industry in the area.

Hardeeville is now home to many Latinos who service all the retirement communities sprouting up in the Lowcountry. Long story short, this means if you're hungry in Hardeeville, go straight to (**Mi Tierrita** (U.S. 17 and I-95, 843/784-5011, $5), an excellent, authentic Mexican restaurant near the I-95/U.S. 17 confluence. It's pretty beat-up on the inside, but the food is delicious and many steps above the typical watered-down Tex-Mex you find in the Southeast.

If barbecue's your thing, go on Highway 170A on the "backside" of Hardeeville in the hamlet of Levy to **The Pink Pig** (3508 South Okatie Hwy., 843/784-3635, www.the-pinkpig.com, Tues.–Wed. and Sat. 11 A.M.–3 P.M., Thurs.–Fri. 11 A.M.–3 P.M. and 5–7 P.M.,

$5–15). They offer three sauces: honey mustard, spicy, and "Gullah." The place is surprisingly hip, with good music piped-in and a suitably cutesy, kid-friendly décor with plenty of the eponymous rosy porcine figures.

SAVANNAH NATIONAL WILDLIFE REFUGE

Roughly equally divided between Georgia and South Carolina, the sprawling, 30,000-acre Savannah National Wildlife Refuge (912/652-4415, www.fws.gov/savannah, daily dawn–dusk, free) is a premier bird-watching and nature-observing locale in the Southeast. As with many refuges in the coastal Southeast, it's located on former plantations. The system of dikes and paddies once used to grow rice now helps make this an attractive stopover for migrating birds.

Bird-watching is best from October–April, with the winter months best for viewing migratory waterfowl. While you can kayak yourself on miles of creeks, you can also call **Swamp Girls Kayak Tours** (843/784-2249, www.swampgirls.com), who work out of nearby Hardeeville, for a guided tour.

To get here, take exit 5 off I-95 onto U.S. 17. Go south to U.S. 170 and look for the Laurel Hill Wildlife Drive.

331

BACKGROUND

The Land

GEOGRAPHY

The story of the coastal Carolinas' geography begins, ironically enough, with the Appalachian Mountain chain. It's in Appalachia where so much of the coast's freshwater—in the form of rain—comes together and flows southeast—in the form of rivers—to the Atlantic Ocean.

Moving east, the next level down from the Appalachians is the **Piedmont** region. The Piedmont is a rolling, hilly area, the eroded remains of an ancient mountain chain now long gone.

At the Piedmont's eastern edge is the **fall line,** so named because it's there where rivers make a drop toward the sea, generally becoming navigable. This slight but noticeable change in elevation—which actually marked the shoreline about 60 million years ago—not only encouraged trade, but has provided water power for mills for hundreds of years. Many inland cities of the region trace their origin and commercial success to their strategic location on the fall line.

Around the fall line zone in the **Upper Coastal Plain** you can sometimes spot **sandhills,** usually only a few feet in elevation, generally thought to be the vestigial remains of primordial sand dunes and offshore

© JIM MOREKIS

sandbars. Well beyond the fall line and the sometimes nearly invisible sandhills lies the **Lower Coastal Plain,** gradually built up over a 150 million-year span by sedimentary runoff from the Appalachian Mountains, which were then as high or even higher than the modern-day Himalayas.

The Coastal Plain was sea bottom for much of the earth's history, and in some eroded areas you can see dramatic proof of this in prehistoric shells, sharks' teeth, and fossilized whale bones and oyster beds, often many miles inland. In some places, calcium from these ancient shells has provided a lush home for distinct groups of unique plants, called **dijuncts.**

At various times over the last 50 million years, the Coastal Plain has submerged, surfaced, and submerged again. At the height of the last major Ice Age, when global sea levels were very low, the east coast of North America extended out nearly 100 miles farther than the present shoreline. (We now call this former coastal region the **continental shelf.**) The Coastal Plain has been in roughly its current form for about the last 15,000 years.

In coastal North Carolina, above about Jacksonville, begins a sort of hybrid geography, mixing characteristics of the Coastal Plain with a series of massive river estuaries. Here the general salt marsh environment gives way to a more windswept, deeper-water topography that will find its ultimate expression in the remote feel and independent lifestyle of the Outer Banks themselves.

Rivers

Visitors from drier climates are sometimes shocked to see how huge the rivers can get in the South, how wide and voluminous as they saunter to the sea, their seemingly slow speed belying the massive power they contain. North and South Carolina's big **alluvial,** or sediment-bearing, rivers originate in the region of the Appalachian mountain chain.

The **blackwater river** is a particularly interesting Southern phenomenon, duplicated elsewhere only in South America and one example each in New York and Michigan. While alluvial

The Edisto River is the longest blackwater river in the world.

rivers generally originate in highlands and carry with them a large amount of sediment, blackwater rivers—the Edisto in South Carolina being a great example, along with North Carolina's Cape Fear River—tend to originate in low-lying areas and move slowly toward the sea, carrying with them very little sediment.

Rather, their dark tea color comes from the tannic acid of decaying vegetation all along their banks, washed out by the slow, inexorable movement of the river toward the sea. While I don't necessarily recommend drinking it, despite its dirty color blackwater is for the most part remarkably clean and hygienic.

Carolina Bays

An interesting regional feature of the Carolinas is the **Carolina Bay,** an elliptical depression rich with biodiversity, thousands of which are found all along the coast from Delaware to Florida. While at least 500,000 have been identified, new laser-based technology is enabling the discovery of thousands more, previously unnoticed.

Though not all Carolina Bays are in the Carolinas, many are and that's where they were first documented. They're called "bays" not for the water within them—indeed, many hold little or no water at all—but for the proliferation of bay trees often found inside. Carolina Bays can be substantially older than the surrounding terrain, with many well over 25,000 years old. Native Americans referred to the distinctive wetland habitat within a Carolina Bay as a *pocosin.*

Theories abound as to their origin. One has it that they're the result of wave action from when the entire area was underwater in primordial times. The most popular, if unproven theory, is that they are the result of a massive meteor shower in prehistoric times. Certainly their similar orientation, roughly northwest-southeast, makes this intuitively possible as an impact pattern. Further bolstering this theory is the fact that most Carolina Bays are surrounded by sand rims, which tend to be thicker on the southeast edge.

An old, once-discredited theory now gaining new credence is that Carolina Bays are the result of a disintegrating comet, which exploded upon entry into the earth's atmosphere somewhere over the Great Lakes. Apparently if you extend the axes of all the Carolina Bays, that's where they all converge. This theory takes on an ominous edge when one realizes that the same comet is also blamed for a mass extinction of prehistoric animals such as the mammoth.

The Intracoastal Waterway

You'll often see its acronym ICW on signs—and sadly you'll probably hear the locals mispronounce it "Intercoastal Waterway"—but the casual visitor might actually find the Intracoastal Waterway difficult to spot. Relying on a natural network of interconnected estuaries and channels, combined with manmade **cuts,** the ICW often blends in rather subtly with the already extensive network of creeks and rivers in the area.

Mandated by Congress in 1919 and maintained by the U.S. Army Corps of Engineers, the Atlantic portion of the ICW runs from Key West to Boston and carries recreational

and barge traffic away from the perils of offshore currents and weather. Even if they don't use it specifically, kayakers and boaters often find themselves on it at some point during their nautical adventures.

Estuaries

Most biologists will tell you that the Coastal Plain is where things get interesting. The place where a river interfaces with the ocean is called an estuary, and it's perhaps the most interesting place of all. Estuaries are heavily tidal in nature (indeed, the word derives from *aestus,* Latin for tide), and feature brackish water and heavy silt content.

The Carolinas typically have about a six- to eight-foot tidal range, and the coastal ecosystem depends on this steady ebb and flow for life itself. At high tide, shellfish open and feed. At low tide, they literally clam up, keeping saltwater inside their shells until the next tide comes.

Waterbirds and small mammals feed on shellfish and other animals at low tide, when their prey is exposed. High tide brings an influx of fish and nutrients from the sea, in turn drawing predators like dolphins, who often come into tidal creeks to feed.

It's the estuaries that form the most compelling and beautiful sanctuaries for the area's incredibly rich diversity of animal species. Many estuaries are contiguous with those of other rivers.

Salt Marsh

All this water action in both directions—freshwater coming from inland, saltwater encroaching from the Atlantic—results in the phenomenon of the salt marsh, the single most recognizable and iconic geographic feature of the Carolina coast, also known simply as "wetlands." (Freshwater marshes are more rare, Florida's Everglades being perhaps the premier example.)

Far more than just a transitional zone between land and water, marsh is also nature's nursery. Plant and animal life in marshes tends to be not only diverse, but encompasses multitudes. Though you may not see its denizens easily, on close inspection you'll find the marsh absolutely teeming with creatures. Visually, the main identifying feature of a salt marsh is its distinctive, reed-like marsh grasses, adapted to survive in brackish water. Like estuaries, marshes and all life in them are heavily influenced by the tides, which bring in nutrients.

The marsh has also played a key role in human history as well, for it was here where the massive rice and indigo plantations grew their signature crops, aided by the natural ebb and flow of the tides. While most marsh you see will look quite undisturbed, very little of it could be called pristine.

In the heyday of the rice plantations of the Carolinas, much of the entire coastal salt marsh was crisscrossed by the canal-and-dike system of the rice paddies. You can still see evidence almost everywhere in the area if you look hard enough (the best time to look is right after takeoff or before landing in an airplane, since many approaches to regional airports take you over wetlands). Anytime you see a low, straight ridge running through a marsh, that's likely the eroded, overgrown remnant of an old rice paddy dike. Kayakers occasionally find old wooden water gates, or "trunks," on their paddles.

In the Lowcountry of South Carolina, you'll often hear the term **pluff mud.** This refers to the area's distinctive variety of soft, dark mud in the salt marsh, which often has an equally distinctive odor that locals love, but some visitors have a hard time getting used to. Extraordinarily rich in nutrients, pluff mud helped make rice a successful crop in the marshes of the Lowcountry.

In addition to their huge role as wildlife incubators and sanctuaries, wetlands are also one of the most important natural protectors of the health of the coastal region. They serve as natural filters, cleansing runoff from the land of toxins and pollutants before it hits the ocean. They also help humans by serving as natural hurricane barriers, their porous nature helping to ease the brunt of the damaging storm surge.

Beaches and Barrier Islands

The beaches of the Carolinas are almost all situated on barrier islands, long islands parallel to the shoreline and separated from the mainland by a sheltered body of water. Because they're formed by the deposit of sediment by offshore currents, they change shape over the years, with the general pattern of deposit going from north to south (i.e., the northern end will begin eroding first).

Most of the barrier islands are geologically quite young, only being formed within the last 25,000 years or so. Natural erosion, by current and by storm, combined with the accelerating effects of dredging for local port activity has quickened the decline of many barrier islands. Many beaches in the area are subject to a mitigation of erosion called **beach renourishment,** which generally involves redistributing dredged material closely offshore so that it will wash up on and around the beach.

As the name indicates, barrier islands are another of nature's safeguards against hurricane damage. Historically, the barrier islands have borne the vast bulk of the damage done by hurricanes in the region. Like the marshes, barrier islands also help protect the mainland by absorbing the brunt of the storm's wind and surging water.

While the barrier islands of South Carolina are certainly much more heavily traveled, the most unique collection of them is off the North Carolina coast. Taking up the entire northern half of the Tarheel State's coast, the **Outer Banks** is a nearly 200-mile-long string of very narrow barrier islands, jutting much farther into the Atlantic Ocean than their southern counterparts.

As a result of this eastward positioning, not only do the Outer Banks have a much more lonely, windswept feel than more southerly barrier islands, they're also virtual hurricane magnets, with hundreds of the storms making contact with the Outer Banks since such records began.

This extreme vulnerability means that, even more than most barrier islands, the geography of the Outer Banks changes with each year's storm patterns. For example, Hatteras Island was literally cut in half by Hurricane Isabel in 2003. (The damage was later repaired by a U.S. Army Corps of Engineers' project).

The relative solitude of the Outer Banks has also contributed to its status as the "Graveyard of the Atlantic," a place where at least 2,000 shipwrecks have occurred in its nearly 500 years of recorded history.

Wiregrass and Longleaf Ecosystems

In prehistoric times, most of Carolina Upper Coastal Plain was covered by what's known as a wiregrass or longleaf pine ecosystem. Wiregrass (*Arista stricta*) is a foot-tall species of hardy grass which often coexists with forests of the longleaf pine (*Pinus palustrist*), a relative of the slash pine now used as a cash crop throughout the South. The longleaf pine is fire-dependent, meaning it only reproduces after wildfire—usually started by lightning—releases its seed cones.

Wiregrass savanna and old-growth forests of longleaf pine once covered most of the Southeast to the tune of about 100 million acres. Within about 200 years, however, settlers had deforested the region to a shadow of its former self. Contrary to Hollywood portrayals, no one ever needed a machete to tear their way through an old-growth forest. Because the high, thick tree canopy allows little but wiregrass to grow on the forest floor, Native Americans and early settlers could simply walk through these primordial forests with ease.

CLIMATE

One word comes to mind when one thinks about Southern climate: hot. That's the first word that occurs to Southerners as well, but virtually every survey of why residents are attracted to the area puts the climate at the top of the list. Go figure.

How hot is hot? The average high for July, the region's hottest month, in Charleston is about 89°F. While that's nothing compared to Tucson or Death Valley, coupled with the region's notoriously high humidity it can have an altogether miserable effect.

Technically most of the Carolina coast has a **humid subtropical** climate. During summer the famous high-pressure system called the **Bermuda High** settles over the entire southeastern United States, its rotating winds pushing aside most weather coming from the west. This can bring drought, as well as a certain sameness that afflicts the area during summer. Heat aside, there's no doubt that one of the most difficult things for an outsider to adjust to in the South is the humidity. The average annual humidity in Charleston is about 55 percent in the afternoons and a whopping 85 percent in the mornings. The most humid months are August and September.

There is no real antidote to humidity—other than air conditioning, that is—though many film crews and other outside workers swear by the use of Sea Breeze astringent. If you and your traveling partner can deal with the strong minty odor, dampen a hand towel with the astringent, drape it across the back of your neck and go about your business. Don't assume that because it's humid you shouldn't drink fluids. Just as in any hot climate, you should drink lots of water if you're going to be out in the Southern heat.

If you're on the Carolina coast, you'll no doubt grow to love the steady ocean breeze during the day. But at night you may notice the wind changing direction and coming from inland. That's caused by the land cooling at night, and the wind rushing toward the warmer waters offshore. This shift in wind current is mostly responsible for that sometimes awe-inspiring, sometimes just plain scary phenomenon of a typical Southern **thunderstorm.** Seemingly within the space of a few minutes on a particularly hot and still summer day, the afternoon is taken over by a rapidly moving stacked storm cloud called a **thunderhead,** which soon bursts open and pours an unbelievable amount of rain on whatever is unlucky enough to be beneath it, along with frequent, huge lightning strikes. Then, almost as quickly as it came on, the storm subsides and the sun comes back out again as if nothing happened.

August and September are the rainiest months in terms of rainfall, with averages well over six inches for each of those months. July is also quite wet, coming in at over five inches on average. Winters here are pretty mild, but can seem much colder than they actually are because of the dampness in the air. The coldest month is January, with about a 58°F high for the month and a 42°F average low.

You're highly unlikely to encounter snow in the area, and if you do it will likely only be skimpy flurries that a resident of the Great Lakes region wouldn't even notice as snow. But don't let this lull you into a false sense of security. If such a tiny flurry were to hit, be aware that most people down here have no clue how to drive in rough weather and will not be prepared for even such a small amount of snowfall. Visitors from snow country are often surprised by how completely a Southern city will shut down when that rare few inches of snow finally hits.

Hurricanes

The major weather phenomenon for residents and visitors alike is the mighty hurricane. These massive storms, with counterclockwise-rotating bands of clouds and winds pushing 200 miles per hour, are an ever-present danger to the southeast coast June–November of each year (the real danger period is around Labor Day).

North Carolina's Outer Banks in particular have seen an incredible number of damaging storms. I remember seeing a map showing all the routes of all the hurricanes in recorded history known to make landfall in the United States. About a third of them crossed over the same point: Cape Hatteras, North Carolina.

As most everyone is aware now from the horrific, well-documented damage from such killer storms as Hugo, Andrew, and Katrina, hurricanes are not to be trifled with. Old-fashioned, drunken "hurricane parties" are a thing of the past for the most part, the images of cataclysmic destruction everyone has seen on TV having long since eliminated any lingering romanticism about riding out the storm.

Local TV, websites, and print media can be counted on to give more than ample warning in the event a hurricane is approaching the area during your visit. Whatever you do, do not discount the warnings. It's not worth it. If the locals are preparing to leave, you should too.

Typically when a storm is likely to hit the area, there will first be a suggested evacuation. But if authorities determine there's an overwhelming likelihood of imminent hurricane damage, they will issue a **mandatory evacuation order.** What this means in practice is that if you do choose to stay behind, you cannot count on any type of emergency services or help whatsoever.

Generally speaking, the most lethal element of a hurricane is not the wind but the **storm surge,** the wall of ocean water that the winds drive before them onto the coast. During Hurricane Hugo, Charleston's Battery was inundated with a storm surge of over 12 feet, with an amazing 20 feet reported farther north at Cape Romain.

ENVIRONMENTAL ISSUES

The Carolina coast is currently experiencing a double whammy, environmentally speaking: Not only are its distinctive wetlands extraordinarily sensitive to human interference, this is one of the most rapidly developing parts of the country. New and often-poorly planned subdivisions and resort communities are popping up all over the place. Vastly increased port activity, too, is taking a devastating toll on the salt marsh and surrounding barrier islands. Combine all that with the South's often skeptical attitude towards environmental activism, and you have a recipe for potential ecological disaster.

Thankfully, there are some bright spots. More and more communities are seeing the value of responsible planning and not greenlighting every new development sight unseen. Land trusts and other conservation organizations are growing in size, number, funding, and influence. The large number of marine biologists in these areas at various research and educational institutions means there's a wealth of education and talent available in advising local governments and citizens on how best to conserve the area's natural beauty.

THE NEW CHARLESTON GREEN

Most people know "Charleston Green" as a unique local color, the result of adding a few drops of yellow to post-Civil War surplus black paint. But these days the phrase might refer to all the environmentally friendly development in Charleston, which you might find surprising considering the city's location in one of the most conservative states in the country's most conservative region.

The most obvious example is the ambitious Navy Yard redevelopment, which seeks to re-purpose the closed-down facility. That project is part of a larger civic vision to re-imagine the entire 3,000-acre historic Noisette community of North Charleston, with an accompanying wetlands protection conservancy. From its inception in 1902 at the command of President Theodore Roosevelt, through the end of the Cold War, the Charleston Navy Yard was one of the city's biggest employers. Closed down in 1995 as part of a national base realignment plan, locals feared the worst.

But a 340-acre section, the **Navy Yard at Noisette** (www.navyyardsc.com), now hosts an intriguing mix of green-friendly design firms, small nonprofits, and commercial maritime companies. The activity centers on the restoration of three huge former naval warehouses at 7, 10, and 11 Storehouse Row. Nearby, on the way to where the CSS *Hunley* is currently being restored, is the big Powerhouse, once the electrical station for the whole yard and now envisioned as the center of a future entertainment and retail district. In the meantime, the Navy Yard's no-frills retro look is so realistic that it has played host to scenes of the Lifetime TV series *Army Wives*.

Also in North Charleston, local retail chain Half Moon Outfitters recently completed a green-friendly warehouse facility in an old Piggly Wiggly Grocery store. The first LEED (Leadership in Energy and Environmental Design) Platinum certified building in South Carolina, the warehouse features solar panels, rainwater reservoirs, and locally harvested or salvaged interiors. There's also the LEED-cer-

tified North Charleston Elementary School, as well as North Charleston's adoption of a "Night Skies" ordinance to cut down on light pollution.

But North Charleston's far from the only place in town going green. On the peninsula the historic meeting house of the Circular Congregation Church, which gave Meeting Street its name, has a green addition with geothermal heating and cooling, rainwater cisterns, and Charleston's first vegetative roof. In addition to walking the historic byways of the Old Village of Mount Pleasant, architecture and design buffs might also want to check out the new 243-acre **I'On** (www.ionvillage.com) "neotraditional" planned community, a successful model for this type of pedestrian-friendly, New Urbanist development.

On adjacent Daniel Island, the developers of that island's 4,000-acre planned residential community were recently certified as an "Audubon Cooperative Sanctuary" for using wildlife-friendly techniques on its golf and recreational grounds. Even ultra-upscale Kiawah Island has gone green in something other than golf – the fabled Kiawah bobcats are making a comeback, thanks to the efforts of the Kiawah Conservancy.

Why has Charleston proven so adept at moving forward? Locals chalk it up to two things: affluent, well-connected Charlestonians who want to maintain the area's quality of life, and the forward-thinking leadership of Mayor Joe Riley in Charleston and Mayor Keith Summey in North Charleston. For many Charlestonians, however, the green movement manifests in simpler things: the pedestrian and bike lanes on the new Ravenel Bridge over the Cooper River; the thriving city recycling program; or the Sustainable Seafood Initiative, a partnership of local restaurants, universities, and conservation groups that brings only the freshest, most environmentally responsible dishes to your table when you dine out in Charleston.

Marsh Dieback

The dominant species of marsh grass, *Spartina alterniflora* (pronounced Spar-TINE-uh) and *Juncus roemerianus* thrive in the typically brackish water of the coastal marsh estuaries, their structural presence helping to stem erosion of banks and dunes. While drought and blight have taken their toll on the grass, increased coastal development and continued channel deepening have also led to a steady creep of ocean saltwater farther and farther into remaining marsh stands.

The Paper Industry

Early in the 20th century, the Southeast's abundance of cheap, undeveloped land and plentiful, free water led to the establishment of massive pine tree farms to feed coastal pulp and paper mills. Chances are if you used a paper grocery bag recently, it was made in a paper mill in the South.

But in addition to making a whole lot of paper bags and providing lots of employment for residents through the decades, the paper industry also gave the area lots of air and water pollution, stressed local water supplies (it takes a lot of water to make paper from trees), and took away natural species diversity from the area by devoting so much acreage to a single crop, pine trees.

Currently the domestic paper industry is reeling from competition from cheaper Asian lumber stocks and paper mills. As a result, an interesting—and not altogether welcome— phenomenon has been the wholesale entering of Southeastern paper companies into the real estate business. Discovering they can make a whole lot more money selling or developing tree farms for residential lots than making paper bags, pulp and paper companies are helping to drive overdevelopment in the region by encouraging development on their land rather than infill development closer to urban areas. So in the long run, the demise of the paper industry in the South may not prove to be the net advantage to the environment that was anticipated.

Aquifers

Unlike parts of the western U.S., where individuals can enforce private property rights to water, the South has generally held that the region's water is a publicly held resource. The upside of this is that everybody has equal claim to drinking water without regard to status or income or how long they've lived there. The downside is that industry also has the same free claim to the water that citizens do—and they use a heck of a lot more of it.

Currently at least half of the population of North and South Carolina gets its water from aquifers, which are basically huge underground caverns made of limestone. Receiving **groundwater** drip by drip, century after century, from rainfall farther inland, the aquifers essentially act as massive, sterile warehouses for freshwater, accessible through wells.

The aquifers have human benefit only if their water remains fresh. Once saltwater from the ocean begins intruding into an aquifer, it doesn't take much to render all of it unfit for human consumption—forever. What keeps that freshwater fresh is natural water pressure, keeping the ocean at bay.

But nearly a century ago, paper mills began pumping millions and millions of gallons of water out of coastal aquifers. Combined with the dramatic rise in coastal residential development, that has decreased the natural water pressure of the aquifers, leading to measurable saltwater intrusion at several points under the coast.

Currently, local and state governments in both states are increasing their reliance on **surfacewater** (i.e., treated water from rivers and creeks) to relieve the strain on the underground aquifer system. But it's too soon to tell if that has contained the threat from saltwater intrusion.

Nuclear Energy

South Carolina has four nuclear power plants, though none on the coast, in the Greenville, Hartsville, and Jenkinsville areas, and in York County. The massive, Cold War–era nuclear bomb plant Savannah River Site is near Aiken, well inland.

North Carolina has three nuclear power plants: one in Brunswick County near the coast, one near Charlotte well inland, and one near Raleigh in the middle of the state.

Air Pollution
Despite growing awareness of the issue, air pollution is still a big problem in the coastal region. Paper mills still operate, putting out

their distinctive rotten-eggs odor, and auto emissions standards are notoriously lax in South Carolina. The biggest culprit, though, are coal-powered electric plants, which are the norm throughout the region and which continue to pour large amounts of toxins into the atmosphere.

Flora and Fauna

FLORA
The most iconic plant life of the coastal region is the **Southern live oak** *(Quercus virginiana).* Named because of its evergreen nature, a live oak is technically any one of a number of evergreens in the *Quercus* genus, many of which reside in the Carolinas, but in local practice almost always refers to the Southern live oak. Capable of living over 1,000 years and possessing wood of legendary resilience, the Southern live oak is one of nature's most magnificent creations. Though the timber value of live oaks has been well known since the earliest days of the American shipbuilding industry—when the oak dominated the entire coast inland of the marsh—their value as a canopy tree has finally been widely recognized by local and state governments as well.

Fittingly, the other iconic plant life of the coastal region grows on the branches of the live oak. Contrary to popular opinion, **Spanish moss** *(Tillandsia usnesides)* is neither Spanish nor moss. It's an air plant, a wholly indigenous cousin to the pineapple. Also contrary to folklore, Spanish moss is not a parasite nor does it harbor parasites while living on an oak tree—though it can after it has already fallen to the ground.

Also growing on the bark of a live oak, especially right after a rain shower, is the **resurrection fern** *(Polypodium polypodioides),* which can stay dormant for amazingly long periods of time, only to spring back to life with the introduction of a little water. You can find live oak, Spanish moss, and resurrection fern anywhere in the **maritime forest** ecosystem of

the coastal Carolinas, a zone generally behind the **interdune meadows,** which is itself right behind the beach zone.

Far and away the region's most important commercial tree is the pine, used for paper, lumber, and turpentine. Rarely seen in the wild today due to tree farming, the dominant species is now the **slash pine** *(Pinus elliottii),* often seen in long rows on either side of rural highways. Before the introduction of large-scale monoculture tree farming, however, a rich variety of native pines flourished in the **upland forest** inland from the maritime forest, chief among them the **longleaf** *(Pinus palustris)* and **loblolly** *(Pinus taeda)* pines. Longleaf forest covered nearly 100 million acres of the Southeast Coastal Plain upon the arrival of the Europeans; within 300 years most of it would be cut down and/or harvested.

Right up there with live oaks and Spanish moss in terms of instant recognition would have to be the colorful, ubiquitous **azalea,** a flowering shrub of the *Rhododendron* genus. Over 10,000 varieties have been cultivated through the centuries, with quite a wide range of them on display during blooming season, March–April. The area's other great floral display comes from the **camellia** *(Camellia japonica),* a large, cold-hardy evergreen shrub with flowers that generally bloom in late winter (January–March). An import from Asia, the southeastern coast's camellias are close cousins to *Camellia sinensis,* from which tea is made (and also an import).

Other colorful ornamentals of the area include the ancient and beautiful **Southern**

longleaf pine, which once covered most of the Southeast

magnolia *(Magnolia grandiflora)*, a native plant with distinctive large white flowers (evolved before the advent of bees); and the **flowering dogwood** *(Cornus florida)*, which despite its very hard wood—great for daggers, hence its original name "dagwood"—is actually quite fragile. An ornamental imported from Asia that has now become quite obnoxious in its aggressive invasiveness is the **mimosa** *(Albrizia julibrissin)*, which blooms March–August.

Moving into watery areas, you'll find the remarkable **bald cypress** *(Taxodium distichum)*, a flood-resistant conifer recognizable by its tufted top, its great height (up to 130 feet), and its distinctive "knees," parts of the root that project above the waterline and which are believed to help stabilize the tree in lowland areas. Much prized for its beautiful, pest-resistant wood, great stands of ancient cypress once dominated the marsh along the coast; sadly, overharvesting and destruction of wetlands has made the magnificent sight of this ancient, dignified species much less common.

Probably the most unique plant on the coast

of the Carolinas—for a variety of reasons—is the **Venus flytrap** *(Dionaea muscipula)*. This fascinating carnivorous species grows only in the bogs of the coastal Carolinas, generally within about a hundred-mile radius of Wilmington, North Carolina. Easily accessible areas where you can find Venus flytraps in the wild include Green Swamp Preserve in Brunswick County and Carolina Beach State Park south of Wilmington.

The acres of **smooth cordgrass** that comprise the coastal marsh are plants of the *Spartina alternaflora* species. (A cultivated cousin, *Spartina anglica,* is considered invasive.) Besides its simple natural beauty, *Spartina* is also a key food source for marsh denizens. Playing a key environmental role on the coast are **sea oats** *(Uniola paniculata)*. This wispy, fast-growing perennial grass anchors sand dunes and hence is a protected species (it's a misdemeanor to pick them).

South Carolina isn't called the "Palmetto State" for nothing. Though palm varieties are not as common up here as in Florida, you'll definitely encounter several types along the coast. The **cabbage palm** *(Sabal palmetto)*, for which South Carolina is named, is the largest variety, up to 50–60 feet tall. Its "heart of palm" is an edible delicacy, which coastal Native Americans boiled in bear fat as porridge. In dunes and sandhills you'll find clumps of the low-lying **saw palmetto** *(Serenoa repens)*. The **bush palmetto** *(Sabal minor)* has distinctive fan-shaped branches. The common **Spanish bayonet** *(Yucca aloifolia)* looks like a palm, but it's actually a member of the agave family.

FAUNA
On Land
Perhaps the most iconic land animal—or semi-land animal, anyway—of the Carolina coast is the legendary **American alligator** *(Alligator mississippiensis)*, the only species of crocodile native to the area. Contrary to their fierce reputation, locals know these massive reptiles, 6–12 feet long as adults, to be quite shy.

If you come in the colder months you won't see one at all, since alligators require an outdoor temperature over 70°F to become active and feed. (Indeed, the appearance of alligators was once a well-known symbol of spring in the area.) Often all you'll see is a couple of eyebrow ridges sticking out of the water, and a gator lying still in a shallow creek can easily be mistaken for a floating log. But should you see one or more gators basking in the sun—a favorite activity on warm days for these cold-blooded creatures—it's best to admire them from afar. A mother alligator, in particular, will destroy anything that comes near her nest. Despite the alligator's short, stubby legs, they run amazingly fast on land—faster than you, in fact.

If you're driving on a country road at night, be on the lookout for **white-tailed deer** *(Odecoileus virginianus)*, which, besides being quite beautiful, also pose a serious road hazard. Because development has dramatically reduced the habitat—and therefore the numbers—of their natural predators, deer are plentiful throughout the area and, as you read this, are hard at work devouring vast tracts of valuable vegetation. No one wants to hurt poor little Bambi, but the truth is that area hunters perform a valuable service by culling the local deer population, which is in no danger of extinction anytime soon—far from it.

North and South Carolina host large populations of playful **river otter** *(Lutra Canadensis)*. Not to be confused with the larger sea otters off the West Coast, these fast-swimming members of the weasel family inhabit inland waterways and marshy areas, with dominant males sometimes ranging as much as 50 miles within a single waterway. As strict carnivores, usually of fish, otters are a key indicator of the health of their ecosystem. If they're thriving, water and habitat quality is likely to be pretty high. If they're not, something's going badly wrong.

While you're unlikely to encounter an otter, if you're camping you might easily run into the **raccoon** *(Procyon lotor)*, an exceedingly intelligent and crafty relative of the bear, sharing that larger animal's resourcefulness in stealing your food. Though nocturnal, raccoons will feed whenever food is available. Raccoons can grow so accustomed to the human presence as to almost consider themselves part of the family, but resist the temptation to get close to them. Rabies is prevalent in the raccoon population and you should always, always keep your distance.

Another common campsite nuisance, the **opossum** *(Didelphis virginiana)* is a shy, primitive creature that is much more easily discouraged. North America's only marsupial, a 'possum's usual "defense" against predators is to play dead. That said, however, they have an immunity to snake venom and often feed on the reptiles, even the most poisonous ones.

Opossums are native to the area, but another similarly slow-witted, slow-moving creature is not: the **nine-banded armadillo** *(Dasypus novemcinctus)*. In centuries past, these armor-plated insect-eaters were mostly confined to Mexico, but they are gradually working their way northward. Obsessive diggers, armadillos cause quite a bit of damage to crops and gardens. Sometimes jokingly called "'possum on the half shell," armadillo, like opossum, are frequent roadkill on Carolina highways.

While you're highly unlikely to actually see a **red fox** *(Vulpes vulpes)*, you might very well see their distinctive footprints in the mud of a marsh at low tide. These nocturnal hunters, a non-native species introduced by European settlers, range the coast seeking mice, squirrels, and rabbits.

Once fairly common in the Carolinas, the **black bear** *(Ursus americanus)* has suffered from hunting and habitat destruction and is extremely rare in the region.

In the Water

Humankind's aquatic cousin, the **Atlantic bottle-nosed dolphin** *(Ursiops truncates)*, is a well-known and frequent visitor to the coast, coming far upstream into creeks and rivers to feed. Children, adults, and experienced seamen alike all delight in encounters with the mammals, sociable creatures who travel in family units. When not occupied with feeding or mating activities—both of which can get surprisingly rowdy—dolphins show great curiosity about human visitors to their habitat. They will gather near boats, surfacing often with the distinctive chuffing sound of air coming from their blowholes. Occasionally they'll even lift their heads out of the water to have a look at you; consider yourself lucky indeed to have such a close encounter. Don't be fooled by their cuteness, however. Dolphins live life with gusto and aren't scared of much. They're voracious eaters of fish, amorous and energetic lovers, and will take on an encroaching shark in a heartbeat.

Another beloved part-time marine creature of the barrier islands of the coast is the **loggerhead turtle** (*Caretta caretta*), which is South Carolina's state reptile. Though the species prefers to stay well offshore the rest of the year, females weighing up to 300 pounds come out of the sea each May–July to dig a shallow hole in the dunes and lay over 100 leathery eggs, returning to the ocean and leaving the eggs to hatch on their own after two months. Interestingly, the mothers prefer to nest at the same spot on the same island year after year. After hatching, the baby turtles then make a dramatic, extremely dangerous (and extremely *slow* trek) to the safety of the waves, at the mercy of various predators.

A series of dedicated research and conservation efforts are working hard to protect the loggerheads' traditional nursery grounds to ensure the survival of this fascinating, loveable, and threatened species. Cape Island within the Cape Romain National Wildlife Refuge accounts for about a quarter of all loggerhead nests in South Carolina, and is the leading nesting site north of Florida. Other key sites in South Carolina include Kiawah, Edisto, and Hilton Head Islands. Though their numbers are lower in the Tarheel State, the loggerheads do like to nest along the entire length of the coast, especially near Cape Hatteras.

Of course the coastal waters and rivers are chock-a-block with fish. The most abundant and sought-after recreational species in the area is the **spotted sea trout** (*Cynoscion nebulosus*), followed by the **red drum** (*Suaenops ocellatus*). Local anglers also pursue many varieties

of **bass, bream, sheepshead,** and **crappie.** It may sound strange to some accustomed to considering it a "trash" fish, but many types of **catfish** are not only plentiful here but are a common and well-regarded food source. Many species of **flounder** inhabit the silty bottoms of estuaries all along the coast. Farther offshore are game and sportfish like **marlin, swordfish, shark, grouper,** and **tuna.**

Each March, anglers jockey for position on coastal rivers for the yearly running of the **American shad** (*Alosa sapidissima*) upstream to spawn. This large (up to eight pounds), catfish-like species is a regional delicacy as a seasonal entrée, as well as for its tasty roe. There's a limit of eight shad per person per season.

One of the more interesting fish species in the area is the endangered **shortnose sturgeon** (*Acipenser brevirostrum*). A fantastically ancient species that has evolved little in hundreds of millions of years, this small, freshwater fish is known to exist in the estuaries of the ACE Basin. Traveling upriver to spawn in the winter, the sturgeons remain around the mouths of waterways the rest of the year, venturing near the ocean only sparingly.

Crustaceans and shellfish have been a key food staple in the area for thousands of years, with the massive shell middens of the coast being testament to Native Americans' healthy appetite for them. The beds of the local variant, the **eastern oyster** (*Crassostrea virginica*), aren't what they used to be due to overharvesting, water pollution, and disruption of habitat. In truth, most local restaurants import the little filter-feeders from the Gulf of Mexico these days. Oysters spawn May–August, hence the old folk wisdom about eating oysters only in months with the letter "r," so as not to disrupt the breeding cycle.

Each year April–January, shrimp boats up and down the southeastern coast trawl for **shrimp,** most commercially viable in two local species, the white shrimp (*Penaeus setiferus*), and the brown shrimp (*Penaeus aztecus*). Shrimp are the most popular seafood item in the United States and account for hundreds of millions of dollars in revenue in the coastal

the horseshoe crab, essentially unchanged in tens of millions of years

© JIM MOREKIS

economy. While consumption won't slow down anytime soon, the Carolina shrimping industry is facing serious threats, both from species decline due to pollution and overfishing and from competition from shrimp farms and the Asian shrimp industry.

Another important commercial crop is the **blue crab** (*Callinected sapidus*), the species used in such Lowcountry delicacies as crab cakes. You'll often see floating markers bobbing up and down in rivers throughout the region. These signal the presence directly below of a crab trap, often of an amateur crabber.

A true living link to primordial times, the alien-looking **horseshoe crab** (*Limulus polyphemus*), is frequently found on beaches of the coast during the spring mating season (it lives in deeper water the rest of the year). More closely related to scorpions and spiders than crabs, the horseshoe has evolved hardly a lick in hundreds of millions of years.

Any trip to a local salt marsh at low tide will likely uncover hundreds of **fiddler crabs** (*Uca pugilator* and *Uca pugnax*), so-named for the way the males wave their single enlarged

claws in the air to attract mates. (Their other, smaller claw is the one they actually eat with.) The fiddlers make distinctive burrows in the pluff mud for sanctuary during high tide, recognizable by the little balls of sediment at the entrances (the crabs spit out the balls after sifting through the sand for food).

One charming beach inhabitant, the **sand dollar** (*Mellita quinquiesperforata*), has seen its numbers decline drastically due to being entirely too charming for its own good. Beachcombers are now asked to enjoy these flat little cousins to the sea urchin in their natural habitat and to refrain from taking them home. Besides, they start to smell bad when they dry out.

The **sea nettle** (*Chrysaora quinquecirrha*), a less-than-charming beach inhabitant, is a jellyfish that stings thousands of people on the coast a year (though only for those with severe allergies are the stings potentially life-threatening). Stinging their prey before transporting it into their waiting mouths, the jellyfish also sting when disturbed or frightened. Most often, people are stung by stepping on the bodies of jellyfish washed up on the sand. If you're stung by a jellyfish, don't panic. You'll probably experience a stinging rash for about half an hour. Locals say applying a little baking soda or vinegar helps cut the sting. (Some also swear fresh urine will do the trick, and I pass that tip along to you purely in the interest of thoroughness.)

In the Air

When enjoying the marshlands of the coast, consider yourself fortunate to see an endangered **wood stork** *(Mycteria americana),* though their numbers are on the increase. The only storks to breed in North America, these graceful, long-lived birds (routinely living over 10 years) are usually seen on a low flight path across the marsh, though at some birding spots beginning in late summer you can find them at a **roost,** sometimes numbering over 100 birds. Resting at high tide, they fan out over the marsh to feed at low tide on foot. Old-timers sometimes call them "Spanish buzzards" or simply "the preacher."

Often confused with the wood stork is the gorgeous **white ibis** *(Eudocimus albus),* distinguishable by its orange bill and black wingtips. Like the wood stork, the ibis is a communal bird that roosts in colonies. Other similar-looking coastal denizens are the white-feathered **great egret** *(Ardea alba)* and **snowy egret** *(Egretta thula),* the former distinguishable by its yellow bill and the latter by its black bill and the tuft of plumes on the back of its head.

Egrets are in the same family as herons. The most magnificent is the **great blue heron** *(Ardea herodias).* Despite their imposing height—up to four feet tall—these waders are shy. Often you hear them rather than see them, a loud shriek of alarm that echoes over the marsh.

So how to tell the difference between all these wading birds at a glance? It's actually easiest when they're in flight. Egrets and herons fly with their necks tucked in, while storks and ibises fly with their necks extended.

Dozens of species of shorebirds comb the beaches, including **sandpipers, plovers,** and the wonderful and rare **American**

oystercatcher *(Haematopus palliates),* instantly recognizable for its prancing walk, dark brown back, stark white underside, and long, bright-orange bill. **Gulls** and **terns** also hang out wherever there's water. They can frequently be seen swarming around incoming shrimp boats, attracted by the catch of little crustaceans.

The chief raptor of the salt marsh is the fish-eating **osprey** *(Pandion haliaetus).* These large grayish birds of prey are similar to eagles but are adapted to a maritime environment, with a reversible outer toe on each talon (the better for catching wriggly fish) and closable nostrils so they can dive into the water after prey. Very common all along the coast, they like to build big nests on top of buoys and channel markers in addition to trees.

The **bald eagle** *(Haliaeetus leucocephalus),* is making a comeback thanks to increased federal regulation and better education of trigger-happy locals. Of course as we all should have learned in school, the bald eagle is not actually bald but has a head adorned with white feathers. Like the osprey, they prefer fish, but unlike the osprey they will settle for rodents and rabbits.

Inland among the pines you'll find the most common area woodpecker, the huge **pileated woodpecker** *(Dryocopus pileatus)* with its huge crest. Less common is the smaller, more subtly marked **red-cockaded woodpecker** *(Picoides borealis).* Once common in the vast primordial pine forests of the southeast, the species is now endangered, its last real refuge being the big tracts of relatively undisturbed land on military bases and on national wildlife refuges.

Insects

Down here they say that God invented bugs to keep the Yankees from completely taking over the South. And insects are probably the most unpleasant fact of life in the southeastern coastal region.

The list of annoying indigenous insects must begin with the infamous **sand gnat** *(Culicoides furens),* scourge of the lowlands. This tiny and persistent nuisance, a member of the midge family, lacks the precision of the mosquito with its long proboscis. No, the sand gnat is more torture-master than surgeon, brutally gouging and digging away at its victim's skin until it hits a source of blood. Most prevalent in the spring and fall, the sand gnat is drawn to its prey by the carbon dioxide trail of its breath.

While long sleeves and long pants are one way to keep gnats at bay, that causes its own discomfort because of the region's heat and humidity. The only real antidote to the sand gnat's assault—other than never breathing—is the Avon skin care product Skin So Soft, which has taken on a new and wholly unplanned life as the South's favorite anti-gnat lotion. Grow to like the scent, because the more of this stuff you lather on the better. And in calmer moments grow to appreciate the great contribution sand gnats make to the salt marsh ecosystem—as food for many species of birds and bats.

Running a close second to the sand gnat are the over three dozen species of highly aggressive **mosquito,** which breed anywhere a few drops of water lie stagnant. Not surprisingly, massive populations blossom in the rainiest months, in late spring and late summer. Like the gnat, the mosquito—the biters are always female—homes in on its victim by trailing the plume of carbon dioxide exhaled in the breath.

More than just a biting nuisance, mosquitoes are now vectoring West Nile disease, signaling a possibly dire threat to public health. Local governments in the region pour millions of dollars of taxpayer money into massive pesticide spraying programs from helicopters, planes, and trucks. While that certainly helps stem the tide, it by no means eliminates the mosquito population. (This is just as well, because like the sand gnat the mosquito is an important food source for many species, such as bats and dragonflies.) Alas, Skin So Soft has little effect on the mosquito. Try over-the-counter sprays, anything smelling of citronella,

and wearing long sleeves and long pants when weather permits.

But undoubtedly the most viscerally loathed of all pests here, especially on the coast, is the so-called "palmetto bug," or **American cockroach** *(Periplaneta americana).* These black, shiny, and sometimes grotesquely massive insects—up to two inches long—are living fossils, virtually unchanged over hundreds of millions of years. And perfectly adapted as they are to life in and among wet, decaying vegetation, they're unlikely to change a bit in 100 million more years.

While they spend most of their time crawling around, usually under rotting leaves and tree bark, the American cockroach can indeed fly—sort of. There are few more hilarious sights than a room full of people frantically trying to dodge a palmetto bug that has just clumsily launched itself off a high point on the wall. Because the cockroach doesn't know any better than you do where it's going, it can be a particularly bracing event—though the insect does not bite and poses few real health hazards.

Popular regional use of the term "palmetto bug" undoubtedly has its roots in a desire for polite Southern society to avoid using the ugly word "roach" and its connotations of filth and unclean environments. But the colloquialism actually has a basis in reality. Contrary to what anyone tells you, the natural habitat of the American cockroach—unlike its kitchen-dwelling, much-smaller cousin the German cockroach—is outdoors, often up in trees. They only come inside human dwellings when it's especially hot, especially cold, or especially dry outside. Like you, the palmetto bug is easily driven indoors by extreme temperatures and by thirst.

Other than visiting the Southeast during the winter, when the roaches go dormant, there's no convenient antidote for their presence. The best way to keep them out of your life is to stay away from decaying vegetation and keep doors and windows closed on especially hot nights.

History

BEFORE THE EUROPEANS

Based on studies of artifacts found throughout the area, anthropologists know the first humans arrived in the Carolinas at least 13,000 years ago, at the tail end of the Ice Age. However, a still-controversial archaeological dig in South Carolina, the Topper Site on the Savannah River inland near Allendale, has found artifacts that some scientists say are about 50,000 years old.

In any case, during this **Paleoindian Period,** sea levels were over 200 feet lower than present levels, and large mammals such as wooly mammoths, horses, and camels were hunted for food and skins. However, rapidly increasing temperatures, rising sea levels, and efficient hunting techniques combined to quickly kill off these large mammals, relics of the Pleistocene Era, ushering in the **Archaic Period** of history in what's now the southeastern United States. Still hunter-gatherers, Archaic Period Indians began turning to small game such as deer, bear, and turkey, supplemented with fruit and nuts.

The latter part of the Archaic era saw more habitation on the coasts, with an increasing reliance on fish and shellfish for sustenance. It's during this time that the great **shell middens** of the Carolina and Georgia coast trace their origins. Basically serving as trash heaps for discarded oyster shells, as the middens grew in size they also took on a ceremonial status, often being used as sites for important rituals and meetings. Such sites are often called **shell rings,** and the largest yet found was over nine feet high and 300 feet in diameter. Hilton Head Island, for example, has two remaining shell rings. Using ground-penetrating radar, archaeologists are finding more and more Archaic era shell middens and rings all the time.

The introduction of agriculture and improved pottery techniques about 3,000 years ago led to the **Woodland Period** of Native American settlement. Extended clan groups were much less migratory, establishing year-round communities of up to 50 people who began the practice of clearing land to grow crops. The ancient shell middens of their forefathers were not abandoned, however, and were continually added onto.

Native Americans had been cremating or burying their dead for years, a practice which eventually gave rise to the construction of the first **mounds** during the Woodland Period. Essentially built-up earthworks sometimes marked with spiritual symbols, often in the form of animal shapes, mounds not only contained the remains of the deceased, but items like pottery to accompany the deceased into the afterlife.

Increased agriculture led to increased population, and with that population growth came competition over resources and a more formal notion of warfare. This period, from about A.D. 800–1600, is termed the **Mississippian Period.** It was the Mississippians who would be the first Native Americans in what's now the continental United States to encounter European explorers and settlers after Columbus.

The Native Americans who would later be called **Creek Indians** were the direct descendants of the Mississippians in lineage, language, and lifestyle. Described by later European accounts as a tall, proud people, the Mississippians often wore elaborate body art and, like the indigenous inhabitants of Central and South America, used the practice of **head shaping,** whereby an infant's skull was deliberately deformed into an elongated shape by tying the baby's head to a board for about a year.

By about A.D. 1400, change came to the Mississippian culture for reasons that are still not completely understood. In some areas, large chiefdoms began splintering into smaller subgroups in an intriguing echo of the medieval feudal system going on concurrently in Europe. In other areas, however, the rise of a handful of more powerful chiefs subsumed smaller communities under their influence. In either case, the result was the same: The landscape of the Southeast became less peopled as many of the old villages, built around huge central mounds, were abandoned, some suddenly.

As tensions increased, the contested land became more and more dangerous for the poorly armed or poorly connected. Indeed, at the time of the Europeans' arrival much of the coastal area was more thinly inhabited than it had been for many decades.

THE EUROPEANS ARRIVE

The record of white European contact in the coastal Carolinas begins, suitably enough, with Amerigo Vespucci, the man for whom America was named. The Italian explorer came ashore somewhere in the Cape Hatteras area during his long-ranging first voyage to the new world in the 1490s.

Later, the Spanish arrived on the South Carolina coast in 1521, roughly concurrent with Cortez's conquest of Mexico. A party of Spanish slavers, led by Francisco Cordillo (sometimes spelled Gordillo), ventured to what's now Port Royal Sound from Santo Domingo in the Caribbean. Naming the area Santa Elena, he kidnapped a few dozen Indian slaves and left, ranging as far north as the Cape Fear River in present-day North Carolina, and by some accounts even further up the coast.

The first serious exploration of the coast came in 1526, when Lucas Vazquez de Ayllon and about 600 colonists made landfall at Winyah Bay near present-day Georgetown, South Carolina. They didn't stay long, however, immediately moving down the coast and trying to establish roots in the St. Catherine's Sound area of modern-day Georgia. That colony—called San Miguel de Gualdalpe—was the first European colony in America. (The continent's oldest continuously occupied settlement, St. Augustine, Florida, wasn't founded until 1565.) The colony also brought with it the seed of a future nation's dissolution: slaves from Africa. San Miguel lasted only six weeks due to political tension and a slave uprising.

Hernando de Soto's infamous expedition of 1539–1543 began in Florida and went through southwest Georgia before crossing the Savannah River somewhere near modern-day North Augusta, South Carolina. He immediately came in contact with emissaries from the Cofitachequi empire of Mississippian Indians. His subsequent route took him through the central Carolinas, westward over the Appalachians, and eventually to the Gulf of Mexico, where de Soto died of fever.

Long after his departure, de Soto's legacy was felt throughout the Southeast in the form of various diseases for which the Mississippian tribes had no immunity whatsoever: smallpox, typhus, influenza, measles, yellow fever, whooping cough, diphtheria, tuberculosis, and bubonic plague. While the barbaric cruelties of the Spanish certainly took their toll, far more damaging were these deadly diseases to a population totally unprepared for them. As the viruses they introduced ran rampant, the Europeans themselves stayed away for a couple of decades after the ignominious end of de Soto's quest. During that quarter-century, the once-proud Mississippian culture, ravaged by disease, disintegrated into a shadow of its former greatness.

The French Misadventure

The Spanish presence in the Carolinas was briefly threatened by the ill-fated establishment of Charlesfort in 1562 by French Huguenots under Jean Ribault. Part of a covert effort by the Protestant French Admiral Coligny to send Huguenot colonizing missions around the globe, Ribault's crew of 150 first explored the mouth of the St. Johns River near present-day Jacksonville, Florida before heading north to Port Royal Sound and present-day Parris Island, South Carolina.

After establishing Charlesfort, Ribault returned to France for supplies. During his absence, religious war had broken out in his home country. Ribault sought sanctuary in England but was clapped in irons anyway. Meanwhile, most of Charlesfort's colonists grew so demoralized they joined another French expedition led by Rene Laudonniere at Fort Caroline on the St. Johns River. The remaining 27 built a ship to sail from Charlesfort back to France. Only 20 of them survived the journey, which was cut short in the English Channel when they had to be rescued.

Ribault himself was dispatched to reinforce Fort Caroline, but was headed off by a contingent from the new Spanish fortified settlement at St. Augustine. The fate of the French presence on the southeast coast was sealed when not only did the Spanish take Fort Caroline, but a storm destroyed Ribault's reinforcing fleet. Ribault and all survivors were massacred as soon as they struggled ashore.

To keep the French away for good and cement Spain's hold on this northernmost part of their province of *La Florida,* the Spanish built the fort of Santa Elena directly on top of Charlesfort. Both layers are currently being excavated and studied today on Parris Island, near a golf course on the U.S. Marine camp.

The Mission Era

With Spanish dominance ensured for the near future, the lengthy mission era began. While it's rarely mentioned as a key part of U.S. history, the truth is that the Spanish missionary presence in Florida and on the Georgia coast was longer and more comprehensive than its much more widely known counterpart in California.

While the purpose of the missions was to convert as many Indians as possible to Christianity, they also served to further consolidate Spanish political control. It was a dicey proposition, as technically the mission friars served at the pleasure of the local chiefs. But the more savvy of the chiefs soon learned that cooperating with the militarily powerful Spanish led to more influence and more supplies. Frequently it was the chiefs themselves who urged for more expansion of the Franciscan missions.

The looming invasion threat to St. Augustine from the great English adventurer and privateer Sir Francis Drake was a harbinger of trouble to come. The Spanish consolidated their positions near St. Augustine and Santa Elena

on Parris Island was abandoned. As Spanish power waned, in 1629 Charles I of England laid formal claim to what's now the Carolinas, Georgia, and much of Florida, but made no effort to colonize the area.

By 1706 the Spanish mission effort in the southeast had fully retreated to Florida. In an interesting postscript, 89 Native Americans—the sole surviving descendants of Spain's southeastern missions—evacuated to Cuba with the final Spanish exodus from Florida in 1763.

THE LOST COLONY

The first English settlement in the New World, the ill-fated "Lost Colony" of Roanoke Island, was in modern-day North Carolina. Somewhat confusingly, however, it was considered part of Virginia at the time. (The first permanent English settlement, Jamestown, happened two decades later in Virginia proper.)

Famed English maritime adventurer Sir Walter Raleigh received a charter from Queen Elizabeth I in the 1580s to establish a colony—to be called Virginia after the "Virgin Queen" herself—that would provide a base of operations from which to plunder Spanish treasure ships crossing the Atlantic.

The Outer Banks were considered the ideal place for such a naval base, and Raleigh sent an expedition to the modern-day Manteo area on Roanoke Island commanded by Phillip Amadas and Arthur Barlowe, followed a few months later in spring 1585 by Sir Richard Grenville's larger colonizing expedition.

While first contact between the English and the resident Native Americans went reasonably well, a bad omen came early, when a dispute over a silver cup stolen from the colonists led to the ransacking of an Indian village and the brutal execution by fire of the local chief.

Despite this, Grenville went ahead with his plan to leave about 75 colonists behind while he and his crew went back to England to re-provision. Though he promised to be back by April 1586, the only Englishman to visit during that time was the wide-ranging privateer Sir Francis Drake, who simply took the bulk of the colonists back to England with him.

That group, however, was not the Lost Colony. Raleigh—who eventually did return, albeit finding no one there—sent a second group of 117 settlers to the same spot, making landfall July 22, 1587. In a chilling harbinger of what was to come, this group found no trace of the 15 men left behind to maintain the Queen's claim to Virginia—save for the bones of a single man.

The group of 117 settlers—their ranks expanded by one with the birth of the first English baby in the Americas, Virginia Dare—immediately ran into trouble with some of the local tribes, whose memory of the violence of a year before was still vivid. Though relations were good with the Croatan tribe, others in the area were less friendly, and a dispute led to the killing of a colonist, George Howe.

In response, the colonists asked their leader, John White, to return to England to bring reinforcements. The timing couldn't have been worse.

The crisis induced by the attack of the Spanish Armada on England in 1588 meant White could find no decent ship in which to return to Roanoke. In desperation he contracted with the captains of two very small vessels. On the way back to America, the captains decided to indulge in a little piracy of their own, only to have the tables turned and have their own supplies taken from them. Thus humbled, White had to sail back to England.

Continuing war with the Spanish further delayed White's return to Roanoke by another three years. Finally hitching a ride with a privateer headed for the Caribbean, White made landfall in Roanoke on August 18, 1590.

The colony was totally deserted, with no sign of struggle and the fortifications carefully dismantled. The only clue he found was a cryptic word carved into a tree that would resonate through history: "Croatoan." On a nearby tree was apparently another attempt to write the same word: "Cro."

The tree-carvings weren't without context. Before he had left the colonists, White had told them to carve a Maltese cross into a tree as a sign that they'd left under duress.

Finding no such symbol, White could only assume that the colonists were trying to tell him they'd decamped for some reason to be near the Croatan tribe. He wanted to head north to find them, but a storm was brewing and White's men refused to go any further. Later fact-finding expeditions out of the Jamestown colony farther north were also fruitless.

Why did they leave? With no sign of struggle, it's hard to blame friction with local tribes for the move. However, scientists have proven through tree-ring study that the period of the colonists' departure coincided exactly with one of the worst droughts ever recorded.

Where did these possibly drought-stricken colonists go? To this day no one knows. The modern-day Lumbee Indians of southeastern North Carolina insist they are descended from Roanoke colonists who intermarried with their tribe, and indeed they still bear many of the historical surnames of the colonists.

Chief Powhatan of Virginia, however, told English settlers that the colonists had taken up with a tribe in his area, and that he had destroyed that tribe as well as the colonists wholesale.

Another theory has it that the colonists became assimilated into the Tuscarora tribe of the Carolinas, or maybe the Indians of Person County, long known for their European look and characteristics.

DNA testing is now ongoing, and so far the most promising explanation favors the longest-running claim of all—that of the Lumbees.

THE FOUNDING OF CAROLINA

With the settlement of Jamestown, Virginia, in 1607, the English focus moved farther north for awhile. Activity in what would later be called the Carolinas was further limited by continuing political unrest in England, which culminated in the savage English Civil War.

The colony of Carolina was a product of the **English Restoration,** when the monarchy returned to power after the grim 11-year tenure of Oliver Cromwell, who had defeated Royalist

HENRY WOODWARD, COLONIAL INDIANA JONES

He's virtually unsung in the history books. There are no movies made about him. But Dr. Henry Woodward, the first English settler in the Carolinas, lived a life that is the stuff of novels and screenplays.

Educated in medicine in London, Woodward first tried his hand in the colony of Barbados. But Barbados, crowded and run by an elite, was no place for a young man with a sense of adventure but no contacts in the sugar industry. Still in his teens, Woodward left Barbados in Captain Robert Sandford's 1664 expedition to Carolina. Landing in the Cape Fear region, Sandford's cohort made its way down to Port Royal Sound to contact the Cusabo tribe. In 1666, in what is perhaps the New World's first "cultural exchange program," Woodward volunteered to stay behind while the rest of the expedition returned to England with a Native American named Shadoo.

Woodward learned the local language and established political relations with surrounding tribes, actions for which the Lords Proprietors granted him temporary "formall possession of the whole Country to hold as Tennant att Will." The Spanish had different plans, however. They came and kidnapped the young Englishman, taking him to what turned out to be a very permissive state of house arrest at the Spanish stronghold of St. Augustine in Florida.

Surprising the Spanish with his request — in Latin, no less — to convert to Catholicism, Woodward was popular and well-treated. An excellent student of the Catechism, Woodward became a favorite of the Spanish governor, and was even promoted to official surgeon. During that time, he studied Spanish government, commerce, and culture, with the same diligence with which he studied the Indians a year earlier.

In 1668, Woodward was "rescued" by English privateers — pirates, really — under the command of Robert Searle, who'd come to sack St. Augustine. Woodward's sojourn with the pirates would last two years, during which he was kept on board as ship's surgeon. Was the pirate raid a coincidence? Or, as some schol-

ars suggest, was Woodward really one of history's greatest spies? We will probably never know. Incredibly, the plot thickens. In another coincidence, in 1670 Woodward was rescued when the pirates shipwrecked on the Caribbean island of Nevis. His rescuers were none other than the settlers on their way to found Charles Town.

On landfall, Woodward asserted his previous experience in the area to direct the colonists away from Port Royal to an area of less Spanish influence. That same year he began a series of expeditions to contact tribes in the Carolina interior — the first non-Spanish white person to set foot in the area. Using economic espionage gained from the Spanish, Woodward's goal was to jumpstart the trade in deerskins that would be the bulwark of the Charles Town colony. Woodward's unlikely 1674 alliance with the aggressive Westo tribe was instrumental in this burgeoning trade. As if all this weren't enough, in 1680 Woodward, now with property of his own on Johns Island, would introduce local farmers to a certain strange crop recently imported from Madagascar: rice!

Woodward made enemies, however, of settlers who were envious of his growing affluence and suspicious of his friendship with the Westo. His outspoken disgust with the spread of Indian slavery brought a charge against him of undermining the interests of the crown. But Woodward, by now a celebrity of sorts, returned to England to plead his case directly to the Lords Proprietors. They not only pardoned him, but made him their official Indian agent — with a 20 percent share of the profits.

Woodward would never again see the land of his birth. He returned to America to trek inland, making alliances with Creek tribes in Spanish-held territory. Hounded by Spanish troops, Woodward fell ill of a fever somewhere inland in the Savannah River Valley. He made it to Charleston and safety, but never fully recovered and died around 1690 — after living the kind of life you usually only see in the movies.

forces in the English Civil War. The attitude of the Restoration era was expansionist, confident, and mercantile.

Historians dispute exactly how close-minded Cromwell himself was, but there's no debating the puritanical tone of his reign as British head of state. Theater was banned, as was most music except for religious hymns. Hair was close-cropped and dress was extremely conservative. Most disturbing of all for the holiday-loving English, the observation of Christmas and Easter was strongly discouraged because of their supposedly pagan origins.

Enter Charles II, son of the beheaded Charles I. His ascent to the throne in 1660 signaled a release of all the pent-up creativity and energy of the British people, stagnant under Cromwell's repression. The arts returned to their previous importance. Foreign policy became aggressive and expansionist. Capitalists again sought profit. Fashion made a comeback, and dandy dress and long hair for both men and women were all the rage.

This then, is the backdrop for the first English settlement of the deep South. The first expedition was by a Barbadian colonist, William Hilton, in 1663. While he didn't establish a new colony, he did leave behind his name on the most notable geographic feature he saw—Hilton Head Island.

In 1665 King Charles II gave a charter to eight Lords Proprietors to establish a colony in the area, generously to be named Carolina after the monarch himself. (One of the Proprietors, Lord Ashley Cooper, would see not one but both rivers in the Charleston area named after him.) Remarkably, none of the Proprietors ever set foot in the colony they established for their own profit.

Before their colony was even established, the Proprietors themselves set the stage for the vast human disaster that would eventually befall it. They encouraged slavery by promising that each colonist would receive 20 acres of land for every black male slave and 10 acres for every black female slave brought to the colony within the first year.

In 1666 explorer Robert Sandford officially claimed Carolina for the king, in a ceremony on modern-day Seabrook or Wadmalaw Island. The Proprietors then sent out a fleet of three ships from England, only one of which, the *Carolina*, would make it the whole way. After stops in the thriving English colonies of Barbados and Bermuda, the ship landed in Port Royal. They were greeted without violence, but the fact that the local indigenous people spoke broken Spanish led the colonists to conclude that perhaps the site was too close to Spain's sphere of influence for comfort. A Kiawah chief, eager for allies against the fierce, slave-trading Westo tribe, invited the colonists north to settle instead.

So the colonists—148 of them, including three African slaves—moved 80 miles up the coast, and in 1670 pitched camp on the Ashley River at a place they dubbed Albemarle Point after one of their lost ships. Living within the wooden palisades of the camp, the colonists farmed 10-acre plots outside the walls for sustenance. The Native Americans of the area were of the large and influential Cusabo tribe of the Creeks, and are sometimes even today known as the Settlement Indians. Subtribes of the Cusabo whose names live on today in South Carolina geography were the Kiawah, Edisto, Wando, Stono, and Ashepoo.

A few years later some English colonists from the Caribbean colony of Barbados, which was beginning to suffer overpopulation, joined the Carolinians. The Barbadian influence, with an emphasis on large-scale slave labor and a caste system, would have an indelible imprint on the colony in years to come. Indeed, within a generation a majority of settlers in the new colony would be African slaves.

By 1680, however, Albemarle Point was feeling growing pains as well, and the Proprietors ordered the site moved to Oyster Point at the confluence of the Ashley and Cooper Rivers (the present-day Battery). Within a year Albemarle Point was completely abandoned, and the walled fortifications of Charles Town were built a few hundred yards up from Oyster Point on the banks of the Cooper River.

The original Anglican settlers were quickly

joined by various Dissenters, among them French Huguenots, Quakers, Congregationalists, and Jews. A group of Scottish Presbyterians established the short-lived Stuart Town near Port Royal in 1684. Recognizing this diversity, the colony in 1697 granted religious liberty to all "except Papists." The Anglicans attempted a crackdown on Dissenters in 1704, but two years later Queen Anne stepped in and ensured religious freedom for all Carolinians (again with the exception of Roman Catholics, who wouldn't be a factor in the colony until after the American Revolution).

The English settlements quickly gained root as the burgeoning deerskin trade increased exponentially. Traders upriver, using an ancient network of trails, worked with local Native Americans, mostly Cherokees, to exploit the massive numbers of deer in the American interior.

The Tuscarora War

The Tuscarora War was a remarkably bloody conflict in present-day North Carolina between settler and Indian that had the result of cementing the control of white settlers on the region.

In a similar story repeated throughout the region, the Tuscarora—demoralized by disease and tired of unscrupulous white traders—decided to take a stand and coordinate an attack. On Sept. 22, 1711, came the first attacks, near the town of Bath and the plantations on the Neuse and Trent rivers. Hundreds of settlers died.

The response was even more devastating. Gov. Edward Hyde called out the militia, and a combined force of settlers and Indian allies attacked the southern Tuscarora Indians at Fort Narhantes in Craven County in 1712. Over 300 Tuscarora were killed. Unrest continued, resulting in a clash at Fort Neoheroka in Greene County in which over a thousand Tuscarora were killed or captured.

By this time the tribe began emigrating to the New York area to escape further destruction. The remaining tribespeople signed a peace treaty in 1718, one of the terms of which was their removal to a tract of land in Bertie County.

The Yamasee War

South Carolina would have its own bloody conflict with Native Americans, also named after the tribe in opposition to the settlers.

Within 20 years the English presence expanded throughout the Lowcountry to include Port Royal and Beaufort. Charles Town became a thriving commercial center, dealing in deerskins with independent traders in the interior and with foreign concerns from England to South America. Its success was not without a backlash, as the local Yamasee tribe of the Creek Indians became increasingly disgruntled at the settlers and their allies' growing monopolies on deerskin and the slave trade.

Slavery was a sad and common fact of life from the earliest days of white settlement in the region. Indians were the most frequent early victims, with not only white settlers taking slaves from the tribes, but the tribes themselves conducting slaving raids on each other, often selling their hostages to eager colonists.

As rumors of war spread, on Good Friday, 1715, a delegation of six white Carolinians went to the Yamasee village of Pocataligo to address some of the tribe's grievances in the hopes of forestalling violence. Their effort was in vain, however, as Yamasee warriors murdered four in their sleep, the remaining two escaping to sound the alarm. The treacherous attack signaled the beginning of the two-year Yamasee War, which would claim the lives of nearly 10 percent of the colony's population and an unknown number of Native Americans—making it one of the bloodiest conflicts in American history.

Energized and ready for war, the Yamasee attacked Charles Town itself and killed about 90 of the 100 or so white traders in the interior, effectively ending all commerce in the area. As Charles Town began to swell with refugees from the hinterland, water and supplies ran low and the colony was in peril.

After an initially poor performance by the Carolina militia, a professional army—including armed African slaves—was raised. Well

PIRATES OF THE CAROLINA COAST

Pirates, along with their close cousins, slavers, were among the earliest explorers of the Atlantic seaboard of America, and other than Native American chiefs, were the only real authority in the area for decades. The creeks and barrier islands of the Carolina coast provided important, hard-to-find sanctuaries off the regular pirate circuit down in the booty-laden Spanish Caribbean.

For most of us, pirate stories and movies are a form of escapism, in which the most unlikely scenarios happen with ease. But a real-life pirate story from the earliest days of Charleston would almost seem too unbelievable even for Hollywood.

The encounter was at the hands of the infamous Edward Teach, a.k.a. Blackbeard. A tall, terrifying bully of a man, the legendary pirate also had a flair for the dramatic, as all proper pirates should. Given to twisting flaming wads of cloth into his beard when he attacked his prey, Blackbeard was also quite eccentric, as his Charleston escapade shows.

In June 1718, Blackbeard, driven northward from his usual haunting grounds in the Bahamas by a concerted effort from the British Navy, approached Charleston harbor in his flagship *Queen Anne's Revenge*, accompanied by three smaller vessels. He immediately seized several ships and kidnapped several leading citizens, including Councilman Samuel Wragg and his four-year-old son. He sent one captive ashore with the message that unless his demand was met, the heads of Wragg and son would soon be delivered to the colonial governor's doorstep.

Blackbeard's demand? A chest of medicine. For what purpose, we still aren't sure, but apparently it really was all he wanted. The medicines were delivered in short order, Blackbeard then released his hostages, and sailed to North Carolina. He grounded his ships in Beaufort Inlet and went to the then-capital of Bath to officially receive a royal pardon he'd been promised.

One of the pirates serving under Blackbeard during the Charleston escapade was Stede Bonnet, quite a contrasting figure in his debonair nature and posh finery. When Charleston's Colonel William Rhett – his house at 54 Hasell Street is still standing, the city's oldest – got wind that Bonnet and crew were still a-pirating off Cape Fear, North Carolina, he set out with a fleet to bring him to justice.

And that he did, bringing pirate and crew back to Charleston for a trial that almost didn't happen after Bonnet escaped from custody dressed as a woman (he was captured on Sullivan's Island). The dashing Bonnet actually garnered quite a bit of public sympathy – especially when he begged not to be hanged – but it wasn't enough to forestall the grim fate of the pirate and his crew: public execution at White Point, the bodies left to dangle as a warning to other buccaneers.

Another coastal menace, Richard Worley, was also hanged in Charleston. He supposedly was buried in a marshy creek downtown, where Meeting and Water Streets intersect today.

As for Blackbeard, his retirement plans were interrupted by the royal governor of Virginia, who decided to nullify the pirate's pardon out of concern for public safety. Motivated by the promise of a sizable bounty, Lt. Robert Maynard and a British naval contingent tracked Blackbeard and his band of pirates down near Beaufort, North Carolina, in November 1718.

A running gun battle ensued in the area of Ocracoke Island, with Blackbeard aboard the *Adventure* and Maynard on the *Ranger*. The violence climaxed with Blackbeard boarding Maynard's ship, which was preceded by a barrage of makeshift hand grenades made from gunpowder in rum bottles.

But it was a trap – Maynard and his men burst from below deck and counterattacked. According to legend, Blackbeard had to be shot five times and stabbed more than 20 times before he died. He was decapitated, and his head was mounted on the bowsprit of a British vessel as an example to others – and so that Maynard could claim his prize money! Today you can see a few artifacts from what is believed to be the wreck of *Queen Anne's Revenge* at the North Carolina Maritime Museum in Beaufort.

trained and well led, the new army more than held its own despite being outnumbered. A key alliance with local Cherokees was all the advantage the colonists needed to turn the tide for good. While the Cherokee never received the overt military backing from the settlers that they sought, they did garner enough supplies and influence to convince their Creek rivals, the Yamasee, to begin the peace process.

The war-weary settlers, eager to get back to life and to business, were eager to negotiate with them, offering goods as a sign of their earnest intent. By 1717 the Yamasee threat had subsided and trade in the region began flourishing anew.

No sooner had the Yamasee War ended, however, when a new threat emerged: the dread pirate Edward Teach, a.k.a. Blackbeard. Entering Charleston harbor in May 1718 with his flagship *Queen Anne's Revenge* and three other vessels, he promptly plundered five ships and began a full-scale blockade of the entire settlement. He took a number of prominent citizens hostage before finally departing northward along the coast, thinking he had a royal pardon. However, a Royal Navy flotilla tracked him down near Ocracoke Island in the Outer Banks and killed him.

Slavery Expands

While it was the Spanish who introduced slavery to America—of Indians as well as Africans—it was the English-speaking settlers who dramatically expanded the institution.

For the colonists of South Carolina, the Blackbeard episode was the final straw. Already disgusted by the lack of support from the Lords Proprietors during the Yamasee War, the humiliation of the pirate blockade was too much to take. So to almost universal agreement in the colony, the settlers threw off the rule of the Proprietors and strenuously lobbied in 1719 to become a crown colony, an effort that came to final fruition in 1729. While this outward-looking and energetic place—whose name would morph into Charlestown, and then simply Charleston—was originally built on the backs of merchants, with the introduction of the rice

and indigo crops in the early 1700s it would increasingly be built on the backs of slaves.

For all the wealth gained through the planting of indigo, rice, and cotton seeds, another seed was sown by the Lowcountry plantation culture. The area's total dependence on slave labor would soon lead to a disastrous war, a conflict signaled for decades to those smart enough to read the signs.

By this time Charleston was firmly established as the key American port for the importation of African slaves, accounting for about 40 percent of the trade. As a result, the black population of the coast outnumbered the white population by more than three-to-one. The very real fear of violent slave uprisings had great influence over not only politics, but day-to-day affairs. These fears were eventually realized in the **Stono Rebellion.**

On September 9, 1739, 20 slaves, led by an Angolan known only as Jemmy, met near the Stono River 20 miles southwest of Charleston. Marching with a banner that read "Liberty," they seized guns from a store, killing the proprietors, with the eventual plan of marching all the way to Spanish Florida and sanctuary in the wilderness. On the way they burned seven plantations and killed 20 more whites. A militia eventually caught up with them, killing 44 escaped slaves and losing 20 of their own. The prisoners were decapitated and had their heads spiked on every milepost between the spot of that final battle and Charleston.

The result was not only a 10-year moratorium on slave importation into Charleston, but a severe crackdown on the education of slaves—a move that would have damaging implications for generations to come.

Spain Vanquished

In 1729, Carolina was divided into north and south. In 1731, a colony to be known as Georgia, after the new English king, was carved out of the southern part of the Carolina land grant specifically to provide a military buffer to protect Carolina.

A young English general, aristocrat, and humanitarian named James Edward Oglethorpe gathered together a group of Trustees—similar to Carolina's Lords Proprietors—to take advantage of that grant. Like Carolina the Georgia colony also emphasized religious freedom. While to modern ears Charleston's antipathy towards "papists" and Oglethorpe's original ban of Roman Catholics from Georgia might seem incompatible with this goal, the reason was a coldly pragmatic one for the time: England's two main global rivals, France and Spain, were both staunchly Catholic countries.

In 1742 Oglethorpe defeated a Spanish force on St. Simons Island, Georgia in the **Battle of Bloody Marsh.** That clash marked the end of Spanish overtures on England's colonies in America. With first the French and then the Spanish effectively shut off from the American East Coast, the stage was set for an internal battle between England and its burgeoning colonies across the Atlantic.

REVOLUTION AND A NEW NATION

It's a persistent but inaccurate myth that the affluent elite on the southeastern coast were reluctant to break ties with England. While the coast's cultural and economic ties to England were certainly strong, the **Stamp Act** and the **Townshend Acts** combined to turn public sentiment against the mother country there as elsewhere in the colonies.

Militarily, the Carolinas were the key to the colonist's eventual victory. With George Washington in a stalemate with British troops in the northeast, the war hinged on the success or failure of the British **"Southern Strategy,"** an attempt to expand Redcoat ranks by enlisting support from loyalists in the area.

South Carolinian planters like Christopher Gadsden, Henry Laurens, John Rutledge, and Arthur Middleton were early leaders in the movement for independence. In 1773, North Carolina installed nonimportation agreements that forced local merchants to drop trade with Great Britain. The next year, North Carolina planters sent food and supplies to Massachusetts, then facing the brunt of the British crackdown.

At war's outbreak, North Carolina saw its first engagement at the Battle of Moore's Creek Bridge near Wilmington in early 1776. This clash of loyalist and patriot forces was a clear-cut patriot victory, and little fighting occurred on the North Carolina coast through the end of the conflict.

The poor showing of the loyalists prompted British General Sir Henry Clinton to head further south to attempt to take Charleston, South Carolina—fourth-largest city in the colonies—in June 1776. The episode gave South Carolina its "Palmetto State" moniker when Redcoat cannonballs bounced off the palm tree–lined walls of Fort Moultrie on Sullivan's Island. The British successfully took the city, however, in 1780, holding it until 1782.

Though the southeast coast's two major cities were captured—Savannah fell to the British in 1778—the war raged on throughout the surrounding area. With over 130 known military engagements occurring in South Carolina, that colony sacrificed more men during the war than any other—including Massachusetts itself.

The struggle became a guerrilla war of colonists vs. the British as well as a civil war between patriots and loyalists, or **Tories.** Committing what would today undoubtedly be called war crimes, the British routinely burned homes, churches, and fields, and killed recalcitrant civilians. In response, patriots of the Lowcountry bred a group of deadly guerrilla soldiers under legendary leaders such as Francis Marion, "the Swamp Fox," and Thomas Sumter, "the Gamecock." Using unorthodox tactics perfected in years of backcountry Indian fighting, the patriots of the Carolinas attacked the British in daring hit-and-run raids staged from the swamps and marshes, from the hills and forests.

The Cotton Boom

True to form, the new nation wasted no time in asserting its economic strength. Rice planters from Wilmington, North Carolina, on down to the St. Johns River in Florida built on their already-impressive wealth, becoming America's richest men by far—with fortunes built, of course, on the backs of the slaves working in the fields and paddies.

Charleston was still by far the largest, most powerful, and most influential city in the southeast. While most Lowcountry planters spent the warmer months away from the mosquito-and-malaria-infested coast, Charleston's elite grew so fond of their little peninsula that they took to living in their "summer homes" year-round, becoming absentee landlords of their various plantations. As a result of this affluent, somewhat hedonistic atmosphere, Charleston became an early arts and cultural center for the United States.

In 1786, a new crop was introduced that would only enhance the financial clout of the coastal region: cotton. A former loyalist colonel, Roger Kelsal, sent some seed from Anguilla in the West Indies to his friend James Spaulding, owner of a plantation on St. Simons Island, Georgia. This crop, soon to be known as **Sea Island cotton** and considered the best in the world, would eventually supplant rice as the crop of choice for coastal plantations. Plantations on Hilton Head, Edisto, Daufuskie, and Kiawah islands would make the shift to this more profitable product and amass even greater fortunes for their owners.

With the boom in cotton there needed to be a better way to get that cash crop to market quickly. In 1827, the South Carolina Canal and Rail Road Company was chartered to build a line that would expedite cotton trade from the Upcountry down to the port of Charleston. The resulting 137-mile Charleston-Hamburg line, begun in 1833, was at the time the longest railroad in the world.

Up in North Carolina, New Bern was at this time the state's most populous city, though it had lost its capital status to Raleigh in 1794.

Secession

Though much of the lead-in to the Civil War focused on whether or not slavery would be allowed in America's newest territories in the West, all figurative roads eventually led to South Carolina.

During Andrew Jackson's presidency in the 1820s, his vice president, South Carolina's John C. Calhoun, became a thorn in Jackson's side with his aggressive advocacy for the concept of **nullification,** which Jackson strenuously rejected. In a nutshell, Calhoun said that if a state decided that the federal government wasn't treating it fairly—in this case with regards to tariffs that were hurting the cotton trade in the Palmetto State—it could simply nullify the federal law, superseding it with law of its own.

As the abolition movement gained steam and tension over slavery rose, South Carolina Congressman Preston Brooks took things to the next level. On May 22, 1856, he beat fellow Senator Charles Sumner of Massachusetts nearly to death with his walking cane on the Senate floor. Sumner had just given a speech criticizing pro-slavery forces—including a relative of Brooks—and called slavery "a harlot." (In a show of support, South Carolinians sent Brooks dozens of new canes to replace the one he broke over Sumner's head.)

In 1860, the national convention of the Democratic Party, then the dominant force in U.S. politics, was held in—where else?—Charleston. Rancor over slavery and state's rights was so high that they couldn't agree on a single candidate to run to replace President James Buchanan. Reconvening in Maryland, the party split along sectional lines, with the northern wing backing Stephen A. Douglas. The southern wing, fervently desiring secession above all else, deliberately chose its own candidate, John Breckenridge, in order to split the Democratic vote and throw the election to Republican Abraham Lincoln, an outspoken opponent of slavery.

During that so-called **Secession Winter** before Lincoln took office, seven states seceded from the union, first among them the Palmetto State, followed by Mississippi, Florida, Alabama, Georgia, Louisiana, and Texas.

Ironically, South Carolina's neighbor to the north was the last Southern state to secede, leaving the union after the war had already begun. Known as being quite reluctant to the cause, the Tarheel State may have even gotten its nickname for having metaphorical feet that were too sticky to take a step.

Not nearly as dependent on slave labor as South Carolina, North Carolinians for the most part saw no reason to be hasty about dissolving a union that for the most part had been quite good to it. Once committed, however, they were fully devoted to the Confederacy, and indeed lost more troops in the conflict than any other Southern state.

A UNION DISSOLVED

Five days after South Carolina's secession on December 21, 1860, U.S. Army Major Robert Anderson moved his garrison from Fort Moultrie in Charleston harbor to nearby Fort Sumter. Over the next few months and into the spring, Anderson would ignore many calls to surrender the fort and Confederate forces would prevent any Union resupply or reinforcement. Shortly before dawn on April 12, 1861, Confederate batteries around Charleston—ironically none of which were at the Battery itself—opened fire on Fort Sumter for 34 straight hours, until Anderson surrendered on April 13.

In a classic example of why you should always be careful what you wish for, the secessionists had been too clever by half in pushing for the election of Lincoln. Far from prodding the North to sue for peace, the fall of Fort Sumter instead caused the remaining states in the Union to rally around the previously unpopular tall man from Illinois. Lincoln's skillful—some would say cunning—management of the Fort Sumter standoff meant that from then on out, the South would bear history's blame for initiating the conflict that would claim over half a million American lives.

After Fort Sumter, the remaining four states of the Confederacy—Arkansas, Tennessee, North Carolina, and Virginia—seceded. The Old Dominion was the real prize for the secessionists, as Virginia had the South's only ironworks and by far its largest manufacturing base.

War on the Coast

In November 1861, a massive Union invasion armada landed in Port Royal Sound in South Carolina, effectively taking the entire Lowcountry and Sea Islands out of the war. Charleston, however, did host two battles in the conflict. The **Battle of Secessionville** came in June 1862, when a Union force attempting to take Charleston was repulsed on James Island with heavy casualties. The next battle, an unsuccessful Union landing on Morris Island in July 1863, was immortalized by the movie *Glory*.

The 54th Massachusetts Regiment, an African American unit with white commanders, performed so gallantly in its failed assault on the Confederate Battery Wagner that it inspired the North and was cited by abolitionists as further proof that African Americans should be given freedom and full citizenship rights. Another invasion attempt on Charleston would not come, but it was besieged and bombarded for nearly two years (devastation made even worse by a massive fire, unrelated to the shelling, which destroyed much of the city in 1861).

In other towns, white Southerners evacuated the coastal cities and plantations for the hinterland, leaving behind only slaves to fend for themselves. In many coastal areas, African Americans and Union garrison troops settled into an awkward but peaceful coexistence.

While the ironclad *USS Monitor* gained fame for its sea battle with the Confederate ironclad *CSS Virginia* (formerly the *Merrimac*) farther north in Virginia waters, it was actually lost at sea off Cape Hatteras in December 1862. The underwater site is now a National Historic Landmark.

In Savannah to the south, General William Sherman concluded his **March to the Sea** in 1864, famously giving the city to Lincoln as a Christmas present. While staunch Confederates, city fathers were wise enough to know what would happen to their accumulated wealth and fine homes should they be foolhardy enough to resist Sherman's army of war-hardened veterans, most of them farm boys from the Midwest with a pronounced distaste for the "peculiar institution" of slavery.

In North Carolina, Wilmington remained in Confederate hands until very late in the war, February 1865, acting as the South's de facto main base for blockade runners due to the quick fall of New Orleans and the effective blockading of Charleston, Beaufort, and Savannah.

Aftermath

The only military uncertainty left was in how badly Charleston, the "cradle of secession," would suffer for its sins. Historians and local wags have long debated why Sherman spared Charleston, the hated epicenter of the Civil War. Did Sherman fall in love with the city during his brief posting there as a young lieutenant? Did he *literally* fall in love there, with one of its legendarily beautiful and delicate local belles?

We may never know for sure, but it's likely that the Lowcountry's marshy, mucky terrain simply made it too difficult to move large numbers of men and supplies from Savannah to Charleston proper. So Sherman turned his terrifying, battle-hardened army inland toward the state capitol of Columbia, which would not be so lucky. Most of Charleston's outlying plantation homes, too, would be put to the torch.

For the African American population of South Carolina, however, it was not a time of sadness but the great Day of Jubilee. Soon after the Confederate surrender, black Charlestonians held one of the largest parades the city has ever seen, with one of the floats being a coffin bearing the sign, "Slavery is dead."

As for the place where it all began, a plucky Confederate garrison remained underground at Fort Sumter throughout the war, as the walls above them were literally pounded into dust by the long Union siege. The garrison quietly left the fort under cover of night on February 17, 1865. Major Robert Anderson, who surrendered the fort at war's beginning, returned to Sumter in April 1865 to raise the same flag he'd lowered exactly four years earlier. Three thousand African Americans attended the ceremonies, including the son of Denmark Vesey himself.

Later that same night, Abraham Lincoln was assassinated in Washington, D.C.

Reconstruction

A case could be made that slavery need not have led America into Civil War. The U.S. had banned the importation of slaves long before, in 1808. The great powers of Europe would soon ban slavery altogether (Spain in 1811, France in 1826, and Britain in 1833). Visiting foreign dignitaries in the mid-1800s were often shocked to find the practice in full swing in the American South. Even Brazil, the world center of slavery, where four out of every 10 African slaves were brought (less than 5 percent came to the U.S.), would ban slavery in 1888.

Still, the die was cast, the war was fought, and everyone had to deal with the aftermath. For a brief time, Sherman's benevolent dictatorship on the coast held promise for an orderly post-war future. In 1865, he issued his sweeping "40 Acres and a Mule" order seeking dramatic economic restitution for free blacks of the Sea Islands of South Carolina and Georgia. However, politics reared its ugly head in the wake of Lincoln's assassination and the order was rescinded, ushering in the chaotic Reconstruction era, echoes of which linger to this day.

Nonetheless, that period of time in the South Carolina and Georgia Sea Islands served as an important incubator of sorts for the indigenous African American culture of the coast—called Gullah in South Carolina and Geechee in Georgia. Largely left to their own devices, these insulated farming and oystering communities held to their old folkways, many of which exist today.

Even as the trade in cotton and naval stores hit even greater heights than before, urban life and racial tension became more and more problematic. Urban population swelled as freed blacks from all over the depressed countryside rushed into the cities. As one, his name lost to history, famously said: "Freedom was free-er in Charleston."

It was during this time that some gains were made by African Americans, albeit with little support from the indigenous white population. Largely under duress, the University of South Carolina became the first Southern university to grant degrees to black students. The historically black, Methodist-affiliated Claflin College in Orangeburg was founded in 1869.

While the coast and urban areas saw more opportunity for African Americans, tension remained high in the countryside.

Largely with the support of white militia groups, in 1876 the old guard of the Democratic Party returned to power in South Carolina with the election of former Confederate General Wade Hampton III to the governor's office. Supported by a violent paramilitary group called the "Red Shirts," Hampton used his charisma and considerable personal reputation to attempt to restore South Carolina to its antebellum glory—and undo Reconstruction in the process.

The Wilmington Insurrection

Despite its laidback, friendly reputation, Wilmington was the site of one of the bloodiest racial incidents in American history, and by some accounts the only time a U.S. municipal government has ever been removed by force.

In the late 19th century, Wilmington was North Carolina's largest city and had a reasonably well-functioning Republican-led government that featured the input of many free African American citizens. One was Alexander Manly, editor of the *Wilmington Daily Record*, at the time the only black-owned newspaper in the United States.

On the morning of November 10, 1898, a mob largely comprising former Confederate soldiers attacked the newspaper office, motivated by Manly's recent rebuttals against accusations that local African American men were guilty of raping white women. Manly left town in fear of his life as the mob burned the newspaper building down.

Led by Alfred Moore Waddell, the mob then gave the elected city government, which included both white and black officials, an ultimatum: Resign or face a similar fate. Literally at gunpoint, the municipal government was dissolved and a new city council "appointed." By four o'clock in the afternoon of the same day, Waddell was declared mayor.

RENAISSANCE

While the aftermath of the Civil War was painful, it was by no means bereft of activity or profit. The reunion of the states marked the coming of the Industrial Revolution to America, and in many quarters of the South the cotton, lumber, and naval stores industries not only recovered, but exceeded antebellum levels.

A classic South Carolina example was in Horry County, where the town of Conway exploded as a commercial center for the area logging industry. By 1901 the first, modest resort had been built on nearby Myrtle Beach, and the area rapidly became an important vacation area—a role it serves to this day.

The **Spanish-American War of 1898** was a major turning point for the South. For most Southerners, it was the first time since the Civil War that they were enthusiastically patriotic about being Americans. The southeastern coast felt this in particular, as it was a staging area for the invasion of Cuba. Charlestonians cheered the exploits of their namesake heavy cruiser the USS *Charleston*, which played a key role in forcing the Spanish surrender of Guam.

A South Carolinian himself, Wall Street financial wizard and presidential advisor Bernard Baruch would make many Americans more familiar with the state's natural beauty. After his acquisition of the old Hobcaw Barony near Georgetown in 1905, he hosted many a world leader there, including President Franklin D. Roosevelt and British Prime Minister Winston Churchill.

Charleston would elect its first Irish-American mayor, John Grace, in 1911. Though it wouldn't open until 1929, the first Cooper River Bridge joining Charleston with Mount Pleasant was the child of the Grace administration, which is credited today for modernizing the Holy City's infrastructure (as well as tolerating high levels of vice during Prohibition) and making possible much of the civic gains to follow.

A major change that came during this time is rarely remarked upon in the history books:

This was when South Carolina became a majority white state. With thousands of African Americans leaving for more tolerant pastures and more economic opportunity in the North and the West—a move known as the **Great Migration**—the demographics of the state changed accordingly.

The arrival of the tiny but devastating boll weevil all but wiped out the cotton trade on the coast after the turn of the century, forcing the economy to diversify. Naval stores and lumbering were the order of the day at the advent of **World War I,** the combined patriotic effort for which did wonders in repairing the wounds of the Civil War, still vivid in many local memories.

A major legacy of World War I that still greatly influences life in the Lowcountry is the Marine Corps Recruiting Depot Parris Island, which began life as a small Marine camp in 1919.

First in Flight

The lonely Outer Banks of North Carolina hosted one of the seminal events in human history, with the **Wright Brothers'** first powered flight.

Born in Indiana and raised in Dayton, Ohio, neither Orville and Wilbur Wright graduated from college. They opened a bicycle shop in Dayton and used the profits to fund their growing interest in aviation.

Wilbur, the more aggressive of the two, was inspired by the flight of birds to make groundbreaking research into wing design. Another key difference between the Wrights' work and other concurrent aviation minds was that the brothers insisted on the pilot having total control over the aircraft, as opposed to being totally dependent on prevailing winds.

To bring their ideas to fruition, in 1900 the Wrights traveled to remote and then barely-inhabited Kitty Hawk, North Carolina, which they picked for two reasons: First, the sea breeze and soft sand were conducive to flight experiments; and just as importantly, no reporters were likely to follow them there and prematurely reveal their designs and methods.

For two full years, they worked on nothing but gliders, launching them off of Kill Devil Hill, the highest point on this part of the Outer Banks. In late 1903, however, the "Wright Flyer One" was ready for takeoff. Wilbur won a coin toss to see who would pilot the first flight, an ill-fated three-second trip that damaged the craft.

When the Flyer was repaired, it was quiet Orville who would pilot the historic "real" first flight, a 12-second, 120-foot trip across the sandy scrub at the base of Kill Devil Hill on December 17, 1903. It is this flight which is recorded in the famous photograph instantly recognizable the world over.

Fame was long in coming, however. Despite the presence of a handful of witnesses—not to mention the photo—no one quite believed the Wright Brothers had actually managed controlled, powered flight.

For a time, this suited the Wrights just fine, since they had not yet received a patent for their revolutionary wing design and were still fearful their work would be pirated by others. They continued working in relative anonymity back in Dayton, until finally receiving a patent in 1906, after which a whirlwind of transatlantic business negotiations followed.

The skeptical French were wowed by a display in August 1908, which stunned a crowd at Le Mans with a nearly two-minute powered flight that included several graceful banked turns.

The famously protective Wrights continued to defend their patents, with mixed results, against other businesspeople. While they never profited as much as they wanted from their invention, history still reveres the brilliant, oddball brothers as the fathers of aviation.

In the kind of win-win situation that was unfortunately lacking in the Wright Brothers' business activities, the states of Ohio and North Carolina have worked out a compromise of sorts to share the Wright legacy. Ohio calls itself "The Birthplace of Aviation Pioneers" (a nod to the fact that astronauts John Glenn and Neil Armstrong are also Ohioans), whereas the Tarheel State claims as its motto "First in Flight."

The Roaring Twenties

In the boom period following World War I,

North Carolina was the most industrialized state in the South, chiefly due to its healthy textile trade. The tobacco crop as well was particularly profitable.

During this time, Charleston, South Carolina, entered the world stage and made some of its most significant cultural contributions to American life. The "Charleston" dance, originated on the streets of the Holy City and popularized in New York, would sweep the world. The Jenkins Orphanage Band, often credited with the dance, traveled the world, even playing at President Taft's inauguration.

In the visual arts, the "Charleston Renaissance" took off, specifically intended to introduce the Holy City to a wider audience. Key work included the Asian-influenced work of self-taught painter Alice Ravenel Huger Smith and the etchings of Elizabeth O'Neill Verner. Edward Hopper was a visitor to Charleston during that time and produced several noted watercolors. The Gibbes Art Gallery, now the Gibbes Museum of Art, opened in 1905.

Recognizing the cultural importance of the city and its history, in 1920 socialite Susan Pringle Frost and other concerned Charlestonians formed the Preservation Society of Charleston, the oldest community-based historic preservation organization in America.

In 1924, lauded Charleston author DuBose Heyward wrote the locally set novel *Porgy*. With Heyward's cooperation, the book would soon be turned into the first American opera, *Porgy and Bess,* by George Gershwin, who labored over the composition in a cottage on Folly Beach, South Carolina. Ironically, *Porgy and Bess,* which premiered with an African American cast in New York in 1935, wouldn't be performed in its actual setting until 1970 because of segregation laws.

And in a foreshadowing of a future tourist boom to come, the Pine Lakes golf course opened in Myrtle Beach, South Carolina, in 1927, the first on the Grand Strand.

A NEW DEAL

Alas, the good times didn't last. The Great Depression hit the South hard, but since wages and industry were already behind the national average, the economic damage wasn't as bad as elsewhere in the country. As elsewhere in the South and indeed across the country, public works programs in President Franklin D. Roosevelt's New Deal helped not only to keep locals employed, but contributed greatly to the cultural and archaeological record of the area.

The Public Works of Art Project stimulated the visual arts. The Works Progress Administration renovated the old Dock Street Theatre in Charleston, and theatrical productions once again graced that historic stage. You can still enjoy the network of state parks built in South Carolina by the Civilian Conservation Corps.

As important and broadly supported as the New Deal was in the Carolinas, the primarily rural nature of both states meant a less vigorous and concentrated lobbying effort in Washington DC, to free up funding. Hence, the per capita benefit of the New Deal in the Carolinas was actually significantly less than for other states.

WORLD WAR II AND THE MODERN ERA

With the attack on Pearl Harbor and the coming of World War II, life in America and the Carolinas would never be the same. Military funding and facilities swarmed into the area, and populations and long-depressed living standards rose as a result. Here are some key wartime developments on the coast:

- In 1941 construction began in Onslow County on what would become Marine Corps Base Camp Lejeune near Jacksonville, North Carolina. A satellite facility of Camp Lejeune, Montford Point (now called Camp Gilbert H. Johnston), trained 20,000 African American Marines 1942–1947, when the U.S. military was still segregated.

- Also in 1941, construction began on what would become Marine Corps Air Station Cherry Point, which trained Marine aviators for service in the Pacific theater of operations.

TORPEDO JUNCTION

The Outer Banks of North Carolina bore grim witness to one of the darkest times of World War II, when German submarines"– known as U-boats after their German name, *untersee-booten*"– wreaked havoc just offshore. The episode gave rise to the nickname "Torpedo Junction" for the entire area of the coast from the Virginia border down to Morehead City.

Just after Pearl Harbor, the United States was eager to enter the war but woefully underequipped to fight it. Before more effective countermeasures were developed later in the war, U-boats had nearly free reign off the entire U.S. eastern seaboard for the first six months of 1942, sinking merchant ships at will. During this "Happy Time," as the U-boat commanders called it, the subs sunk nearly 400 cargo vessels, at least 80 of them off the Outer Banks.

Older residents still recall hearing the explosions offshore, as merchant ships were hit by torpedoes and sunk, usually bursting into flames as flammable cargo and fuel ignited. Some remember even being knocked out of bed by the force of the blasts.

Because U-boats usually attacked at night, the first evidence to those ashore was the noise of the blast followed by a massive fireball visible for miles. In the mornings residents could still see the plume of dark smoke marking the cargo ship's demise. Later more palpable results would come washing ashore: oil, wreckage, and bodies.

The rumor mill was quite active during this time, and stories circulated of German spies being let off by the submarines, or more outlandishly, of English-speaking U-boat crewmen coming ashore to buy groceries! However, none of these stories was ever substantiated.

While technically the entire coast was supposed to be under blackout conditions during wartime"– with lights turned off at night to hinder enemy navigation"– these rules were mostly ignored, and in any case the "blackout" certainly didn't seem to hinder the U-boats very much.

The U-boat attacks didn't slow down until later in 1942, when the Allies began using new tactics to fight them, including grouping merchant ships in convoys with naval escorts and striking located U-boats with combined attacks by airplanes and depth charge–equipped destroyers.

At least four U-boats were sunk off the North Carolina coast, including U-85, U-701, and by far the most popular and accessible, the U-352 (U-boats were known to friends and foe alike only by their numbers). Recreational divers today frequently dive on the wrecks. If you go, don't expect to salvage any artifacts"– most all of them have long since been picked clean.

Dive charters in the Morehead City, North Carolina, area can take you to the subs, as well as to the poignant wrecks of many of the Allied cargo vessels"– final resting places of thousands of the war's unsung heroes.

- Though Fort Bragg in Fayetteville, North Carolina, was begun in 1918, it really got on the map during World War II as a major training facility. Immediately following World War II, Fort Bragg became the operations and training center for the U.S. Army Special Forces, and it remains so to this day.

- The Charleston Navy Yard became that city's largest employer, and the population soared as workers crowded in.

- Down in Walterboro, South Carolina, the Tuskegee Airmen, a highly-decorated group of African American fighter pilots, trained for their missions escorting bombing raids over Germany. Walterboro also hosted a large German POW camp.

- The Marine Corp Recruiting Depot Parris Island in South Carolina expanded massively, training nearly a quarter-million recruits 1941–1945.

- The entire 1944 graduating class of The Citadel in Charleston was inducted into the armed forces—possibly the only time an entire class was drafted at once.

The war particularly hit home in North Carolina, which trained more soldiers than any other state in its 24 bases. The hottest spot for German U-boat attacks on the U.S. eastern seaboard was off the Outer Banks. Residents—living in blackout conditions at night—would often see explosions just offshore as American merchant ships were sunk by the submarines. To this day the sea bottom on the coast is littered with over 60 sunken vessels from this dark time—including at least three destroyed U-boats.

Then of course there's the famous battleship *USS North Carolina,* which participated in every major naval campaign of the war's Pacific theater of operations. When commissioned in April 1941, it was considered the most advanced, if not the largest, battleship in the world. Decommissioned after the war, the ship spent 14 years anchored in New Jersey. Scheduled to be scrapped, it was saved by a conservation and fundraising effort in the late 1950s, which brought the great warship back to its namesake state in 1961. Today berthed in Wilmington, the *North Carolina* is a major tourist attraction and a stirring tribute to a key chapter in U.S. naval history.

The Postwar Boom

Myrtle Beach and the Grand Strand were already the breeding ground of that unique South Carolina dance called the shag. The postwar era marked the shag's heyday, as carefree young South Carolinians flocked to beachfront pavilions to enjoy this indigenous form of music, sort of a white variation on the regional black rhythm 'n' blues of the time.

America's post-war infatuation with the automobile—and its troublesome child, the suburb—brought exponential growth to the great cities of the coast. The first bridge to Hilton Head Island was built in 1956, leading to the first of many resort developments on the island, Sea Pines, in 1961. In many outlying Sea Islands, electricity came for the first time.

With rising coastal populations came pressure to demolish more and more fine old buildings to put parking lots and high-rises in their place;

a backlash grew among the cities' elites, aghast at the destruction of so much history. The immediate postwar era brought about the formation of the Historic Charleston Foundation, which began the financially and politically difficult work of protecting the historic districts from the wrecking ball of "progress."

They weren't always successful, but the work of these organizations—mostly comprising older women from the upper crust—laid the foundation for the successful coastal tourist industry to come, as well as preserved important American history for the ages.

Civil Rights

Contrary to popular opinion, the civil rights era wasn't just a blip in the 1960s. The gains of that decade were the fruits of efforts begun decades prior.

Many of the efforts involved expanding black suffrage. Though African Americans secured the nominal right to vote years before, primary contests were not under the jurisdiction of federal law. As a result, Democratic Party primary elections—the *de facto* general elections because of that party's total dominance in the South at the time—were effectively closed to African American voters.

In Charleston, the Democratic primary was opened to African Americans for the first time in 1947. In 1960, the Charleston Municipal Golf Course voluntarily integrated to avoid a court battle. Lunch counter sit-ins happened all over South Carolina, including the episode of the "Friendship Nine" in Rock Hill. Martin Luther King Jr. visited South Carolina in the late 1960s, speaking in Charleston in 1967 and helping reestablish the Penn Center on St. Helena Island as not only a cultural center, but a center of political activism as well.

The hundred-day strike of hospital workers at the Medical University of South Carolina in 1969—right after King's assassination—got national attention and was the culmination of Charleston's struggle for civil rights. By the end of the 1960s, the city council of Charleston had elected its first black alderman, and the next phase in local history began.

A Coast Reborn

While the story of the South Carolina coastal boom actually begins in the 1950s with Charles Fraser's development of Sea Pines Plantation on Hilton Head—forever changing that barrier island—the decade of the 1970s was pivotal to the future success of the South Carolina coast.

In Charleston, the historic tenure of Mayor Joe Riley began in 1975, continuing to this day as of this writing. The Irish American would break precedents and forge key alliances, reviving not only the local economies but tamping down age-old racial tensions. Beginning with downtown's Charleston Place, Riley embarked on a series of high-profile public works projects to reinvigorate the then-moribund Charleston historic area. King Street would soon follow. In the years 1970–1976, tourism in the Holy City would increase 60 percent.

The coast's combination of beautiful scenery and cheap labor proved irresistible to the movie and TV industry, which began filming many shows and films in the area in the 1970s, and continue to do so to this day.

Wilmington, North Carolina, remains a key movie location, often calling itself "Hollywood East." Some of the 300 feature films made there include *Blue Velvet, I Know What You Did Last Summer, Enchanted, Weekend at Bernies,* and *Divine Secrets of the Ya-Ya Sisterhood.* Beaufort, South Carolina, would also emerge from its stately slumber as the star of several popular films, such as *The Great Santini* and *The Big Chill.*

Of course, Myrtle Beach had been a leisure getaway for generations. But with the 1980s and the building of the Barefoot Landing retail/lodging development—followed by many others like it—the Grand Strand entered the first tier of American tourist destinations, where it remains.

Charleston received its first major challenge since the Civil War in 1989 when Hurricane Hugo slammed into the South Carolina coast just above Charleston. The Holy City, including many of its most historic locations, was massively damaged, with hardly a tree left standing. However, in a testament to the toughness beneath Charleston's genteel veneer, the city not only rebounded but came back stronger. In perhaps typically mercantile fashion, Charlestonians used the devastation of Hugo as a reason to introduce a new round of residential construction to the entire area, particularly the surrounding islands.

Government and Economy

GOVERNMENT

For many decades, the South was completely dominated by the Democratic Party. Originally the party of slavery and segregation, the Democratic Party began attracting Southern African American voters in the 1930s with the election of Franklin D. Roosevelt. The allegiance of black voters was further cemented in the Truman, Kennedy, and Johnson administrations.

The region would remain solidly Democratic until a backlash against the civil rights movement of the 1960s drove many white Southerners, ironically enough, into the party of Lincoln, the Republicans. This added racial element, so confounding to Americans from other parts of the country, remains just as potent today.

The default mode in the South is that white voters are massively Republican, and black voters massively Democratic. Since South Carolina is 69 percent white, doing the math translates to an overwhelming Republican dominance in the state. The GOP currently controls the governor's mansion and both houses of the state legislature, and Republican Senator John McCain easily won the Palmetto State's electoral votes in the 2008 presidential election.

North Carolina is a very different story, at least on paper. It has a new Democratic governor, and both houses of its legislature are controlled by Democrats. In 2008, in a development that stunned many political observers,

Democrat Barack Obama prevailed in the state over John McCain.

However, North Carolina's progressivism is relative, and the state is still quite conservative compared to other areas of the country. Democrats in the state are often quite different from their counterparts in more liberal areas of the United States.

Similarly, don't make the mistake of assuming that local African Americans are particularly liberal because of their voting habits. Deeply religious and traditional in background and upbringing, African Americans in the Carolinas are among the most socially conservative people in the region, even if their choice of political party does not always reflect that.

ECONOMY

Even before the recent economic downturn, the coastal Carolinas had experienced a century's worth of profound changes in economy and business. The rice crop moved offshore in the late 1800s and the center of the cotton trade moved to the Gulf states in the early 1900s. That left timber as the main cash crop all up and down the coast, specifically huge pine tree farms to feed the pulp and paper business.

For most of the 20th century, the largest employers along the coast were massive, sulfur-smelling paper mills, which had as big an effect on the local environment as on its economy. But even that's changing, as Asian competition is driving paper companies to sell off their tracts for real estate development—not necessarily a more welcome scenario from an environmental perspective.

Since World War II, the U.S. Department of Defense has been a major employer and economic driver in the entire South. Despite the closing of the Charleston Naval Yard in the mid-1990s, the grounds now host the East Coast headquarters of SPAWAR (Space and Naval Warfare Systems Center), which provides high-tech engineering solutions for the Navy. Charleston also retains a large military presence in the Charleston Air Force Base near North Charleston, which hosts two airlift wings and employs about 6,000.

Myrtle Beach went through a similarly anxious state of events in the mid-1990s with the closing of Myrtle Beach Air Force Base. As with Charleston, the local economy appears to have weathered the worst effects of the closing.

Farther down the coast, Beaufort is home to the Naval Hospital Beaufort and the Marine Corps Air Station Beaufort and its six squadrons of FA-18 Hornets. On nearby Parris Island is the legendary Marine Corps Recruit Depot Parris Island, which puts all new Marine recruits from east of the Mississippi River through rigorous basic training.

Coastal North Carolina also has an expansive military presence, especially the U.S. Marines, who train at Camp Lejeune and its satellite facilities. Havelock, North Carolina, hosts Marine Corps Air Station Cherry Point.

A little farther inland, Fayetteville is of course the home of sprawling Fort Bragg, home of the 82nd Airborne Division and U.S. Army Special Forces. Pope Air Force Base is directly adjacent.

Of course, tourism is also an important factor in the local economies of the area, particularly in seasonal, resort-oriented areas like Hilton Head, Myrtle Beach, Kiawah, and Seabrook Islands. Charleston also has a well-honed tourist infrastructure, bringing at least $5 billion a year into the local economy, and is routinely voted as one of the top three American cities to visit.

Almost all parts of the Carolina coast have become havens for transplants and retirees looking for better weather and/or cheaper housing, as well as generally high quality of life (except for the hurricanes!). The so-called Inner Banks of North Carolina—actually a recent term concocted by Chamber of Commerce–types and the real estate industry—is particularly bullish on attracting retirees from other areas of the country, as is the Beaufort–Bluffton–Hilton Head area of South Carolina.

Another huge economic development on the coast has been the exponential growth of the Charleston seaport. From the 1990s on, the quickened pace of globalization has brought enormous investment, volume, and expansion to area port facilities. Charleston's port experienced record volume in 2006–2007, though the recent economic downturn has hurt business.

People and Culture

Contrary to how they are often portrayed in the media, the Carolinas are hardly exclusive to natives with thick, flowery accents who still obsess over the Civil War and eat grits three meals a day. As you will quickly discover, the entire coastal area is becoming heavily populated with transplants from other parts of the country. In some of these places you can actually go quite a long time without hearing even one of those Scarlett O'Hara accents.

Some of this is due to the region's increasing attractiveness to professionals and artists, drawn by the temperate climate, natural beauty, and business-friendly environment. Part of it is due to its increasing attractiveness to retirees, most of them from the frigid Northeast. Indeed, in some places, chief among them Hilton Head, the most common accent is a New York or New Jersey one, and a Southern accent is rare.

In any case, don't make the common mistake of assuming you're coming to a place where footwear is optional and electricity is a recent development (though it's true that many of the islands didn't get electricity until the 1950s and '60s). Because so much new construction has gone on in the South in the last quarter-century or so, you might find some aspects of the infrastructure—specifically the roads and the electrical utilities—actually superior to where you came from.

POPULATION

A 2008 U.S. Census estimate had South Carolina's population at 4,480,000, 24th among U.S. states. Population statistics for individual cities in the state can be misleading because of South Carolina's notoriously strict annexation laws, which make it nearly impossible for a city to annex growing suburbs.

In rough order of rank, the largest official metropolitan areas in South Carolina are Columbia (720,000), Charleston/North Charleston/Summerville (630,000), Greenville/Mauldin/Easley (620,000), Myrtle Beach/North Myrtle Beach/Conway (240,000), Florence (200,000), and Hilton Head/Beaufort (165,000).

Although its coast often seems less populated than the Palmetto State's, North Carolina is actually a much more populous state, coming in at number 10 in the nation with a total population of 9,222,000. Its largest metro areas tend to be clusters of several cities, for example Charlotte–Gastonia–Salisbury (population 2.3 million), Raleigh–Durham–Chapel Hill (1.6 million), and Greensboro–Winston-Salem–High Point (1.5 million).

The Fayetteville metropolitan area (population just over 350,000) and the Wilmington metro area (just under 350,000) are the two most populous North Carolina cities covered in this book. Otherwise coastal North Carolina is quite sparsely populated compared to the middle of the state. New Bern, a large town for the area, has only about 120,000 people. The entire Outer Banks has a year-round population of less than 60,000.

Racial Makeup

Its legacy as the center of the U.S. slave trade and plantation culture means that South Carolina continues to have a large African-American population, nearly 30 percent of the total. The coastal percentage is generally higher, with Charleston being about 31 percent African American and Georgetown about 40 percent.

North Carolina's African American population comes in around 21 percent, but again, the number is higher along the coast.

One unfortunate legacy of the Carolinas' history is the residual existence, even to this day, of a certain amount of *de facto* segregation. Visitors are often shocked to see how some residential areas even today still break sharply on racial lines—as do schools, with most public schools in the area being majority black and most private schools overwhelmingly white.

However, despite persistent media portrayals,

SEPHARDIC JEWS

Visitors are sometimes surprised to discover that the Anglo-Saxon Protestant South has a rich and early history of an active Jewish presence – specifically, Sephardic Jews (i.e., those with a Spanish or Portuguese background).

Contrary to modern political trends, Jews and Muslims on the Iberian Peninsula actually got along quite well while the Islamic Moors of North Africa dominated the area. But after Ferdinand and Isabella's completion of the Reconquista in that pivotal year of 1492 – also the date of Columbus's famous voyage – the Jews of Spain went from being respected citizens to persecuted pariahs nearly overnight. Five years later, Portugal followed suit, expelling all Jews on pain of death unless they became "New Christians," or *conversos*. As a result many fled for points beyond to practice their faith openly, whether to London or the Ottoman Empire or to Morocco.

A sizeable proportion of conversos, however, were actually so-called "crypto-Jews," who publicly practiced Roman Catholicism while secretly remaining devout Jews. Many synagogues of Sephardic origin today have their floors covered in sand to remember that dark time when Jewish congregations practiced their faith in basements covered with sand to muffle the sounds of their feet.

The diaspora of the Sephardic Jews, ironically, contributed greatly to the health of the global Jewish community, as skilled tradesmen, doctors, and men of letters spread out to Spanish, Portuguese, English, and Dutch colonies where the Inquisition had little sway. It was primarily from the ranks of this Sephardic diaspora that the Jewish settlers of the Lowcountry and Georgia coast came.

The first Jewish presence in Charleston was recorded in 1695, with Jews voting in local elections as early as 1702. Stimulated by the busy port trade of that city, the initially overwhelmingly Sephardic Charleston Jewish community quickly grew and prospered with the addition of Ashkenazi, or Eastern European, Jews in the late 1700s. By 1820, Charleston boasted the biggest American Jewish population in the United States.

In one of the great tales of the American melting pot, the assimilation of the Jews into Southern society was so complete that the Secretary of State of the Confederate States of America, Judah Benjamin, was a practicing Jew of Sephardic origin.

This assimilation also had a flip side, however, in that the Sephardic Jews were generally just as enthusiastic about owning slaves as any other white citizens of the area. In 1830, about 83 percent of Jewish households in Charleston had slaves, as compared to an almost-identical percentage of 87 percent of white Christian Charlestonians.

---

overt racism is extremely rare in the areas covered in this book. In remote areas an interracial couple might get some disapproving looks, but in any urban area of real size, hardly anyone will bat an eye.

The Hispanic population, as elsewhere in the U.S., is growing rapidly in the coastal Carolinas. But statistics can be misleading. Though Hispanics are growing at a triple-digit clip throughout the region, they still remain under 3 percent of South Carolina's total population and about 7 percent of North Carolina's, with most of the latter population not along the coast at all. Bilingual signage is becoming more common but is still quite rare.

RELIGION

The South Carolina Lowcountry, and Charleston in particular, is unusual in the Deep South for its wide variety of religious faiths. While South Carolina remains overwhelmingly Protestant—over 80 percent of all Christians in the state are members of some Protestant denomination, chief among them Southern Baptist and Methodist—the coast's cosmopolitan, polyglot history has made it a real melting pot of faith.

Though the Lowcountry was originally dominated by the Episcopal Church (known as the Anglican Church in England), from early on they were also havens for those of other

VOODOO AND HOODOO

The spiritual system we know as voodoo – the word is a corruption of various West African spellings – came to the western hemisphere with the importation of slaves. Contrary to popular opinion, voodoo isn't a mere collection of primitive superstitions but is a clearly defined religion in its own right and is still the dominant religion of millions of West Africans.

Like many ancient belief systems, voodoo is based on the veneration of ancestors and the possibility of continued communication with them, and it's perhaps this characteristic that is responsible for so much misunderstanding. For example, up until fairly recently the African American Gullah and Geechee populations of the South Carolina and Georgia Sea Islands still had a common belief that the older slaves who were born in Africa could actually fly in spirit form back to the continent of their birth and back again.

While voodoo has always been unfairly sensationalized – the most notable recent example being the "voodoo priestess" Minerva in *Midnight in the Garden of Good and Evil* – it's not necessarily as malevolent in actual practice as in the overactive imaginations of writers and directors. For example, the stereotypical practice of sticking pins in dolls to bring pain to a living person actually has its roots in European and Native American folklore. But sensationalism sells, so you'll sometimes find such items being hawked to gullible tourists as "voodoo dolls."

Much of what the layperson thinks is voodoo is actually hoodoo, a body of folklore – not a religion – indigenous to the American South. Hoodoo combines elements of voodoo (communicating with the dead) and fundamentalist Christianity (extensive Scriptural references). In the United States, most African American voodoo tradition was long ago subsumed within Protestant Christianity, but the Gullah populations of the Sea Islands of South Carolina and Georgia still keep alive the old ways. In the Gullah/Geechee areas of the Georgia and Carolina Sea Islands, the word "conjure" is generally the preferred terminology for this hybrid belief system, which has good sides and bad sides and borrows liberally from African lore and Christian folkways.

The old Southern practice of painting shutters and doors blue to ward off evil comes from hoodoo, where the belief in ghosts, or "haints," is largely a byproduct of poorly understood Christianity (Mediterranean countries also use blue to keep evil at bay, and the word "haint" is of Scots-Irish origin). If you keep your eyes attuned, you can still see this particular shade of "haint blue" on rural and vernacular structures throughout the South Carolina Lowcountry. (Were you to enter one of these homes, you would almost certainly find a horseshoe tacked over the front door as well.)

Another element of hoodoo that you can still encounter today is the role of the "root doctor," an expert at folk remedies who blends together various indigenous herbs and plants in order to produce a desired effect or result. In *Midnight in the Garden of Good and Evil,* this role belongs to the fabled Dr. Buzzard, who teaches Minerva everything she knows about "conjure work." However, a root doctor is not to be confused with a "gifted reader," a fortuneteller born with the talent to tell the future.

From the no-doubt embellished account in John Berendt's *Midnight,* scholars would put Minerva squarely into the category of root doctor or "conjurer" rather than the undeniably more compelling "voodoo priestess."

faiths. Various types of Protestant offshoots soon arrived, such as French Huguenots and Congregationalists. Owing to vestigial prejudice from the European *realpolitik* of the founding era, the Roman Catholic presence in South Carolina was late in arriving, but once it came it was there to stay, especially on the coast.

Most unusually of all for the deep South, Charleston had not only a large Jewish population, but one that was a key participant in the city from the very first days of settlement. Sephardic Jews of primarily Portuguese descent were among the first settlers. One of them, Judah Benjamin, spent a lot of time in the Carolinas and became the Confederacy's secretary of state. Indeed, up to about 1830 South Carolina had the largest Jewish population of any state in the union.

The North Carolina coast also has an interesting religious history. While the Southern Baptist and Methodist churches are the top two Christian denominations in the state, the coast—as is the case in South Carolina—has quite a large Episcopal representation, a legacy of the original English colonization.

In and around the New Bern area there is a large concentration of Calvinist-affiliated churches, a legacy of the original Swiss and German settlers of this second-oldest city in North Carolina.

More recently, Roman Catholicism has been on the increase along the North Carolina coast, due to the influx of northeastern transplants as well as a growing Latino population. An exception exists in certain counties on the sparsely populated extreme northeast coast, where there are no reported Catholic congregations at all.

MANNERS

The prevalence and importance of good manners is the main thing to keep in mind about the South. While it's tempting for folks from more outwardly and assertive parts of the world to take this as a sign of weakness, that would be a major mistake. Bottom line: Good manners will take you a long way here.

Southerners use manners, courtesy, and chivalry as a system of social interaction with one goal above all: to maintain the established order during times of stress. A relic from a time of extreme class stratification, etiquette and chivalry are ways to make sure that the elites are never threatened—and on the other hand, that even those on the lowest rungs of society are afforded at least a basic amount of dignity.

But as a practical matter, it's also true that Southerners of all classes, races, and backgrounds rely on the observation of manners as a way to sum up people quickly. To any Southerner, regardless of class or race, your use or neglect of basic manners and proper respect indicates how seriously they should take you—not in a socio-economic sense, but in the big picture overall.

The typical Southern sense of humor—equal parts irony, self-deprecation, and good-natured teasing—is part of the code. Southerners are loathe to criticize another individual directly, so often they'll instead take the opportunity to make an ironic joke. Self-deprecating humor is also much more common in the South than in other areas of the country. Because of this, you're also expected to be able to take a joke yourself without being too sensitive.

Etiquette

The most basic rules are that it's rude here to inquire about personal finances, along with the usual no-go areas of religion and politics. Here are some other specific etiquette tips.

Basics: Be liberal with "please" and "thank you," or conversely, "no, thank you" if you want to decline a request or offering.

Eye contact: With the exception of elderly African Americans, eye contact is not only accepted in the South, it's encouraged. In fact, to avoid eye contact in the South means you're likely a shady character with something to hide.

Handshake: Men should always shake hands with a *very* firm, confident grip and appropriate eye contact. It's okay for women to offer a handshake in professional circles, but otherwise not required.

Chivalry: When men open doors for women here—and they will—it is not thought of as a patronizing gesture, but as a sign of respect. Accept graciously and walk through the door.

The elderly: Senior citizens—or really anyone obviously older than you—should be called "sir" or "ma'am." Again, this is not a patronizing gesture in the South, but is considered a sign of respect. Also, in any situation where you're dealing with someone in the service industry, addressing them as "sir" or "ma'am" regardless of their age will get you far.

Bodily contact: Interestingly, though public displays of affection by romantic couples are generally frowned upon here, Southerners are otherwise pretty touchy-feely once they get to know you. Full-on body hugs are rare, but

Southerners who are well acquainted often say hello or goodbye with a small hug.

Driving: With the exception of the interstate perimeter highways around the larger cities, drivers in the South are generally less aggressive than in other regions. Cutting sharply in front of someone in traffic is taken as a personal offense. If you need to cut in front of someone, poke the nose of your car a little bit in that direction and wait for a car to slow down and wave you in front. Don't forget to wave back as a thank-you! Similarly, using a car horn can also be taken as a personal affront, so use your horn sparingly, if at all. In rural areas, don't be surprised to see the driver of an oncoming car offer a little wave. This is an old custom, sadly dying out. Just give a little wave back; they're trying to be friendly.

THE GUN CULTURE

One of the most misunderstood aspects of the South is the value the region places on the personal possession of firearms. No doubt, the Second Amendment to the U.S. Constitution ("A well regulated Militia, being necessary to the security of a free State, the right of the people to keep and bear Arms, shall not be infringed") is well known here and fiercely protected, at the governmental and at the grassroots level.

But while guns are indeed more casually accepted in everyday life in the South, the reason for this has less to do with personal safety than with the rural background of the region and its long history of hunting. If you're traveling a back road and you see a pickup truck with a gun rack in the back containing one or more rifles or shotguns, this is not intended to be menacing or intimidating. Chances are the driver is a hunter, nothing more.

State laws do tend to be significantly more accommodating of gun owners here than in much of the rest of the country. It is legal to carry a concealed handgun in North and South Carolina with the proper permit, and you need no permit at all to possess a weapon for self-defense. However, there are regulations regarding how a handgun must be conveyed in automobiles.

Both North Carolina and South Carolina feature versions of the so-called "stand your ground" law, whereby if you're in imminent lethal danger you do not have to first try to run away before resorting to deadly force to defend yourself. South Carolina's goes one step further, however, in that their stand-your-ground law extends to lethal danger in public places as well as in the home or car.

ESSENTIALS

Getting There and Around

BY AIR

There are five international airports serving the coastal Carolinas.

Norfolk International Airport (airport code NIA, 2200 Norview Ave., Norfolk, Virginia, 757/857-3351, www.norfolkairport.com), served by American Airlines (www.aa.com), Continental Airlines (www.continental.com), Delta (www.delta.com), Northwest Airlines (www.nwa.com), Southwest Airlines (www.southwest.com), United Airlines (www.ual.com), and US Airways (www.usairways.com).

Though in Virginia, this airport is close enough to the northern portion of North Carolina to make it a good choice for those wanting to concentrate on that area.

Wilmington International Airport (1740 Airport Blvd., 910/341-4125, airport code ILM, www.flyilm.com), served by Allegiant Air (www.allegiantair.com), Delta (www.delta.com), and US Airways (www.usairways.com). This is a good choice for those needing a central embarkation point on the Carolina coast.

COURTESY OF CHARLESTON AREA CVB, WWW.EXPLORECHARLESTON.COM

Charleston International Airport (airport code CHS, 5500 International Blvd., 843/767-1100, www.chs-airport.com) is served by AirTran (www.airtran.com), American Airlines (www.aa.com), Continental Airlines (www.continental.com), Delta (www.delta.com), Northwest Airlines (www.nwa.com), United Airlines (www.ual.com), and US Airways (www.usairways.com). Recommended mostly for those visiting Charleston and vicinity.

Myrtle Beach International Airport (airport code MYR, 1100 Jetport Rd., 843/448-1589, www.flymyrtlebeach.com) is served by Continental Airlines (www.continental.com), Delta (www.delta.com), Myrtle Beach Direct Air (www.mb-directair.com), Northwest Airlines (www.nwa.com), Spirit Airlines (www.spiritair.com), United Express Airlines (www.ual.com), and US Airways (www.usairways.com). This airport serves the Grand Strand region of South Carolina but is reasonably close to the North Carolina border.

Savannah/Hilton Head International Airport (airport code SAV, 400 Airways Ave., 912/964-0514, www.savannahairport.com) off I-95 in Savannah, Georgia, is served by AirTran (www.airtran.com), American Eagle (www.aa.com), Continental (www.continental.com), Delta (www.delta.com), Northwest Airlink (www.nwa.com), United Express (www.ual.com), and US Airways (www.airways.com). Though located in Georgia, because of its location at the extreme southern tip of South Carolina, this airport is a short drive from Hilton Head and Beaufort, South Carolina, and is a good point of entry for the southern portion of the South Carolina coast.

BY CAR

The distance between the Great Dismal Swamp in North Carolina to Hilton Head Island, South Carolina, is about 500 miles, roughly 10–12 hours of drive time. Due to the spread-out nature of the coastal Carolinas and the general lack of public transportation, auto travel is integral to enjoying the region.

While the road infrastructure in the Outer and Inner Banks regions of North Carolina is in pretty good shape, driving from one place to another always takes longer than it looks on a map because there are so many waterways to cross and so few direct routes anywhere. Always budget more time than you think you'll need for auto travel in this area.

The main interstate arteries into and through the region are the north-south I-95 and the east-west I-26 and I-40. The bulk of your travel, however, will not be on interstate highways, but rather various state highways, most of which are quite well maintained and which I do recommend using, for the most part.

Keep in mind that despite being very heavily traveled, the Myrtle Beach area is not served by any interstate. A common landmark road throughout the coastal region is U.S. 17, which used to be known as the Coastal Highway and currently goes by a number of local incarnations as it winds its way along the coast.

Unfortunately, the stories you've heard about speed traps in small towns in the South are often correct. Always strictly obey the speed limit, and if you're pulled over always deal with the police respectfully and truthfully, whether or not you agree with their judgment.

Car Rentals

Unless you're going to hunker down in one city, you will need auto transportation to enjoy the coastal Carolinas. Renting a car is easy and fairly inexpensive as long as you play by the rules, which are simple. You need either a valid U.S. driver's license from any state or a valid International Driving License from your home country, and you must be at least 25 years old.

If you do not either purchase insurance coverage from the rental company or already have insurance coverage through the credit card you rent the car with, you will be 100 percent responsible for any damage caused to the car during your rental period. While purchasing insurance at the time of rental is by no means mandatory, it might be worth the extra expense just to have that peace of mind.

Some rental car locations are in cities proper, but the vast majority of outlets are in airports, so plan accordingly. The airport locations have the bonus of generally holding longer hours than their in-town counterparts.

BY TRAIN

Passenger rail service in the car-dominated United States is far behind other developed nations, both in quantity and quality. For the most part, the national rail system, **Amtrak** (www.amtrak.com), runs well inland from the areas covered by this book. Exceptions include Amtrak stations in Charleston and Yemassee in South Carolina and Fayetteville, Wilson, and Rocky Mount in North Carolina. You could use this quasi-coastal route to access points of entry for the coast, but you would need other transportation to make it the rest of the way.

BY BUS

With the exception of the Outer Banks, the large bus service, **Greyhound** (www.greyhound.com), has decent coverage in coastal North Carolina, including stations in Elizabeth City, Fayetteville, Jacksonville, New Bern, and Wilmington. In coastal South Carolina, the bus company has stations in Beaufort, Charleston, Georgetown, Myrtle Beach, and Walterboro. Due to the frequent stops and relatively leisurely pace, this is by far the slowest form of travel in the region—as well as somewhat rustic—and should only be considered as an extreme budget option.

BY BOAT

One of the coolest things about the coastal Carolinas is the prevalence of the Intracoastal Waterway, a combined manmade/natural sheltered seaway going from Miami to Maine. Many boaters enjoy touring the coast by simply meandering up or down the Intracoastal, putting in at marinas along the way.

Key cities and towns along the ICW in North Carolina are Wilmington, Swansboro, Southport, Morehead City, Hatteras, Elizabeth City, Calabash, Belhaven, and Beaufort.

Key cities and towns along the ICW in South Carolina are Beaufort, Charleston, Georgetown, Hilton Head, Murrells Inlet, Myrtle Beach, and Port Royal.

If you've got a boat, you might want to traverse the entire coast for yourself. An excellent online resource is www.cruisingtheicw.com, which includes comprehensive marina and docking information. You can sleep onboard the whole time or occasionally tie up for the night and go into town for a stay at a nearby B&B.

For a hilarious and informative account of an oddball journey down the ICW in a restored English canal boat (or "narrow dog"), read Terry Darlington's 2009 account, *Narrow Dog to Indian River*.

Recreation

STATE PARKS AND NATURAL AREAS

The Carolinas have two of the best state park systems in the United States, many built by the Civilian Conservation Corps during FDR's New Deal and boasting distinctive, rustic, and well-made architecture.

While primitive camping is available, the general preference here is for more plush surroundings more conducive to a family vacation. Many state parks offer fully-equipped rental cabins with modern amenities that rival a hotel's. Generally speaking, such facilities tend to sell out early in the calendar, so make reservations as soon as you can. Keep in mind that during the high season, March–November, there are minimum rental requirements.

Dogs are allowed in state parks, but they must be leashed at all times.

NATIONAL WILDLIFE REFUGES

Coastal North Carolina has the following U.S. Fish and Wildlife Service National Wildlife Refuges (NWR), from north to south:

- **Mackay Island NWR**
  (www.fws.gov/mackayisland)

- **Currituck NWR**
  (www.fws.gov/currituck)

- **Pocosin Lakes NWR**
  (www.fws.gov/pocosinlakes)

- **Roanoke River NWR**
  (www.fws.gov/roanokeriver)

- **Alligator River NWR**
  (www.fws.gov/alligatorriver)

- **Pea Island NWR**
  (www.fws.gov/peaisland)

- **Mattamuskeet NWR**
  (www.fws.gov/mattamuskeet)

- **Swanquarter NWR**
  (www.fws.gov/swanquarter)

- **Cedar Island NWR**
  (www.fws.gov/cedarisland)

Coastal South Carolina has the following National Wildlife Refuges, from north to south:

- **Waccamaw NWR**
  (www.fws.gov/waccamaw)

- **Cape Romain NWR**
  (www.fws.gov/caperomain)

- **ACE Basin NWR**
  (www.fws.gov/acebasin)

- **Pinckney NWR**
  (www.fws.gov/pinckneyisland)

- **Savannah NWR**
  (www.fws.gov/savannah)

Admission is generally free. Access is limited to daytime hours, from sunrise to sunset. Keep in mind that some hunting is allowed on some refuges.

ZOOS AND AQUARIUMS

There are plenty of opportunities for kids and nature-lovers to learn about and enjoy animals up close and personal in the coastal Carolinas. Chief among them are the **North Carolina Aquariums** (www.ncaquariums.com) on Roanoke Island near the Outer Banks, Pine Knoll Shores on the central coast, and Fort Fisher near Wilmington. The **South Carolina Aquarium** (www.scaquarium.org) is in downtown Charleston.

For a more land-oriented experience, there is **Charles Towne Landing** (www.charlestowne. org) in Charleston and **Alligator Adventure** (www.alligatoradventure.com) and **T.I.G.E.R.S.** (www.tigerfriends.com), both in Myrtle Beach.

BEACHES

Some of the best beaches in America are in the region covered in this book. While the upscale amenities aren't always there and they aren't very surfer-friendly, the area's beaches are outstanding for anyone looking for a relaxing, scenic getaway.

By law, beaches in the United States are fully accessible to the public up to the high-tide mark during daylight hours, even if the beach fronts are private property and even if the only means of public access is by boat.

It is a misdemeanor to disturb the sea oats, those wispy, waving, wheat-like plants among the dunes. Their root system is vital to keeping the beach intact. Also never disturb a turtle nesting area, whether it is marked or not.

The North Carolina Outer Banks feature many miles of long, comparatively uncrowded beaches. For a more commercial experience, there's Nags Head, but for something more wild, check out the National Seashores of Cape Hatteras and Cape Lookout.

The Wilmington area features several fun, beautiful, and high-trafficked beach areas, especially Wrightsville Beach, Kure Beach, and Carolina Beach.

The busy Grand Strand, of course, has many miles of beach, from North Myrtle Beach on down to Huntington Beach State Park. Charleston-area beaches, generally less crowded, include **Folly Beach, Sullivan's Island,** and **Isle of Palms.** Moving down the coast, some delightful beaches are at **Edisto Island** and **Hunting Island,** which both feature state parks with lodging.

Hilton Head Island has about 12 miles of beautiful, family-friendly beaches, and while most of the island is devoted to private golf resorts, the beaches remain accessible to the general public at four points with parking: Driessen Beach Park, Coligny Beach Park, Alder Lane Beach Access, and Burkes Beach Road.

KAYAKING AND CANOEING

In North Carolina, sea kayakers enjoy many areas in the Outer Banks, including Bald Head Island, Cape Hatteras, and Ocracoke Island. Just to the north is the Great Dismal Swamp, a haven for kayaking and canoeing.

Down the coast, hot spots include Albemarle Sound, Alligator River NWR, and the Cape Fear and Cashie Rivers.

In the Grand Strand of South Carolina, you can enjoy kayaking on the Waccamaw River and Winyah Bay. Some key kayaking and canoeing areas in the Charleston area are Cape Romain National Wildlife Refuge, Shem Creek, Isle of Palms, Charleston Harbor, and the Stono River.

Farther south in the Lowcountry are the Ashepoo, Combahee, and Edisto blackwater rivers, which combine to form the ACE Basin. Next is Port Royal Sound near Beaufort.

The Hilton Head/Bluffton area have good kayaking opportunities at Hilton Head's Calibogue Creek and Bluffton's May River.

FISHING AND BOATING

In the coastal Carolinas, because of the large number of islands and wide area of salt marsh, life on the water is largely inseparable from life on the land. Fishing and boating are very common pursuits, with species of fish including spotted sea trout, channel bass, flounder, grouper, mackerel, sailfish, whiting, shark, amberjack, and tarpon.

Freshwater anglers will find largemouth bass, bream, catfish, and crappie, among many more.

To fish legally in North Carolina, if you're over 16 years old you'll need to get a Coastal Recreational Fishing License. A 10-day nonresident license is $15. Go to www.ncwildlife.org for more information or to purchase a license online.

In South Carolina, if you're over 16 years old, you'll need to get a nonresident fishing license. A seven-day license is $11. Go to www.dnr.sc.gov for more information or to purchase a license online.

Fishing charters and marinas are ample throughout the region, for both inshore and offshore trips. Details for each destination are in their dedicated chapters.

GOLF

The first golf club in America was formed in Charleston, and South Carolina as a whole is one of the world's golf meccas. There is a great variety of courses to choose from here, from tony courses like the Pete Dye–designed Ocean Course at the **Kiawah Island Golf Resort** or **Harbour Town** on Sea Pines Plantation in Hilton Head, to the more **budget-conscious courses** in the Santee Cooper region, Myrtle Beach, and North Myrtle Beach.

Don't be shy about pursuing golf packages which combine lodging with links. South Carolina, especially the coastal area, is currently suffering from something of a glut in courses, and you can find some great deals online.

Tips for Travelers

TRAVELING WITH CHILDREN

The coastal Carolinas are extremely kid-friendly, with the possible exception of some B&Bs that are clearly not designed for younger children. If you have any doubts about this, feel free to inquire. Otherwise, there are no special precautions unique to this area.

WOMEN TRAVELING ALONE

Women should take the same precautions they would take anywhere else. Many women traveling to this region have to adjust to the prevalence of traditional chivalry. In the South, if a man opens a door for you, it's considered a sign of respect, not condescension.

Another adjustment is the possible assumption that two or three women who go to a bar or tavern together might be there to invite male companionship. This misunderstanding can happen anywhere, but in some parts of the South it might be slightly more prevalent.

While small towns in the Carolinas are generally very friendly and law-abiding, some are more economically depressed than others and hence prone to higher crime. Always take common-sense precautions, no matter how bucolic the setting may be.

TRAVELERS WITH DISABILITIES

While the vast majority of attractions and accommodations make every effort to comply with federal law regarding those with disabilities, as they're obliged to do, the very historic nature of this region means that some structures simply cannot be retrofitted for maximum accessibility. This is something you'll need to find out on a case-by-case basis, so call ahead. The sites administered by the National Park Service in this book are as wheelchair-accessible as possible.

GAY AND LESBIAN TRAVELERS

North Carolina is one of the more progressive Southern states, and gay and lesbian travelers will generally feel quite comfortable there. Because of its large college-age population and heavy arts component, Wilmington is particularly gay-friendly.

While South Carolina is typically more conservative in outlook, Charleston, in particular, is quite accepting, and generally speaking, gay and lesbian travelers shouldn't expect anything untoward to happen.

In small towns all over the Carolinas, the best approach is to simply observe dominant Southern mores for anyone here, gay or straight. In a nutshell, that means keep public displays of affection and politics to a minimum. Southerners in general have a low opinion of anyone who flagrantly espouses a viewpoint too obviously or loudly.

SENIOR TRAVELERS

Both because of the large proportion of retirees in the region and because of the South's traditional respect for the elderly, the area is quite friendly to senior citizens. Many accommodations and attractions offer a senior discount, which can add up over the course of a trip. Always inquire *before* making a reservation, however, as check-in time is sometimes too late.

PACKING TIPS

- The coast can get hot and humid at just about any time of year, so pack lots of **natural fabric.**

- In all parts of the region, thundershowers can approach with little warning, especially on spring and summer afternoons. While they rarely last long, you don't want to be without an **umbrella** when one breaks out.

- If you're going to spend any time in Charleston, you'll be doing lots of walking. Bring

comfortable shoes; this will come in doubly handy when traversing the old cobblestone streets on the waterfront.

- While jackets are almost never a requirement in restaurants, keep in mind that Southerners in general like a well-dressed person. **Tourist-casual clothing** is fine, but don't overdo it. With the notable exception of Myrtle Beach, overly revealing clothing is frowned upon most places, especially small towns.

TRAVELING WITH PETS

While the United States is very pet-friendly, that friendliness rarely extends to restaurants and other indoor locations. More and more accommodations are allowing pet owners to bring pets, often for an added fee, but please inquire *before* you arrive. In any case, keep your dog on a leash at all times. Some beaches in the area permit dog-walking at certain times of the year, but as a general rule keep dogs off beaches unless you see signage saying otherwise.

Health and Safety

CRIME

While crime rates are indeed above national averages in much of the Carolinas, especially in inner city areas, incidents of crime in the more heavily trafficked tourist areas are no more common than anywhere else. In fact, these areas might be safer because of the amount of foot traffic and police attention.

By far the most common crime against visitors here is simple theft, primarily from cars. (Pickpocketing, thankfully, is quite rare in the United States). Always lock your car doors. Conversely, only leave them unlocked if you're absolutely comfortable living without whatever's inside at the time. As a general rule, I try to lock valuables—such as CDs, a recent purchase, or my wife's purse—in the trunk. (Just make sure the "valet" button, allowing the trunk to be opened from the driver's area, is disabled.)

Should someone corner you and demand your wallet or purse, just give it to them.

Unfortunately, the old advice to scream as loud as you can is no longer the deterrent it once was, and in fact may hasten aggressive action by the robber.

If you are the victim of a crime, *always call the police.* Law enforcement wants more information, not less, and the worst thing that can happen is you'll have an incident report in case you need to make an insurance claim for lost or stolen property.

Remember that in the United States as elsewhere, no good can come from a heated argument with a police officer. The place to prove a police officer wrong is in a court of law, perhaps with an attorney by your side, not at the scene.

For emergencies, always call 911.

AUTO ACCIDENTS

If you're in an auto accident, you're bound by law to wait for police to respond. Failure to do so can result in a "leaving the scene of an accident" charge, or worse. In the old days, cars in accidents had to be left exactly where they came to rest until police gave permission to move or tow them. However, many U.S. states have recently loosened regulations so that if a car is blocking traffic as a result of an accident, the driver is allowed to move it enough to allow traffic to flow again. That is, if the car can be moved safely. If not, you're not required to move it out of the way.

Since it's illegal to drive without auto insurance, I'll assume you have some. And because you're insured, the best course of action in a minor accident, where injuries are unlikely, is to patiently wait for the police and give them your side of the story. In my experience, police react negatively to people who are too quick to start making accusations against other people. After that, let the insurance companies deal with it. That's what they're there for.

If you suspect any injuries, call 911 immediately.

ILLEGAL DRUGS

Marijuana, heroin, methamphetamine, and cocaine and all its derivatives are illegal in the United States with only a very few, select exceptions, none of which apply to the areas covered by this book. The use of ecstasy and similar mood-elevators is also illegal. The penalties for illegal drug possession and use in the Carolinas are *extremely severe*. Just stay away from them entirely.

ALCOHOL

The drinking age in the United States is 21. Most restaurants that serve alcoholic beverages allow those under 21 inside. Generally speaking, if only those over 21 are allowed inside, you will be greeted at the door by someone asking to see identification. These people are often poorly trained and anything other than a state driver's license may confuse them, so be forewarned.

Drunk driving is a problem on the highways of America, and the Carolinas are no exception. Always drive defensively, especially late at night, and obey all posted speed limits and road signs—and never assume the other driver will do the same. You may *never* drive with an opened alcoholic beverage in the car, even if it belongs to a passenger.

Generally speaking, both Carolinas have so-called **blue laws** allowing Sunday retail purchase of beer and wine after noon, but no hard liquor the entire day. Closing times at bars generally vary by municipality.

Both Carolinas feature ABC, or **Alcohol Beverage Control,** stores, which are the only places to buy liquor outside a restaurant or bar setting.

GETTING SICK

Unlike most developed nations, the United States has no comprehensive national health care system (there are programs for the elderly and the poor). Visitors from other countries who need non-emergency medical attention are best served by going to free-standing medical clinics. The level of care is typically very good, but you'll be paying out of pocket for the service, unfortunately.

For emergencies, however, do not hesitate to go to the closest hospital emergency room, where generally the level of care is also quite good, especially for trauma. Worry about payment later. Emergency rooms in the United States are required to take true emergency cases whether or not the patient can pay for services.

Pharmaceuticals

Unlike many European nations, antibiotics are available in the United States only on a prescription basis and are not available over the counter. Most cold, flu, and allergy remedies are available over the counter. While homeopathic remedies are gaining popularity in the United States, they are nowhere near as prevalent as in Europe.

Drugs with the active ingredient ephedrine are available in the United States without a prescription, but their purchase is often tightly regulated to cut down on the use of these products to make the illegal drug methamphetamine.

NOT GETTING SICK
Vaccinations

As of this writing, there are no vaccination requirements to enter the United States. Contact your embassy before coming to confirm this before arrival, however.

In the autumn, at the beginning of flu season, preventive influenza vaccinations, simply called "flu shots," often become available at easily accessible locations like clinics, health departments, and even supermarkets.

Humidity, Heat, and Sun

There is only one way to fight the South's high heat and humidity, and that's to drink lots of fluids. A surprising number of people each year refuse to take this advice and find themselves in various states of dehydration, some of which can land you in a hospital. Remember: If you're thirsty, you're already suffering from dehydration. The thing to do is keep drinking fluids *before* you're thirsty, as a preventative action rather than a reaction.

Always use sunscreen, even on a cloudy day. If you do get a sunburn, get a pain relief product with aloe vera as an active ingredient. On extraordinarily sunny and hot summer days, don't even go outside between the hours of 10 A.M. and 2 P.M.

HAZARDS
Insects

Because of the recent increase in the mosquito-borne and often deadly West Nile virus, the most important step to take in staying healthy in the coastal Carolinas is to keep **mosquito bites** to a minimum. Do this with a combination of mosquito repellent and long sleeves and long pants, if possible. Not every mosquito bite will give you the virus; in fact, chances are quite slim that one will. But don't take the chance if you don't have to.

The second major step in avoiding insect nastiness is to steer clear of **fire ants,** whose large, gray or brown-dirt nests are quite common in this area. They attack instantly and in great numbers, with little or no provocation. They don't just bite, they inject you with

poison from their stingers. In short, fire ants are not to be trifled with.

While the only real remedy is the preventative one of never coming in contact with them, should you find yourself being bitten by fire ants, the first thing is to stay calm. Take off your shoes and socks and get as many of the ants off you as you can. Unless you've had a truly large amount of bites—in which case you should seek medical help immediately—the best thing to do next is wash the area to get any venom off, and then disinfect with alcohol if you have any handy. Then a topical treatment such as calamine lotion or hydrocortisone is advised. A fire ant bite will leave a red pustule that lasts about a week. Try your best not to scratch it so that it won't get infected.

Outdoor activity, especially in woodsy, undeveloped areas, may bring you in contact with another unpleasant indigenous creature, the tiny but obnoxious **chigger,** sometimes called the redbug. The bite of a chigger can't be felt, but the enzymes it leaves behind can lead to a very itchy little red spot. Contrary to folklore, putting fingernail polish on the itchy bite will not "suffocate" the chigger, because by this point the chigger itself is long gone. All you can do is get some topical itch or pain relief and go on with your life. The itching will eventually subside.

For **bee stings,** the best approach for those non-allergic to them is to immediately pull the stinger out, perhaps by scraping a credit card over the bite, and apply ice if possible. A topical treatment such as hydrocortisone or calamine lotion is advised. In my experience the old folk remedy of tearing apart a cigarette and putting the tobacco leaves directly on the sting does indeed cut the pain. But that's not a medical opinion, so do with it what you will. A minor allergic reaction can be quelled by using an over-the-counter antihistamine. If the sting victim is severely allergic to bee stings, go to a hospital or call 911 for an ambulance.

Threats in the Water

While enjoying area beaches, a lot of visitors

become inordinately worried about **shark attacks.** Every couple of summers there's a lot of hysteria about this, but the truth is that you're much more likely to slip and fall in a bathroom than you are to even come close to being bitten by a shark in these shallow Atlantic waters.

A far more common fate for area swimmers is to get stung by a **jellyfish,** or sea nettle. They can sting you in the water, but most often beachcombers are stung by stepping on beached jellyfish stranded on the sand by the tide. If you get stung, don't panic; wash the area with saltwater, not freshwater, and apply vinegar or baking soda.

Lightning

The southeastern United States is home to some vicious, fast-moving thunderstorms, often with an amazing amount of electrical activity. Death by lightning strike occurs often in this region and is something that should be taken quite seriously. The general rule of thumb is if you're in the water, whether at the beach or in a swimming pool, and hear thunder, get out of the water immediately until the storm passes. If you're on dry land and see lightning flash a distance away, that's your cue to seek safety indoors. Whatever you do, do not play sports outside when lightning threatens.

Information and Services

TOURIST INFORMATION

Outer Banks

The **Aycock Brown Welcome Center** at Kitty Hawk (U.S. 158, MP 1.5, 252/261-464, www.outerbanks.org, 9 A.M.–5 P.M. daily Dec.–Feb., 9 A.M.–5:30 P.M. daily Mar.–May and Sept.–Nov., 9 A.M.–6 P.M. daily June–Aug.), Outer Banks Welcome Center at Manteo, and Cape Hatteras National Seashore Visitors Center on Ocracoke are all clearinghouses for regional travel information. The **Outer Banks Visitors Bureau** (www.outerbanks.org) can be reached directly at 877/629-4386.

North Carolina Central Coast

In New Bern, the **New Bern/Craven County Convention and Visitors Bureau** (800/437-5767) is at 203 S. Front St. within the Convention Center.

The **Crystal Coast Visitor Center** (3409 Arendell St., 252/726-8148) is in Morehead City, North Carolina.

Wilmington and the Cape Fear Region

Extensive tourism and travel information is available from local convention and visitors bureaus:

the **Wilmington/Cape Fear Coast CVB** (23 N. 3rd St., Wilmington, 877/406-2356, www.cape-fear.nc.us, 8:30 A.M.–5 P.M. Mon.–Fri., 9 A.M.–4 P.M. Sat., and 1–4 P.M. Sun.), and the **Brunswick County Chamber of Commerce** (4948 Main St., 800/426-6644, www.brunswickcountychamber.org, 8:30 A.M.–5 P.M. Mon.–Fri.) in Shallotte.

For Fayetteville, try the **Fayetteville Area Convention and Visitors Bureau** (www.visitfayettevillenc.com).

Myrtle Beach and the Grand Strand

The main visitors center is the **Myrtle Beach Area Chamber of Commerce and Visitor Center** (1200 N. Oak St., 843/626-7444, www.visitmybeach.com, Mon.–Fri. 8:30 A.M.–5 P.M., Sat. 10 A.M.–2 P.M.) There's an airport welcome center as well (1180 Jetport Rd., 843/626-7444).

The **North Myrtle Beach Chamber of Commerce and Convention and Visitors Bureau** is at 270 Hwy. 17 (843/281-2662, www.northmyrtlebeachchamber.com).

Charleston

The main visitors center is the **Charleston**

Visitor Reception and Transportation Center (375 Meeting St., 800/774-0006, www.charlestoncvb.com, Mon.–Fri. 8:30 A.M.–5 P.M.). Outlying visitors centers are the **Mt. Pleasant-Isle of Palms Visitor Center** (Johnnie Dodds Blvd., 843/853-8000, 9 A.M.–5:30 P.M.), and the **North Charleston Visitor Center** (4975-B Centre Pointe Dr., 843/853-8000, Mon.–Sat. 10 A.M.–5 P.M.).

South Carolina Lowcountry

The Beaufort **Visitors Information Center** is at 1006 Carteret St. (843/524-3163, www.beaufortsc.org, 9 A.M.–5:30 P.M. daily).

In Hilton Head, get information, book a room, or secure a tee time just as you come onto the island at the **Hilton Head Island Chamber of Commerce Welcome Center** (100 William Hilton Pkwy., 843/785-3673, www.hiltonheadisland.org, 9 A.M.–6 P.M. daily), in the same building as the Coastal Discovery Museum.

You'll find Bluffton's visitors center in the **Heyward House Historic Center** (70 Boundary St., 843/757-6293, www.heywardhouse.org, 10 A.M.–3 P.M. Mon.–Fri., 11 A.M.–2 P.M. Sat.).

MONEY

Automated Teller Machines (ATMs) are available in all urban areas covered in this book. Be aware that if the ATM is not owned by your bank, not only will that ATM likely charge you a service fee, but your bank may charge you one as well.

While ATMs have made travelers checks less essential, travelers checks do have the important advantage of accessibility, as some rural and less-developed areas covered in this book have few-to-no ATMs. You can purchase travelers checks at just about any bank.

Establishments in the United States only accept the national currency (the U.S. dollar). To exchange foreign money, go to any bank.

Generally, establishments that accept credit cards will feature stickers on the front entrance with the logo of the particular cards they accept, though this is not a legal requirement. The use of debit cards has dramatically increased in the United States. Most retail establishments and many fast-food chains are now accepting them. Make sure you get a receipt whenever you use a credit card or a debit card.

INTERNET ACCESS

Visitors from Europe and Asia are likely to be disappointed at the quality of Internet access in the United States, particularly the area covered in this book. Fiber optic lines are still a rarity, and while many hotels and B&Bs now offer in-room Internet access—some charge, some don't, make sure to ask ahead—the quality and speed of the connection might prove poor.

Wireless (Wi-Fi) networks also are less than impressive, though that situation continues to improve on a daily basis in coffeehouses, hotels, and airports. Unfortunately, many hot spots in private establishments are for rental only.

PHONES

Generally speaking, the United States is behind Europe and much of Asia in terms of cell phone technology. Unlike Europe, where "pay-as-you-go" refills are easy to find, most American cell phone users pay for monthly plans through a handful of providers. Still, you should have no problem with cell phone coverage in urban areas. Where it gets much less dependable is in rural areas and on beaches. Bottom line, don't depend on having cell service everywhere you go.

As with a regular landline, any time you face an emergency call 911 on your cell phone.

All phone numbers in the United States are seven digits preceded by a three-digit area code. You may have to dial a "1" before a phone number if it's a long-distance call, even within the same area code.

RESOURCES

Suggested Reading

NONFICTION

Carlson, Tom. *Hatteras Blues: A Story from the Edge of America*. Chapel Hill, NC: University of North Carolina Press, 2005. A poignant chronicle of the ups and downs of one family's sportfishing business on the Outer Banks.

Click, Patricia. *Time Full of Trial: The Roanoke Island Freedmen's Colony, 1862-1867*. Chapel Hill, NC: University of North Carolina Press, 2001. An insightful exploration, based on primary sources, of this underreported, major chapter of African-American history in coastal North Carolina.

Darlington, Terry. *Narrow Dog to Indian River*. New York, NY: Delta, 2009. A British couple and their whippet dog Jim navigate an English canal boat down the Intracoastal Waterway from Virginia to Florida, with long, hilarious sections about their travels in North and South Carolina.

Ferling, John E. *Almost a Miracle: The American Victory in the War of Independence*. New York, NY: Oxford University Press, 2007. Not only perhaps the best single volume detailing the military aspects of the Revolutionary War, but absolutely indispensable for learning about the Carolinas' key role in it. In a dramatic departure from most New England-focused books of this genre, fully half of *Almost a Miracle* is devoted to an in-depth look at the Southern theater of the conflict.

Hudson, Charles M. *The Southeastern Indians*. Knoxville, TN: University of Tennessee Press, 1976. Though written decades ago, this seminal work by the noted University of Georgia anthropologist remains the definitive work on the life, culture, art, and religion of the Native Americans of the Southeast region.

Klein, Maury. *Days of Defiance: Sumter, Secession, and the Coming of the Civil War*. New York, NY: Vintage, 1999. A gripping and vivid account of the lead-up to war, with Charleston as the focal point.

Pilkey, Orrin H. *How to Read a North Carolina Beach: Bubble Holes, Barking Sands, and Rippled Runnels*. Chapel Hill, NC: University of North Carolina Press, 2006. Fascinating and user-friendly guide to taking an up-close look at the ebb and flow of the typical North Carolina maritime ecosystem.

Reed, John Shelton. *Holy Smoke: The Big Book of North Carolina Barbecue*. Chapel Hill, NC: University of North Carolina Press, 2009. The title says it all: everything you ever needed or wanted to know about North Carolina 'cue.

Robinson, Sally Ann. *Gullah Home Cooking the Daufuskie Island Way*. Chapel Hill, NC: University of North Carolina Press, 2007. Subtitled "Smokin' Joe Butter Beans, Ol' 'Fuskie Fried Crab Rice, Sticky-Bush Blackberry Dumpling, and Other Sea Island Favorites," this cookbook by a native Daufuskie Islander features a foreword by Pat Conroy.

Rogers Jr., George C. *Charleston in the Age of the Pinckneys,* Columbia, SC: University of South Carolina Press, 1980. This 1969 history is a classic of the genre.

Rosen, Robert. *A Short History of Charleston.* Columbia, SC: University of South Carolina Press, 1997. Quite simply the most concise, readable, and entertaining history of the Holy City I've found.

Whedbee, Charles Harry. *Blackbeard's Cup and Stories of the Outer Banks.* Winston-Salem, NC: John F. Blair, 1989. Funny and engaging collection of folklore in and around the Outer Banks.

Woodward, C. Vann (ed.). *Mary Chesnut's Civil War.* New Haven, CT: Yale University Press, 1981. The Pulitzer Prize–winning classic compilation of the sardonically funny and quietly heartbreaking letters of Charleston's Mary Chesnut during the Civil War.

FICTION

Conroy, Pat. *The Lords of Discipline.* New York, NY: Bantam, 1985. For all practical purposes set at the Citadel, this novel takes you behind the scenes of the notoriously insular Charleston military college.

Conroy, Pat. *The Water is Wide.* New York, NY: Bantam, 1987. Immortal account of Conroy's time teaching African-American children in a two-room schoolhouse on "Yamacraw" (actually Daufuskie) Island.

Frank, Dorothea Benton. *Sullivan's Island.* New York, NY: Berkley, 2004. This South Carolina native's debut novel, and still probably her best, chronicles the journey of a Charleston woman through the breakup of her marriage to eventual redemption.

Kidd, Sue Monk. *The Secret Life of Bees.* New York, NY: Penguin, 2003. Set in South Carolina in the 1960s, this best-seller delves into the role of race in the regional psyche. It gained critical acclaim due to the unusual fact that the author, a white woman, features many African-American female characters.

Poe, Edgar Allan. *The Gold Bug.* London: Hesperus Press, 2007. Inspired by his stint there with the U.S. Army, the great American author set this classic short story on Sullivan's Island, South Carolina, near Charleston.

Siddons, Anne Rivers. *Outer Banks.* New York, NY: HarperTorch, 1992. The Outer Banks are the backdrop for this gripping, character-driven novel by this best-selling author.

Internet Resources

RECREATION

North Carolina Department of Natural Resources
www.ncwildlife.org

A great one-stop-shop for detailed, user-friendly information on North Carolina nature and nature-based tourism, including a separate kid's section.

South Carolina Department of Natural Resources
www.dnr.sc.gov

More than just a compendium of license and fee information—though there's certainly plenty of that—this site features a lot of practical advice on how best to enjoy South Carolina's great outdoors.

South Carolina State Parks
www.southcarolinaparks.com

This site offers vital historical and visitors' information for South Carolina's excellent, underrated network of state park sites, including camping reservations.

Dozier's Waterway Guide
www.waterwayguide.com

A serious boater's guide to stops on the Intracoastal Waterway, this site features a lot of solid navigational information.

Cruising the ICW
www.cruisingtheicw.com

Another great resource for boaters wanting to traverse the Intracoastal Waterway along the coast.

NATURE AND ENVIRONMENT

Francis Beidler Forest Blog
http://beidlerforest.blogspot.com

This site features an informative blog by a nature expert with Francis Beidler Forest, a jointly owned conservation venture of the South Carolina Audubon Society and the Nature Conservancy.

North Carolina Audubon Society
http://ncaudubon.org

The go-to site for birding information in the Tarheel State.

Go Green Charleston
www.gogreencharleston.org

The latest environmental and sustainable living news in Charleston, this site features a lot of practical and fun visitors' information and links.

Charleston Green Map
www.charlestongreenmap.org

Here you'll find a painstakingly compiled guide to green businesses, restaurants, and organizations in the Holy City.

FOOD

Charleston Chow
http://charlestonchow.blogspot.com

This site provides an unvarnished take on the local food and bev scene by a professional chef and former food critic for the Charleston *Post and Courier.*

South Carolina Foodie
www.scfoodie.net

Stephanie Nettis gives you an enthusiastic insider's look at the Charleston restaurant scene, with an emphasis on what's new and hot.

Kent Craig's Barbecue
http://hkentcraig.com/bbq.html

Kent Craig's compendium of North Carolina barbecue background and favorite hotspots, with a healthy helping of them on the coast, featuring the distinctive, vinegary Eastern North Carolina brand of the culinary art form.

HISTORY AND BACKGROUND

South Carolina Information Highway
www.sciway.net

An eclectic cornucopia of interesting South

Carolina history and assorted background facts makes for an interesting Internet portal into all things Palmetto State.

Outer Banks History Center
www.obhistorycenter.ncdcr.gov
The online presence of this archives and research library administered by the North Carolina State Archives and based in Manteo.

Searching for the Lost Colony
http://the-lost-colony.blogspot.com
The engaging and active blog of the Lost Colonies of Roanoke DNA Project, which uses genetic research to try and find out what became of the vanished English colonists of 1585.

TOURIST INFORMATION

Outer Banks Conventions and Visitors Bureau
www.outerbanks.org
The official travel website for visitors to the Outer Banks Region.

Wilmington and the Cape Fear Coast Conventions and Visitors Bureau
www.capefearcoast.com
The official travel website for those visiting Wilmington and surrounding area.

Myrtle Beach Conventions and Visitors Bureau
www.visitmyrtlebeach.com
There is a plethora of websites having to do with Myrtle Beach tourism, some making a conscious attempt to masquerade as an official website. This is the only official tourism website for the Myrtle Beach area.

Charleston Convention and Visitors Bureau
www.charlestoncvb.com
This very professional and user-friendly tourism site is perhaps the best and most practical Internet portal for visitors to Charleston.

Index

List of Maps

Acknowledgments

I had a lot of help and advice in gathering information for this project. In South Carolina, Erin Coy of the Charleston Area Convention and Visitors Bureau was invaluable in my explorations of the Holy City, and Kimberly Miles of the Myrtle Beach Area Chamber of Commerce/Convention and Visitors Bureau was vital in my research of the Grand Strand.

In the Tarheel State, I thank the Milton family of Wilmington's matchless Rosehill Inn and Joe Cowling at the Colony IV by the Sea in Kill Devil Hills for their gracious hospitality. Many thanks also go to Connie Nelson of the Wilmington/Cape Fear Coast Convention & Visitors Bureau and Aaron Tuell of the Outer Banks Visitors Bureau.

My stable of go-to experts for the book included Dee Hope of the South Carolina Association of Naturalists, who provided key insight into the Palmetto State's natural beauty and ecology; Stephanie Nettis of sc-foodie.net, who delivered up-to-the-minute observations of the Charleston cuisine scene; and golf writer Joel Zuckerman, who provided input on the state of South Carolina golf.

As always, I thank the editorial, creative, and marketing staff at Avalon Travel for their extraordinary professionalism, good humor, and attention to detail: Grace Fujimoto, Naomi Adler Dancis, Jehan Seirafi, Elizabeth Jang, Brice Ticen, Jamie Andrade, and everyone else who helped in putting together this project.

I could not have written the book without the strong encouragement of my entire family, and I thank them all for their continuing love and support.

www.moon.com

MOON.COM is all new, and ready to help plan your next trip! Filled with fresh trip ideas and strategies, author interviews, informative blogs, a detailed map library, and descriptions of all the Moon guidebooks, Moon.com is all you need to get out and explore the world—or even places in your own backyard. As always, when you travel with Moon, expect an experience that is uncommon and truly unique.